DISCRETE WAVELET TRANSFORMS: ALGORITHMS AND APPLICATIONS

Edited by **Hannu Olkkonen**

Discrete Wavelet Transforms: Algorithms and Applications
Edited by Hannu Olkkonen

Published by InTech
Janeza Trdine 9, 51000 Rijeka, Croatia

Publishing Process Manager Ivana Lorkovic

Technical Editor Teodora Smiljanic

Cover Designer InTech Design Team

Additional hard copies can be obtained from orders@intechopen.com

Discrete Wavelet Transforms: Algorithms and Applications, Edited by Hannu Olkkonen
p. cm.
ISBN 978-953-307-482-5

For EU product safety concerns:
IN TECH d.o.o., Prolaz Marije Krucifikse Kozulić 3, 51000 Rijeka, Croatia,
info@intechopen.com or visit our website at intechopen.com.

Meet the editor

Dr. Hannu Olkkonen received his Ph.D. degree in year 1982 from the University of Kuopio, Finland. Since then he has worked as a Professor of Physics and Electronics at the Department of Applied Physics, University of Kuopio, Finland. He is authored more that 260 reviewed journal articles and served as an editor of several scientific books and book chapters. His research interests include wide range of digital signal processing applications in research and industry, biomedical instrumentation, wireless multisensor networks and discrete wavelet transform algorithms.

Contents

Preface

The discrete wavelet transform (DWT) algorithms have a firm position in processing of signals in several areas of research and industry. As DWT provides both octave-scale frequency and spatial timing of the analyzed signal, it is constantly used to solve and treat more and more advanced problems. The DWT algorithms were initially based on the compactly supported conjugate quadrature filters (CQFs). However, a drawback in CQFs is due to the nonlinear phase effects such as spatial dislocations in multi-scale analysis. This is avoided in biorthogonal discrete wavelet transform (BDWT) algorithms, where the scaling and wavelet filters are symmetric and linear phase. The BDWT algorithms are usually constructed by a ladder-type network called lifting scheme. The procedure consists of sequential down and uplifting steps and the reconstruction of the signal is made by running the lifting network in reverse order. Efficient lifting BDWT structures have been developed for VLSI and microprocessor applications. Only register shifts and summations are needed for integer arithmetic implementation of the analysis and synthesis filters. In many systems BDWT-based data and image processing tools have outperformed the conventional discrete cosine transform (DCT) -based approaches. For example, in JPEG2000 Standard the DCT has been replaced by the lifting BDWT.

A difficulty in multi-scale DWT analyses is the dependency of the total energy of the wavelet coefficients in different scales on the fractional shifts of the analysed signal. This has led to the development of the complex shift invariant DWT algorithms, the real and imaginary parts of the complex wavelet coefficients are approximately a Hilbert transform pair. The energy of the wavelet coefficients equals the envelope, which provides shift-invariance. In two parallel CQF banks, which are constructed so that the impulse responses of the scaling filters have half-sample delayed versions of each other, the corresponding wavelet bases are a Hilbert transform pair. However, the CQF wavelets do not have coefficient symmetry and the nonlinearity disturbs the spatial timing in different scales and prevents accurate statistical analyses. Therefore the current developments in theory and applications of shift invariant DWT algorithms are concentrated on the dual-tree BDWT structures.

This book reviews the recent progress in discrete wavelet transform algorithms and applications. The book covers a wide range of methods (e.g. lifting, shift invariance, multi-scale analysis) for constructing DWTs. The book chapters are organized into four major parts. Part I describes the progress in hardware implementations of the DWT algorithms. Applications include multitone modulation for ADSL and equalization techniques, a scalable architecture for FPGA-implementation, lifting based algorithm for VLSI implementation, comparison between DWT and FFT based OFDM and modified SPIHT codec. Part II addresses image processing algorithms such as multiresolution approach for edge detection, low bit rate image compression, low complexity implementation of CQF wavelets and compression of multi-component images. Part III focuses watermaking DWT algorithms. Finally, Part IV describes shift invariant DWTs, DC lossless property, DWT based analysis and estimation of colored noise and an application of the wavelet Galerkin method.

The chapters of the present book consist of both tutorial and highly advanced material. Therefore, the book is intended to be a reference text for graduate students and researchers to obtain state-of-the-art knowledge on specific applications. The editor is greatly indebted to all co-authors for giving their valuable time and expertise in constructing this book. The technical editors are also acknowledged for their tedious support and help.

Hannu Olkkonen, Professor
University of Eastern Finland, Department of Applied Physics, Kuopio, Finland

Part 1

Discrete Wavelet Transform Based Hardware Algorithms

1

Discrete Wavelet Multitone Modulation for ADSL & Equalization Techniques

Sobia Baig[1], Fasih-ud-Din Farrukh[2] and M. Junaid Mughal[2]
[1]Electrical Engineering Department,
COMSATS Institute of Information Technology, Lahore
[2]Faculty of Electronic Engineering,
GIK Institute of Engineering Sciences and Technology, Topi
[1,2]Pakistan

1. Introduction

The reliable delivery of information over severe fading wireless or wired channels is a major challenge in communication systems. At the heart of every communication system is the physical layer, consisting of a transmitter, a channel and a receiver. A transmitter maps the input digital information into a waveform suitable for transmission over the channel. The communication channel distorts the transmitted waveform. One of the many sources of signal distortion is the presence of multipath in the communication channel. Due to the effect of the multipath signal propagation, inter-symbol interference (ISI) occurs in the received waveform. Moreover, the transmitted signal gets distorted due to the effect of various kinds of interference and noise, as it propagates through the channel. ISI and the channel noise distort the amplitude and phase of the transmitted signal, which lead to erroneous bit detection at the receiver. It is desirable for a good communication system that its receiver is able to retrieve the digital information from the received waveform, even in the presence of channel impairments such as, multipath effect and noise.

Orthogonal Frequency Division Multiplexing (OFDM) is a Multi-Carrier Modulation (MCM) technique that enables high data rate transmission and is robust against ISI (Saltzberg, 1967), (Weinstein and Ebert, 1971), (Hirosaki, 1981). It is a form of frequency division multiplexing (FDM), where data is transmitted in several narrowband streams at various carrier frequencies. The sub-carriers in an OFDM system are orthogonal under ideal propagation conditions. By dividing the input bit-stream into multiple and parallel bit-streams, the objective is to lower the data rate in each sub-channel as compared to the total data rate and also to make sub-channel bandwidth lower than the coherence bandwidth of the communication channel. Therefore, each sub-channel will experience flat-fading and will have small ISI. Hence an OFDM system requires simplified equalization techniques, to mitigate the inter-symbol interference. The ISI can be completely eliminated in OFDM transceivers by utilizing the principle of cyclic prefixing (CP). Therefore, high data rate communication systems prefer to apply multicarrier modulation techniques. OFDM has been standardized for many digital communication systems, including ADSL, the 802.11a and 802.11g Wireless LAN standards, Digital audio broadcasting including EUREKA 147 and Digital Radio Mondiale, Digital Video Broadcasting (DVB), some Ultra Wide Band (UWB) systems, WiMax, and Power Line Communication (PLC) (Sari, et al., 1995) (Frederiksen and Prasad, 2002), (Baig and Gohar, 2003).

Over the years, OFDM has evolved into variants, such as Discrete Multitone (DMT), and hybrid modulation techniques, such as multi-carrier code division multiple access (MC-CDMA), Wavelet OFDM and Discrete Wavelet Multitone (DWMT). Several factors are responsible for the development of these variants, especially Wavelet based OFDM techniques, which target several disadvantages associated with Multicarrier modulation (MCM) techniques. Some of these drawbacks are:

- the spectral inefficiency associated with the guard interval insertion, which includes the cyclic prefix
- the high degree of spectral leakage due to high magnitude side lobes of pulse shape of sinusoidal carriers
- OFDM based communication system's sensitivity to inter-carrier interference (ICI) and narrowband interference (NBI)

Therefore, a Discrete Wavelet Transform (DWT) based MCM system was developed as an alternative to DFT based MCM scheme (Lindsey, 1995). DWT based MCM techniques came to be known as Wavelet-OFDM in wireless communications and as Discrete Wavelet Multitone (DWMT) for harsh and noisy wireline communication channels such as Digital Subscriber Line (DSL) or Power Line Communications (PLC) (Baig and Mughal, 2009).

This chapter describes the application of DWT in Discrete Multitone (DMT) transceivers and its performance analysis in Digital Subscriber Line (DSL) channel, in the presence of background noise, crosstalk etc. Time domain equalization techniques proposed for DWT based multitone that is DWMT are discussed, along with the simulation results. The pros and cons of adopting DWT instead of DFT in DMT transceivers will also be discussed, highlighting the open areas of research.

2. Basics of wavelet filter banks & multirate signal processing systems

Wavelets and filter banks play an important role in signal decomposition into various subbands, signal analysis, modeling and reconstruction. Some areas of DSP, such as audio and video compression, signal denoising, digital audio processing and adaptive filtering are based on wavelets and multirate DSP systems. Digital communication is a relatively new area for multirate DSP applications. The wavelets are implemented by utilizing multirate filter banks (Fliege, 1994). The discovery of Quadrature Mirror Filter banks (QMF) led to the idea of Perfect Reconstruction (PR), and thus to subband decomposition. Mallat came up with the idea of implementing wavelets by filter banks for subband coding and multiresolution decomposition (Mallat, 1999). DWT gives time-scale representation of a digital signal using digital filtering techniques. The DWT analyzes the signal at different frequency bands with different resolutions by decomposing the signal into approximation and detail coefficients. The decomposition of the signal into different frequency bands is obtained simply by successive high pass and low pass filtering of the time domain signal.

2.1 Analysis and synthesis filter banks

Analysis filter banks decomposes input signal into frequency subbands. A two channel analysis filter bank, as shown in Fig. 1, splits the input signal $X(z)$ into a high frequency component $U_0(z)$ and a low frequency component $U_1(z)$. The input signal $X(z)$ is passed through a low pass filter $H_0(z)$ and a high pass filter $H_1(z)$, yielding the $U_0(z)$ and $U_1(z)$ respectively.

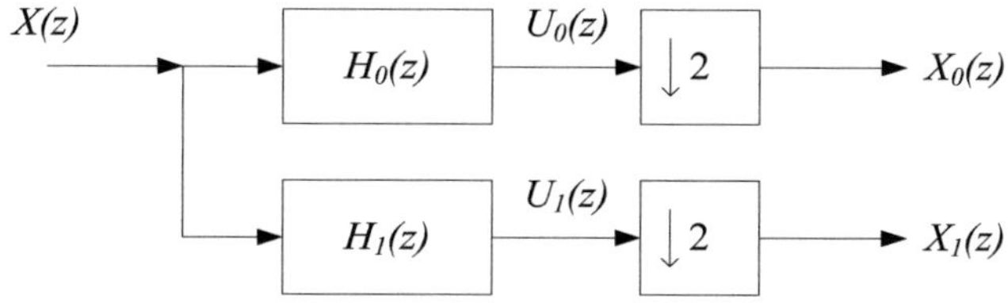

Fig. 1. Two-channel Analysis filter bank.

Consequently, with the sampling frequency, $F_s = 2\pi$, the available bandwidth from 0 to π, is divided into two halves, $0 \leq f \leq {}^{F_s}/_4$ for the lower frequency signal $U_0(z)$and ${}^{F_s}/_4 \leq f \leq {}^{F_s}/_2$ for the high frequency signal $U_1(z)$. Therefore, the filtered signals $U_0(z)$and $U_1(z)$have half the bandwidth of the input signal after being convolved with the low pass filter and high pass filter respectively.The filtered and downsampled signal spectra are shown in Fig. 2. In matrix form the sub-band signals are represented as (Fliege, 1994),

$$\begin{bmatrix} X_0(z) \\ X_1(z), \end{bmatrix} = \frac{1}{2}\begin{bmatrix} H_0(z^{1/2}) & H_0(-z^{1/2}) \\ H_0(z^{1/2}) & H_0(-z^{1/2}) \end{bmatrix}\begin{bmatrix} X(z^{1/2}) \\ X(-z^{1/2}) \end{bmatrix} \quad (1)$$

The two signal spectra overlap. The downsampling will produce aliased components of the signals, that are functions of $X(-z^{1/2})$ in Eq. 1, since the filtered signals are not bandlimited to π. Two-channel synthesis filter bank is the dual of analysis filter bank, as shown in Fig. 3. $G_0(z)$ and $G_1(z)$ denote the lowpass and highpass filters, which recombine the upsampled signals $U_0(z)$ and $U_1(z)$ into $X(z)$, the reconstructed version of the input signal. The aliased images are removed by the filter $G_0(z)$ in the frequency range ${}^{F_s}/_4 \leq f \leq {}^{F_s}/_2$, while the filter $G_1(z)$ eliminates the images in the upsampled signal $U_1(z)$ in the frequency range $0 \leq f \leq {}^{F_s}/_4$. Therefore, the signal $X(z)$, output from the synthesis filter bank is (Fliege, 1994),

$$X(z) = [G_0(z) \quad G_1(z)]\begin{bmatrix} X_0(z^2) \\ X_1(z^2) \end{bmatrix} \quad (2)$$

(a)

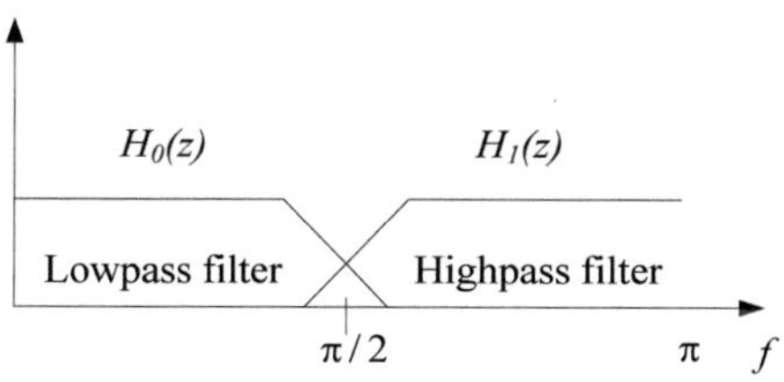

Fig. 2. (Continued)

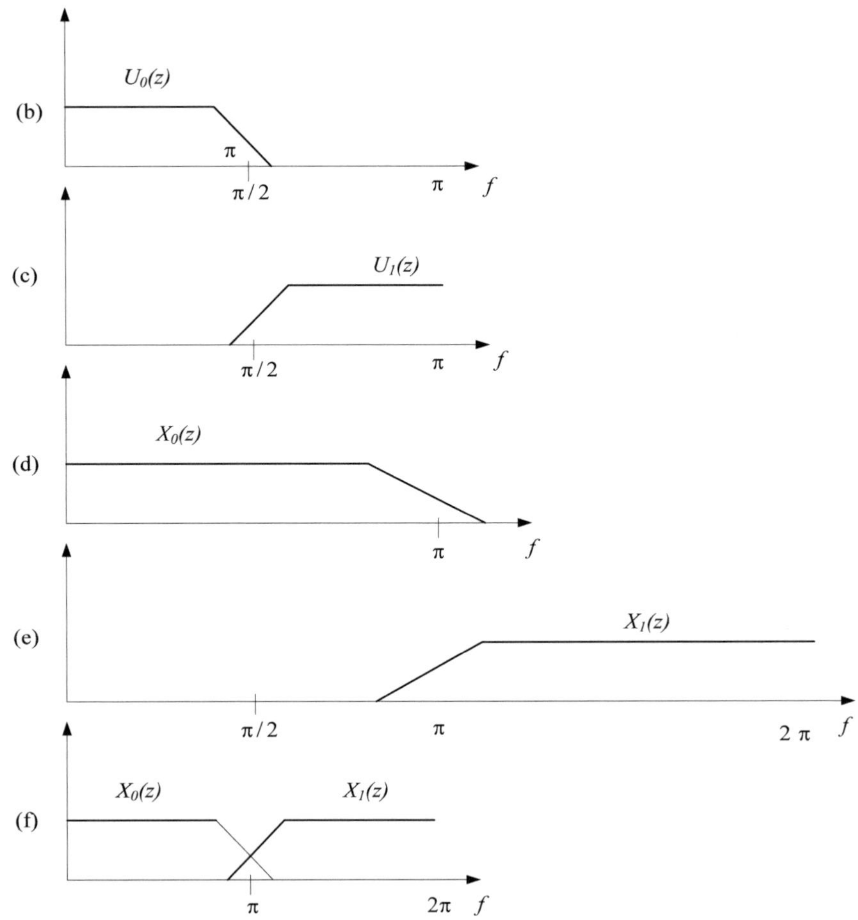

Fig. 2. Signal spectra in two-channel analysis filter bank. (a) Low pass & high pass filter transfer functions. (b) low pass filtered signal spectrum $U_0(z)$. (c) high pass filtered signal spectrum $U_1(z)$. (d) downsampled signal $X_0(z)$spectrum. (e) downsampled signal $X(z)$ spectrum (f) output signal spectra.

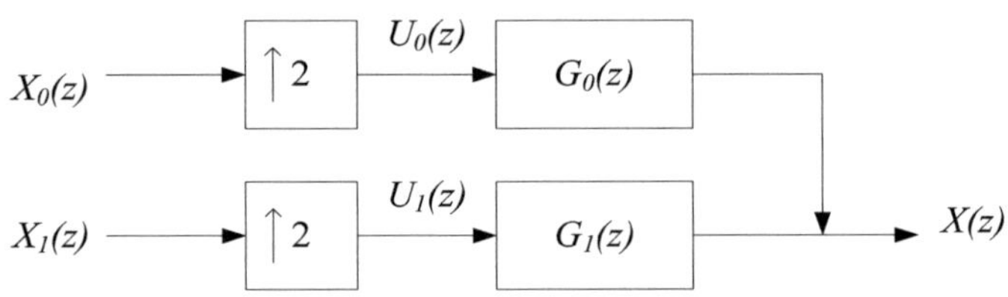

Fig. 3. Two-channel Synthesis filter bank.

2.2 Quadrature mirror filter bank

The analysis and the synthesis filter banks combine to form a structure commonly known as the two-channel quadrature mirror filter (QMF) bank. QMF bank serves as the basic building block in many multirate systems. A two-channel QMF bank is shown in Fig. 4. The constituent analysis and synthesis filter banks have power complementary frequency responses. The low pass and high pass filters in the analysis filter bank decompose the input signal into sub-bands, and the decimation introduces a certain amount of aliasing, due to the non-ideal frequency response of the analysis filters. However, the synthesis filters characteristics are chosen with such frequency response, that the aliasing introduced by the analysis filter bank is canceled out in the reconstruction process. The output signal $\widehat{X}(z)$ is the recovered version of the input signal $X(z)$. Therefore, the output signal $\widehat{X}(z)$ is expressed as,

$$\widehat{X}(z) = [G_0(z) \quad G_1(z)]\frac{1}{2}\begin{bmatrix} H_0(z) & H_0(-z) \\ H_1(z) & H_1(-z) \end{bmatrix}\begin{bmatrix} X(z) \\ X(-z) \end{bmatrix} \tag{3}$$

$$\widehat{X}(z) = F_0(z)X(z) + F_1(z)X(-z) \tag{4}$$

The reconstructed signal $\widehat{X}(z)$ consists of two terms, the first term that is the product of the transfer function $F_0(z)$ and $X(z)$ is the desired QMF output, while the second term is the product of the transfer function $F_1(z)$ and $X(-z)$ is the aliasing term $F_1(z)$ denotes the aliasing components produced by the overlapping frequency responses of the analysis and synthesis filter banks. For an alias-free filter bank, $F_1(z)$ must be equal to zero. This condition is mathematically expressed as (Vaidyanthan, 1993),

$$F_1(z) = \frac{1}{2}[G_0(z)H_0(-z) + G_1(z)H_1(-z)] = 0 \tag{5}$$

This condition may be satisfied by choosing $G_0(z) = H_1(-z)$ and $G_1(z) = H_0(-z)$, then the desired QMF output is represented as (Fliege, 1994),

$$F_1(z) = \frac{1}{2}[H_0(z)H_1(-z) - H_1(z)H_0(-z)] \tag{6}$$

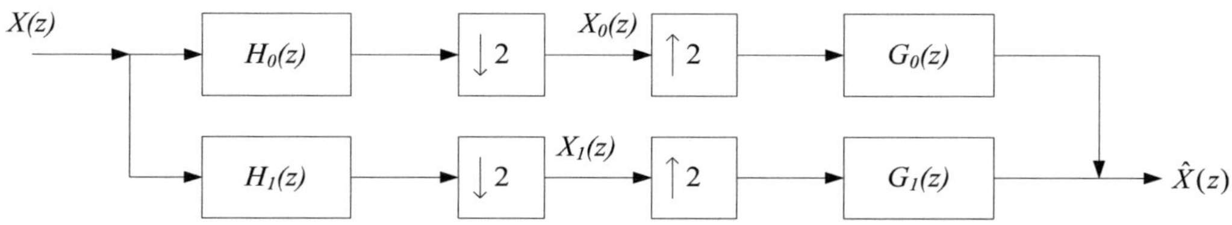

Fig. 4. Two-channel QMF bank.

The filter banks, which are able to perfectly reconstruct the input signal are the perfect reconstruction filter banks, that satisfy the perfect reconstruction condition. The desired QMF output includes the function $F_0(z)$ which gives perfect reconstruction of the input signal if it is a mere delay, that is $F_0(z) = z^{-K}$(Fliege, 1994). Two-channel filter bank, shown in Fig. 4, can be utilized to construct an octave-spaced wavelet filter bank with the help of a tree type structure. Octave filter bank is constructed by the successive decomposition of the low pass signal into constituent sub-bands, every time using the two-channel filter bank (Qian, 2002). A three-level octave-spaced analysis filter bank is shown in Fig. 5 (a) and a three-level octave-spaced synthesis filter bank is shown in Fig. 5 (b).

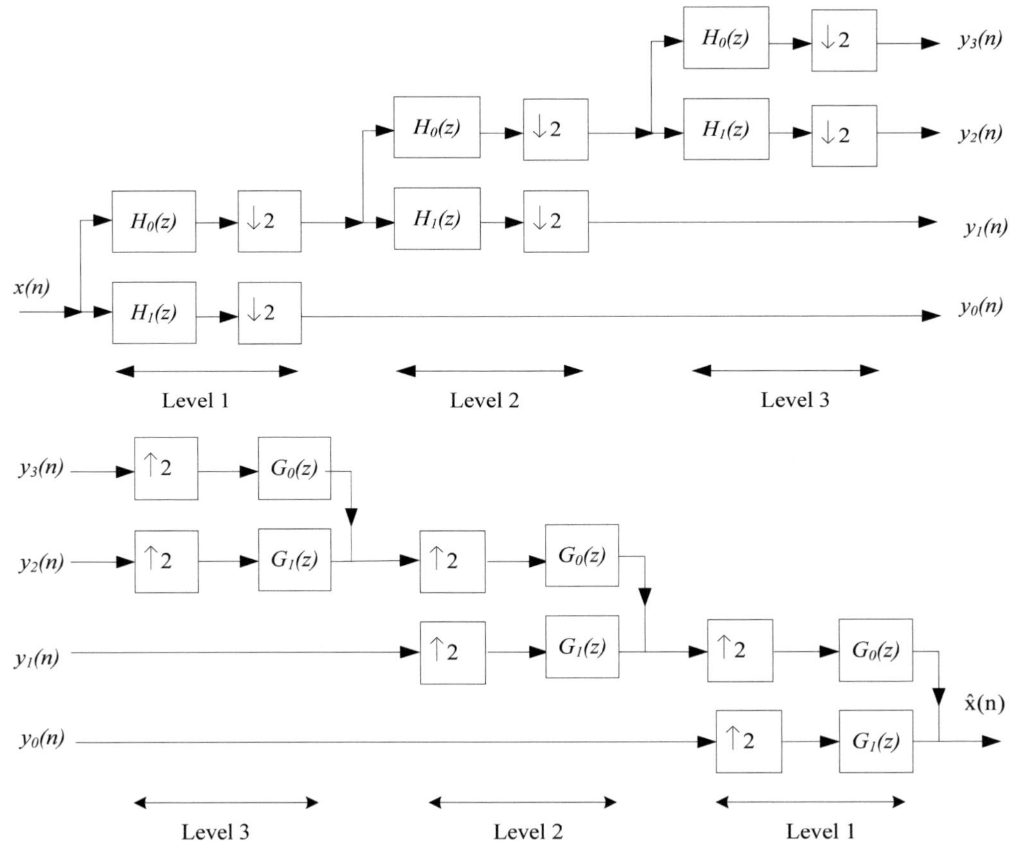

Fig. 5. (a) Three-level analysis filter bank (b) Three-level synthesis filter bank.

2.3 Transmultiplexer

Transmultiplexers form an integral part of modems and transceivers based on filter banks that work on the principle of perfect reconstruction. A simple two-channel filter bank can be utilized to illustrate the perfect reconstruction condition. A transmultiplexer is the dual of Sub-band coder (SBC) in structure. Fig. 6 shows a two-channel transmultiplexer filter bank, which converts a time-interleaved signal at its input to a FDM signal, having separate bands of spectrum multiplexed together and then converts it back into TDM signal at its output. Transmultiplexers find application in modems and transceivers for digital communication (Vaidyanthan, 1993).

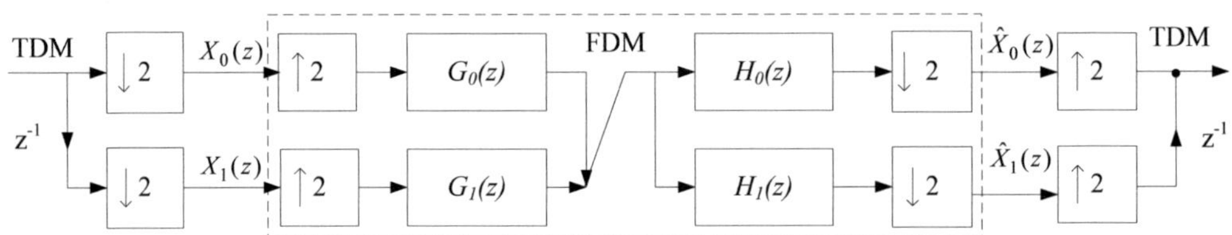

Fig. 6. Two-channel Transmultiplexer.

3. Discrete multitone modulation technique

Discrete Multitone (DMT) modulation is a variant of OFDM associated with various loading algorithms, so as to optimize a transceiver's performance in wireline channels like Asymmetrical Digital Subscriber Line (ADSL) and power line (Chow, et al., 1991). In literature, several loading algorithms have been developed; allocating resources such as data bits, or power in order to optimize high data rate, low average transmitting power, or low bit error rate. Typically two of these parameters are kept constant and third is the goal of optimization.

A conventional DFT based DMT transceiver block diagram is shown in Fig. 7. The channel bandwidth is divided into N sub-channels. The input serial bit-stream is also split into N parallel sub-streams. The data bits assigned to sub-channels are according to a loading algorithm. For water-filling bit-loading algorithm, greater number of bits is assigned to higher SNR sub-channels. If the value of SNR of a sub-channel is below a pre-assigned threshold, then no bits are allocated to that sub-channel. The assigned bits are mapped onto Quadrature amplitude modulation (QAM) constellation forming a complex symbol. The QAM symbols are then modulated onto orthogonal sub-carriers using Inverse Fast Fourier Transform (IFFT). The N QAM symbols are duplicated with their conjugate symmetric counterparts and subjected to $2N$ point IFFT, in order to generate real samples for transmission through the channel. A DMT symbol is thus formulated.

A guard band consisting of a few samples of the DMT symbol is pre-appended to the symbol. This is the cyclic prefix, which consists of the last v samples of the DMT symbol, circularly wrapped to the $2N$ DMT symbol. The length of cyclic prefix v is chosen such that it will be longer than the length of the channel response. The cyclic prefix added to a DMT symbol lengthens the symbol period, making it longer than the worst possible delay spread, which is caused by time delayed reflections of the original symbol arriving at the receiver. Consequently, the cyclic prefix serves the purpose of absorbing any multipath interference. Due to this cyclic extended symbol, the samples required for performing the FFT can be taken anywhere over the length of the symbol, without degradation by the neighboring symbols. However, the information sent in the cyclic prefix is redundant and reduces the transceiver throughput by $(2N + v)/2N$. Between the transmitter and receiver lies the communication channel, which introduces both noise and distortion (mainly due to multipath propagation) to the composite transmit signal. The channel can be modeled as a finite impulse response (FIR) filter that possesses a frequency-selective fading characteristic. The cyclic prefixed signal is transmitted through the channel, the output of which gives the product of the channel impulse response and the transmitted symbols in frequency domain. DMT receiver is basically the dual of the DMT transmitter, with the exception of the equalization part. The equalization block consists of two parts, the time-domain equalizer (TEQ) and the frequency-domain equalizer (FEQ). The purpose of TEQ is channel-shortening and it immediately follows the channel, as shown in the Fig. 7. It serves to shorten the channel impulse response, so that the equalized channel impulse response is less than the length of the cyclic prefix v. At the receiver the cyclic prefix samples are discarded and remaining samples are subject to Fast Fourier transform (FFT). The frequency domain equalizer divides the received sub-symbols by the FFT coefficients of the shortened channel impulse response. The resulting signal is demodulated to recover the original data bits and converted into a serial bit stream.

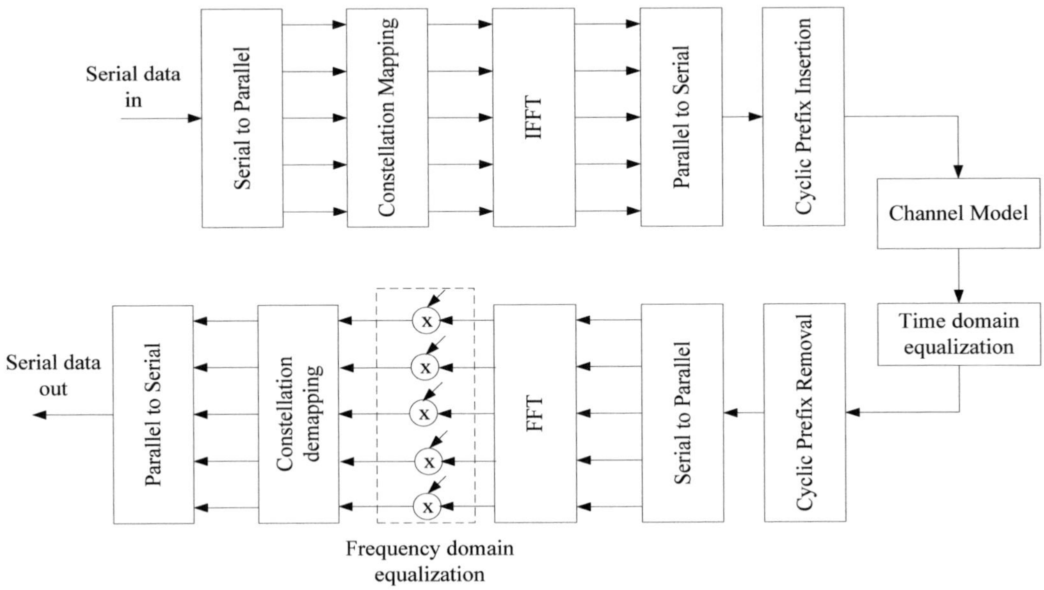

Fig. 7. Functional block diagram of a DMT transceiver.

3.1 Evolution of discrete wavelet multitone modulation

A major drawback of DFT-DMT is that the rectangular low-pass prototype filter results in *sinc* shaped sub-band spectral response, the first side lobes of which are only 13dB down, as pointed out by Sandzberg (Sandzberg, 1995). A dispersive channel will thus introduce Inter-Carrier Interference (ICI) at significant levels. To mitigate this we can increase filter bank genus, and design sub-channels with greater spectral isolation. We call this a lapped transform, and much work has been done on the particular case of the Lapped Orthogonal Transform (LOT) (Malvar, 1992). General Extended Lapped Transform (ELT) design is computationally prohibitive, however Cosine Modulated Filter Banks (CMFB) can be efficiently implemented utilizing Discrete Cosine Transform (DCT). In this way the design procedure is simplified if we allow the transmultiplexer filters to be modulated versions of a low pass, linear-phase prototype. Therefore, instead of designing N filters, we now only design one prototype filter. Modulated filter banks implementing lapped transforms with applications to communications are generally referred to as Discrete Wavelet Multitone (DWMT), to distinguish from DMT which uses a rectangular prototype.

Many contributions in literature have emphasized the need for DWMT in specific channel conditions. Tzannes and Proakis have proposed DWMT in (Tzannes, et al., 1994), and shown it to be superior to DFT-DMT. Authors suggest implementing DWMT in DSL channel for improved performance (Doux et al., 2003). Studies have compared DMT and DWMT performance in DSL channel (Akansu and Xueming 1998).

DWT exhibits better spectral shaping compared to the rectangular shaped subcarriers of OFDM. Therefore, it offers much lower side lobes in transmitted signal, which reduces its sensitivity to narrowband interference (NBI) and inter-carrier interference (ICI). However, it cannot utilize CP to mitigate ISI created by the frequency-selective channel, as various DWT symbols overlap in time domain (Vaidyanathan, 1993). Nevertheless, such MCM systems based on DWT require an efficient equalization technique to counter the ISI created by the channel.

4. Discrete Wavelet Multitone (DWMT) in Digital Subscriber Line (DSL)

A system based on Discrete Wavelet Multitone (DWMT) for modulating and demodulating the required signal using Discrete Wavelet Transform as a basis function has been suggested in wireless applications (Jamin andMähönen, 2005). The importance of DWMT in wireless communication is a recognized area of research and on similar lines a DWMT system can be implemented in wireline communication. It can be used as a maximally decimated filter bank with its overlapping symbols in time-domain. Therefore, this structure does not require the addition of CP which is an overhead in DMT and DWMT based wireline systems (Vaidyanathan, 1993). On the other hand, the wavelet filters also possess the advantages of having greater side-lobe attenuation and requires no CP (Bingham, 1990). Therefore, the DWMT systems are bandwidth efficient by not using the CP which creates the problem of bandwidth containment in DMT based systems. However, application of the DWMT systems in a dispersive channel like ADSL necessitates a robust channel equalization technique (Sandberg and Tzannes, 1995). In literature some equalization techniques for DMT based multicarrier systems have been suggested by many authors (Pollet and Peeters, 2000); (Acker et al., 2001); (Acker et al., 2004); (Karp et al.,2003) and DWMT based multicarrier systems (Viholainen et al., 1999). Equalization is a key factor in the design of modems based on DWMT modulation technique and till date, it remains an open research area. When using the Discrete Wavelet Packet Transform (DWPT) as a basis function in DWMT systems, it is difficult to equalize the overlapped symbols in time domain. We emphasize on the design of equalizer for DWPT based DWMT multicarrier systems. The proposed system is based on DWPT for DWMT wireline systems and time-domain equalization is suggested for the equalization process of overlapped symbols.

In this chapter, the time-domain equalization through a linear transversal filter is applied. The equalization algorithms are based on Zero-Forcing (Z-F) and minimum mean squared error (MMSE) criterion to a discrete wavelet-packet transform based DWMT transceiver for a wireline ADSL channel. It is then compared with the system's performance of a DMT based ADSL system. For a fair comparison between the two systems, the DMT system also utilizes the same time-domain equalization. The performance of the proposed wavelet-packet based transceiver is also evaluated in the presence of near-end crosstalk (NEXT) and far-end crosstalk (FEXT) for downstream ADSL. It is shown that the DWMT system conserves precious bandwidth by not utilizing any CP, and gives improvement in bit error rate (BER) performance over the DMT system with time-domain equalization (TEQ).

4.1 System model of DWMT

The DWMT system model's block diagram is shown in Fig. 8. It divides the input data bit-stream into multiple and parallel bit-streams. The proposed DWMT transceiver is based on discrete wavelet packet transform (DWPT). The DWPT is implemented through a reverse order perfect reconstruction filter bank transmultiplexer. Wavelet packets can be implemented as a set of FIR filters, which leads to the filter bank realization of wavelet transform, according to Mallat's algorithm (Mallat, 1998). The blocked version of the input signal $x_k(n)$ is mapped to a variable QAM constellation according to the number of bits loaded. This is interpolated and filtered by the kth branch synthesis filter $F_k(z)$. The combined signal is sent through the channel, and the received signal is filtered by an equalizer filter. The equalized signal is passed through the corresponding analysis filter $H_k(z)$ and decimated to retrieve the QAM encoded version of the transmitted signal. The transmitted signal is recovered after QAM decoding.

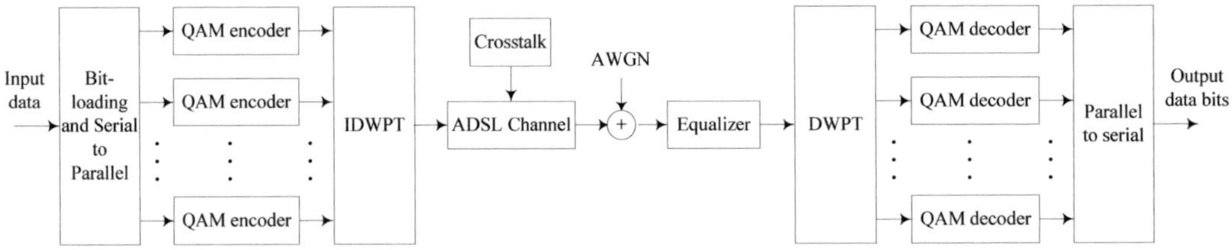

Fig. 8. Functional Block diagram of DWMT system.

4.1.1 Water filling bit loading

Bit loading is usually applied to DMT modulated systems applied to wireline channels, by first estimating the signal-to-noise ratio (SNR) of each sub-channel through channel estimation techniques, which is followed by the distribution of bits to these sub-channels according to their respective SNR. Water-Filling bit loading algorithm applied in the proposed system is rate adaptive and it is suitable for achieving maximum bit rate and also useful when considering the large number of sub-channels and variable QAM constellation (Leke and Cioffi, 1997);(Yu and Cioffi, 2001). A discrete version of this algorithm is applied, in which the bit-loading procedure initiates by determining the sub-channels that should be turned off, due to very low SNR. The bits are assigned to channels according to their capacity, expressed mathematically as (Thomas et al., 2002),

$$b = \frac{1}{2}\log_2\left[1 + \frac{SNR}{\Gamma.\gamma_m}\right] \tag{7}$$

where $SNR = \varepsilon_n.g_n$ is the SNR of each sub-channel, ε_n is the sub-channel energy and g_n is the sub-channel SNR and it can be calculated as,

$$g_n = \frac{|H_n|^2}{\sigma^2} \tag{8}$$

where H_n is the ADSL channel impulse response and σ^2 is the noise power, Γ is the SNR gap and γ_m is the performance margin, which is the amount by which SNR can be reduced (Yu and Cioffi,2001). The water filling bit-loading for the proposed system is shown in Fig. 9. While considering the DWMT based communication system for the ADSL channel, it is necessary to consider its frequency response and the effect of crosstalk, near-end crosstalk (NEXT), and far-end crosstalk (FEXT) in system simulation. The ADSL channel impairments and crosstalk is briefly discussed in the following section.

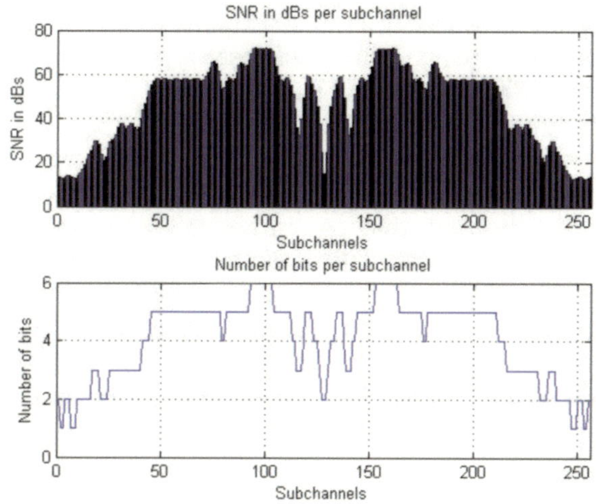

Fig. 9. ADSL channel frequency response & number of bits loaded according to discrete water-filling algorithm.

4.2 ADSL channel

Digital Subscriber Line, commonly known as DSL is the most popular and ubiquitously available wireline medium which provides high-speed Internet access over the twisted pair telephone network. Fig. 10 shows a typical DSL network, which consists of copper lines extending all the way from the central office (CO) to the customer's premises. Current and future applications such as Interactive Personalized TV, high definition TV (HDTV) and video-on-demand through high-speed Internet access, will require more bandwidth. Researchers are exploring cost-effective ways to exploit the existing copper infrastructure to deliver greater bandwidth.

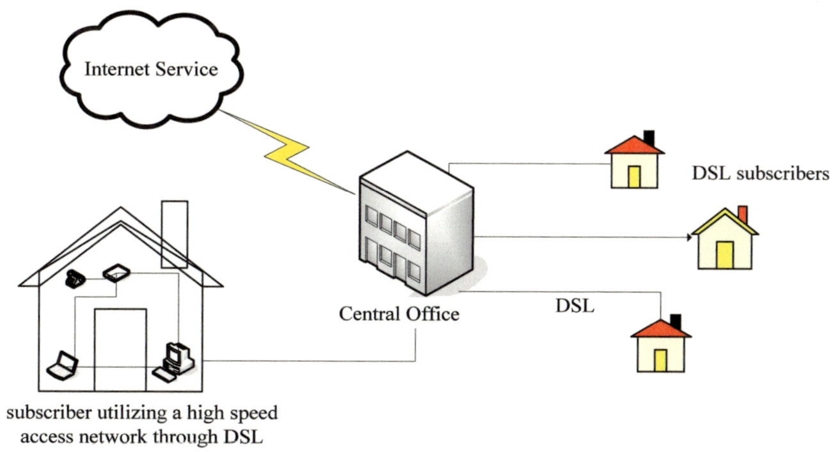

Fig. 10. A typical DSL network connecting subscribers to internet services through DSL to the Central Office.

Although the DSL channel offers the advantage of utilizing the already in place telephone lines to carry digital data, however there are different channel impairments that pose difficulties in achieving the objective of high-speed and reliable communication (Cook, et al.,1999). These channel impairments include different types of noise and interference. The noise sources include crosstalk, impulse noise and narrow band noise (Thomas Starr, et al., 2002). Also, interference in the communication signal may occur due to the electromagnetic conduction (EMC) in the unshielded twisted pair (UTP) and DSL operating in the vicinity of transmitters may pick up radio frequency interference (RFI) (Cook, et al.,1999). Moreover, signal reflection may be induced due to bridge tabs, unterminated lines and load mismatching in the telephone network. This leads to multipath signal propagation, due to ISI occurs (Bingham, 2000). BER deterioration, due to ISI is a significant problem in the communication systems utilizing the DSL channel. A typical telephone line frequency response and its impulse response are shown in Fig. 11 and Fig. 12 respectively. Multicarrier modulation is a possible solution to the ISI problem in DSL, which is already standardized in Asymmetric digital subscriber line (ADSL), in the form of DMT modulation, as G.DMT and G.lite ADSL.

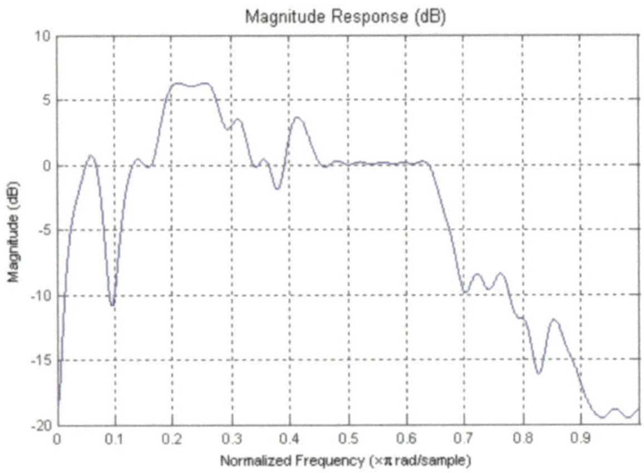

Fig. 11. Frequency response of telephone line FIR channel.

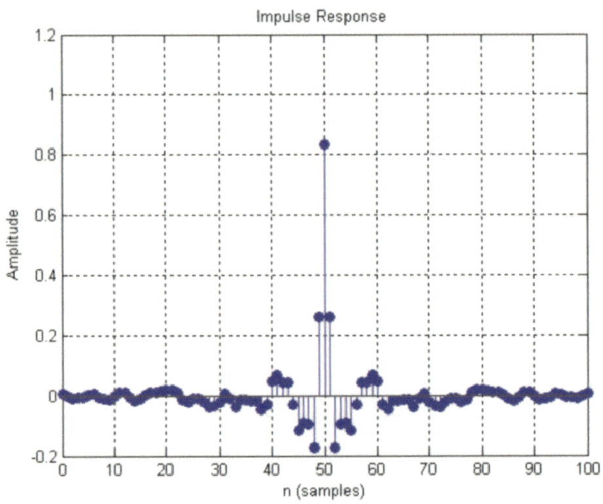

Fig. 12. DSL channel impulse response.

4.2.1 Crosstalk

In a telephone network, each subscriber is connected to the CO through a twisted pair, however, hundreds of such pairs are bound together in a cable. The twisting in the wires keeps the electromagnetic coupling between them to a minimum, however, when the pairs are numerous, all crosstalk between the pairs cannot be completely removed. Therefore, this crosstalk constitutes a dominant impairment, where DSL channel is concerned. The DSL crosstalk types, namely near end crosstalk (NEXT) and far-end crosstalk (FEXT) are illustrated in Fig. 13 (Thomas Starr, et al., 2002). NEXT is the crosstalk due to the neighboring transmitter on a different twisted pair line and its power increases with increase in frequency. FEXT is the noise detected by the receiver located at the far end of the cable from the transmitter. FEXT is typically less severe than NEXT, because FEXT is attenuated as the cable length increases.

In this chapter, the performance of DWMT transceiver is evaluated for the downstream ADSL channel. For this purpose, the NEXT and FEXT are modeled using the ADSL standard G.992.1/G.992.2(ITU-T, 2003).

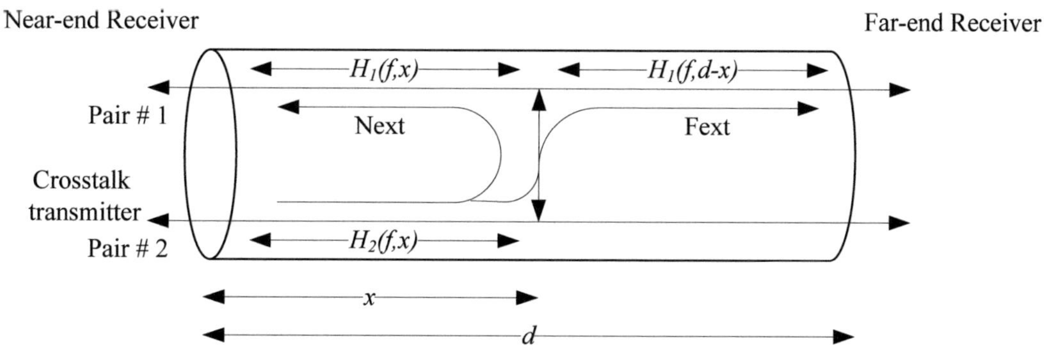

Fig. 13. NEXT and FEXT, the DSL crosstalks illustrated (Thomas Starr, et al., 2002).

The PSD of the ADSL transceiver disturbers for downstream is given by (ITU-T, 2003),

$$PSD_{ADSL,ds-Disturber} = K_{ADSL,ds} \times \frac{2}{f_o} \times \frac{\left[\sin\left(\pi \frac{f}{f_o}\right)\right]^2}{\left(\pi \frac{f}{f_o}\right)^2} \times \frac{1}{1+\left(\frac{f}{f_{HP3dB}}\right)^{12}} \times \frac{1}{1+\left(\frac{f_{HP3dB}}{f}\right)^{16}},$$

$$(0 \le f < \infty) \tag{9}$$

where f is in Hz and the remaining parameters are defined in Table 1. The PSD of the ADSL transceiver downstream NEXT is given by (ITU-T, 2003),

$$PSD_{ADSL,ds-NEXT} = PSD_{ADSL,ds-Disturber} \times \left[10^{-\frac{NPSL_n}{10}} \times f_{NXT}^{-1.5}\right] \times f^{1.5}, (0 \le f < \infty) \tag{10}$$

where f is in Hz and the remaining parameters are also given in Table 1. The PSD of the ADSL transceiver downstream FEXT is given by (ITU-T, 2003),

$$PSD_{ADSL,ds-FEXT} = PSD_{ADSL,ds-Disturber} \times \left|H_{channel}(f)\right|^2 \times \left[10^{-\frac{FPSL_n}{10}} \times d_{FXT}^{-1} \times d_{FXT}^{-2}\right] \times d \times f^2,$$

$$(0 \le f < \infty) \qquad (11)$$

where f is in Hz, and $H_{\text{channel}}(f)$ is the channel transfer function and the remaining parameters are given in Table 1.
PSD of disturbers and NEXT is shown in Fig. 14(a) and Fig. 14 (b) displays the FEXT PSD for downstream ADSL (ITU-T, 2003). The NEXT and FEXT for upstream can be computed in a similar manner (ITU-T, 2003).

Parameter	**WPT-DWMT**	**DFT-DMT**
Number of disturbers	24	24
f_{LP3dB}	fs/2	fs/2
f_{HP3dB}	138 kHz	138 kHz
K_{ADSL}	0.1104 watts	0.1104 watts
f_{NXT}	160 kHz	160 kHz
NPSL	47.0 dB	47.0 dB
f_{FXT}	160 kHz	160 kHz
d_{FXT}	1.0 km	1.0 km
FPSL	45.0 dB	45.0 dB

Table 1. NEXT & FEXT Simulation Parameters.

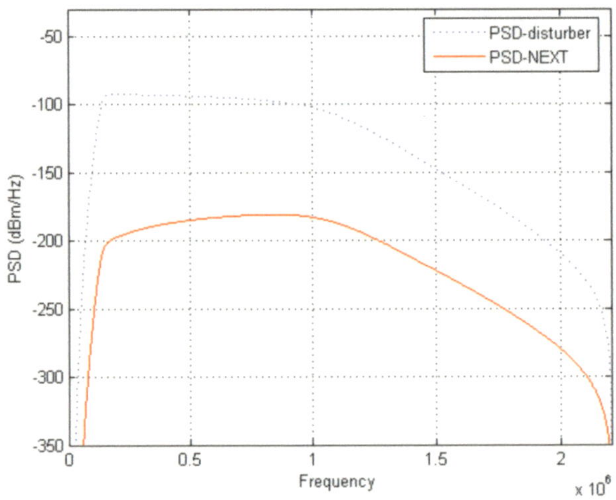

Fig. 14. (a) PSD-disturber & PSD-NEXT for downstream ADSL in G.992.1/G.992.2 standard.

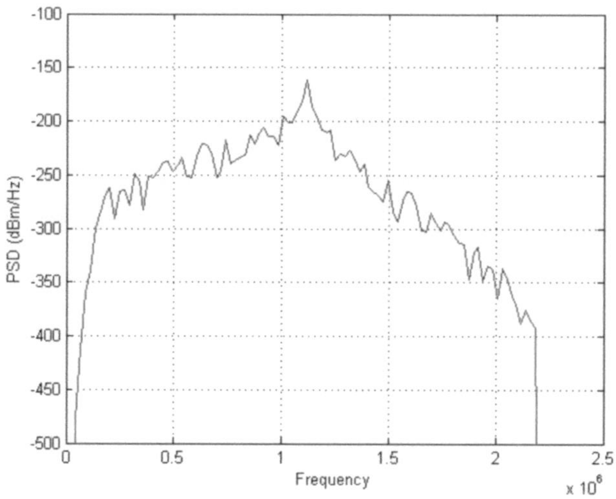

Fig. 14. (b) PSD-FEXT for downstream ADSL in G.992.1/G.992.2 standard.

The wavelet packet transform (WPT) transmultiplexer in the proposed DWMT transceiver gives perfect reconstruction of the transmitted signal, if ideal channel conditions are assumed. However, an actual channel like ADSL is far from ideal, and therefore requires some form of equalization to reliably retrieve the transmitted signal. Time domain equalization is proposed here for DWMT based transceiver for ADSL. There are some equalization techniques for ADSL proposed in literature (Acker et al., 2004);(SMÉKAL et al., 2003);(Trautmann and Fliege, 2002); (Yap and McCanny, 2002).

4.3 Time domain equalization

In order to equalize the signal after it has been dispersed by the ADSL channel, time domain equalization is proposed, and it is implemented through a linear transversal filter. The equalizer filter is a linear function of the channel length L, and the filter coefficients are optimized using the zero-forcing (ZF) and mean squared error (MSE) criterion (Farrukh et al., 2007); (Farrukh et al., 2009).

4.3.1 ZF finite length equalizer

In ZF algorithm it cancels out the channel effect completely by multiplying the received signal with the inverse of the channel impulse response, as shown in Fig. 15. With an infinite length equalizer filter, it is possible to force the system impulse response to zero at all sampling points (Proakis, 1995). However, since an infinite length filter is unrealizable. Therefore, a finite length filter is considered that approximates the infinite length filter (Proakis, 1995). The received signal $\mathbf{y}$ is the distorted version of the transmitted signal $\mathbf{x}$ after convolution with the channel $\mathbf{c}_h$ plus the channel noise $\mathbf{r}$. The received signal can be expressed in vector notation as,

$$\mathbf{y} = \mathbf{x}\mathbf{c}_h + \mathbf{r} \tag{12}$$

The equalizer output vector **z** can be found by convolving a set of a training sequence input samples **h** and equalizer tap weights **c** (Sklar, 2001),

$$\mathbf{z} = \mathbf{hc} \tag{13}$$

However, we continue with the assumption that channel state information is entirely known at the receiver. Therefore, a square matrix **h**, consisting of channel coefficients is formulated with the help of ZF criterion. The ZF algorithm defines that in order to minimize the peak ISI distortion by selecting the equalizer filter weights **c** such that the equalizer output is enforced to zero at sample points other than at the desired pulse. The weights are chosen such that (Sklar, 2001)

$$z(k) = \begin{cases} 1 & for\ k = 0 \\ 0 & for\ k = \pm1, \pm2, \ldots, N \end{cases} \tag{14}$$

The equalizing filter has *L=2N+1* taps. Equalizer filter coefficients are computed by (Sklar, 2001)

$$\boldsymbol{c} = \boldsymbol{h}^{-1}\boldsymbol{z} \tag{15}$$

The job of equalizing filter is to recover the transmitted signal $\hat{\mathbf{x}}$ from the received channel-distorted signal **y**, as follows,

$$\begin{aligned} \hat{\mathbf{x}} &= \mathbf{yc} \\ &= \mathbf{x}\mathbf{c}_{\mathrm{h}}\mathbf{c} + \mathbf{rc} \end{aligned} \tag{16}$$

where $\hat{\mathbf{x}}$ is the distorted received signal which was transmitted through ADSL channel and recovered after ZF equalization.

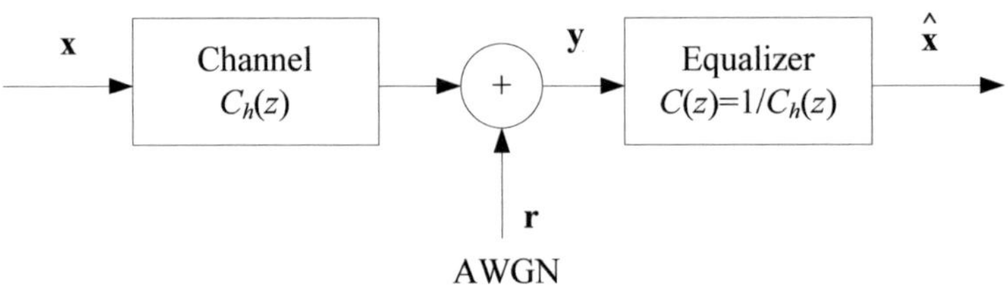

Fig. 15. A Linear transversal equalizer with coefficients optimized by Zero-Forcing criterion.

4.3.2 MMSE criterion

The MMSE criterion represents a more robust solution compared to the ZF since it considers the effect of additive channel noise (Proakis, 1995);(Sklar, 2001). The MMSE criterion of transversal equalizer filter coefficients optimizes the mean squared error of all the ISI terms plus the noise at the equalizer output. A set of over determined equations is formed, in order to derive a minimum MSE solution of the equalizer filter (Sklar, 2001). Therefore, for a *2N+1* tap filter, the matrix **h** will have dimensions of *4N+1* by *2N+1*. Multiplying Eq. (13) by $\mathbf{h}^T$ (Sklar, 2001),

$$\mathbf{h}^T\mathbf{z} = \mathbf{h}^T\mathbf{hc} \tag{17}$$

$$\mathbf{R_{hz}} = \mathbf{R_{hh}c} \tag{18}$$

where $\mathbf{R_{hz}}$ is the cross correlation matrix and $\mathbf{R_{hh}} = \mathbf{h^T h}$ is the autocorrelation matrix of the input noisy signal, which are used to determine the equalizer coefficients **c**,

$$\mathbf{c} = \mathbf{R_{hh}^{-1} R_{hz}} \tag{19}$$

For the MMSE solution of the equalizing filter, an over sampled non-square matrix **h** is formed which is transformed to a square autocorrelation matrix $\mathbf{R_{hh}}$, yielding the optimized filter coefficients.

4.4 Simulation results

An ADSL system is investigated which is based on DWPT transmultiplexer. The system utilizes M = 256 sub-channels and rate adaptive bit-loading algorithm is applied for bit allocation to each sub-channel in channel environment which is based on ADSL along with the crosstalk noise standards G.992.1/G.992.2 (ITU-T, 2003). For fair comparison, two systems are simulated, which are based on DWMT and DMT transceiver using time-domain equalization (TEQ) techniques for ADSL channel in the presence of AWGN and crosstalk noise. The channel is considered to be stationary during symbol duration. MatLab is used for all this simulation purpose and the parameters for simulation are specified in Table 2.

Parameter	WPT-DWMT	DFT-DMT
Data rate	1 Mbps	1 Mbps
Sampling Frequency	2.208 MHz	2.208 MHz
Modulation	*M*-QAM (2, 4, 8, 16, 32, 64)	*M*-QAM (2, 4, 8, 16, 32, 64)
Cyclic Prefix	None	20%
FFT size (N)	-	512
Wavelet-level	2	-
Number of bits/sub-channel	1 to 6	1 to 6

Table 2. DWMT & DMT System Simulation Parameters.

This corresponds to a system bandwidth of 2 MHz with data rate of 1 Mbps with discrete wavelet packet filter which is used for transmitter and receiver end. The channel equalization is performed by applying a linear equalizing filter in time-domain. The filter coefficients for equalization are optimized by ZF algorithm and MMSE criterion. The ADSL channel is simulated by an FIR filter of 100 taps.

The prototype filter for the synthesis and analysis part of the transmultiplexer is a discrete wavelet filter using 2-level wavelet packet. The input symbols $x_k(n)$ are M-QAM modulated. The equalizer frequency response of ZF equalizer FIR filter is shown in Fig. 16. Initially DWMT transceiver and DMT systems are compared regarding the bit error rate (BER) performance in AWGN channel, having identical time-domain zero-forcing channel equalization. Although, the conventional DMT system equalization is a combination of time-domain equalization (TEQ) and frequency-domain equalization (FEQ) techniques, in this case DMT is equalized with a time-domain Zero-Forcing for fair comparison between the two systems. The DWPT transform is applied utilizing Haar wavelet. Fig. 17 shows the comparative performance of two systems in the presence of AWGN without crosstalk. The

BER curve, shown in Fig. 17, presents the fact that the two systems give almost identical performance for lower SNR, and at higher SNR, the DWMT system exhibits an improvement of 1 dB in E_b/N_o over the DMT system for an AWGN channel, at a BER of 1E-6. It shows that both techniques using DMT and DWPT based ADSL without crosstalk perform identically except at higher SNR. In the next step, the simulation is performed according to the ADSL standard with crosstalk from G.992.1/G.992.2 (ITU-T, 2003).

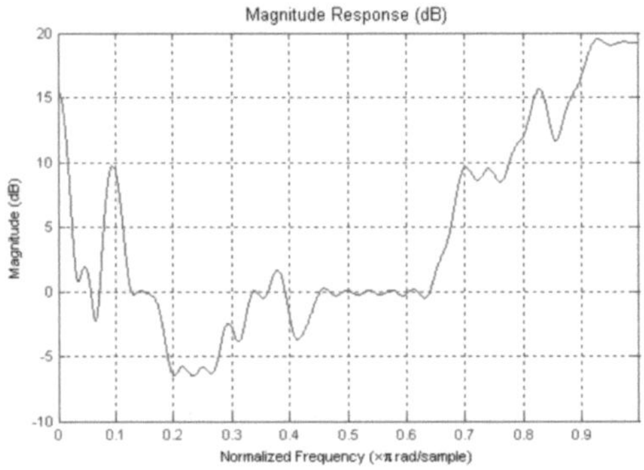

Fig. 16. Equalizing Zero-Forcing filter frequency response.

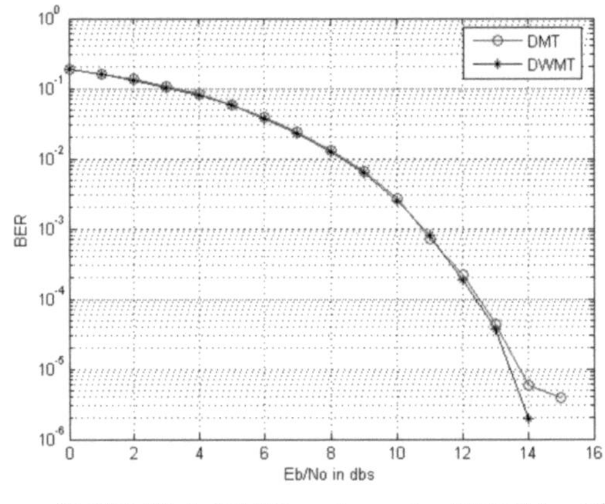

Fig. 17. BER Comparison of DWMT & DMT systems in AWGN with ZF Equalization techniques.

Fig. 18 shows the performance of DWMT and DMT systems in ADSL channel with AWGN, NEXT and FEXT (crosstalk), utilizing time-domain equalization (TEQ) techniques. The NEXT & FEXT represent the downstream crosstalk in ADSL channel according to the G.992.1/G.992.2 standard (ITU-T, 2003), with the simulation parameters as described in Table 1. DMT system is still equalized by ZF-TEQ, while the DWMT transceiver is equalized by ZF-TEQ, time-domain MMSE (MMSE-TEQ). The BER curves shown in Fig. 18 validate the fact that the wavelet packet transmultiplexer improves the performance of DWMT transceiver, having ZF-TEQ by E_b/N_o margin of 1.0 db for BER of 1E-4, over a DMT transceiver, having an identical equalizer. Moreover the MMSE-TEQ technique for DWMT system shows an improvement of 2 dBs in E_b/N_o over ZF-TEQ technique for DWMT and a 3 dB gain over the ZF-TEQ equalized DMT system, at a BER of 1E-4.

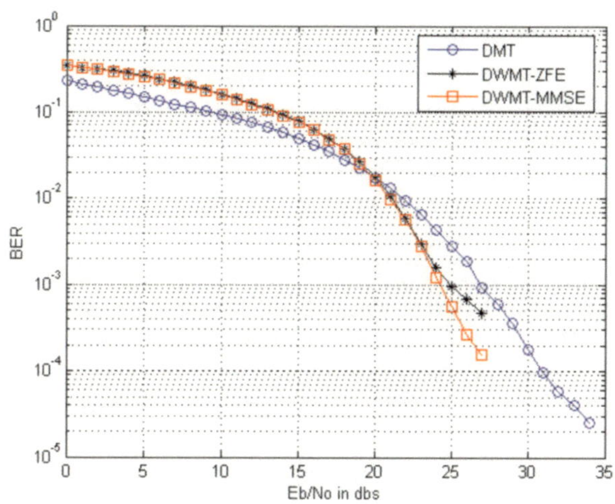

Fig. 18. BER Comparison of DWMT & DMT systems for ADSL channel with AWGN, NEXT & FEXT.

5. Pros & cons of applying DWT in multicarrier modulation techniques

DWMT modulation based transceiver, appears to be an interesting choice, when utilizing multi-carrier modulation techniques in wireline systems. It not only recommends the unique time-frequency localization advantage over the conventional frequency localized DMT systems, but also preserves precious bandwidth, which is wasted in DMT based systems in the form of cyclic prefix. However, when utilized in time dispersive channel like ADSL, DWMT transceiver cannot do without an equalization technique because of the time overlapped symbols. In this chapter DWMT based transceiver is discussed and its performance analyzed for the ADSL channel, in comparison with a conventional DMT modulation with ZF and MMSE algorithms using the time-domain equalization. DWMT system based on WPT performs well in the presence of AWGN and crosstalk in comparison with the DMT system for ADSL. ZF equalization algorithm does not consider noise, while the MMSE criterion of optimizing the equalizer coefficients takes into account the effect of channel noise. Therefore MMSE algorithm based DWMT transceiver gives better BER performance in comparison with ZF criterion, since ZF is known to enhance channel noise. The time-domain equalization is computationally complex in comparison to frequency domain equalization, however it offers improved bit error rate.

6. Conclusion

The multirate digital signal processing techniques, including wavelets and filter banks are part of new emerging technologies, which are finding applications in the field of digital communications. DWT based Multicarrier modulation techniques have opened new avenues for researchers, to avoid the spectral leakage and spectral inefficiency associated with Fourier Transform based MCM techniques. Time domain equalizers based on ZF and MMSE algorithms are utilized for DSL channel equalization in DWMT transceivers. MMSE based equalizers outperform the ZF equalizers in terms of BER. The equalization techniques adopted for DWMT transceiver is a topic of active research. Moreover, simulation results found in literature have shown that DWT based MCM systems exhibit higher immunity to narrowband interference (NBI). Therefore, WOFDM/DWMT can be considered as a viable alternative to spectrally inefficient OFDM/DMT, however at the cost of higher computational complexity of equalization.

7. References

Acker, K. V. , Leus, G. Moonen, M. van de Wiel, O. and Pollet, T. (2001). Per tone equalization for DMT-based systems, *IEEE Trans. on Communications*, vol. 49, no. 1, pp. 109-119.

Akansu, A.N.; Xueming Lin. (1998).A comparative performance evaluation of DMT (OFDM) and DWMT (DSBMT) based DSL communications systems for single and multitone interference. *Proceedings of IEEE International Conference onAcoustics, Speech and Signal Processing, 1998.*, vol.6, no., pp.3269-3272 vol.6, 12-15.

Alliance for Telecommunications Industry Solutions, (1995). American National Standard for Telecommunications - Network and Customer Installation Interfaces - Asymmetric Digital Subscriber Line (ADSL) Metallic Interface. ANSI T1.413 1995 ANSI. New York.

Jamin, A. Mähönen, P. (2005). Wavelet packet modulation for wireless communications, *Wireless Communications and Mobile Computing* 5 (2): pp. 123-137.

Baig, S. and Gohar, N. D. (April 2003). Discrete Multi-Tone Transceiver atthe Heart of PHY Layer of an In-Home Powerline Communication Local Area Network.*IEEE Communications Magazine*,pp. 48-53.

Baig, S. and Mughal, M.J. (2009). Multirate signal processing techniques for high-speed communication over power lines, *IEEE Communications Magazine,* vol.47, no.1, pp.70-76, January 2009

Bingham, J. C. (2000). *ADSL, VDSL, and Multicarrier Modulation*, Wiley & Sons.

Chow, P. S., Tu, J. C. and Cio, J. M. (1991). Performance Evaluation ofa Multichannel Transceiver System for ADSL and VHDSL Services.*IEEE Journal on Select. Areas in Commun.*, 9(6):909-919.

Cook, J.W.; Kirkby, R.H.; Booth, M.G.; Foster, K.T.; Clarke, D.E.A.; Young, G. (1999). The noise and crosstalk environment for ADSL and VDSL systems.*IEEE Communications Magazine*,vol.37, no.5, pp.73-78, May 1999.

Doux, C., V.; Lienard, J.; Conq, B.; Gallay, P.(2003). Efficient implementation of discrete wavelet multitone in DSL communications.*Video/Image Processing and Multimedia Communications, 2003. 4th EURASIP Conference focused on* , vol.1, no., pp. 393- 398.

Farrukh,F., Baig, S. and Mughal, M.J. (2007). Performance Comparison of DFT-OFDM and Wavelet-OFDM with Zero-Forcing Equalizer for FIR Channel Equalization, *Proc. of IEEE International Conference on Electrical Engineering*, LHR, Pakistan.

Farrukh,F., Baig, S. and Mughal, M.J. (2009). MMSE Equalization for Discrete Wavelet Packet Based OFDM, *Proc. of IEEEInternational Conference on Electrical Engineering, ICEE'09*, LHR, Pakistan.

Frederiksen, F.B. Prasad, R. (2002). An overview of OFDM and relatedtechniques towards development of future wireless multimedia communications.*Proceedingsof IEEE Radio and Wireless Conference, RAWCON*.pp. 19- 22.Aug. 11-14 Boston, Massachusetts, USA.

Fliege, N.J.(1994). *Multirate Digital Signal Processing-Multirate Systems-Filter Banks-Wavelets,* Wiley, New York.

H. S. D. (June 1988). The LOT: a link between block transform coding and multirate filter banks.*IEEE International Symposium on Circuits and Systems.* pp. 835–838.Espoo, Finland.

Hirosaki, B. (Jul 1981). An Orthogonally Multiplexed QAM System Using the Discrete Fourier Transform.*IEEE Transactions onCommunications,* Volume 29, Issue 7, pp. 982-989.

Karp, T. , Wolf, M. Trautmann, S. and Fliege, N. J. (2003). Zero-Forcing Frequency Domain Equalization for DMT Systems with Insufficient Guard Interval, *Proceedings of IEEE International Conference on Acoustics, Speech, and Signal Processing,* pp. IV221- IV224, Hong Kong, China.

Leke, A.and Cioffi, I. M. (1997). A Maximum Rate Loading Algorithm for Discrete Multitone Modulation System, *Proc. IEEE GLOBECOM '36.*London. U.K., "01.3.DD. 1514-18.

Lindsey, A. R. and Dill, J. C. (1995). Wavelet packet modulation: a generalized method for orthogonally multiplexed communications.*Proceedings of IEEE 27th Southeastern Symposium on System Theory,* pp. 392–396.March *1995.* Starkville,. Mississippi, USA.

Mallat, S. (1999) *A Wavelet Tour of Signal Processing,* 2nd ed. Academic Press New York.

Malvar, H. S. (1992). Extended lapped transforms: Properties, applications and fast algorithms.*IEEE Transactions on Signal Processing.* Vol. 40, no. 11, pp. 2703–2714.

Pollet, Thierry and Peeters, Miguel. (2000). Equalization for DMT-Based Broadband Modems, *IEEE Comm. Mag.*

Proakis, J. G. (1995). *Digital Communications,* 3rd edition, McGraw-Hill International Editions.

Qian, Shie, (2002). *Introduction to Time-Frequency and Wavelet Transforms,*1st Ed, Prentice Hall PTR.

Saltzberg, B. (Dec 1967). Performance of an Efficient Parallel Data Transmission System.*IEEE Transactions on Communications,* Volume 15, Issue 6, Page(s):805 – 81

Sandberg, S. D. and Tzannes, M. A. (1995).Overlapped discrete multitone modulation for high speed copper wire communications, *IEEE J. Select. Areas Commun.,* vol. 13, no. 9, pp. 1571--1585.

Sari, H. Karam, G. and Jeanclaude, I. (1995). Transmission techniquesfor digital terrestrial TV broadcasting.*IEEE Comms. Mag,*Vol. 33, pp. 100–109.

Sklar, B. (2001). *Digital Communications: Fundamentals and Applications,* 2nd Ed. Ch. 3, Englewood Cliffs, NJ: Prentice Hall.

Starr,T. Sorbara,M. Cioffi,J.M. Silverman,P.J. (2002). *DSL Advances,* Prentice Hall PTR.

Tzannes, M.A.; Tzannes, M.C.; Proakis, J.; Heller, P.N. (1994). DMT systems, DWMT systems and digital filter banks.*Proceedings of ICC '94,* pp. 311 - 315 Vol.1.New Orleans.

Van Acker K., Leus G., Moonen M., Pollet T., (2004). Improved initialization for time domain equalization in ADSL, Signal Processing, vol. 84, pp. 1895-1908.

Vaidyanathan, P.P.. (1993).*Multirate Systems and Filter Banks.* Prentice-Hall, Inc.UpperSaddle River, NJ.

Viholainen, A., J. Alhava, J. Helenius, J. Rinne, and M. Renfors, (1999).Equalization in filter bank based multicarrier systems, in *Proc. Int. Conf. on Electronics, Circuits and Systems,* Pafos, Cyprus, pp. 1467-1470.

Weinstein, S.; Ebert, P. (Oct 1971). Data Transmission by Frequency-Division Multiplexing Using the Discrete Fourier Transform. *IEEE Transactions on Communications,*Volume 19, Issue 5,Part 1, pp:628 - 634.

Yap, K.S. and J.V. McCanny, (2002). A mixed cost-function adaptive algorithm for ADSL time-domain equalization, *Proc. of the IEEE International Conference on Communication (ICC 2002),* Vol. 3, New York, pp. 1798-1802.

Yu, W. and Cioffi, J. M. (2001). On Constant Power Water-Filling, *IEEE ICC.*

2

A Scalable Architecture for Discrete Wavelet Transform on FPGA-Based System

Xun Zhang
Institut Superieur d'Electronique de Paris-ISEP
France

1. Introduction

In recent year, the Forward and Inverse Discrete Wavelet Transform (FDWT/IDWT) (S.Mallet, 1999) has been widely used as an alternative to the existing time-frequency representations such as DFT and DCT. It has become a powerful tool in many areas, such as image compression and analysis, texture discrimination, fractal analysis, pattern recognition and so on. The recent and future developments of high definition digital video and the diversity of the terminals had led to consider a multi-resolution codec. In this context, the FDWT/IDWT as well as the others computational functions such as Motion Estimation (ME) are required to be scalable and flexible to support rich multimedia applications and adapt to the fast changing of standards requirement. In this background, a universal, extremely scalable and flexible computational architecture which can adapt to variable workload would be more and more important and suitable for the multimedia application in the future.

In the literature, there have been several proposals devoted to the hardware implementation of FDWT/IDWT. Some proposals(M.A.Trenas et al., 2002) (et al, 2002) (Lee & Lim, 2006)(Ravasi, 2002)(P.Jamkhandi et al., 2000)(Tseng et al., 2003)addressed the importance of flexibility and proposed programmable DWT architectures based on two types: VLSI or FPGA architecture. The VLSI architectures have large limitations in terms of flexibility and scalability compared to the FPGA architectures. Even though some recent solutions proposed programmable and scalable for either variable wavelet filters(Olkkonen & T.Olkkonen, 2010) (Lee & Lim, 2006) or the structure of FDWT, they remind, in addition to their cost, dedicated to specifics algorithms and cannot be adapted to future solutions. In another hand, the existing FPGA architectural solutions are mainly ASIC like architectures and use external off-the-shelf memory components which represent a bottleneck for data access. The possibility of parallelizing the processing elements offered by FPGAs associated to a sequential access to data and bandwidth limitations do not enhance the overall computing throughput. The very powerful commercial VLIW digital signal processor obtains its performance thanks to a double data-path with a set of arithmetic and logic operators with a possibility of parallel executions and a wide execution pipeline. However, these performances are due to a high frequency working clock. Even though these DSP has a parallel but limited access to a set of instructions, the data memory access remains sequential. The performance requirement is paid by high circuit complex and power consumption. Most of work focuses on the reuse of devices likes FPGAs for different applications or different partitions of one applications.

In order to square up these needs, we propose a novel DWT architecture and implementation method. The proposed architecture can support multi-standard by reconfiguring the

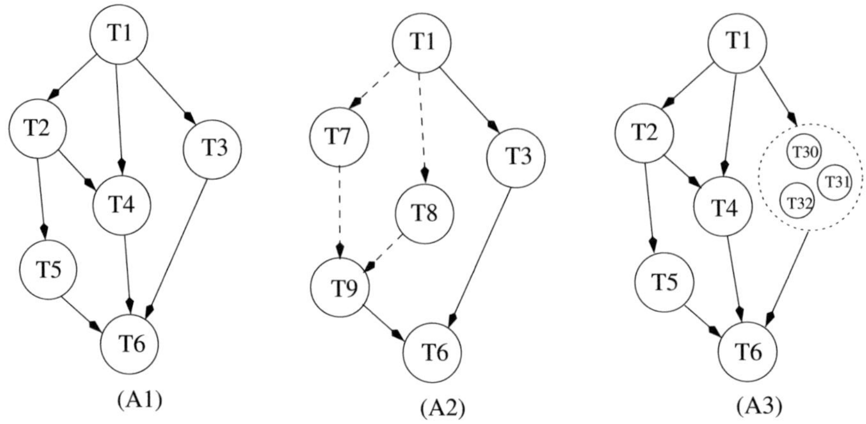

Fig. 1. Application adaptive configuration

interconnection between date memories and processing elements. Moreover, the number of processing element and its working frequency could be reconfigured dynamically. A controller plays a key role as a reconfigurable interface allowing multiple accesses to local memory, external memory through a DMA and feeding the processing element in an optimal fashion. An implementation method is developed to identify parallelism level of processing element and working frequency as well as to find out the tradeoff between power consumption and performance. In comparing with others VLSI and ASIC architecture, double size of memory can be economic in using our novel architecture.

In the following paper, we start, in Section2 by presenting a definition of adaptation in two manners: the application adaptive and task adaptive, within the system complexe context. We then give a brief overview of DWT algorithm in Section 3 where we detail a reconfigurable DWT hardware processor architecture. In order to experimentally explicit our proposed system, Section 4 focus on the detail of our proposed reconfigurable architecture which supports our DWT algorithm implementation. Section 5 focus on the implmentation, analysis and validation of system. Finally, Section 6 summarizes and concludes this work.

2. Levels of adaptation

In the multimedia computing environment, adaptation can be seen in two manners: the application adaptive and task adaptive. Following the adaptation of computing environement the different applications or different standard of one application can be switched in run-time. For example, the multimedia terminal switches it use from playing a movie to answering a video call. The task adaptive consists of the switching different versions of a task of an application, this situation can occur for instance in down scaling or up scaling situations.

2.1 Application adaptive

For a given domain, applications can be described by a set of processing tasks and sub tasks. The difference between the applications could be represented with common processing tasks and specific processing tasks. Figure 1-A2 shows an example of two applications A1 and A2 featuring common tasks (continuous lines) and specific tasks (dash lines). Switching from application A1 to application A2requires replacement of specific tasks and the communication between newly loaded tasks and common tasks. In some cases, the simultaneous execution of two applications is required. To achieve this, different versions of specific tasks must be available.

2.2 Task adaptive

Each task of an application commonly consists of a set of sub-tasks or a set of operators depending on the complexity of task as shown in figure1-A3. To enable task adaptivity, different versions of a task for a given algorithm must be defined and characterised in terms of power, area, throughput, efficiency and other objectives. For the same task, it must be also possible to change the type of algorithm in order to adapt the application to the future standards.

In this background, the adaptability of application helps us to configure partially one part of application for adapting to a new application. The task adaptive level permits us mainly to make a small change in the task to make the application adapt to different sceneries. In this paper, we focus on the task adaptive so as to realize muti DWT processing algorithms by using partial reconfiguration technique.

3. 2-D DWT processing algorithm

A survery of 2-D DWT architecture can be referenced in the paper Olkkonen & T.Olkkonen (2010). The two dimensional ($2D$) forward discrete wavelet transform (FDWT) is a rapid decomposition in the multimedia application domain. The FDWT is computed by successive low-pass and high-pass filtering. The output of each filter is decimated that is every second value is removed halving de length of the output S.Mallet (1999). The output of each filter stage is made of transform coefficients and each filter stage represents a level of transform. The low pass result is then transformed by the same process and this is repeated until the desired level is reached. In the Inverse discrete wavelet transform (IDWT), the approximation and detail coefficients at every level are up-sampled by two, passed through the low pass and high pass filters and then added. This process is continued through the same number of levels as in the decomposition process to obtain the original signal. In this paper we will focus on the implementation of IDWT, the same approach will be applied to FDWT.

3.1 Classical processing approach

The classical approach to $2D$ decoding is to process each layer in the tree decomposition separately and to process the vertical and horizontal layers successively one after the other. The performance of this approach is strongly limited by the management of temporary data required between two successive layers and between horizontal and vertical filtering. For a $2D$ image with N rows and N columns and L levels, the amount of data to be filtered on each layer increase (for IDWT) by a factor of four from one layer to the next, and the total amount of processed data along the whole tree reconstruction process is given by the following equation:

$$D = \sum_{i=1}^{L} \frac{N \times N}{4^{i-1}} = \frac{4^L - 1}{3 \times 4^{L-1}} \times N \times N \tag{1}$$

To process a $N \times N$ image, a temporal memory of size

$$D - N \times N = (\frac{4^L - 1}{3 \times 4^{L-1}}) \times N \times N \tag{2}$$

is required. As an example, for 2 level resolution a temporal memory of 0.25 $N \times N$ size is required. For a given layer, the filtering process is achieved horizontally and vertically; thus two read accesses and two writes accesses are necessary and the total amount of data read and written is expressed as $D_w = D_r = 2 \times D$. The memory bandwidth B, in bidirectional access case, can be considered as the production of the total amount of data processed for a frame per second (fps) $T_{df} = (D_r + D_w) \times fps$ and the number of bits N_b of a coefficient:

$$B = T_{df} \times N_b \tag{3}$$

As an example, for a gray level image of 512 × 512 pixels with 25 frame per second, 8 bits per pixel and 2 levels of reconstruction, a bandwidth of 260 Mb/s is required. These results illustrate the memory management problem as the main bottleneck of the classical approach.

3.2 Proposed processing approach

In order to reduce the memory size and to optimize the overall system performance, the wavelet algorithm is redesigned to exploit efficiently the inherent processing parallelism. This processing parallelism is possible if the required data is accessible in parallel, accordingly a data partitioning is used. The degree of parallelism and thus of the data partitioning will depend on the level of transformation, the number of levels and data dependency.
The proposed organization is shown in figure 2 depicting the memory fragmentation (2-a) and tasks allocation (2-b) on processing elements for two level IDWT. It is a compromise and intermediate solution between a massive parallelism and a sequential execution. The processing tasks are mainly filtering operations witch are organized and allocated to a processing element so that the among of data processed is the same. Indeed, if we consider a $W \times W$ bloc, an IDWT will be processed in three phases as shown in figure (3). In phase Φ_1 The processing element $PE1$ requires $2 \times \frac{W}{2} \times \frac{W}{2} = \frac{W \times W}{2}$ data accesses to reconstruct the LL bloc meanwhile the processing element $PE2$ can process vertically the $\frac{W \times W}{2}$ remaining data (HL and HH). In phase Φ_2, when the two processing elements terminate their executions, the LL bloc is reconstructed and the pressing element $PE2$ can resume its vertical executions on the $\frac{W \times W}{2}$ available data. In phase Φ_3, after the termination of $PE2$, data is available to process the horizontal pass on a bloc of $W \times W$data. Using $PE1$ and $PE2$ in parallel, the data processed by each PE is of $\frac{W \times W}{2}$. This architecture is scalable and can be extended to different levels of resolutions by an adequate choice of processing elements.

4. System overall architecture

With the down scaling technology, the modern chips can integrate a huge quatity of mixed grain hardware resources ranging from several hard microprocessors, hard arith- metic operators to hundred of thousand of simple gates allowing the integration of various soft cores. The prob- lem of resources management becomes then very acute especially in reconfigurable systems. In these systems, the management of reconfigurations is a very important part in the design phase due to the complexity of hardware reconfigurations and the reconfigurability needs of an aplication.
In the different proposed solutions, the two parts of reconfiguration that are reconfigurable capabilities of the hardware and the different reconfigurations possibilities of an application are not taken into account. A layered reconfiguration management approach through a hierarchical decomposition of a system will allow us to solve this problem.
The proposed adaptable architectue shown in figure 1- c, allowing the adaptation of differents applications and an application in different conditions, is organised as a set of clusters. Each cluster is designed to execute a sub-set of tasks. This clusters are parallelisable, so that the

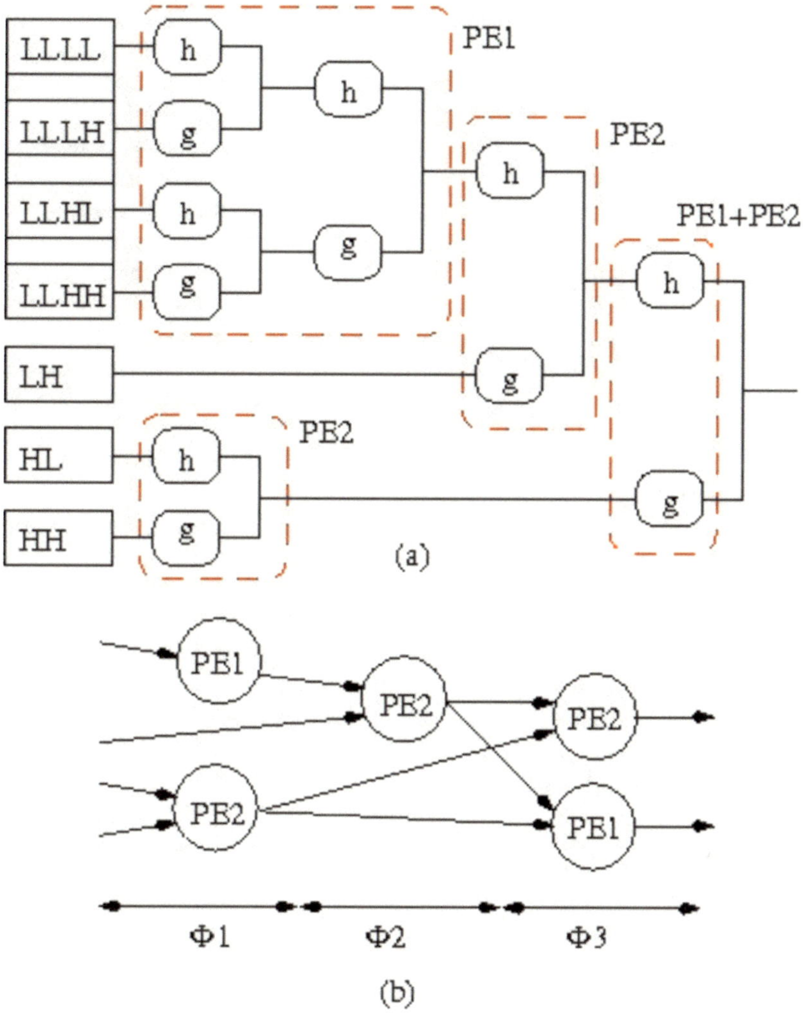

Fig. 2. Processing approach in 2*D* IDWT onto two-level(a); task allocation(b)

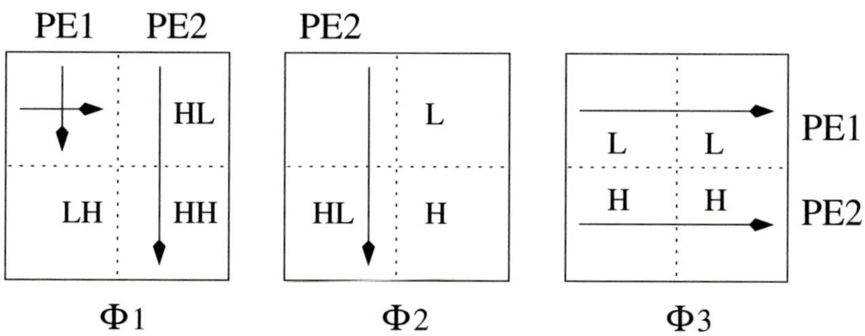

Fig. 3. 2-D IDWT Processing phases

same set of processing are performed on multiple data blocs. Each cluster is composed of an heterogeneous multiprocessor cores that allow software reuse, one or several Reconfigurable Processing Modules (RPU), a Reconfigurable Communication Module (RCM), and on chip memory. The RPM allows hardware acceleration and can be configured in a way that supports different versions of a task. The reconfigurable interface (RIF) is used to build the inter- connection between differents modules. Each RPM can be reconfigured at runtime.
Each cluster has a local configuration manager implemented in an on chip processor that controls the sequences of reconfigurations of the cluster. In this local configuration level, all clusters are configurable in parallel and independently. The reconfiguration process allocates dynamicaly to differents tasks of an application the adequate hard- ware ressources and optimal operation frequency and voltage. The presence of local configuration managers allows the acceleration of the adaptation process. To control the overall system, a global reconfiguration level is necessary. In this level, the necessary informations are managed in order to modify the global organisation of the system by configuring the communication between clusters and the elements of a cluster, allowing for instance to switch from an application to another.
The overall architectureM.Guarisco et al. (2007) is depicted in figure 4. Three memory blocks are present, while the first one and the last one repectively store original data image and deliver computed data, the second block feeds the processing elements. In addition to these three blocks, the system is composed of a reconfigurable processing unit two data organization units and control unit. This last one unit allows to connect the right memory to the right Unit at the right time. Once the memory bloc 1 is full (and as a consequence memory bloc 3 is empty, or at least, all his bytes are read or store in external memory), each memory datapath is switch allowing new picture datas to be treated. A new cycle begins, memory 3 is this time filled and datas in memory 1 are transforming.

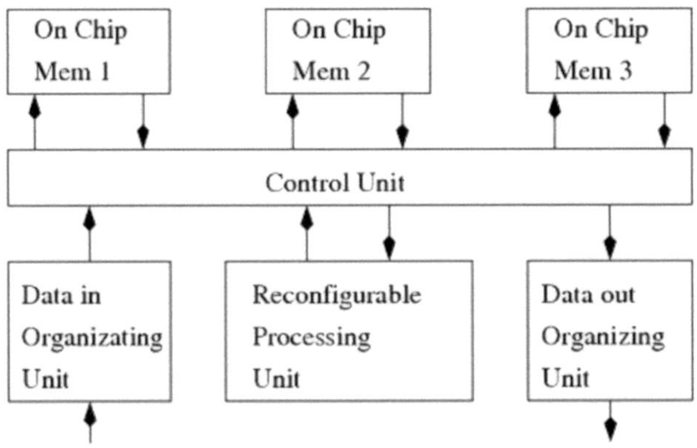

Fig. 4. Porposed DWT processing system architecture

4.1 RPU instance

The reconfigurable Processing Unit (RPU) allows the implementation of different types of wavelet filter. A filter (task) is a set of arithmetic and logic operators. A configuration of RPU consists of a type of filter or a version of a filter. For a given filter, corresponding operators can be connected by different ways in order to carry out different filter versions. These different

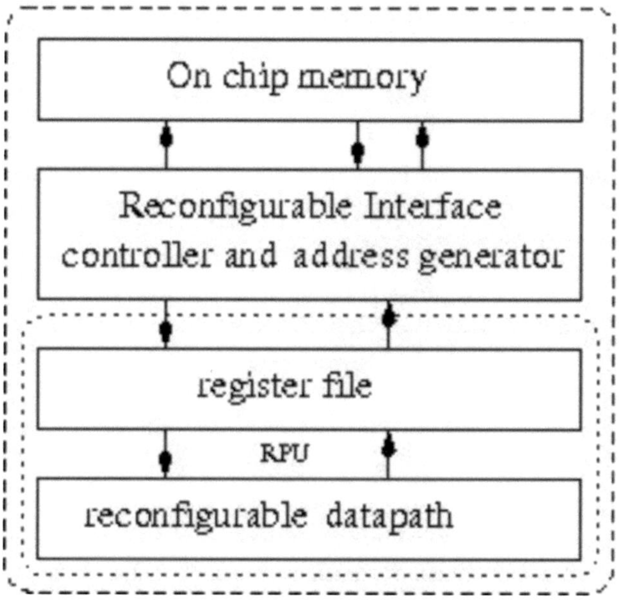

Fig. 5. General architecture of a RPU

versions can be parallel, in pipeline, sequential or an association of both methods. A possible architecture of the RPU and conction with reconfigurable interface is shown in the figure5 Chart1 lists number of computation operators needed (number of additioner, shifter, multiplier by filtering operation). We have choose two filters in order to illustrate adaptation at task level.

Filters	Additions	Shifts	Multiplications
5/3	5	2	0
2/6	5	2	0
SPB	7	4	1
9/7-M	8	2	1
2/10	7	2	2
5/11-C	10	3	0
5/11-A	10	3	0
6/14	10	3	1
SPC	8	4	2
13/7-T	10	2	2
13/7-C	10	2	2
9/7-F	12	4	4

Table 1. Different filter types of wavelet transform

Table 1 lists the number of main computational requirements (the number of additions, shifts, and multiplications per filtering operation). We choose two filters to illustrate the task adaptive level.

4.1.0.1 The 5/3 lifting based wavelet transform

The IDWT 5/3 lifting based wavelet transform has short filter length for both low-pass and high-pass filter. They are computed through following equations :

$$D[n] = S_0[n] - [1/4(D[n] + D[n-1]) + 1/2] \quad (4)$$

$$S[n] = D_0[n] + [1/2(S_0(n+1) + S_0[n])] \quad (5)$$

The equations for FDWT 5/3 are given bellow:

$$D[n] = D_0[n] - [1/2(S_0(n+1) + S_0[n])]] \quad (6)$$

$$S[n] = s_0[n] + [1/4(D[n] + D[n-1]) + 1/2] \quad (7)$$

$D[n]$ is the even term and $S[n]$ is the odd term. The corresponding data flow graph(DFG) is shown in figure 6. It is composed of two partitions: odd and even. Each partition is implemented in the corresponding data path of the RPU. The register file is used to hold intermediate computation results.

4.1.0.2 The $9/7 - F$ based FDWT

The 9/7-F FDWT is an efficient approach which is computed through following equations:

$$D_1[n] = D_0[n] + [\frac{203}{128}(-S_0[n+1] - S_0[n]) + 0.5] \quad (8)$$

$$S_1[n] = S_0[n] + [\frac{217}{4096}(-D_1[n] - D_1[n-1]) + 0.5] \quad (9)$$

$$D[n] = D_1[n] + [\frac{113}{128}(D_1[n+1] + D_1[n]) + 0.5] \quad (10)$$

$$S[n] = S_1[n] + [\frac{1817}{4096}(D_1[n] + D_1[n-1]) + 0.5] \quad (11)$$

There is similarities between equations of 5/3 filter and those of $9/7 - F$ filter which implies same similarities between the data flow graph of the two filters. It is clear that by duplicating the dataflow graph of filter 5/3 and inserting four multipliers we obtain the data flow graph of the 9/7 filter. Moreover, if we consider the table 1, we can see that by partially reconfiguring the 9/7 filter we can implement all the list of the table. The reconfiguration of 9/7 filter consists of suppressing or disconnecting unused operators and generation of an adequate control and an efficient data management.

4.2 Reconfigurable interface

The reconfigurable interface is the key element of Reconfigurable Prcessing Unit (RPU). One of its functionality is to connect together the RPU and control communication protocol between the RPU and internal memory. Th controler has to generate adresses for writing and reading operations in memory. A reconfigurable sequencer is used in order to manage the operation and communication sequence. The reconfigurable interface is composed of a three levels pipelined structure for calcul units apart from the one of the first level. Steps of pipeline are : reading (R), execution (E), and writing (W). In our bench test, two versions of interfaces holding different filters implementation are defined. The pipeline stages are :

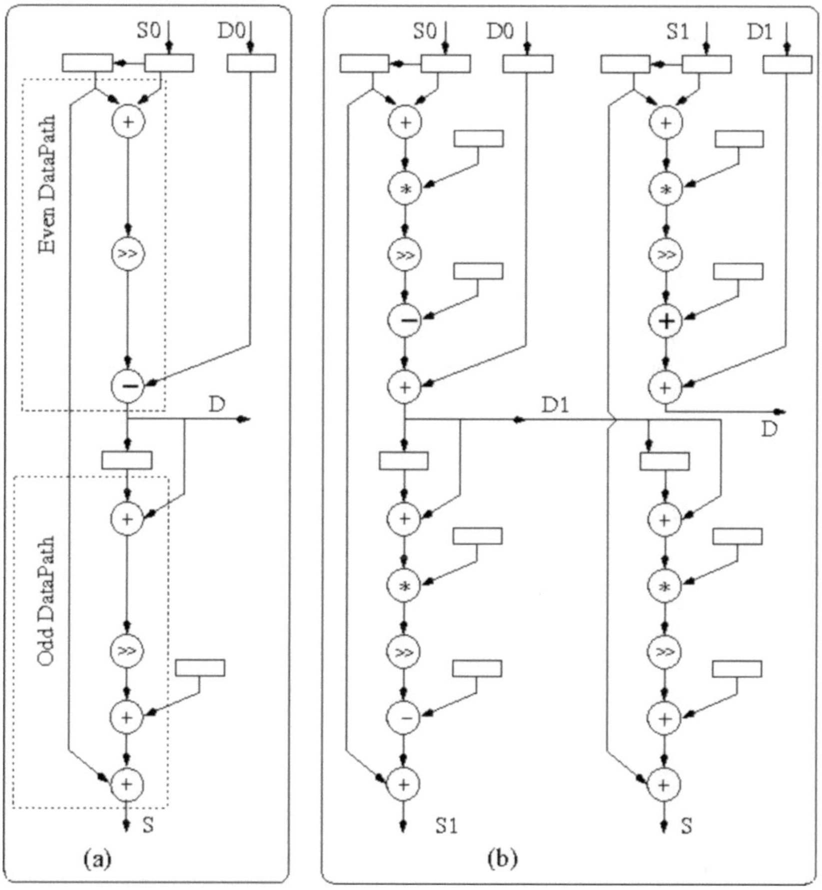

Fig. 6. IDWT 5/3 (a) and 9/7 DFG (b)

- Read (R): The source operands from the on chip memory are sent to the register file. The contro module gives an order to the reading file address generator integrated into the control module for reading the row or column resource from the memory module (SRAM) to the RPU at the address pointed to be by a read counter. Two data are read in one clock cycle.
- Execution (E): The data available in the regiter file is used bythe data-path to process in parallel the two parts of the filter. As the high pass filter part requires the previous result of low pass filter part, the execution is delayed by one clock cylce for high pass filter results. This operation is executed in one clock cycle.
- Writeback (W): The results of computation are written back to on chip memory at the address pointed to by a write counter.

The figure7 illustrates the operating mode of the three stages pipeline. Because of sequential acces to one memory bloc, the computations of the first level are performed as shown in (a) allowing the exection of three operations in one clock cycle. For the remaining porcessing, thanks to the parallel read, execute and write, six operations are executed in one clock cycle (b).

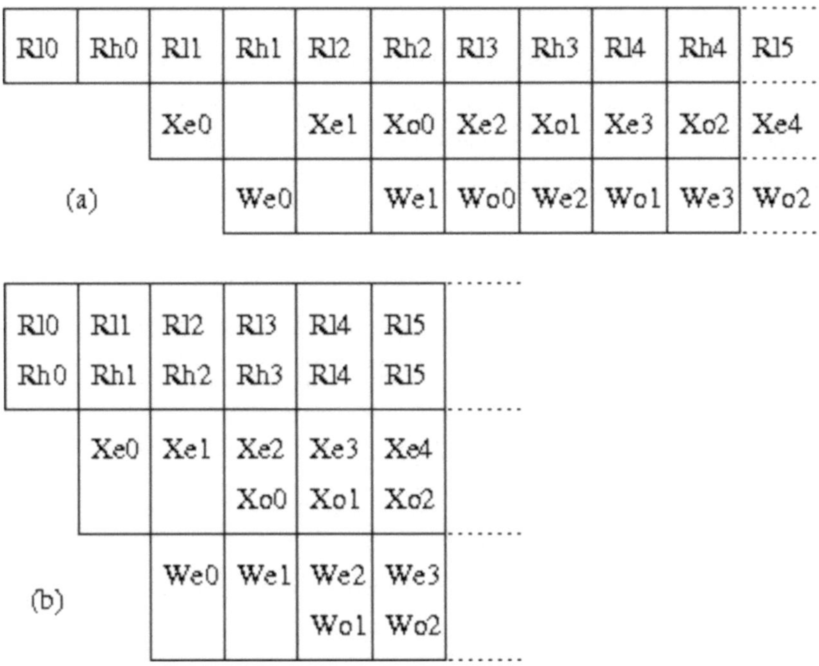

Fig. 7. Pipeline organization: special case (a) and normal case(b)

4.3 Memory access

Seemless memory is make up of several fixed size blocks. Each block is a dual port memory with simultaneous read-write access. Size of memory block correspond to image size in the first level of transformation in the case of the iDWT (inverse DWT). In our experimentation we choose an image of 32x32 pixels or bytes (we work on grey level pictures, that's why a pixel is constitued by one byte only). Because of this organisation, when the first level is proceded, the two data paths of the processing elements are sequentially feeded, that require two memory access cycles. However, for others, datas are read from (or ordered in) two different parallel memory blocks for one processing element in parallel.

4.4 Detailed operations

To explain the operating details of the system, consider an original 8x8 image as shown in figure 8-a. One of the task of this architecture is to rearrange the the pixels in the memory bloc. In order to benefit from the parallelism, Data organizing mudule arranges the pixels as shown in figure 8-b. So, due to the utilisation of memory bloc divided in four independent dual port memories, the processing controller can reach, for a given i, Si and Di which are normally two consecutive pixel in the image and those which we need to calculate at the same time the two coefficient of the DWT. If we want to calculate two new samples at each clock cycle, we have to reach two consecutive elements (Si and Di) at the same cycle.
So, in a first time, each processing element can calculate 1D-DWT in line. As we have two element, the system can compute two 1D-DWT in the same time. In a second time, the system computes the 1D-DWT, but now, in columns. Thus, we save a precious time and we can theoretically achieve an infinite number of levels. Let be T_{load}, the needed time to fill a memory bloc at the frequency of the data (it corresponds to the time of a complete reading or writing, pixel after pixel, of the whole memory bloc), we can say that the execution time of the first

S00	D00	S01	D01	S02	D02	S03	D03
S04	D04	S05	D05	S06	D06	S07	D07
S08	D08	S09	D09	S10	D10	S11	D11
S12	D12	S13	D13	S14	D14	S15	D15
S16	D16	S17	D17	S18	D18	S19	D19
S20	D20	S21	D21	S22	D22	S23	D23
S24	D24	S25	D25	S26	D26	S27	D27
S28	D28	S29	D29	S30	D30	S31	D31

S00	S01	S02	S03	D00	D01	D02	D03
S08	S09	S10	S11	D08	D09	D10	D11
S16	S17	S18	S19	D16	D17	D18	D19
S24	S25	S26	S27	D24	D25	D26	D27
S04	S05	S06	S07	D04	D05	D06	D07
S12	S13	S14	S15	D12	D13	D14	D15
S20	S21	S22	S23	D20	D21	D22	D23
S28	S29	S30	S31	D28	D29	D30	D31

Fig. 8. Original Image(a); Reorganized Image(b)

level is $\frac{T_{load}}{2}$ (we reach two pixels at one clock cycle, so, it divides by two T_{load}, we have two PE that divides again by two Tload but we have to achieve two time the 1D-DWT. Finally the execution time is of $\frac{T_{load}}{2}$). Moreover, we know that for the next level, we need only the low frequency coefficients which represent only a quarter of the total result of the previous level. The execution time is then the result of an arithmetic suite which is represented in equation 4.

$$T^n_{exec} = \sum i = 1^n \frac{1}{4^{i-1}} \frac{T_{load}}{2} \quad (12)$$

If the number of level tends towards infinite, the execution time is then of $\frac{2*T_{load}}{3}$. A data-out unit allows getting back the DWT coefficients in an ordered way. This controller can be easily modified to adapt the structure of the data flow to the system.

4.5 Target platform

In order to demonstrate the feasibility of the proposed FDWT/IDWT architecture, we have implemented a reconfigurable architecture IDWT targeting an FPGA Xilinx from the Virtex 4 family. The virtex-4 circuit hold partial reconfiguration. Partial reconfiguration of Xilinx FPGA's is achieved using partial configuration datas Inc. (2004). The target architecture, as shown as in the figure 9, is make up of static modules (PowerPC, ICAP, BRAM, PLB Bus) and reconfigurable units(the scalable RPU and hierarchic on-chip memory). ICAP is used to achieve the partial reconfiguration through the embeded processor PowerPC. The reconfiguration datas are stocked in BRAM memory of FPGA and are loaded via ICAP.

5. Implementation results

We have modeled the architecture in HDL in the sofware suite ISE from Xilinx. The simulation results agree with our theoretical waiting. Indeed, we can perform with this architecture a very high number of levels. According to the simulation results, we can run a working frequency of 67MHz. But as we use the internal memory of an FPGA, we are limited and we can reach an image size of only 128x128 pixels. The solution consists of a small modification of the data organizing units to allow the architecture to treat macro-bloc instead of a whole picture.

Figure10 illustrates the placement and routing of one RPU on Xilinx Virtex-4 FPGA. Three mains parts of system like: reconfigurable interface(middle bloc), four registre blocs and two datapaths of IDWT algorithm. The configuration file of each is independant, which is named

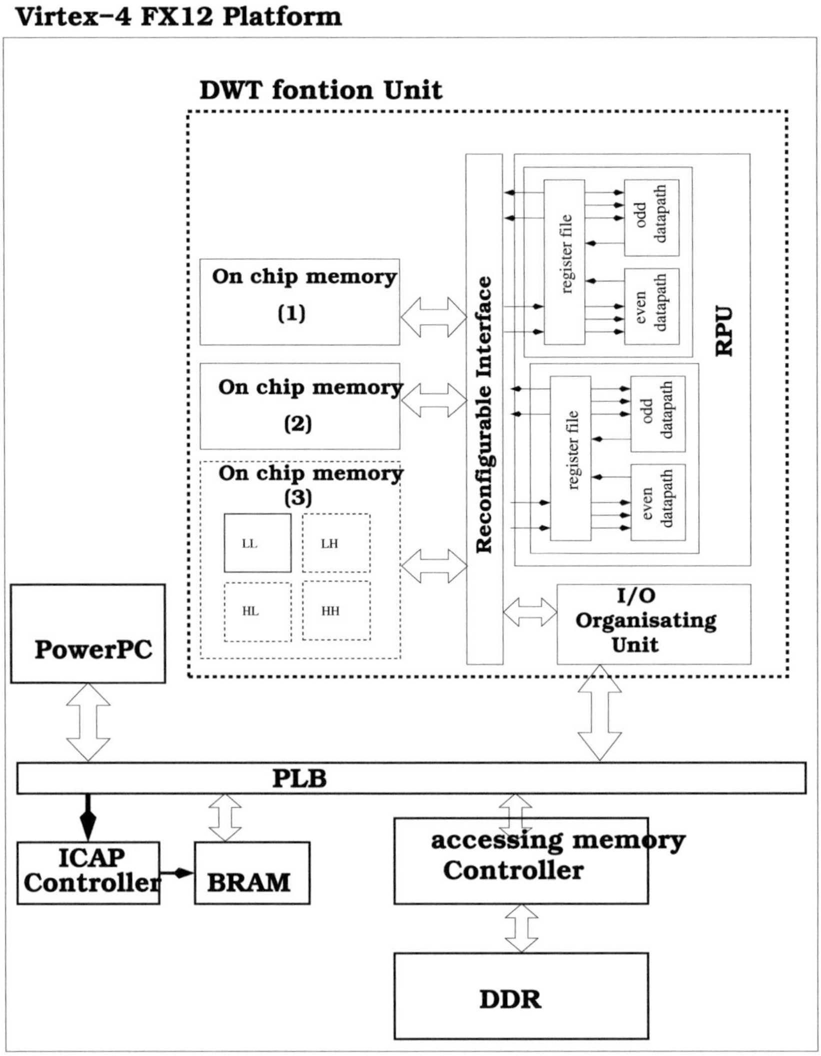

Fig. 9. Target architecture.

Partial bitstreams	RPU	bitstream size(Kbyte)	Reconfiguration time
		Ko	ms
	static part	582 Ko	21 sec (JTAG)
Partial bitstream 1	R_com_1	33Ko	0.57 ms
Partial bitstream 2	R_com_2	63Ko	0.67 ms
Partial bitstream 3	R_f_53	28Ko	0.26 ms
Partial bitstream 3	R_d_97	11Ko	0.16 ms

Table 2. Measured reconfiguration time of different bitstream files for 2-D IDWT.

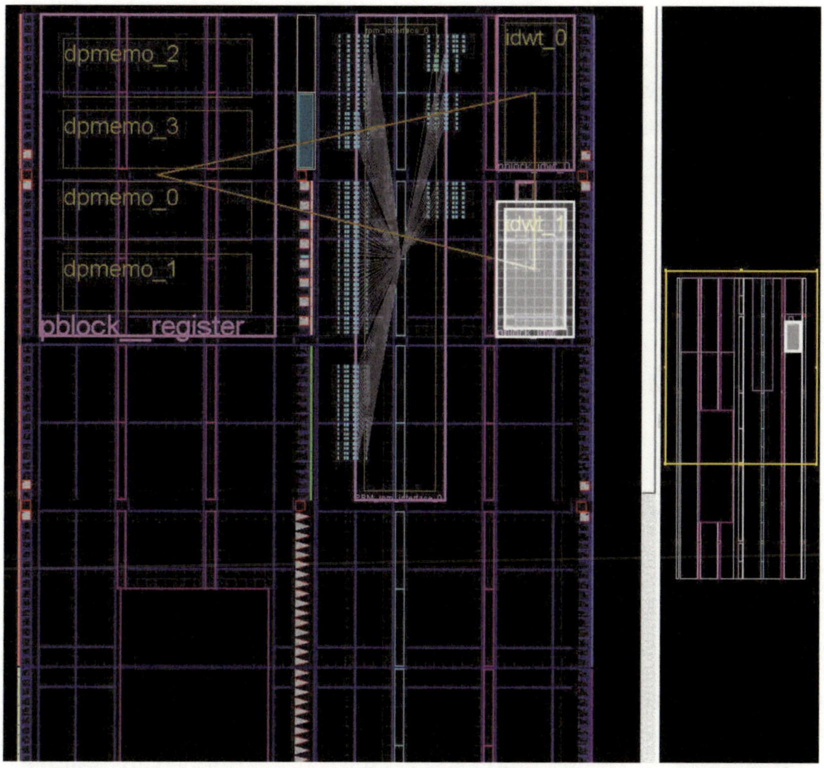

Fig. 10. placement and routing schema of DWT processing unit with Xilinx PlanAhead tool

as partial bitstreams. The different partial bitstreams are stored in the on chip BRAM. The static bitstream is loaded using cable. To measure the execution time of each partial bitstream, a free running hardware timer is used. The measurement results are in table 2. In this table, the mains modules are : the different part between filter 5/3 and 9/7 (R_d_97), 5/3 filter functional module (R_f_53), interface for 5/3 filter (R_com_1) and: communication interface for 9/7 filter (R_com_2).

The on chip PowerPC processor is used for autoconfiguration through HWICAP. As the PowerPC is an element of the system, it is used to detect external or internal events and accordingly loads automatically the adequate configuration to adapte the system to the given situation and then making the auto-adaptive. The HWICAP makes auto-configuration easier, in fact a C program on PowerPC allows the transfer of 512x32 bit blocks of the partial bitstream from the configuration memory to a fixed size buffer of the HWICAP peripheral, which the transfer from the buffer to the ICAP. The total reconfiguration time can approximated by the following equation:

$$T_{config} = T_{ICAP} + T_{BRAM} \tag{13}$$

Where T_{ICAP} is the time required to transfer configuration from the buffer to the ICAP, and T_{BRAM} is the time required to transfer data from configuration memory to the HWICAP buffer. Table 2 shows different parts of the system, the size of corresponding bitstream file and their configuration time. The system consists of a static part and reconfigurable parts ($Part_1$ and $Part_2$ are the two versions of reconfigurable communication allowing the switching between two filters, $Part_3$ corresponds to 5/3 filter, and $Part_4$ is the difference between 5/3 filter and 9/7 filter). The configuration time is measured using a free running counter (timer) incremented every system clock cycle, and capturing the start time and the end time. We see that the configuration time as expected depends linearly on the size of bitstream.

Type of architecture	Resolution	Area(mm2 for VLSI and ASIC)(CLB for FPGA)	Max frequency of operation(MHz)	Memory Requirement (KB)
Proposed architecture	32x32	153 CLBs	50	1.024
	64x64	538 CLBs	50	4.960
ASICs based(Tseng et al., 2003)	one image frame	8.796 mm2	50	2 memory frames
Zero-padding scheme (et al, 2002)	32x32	4.26mm2	50	6.99

Table 3. Implementation results

To compare the measured configuration time with the minimum possible value, the value for the reconfiguration of Virtex-4 FPGA could be obtained with this equation: $T_{config} = L/r$, where L is the length of the configuration and r is the transfer rate. As an example, for a file of 63KB size, and a clock frequency of 100 MHz as used in our experimentation, the minimum theoretical time is 0.63 ms, which is much less than 90 ms that as given in table 2. This is due to PowerPC that acts as the configuration manager in our system. Large part of time is spent to copy reconfiguration data from on chip or external memory to HWICAP buffer. The difference between the measured configuration time (0.97 ms) and the computed time (0.63 ms) is due to the imprecision of the measurement method. In fact, the capture of start and stop time is achieved using software, which tacks additional clock cycles. In table 2 we can see also that the main part of reconfiguration time is wasted for the transmission of reconfiguration files.
The reconfiguration time includes two part times: T_{bram}, the total load time for transferring the reconfiguration bitstreams from memory on chip to buffer of ICAP with package $512byte$. T_{icap}, the total configuration time through the ICAP port is grouped by the sum of configuration time for one package. Hence, the reconfiguration time is decided largely by the size of reconfiguration bit files and the number of reconfiguration bit files. The reconfiguration manager makes possible to reduce the reconfiguration time through hiding partial reconfiguration process in the execution process. It is obvious that the configuration time can be improved. A solution we are studying is based on a specific hardware reconfiguration manager capable to transfers the configuration data from on chip memory to ICAP.
Moreover, the chart 3 compare our approach with the other architecture. We observe primary two parameters based on different resolution of image. At the same working condition, the area of DWT computing module is variety according to the size of image(153CLBs for 32x32 and 538CLBs for 64x64) where including the adding of memory requirement(1,024KB for 32x32 and 4,960KB for 64x64). Thus the area of circuit can be used efficiently according to

the defnite size of image. The size of of memory requirment is scalable and thus the correcte size of memory can be configured dynamically to adapt to the requirement of bandwidth of memory. The other work shown in this table are based on ASIC(Tseng et al., 2003)and VLSI (et al, 2002). the area of circuit and the size of memory are fixed and thus the maximum size of memory must be previewered, which may lead to the urgent or surplus of memory access.
This proposed architecture features small area and low momory requirments. Processing time for a $32x32$ image blocks is $43s$ which is lower than others traditional design. Using a $64X64$ image blocks gives a good performance throughput which takes $86s$ for the transformation, for two-level 2D IDWT, which is capable to perform the image CCIR(720X576) format image signal at 50 $frame/s$.

6. Conclusion

In this book chapter, , we have described auto-adaptive and reconfigurable hybrid architecture for F/IDWT signal processing application. Two levels of auto adaptation are defined in order to minimize the reconfiguration overhead. The application adaptive level in which different applications of a domain are classified and characterized by a set of tasks. The task adaptive level in which for a given task, a set of versions are defined and characterized for use in a situation to adapt the application to different constraints like energy, and bandwidth requirement.
The proposed architecture is a universal, scalable and flexible featuring two levels of reconfiguration in order to enable the application adaptivity and task adaptivity. We demonstrated through the case study that it can be used for any types of filters, any size of image and any level of transformation. The memory is organized as a set of independent memory blocks. Each memory block is a reconfigurable module. The high scalability of the architecture is achieved through the flexibility and ease of choosing the number of memory blocks and processing elements to match the desired resolution. The on-chip memory is used not only to hold the source image, but also to store the temporary and final result. Hence, there is no need of temporal memory. The processor has no instructions and then no decoder, in fact, the hardware reconfigurable controller plays the role of a specific set of instructions and their sequencing. For a given set of tasks, a set of configurations are generated at compile time and loaded in run time by the configuration manager via configuration memory. The prototype has been tested on FPGA developpment cart of Xilinx with 65nm CMOS technology. The prototyping chip can be reconfigured to adapte 5/3 filter or 9/7 filter. In comparing with others ASIC architecture at the same working frequency, our proposed architecture requires less memory bloc and fewer hardware resource than the others.

7. References

et al, S. (2002). Vlsi implmentation of 2-d dwt/idwt cores using 9/7-tap filter banks based on the non-expansive symmetric extension scheme, *in* IEEE (ed.), *Proceedings of the 15th International Conference on VLSI Design*, number 435 in *ASP-DAC '02*, IEEE Computer Society, Washington, DC, USA.

Inc., X. (ed.) (2004). *Two flows for partial reconfiguration: module-based or different based*, Xilinx.

Lee, S.-W. & Lim, S.-C. (2006). Vlsi design of a wavelet processing core, *in* IEEE (ed.), *IEEE Transactions on Circuits and Systems for Video Technology*, Vol. 16.

M.A.Trenas, J.Lopez & E.L.Zapata (2002). A configurable arechitecture for the wavelet packet transform, *The journal of VLSI Signal Processing*, Vol. 32, pp. 151–163.

M.Guarisco, X.Zhang, H.Rabah & S.Weber (2007). An efficient implementation of scalable architecture for discrete wavelet transform on fpga, *in* IEEE (ed.), *6th IEEE Dallas Circuits and Systems workshop*, pp. 1–3.

Olkkonen, H. & T.Olkkonen, J. (2010). *Discrete Wavelet Transform Structures for VLSI Architecture Design*, intech, Hannu Olkkonen and Juuso T. Olkkonen (2010). Discrete Wavelet Transform Structures for VLSI Architecture Design, VLSI, Zhongfeng Wang (Ed.), ISBN: 978-953-307-049-0, InTech, Available from: http://www.intechopen.com/articles/show/title/discrete-wavelet-transform-structures-for-vlsi-architecture-design.

P.Jamkhandi, A.Mukherjee, K.Mukherjee & Franceschini, R. (2000). Parallel hardware/software architecture for computation of discret wavelet tranform using the recursive merge filtering algorithm, *Proceeding International Parallel Distrib. workshop*, pp. 250–256.

Ravasi, M. e. a. (2002). A scalable and programmable architecture for 2-d dwt decoding, *IEEE Transactions on Circuits and Systems for Video Technology*, Vol. 12, pp. 671–677.

S.Mallet (1999). A theory for multi-resolution signal decomposition: The wavelet representation, number 7, IEEE, pp. 674–693.

Tseng, P.-C., Huang, C.-T. & Chen, L.-G. (2003). Reconfigurable discrete wavelet transform architecture for advancedmultimedia, *in* IEEE (ed.), *Signal Processing Systems*, number 137-141.

3

VLSI Architectures of Lifting-Based Discrete Wavelet Transform

Sayed Ahmad Salehi and Rasoul Amirfattahi
Isfahan University of Technology, Department of Electrical and Computer Engineering, Digital Signal Processing Research Lab., Isfahan Iran

1. Introduction

The advantages of the wavelet transform over conventional transforms, such as the Fourier transform, are now well recognized. Because of its excellent locality in time-frequency domain, wavelet transform is remarkable and extensively used for signal analysis, compressing and denoising. Defining DWT by Mallat [1] provided possibility of its digitally hardware or software implementation. The discrete wavelet transform (DWT) performs a multiresolution signal analysis which has adjustable locality in both the space (time) and frequency domains [1]. Unlike the Fourier transform, the wavelet transform has many possible sets of basis functions. A trade-off can be made between the choice of basis functions and the complexity of the corresponding hardware implementations. Using finite impulse response (FIR) filters and then subsampling is the classical method for implementing the DWT. Due to the large amount of computations required, there have been many research efforts to develop new rapid algorithms [2]. In 1996, Sweldens presented a lifting scheme for a fast DWT, which can be easily implemented by hardware due to significantly reduced computations [3]. This method is entirely based on a spatial interpretation of the wavelet transform. Moreover, it provides the capability of producing new mother wavelets for the wavelet transform, based on space domain features. Due to recent advances in the technology, implementation of the DWT on field programmable gate array (FPGA) and digital signal processing (DSP) chips has been widely developed. As described in Sect. 3, in the lifting scheme the structural processing elements, including multipliers, are arranged serially; hence, the number of multipliers in each pipeline stage determines the clock speed of the structure. Based on [4], the main challenges in the hardware architectures for 1-D DWT are the processing speed and the number of multipliers, while for 2-D DWT it is the memory issue that dominates the hardware cost and the architectural complexity. The reason is the limitation of the on-chip memory and the power consumption [4,5].

2. DWT structures

The wavelet transform provides a time-frequency domain representation for the analysis of signals. Therefore, there are two main methods to produce and implement wavelet transforms. These methods are based on time domain or frequency domain features. The frequency based method is Filter Banks (FB) and the time based one is called Lifting Scheme (LS). We will describe them in following sections.

2.1 Filter banks structure

In the FB method, for one level of wavelet decomposition, the input signal is divided into two separate frequency parts by passing it simultaneously through a pair of low pass, $H(z)$, and high pass, $G(z)$, filters, as shown in Fig. 1. Then, subsampling the filter's output to produce the low pass and high pass outputs (s,d). Therefore, the FB method performs the DWT based on convolving filter taps and samples of the input signal. $H(z)$ and $G(z)$ can be written in this form:

$$H(z) = h_0 + h_1 z^{-1} + h_2 z^{-2} + ... + h_N z^{-N}$$
$$G(z) = g_0 + g_1 z^{-1} + g_2 z^{-2} + ... + g_M z^{-M}.$$

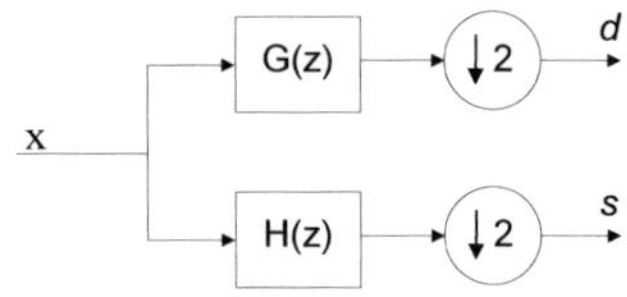

Fig. 1. *Filter Banks Block diagram*

As an example consider the CDF(2,2) wavelet. $H(z)$ and $G(z)$ for this transform are

$$H(z) = \frac{-1}{4\sqrt{2}}z^2 + \frac{1}{2\sqrt{2}}z + \frac{3}{2\sqrt{2}} + \frac{1}{2\sqrt{2}}z^{-1} + \frac{-1}{4\sqrt{2}}z^{-2}.$$

$$G(z) = \frac{-1}{2\sqrt{2}}z^2 + \frac{1}{\sqrt{2}}z + \frac{-1}{2\sqrt{2}}$$

The low pass filter has 5 taps and the high pass has 3 taps, so we call it 5/3 wavelet. Although FB structure is the prior one but it is only capable of providing wavelet transforms in the frequency domain and not in the time domain. Moreover, in general, the FB filter coefficients are not integer numbers; hence, they are not appropriate for hardware implementation. In addition, the number of arithmetic computations in the FB method is very large.

2.2 Lifting structure

The LS method is a new method for constructing and performing wavelets based on the time (space) domain [3].

As shown in Fig. 2, at first the LS structure splits the input signal samples into even and odd samples. Then P function is applied on even samples as a prediction function. The word prediction is used here because P function predicts odd samples using even samples.The difference between this prediction and the actual value of odd sample, creates the high frequency part of the signal which is called "detail" coefficients (d). Then applying the U function on detail signal and combining the result with even samples update them so that the output coefficients (s) have the desired properties. Usually the desired properties of s is the same as the properties of input signal (x) but with half size. So the s signal is an approximation for x and is called approximation coefficient.

Note that the details and approximation coefficients (d,s) in lifting scheme, respectively, are the same as high pass and low pass outputs in FB.

Based on the above description we have

$$d = x_{odd} - P(x_{even}),$$

for prediction block and

$$s = x_{even} + U(d)$$

for update block.
Equations for P and U functions are determined based on the implemented wavelet, also the number and arrangement of P and U blocks in the lifting structure are different for various types of wavelets.

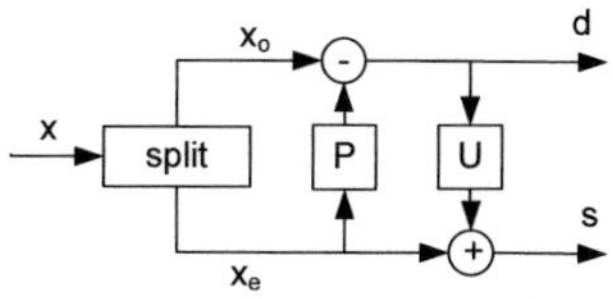

Fig. 2. Block diagram of a lifting stage

We can write matrix equations for P and U blocks respectively as following:

$$\begin{bmatrix} x_{even}(z) \\ d(z) \end{bmatrix} = \underbrace{\begin{bmatrix} 1 & 0 \\ t(z) & 1 \end{bmatrix}}_{P} \begin{bmatrix} x_{even}(z) \\ x_{odd}(z) \end{bmatrix}$$

$$\begin{bmatrix} s(z) \\ d(z) \end{bmatrix} = \underbrace{\begin{bmatrix} 1 & s(z) \\ 0 & 1 \end{bmatrix}}_{U} \begin{bmatrix} x_{even}(z) \\ d(z) \end{bmatrix}.$$

Generally speaking, if we have more than one lifting step, the matrix equation is(3):

$$\begin{bmatrix} s(z) \\ d(z) \end{bmatrix} = \begin{bmatrix} k & 0 \\ 0 & 1/k \end{bmatrix} \prod_{i=1}^{m} \begin{bmatrix} 1 & s_i(z) \\ 0 & 1 \end{bmatrix} \begin{bmatrix} 1 & 0 \\ t_i(z) & 1 \end{bmatrix} \begin{bmatrix} x_{even}(z) \\ x_{odd}(z) \end{bmatrix} \tag{1}$$

In (1), k and $1/k$ are normalization factors. The last matrix is used only for normalization and may be omitted in many applications such as compression. The relation between FB coefficients and LS equations is (3):

$$E(z) = \begin{bmatrix} h_e(z) & h_o(z) \\ g_e(z) & g_o(z) \end{bmatrix} = \begin{bmatrix} k & 0 \\ 0 & 1/k \end{bmatrix} \prod_{i=1}^{m} \begin{bmatrix} 1 & s_i(z) \\ 0 & 1 \end{bmatrix} \begin{bmatrix} 1 & 0 \\ t_i(z) & 1 \end{bmatrix}$$

Matrix $E(z)$ is called a polyphase matrix, where according to the FB structure, h_e and h_o are even and odd taps of the low pass filter and g_e and g_o are even and odd taps of the high pass filter, respectively. $s_i(z)$ and $t_i(z)$ are related to filter coefficients in FB structure. In other words $s_i(z)$ and $t_i(z)$ can be obtained from FB by factorization algorithm presented in [5].
Example: Let consider the previous example, 5/3 wavelet, in LS. This wavelet consist of one lifting step (one P unit and one U unit together is a lifting step). For this wavelet the prediction of each odd sample in signal is the average of two adjacent even samples. Then P block calculates the difference between the real value of signal sample and its prediction:

$$d(n) = x(2n+1) - \frac{1}{2}[x(2n) + x(2n+2)].$$

U block updates even samples to have the same property as the original signal. It uses two most recently computed differences for update procedure:

$$s(n) = x(2n) + \frac{1}{4}(d(n-1) + d(n)).$$

So the matrix equation for 5/3 wavelet is

$$\begin{bmatrix} s(z) \\ d(z) \end{bmatrix} = \underbrace{\begin{bmatrix} \sqrt{2} & 0 \\ 0 & \frac{1}{\sqrt{2}} \end{bmatrix} \begin{bmatrix} 1 & \frac{1}{4}(1+z^{-1}) \\ 0 & 1 \end{bmatrix} \begin{bmatrix} 1 & 0 \\ \frac{-1}{2}(1+z) & 1 \end{bmatrix}}_{\text{E(z)}} \begin{bmatrix} x_{even}(z) \\ x_{odd}(z) \end{bmatrix}$$

and the polyphase matrix is

$$E(z) = \begin{bmatrix} \frac{-1}{4\sqrt{2}} z^{-1} + \frac{3}{2\sqrt{2}} - \frac{1}{4\sqrt{2}} z & \frac{1}{2\sqrt{2}} z^{-1} + \frac{1}{2\sqrt{2}} \\ \frac{-1}{2\sqrt{2}} - \frac{1}{2\sqrt{2}} z & \frac{1}{\sqrt{2}} \end{bmatrix}.$$

We propose the following lemma for using in hardware implementation of LS as will be describe in section 3.1.

Lemma1: Factorization can be done so that $s_i(z)$ and $t_i(z)$ are first-order or lower-order polynomials.

Proof sketch: After a polyphase matrix representing a wavelet transform with finite filters is factored into lifting steps, each step becomes a Laurent polynomial. Since the difference between the degrees of the even and odd parts of a polynomial is never greater than 2, it is always possible to find the common divisor of the first-order or lower-order polynomials. Also, the lifting factorization process is non-unique and so there is freedom in the form of factorization. Hence, a classical wavelet filter can always be factored into first-order or lower-order Laurent polynomials (i.e., $s_i(z)$ or $t_i(z)$).□

Compared to the FB method, the LS method has many advantages [6,7]. The most important one is the number of arithmetic computations. In the LS method, the number of arithmetic operations, additions and multiplications, is nearly one-half of that of the FB, which is why the LS structure is more efficient. Even the amount of computations in some types of DWT can be reduced to a quarter of that needed for FB [8]. Furthermore the LS structure has the advantage of implementing the Integer Wavelet Transform (IWT) efficiently. IWT is a wavelet-like transform in which all of the decomposition coefficients are integer [9]. The IWT is appropriate for hardware implementation of the DWT [10]. The practical advantages of using the lifting-based IWT have been described in [11]. Moreover, by using the LS, it is easy to implement the DWT in a fully in-place method, which is memory efficient [2,12].

Regarding the above explanation, the LS structure is used to implement 5/3 and 9/7 wavelets, which are used, respectively, for lossless and lossy compression in the JPEG 2000 standard.

3. 1-DDWT

In this section, some types of lifting-based DWT processing elements and 1-D structures are explained.

3.1 Basic functional units for lifting scheme

As pointed out in Lema1, factorization can be done so that si(z) and ti(z) are first order or lower-order polynomials. Figure 3 shows three possible categories of the basic processing unit and the related polynomials in such a factorization. Different kinds of lifting-based DWT architectures can be constructed by combining the three basic lifting elements. Most of the applicable DWTs like 9/7 and 5/3 wavelets consist of processing units, as shown in Fig. 3(a), which is simplified as Fig. 4. This unit is called the processing element (PE). In Fig. 4, A, B and C are input samples which arrive successively. To implement the P unit, A and C receive

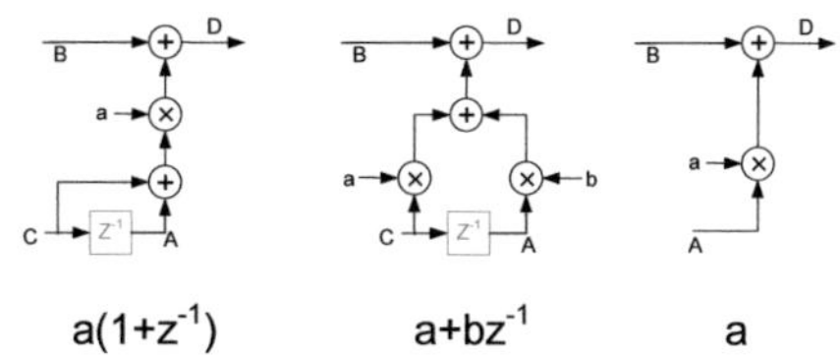

Fig. 3. Basic functional units for LS

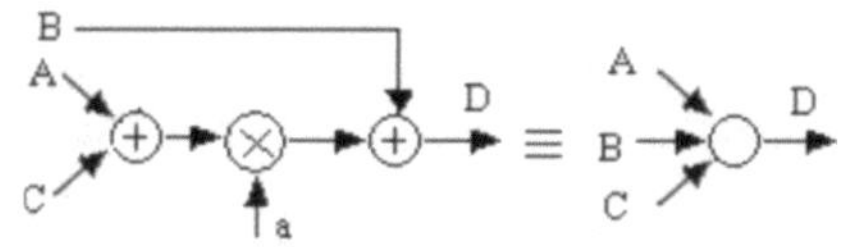

Fig. 4. Most convenient basic PE for LS

even samples while B receives odd samples. On the other hand, for the U unit, A and C are odd samples and B receives even samples. Now, the structure of Fig. 4 can be used to implement 5/3 and 9/7 wavelets. For instance, Fig. 5 and Fig. 6 shows the architecture of the 5/3 and 9/7 wavelets respectively, where each white circle represents a PE. In Fig. 6, the

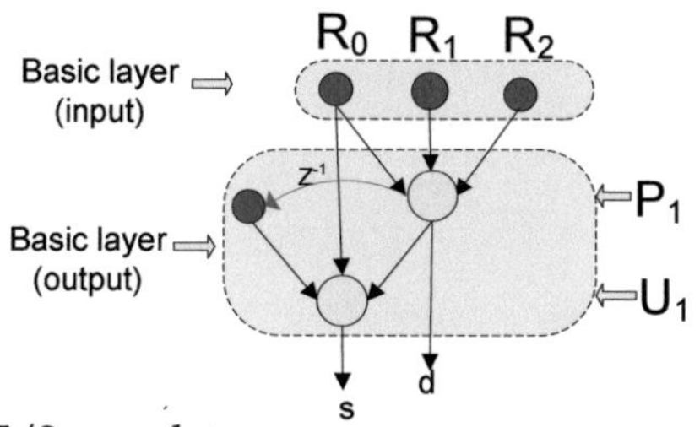

Fig. 5. Lifting Structure for 5/3 wavelet

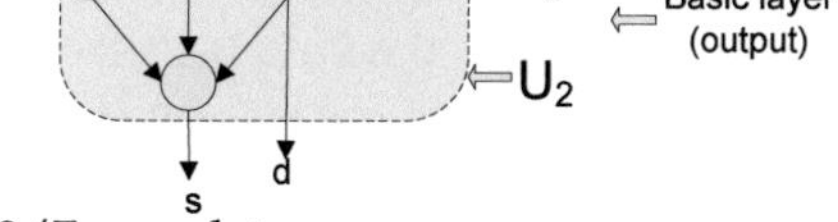

Fig. 6. Lifting Structure for 9/7 wavelet

input and output layers are essential (basic) layers and are fixed for each wavelet type, while by changing the number of extended layers, the type of wavelet can be changed accordingly. For example, omission of a single extended (added) layer in Fig. 6 will change the related architecture from 9/7 type to 5/3 type. The black circles in Fig. 6 represent needed stored data for computing outputs (*s*,*d*). R_0, R_1 and R_2, are registers that get their values from new input samples and are called data memory. The other three black circles which store the results of previous computations are known as temporary memory. The number of data memory registers is constant and is equal to 3, while the number of temporary memory registers is $(2e + 1)$, where e is the number of extended layers [13]. This structure can be implemented by using combinatorial circuits so that, when the input samples are fed to the architecture, outputs are ready to be used after a delay time. Also, the implementation of the structure can be performed via a pipelined structure by adding some registers. The number of pipeline stages depends on the added registers. Increasing the pipeline stages results in increases in the clock frequency, system latency and number of required registers [4]. Note that 2-D DWT architectures are constructed from 1-D DWT units as row-wise and column-wise DWT units. The data of a complete row is saved for each memory in a column-wise unit. So, the sum of the data and temporary memories in the column-wise DWT unit determines the amount of needed internal memory [14,15,16]. The pipeline registers do not affect the required internal memory [17].

3.2 1-D DWT structures

By combining the functional units described in previous section we can construct 1 dimensional DWT. The architectures presented in Fig. 7 can be applied to implement the lifting-based 1-D DWT. The structure shown in Fig. 7(a) processes all input samples concurrently, in parallel form. In Fig. 7(b), input samples arrive in pairs at consecutive clock pulses and the results for each pair are ready after five cycles. However, due to the pipelined structure, the clock frequency of Fig. 7(b) is higher than that of Fig. 7(a). There is a trade-off between the clock speed and the number of pipeline stages.

4. Hardware architectures

4.1 Simple hardware implementation

Figure 7 shows an architecture proposed in [18] for the 9/7 wavelet. Indeed, it is the hardware Implementation of Fig. 6. Accordingly, the architecture presented in Fig. 9 can be used for the 5/3 wavelet.

4.2 Minimizing hardware architectures

In the structure of Fig. 8, there are two similar cascaded blocks which are different only in the multiplier's coefficients. According to [19], one of the similar blocks may be omitted as shown in Fig. 10. Note that in Figs. 7 and 8, the delay unit represented by z^{-1} is implemented by one register, while in Fig. 10 each delay unit contains two consecutive registers. Investigation on the architecture depicted in Fig. 10 shows that this hardware contains one P and one U unit. Note that, as mentioned in Sect. 2, both the P and U units can be implemented with the functional unit depicted in Fig. 4. Therefore, the structure shown in Fig. 10 is implemented by two similar sections which can be reduced to one section. The resulting architecture for the 9/7 wavelet is shown in Fig. 11. In this structure, U1(0) represents the current output of the U1 unit and P1(-1) represents the previous output of the P1 unit, and so on. The control signal, "S", which has four states, selects the inputs of the multiplexers sequentially. In the first state, two consecutive input samples arrive and the P1 function with α coefficient is performed on them. In the second state, the U1 function with β coefficient will be imposed on the result of the previous state (first state's output). Similarly, in the third and fourth states, computations for P2 and U2 units will be performed on the results of the previous states. Thus, P2 and U2 produce final outputs for the structure. The data flow for achieving a pair of wavelet coefficients using the proposed structure is shown in Table 1.

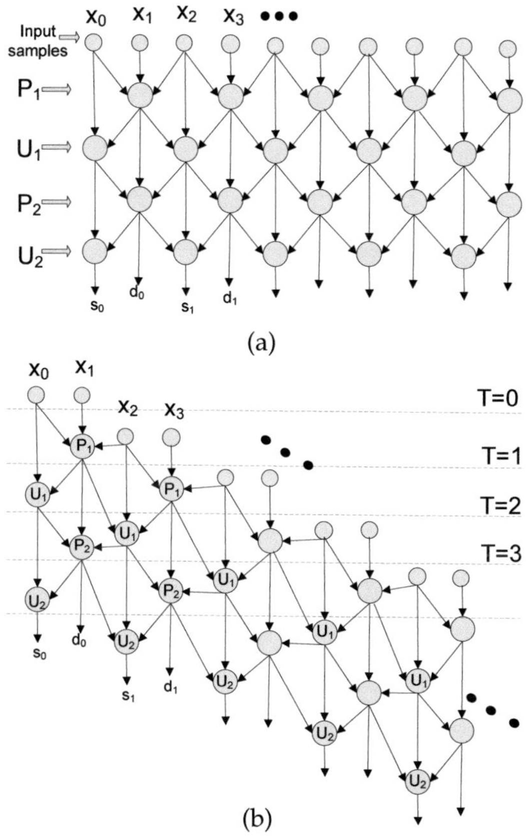

Fig. 7. 1-D DWT structures based on lifting a)parallel architecture b) sequential-pipelined architecture

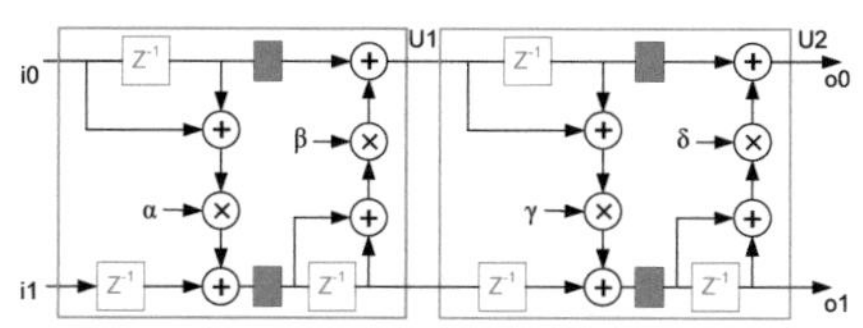

Fig. 8. Lifting-based hardware architecture for 9/7 wavelet

S	in1	in2	out	F(factor)
0	i1	i0	P_1	α
1	i0(-1)	P_1	U_1	β
2	$P_1(-1)$	U_2	P_2	γ
3	$U_1(-1)$	P_2	U_2	ζ

Table 1. Time sequence for structure of Fig. 11

The calculation of consecutive wavelet coefficients is periodic and continuous; therefore, the sequence of control signal "S" for data flow can be easily generated by a simple logic circuit. Figure 11 shows the hardware architecture for Fig. 11. The 5/3 wavelet implementation of the proposed architecture is depicted in Fig. 13. It is clear that only the number of coefficients

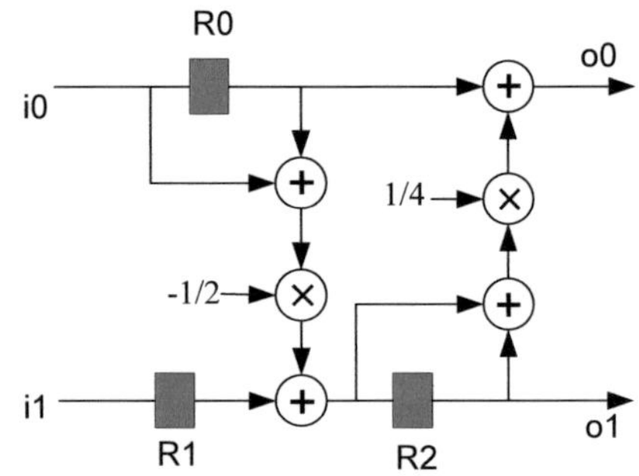

Fig. 9. Lifting-based hardware architecture for 5/3 wavelet

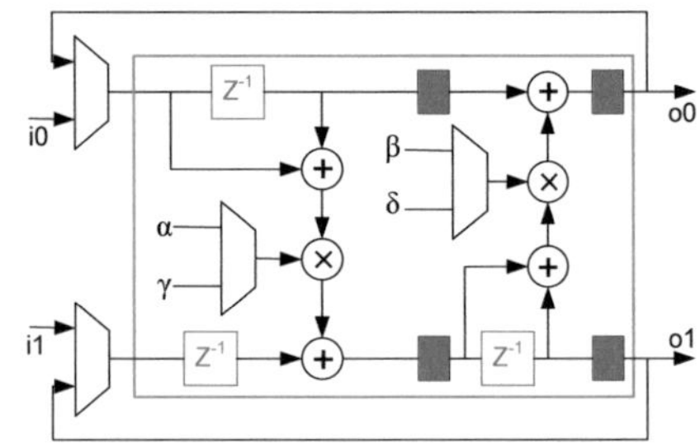

Fig. 10. Propose architecture in [19]

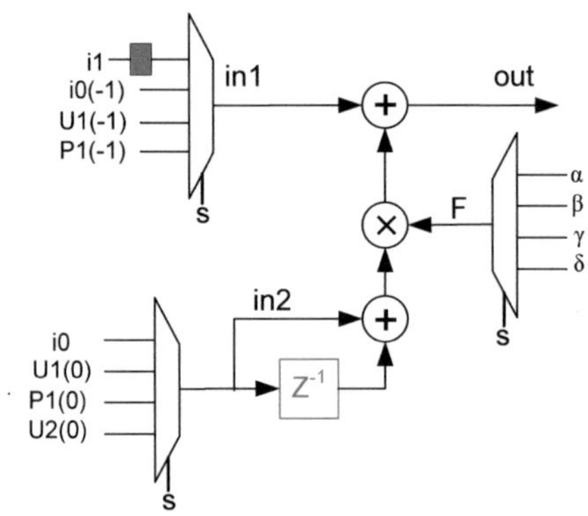

Fig. 11. Minimized structure

and delay block registers, that is, the z^{-1} blocks, have been modified from four to two. So, changing the wavelet type changes these two quantities, coefficients and registers, only. Both P and U units in LS can be implemented by means of the PE shown in Fig. 4. We explored this feature in the previous section and implemented a 1-D DWT structure containing only one PE. We call this method the "folded method". The folded structure is an alternative for the proposed method in [12] by which the lifting-based structures can be designed systematically. As shown in Fig. 14 for 9/7 wavelet, the method in [12] produces systolic architecture, but folded method produces folded architecture. In folded structure, the output of the PE unit is fed back through the delay registers to the PE's input. By incorporating different numbers of delay registers and coefficients with PE, the structure for different wavelets can be designed. For example the folded structure for 5/3 and 9/7 wavelets has two and four delay registers, respectively. Also the coefficients for 5/3 wavelet are $\frac{-1}{2}$ and $\frac{1}{4}$while for 9/7 they are $\alpha, \beta, \gamma, \delta$.

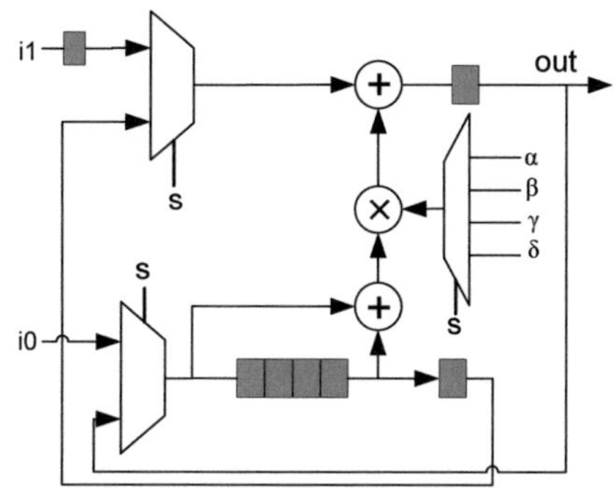

Fig. 12. Hardware implementation for Fig.10

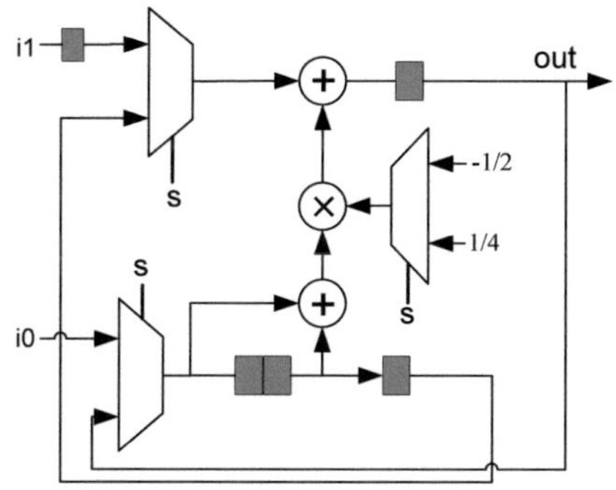

Fig. 13. Minimized architecture for 5/3 wavelet

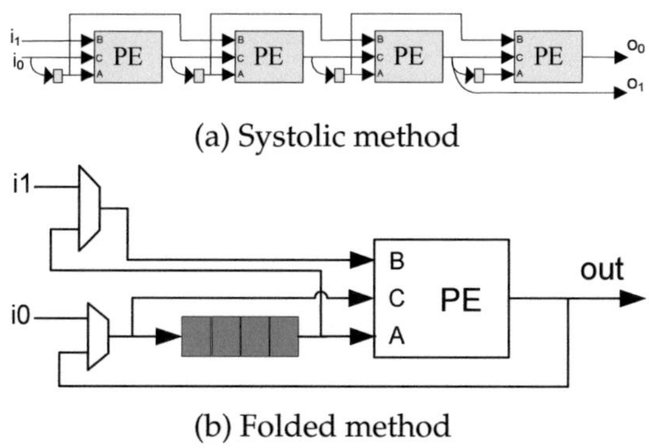

Fig. 14. 1-D Lifting-Based DWT for 9/7 wavelet by Systematic Design Method

In order to show the efficiency of our architecture, several architectures are chosen for comparison. Ignoring the pipeline registers, the results of comparison for the 9/7 wavelet are given in Table 2. It is obvious that compared to other architectures, the number of processing units is reduced in the folded architecture, thus requiring less area to implement the DWT. Having smaller 1-D DWT units is very effective in multidimensional architectures or in 2-D DWT, where it is needed to increase the number of 1-D DWT units to achieve a higher performance [20]. The cost is that, in the proposed architecture, the clock pulses required to compute outputs are more than those in the previous architectures. This requirement is due to the sequential states required to complete the computation of each output.

Architecture	Multiplier	Adder	Register
Lifting[18]	4	8	6
Proposed in [19]	2	4	6
Systolic[12]	4	8	4
Folded [30]	1	2	4

Table 2. Comparison of some different 1-D DWT architectures for 9/7 wavelet ($J \longrightarrow \infty$)

5. 2-D DWT structures

In this section, we review four convenient structures for 2-D DWT. It is assumed that the 2-D wavelets reviewed in the following structures are separable, so that the 2-D wavelet transform can be reduced to a 1-D wavelet transform performed on rows and columns, respectively.
In the direct method (step-by-step method), shown in Fig. 15, the input frame, stored in external memory, arrives at the 1-D DWT, row by row. The primary outputs are wavelet coefficients in the row direction and are stored in the external memory. After scanning all the rows of the frame, again the coefficients are transferred from the external memory to the 1-D DWT block, but this time in the column-wise direction. The secondary outputs of the 1-D DWT block are 2-D DWT coefficients of the input frame, which are stored in the external memory again. If computation of coefficients for one more decomposition level is needed, this procedure must be repeated for the LL part of the previous level, whose size is a quarter of the input frame size. This routine will be repeated for higher levels. The direct method hardware is simple, but its latency and the number of external memory accesses are large. The number of external memory accesses for computing a J-level 2-D DWT of an $N \times N$ input image can be calculated by the expression below, where half of the sum is related to the external memory reads and the other half is related to the external memory writes

$$4 \times (1 + \frac{1}{4} + \frac{1}{16} + \cdots + (\frac{1}{4})^{J-1}) \times N^2 \tag{2}$$

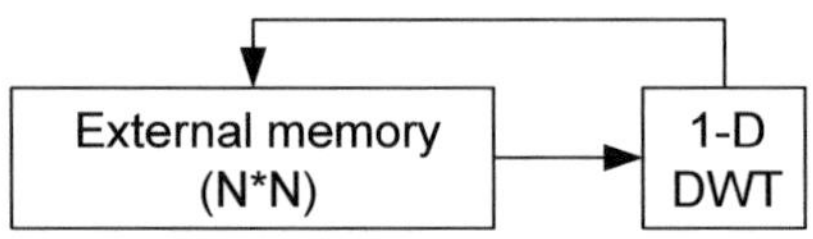

Fig. 15. Direct method

The line-based method can be implemented in two forms: single level and multilevel. In the line-based single level method, which is shown in Fig. 16, each level of DWT is performed by a 2-D DWT block. In this method, only internal memory is used to compute one level DWT for both the row and column directions, hence, there is no external memory access during the computation of one level 2-D DWT (except for reading rudimentary inputs and writing final results for that level). The required internal memory is the sum of the data memory and the temporal memory (black circles shown in Fig. 6) for each line. So the amount of needed internal memory is 6N for 9/7 wavelet and 4N for 5/3 wavelet [13,21]. But the results of the DWT in the row direction for even rows can be used for the computation of the DWT in the column direction without storing them. Hence, the required internal memory for 9/7 and 5/3 2-D wavelets is reduced to 5N and 3N, respectively. Recently, some new modifications have been made for the 2-D DWT block. For example, in [20] the number of data entrances has been increased by using more 1-D DWT units in the 2-D DWT block. Although this modification

increases the speed, it requires more internal memory and the size of the circuit is increased. In [22], by replacing registers with line buffers and controlling data flow in a structure like Fig. 13, with 5 more registers, a 2-D DWT block for 5/3 wavelet has been proposed.
Obviously, for a higher-level 2-D DWT, only LL coefficients of the previous level are used, so the total number of external memory access for a J-level 2-D DWT on an $N \times N$ image is

$$2 \times (1 + \frac{1}{4} + \frac{1}{16} + \cdots + (\frac{1}{4})^{J-1}) \times N^2 \tag{3}$$

The structure of Fig. 17 performs all levels of 2-D DWT, using only internal memory. So,

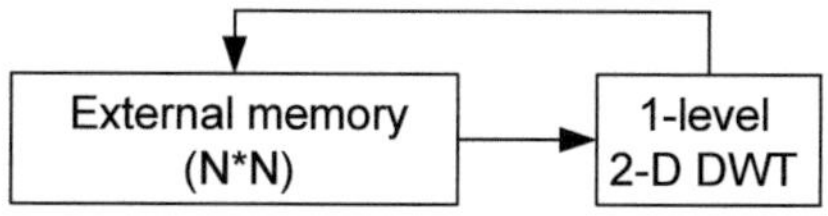

Fig. 16. Single level line-based method

the total number of external memory accesses for a J-level 2-D DWT is limited to $2N^2$, which corresponds to reading the input image for the first level and writing the final DWT results. The line-based multilevel structure, shown in Fig. 17, is much faster than the previous structures, but it needs a larger amount of hardware and so its hardware utilization (i.e., the average value of the area of working parts versus the whole area of the hardware) is low [23], but the 2-D recursive architecture proposed in [24] improves the hardware utilization for the J-level 2-D DWT. In Fig. 17, the required internal memory for the 9/7 wavelet is obtained from equation (4).

$$5N \times (1 + \frac{1}{2} + \frac{1}{4} + \cdots + (\frac{1}{2})^{J-1}) \tag{4}$$

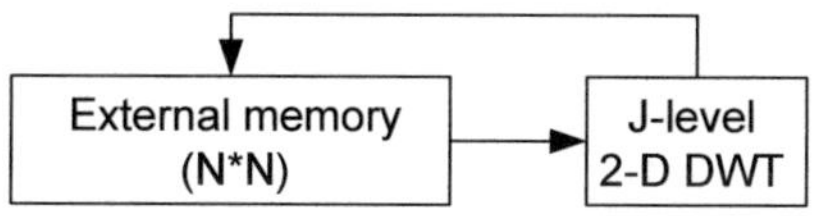

Fig. 17. Multilevel line-based method

There is a trade-off between the size of the internal memory and the number of external memory accesses in the 2-D DWT structures mentioned previously. Now, a block-based structure that parameterizes the aforementioned trade-off is introduced. The block-based structure is similar to the line-based method, but instead of considering the total length of a row for DWT in the row direction, only a part of it with length M pixels is considered (Fig. 18). It means that the first M columns of the main frame (the gray area in Fig. 18) are used as the input frame and 2-D DWT coefficients are computed for them. So the required internal memory, which is determined by the length of the rows, is decreased. As an example, for the 9/7 wavelet the internal memory size will be decreased from 5N to 5M (where M is a fraction of N). It is possible to consider a block of image by partitioning the image in both the row and column directions. In this method, the block (or window) slides across the image and both the row- and column-wise 1-D DWT will be performed on them [25]. The size of tile windows may be reduced to 2×2 pixels [26].

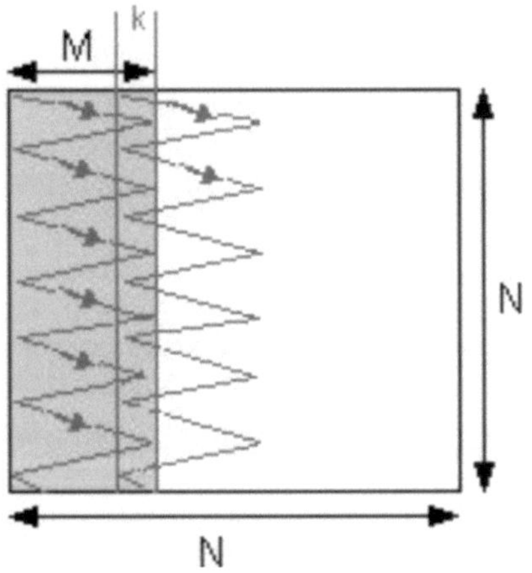

Fig. 18. Scan method in block-based structure

6. Scan methods for block-based structure

However, in the above-mentioned method, there is a problem in the boundary region between two M-pixel sections. To compute the DWT for the beginning pixel of the nextM-pixel section, values of K previous pixels are needed. These K pixels produce values of temporary memory (black circles shown in Fig. 19). K is equal to $n_t - 2$, where nt is the number of filter taps corresponding to the desired DWT. For the 9/7 wavelet, as shown in Fig. 19, K is equal to 7 (shaded circles). To solve the boundary problem, the overlapped scan method has been

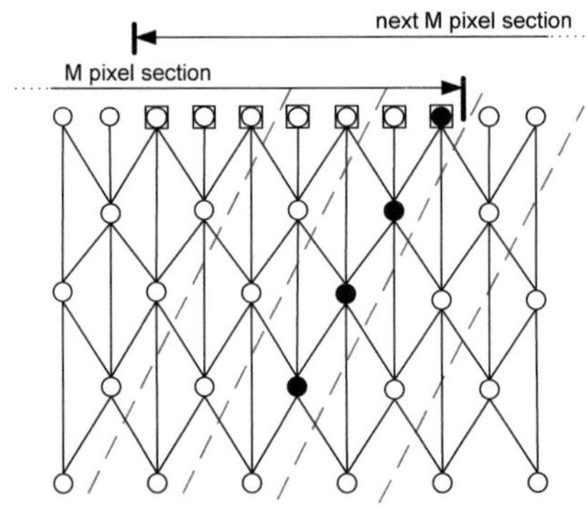

Fig. 19. Boundary region for 9/7 wavelet

proposed in [27]. A new M-pixel section begins from the last K pixels in the previous section. So two sections are overlapped in K pixels, and this causes the number of external memory reads to be $\frac{N^2 M}{(M-K)}$ instead of N^2. The number of external memory writes is limited to writing the output results and is equal to N^2.

We can use an alternate scan method for the overlapped region at the boundary between two M-pixel sections. The relationships for the new scan method are different from the previous method. The temporary memory at the boundary of two M-pixel sections (black circles in Fig. 19) can be saved for the computation of the next section. These saved values will be used for the computation of the next M pixels. Hence, a new M-pixel section begins without any overlap with the previous section. The required memory to save temporary data is $L \times N$, where L is the value of the temporary memory in the related DWT core. For example, in Fig.

	Direct	Single level line-based	Block-Based	
Internal Memory Size	0	$5N$	$5M$	$5M$
External Memory Reads	$2N^2$	N^2	$\frac{N^2M}{M-K}$	$N^2(1+\frac{4}{M})-4N$
External Memory Write	$2N^2$	N^2	N^2	$N^2(1+\frac{4}{M})-4N$
Control complexity	Low	Medium	Medium	Medium

Table 3. Comparison of different 2-D DWT structures for one level 9/7 wavelet

19, L is 4 for the 9/7 wavelet without pipelining. The storage of temporary memory may be fulfilled in internal or external memory. If internal memory is used to save temporary data, the number of external memory accesses is equal to N^2 read and N^2 write operations. However, if external memory is used to save temporary memory, both of the external memory reads and writes are increased by an amount of $(\frac{N}{M}-1)N \times L$. Hence, the number of external memory reads as well as the number of external memory writes is equal to $N^2 + (\frac{N}{M}-1)N \times L$. In this expression, the $(\frac{N}{M}-1)$ coefficient is the number of M-pixel sections. Due to hardware limitations (the limit size of internal memory on FPGA ICs), we select the second case for implementation. Comparisons of the aforementioned methods for one level 2-D DWT are given in Table 3. The table shows the values of the internal memory size and external memory accesses for the three algorithms. It is shown that in our proposed algorithm the internal memory size is between those of two other algorithms (the direct method and the line-based method). The same conclusion is true for the external memory size. The table also shows the order of complexity for the control circuits of these methods based on [28]. Similar comparisons for J-level ($J \longrightarrow \infty$) 2-D DWT are given in Table 4. Note that M has been considered to be fixed for all levels of 2-D DWT. It means that the width of the M-pixel section for the current level is the same as the one in the previous level. The J-level structure can be implemented either in the form of a single level (Fig. 15) or multilevel structure (Fig. 16), and the relevant values are listed in Table 4. We observe that the parameter M can be determined according to hardware limitations, such as internal memory. The conclusion from the two tables is that the block-based structure with the new scan method, in comparison with the direct method, needs more internal memory, but needs only about one-half of the external memory accesses. Due to the shorter access time for internal memory, the clock pulse frequency will increase, and based on the energy model in [5] the power consumption will decrease. In comparison with other methods, the new method remarkably decreases the needed internal memory at the cost of a soft increase in the number of external memory accesses.

7. Experimental results

The folded 1-D DWT architecture was described in VHDL code and simulated by Active-HDL6.3 software. Then the relevant VHDL code was synthesized by the Synplify7.5.1 software tool to be implemented on IC XC2V40 (from the VirtexII family of Xilinx FPGAs). The maximum estimated frequency for implementing Fig. 12 on this IC is 122.4 MHz, which is practical for real-time implementation of the 9/7 wavelet for large images. The maximum frequency to implement the 5/3 wavelet on the IC is 163.1 MHz. Also, the block-based architecture with the new scan method was modeled and simulated for the 5/3 wavelet with N = 1024 and 8-bit pixels. The code was synthesized by Synplify7.5.1 for implementation on VirtexII. After post place and route simulation, the clock pulse frequency achieved was 97 MHz. The structure receives one pixel as input per each clock pulse. So, according to the

	Direct	Line-Based		Block-Based			
				Single Level Line-Based		Multilevel Line-Based	
		Single Level	Multi-level	(27)	(30)	(27)	(30)
Internal Memory Size	0	$5N$	$10N$	$5M$	$5M$	$(5M)^J$	$(5M)^J$
External Memory Reads	$\frac{8}{3}N^2$	$\frac{4}{3}N^2$	N^2	$\frac{4}{3}(\frac{N^2M}{M-K})$	$\frac{4}{3}N^2(1+\frac{4}{M})-8N$	$N^2+\frac{4}{3}\frac{N^2K}{M-K}$	$N^2+\frac{16N^2}{M}-8N$
External Memory Write	$\frac{8}{3}N^2$	$\frac{4}{3}N^2$	N^2	$\frac{4}{3}N^2$	$\frac{4}{3}N^2(1+\frac{4}{M})-8N$	N^2	$N^2+\frac{16N^2}{M}-8N$

Table 4. Comparison of different 2-D DWT structures for J level 9/7 wavelet ($J \longrightarrow \infty$)

calculations below, the folded structure can be used to perform 3 levels of 2-D DWT for 70 frames (1024×1024 pixels) per second, and it is suitable for use in real-time hardware video codec.

$$t = \frac{1024 \times 1024 \times (1 + \frac{1}{4} + \frac{1}{16})}{97MHz} = 14.2ms,$$

$$n_f = \frac{1}{t} = \frac{1}{14.2ms} \simeq 70(frame/s).$$

8. Conclusion

Lifting Scheme and some different lifting based architectures for DWT presented in this chapter. Then we focused on the size (area) of the architecture. An architecture to minimize the number of multipliers and adders has been investigated for implementation of 1-D DWTs. All types of 1-D DWTs can be implemented by modifying only the number of registers and coefficients of the architecture. Thus, the folded architecture, which has fixed form units for all DWT types, presents a new folded method for systematic implementation of DWT. It is possible to design a software program to produce the folded architecture for different types of wavelets. What is needed is to define coefficients ($\alpha, \beta, ...$) required for each step of the desired wavelet in the lifting scheme. The folded method can be extended for large and complex structures such as multilevel discrete wavelet packet transforms [29] to reduce the area. Also, we have reviewed the 2-D DWT block-based structure and shown its power to trade off between the internal memory size and the number of external accesses by a controlling parameter.

9. References

[1] S. Mallat, A theory for multiresolution signal decomposition: the wavelet representation. IEEE Trans. Pattern Anal. Mach. Intell. 11, 674–693 (1989)

[2] T. Acharya, C. Chakrabarti, A survey on lifting-based discrete wavelet transform architectures. J. VLSI Signal Process. 42, 321–339 (2006)

[3] I. Daubechies, W. Sweldens, Factoring wavelet transform into lifting steps. J. Fourier Anal. Appl. 4, 247–269 (1998)

[4] C.-T. Huang, P.-C. Tseng, L.-G. Chen, Flipping structure: an efficient VLSI architecture for liftingbased discrete wavelet transform, IEEE Trans. Signal Process. 52 (2004), pp. 1080–1089
[5] N.D. Zervas et al., Evaluation of design alternatives for the 2-D-discrete wavelet transform. IEEE Trans. Circuits Syst. Video Technol. 11(12), 1246–1262 (2001)
[6] K. A. Kotteri, S. Barua, A. E. Bell, and J. E. Carletta, "A comparison of hardware implementations of the biorthogonal 9/7 DWT: convolution versus lifting," IEEE Trans. Circuits Syst. II, Expr. Br., vol. 52, no. 5, pp. 256-260, 2005.
[7] M. Maurizio, M. Guido, P. Gianluca, and Z. Maurizio, "Novel JPEG 2000 compliant DWT and IWT VLSI implementations," J. VLSI Signal Process., vol. 35, no. 2, pp. 137-153, Sep. 2003.
[8] J. Reichel, On the arithmetic and bandwidth complexity of the lifting scheme, in Proc. of International Conference on Image Processing (2001), pp. 198–201
[9] R. Calderbank, I. Daubechies, W. Sweldens, B.-L. Yeo, Wavelet transforms that map integers to integers. Appl. Comput. Harmon. Anal. 5(3), 332–369 (1998)
[10] A. Jensen, A. La Cour-Harbo, Ripples in Mathematics: The Discrete Wavelet Transform (Springer, Berlin, 2001)
[11] K.G. Oweiss et al., A scalable wavelet transform VLSI architecture for real-time signal processing in high-density intra-cortical implants. IEEE Trans. Circuits Syst. 54(6), 1266–1278 (2007)
[12] C.-T. Huang, P.-C. Tseng, L.-G. Chen, Efficient VLSI architectures of lifting-based discrete wavelet transform by systematic design method, in IEEE International Symposium on Circuits and Systems, vol. 5 (2002), pp. 565–568
[13] W.-H. Chang, Y.-S. Lee, W.S. Peng, C.-Y. Lee, A line-based, memory efficient and programmable architecture for 2D DWT using lifting scheme, in IEEE International Symposium on Circuits and Systems, vol. 4 (2001), pp. 330–333
[14] K. Andra, C. Chakrabarti, T. Acharya, A VLSI architecture for lifting-based forward and inverse wavelet transform. IEEE Trans. Signal Process. 50(4), 966–977 (2002)
[15] O. Fatemi, S. Bolouki, Pipeline memory-efficient and programmable architecture for 2D discrete wavelet transform using lifting scheme, in Proceedings of IEE Circuits, Devices and Systems, December 2005, pp. 703–708
[16] Lan, N. Zheng, Y. Liu, Low power and high-speed VLSI architecture for lifting-based forward and inverse wavelet transform. IEEE Trans. Consumer Electron. 51(2), 379–385 (2005)
[17] C.Y. Xiong, J.W. Tian, J. Liu, A note on Şflipping structure: an efficient VLSI architecture for liftingbased discrete wavelet transformŤ. IEEE Trans. Signal Process. 54(4), 1910–1916 (2006)
[18] J.M. Jou, Y.H. Shiau, C.C. Lio, Efficient VLSI architectures for the biorthogonal wavelet transform by filter bank and lifting scheme, in Proceedings of IEEE ISCAS 2001, pp. 529–533
[19] C.J. Lian, K.F. Chen, H.H. Chen, L.G. Chen, Lifting based discrete wavelet transform architecture for JPEG2000, in IEEE International Symposium on Circuits and Systems (ISCAS 2001) Sydney, May 2001
[20] C.Y. Xiong, J.W. Tian, J. Liu, Efficient architectures for two-dimensional discrete wavelet transform using lifting scheme. IEEE Trans. Image Process. 16(3), 607–614 (2007)

[21] P.-C. Tseng, C.-T. Huang, L.-G. Chen, Generic RAM-based architecture for two-dimensional discrete wavelet transform with line-based method, in Asia-Pacific Conference on Circuits and Systems (2002), pp. 363–366
[22] H. Varshney, M. Hasan, S. Jain, Energy efficient novel architectures for the lifting-based discrete wavelet transform. IET Image Process. 1(3), 305–310 (2007)
[23] C.-T. Huang, P.-C. Tseng, L.-G. Chen, Hardware implementation of shape-adaptive discrete wavelet transform with the JPEG2000 defaulted 9/7 filter bank, in IEEE International Conference on Image Processing, vol. 3 (2003), pp. 571–574
[24] L.Hongyu, M.K. Mandal, B.F. Cockburn, Efficient architectures for 1-D and 2-D lifting-based wavelet transforms. IEEE Trans. Signal Process. 52(5), 1315–1326 (2004)
[25] C.H. Yang et al., A block-based architecture for lifting scheme discrete wavelet transform. IEICE Trans. Fundam. 90(5), 1062–1071 (2007)
[26] J.W. Kim et al., Tiled interleaving for multi-level 2-D discrete wavelet transform, in IEEE Int. Symp. Circuits Syst., May 2007, pp. 3984–3987
[27] C.-T. Huang, P.-C. Tseng, L.-G. Chen, Memory analysis and architecture for two-dimensional discrete wavelet transform, in IEEE International Symposium on Circuits and Systems (ISCAS 2004)
[28] C.-T. Huang, P.-C. Tseng, L.-G. Chen, Analysis and VLSI architecture for 1-D and 2-D discrete wavelet transform. IEEE Trans. Signal Process. 53(4), 1575–1586 (2005)
[29] C. Wang, W.S. Gan, Efficient VLSI architecture for lifting-based discrete wavelet packet transform. IEEE Trans. Circuits Syst. 54(5), 422–426 (2007)
[30] S.A. Salehi, S. Sadri, "Investigation of Lifting-Based Hardware Architectures for Discrete Wavelet Transform," Journal of Circuits Systems and Signal Processing, vol. 28, N.1, pp1-16, 2009.

4

Simulation of Models and BER Performances of DWT-OFDM versus FFT-OFDM

Khaizuran Abdullah[1] and Zahir M. Hussain[2,3]
[1]*Electrical and Computer Engineering Department, International Islamic University Malaysia,*
[2]*Department of Electrical Engineering, University of Kufa,*
[3]*School of Electrical and Computer Engineering, RMIT University,*
[1]*Malaysia*
[2]*Iraq*
[3]*Australia*

1. Introduction

Orthogonal Frequency Division Multiplexing (OFDM) is a multicarrier modulation system. The transmission channel is divided into a number of subchannel in which each subchannel is assigned a subcarrier. Conventional OFDM systems use IFFT and FFT algorithms at the transmitter and receiver respectively to multiplex the signals and transmit them simultaneously over a number of subcarriers. The system employs guard intervals or cyclic prefixes (CP) so that the delay spread of the channel becomes longer than the channel impulse response (Peled & Ruiz, 1980; Bahai & Saltzberg, 1999; Kalet, 1994; Beek et al.,1999; Bingham, 1990; Nee and Prasad, 2000). The system must make sure that the cyclic prefix is a small fraction of the per carrier symbol duration (Beek et al.,1999; Steendam & Moeneclaey, 1999). The purpose of employing the CP is to minimize inter-symbol interference (ISI). However a CP reduces the power efficiency and data throughput. The CP also has the disadvantage of reducing the spectral containment of the channels (Ahmed, 2000; Dilmirghani & Ghavami, 2007, 2008). Due to these issues, an alternative method is to use the wavelet transform to replace the IFFT and FFT blocks (Ahmed, 2000; Dilmirghani & Ghavami, 2007, 2008; Akansu & Xueming, 1998; Sandberg & Tzannes, 1995). The wavelet transform is referred as Discrete Wavelet Transform OFDM (DWT-OFDM). By using the transform, the spectral containment of the channels is better since they are not using CP (Ahmed, 2000; Dilmirghani & Ghavami, 2007, 2008). The illustration of the superior subchannel containment attributes in wavelet has been described in detailed by (Sandberg & Tzannes, 1995) as compared to Fourier. The wavelet transform also employs Low Pass Filter (LPF) and High Pass Filter (HPF) operating as Quadrature Mirror Filters satisfying perfect reconstruction and orthonormal bases properties. It uses filter coefficients as approximate and detail in LPF and HPF respectively. The approximated coefficients is sometimes referred to as scaling coefficients, whereas, the detailed is referred to wavelet coefficients (Abdullah et al., 2009; Weeks, 2007). In some literatures, these two filters are also called subband coding since the signals are divided into sub-signals of low and high frequencies respectively. The purpose of this chapter is to show the simulation study of using the Matrices Laboratory (MATLAB) on the wavelet based OFDM particularly DWT-

OFDM as alternative substitutions for Fourier based OFDM. MATLAB is preferred for this approach because it offers very powerful matrices calculation with wide range of enriched toolboxes and simulation tools. To the best of the authors' knowledge, there is no study on the descriptive procedures of simulations using MATLAB with regards of flexible transformed models in an OFDM system, especially when dealing with wavelet transform. Therefore, this chapter is divided into three main sections: section 2 will explain conventional FFT-OFDM, section 3 will describe in detail the models for DWT-OFDM, and section 4 will discuss the Bit Error rate (BER) result regarding those two transformed platforms, DWT-OFDM versus FFT-OFDM.

2. Fourier-based OFDM

A typical block diagram of an OFDM system is shown in Figure 1. The inverse and forward blocks can be FFT-based or DWT-based OFDM.

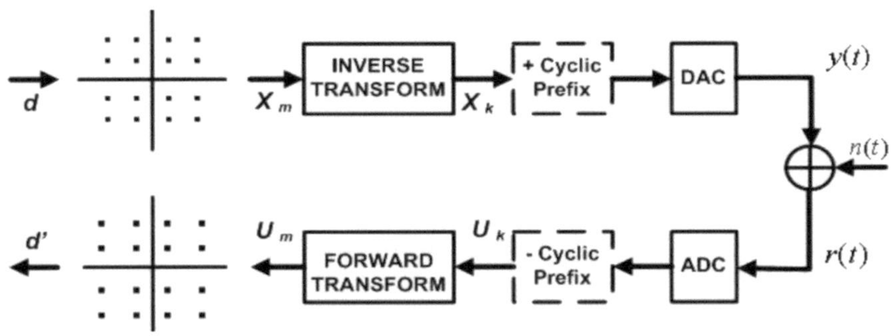

Fig. 1. A Typical model of an OFDM transceiver with inverse and forward transformed blocks which can be substituted as FFT-OFDM or DWT-OFDM.

The system model for FFT-based OFDM will not be discussed in detail as it is well known in the literature. Thus, we merely present a brief description about it. The data d_k is first being processed by a constellation mapping. *M*-ary QAM modulator is used for this work to map the raw binary data to appropriate QAM symbols. These symbols are then input into the IFFT block. This involves taking *N* parallel streams of QAM symbols (*N* being the number of sub-carriers used in the transmission of the data) and performing an IFFT operation on this parallel stream. The output in discrete time domain is as follows:

$$X_k(n) = \frac{1}{\sqrt{N}} \sum_{i=0}^{N-1} X_m(i) e^{j2\pi \frac{n}{N} i} \tag{1}$$

Where $x_k(n) \mid 0 \le n \le N-1$, is a sequence in the discrete time domain and $X_m(i) \mid 0 \le i \le N-1$ are complex numbers in the discrete frequency domain. The cyclic prefix (CP) is lastly added before transmission to minimize the inter-symbol interference (ISI). At the receiver, the process is reversed to obtain the decoded data. The CP is removed to obtain the data in the discrete time domain and then processed to FFT for data recovery. The output of the FFT in the frequency domain is as follows:

$$U_m(i) = \sum_{i=0}^{N-1} U_k(n) e^{j2\pi \frac{n}{N} i} \tag{2}$$

3. Wavelet-based OFDM

As mentioned in the previous section, the inverse and forward block transforms are flexible and can be substituted with FFT or DWT-OFDM. We have discussed briefly about FFT-OFDM. Thus, this section will describe wavelet based OFDM particularly about DWT-OFDM transceiver. This section is divided into three parts: a description of the DWT-OFDM transmitter and receiver models as well as the Perfect Reconstruction properties' discussion.

3.1 Discrete Wavelet Transform (DWT) transmitter

From Figure 1, it is obvious that the transmitter first uses a 16 QAM digital modulator which maps the serial bits *d* into the OFDM symbols X_m, within *N* parallel data stream $X_m(i)$ where $X_m(i) \mid 0 \le i \le N - 1$. The main task of the transmitter is to perform the discrete wavelet modulation by constructing orthonormal wavelets. Each $X_m(i)$ is first converted to serial representation having a vector *xx* which will next be transposed into *CA* as shown in details as in Figure 2. This means that *CA* not only its imaginary part has inverting signs but also its form is changed to a parallel matrix. Then, the signal is up-sampled and filtered by the LPF coefficients or namely as approximated coefficients. This coefficients are also called scaling coefficients. Since our aim is to have low frequency signals, the modulated signals *xx* perform circular convolution with LPF filter whereas the HPF filter also perform the convolution with zeroes padding signals *CD* respectively. Note that the HPF filter contains detailed coefficients or wavelet coefficients. Different wavelet families have different filter length and values of approximated and detailed coefficients. Both of these filters have to satisfy orthonormal bases in order to operate as wavelet transform. The number of *CA* and *CD* depends on the OFDM subcarriers *N*. Samples of this processing signals *CA* and *CD* that pass through this block model is shown in Figure 4. The above mentioned signals are simulated using MATLAB command $[X_k] = idwt(CA;CD;wv)$ where *wv* is the type of wavelet family.

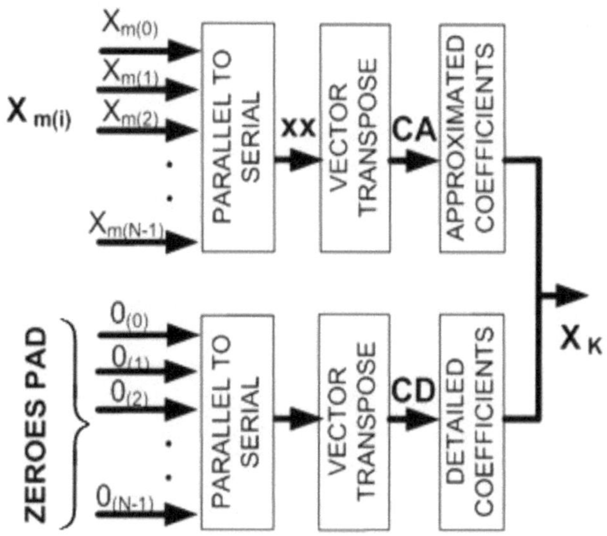

Fig. 2. Discrete Wavelet Transform (DWT)-OFDM transmitter model.

The detailed and approximated coefficients must be orthogonal and normal to each other. By assigning g as LPF filter coefficients and h as HPF filter coefficients, the orthonormal bases can be satisfied via four possible ways (Weeks, 2007): $<g, g^*> = 1$, $<h, h^*> = 1$, $<g, h^*> = 0$ and $<h, g^*> = 0$. The symbol * indicates its conjugate, and the symbol $< , >$ is referring to the dot product. The result which yields to 1 is related to the normal property whereas the result yielding to 0 is for orthogonal property accordingly.

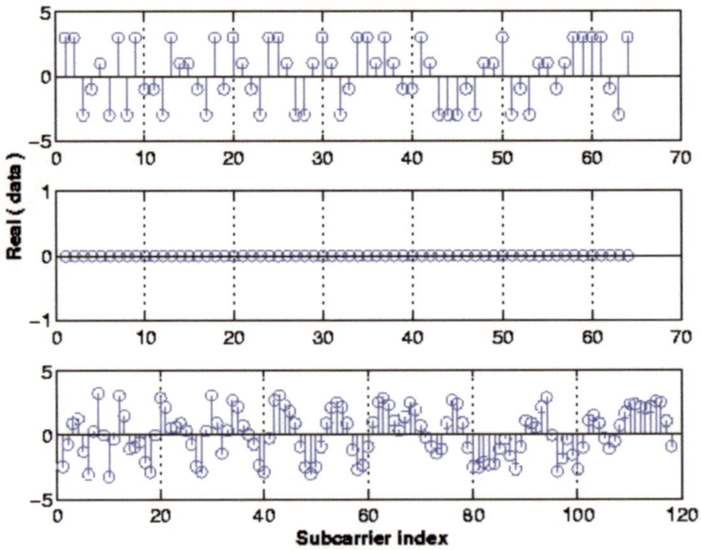

Fig. 3. The processed signals of one symbol DWT-OFDM system using bior5.5 in DWT transmitter. Top: data CA, Middle: data CD, Bottom: data X_k, corresponding to Figure 2.

Both filters are also assumed to have perfect reconstruction property. The input and output of the two filters are expected to be the same. A further discussion can be found in section 3.3.

3.2 Discrete Wavelet Transform (DWT) receiver

The DWT receiver is the reverse process which is simulated using the MATLAB command $[ca; cd] = dwt(U_k;wv)$. The receiver system model that processes the data *ca*, *cd* and U_k is shown in Figure 4. The parameter *wv* is to indicate the wavelet family that is used in this simulation. U_k is the front-end receiver data. This data is decomposed into two filters, high and low pass filters corresponding to detailed and approximated coefficients accordingly. The *ca* signal which is the output of the approximated coefficients or low pass filter will finally be processed to the QAM demodulator for data recovery. To perform that operation, data is first transposed before converting into parallel representation. The output $U_{m(i)}$ is passed to QAM demodulator. The index i depends on the number of OFDM subcarriers. The data *cd* is explained next. Due to the effect of CD data generated in the transmitter, U_k has some zeroes elements which is decomposed as the detailed coefficients. The signal output of these coefficients is *cd*. Comparing to *ca*, the *cd* signal is discarded because it does not contain any useful information instead. Samples of this processing signals that pass through the DWT-OFDM receiver model is shown in Figure 5.

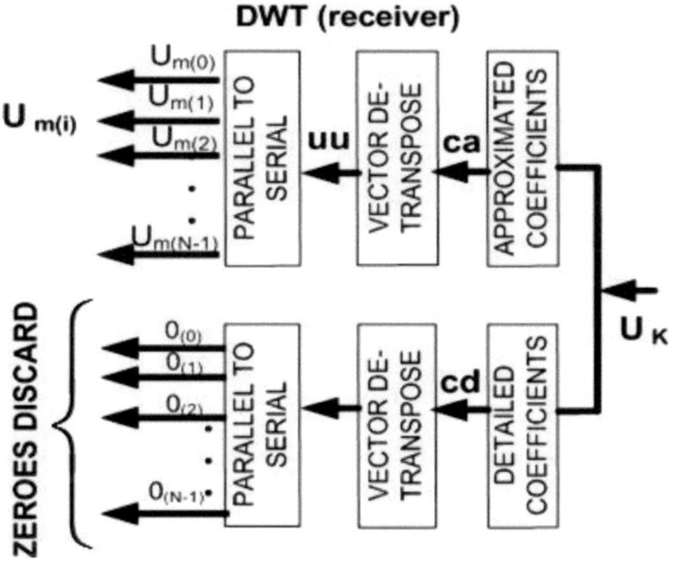

Fig. 4. Discrete Wavelet Transform (DWT)-OFDM receiver model.

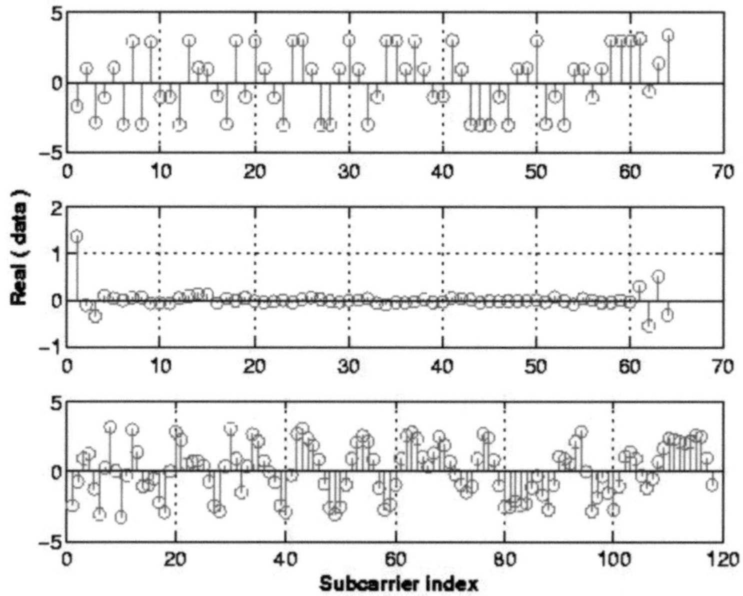

Fig. 5. The processed signals of one symbol DWT-OFDM system using bior5.5 in DWT receiver. Top: data ca. Middle: data cd. Bottom: data U_k, corresponding to Figure 4.

3.3 Perfect reconstruction

A block diagram of perfect reconstruction (PR) system operation is illustrated in Figure 6. The PR property is performed by a two-channel filter bank which is represented by the LPF and HPF. The first level of analysis filter in the receiver part can be folded and the decimator and the expander are cancelled out by each other.

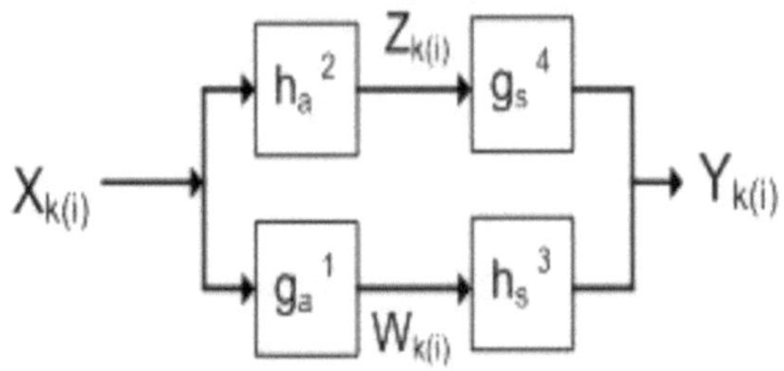

Fig. 6. A simple and modified model of two-channel filter bank illustrating a perfect reconstruction property with the superscript number is referring to the steps.

To satisfy a perfect reconstruction operation, the output $Y_k(i)$ is expected to be the same as $X_k(i)$. With the exception of a time delay, the input can be considered as $Y_k(i) = X_k(i\text{-}n)$ where n can be substituted as 1 to describe this simple task. The steps to perform the mathematical operation of PR can be summarized as follows (Weeks, 2007):

1. Selecting the filter coefficients for g_a, i.e., a and b. Thus, $g_a = \{a; b\}$.
2. h_a is a reversed version of g_a with every other value negated. Thus, $h_a = \{b; -a\}$. If the system has 4 filter coefficients with $g_a = \{a; b; c; d\}$, then $h_a = \{d; -c; b; -a\}$.
3. h_s is the reversed version of g_a, thus $h_s = \{b; a\}$.
4. g_s is also a reversed version of h_a, therefore $g_s = \{-a; b\}$.

The above steps can be rewritten as follows:

$$g_a = \{a,b\},\ h_a = \{b,-a\},\ h_s = \{b,a\},\ g_s = \{-a,b\} \tag{3}$$

Considering that the input with delay are applied to h_a and g_a in Figure 4, then the output of these filters are

$$Z_k(i) = b(X_k(i) - a(X_k(i\text{-}1)) \tag{4}$$

$$W_k(i) = a(X_k(i) + b(X_k(i\text{-}1)) \tag{5}$$

Considering also that $Z_k(i)$ and $W_k(i)$ are delayed by 1, then i can be replaced by (i-1) as follows

$$Z_k(i\text{-}1) = a(X_k(i\text{-}1) + b(X_k(i\text{-}2)) \tag{6}$$

$$W_k(i\text{-}1) = b(X_k(i\text{-}1) - a(X_k(i\text{-}2)) \tag{7}$$

The output $Y_k(i)$ can be written as

$$Y_k(i) = g_s Z_k(i) + h_s W_k(i) \tag{8}$$

or,

$$Y_k(i) = -aZ_k(i) + bZ_k(i\text{-}1) + bW_k(i) + aW_k(i\text{-}1) \tag{9}$$

Substituting equations (5), (6), (7) and (8) into (9) yields to

$$Y_k(i) = 2(a2 + b2)X_k(i\text{-}1) \quad (10)$$

The output $Y_k(i)$ is the same as the input $X_k(i)$ except that it is delayed by 1 if we substitute the coefficient factor $2(a2 + b2)$ by 1. The PR condition is satisfied.

4. Simulation results

Simulation variables and their matrix values are shown in Table I. The number of samples for the subcarriers N is 64, and the number of samples for the symbols ns is 1000. Data is similar between FFT and DWT OFDM in all parameters except the multiplexed one. For DWT-OFDM, it is required the transmitted signal to have double the data of FFT-OFDM. This is due to the fact that the DWT transmitter has zeroes padding component. An element value in the table that has a multiplier is referred to its matrix representation of row and column. If the element has 64 x 1000, it means that it has 64 numbers of rows and 1000 numbers of columns.

	Variables and Parameters	FFT-OFDM	DWT-OFDM
Minimum requirement	Subcarriers	64	64
	OFDM symbols	1000	1000
Transmitter	input binary generated	64 x 1000	64 x 1000
	parallel transmitted data	64 x 1000	64 x 1000
	serial transmitted data	1 x 64000	1 x 64000
	multiplexed data transmitted	64000 x 1	128000 x 1
Receiver	multiplexed data received	64000 x 1	128000 x 1
	serial received data	1 x 64000	1 x 64000
	parallel received data	64 x 1000	64 x 1000
	output binary recovered	64 x 1000	64 x 1000

Table 1. Simulation variables and their matrix values.

The curves in Figure 8 could have been better if we used more number of samples for the symbols. However, this yields longer time of running the simulations. Other variables are listed according to their use as in Figures 1, 2 and 3. Figure 7 shows the OFDM symbols in time domain for the two transformed platforms FFT and DWT. Some of the simulation parameters related to this figure are: the OFDM symbol period T_o = 9 ms, the total simulation time $t = 10 \times T_o$ = 90 ms, the sampling frequency f_s = 71.11 kHz, the carriers spacing ΔN = 1.11 kHz and the bandwidth $B = \Delta N \times 64$ = 71.11 kHz. Thus, the simulation satisfied the Nyquist criterion where $f_s < 2B$. Both platforms used the same parameters. It is interesting to observe that the DWT-OFDM symbol is less in term of the mean of amplitude vectors as compared to FFT-OFDM. The mean of FFT is 1.4270, whereas, the mean of DWT is -9.667E-04. This is due to the fact that zero - padding was performed in the DWT

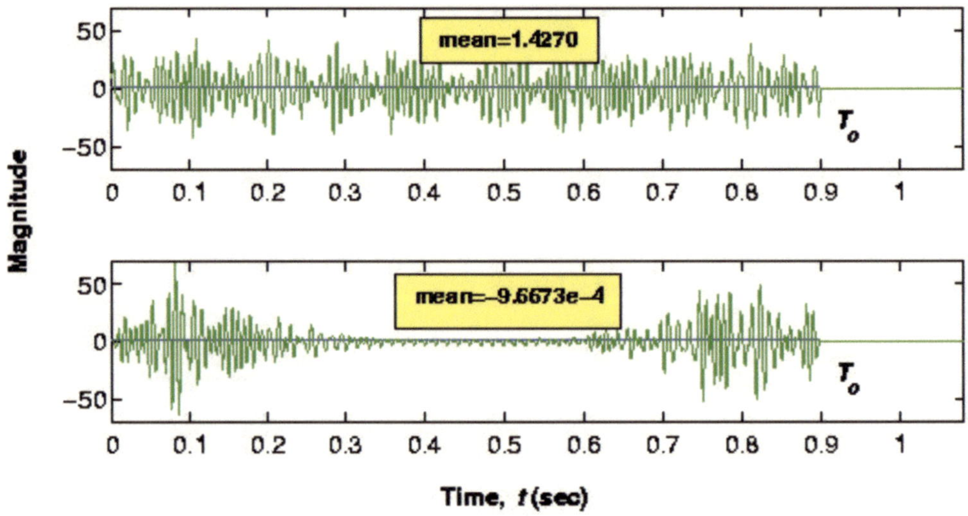

Fig. 7. An OFDM symbol in time domain: FFT-OFDM (Top), DWT-OFDM (Bottom).

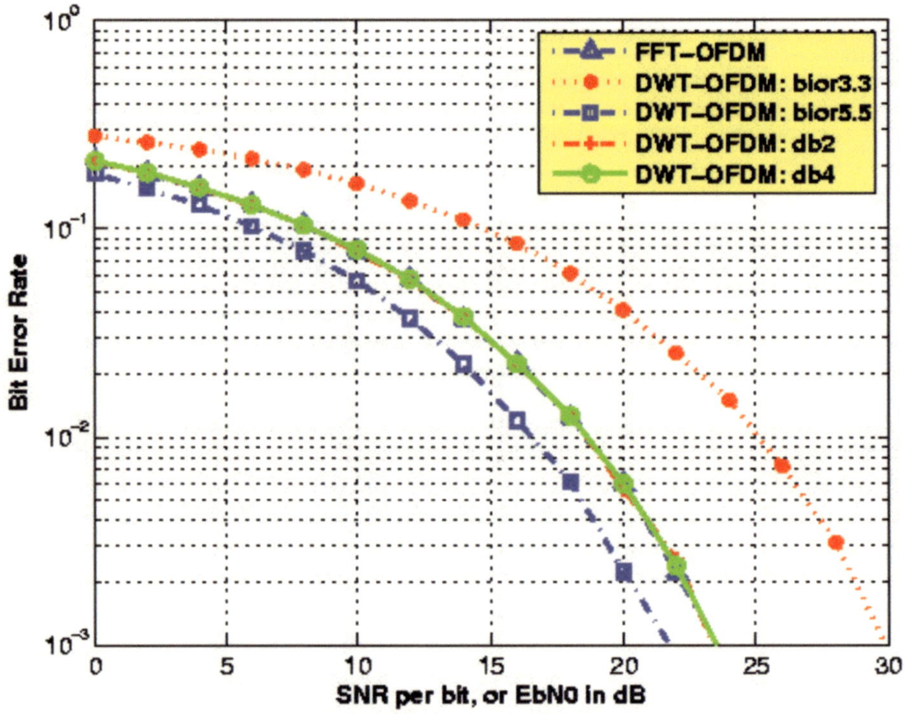

Fig. 8. BER performance for DWT-OFDM.

(transmitter) system model. As a result, most samples in the middle of DWT-OFDM symbol is almost zeroes. The DWT-OFDM performance can be observed from Figure 8. The wavelet families Biorthogonal and Daubechies are compared with FFT-OFDM. It is shown that bior5.5 is superior among all others. It outperforms FFT and Daubechies by about 2 dB and bior3.3 by 8 dB at 0.001 BER.

5. Conclusions

Simulation approaches using MATLAB for wavelet based OFDM, particularly in DWT-OFDM as alternative substitutions for Fourier based OFDM are presented. Conventional OFDM systems use IFFT and FFT algorithms at the transmitter and receiver respectively to multiplex the signals and transmit them simultaneously over a number of subcarriers. The system employs guard intervals or cyclic prefixes so that the delay spread of the channel becomes longer than the channel impulse response. The system must make sure that the cyclic prefix is a small fraction of the per carrier symbol duration. The purpose of employing the CP is to minimize inter-symbol interference (ISI). However a CP reduces the power efficiency and data throughput. The CP also has the disadvantage of reducing the spectral containment of the channels. Due to these issues, an alternative method is to use the wavelet transform to replace the IFFT and FFT blocks. The wavelet transform is referred as Discrete Wavelet Transform OFDM (DWT-OFDM). By using the transform, the spectral containment of the channels is better since they are not using CP. The wavelet based OFDM (DWT-OFDM) is assumed to have ortho-normal bases properties and satisfy the perfect reconstruction property. We use different wavelet families particularly, Biorthogonal and Daubechies and compare with conventional FFT-OFDM system. BER performances of both OFDM systems are also obtained. It is found that the DWT-OFDM platform is superior as compared to others as it has less error rate, especially using bior5.5 wavelet family.

6. References

Abdullah, K.; Mahmoud, S. & Hussain, Z.M. (2009). Performance Analysis of an Optimal Circular 16-QAM for Wavelet Based OFDM Systems. *International Journal of Communications, Network and System Sciences (IJCNS)*, Vol. 2, No. 9, (December 2009), pp 836-844, ISSN 1913-3715.

Ahmed, N. (2000). Joint Detection Strategies for Orthogonal Frequency Division Multiplexing. Dissertation for Master of Science, Rice University, Houston, Texas. pp. 1-51, April.

Akansu, A. N. & Xueming, L. (1998). A Comparative Performance Evaluation of DMT (OFDM) and DWMT (DSBMT) Based DSL Communications Systems for Single and Multitone Interference, Proceedings of the IEEE International Conference on Acoustics, Speech and Signal Processing, vol. 6, pp. 3269 - 3272, May.

Bahai, A. R. S. & Saltzberg, B. R. (1999). *Multi-Carrier Digital Communications - Theory and Applications of OFDM*. Kluwer Academic. ISBN: 0-306-46974-X 0-306-46296-6. New York.

Baig, S. R.; Rehman, F. U. & Mughal, M. J. (2005). Performance Comparison of DFT, Discrete Wavelet Packet and Wavelet Transforms in an OFDM Transceiver for Multipath Fading Channel. 9th IEEE International Multitopic Conference, pp. 1-6, December.

Bingham, J. A. C. (1990). Multicarrier Modulation for Data Transmission: An Idea Whose Time Has Come. *IEEE Communications Magazine*, Vol. 28, no 5, pp. (5-14).

Dilmirghani, R. & Ghavami, M. (2007). Wavelet Vs Fourier Based UWB Systems, 18th IEEE International Symposium on Personal, Indoor and Mobile Radio Communications, pp.1-5, September.

Kalet, I. (1989). The multitone Channel. *IEEE Transactions on Communications*, Vol. 37, No. 2, (Feb 1989), pp. (119-124).

Mirghani, R. & Ghavami, M. (2008). Comparison between Wavelet-based and Fourier-based Multicarrier UWB Systems. *IET Communications*, Vol. 2, Issue 2, pp. (353-358).

Nee, R. V. & Prasad, R. (2000). *OFDM for Wireless Multimedia Communications*, Boston: Artech House. ISBN 0-89006-530-6.

Peled, A. & Ruiz, A. (1980). Frequency Domain Data Transmission Using Reduced Computational Complexity Algorithms, Proceedings IEEE International Conference on Acoustics, speech and Signal Processing (ICASSP 1980), Denver, pp. 964-967.

Sandberg, S. D. & Tzannes, M. A. (1995). Overlapped Discrete Multitone Modulation for High Speed Copper Wire Communications. *IEEE Journal on Selected Areas in Communications*, vol. 13, no. 9, pp. (1571-1585).

Steendam, H. & Moeneclaey, M. (1999). Analysis and Optimization of the Performance of OFDM on Frequency-Selective Time-Selective Fading Channels. *IEEE Transactions on Communications,* Vol. 47, No. 12, (Dec 99), pp. (1811- 1819).

Van de Beek, J. J.; Dling, P.; Wilson, S. K. & Brjesson, P. O. (1999). *Orthogonal Frequency Division Multiplexing (OFDM),* URSI Review of Radio Science 1996-1999, Oxford Publishers.

Weeks, M. (2007). *Digital Signal Processing Using Matlab and Wavelets*, Infinity Science Press LLC. ISBN-10: 0-7637-8422-2.

5

Several Kinds of Modified SPIHT Codec

Wenchao Zhang
Institute of Electronics, Chinese academy of science
People's Republic of China

1. Introduction

SPIHT (**Set Partitioning In hierachical trees**), being an efficient coding method for wavelet coefficients, has acquired more and more widely application, especially in image/video compression fields. But, conventional SPHIT have some obvious limitions. For example, when for the color image compression, polarmetric SAR image compression, or multi-spectrum image compression and other multi-channel image compression, there are only very limited image planes(R,G,B for color image, HH, HV,VVfor polarmetric SAR images) but there exist large amount of information redundancy among the image planes. So, considering the support length of discrete wavelet transform, we can't use the set 8-partition methods such as 3D-SPIHT which has been used for video compression. Another example, when the input image is unsymmetrical such as 16x512 image block even only one line image content, which is very common in hardware design, because it means the larger final chip die size for the many line buffers. But, the traditional SPIHT codec can acquire the best compression performances only for the image is symmetrical in horizontal and vertical dimension. To the above specific applications, I will discuss several kinds of modified SPIHT in this chapter, most of them are the author's newly research result.
In the following section, We will give a simple description about the traditional SPIHT codec, then, we will take the polarimetric SAR intensity image compression as example and give some specific compression method for multi-channel image compression. Certainly, before encoding for the wavelet coefficients, we need a 3D matrix transform to remove the information redundancy among the image plane and in each image plane. For the unsymmetrical image compression used in hardware design, an unsymmetrical SPIHT codec is detailed addressed, at the time, its specific case for only 1 line image compression, 1D SPIHT codec is also given.

2. Traditional SPIHT codec[1]

SPIHT can be used to compress the traditional image, but it need 2D discrete wavelet transform (DWT) before encode the wavelet coefficients. The correlation of DWT coefficients not only exist in each subband inside but also among different subbands. Conventional SPIHT codec is to encode coefficients by SOT (Spatial Orientation Tree), which utilize the correlation of the same subband and different subbands. Conventional SPIHT codec, having many advantages such as simpleness, embedded code stream when compared with other encoders, is a very efficient compression method.

According the SOT structure, the set partitioning can be defined as:

$$\begin{cases} T(i,j) = c(i,j) + D(i,j) \\ D(i,j) = O(i,j) + L(i,j) \\ L(i,j) = \sum D(k,l) \quad (k,l) \in O(i,j) \end{cases} \tag{1}$$

Here, $T(i,j)$ is spatial orientation tree and $c(i,j)$ is a root node of the tree; $D(i,j)$, $O(i,j)$ and $L(i,j)$ are node $c(i,j)$'s descendant node set, direct descendant node set and indirect descendant node set. Direct node set $O(i,j)$ can be further partitioned into 4 nodes just as the following:

$$O(i, j) = \{c(2i, 2j), c(2i, 2j+1), c(2i+1, 2j), c(2i+1, 2j+1)\} \tag{2}$$

Conventional SPIHT encoding process can be divided into sorting pass and refinement pass. During the encoding process, 3 lists are used to record the corresponding encoding information, which include List of insignificant set (LIS), list of insignificant pixel (LIP) and list of significant pixel (LSP). The basic operation is significance test and the significance test function is just as the following:

$$S_n(T) = \begin{cases} 1, & \max\limits_{(i,j)\in T}\left\{\left|c_{i,j}\right|\right\} \geq 2^n \\ 0, & otherwise, \end{cases} \tag{3}$$

The encoding process can be simply described as:
Output the initialized threshold $n = \lfloor \log_2(\max|c(i,j)|\rfloor$; set LSP as NULL; add the root nodes having and no having descendant nodes to LIS and LIP respectively.
For a spatial orientation tree $T(i,j)$, its nodes are partitioned into nodes $c(i,j)$ and descendant nodes $D(i,j)$ according to formula 1. If node $c(i,j)$ is significant, move it from LIP into LSP. If $D(i,j)$ is significant, then partition $D(i,j)$ into $O(i,j)$ and $L(i,j)$. The significant nodes of $O(i,j)$ will also be moved to LSP according to the significance test. If $L(i,j)$ is significant, then $L(i,j)$ will also be partitioned 4 set and test the significance of every set. This process will be continued on.
Sorting pass is for every element $c(i,j)$ of LSP; output the nth efficient bit of $c(i,j)$ for the current threshold n.
Decrease the n and continue the sorting pass and refinement pass until meet the required bit number or the end of encoding.
The decoding process is same to the encoding process, which, compared with EZW, make it un-necessary to transmit position information because the position information is embedded in the encoding process.

3. Multi-channel image compression

SPIHT, utilizing the information redundancy of 2D wavelet coefficients and adopting set 4 division, can be used to compress 2D image data. Naturally, it can be enlongated to 3D video compression, that is to say, if we adopt 3D DWT to remove the information redundancy of video data and choose set 8-partition instead of set 4-partition to encode 3D wavelet transform coefficients, this method is called 3D-SPIHT. But at some cases, we only need to compress multi-channel image, such as color images (R,G, B), polarimetric SAR image (HH,HV,VV), multi-spectrum image, ect. Because the third dimension usually have only limited image planes and can't be processed by supported discrete wavelet transform, however there exist much information redundancy among each image channel. In this case, consider it's simplity, 2D DWT for each image plane and 1D DCT can be used to remove the information redundancy. In the following section 3.1-3, taking polarimetric SAR image as example, 3D matrix transform and the related compression method including bit allocation based encoding method and 3D SPIHT Embedded method will be addressed.

3.1 3D matrix transform for multi-channel image

At first, 3D-matrix [2-3] is adopted to represent the multi-polarimetric SAR intensity images. The 1st, 2nd and 3rd planes represent the HH, HV and VV polarimetric SAR intensity image respectively. Assuming the image dimensions are: $M \times N$, the multi-polarimetric SAR images can be written as a $M \times N \times 3$ matrix $f(x,y,z)$ $(x = 0,1,2,\cdots M-1;$ $y = 0,1,2\cdots N-1; z = 0,1,2)$. In order to remove the redundancy of the matrix, DWT, KLT, DCT and other linear transforms can be used.

Because there are only 3 components in polarimetric channel and KLT is dependent on the statistic properties of data, DCT other than DWT or KLT or other linear transforms is chosen to remove the redundancy of polarimetric channels. According to DCT transform definition, the DCT transform can be represented as:

$$
\begin{aligned}
F(x,y,0) &= \frac{1}{\sqrt{3}}\sum_{z=0}^{2} f(x,y,z) \\
F(x,y,Z) &= \sqrt{\frac{2}{3}}\sum_{z=0}^{2} f(x,y,z)\cos\frac{(2z+1)Z\pi}{6} \qquad (Z=1,2)
\end{aligned} \tag{4}
$$

The 3D-matrix can be composed in other orders, such as HH, VV, HV acted as the 1st, 2nd and 3rd planes respectively. The components of like-polarimetric(HH and VV) have strong correlation, while the components of cross-polarimetric (HH/VV and HV) have weak correlation. Both the DCT theory and experiment results prove that the DCT coefficients of the matrix composed of HH, HV and VV are the most concentrated and that the decoded images have the least loss at the same coding rate

After 1D-DCT transform, the data power of the 3D-matrix is concentrated into the 1st plane and the redundancy among three data planes decreases greatly. In order to remove the redundancy in every data plane of the 3D matrix, 2D-DWT is chosen. According to the definition of 2D-DWT transform, the image data can be decomposed into horizontal, vertical, diagonal and low frequency components after horizontal and vertical filtering. The low frequency component can be decomposed further. After many level discrete wavelet transform, the data power is concentrated to the low frequency components. After 1D-DCT transform and 2D-DWT transform, the power of the whole 3D-matrix is concentrated onto the top left corner. 3 level wavelet transform is adopted, so each data plane is decomposed into 10 subbands including LL_3, HL_3, LH_3 HH_3, HL_2, LH_2, HH_2, HL_1, LH_1, HH_1. Of all the subbands, the LL_3 subband of the 1st plane has the highest power.

The 3D-matrix transform of Multi-polarimetric SAR intensity images (1D-DCT among polarimetric channel and 2D-DWT in each polarimetric plane) is illustrated in Figure.1. The

1D-DCT and 2D-DWT are linear transform, so, the operation $1DCT_z$ and $2DWT_{x,y}$ can be inverted in sequence, that is:

$$1DCT_z(2DWT_{x,y}(f(x,y,z))) = 2DWT_{x,y}(1DCT_z(f(x,y,z))) \quad (5)$$

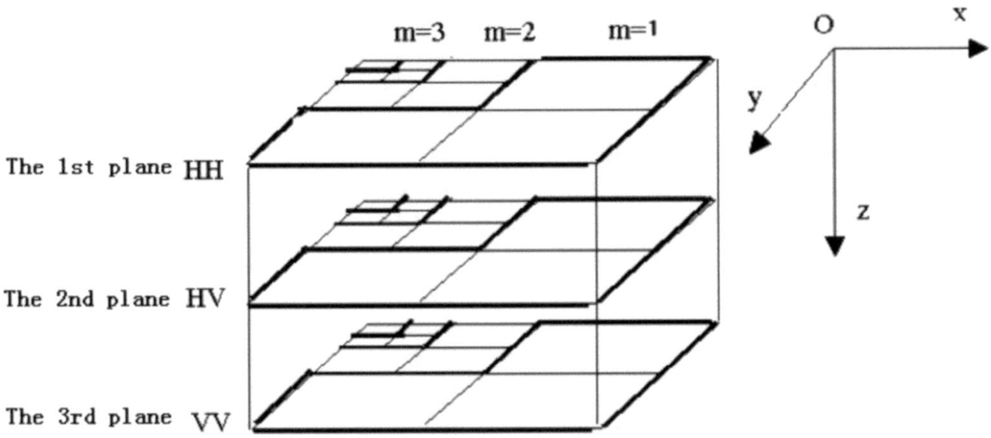

Fig. 1. Illustration of 3D-matrix transform of multi-polarimetric SAR intensity images.

3.2 Bit allocation based on differential entropy encoding

The three mixed coefficient planes have different energy, which means different importance. Different bit allocation scheme will greatly affect the quality of decoding images even at the same mean quantization bit rate. Our aim is to find the optimal quantization bits allocation to make the decoding images have the least distortion, which is a constrained optimal problem. The rate distortion function *R(D)* is unknown in most cases, so its solutions have become a hot research issue. Two variant iterate search [4], Dynamic programming [5] and R/D curve modeling [6] are proposed, but these methods yet haven't been adopted for its enormous computation complexity or the local optimal not the whole optimal bit allocation searched. In this subsection, a new bit allocation method based on differential entropy is proposed. Compared with the existing bit allocation methods, it is easy to find a better bit allocation in whole with the proposed method. At the same time, the computation is not very complex.

Let R_1, R_2, R_3 be the optimal bit rate for the three mixed coefficient plane respectively and R_T be the mean bit rate; Let $D(R)$ be distortion rate function. So, the optimal bit allocation problem can be represented as:

$$\begin{cases} \min\limits_{R_1,R_2,R_3} (D_1(R_1)+D_2(R_2)+D_3(R_3)) \\ \text{subject to } \; R_1+R_2+R_3 = 3R_T \end{cases} \quad (6)$$

Adopt the Lagrangian multiplier,

$$F(R_1,R_2,R_3) = D_1(R_1)+D_2(R_2)+D_3(R_3)+\lambda(3R_T - R_1 - R_2 - R_3) \quad (7)$$

From
$$\begin{cases} \dfrac{\partial F}{\partial R_1} = 0 \\ \dfrac{\partial F}{\partial R_2} = 0 \\ \dfrac{\partial F}{\partial R_3} = 0 \end{cases}$$

we can acquire

$$\begin{cases} \dfrac{\partial D_1(R_1)}{\partial R_1} = \lambda \\ \dfrac{\partial D_2(R_2)}{\partial R_2} = \lambda \\ \dfrac{\partial D_3(R_3)}{\partial R_3} = \lambda \end{cases} \quad (8)$$

According to the inequation of rate distortion function for non-Gauss continuous information source, we have:

$$h(U) - \frac{1}{2}\log 2\pi e D \le R(D) \le \frac{1}{2}\log\frac{\sigma^2}{D} \quad (9)$$

where $h(U)$ is the differential entropy of information source and σ^2 is its mean square error.

At high bit rate, the lower bound of the inequation approaches the real rate distortion function for most probability distributed information source. So, we can let the lower bound equal to the real rate distortion function and then acquire:

$$R(D) = h(U) - \frac{1}{2}\log 2\pi e D \quad (10)$$

Further, we can acquire

$$D(R) = \frac{e^{2(h(U)-R)}}{2\pi e} \quad (11)$$

and

$$\frac{\partial D(R)}{\partial R} = \frac{-e^{2(h(U)-R)}}{\pi e} \quad (12)$$

For every mixed coefficient plane:

$$\begin{cases} R_1 = h(U_1) - \dfrac{1}{2}\log(-\pi e \lambda) \\ R_2 = h(U_2) - \dfrac{1}{2}\log(-\pi e \lambda) \\ R_3 = h(U_3) - \dfrac{1}{2}\log(-\pi e \lambda) \end{cases} \quad (13)$$

According to the constrain condition $R_1 + R_2 + R_3 = 3R_T$, we can acquire the final bit allocation for every coefficient plane:

$$\begin{cases} R_1 = R_T + \dfrac{2h(U_1) - h(U_2) - h(U_3)}{3} \\ R_2 = R_T + \dfrac{2h(U_2) - h(U_1) - h(U_3)}{3} \\ R_3 = R_T + \dfrac{2h(U_3) - h(U_1) - h(U_2)}{3} \end{cases} \tag{14}$$

From formula (14), we can acquire the optimal bit allocation for the three mixed coefficient planes, then the conventional SPIHT can be adopted to encode the coefficients for every plane according to the corresponding allocated bit rate.

3.3 3D-SPIHT embedded encoding

The formula (14) provides a method to compute the bit rate allocation, but the bit allocation accuracy strongly depends on the degree of the lower bound of formula (9) approaches the real rate distortion function. So, in most cases, we only can acquire an approximating optimal bit allocation. In this subsection, a new method named 3D-SPIHT embedded algorithm is proposed, which extends the conventional SPIHT algorithm to 3D case. It avoids bit allocation by adopting 3D-SPIHT to encode the three mixed coefficient plane entirely, so the optimal bit rate allocation can be ensured.

During the 3D-SPIHT encoding process, the following sets and lists will be used:

$H_{iplane}(i,j)$, $D_{iplane}(i,j)$, $O_{iplane}(i,j)$ and $L_{iplane}(i,j)$ represent the $iplane^{th}$ coefficient plane's root node, descendant's nodes of node(i,j), offspring's nodes of node(i,j) and indirect offspring's nodes of node(i,j) respectively. LIS_{iplane}, LIP_{iplane} and LSP_{iplane} represent the $iplane^{th}$ plane's list of insignificant pixel sets, list of insignificant pixels and list of significant pixels respectively, where $iplane = 1,2,3$.

Just as the conventional SPIHT algorithm, the set splitting procedure for every coefficient plane can be defined as following:

$$\begin{cases} T_{iplane}(i,j) = H_{iplane}(i,j) + D_{iplane}(i,j) \\ D_{iplane}(i,j) = O_{iplane}(i,j) + L_{iplane}(i,j) \\ L_{iplane}(i,j) = \sum D_{iplane}(k,l) \quad (k,l) \in O_{iplane}(i,j) \end{cases} \tag{15}$$

The 3D-SPIHT process can be divided into sorting pass and refinement pass, whose basic operations is also significance test of set just as the conventional SPIHT algorithm. That is,

$$S_n\left(T_{iplane}\right) = \begin{cases} 1, & \max\limits_{(i,j)\in T_{iplane}}\left\{\left|C_{iplane}(i,j)\right|\right\} \geq 2^n \\ 0, & otherwise \end{cases} \tag{16}$$

where $C_{iplane}(i,j)$ is the wavelet coefficient of coordinate (i,j) in the $iplane^{th}$ mixed coefficient plane.

The followings are the coding process:

1. Initialization

$$\text{Output} \quad \begin{cases} n\_\max_1 = \left\lfloor \log_2\left(\max_{(i,j)}\{|C_1(i,j)|\}\right)\right\rfloor \\ n\_\max_2 = \left\lfloor \log_2\left(\max_{(i,j)}\{|C_2(i,j)|\}\right)\right\rfloor \\ n\_\max_3 = \left\lfloor \log_2\left(\max_{(i,j)}\{|C_3(i,j)|\}\right)\right\rfloor \\ n \quad = n\_\max_1 \end{cases} \tag{17}$$

(For the HH HV VV combination, $n\_\max_1 > n\_\max_3 > n\_\max_2$ can always be satisfied)
For every coefficient plane, set list of significant pixels (LSP_{iplane}) as NULL, then add the coordinate $(i,j) \in H_{iplane}$ to LIP_{iplane} and those that have descendants to LIS_{iplane}, at the same time, set their type to be A.

2. Sorting pass

If $n\_\max_3 < n$, only sort $C_1(i,j)$ just as conventional SPIHT algorithm.
If $n\_\max_2 < n < n\_\max_3$, sort $C_1(i,j)$ and then sort $C_3(i,j)$ in succession.
If $n < n\_\max_2$, sort $C_1(i,j)$ and then sort $C_2(i,j)$, $C_3(i,j)$ in succession.

3. Refinement pass

If $n\_\max_3 < n$, for any entry (i,j) in LSP_1 except those included in the last sorting pass, output the *n*th most significant bit of $C_1(i,j)$.
If $n\_\max_2 < n < n\_\max_3$, for any entry (i,j) in LSP_1 and LSP_3 except those included in the last sorting pass, output the *n*th most significant bit of $C_1(i,j)$ and $C_3(i,j)$.
If $n < n\_\max_2$, for any entry (i,j) in LSP_1, LSP_2 and LSP_3 except those included in the last sorting pass, output the *n*th most significant bit of $C_1(i,j)$, $C_2(i,j)$ and $C_3(i,j)$.

4. Quantization updating

Decrement *n* by 1 and go to step 2 until acquire the desired compression ratio.
The code stream of embedded 3D-SPIHT encoding can be illustrated as figure.2. The decoding process and encoding process are just the same. So, it's easy to present the decoding process according to the 3D-SPIHT encoding process. The code stream of 3D-SPIHT is more compact and efficient for the three mixed coefficient planes are interleaved during the encoding process.

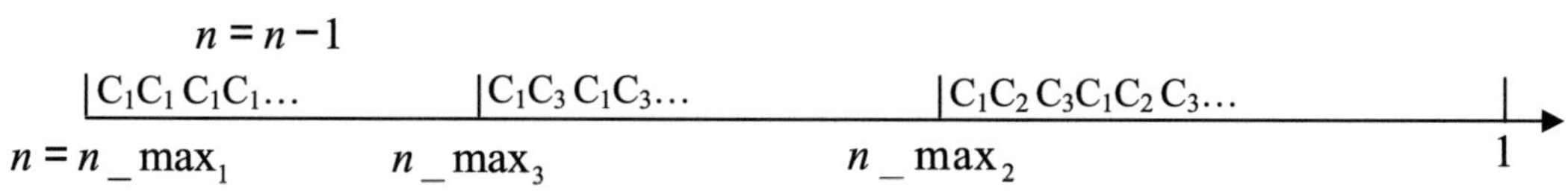

Fig. 2. Code stream illustration for embedded 3D-SPIHT.

Additionally, it is necessary to be mentioned that there have been two kinds of 3D-SPIHT algorithms before. One is proposed for video compression by extending the conventional SPIHT algorithm to 3D case directly and encoding the 3D-DWT wavelet coefficients of video data, so the SOF is defined as 8 splitting [7]. The other is proposed for compression of multispectral images, which make some amendments of the conventional SPIHT by adding one spectral child to every baseband coefficient, so its SOF is still 4 splitting [8]. The proposed 3D-SPIHT embedded coding in this book is very different from the two existing 3D-SPIHT algorithms, which encodes 1 or 2 or 3 coefficient planes of the 3 mixed coefficient plane sequentially by adopting 3 independent thresholds.

4. Unsymmetrical SPIHT codec

It is easy to find that the set partitioning is keeping on 4 partitioning for conventional SPIHT codec, that is to say the same set partitioning in vertical and horizontal direction. This means that the wavelet decomposition only can be implemented under the constraint of the same decomposition level in vertical and horizontal direction, which will affect the redundancy removing of image data efficiently and the final compression performance. The unsymmetrical SPIHT codec, adopting set 2-partitioning or set 4-partitioning according the requirements, doesn't require the same decomposition level in vertical and horizontal direction. So, DWT can be implemented with each highest feasible decomposition level in vertical and horizontal direction respectively and then the spatial redundancy can be removed efficiently.

Because the flow chart of unsymmetrical SPIHT codec is very near to conventional SPIHT codec, only the difference is given.

Assume the image dimensions are $W*H$ and $H=h*2^{HLevel}, W=w*2^{WLevel}$, here $HLevel, WLevel$ are the highest feasible decomposition level in vertical and horizontal direction respectively. Usually, there exists $HLevel \neq WLevel$ when the image size are unsymmetrical. For the conventional SPIHT, the highest feasible decomposition level only can be the lower one of $HLevel$ and $WLevel$, so, $Level = \min(WLevel, HLevel)$. But for unsymmetrical SPIHT codec, the highest wavelet decomposition levels in vertical and horizontal direction are $HLevel$ and $WLevel$ respectively.

All set partitions for conventional SPIHT are set 4 partitioning just as the formula 2, but the set partitions for unsymmetrical SPIHT are set 2-partitioning or set 4-partitioning, just as the following formula:

$$O(i,j)=\begin{cases} c(i,2j), c(i,2j+1) & if\ H_0 \le i < \frac{H}{2} \\ c(2i,j), c(2i+1,j) & if\ \ iW_0 \le j < \frac{W}{2} \\ c(2i,2j), c(2i+1,2j), c(2i,2j+1), c(2i+1,2j+1) & otherwise \end{cases} \tag{18}$$

Here, $H_0 = \frac{H}{2^{HLevel-WLevel+1}}$, $W_0 = \frac{W}{2^{WLevel-HLevel+1}}$.

When $HLevel = WLevel$, the unsymmetrical SPIHT codec will completely degenerate into conventional SPIHT codec. When $HLevel = 1$ or $WLevel = 1$, only set 2-partitioning are implemented in one direction, the coefficients can be encoded line by line independently. The wavelet transform in another direction is only be used as compacting the image energy. Fig 3 and Fig 4 are the illustrations of conventional SPIHT encoding and unsymmetrical SPIHT encoding at $HLevel = 3$ or $WLevel = 5$.

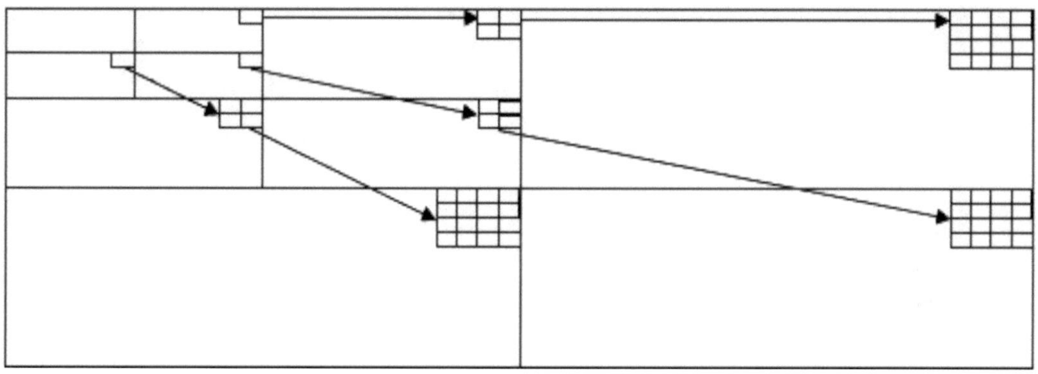

Fig. 3. The illustration of set partitioning using conventional SPIHT encoding for unsymmetrical image size

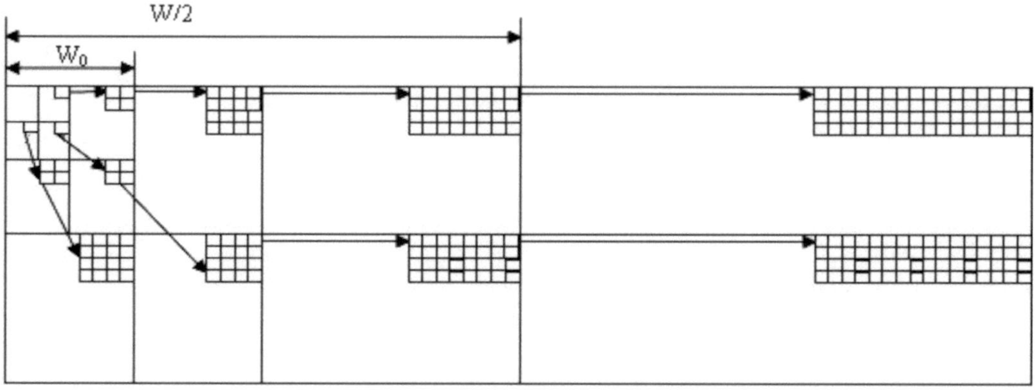

Fig. 4. The illustration of set partitioning with unsymmetrical SPIHT encoding for unsymmetrical image size

5. 1D SPIHT codec

In section 4, unsymmetrical SPIHT codec is detailed described, which also need 2D image data or image block. But, in real time image transmission or scan display system, the image data are usually transmitted or displayed line by line. In order to use conventional SPIHT or unsymmetrical SPIHT, it needs many line buffers to store the previous image data. In hardware, it is a high burden for the costly RAM. So, 1 line image data compression method will have the precedence over other block based compression methods, such as the 1D DWT followed 1D SPIHT codec which will be addressed in the following.
After 1D DWT, the wavelet coefficient also has the natural pyramid characteristic: every pixel of the high frequency subband has its 2 corresponding pixels in its adjacent level high frequency subbands in position, which means that only set 2-partitioning can adopted. The illustration is given in fig3.

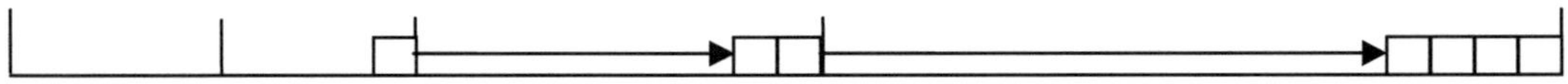

Fig. 5. The illustration of set partitioning with 1D SPIHT encoding for 1 line image.

The SOT and set partitioning can be written as formula 19 and 20.

$$\begin{cases} T(i) = c(i) + D(i) \\ D(i) = O(i) + L(i) \\ L(i) = \sum D(k) \quad (k) \in O(i) \end{cases} \tag{19}$$

$$O(i) = \{c(2i),\ c\ (2i+1)\} \tag{20}$$

From fig 5 and formula 19 and 20, we can see that 1D SPIHT use set 2 partitioning to encode 1D DWT coefficients, which only need 1 line buffer RAM but leave another dimensional redundancy un-removed.

6. Conclusion

In this chapter, SPIHT and it's derivatives or its modification methods, such as 3D-SPIHT, 3D-SPIHT Embedded method, Unsymmetrical SPIHT and 1D-SPIHT are described, which can overcome the disadvantages of traditional SPIHT codec and meet the specific requirements for the real applications. Fig.6 gives the derivative relationship of traditional SPIHT and its several modified methods. We can see that SPIHT is the foundation for traditional symmetrical image, but it can't meet the requirements at some specific applications, such as multi-channel image, strip image (unsymmetrical image), even image line. But, its modified version can meet some specific requirements in real applications.

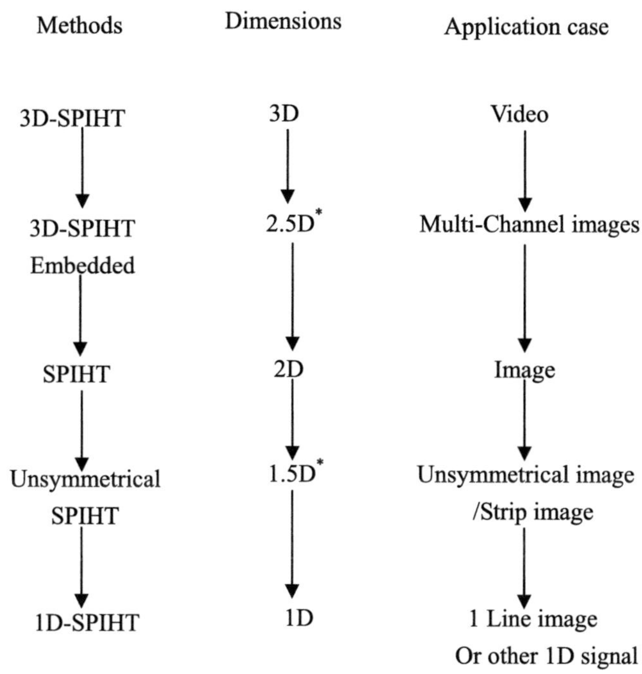

* mean the corresponding dimension is limited compared other dimensions

Fig. 6. Family of SPIHT and its derivatives.

7. References

[1] Said A. and Pearlman W.A., A new fast and efficient image codec based on set partitioning in hierarchal trees, IEEE Trans. on Circuits and Systems for Video Technology, 1996, 6(3): 243-250.

[2] D. E. Dudgen, R. M. Mersereau, Multidimensional digital signal processing, New Jersey：prentice-Hall, Inc.,1984.

[3] Zhu Yanqiu，Chen Hexin，Dai Yisong. Compression Coding of color image via 3-D matrix transform [J] ACTA EI ECTRONICA SINICA，1997，25(7):16-21.

[4] Y. Shoham, A. Gersho, Efficient bit allocation for an arbitrary set of quantizers, IEEE Transaction on Acoustics,Speech, and Signal Processing, 1988,36(9):1445-1453

[5] P. Prandoni, M. Vetterli, R/D optimal linear predication, IEEE Transaction on Speech and Audio Processing, 2000,8(6):646-655.

[6] A. Aminlou, O. Fatemi, Very fast bit allocation algorithm, based on simplified R-D curve modeling, IEEE ICECS 2003, 112-115.

[7] B. J. Kim, Z. Xiong, W. A. Pearlman,Low bit-rate scalable video coding with 3-D set partitioning in hierarchical trees(3-D SPIHT), IEEE Transaction on Circuilt and System for Video technology, 2000, 10(8): 1374-1387.

[8] P. L. Dragotti, G. Poggi and A. R. P. Ragozini, Compression of multispectral images by three-dimensional SPIHT algorithm, IEEE Transaction on Geoscience and Remote sensing, 2000, 38(1):416-428.

[9] W.-C. Zhang, Y.-F. Wang, G.-H. Hu,.Compression of multi-polarimetric SAR intensity images based on 3D-matrix transform, *IET- Image processing,* 2008,2(4):194:202.
[10] Zhang Zhi-hui, Zhang Jun, Unsymmetrical SPIHT Codec and 1D SPIHT Codec, International Conference on Electrical and Control Engineering (ICECE), 2010, wuhan 2498:2501.

Part 2

Image Processing Applications

6

Multiresolution Approaches for Edge Detection and Classification Based on Discrete Wavelet Transform

Guillermo Palacios, J. Ramón Beltrán and Raquel Lacuesta
University of Zaragoza
Spain

1. Introduction

Detecting edges is a very well known subject in the image-processing field. Edge detection is the process of the localization of significant discontinuities in the grey level image and the identification of the physical phenomena that originated them. Those significant intensity changes occur at different resolution or scales for a given image. As suggested by Rosenfeld and Thurston (Rosenfeld & Thurston, 1976) and Marr (Marr, 1982), we can obtain a description of the image changes at different scales combining the information given by an edge detector applied at different resolutions. This is the aim of the work presented in this paper.

The first aspect to be covered by multiresolution analysis is the filter chosen to accomplish the low-pass filtering of the image at different scales. At a single resolution, low pass filtering is imposed because differentiation is an ill-posed problem (Torre & Poggio, 1984). The needed regularization process is implemented by means of a low pass filter. Marr (Marr, 1982) proposed the Gaussian filter because its optimal behaviour in terms of the smoothing and the localization in both the spatial and frequency domains. This filter has been commonly used in edge detectors. In a multiresolution approach the first or second directional derivatives of the low pass filtered image with Gaussians of different widths are used to detect edges. In the Bergholm edge focusing method (Bergholm, 1987) various edge maps extracted at different scales are integrated allowing distinguishing shadows contours from perfect ones using Canny's operator (Canny, 1986) with different widths. Another possibility is to describe the image in terms of the scale space as proposed by Witkin (Witkin, 1983) and to detect edges in terms of the zero crossing of the Laplacian operator with different widths (Park et al., 1995) (Eklundth et al., 1982).

Other multiresolution methods have been proposed. Mallat and Zhong (Mallat & Zhong, 1992) related multiscale edge detection with the discrete wavelet transform (DWT). They proposed a wavelet to perform edge detection and they showed that the evolution of wavelet local maxima across scales characterizes the shape of irregular structures. In our work we will use the wavelet-based algorithm proposed by Mallat and Zhong and we will show the condition that must be satisfied by the Gaussian filter to be comparable with the Mallat and Zhong's wavelet. Our aim is to detect and classify different edge types. Various edge profiles have been proposed. Rosenfeld (Rosenfeld & Kak, 1976) proposed the step, ramp, pulse and stair as the basic edge types. He stated that these profiles are suited for a first intuitive classification of the edges found in the contours of real images.

William and Shah (Williams & Shah, 1990, 1993) have studied these edge types using the first directional derivative of the Gaussian. Some other profiles like the blurred step have also been proposed and analyzed (Ziou & Tabbone, 1993). In a first step of this work we are going to analyze the evolution of the modulus of the wavelet coefficients at the edge position in order to classify the edges into four different profiles: step, ramp, stair and pulse (Beltrán et al., 1994). Then we will propose a general schema to detect, analyze and classify different edge types.

Due to the high pass filtering operation involved in the edge detection algorithms, the noise is always amplified when detecting edges. Thresholding has been the most common way to eliminate the irrelevant or noise detected edges (Canny, 1986; Marr, 1982). To validate the proposed classification schema we will present the noise (Gaussian noise) as a new edge class (Beltrán et al., 1998). Then, we have analyzed this contour type and we have modified the proposed classification algorithm to include the noise as a new edge type. With the noise edges labelled we can easily implement a noise-filtering algorithm. Finally, we have developed a new classification algorithm including other edge profile models, such as the roof, ridge and two non-antisymmetrical step profiles, like the ones proposed by Paillou (Paillou, 1994).

This chapter is divided as follows. Section 2 presents a survey of the wavelet formalism introduced by Mallat and Zhong. Then, we will show the geometrical contour types: step, ramp, pulse and stair. Section 3 presents the edge detection algorithm including the wavelet algorithm implementation. Section 4 presents the classification algorithm implementation details as well as the classification results obtained processing a 256x256 grey level synthetic image with four objects: a circle, a square, a triangle and a narrow line, each one having a different contour type. Section 5 deals with the characterization of the noise as a new type of contour. Section 6 copes with the new contour types just introduced, the modified classification algorithm together with the obtained results. In section 7 we present the main conclusions and the future work.

2. Theoretical basis

Mallat and Zhong (Mallat & Zhong, 1992) introduced the relationship between the wavelet transform and a multiresolution edge detection algorithm. We are going to briefly summarize those results. Let be $f(x,y) \in L^2(R^2)$ an image and $\psi(x,y)$ a wavelet. The bidimensional wavelet transform of f(x,y) is defined as:

$$W_S f(u,v) = \int_{-\infty}^{+\infty}\int_{-\infty}^{+\infty} f(x,y)\frac{1}{s}\psi\left(\frac{x-u}{s},\frac{y-v}{s}\right) \tag{1}$$

If we define the dilation by a factor s as:

$$\psi_S(x,y) = \frac{1}{s}\psi\left(\frac{x}{s},\frac{y}{s}\right) \tag{2}$$

and $\tilde{\psi}(x,y) = \tilde{\psi}(-x,-y)$, we can rewrite (1) as a convolution:

$$W_S f(u,v) = f * \tilde{\psi}_S(u,v) \tag{3}$$

So, as expressed in (3), the wavelet transform can be seen as the filtering of f(x,y) by the filter $\tilde{\psi}_s$ (x,y), that is a variable width bandpass filter (Mallat, 1989). It is possible to define N directional wavelets $\psi^i(x,y)$ $(1 \le i \le N)$, satisfying energy conservation properties. In such a case the directional wavelet transform of f(x,y) is defined as:

$$W_s^i f(u,v) = f * \tilde{\psi}_s^i(u,v) \tag{4}$$

Equation (4) represents the filtering of f(x,y) by the bidimensional, directional and bandpass filter $\tilde{\psi}_s^i$ (x,y).
We can define the Discrete Wavelet Transform (DWT) by selecting the scales inside a dyadic grid; that is to say, the scale could be expressed as $S=2^j$ with $j \in \mathbf{Z}$. Therefore, for discrete signals, we can understand the 2-D wavelet transform as the result of filtering the 2-D signal (the original image) with a bandpass directional FIR filter.
Mallat and Zhong (Mallat & Zhong, 1992) designed a function specially suited for edge detection purposes, which is a wavelet. This function is not a orthogonal wavelet, so the only condition to be satisfied by $\psi(x,y)$ is:

$$\int_{-\infty}^{+\infty}\int_{-\infty}^{+\infty} \psi(u,v)\,du\,dv = 0 \tag{5}$$

We can define two functions $\psi^1(x,y)$ and $\psi^2(x,y)$ as:

$$\psi^1(x,y) = \frac{\partial\theta(x,y)}{\partial x}, \quad \psi^2(x,y) = \frac{\partial\theta(x,y)}{\partial y} \tag{6}$$

Where $\theta(x,y)$ is a smoothing function, that is to say, the integral over x and y is one, and it converges to zero at infinity. With these conditions is easy to show that both $\psi^1(x,y)$ and $\psi^2(x,y)$ satisfy (5), so they are wavelets. Following equation (3) we can say that the wavelet transform of f(x,y) is:

$$\begin{aligned} W_S^1 f(x,y) &= f * \tilde{\psi}_S^1(x,y) \\ W_S^2 f(x,y) &= f * \tilde{\psi}_S^2(x,y) \end{aligned} \tag{7}$$

From (6) and (7) it can be shown that the wavelet transform is the gradient of the image smoothed by a factor or scale s. It can be expressed as:

$$\begin{pmatrix} W_S^1 f(x,y) \\ W_S^2 f(x,y) \end{pmatrix} = s \begin{pmatrix} \frac{\partial}{\partial x}(f * \theta_S) \\ \frac{\partial}{\partial y}(f * \theta_S) \end{pmatrix} = s\vec{\nabla}(f * \theta_S) \tag{8}$$

We can define the modulus **M** and the phase **Φ** of the gradient at scale s as:

$$M\left(\vec{\nabla}(f * \theta_s)\right) = \sqrt{\left|W_s^1 f(x,y)\right|^2 + \left|W_s^2 f(x,y)\right|^2} \tag{9}$$

$$\Phi\left(\vec{\nabla}(f*\theta_s)\right)=\operatorname{atan}\left(\frac{W_s^2 f(x,y)}{W_s^1 f(x,y)}\right) \tag{10}$$

A point (x_0,y_0) will be an edge point of the smoothed image $f*\theta_s(x,y)$ if in this point there is a relative maximum of **M** in the direction addressed by **Φ**. The above statement is the classical definition of edge detection proposed by Canny [5]. In the wavelet case we have a discrete set of scales $s=2^j$ $(0\le j\le J)$, and we can calculate the edges at each scale and not at an only one scale as described in Canny's work. So, we can conclude that we can implement a multiresolution edge detection algorithm by means of the 2-D wavelet transform. The smoothing function could be a new defined function, as in Mallat and Zhong's work, or a Gaussian function, as in Canny's work.

Mallat and Zhong (Mallat & Zhong, 1992) defined $\theta(x,y)$ as a separable bidimensional cubic spline, so $\psi(x,y)$ is a separable bidimensional quadratic spline. Their 1-D expressions are:

$$\hat{\theta}(x)=\begin{cases}\frac{8}{3}x^3+8x^2+8x+\frac{8}{3} & \text{if } -1\le x\le -1/2\\ -8x^3-8x^2+\frac{4}{3} & \text{if } -1/2\le x\le 0\\ 8x^3-8x^2+\frac{4}{3} & \text{if } 0\le x\le 1/2\\ -\frac{8}{3}x^3+8x^2-8x+\frac{8}{3} & \text{if } 1/2\le x\le 1\\ 0 & \text{otherwise}\end{cases} \tag{11}$$

$$\hat{\psi}(x)=\begin{cases}8x^2+16x+8 & \text{if } -1\le x\le -1/2\\ -24x^2-16x & \text{if } -1/2\le x\le 0\\ 24x^2-16x & \text{if } 0\le x\le 1/2\\ -8x^2+16x-8 & \text{if } 1/2\le x\le 1\\ 0 & \text{otherwise}\end{cases} \tag{12}$$

In the 2-D case we can define $\theta(x,y)=\hat{\theta}(x)\hat{\theta}(y)$ and $\psi(x,y)=\hat{\psi}(x)\hat{\psi}(y)$. We can compare the wavelet and the Gaussian functions behaviour. In figure 1 we can observe that both functions present a similar aspect. We have obtained a relationship between the Gaussian width σ and the scale s of the wavelet analysis. The Gaussian normalization constant is:

$N=\frac{1}{\sqrt{2\pi}\cdot\sigma}$, and the smoothing function value at the origin is $\theta(0)=\frac{4}{3}$.

Equating both quantities we obtain σ= 0.3. So, to obtain a similar analysis with the wavelet and the Gaussian function, the Gaussian width and the scale should be related by the aforementioned expression.

Now we will to present the edge profiles considered initially. We have considered that each profile contour is a function that represents a change in the grey level with respect to the image dimensions. In this work we will name U_i the contour height, ω the contour width, x_0 the contour position (at the middle of the contour) and s the scale.

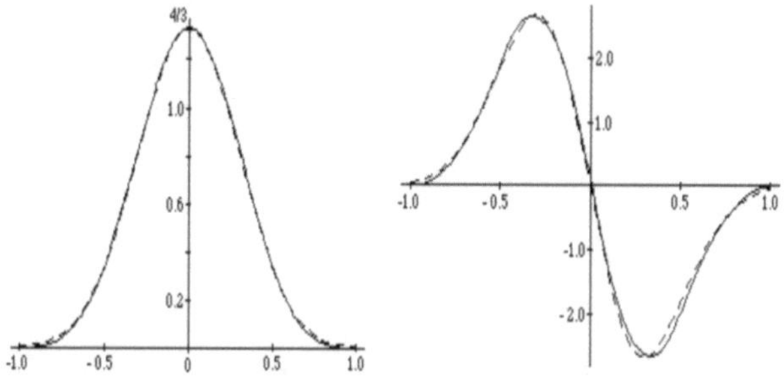

Fig. 1. Left: Solid line: Smoothing function. Dotted line: Gaussian with $\sigma = 0.3$. Right: Solid line: Wavelet. Dotted line: First derivative of Gaussian with $\sigma = 0.3$.

2.1 Step

A step profile is shown in figure 2. We have named x_0 the step location and U_0 the step height. Let be u(x) the step function.

$$u(x) = \begin{cases} U_0 & \text{if } x \geq x_0 \\ 0 & \text{if } x < x_0 \end{cases} \tag{13}$$

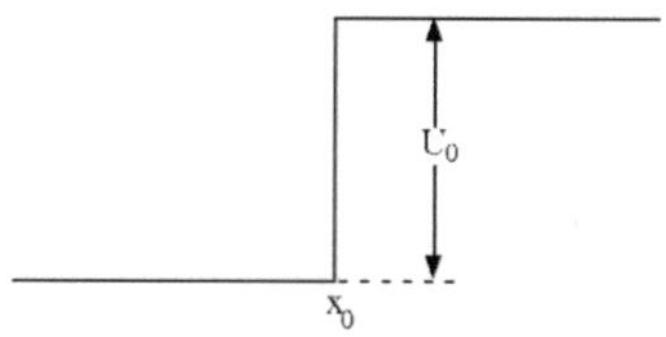

Fig. 2. Step profile. Horizontal axis represents pixels. Vertical axis represents grey level.

2.2 Ramp

The ramp profile is drawn in figure 3. The point x_0 is the middle point of the ramp; U_0 is the height and ω is the ramp width. The ramp slope is $m = U_0/\omega$. Let be r(x) the ramp function.

$$r(x) = \begin{cases} 0 & \text{if } x < x_0 - \dfrac{\omega}{2} \\ mx + r_0 & \text{if } x_0 - \dfrac{\omega}{2} \leq x \leq x_0 + \dfrac{\omega}{2} \\ U_0 & \text{if } x > x_0 + \dfrac{\omega}{2} \end{cases} \tag{14}$$

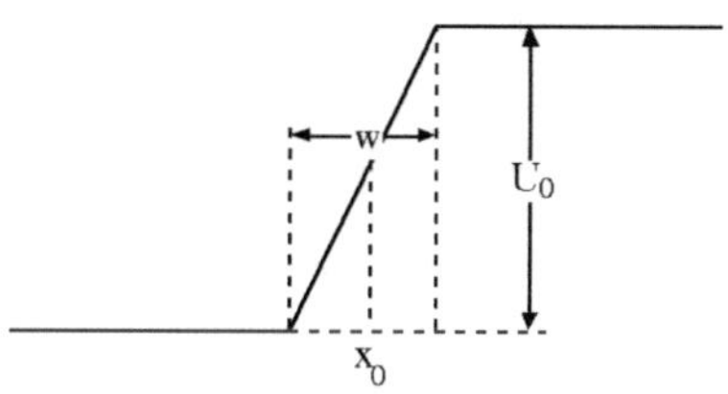

Fig. 3. Ramp profile. Horizontal axis represents pixels. Vertical axis represents grey level.

2.3 Stair

A stair profile with two steps, named s(x), is shown in figure 4. We have named the point x_0 the middle of the stair, ω is the stair width and U_0 and U_1 are, respectively, the steps height.

$$s(x)=\begin{cases}0 & \text{if } x<x_0-\dfrac{\omega}{2}\\ U_1 & \text{if } x_0-\dfrac{\omega}{2}\leq x\leq x_0+\dfrac{\omega}{2}\\ U_0 & \text{if } x>x_0+\dfrac{\omega}{2}\end{cases} \tag{15}$$

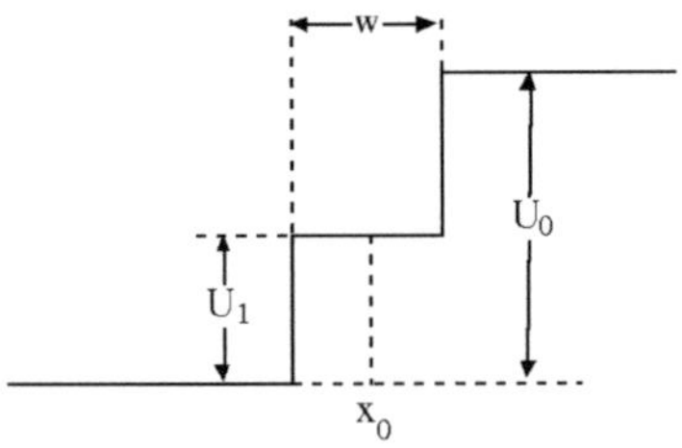

Fig. 4. Stair profile. Horizontal axis represents pixels. Vertical axis represents grey level.

2.4 Pulse

A pulse profile, named p(x), is shown in figure 5. The point x_0 is the middle of the pulse, ω is the width. U_0 and U_1 are, respectively, the maximum and minimum height.

$$p(x)=\begin{cases}0 & \text{if } x<x_0-\dfrac{\omega}{2}\\ U_0 & \text{if } x_0-\dfrac{\omega}{2}\leq x\leq x_0+\dfrac{\omega}{2}\\ U_1 & \text{if } x>x_0+\dfrac{\omega}{2}\end{cases} \tag{16}$$

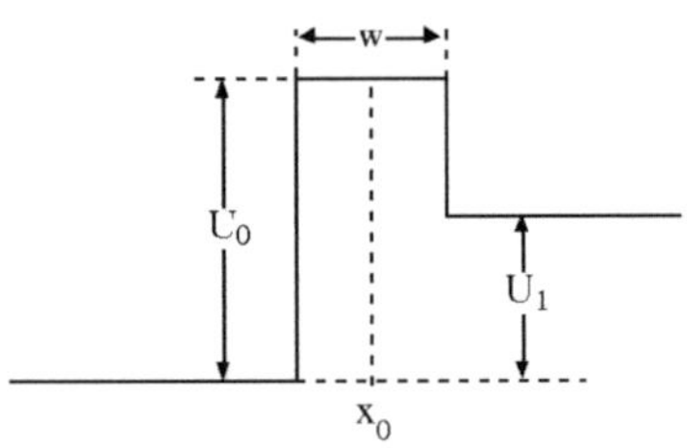

Fig. 5. Pulse profile. Horizontal axis represents pixels. Vertical axis represents grey level.

3. Edge detection algorithm

The processing algorithm we have used is the edge detection algorithm proposed in Mallat and Zhong's work (Mallat & Zhong, 1992). For analysis purposes we have used six of the eight possible scales for a 256x256 grey level image. The scale s forms a dyadic sequence (s = 2j, j = 1..6). The algorithm is summarized in figure 6, and table 1 shows the values of the normalization coefficients λ_j. The algorithm outputs are twelve 256x256 grey level images for each original one, six corresponding to the modulus of the derivative and six to the phase.

As we have pointed out in section 2, it is possible to perform a multiresolution analysis changing the smoothing function. The only difference between a typical Gaussian algorithm and the wavelet one is the filtering stage. In this case, instead of using the filter proposed by Mallat and Zhong, a Gaussian filter with a different size for each scale could be used. It leads to a different way to obtain the derivative of the image at different scales. A more detailed discussion about the Gaussian-based processing algorithm is given in Beltrán (Beltrán et al., 1998). Processing the image with the wavelet filter is faster, in computational cost terms, because the non-zero coefficients are constant independent on scale.

In order to obtain the contour image, a top-down searching algorithm has been implemented. For accepting a maximum at one scale to be an edge, it has been imposed that the maxima have to be propagated to the lowest scale with no change in the gradient direction between scales. When a maximum is found at one scale s we look for extrema in the lower scale within an interval of 2s centered in the extrema position at the scale s, in the direction given by the gradient. This interval is greater than the theoretical one found by Beltrán (Beltrán, 1994), in order to cover the maxima displacement.

The maximum appearing in the lower scale has to have the same direction that the upper one. The best edge position is given at the lowest scale. The first scale to be analyzed depends strongly on the image. Empirically we have noticed that this scale has to be no higher than either the 5th or the 6th. Otherwise, we have a strong blurring in the image that gives us information of global objects rather than finer patterns, like edges. The procedure has been iterated until first scale. A stop could be done at an upper scale, depending on the details we are looking for. If we were looking for finer details we should reach the first scale. A global threshold has been included in order to discard irrelevant edges.

j	λj
1	1.5
2	1.125
3	1.031
4	1.007
5	1.001
6	1

Table 1. Wavelet filtering normalization coefficients.

At the output of this block, we obtain a black and white image with the edge positions, and, for each detected edge, the values of the modulus of the gradient in each scale. The final step is the contour classification, which is made by analyzing the evolution of the modulus of the gradient across scales.

for $j = 1$ *to* 6

$$W_j^1 = \frac{1}{\lambda_j} S_{j-1} * G_{j-1}^1$$

$$W_j^2 = \frac{1}{\lambda_j} S_{j-1} * G_{j-1}^2$$

$$S_j = \left(S_{j-1} * H_{j-1}\right) * H_{j-1}'$$

$$M_j = \sqrt{\left(W_j^1\right)^2 + \left(W_j^2\right)^2}$$

$$P_j = atan \frac{W_j^2}{W_j^1}$$

end

$$H_0 = [0.125 \quad 0.375 \quad 0.375 \quad 0.125]$$

$$G_0^1 = [-2 \quad 2] \quad G_0^2 = \begin{bmatrix} -2 \\ 2 \end{bmatrix}$$

* is the convolution.

F' is the transpose of F.

F_j is the filter F with 2^j -1 zeros between each coefficient

Fig. 6. Wavelet Algorithm.

4. Classification schema

To obtain real evolution patterns in an image we have analyzed the evolution across scales of the value of the wavelet transform modulus for each contour type at the point at which the edge is located in our test image (see figure 7).

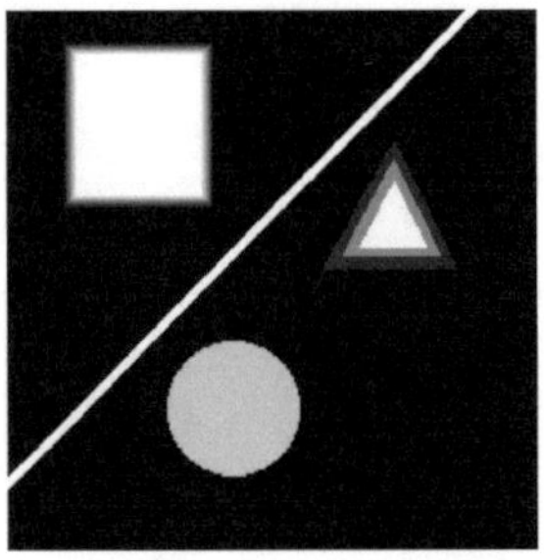

Fig. 7. Test image. Each object has a different contour profile. Circle: step. Square: ramp. Triangle: stair. Straight line: pulse.

In figure 8 we present for each contour class both the median value (normalized to the highest value for each pixel) and the deviation for each scale.

It can be seen a decreasing behavior in the evolution for each contour class in the upper scales due to the interaction between the opposite contours in the image. This decreasing pattern is not present in the 1-D case. From those results we can say that a step profile, figure 8(a), is characterized by an almost constant evolution across scales. The evolution pattern for a ramp, presented in figure 8(b), is a continuous growing from low to high scales. A constant value followed by an increasing in the normalized modulus of the gradient in the

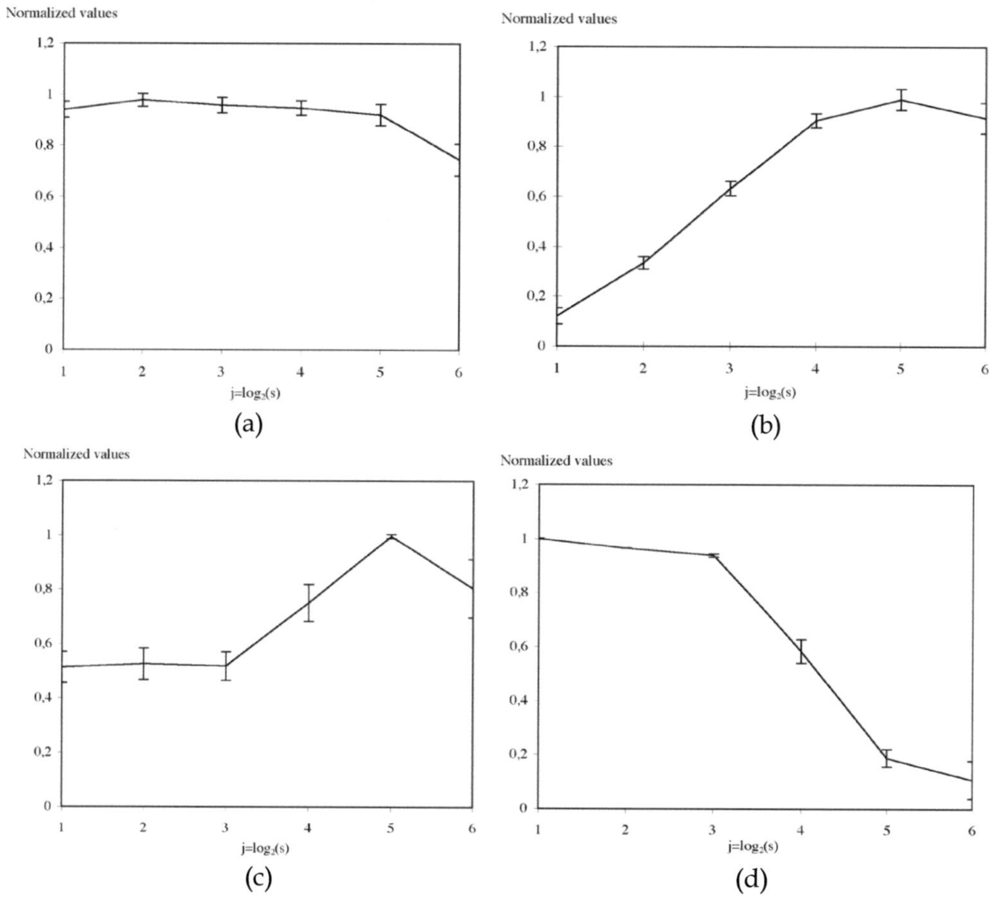

Fig. 8. (a) Step evolution. (b) Ramp evolution. (c) Stair evolution. (d) Pulse evolution. (See text for details)

edge position characterizes a stair contour, figure 8(c). As shown in figure 8(d) the pulse profile presents a sharp decreasing in the upper scales due to the interaction between the positive and negative slopes.

Figure 9 shows a block diagram of the edge detection and classification algorithm. An immediate conclusion is that it is possible to implement an algorithm to detect and classify the above-characterized four profiles using the wavelet transform coefficients. Then, we are able to distinguish one contour type from another one only by looking at the coefficients evolution at the appropriate contour point and with no pre-processing in the coefficient values.

The classification engine is based in a second-order polynomial-fitting algorithm. We have chosen a second order taking into account the easiness of implementation of properties such as derivability, continuity, concavity, and convexity. Analyzing the concavity and convexity, zero crossing and minimum abscissa and ordinate of the fitted polynomial we are able to distinguish between the four profiles presented. Typical values of the coefficients are presented in table 2 and the corresponding polynomial in figure 10. The second order polynomial is of the form: $f(x)=a_0+a_1x+a_2x^2$. We have used a standard polynomial-fitting algorithm with the 6 discrete values obtained for each contour at the edge location.

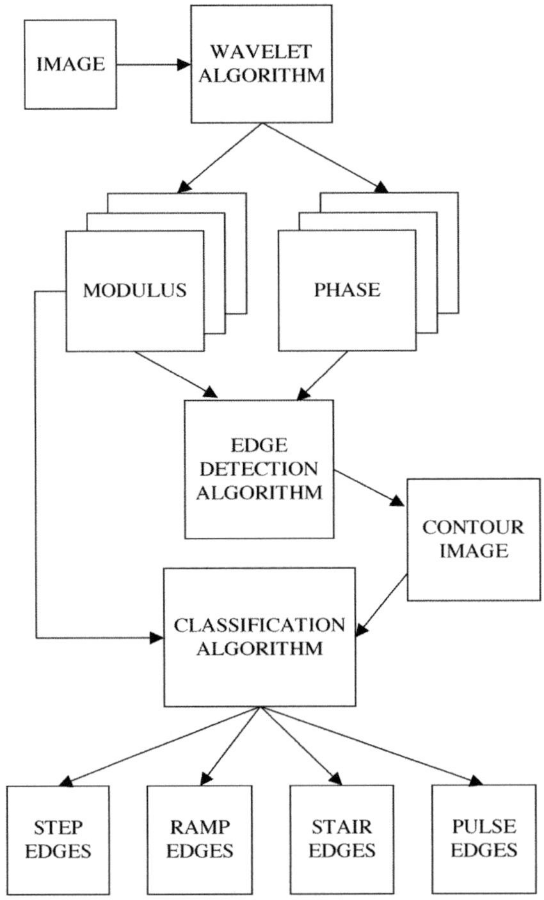

Fig. 9. Edge detection and classification algorithm.

	a_0	a_1	a_2
Step	0.8295	0.1026	-0.0187
Ramp	-0.0249	0.3678	-0.0362
Stair	0.3562	0.0894	0.0005
Pulse	1.0087	-0.0732	-0.0131

Table 2. Typical coefficients values of the fitted polynomial.

The decision algorithm is presented in figure 11. We first analyze the convexity of the polynomial ($a_2>0$), in the affirmative case we have a stair edge. In case of having a concave polynomial we analyze its slope. In case of a positive slope, we will have a ramp edge. In the opposite case, we will have to compute the zero crossing value. If this value is greater than, approximately, 6 the edge will be a step, otherwise it will be a pulse.

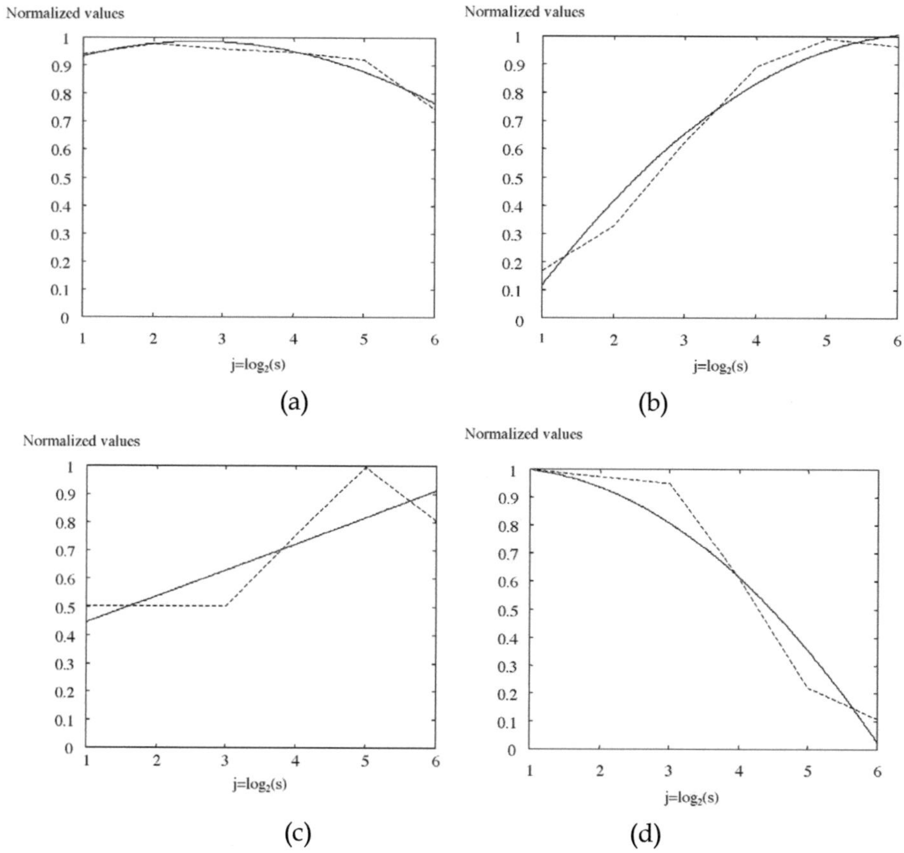

Fig. 10. Dotted lines: Original values. Solid lines: polynomial. (a) Polynomial fitting for the step profile. (b) Polynomial fitting for the ramp profile. (c) Polynomial fitting for the stair profile. (d) Polynomial fitting for the pulse profile.

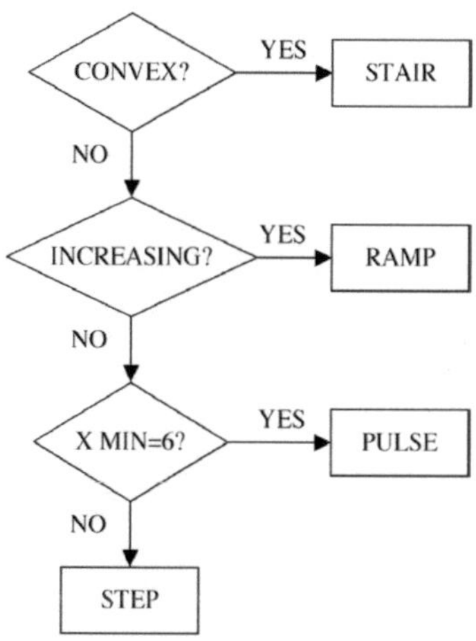

Fig. 11. Decision algorithm for edge classification.

As some preliminary results we can see the correct classification made in figure 12 for our test image. It is important to note that no post-processing (edge tracking, non-maxima suppression, etc.) has been made in the obtained contour image.

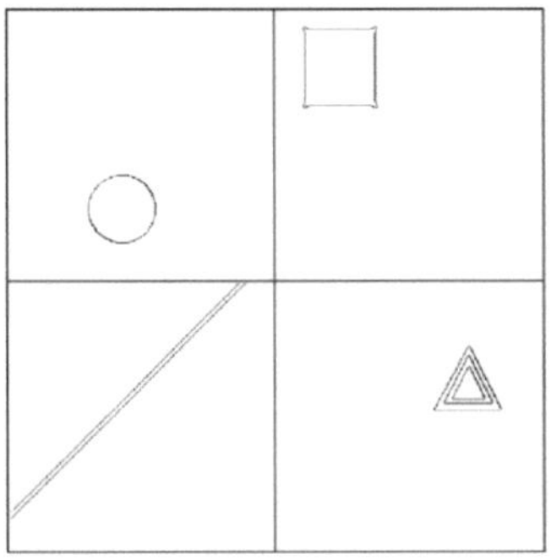

Fig. 12. From left to right and top to bottom: step, ramp, pulse, and stair classified profiles.

5. Noise characterization and polynomial classification

As a first practical result of our processing schema we have analyzed our algorithm behavior with respect to noise. In order to obtain a proper characterization of the noise we have to compare the evolution in the coefficients shown by the noise with that presented by other kind of profiles. Firstly, we have processed a simple image with only Gaussian noise. Secondly, we have analyzed the image with the edge detection and classification algorithm as described in section 4. The mean values of the modulus of the gradient evolution at the edge points are shown in figure 13a. This pattern characterizes isolated Gaussian noise.

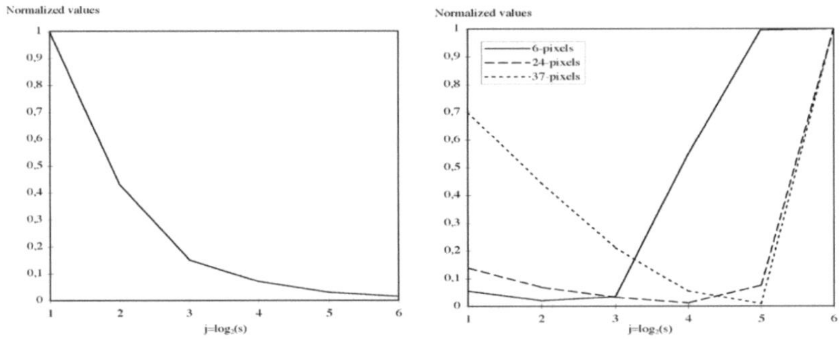

Fig. 13. (a) Mean values of Gaussian noise evolution. (b) Noise dependence on distance.

But noise is rarely presented isolated in a real image, and its evolution depends strongly on the distance between the noise and the contour of the objects present in the image. To obtain the noise evolution we have processed the image of a simple square with a step profile corrupted with Gaussian noise. The evolution in the values of the noise, in terms of the distance between the noise and the square, are presented in figure 13b. These patterns serve us to classify and differentiate the noise from other contour types. We can see that the evolution pattern for a noise contour located very close to a real contour is quite similar to the stair evolution. This is the expected behavior because the stair has been defined as closed steps. We can include this contour type in our classification engine.

The final decision algorithm is presented in figure 14. We have to distinguish between the stair type and the noise one. If we have a convex polynomial ($a_2 > 0$) we have a stair or noise edge. They are differentiated by means of the minimum ordinate value. If the minimum ordinate is close to 0 it is classified as a noise edge.

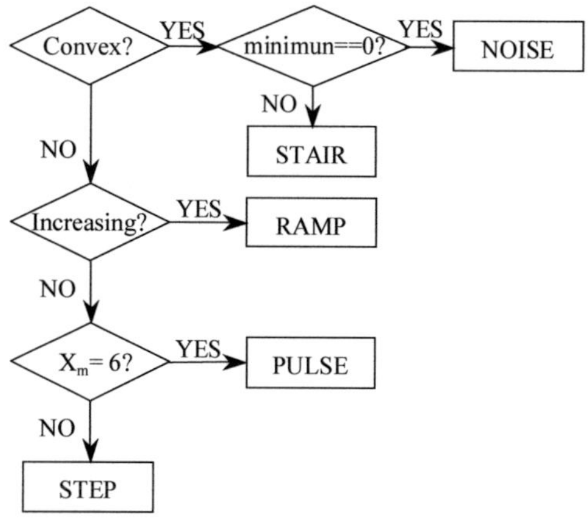

Fig. 14. Decision algorithm for edge classification.

To analyze the robustness of the algorithm we have corrupted our test image with 20 dB of Gaussian noise. The classification results are shown in figures 15 and 16, respectively. No thresholding has been applied to the contour image.

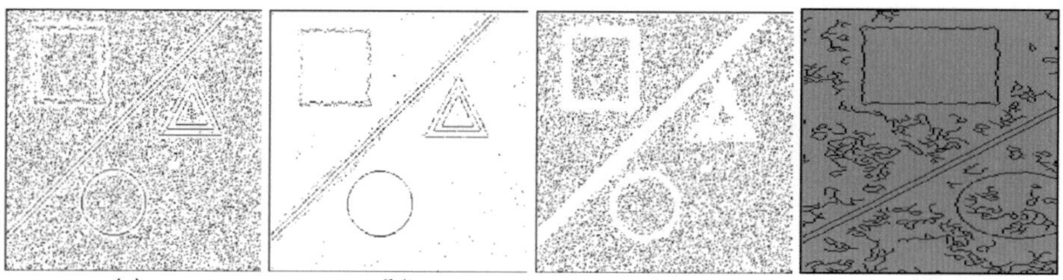

(a) (b) (c) (d)

Fig. 15. Test image corrupted with 20 dB Gaussian noise. (a) Detected edges without thresholding. (b) Non noise edges. (c) Noise edges. (d) Detected edges with Canny algorithm.

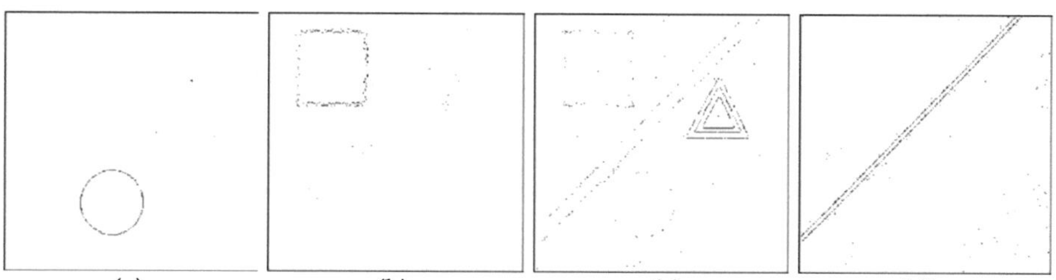

(a) (b) (c) (d)

Fig. 16. Edge profiles detected for the test image corrupted with 20 dB Gaussian noise. (a) Step edges. (b) Ramp edges. (c) Stair edges. (d) Pulse edges.

It can be seen that the noise is perfectly classified (figure 15c) and can be eliminated by simply removing this edge type (figure 15b). Figure 15d shows the output of the Canny edge detector. In this case Canny operator is more sensitive to noise than our algorithm. Figure 16 shows the different edge profiles detected.

6. New contour types

The geometrical characterization of contour types gives us very promising results. To confirm the ability of our algorithm to distinguish different contour types we present here four new types of edge profiles that represent a more general gray-level transition than a simple step. We have included the roof profile, the ridge profile and two non-antisymmetrical step profile models that have been already considered previously by Paillou (Paillou, 1994).

6.1 Roof

A roof profile, named R(x), is shown in figure 17. We have named the point x_0 the middle of the roof, ω is the roof width and U_0 the roof height.

$$r(x)=\begin{cases}0 & \text{if } x<x_0-\dfrac{\omega}{2}\\ mx+k & \text{if } x_0-\dfrac{\omega}{2}\le x\le x_0\\ U_0 & \text{if } x=x_0\\ -mx+k & \text{if } x_0\le x\le x_0+\dfrac{\omega}{2}\\ 0 & \text{if } x>x_0+\dfrac{\omega}{2}\end{cases} \tag{17}$$

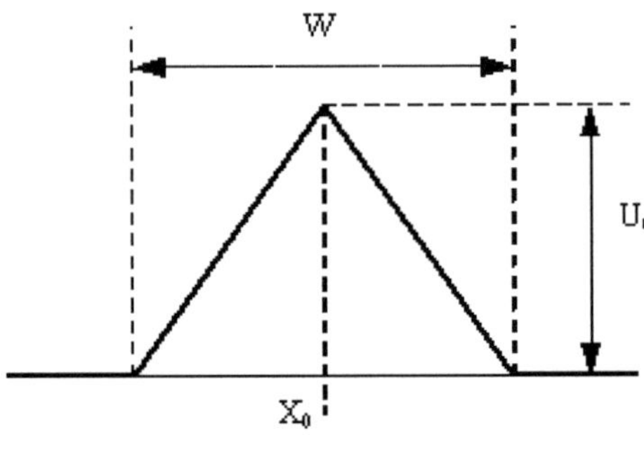

Fig. 17. Roof profile. Horizontal axis represents pixels. Vertical axis represents grey level.

6.2 Ridge

A ridge profile, named R(x), is shown in figure 18. The point x_0 is the middle of the ridge, ω_1 is the width of the first ramp, ω_2 is the width of the plain part, while ω_3 is the width of the second ramp. U_0 is the ridge height.

$$R(x)=\begin{cases}0 & \text{if } x<x_0-\omega_1-\frac{\omega_2}{2}\\ mx+k & \text{if } x_0-\omega_1-\frac{\omega_2}{2}\le x\le x_0-\frac{\omega_2}{2}\\ U_0 & \text{if } x_0-\frac{\omega_2}{2}\le x\le x_0+\frac{\omega_2}{2}\\ -mx+k & \text{if } x_0+\frac{\omega_2}{2}\le x\le x_0+\frac{\omega_2}{2}+\omega_3\\ 0 & \text{if } x>x_0+\frac{\omega_2}{2}+\omega_3\end{cases} \tag{18}$$

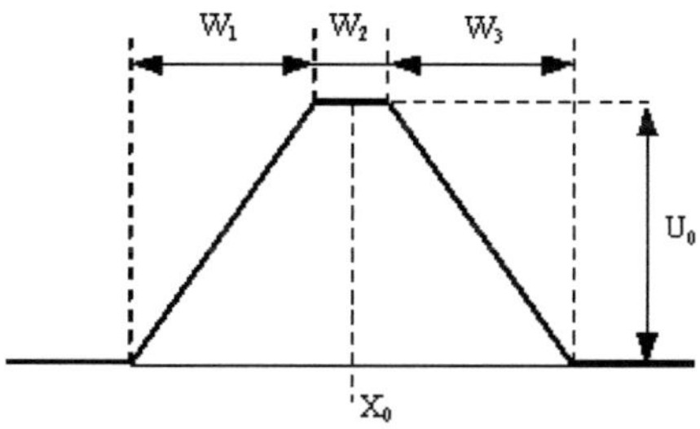

Fig. 18. Ridge profile. Horizontal axis represents pixels. Vertical axis represents grey level.

6.3 First non-antisymmetrical step

The first non-antisymmetrical step profile, named nu(x), is shown in figure 19. The point x_0 is the step location, ω_1 is the width of the first ramp and ω_1 is the width of the second ramp. U_1 and U_3 are their respective heights. U_2 is the step height at position x_0. The first non-antisymmetrical step function can be written as:

$$nu(x)=\begin{cases}0 & \text{if } x<x_0-\omega_1\\ mx+k & \text{if } x_0-\omega_1\le x\le x_0+\omega_1-\omega_2\\ mx+k & \text{if } x_0+\omega_1-\omega_2\le x\le x_0+\omega_1+\omega_2\\ U_3 & \text{if } x>x_0+\omega_1+\omega_2\end{cases} \tag{19}$$

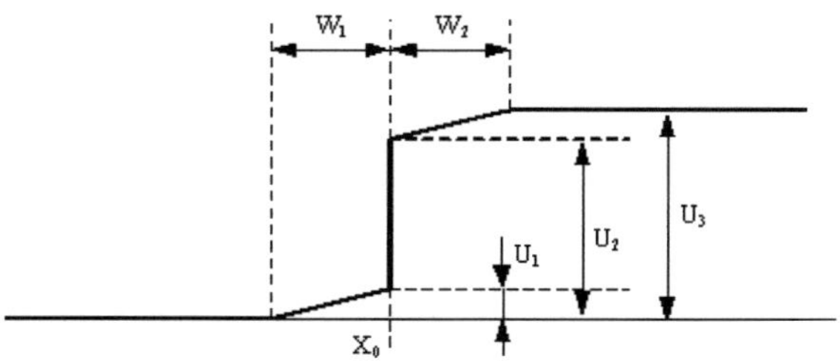

Fig. 19. First non-antisymmetrical step profile. Horizontal axis represents pixels. Vertical axis represents grey level.

6.4 Second non-antisymmetrical step

The second non-antisymmetrical step profile, named nu2(x), is shown in figure 20. The point x_0 is the middle of the main ramp, ω_1 is the width of the first ramp, ω_2 is the width of central ramp and ω_3 is the width of the third ramp, respectively. U_1, U_2 and U_3 are their respective heights (see figure). Let be nu2(x) the second non-antisymmetrical step function.

$$nu2(x)=\begin{cases} 0 & \text{if } x<x_0-\omega_1 \\ mx+k & \text{if } x_0-\omega_1\le x\le x_0+\omega_1-\dfrac{\omega_2}{2} \\ cx+k & \text{if } x_0+\omega_1-\dfrac{\omega_2}{2}\le x\le x_0+\omega_1+\dfrac{\omega_2}{2} \\ mx+k & \text{if } x_0+\omega_1+\dfrac{\omega_2}{2}-\omega_3\le x\le x_0+\omega_1+\dfrac{\omega_2}{2}+\omega_3 \\ U_3 & \text{if } x>x_0+\omega_1+\dfrac{\omega_2}{2}+\omega_3 \end{cases} \tag{20}$$

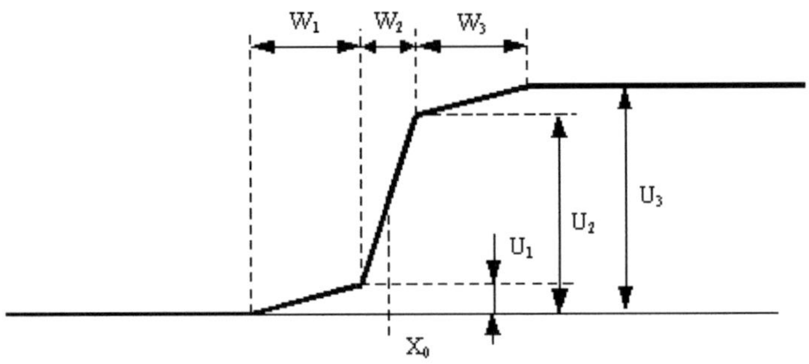

Fig. 20. Second non-antisymmetrical step profile. Horizontal axis represents pixels. Vertical axis represents grey level.

6.5 Modified classification algorithm

Finally, we will include the four contour types in our classification algorithm. We will also work on the basis of the polynomial-fitting algorithm, by following characteristics such as convexity, concavity, zero crossings and minimum abscissa and ordinate as we did beforehand. Furthermore, we have also used a standard polynomial-fitting algorithm with the 6 discrete mean values obtained for each contour at the edge location. However, in this case, a third order polynomial fitting will serve us to classify some of the new profile models introduced above. In particular, the third order coefficient pattern matching will serve us to discriminate among the ridge, roof and ramp profiles, respectively. Maximum value at scales 5 or 6 and comparison between values at two different scales are also used. Figure 21 shows the complete decision algorithm for edge classification.

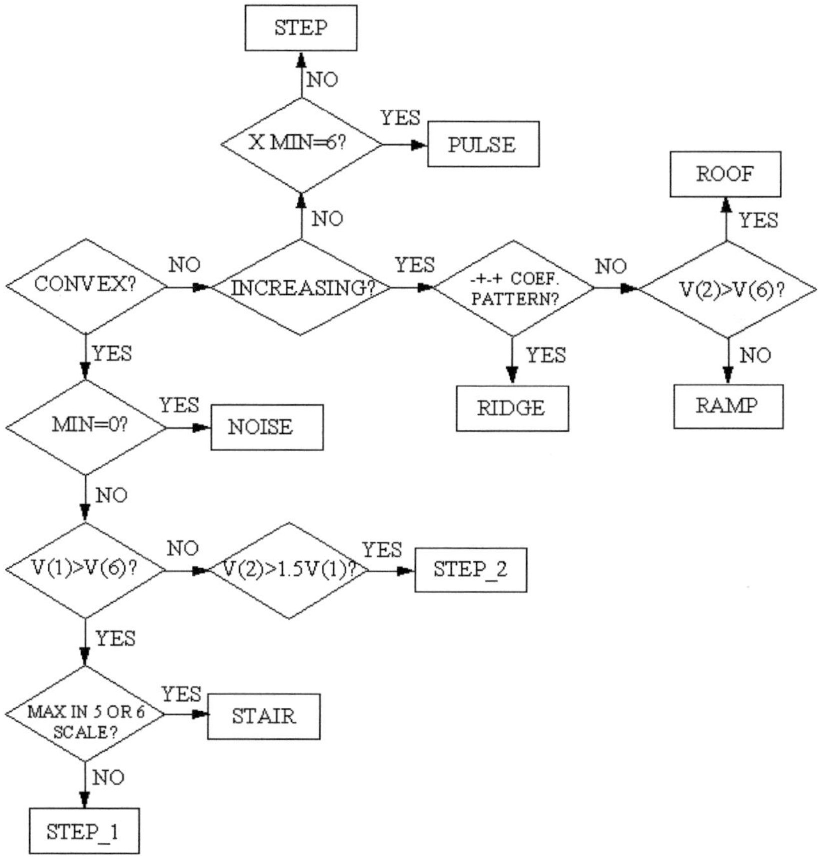

Fig. 21. Modified decision algorithm for edge classification.

The polynomial that characterizes the roof profile (as well as the ridge profile) is concave and with a positive slope in the first three scales, in the same way as the ramp profile does. In order to discriminate among these profile models just mentioned above, it is necessary to calculate the coefficient pattern for several fitting polynomials, third, fourth and fifth order). We find a remarkable difference among the ridge profile on one side, and the ramp and roof profiles on the other side. The coefficient pattern (-,+,-,+) ≡ (a_0,a_1,a_2,a_3), characterizes the ridge profile. In order to distinguish between the ramp and roof profiles, we have realized that the mean value at scale 6 is greater that the one at scale 2 in a ramp profile, whereas both are similar in a roof profile. This is the condition to put aside both profiles.

As far as antisymmetrical step profiles are concerned, we must say that they both have some properties like the stair profile (convexity and minimum greater than zero). It can be shown that if the mean value at scale 6 is smaller than that at scale 1, we will obtain a stair profile, otherwise we will have the first non-antisymmetrical step profile. For the sake of algorithm efficiency, we have included a second condition: a stair profile has the maximum value at scales 5 or 6. In order to obtain the second non-antisymmetrical step profile, we compute whether the mean value at scale 2 is, at least 1.5 times the mean value at scale 1.

In order to show the results of the modified algorithm, we have created a new test image, including the new edge profiles. Figure 22 shows the new test image, together with the different detected edge profiles. Results with a real image are shown in figures 23 and 24.

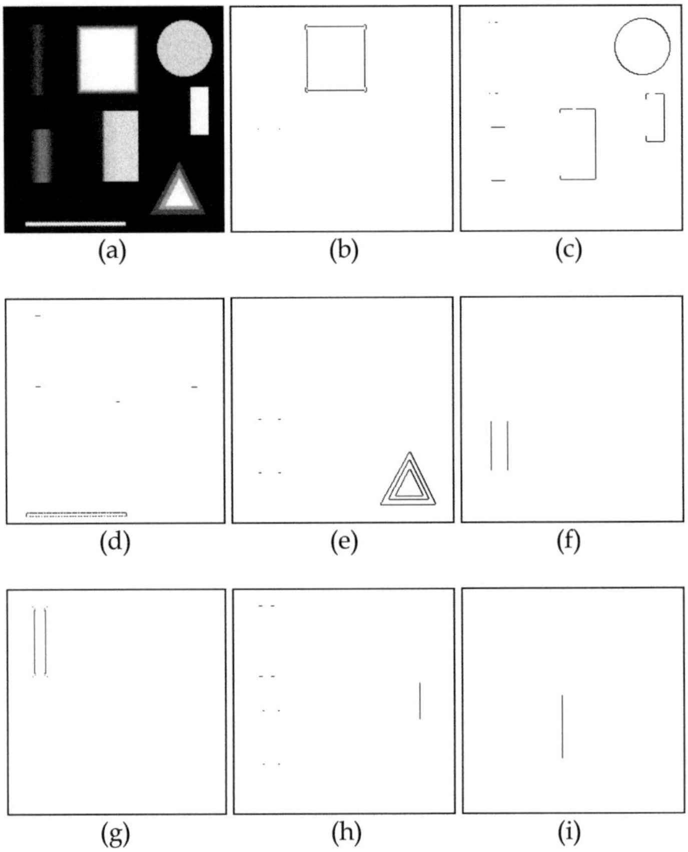

Fig. 22. (a) Test image. (b) Ramp edges. (c) Step edges. (d) Pulse edges. (e) Stair edges. (f) Ridge edges. (g) Roof edges. (h) First non-antisymmetrical step edges. (i) Second non-antisymmetrical step edges.

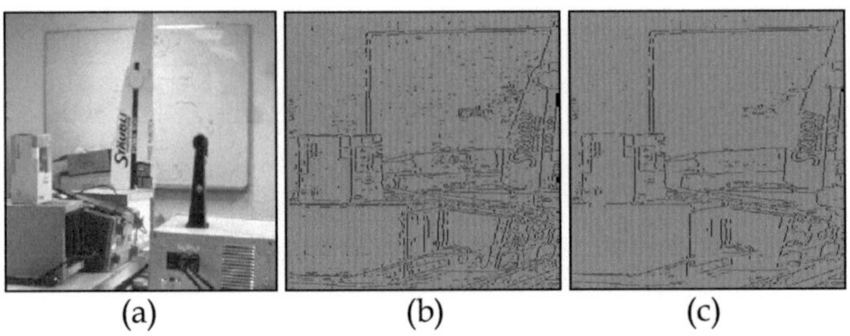

Fig. 23. (a) Original image. (b) Contour image. (c) Contour image after noise filtering.

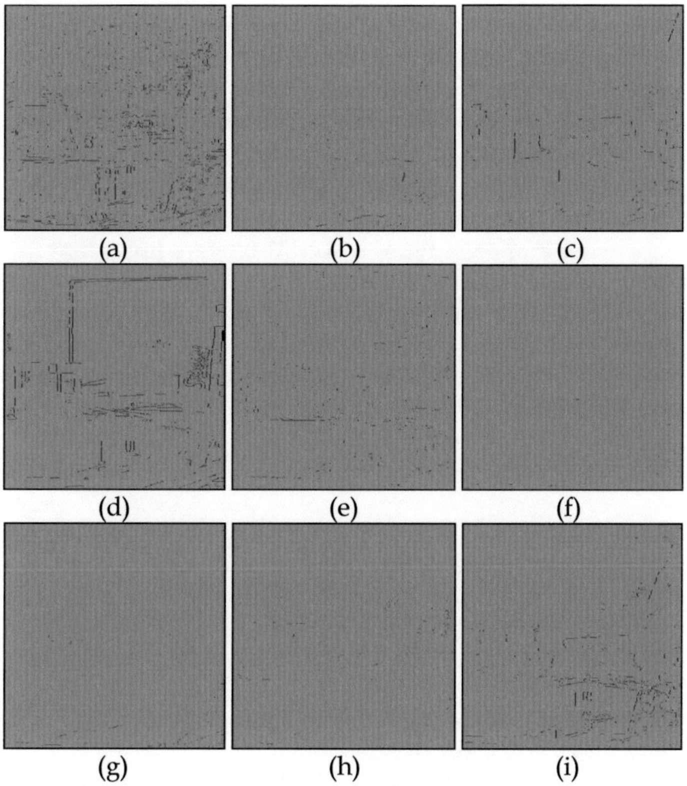

Fig. 24. (a) Noise edges. (b) Ramp edges. (c) Step edges. (d) Pulse edges. (e) Stair edges. (f) Ridge edges. (g) Roof edges. (h) First non-antisymmetrical step edges. (i) Second non-antisymmetrical step edges.

7. Conclusions

In this work, we have developed a new algorithm for edge detection and classification purposes using the coefficients given by the DWT. We have shown that Mallat's wavelet is a very suitable tool to perform both edge detection and contour analysis. We have presented the results obtained with a 256x256 synthetic image with several objects, each one with a different contour profile, obtaining a very good segmentation. At this point, we are not only able to see the evolution across scales of the edges proposed by Rosenfeld (Rosenfeld & Thurston, 1976) like in Williams and Shah's work (Williams & Shah, 1990, 1993), but we are also able to classify them.

A new edge class has been introduced: the noise. This edge type presents a particular evolution across scales. This has allowed us to implement a simply noise filtering algorithm based on edge classification.

The classification algorithm we have developed is based on second order polynomial fitting of the modulus of the wavelet transform coefficients. The mathematical behaviour of the polynomial is a robust indicator of the edge class. This kind of classification is good enough to obtain the five different profiles analyzed: step, ramp, stair, pulse, and noise. The robustness of the proposed classification schema has been tested including other profiles

appeared in the literature: roof, ridge and two kinds of non-antisymmetrical step models. A third order polynomial-fitting algorithm is needed to obtain a proper classification. This algorithm can be viewed as a new framework to classify different contour types.
Some preliminary results, like the behaviour of ramp edges, are promising to obtain a classification of the contours appearing in real images (shadows, changes in illumination, corners and so on). A future work to perform, which has not been covered in this paper, is the study of the evolution across scales of these real edges. If there were some special evolution pattern for these real edge types it would be very important information for the next stages of an image understanding algorithm.
An edge-closing algorithm based on the edge type is under developing in this moment. The extra information provided by the classification stage gives very good indicators to close edges and extract objects in an image. The processing results presented in this work have been obtained using Matlab®.

8. References

Beltrán, J. R., J. García-Lucía, J. & Navarro, J. (1994). Edge detection and classification using Mallat's wavelet. *Proceedings of the ICIP-94*, pp. 293-296

Beltrán, J. R., Beltrán, F & Estopañan A. (1998). Multiresolution edge classification: Noise Characterization, *Proceedings of the IEEE-SMC'98*, pp. 4476-448

Bergholm, F. (1987). Edge Focusing. *IEEE Trans. on Patt. Anal. and Machine Intell*, Vol. 9, No. 6, pp. 726-471

Canny, J. F. (1986). A computational approach to edge detection. I*EEE Trans. on Patt. Anal. And Machine Intell.* Vol. 8, pp. 679-698

Eklundth, J. O., Elfving, T. & Nyberg, S. (1982). Edge detection using the Marr-Hildreth operator whith different sizes. *Procedings of the. 6th. Int. Conf. on Pattern Recognition (ICPR)*, Munich, Germany, pp. 1109-1112

Mallat, S. (1989). A theory for Multiresolution Signal Decomposition: The Wavelet Representation. *Trans. on Patt. Anal. and Machine Intell*, Vol. 11, No. 7, pp. 674-693

Mallat, S. & Zhong, S. (1992). Characterization of Signals from Multiscale Edges. *IEEE Trans. on Patt. Anal. and Machine Intell*, Vol. 14, No. 7, pp. 710-732

Marr, D. (1982). *Vision*. W. H. Freeman. San Francisco

Paillou, Ph. (1994). A non antisymmetrical edge profile detection. *Pattern Recognition Letters* Vol. 15, pp. 595-605

Park, D. J., Nam, Kwon M. & Park, Rae-Hong. (1995). Multiresolution Edge Detection Techniques, *Pattern Recognition*, Vol. 28, No. 2, pp. 211-229

Rosenfeld, A. & Thurston, M. (1971). Edge curve detection for visual scene analysis, *IEEE Transactions Computers*, Vol. 20, pp. 562-569

Rosenfeld, A. & Kak, A. C. (1976). Digital Picture Processing. Academic Press

Torre, V. & Poggio, T. (1984). *On edge detection*. Technical Report 768, MIT

Williams, D. J. & Shah, M. (1990). Normalized Edge Detector. *Proceedings of the 10th Int. Conference On Pattern Recognition*, 1 (16-21), pp. 942-946

Williams, D. J. & Shah, M. (1993). Edge Characterization Using Normalized Edge Detector. *Proceedings of CVGIP*, Vol. 5, No. 4, pp. 311-318

Witkin, A. P. (1983). Scale-space filtering. *Proceedings of the 4th Int. Joint Conference on Artificial Intelligence (IJCAI)*, pp. 1019-1022

Ziou, D. & Tabbone, S. (1993). A Multiescale Edge Detector. *Pattern Recognition*, Vol 26, No. 9, pp. 1305-1314

7

Low Bit Rate Video Compression Algorithm Using 3-D Discrete Wavelet Decomposition

Awad Kh. Al-Asmari
Electrical Engineering Dept., King Saud University, Riyadh
Saudi Arabia

1. Introduction

Video applications, like video teleconferencing, video telephones, and advanced television (ATV), have given the field of compression and transmission of digital video signals a significant importance. It is expected that the advances in video compression technology will play a crucial role in the transmission and display of three-dimensional video signal.
A typical image, for example, of size 512x512 pixels with 8 bits per pixel (bpp) needs storage capacity of about 2 Mbits. A video sequence, on the other hand, with the same frame size with 30 frames per second and a channel transmission rate of 64 kilo bits per second (kbps) would take about 17 minutes of transmission time. The required transmission time would become unmanageable with the continuously increasing demand of image base application. You can't put enough of it over a telephone line and you can't squeeze it into the broadcast bandwidth of available channels[1]. Therefore, image and video compression algorithms became a necessity to store or transmit these images.
Data compression is the science of representing information in a compact form by exploiting the different kinds of statistical structures that may be present in the data[2]. This is to reduce the number of bits per sample while keeping the distortion constant[3]. There is a great deal of correlation between neighboring pixel values of an image. Therefore, removing such redundant information and transmitting only the new information (the changes) enables us to reconstruct the original image. For video signals, redundancy over time between successive images can also be eliminated.
There are two types of compression: lossless and lossy. In the lossless compression the original image can be retrieved without error, while for the lossy compression, the original image can't be retrieved without error; an image copy close to the original can be retrieved.

---

[1] Realtime video compression poses challenge to designers and vendors alike, Computer Design, vol. 32, no. 7, pp. 67-70 (Child, July 1993).
[2] Hybrid coding of images for progressive transmission over a digital cellular channel, CISST'99 International Conference on Imaging Science, Systems and Technology, Monte Carlo resort, Las Vegas, Nevada, USA, PIN 128C (Al-Asmari et al.,June 28 - July 1, 1999).
[3] Introduction to data compression, Morgan Kaufmann Publishers Inc., San Francisco, California (Sayood, 1996).

Motion pictures expert group (MPEG) video standard is the most prevalent and widely used for video compression[3-6]. Also, the MPEG is an application specific standard and different versions of MPEG (Such as MPEG-1, MPEG-2, MPEG-4, and MPEG-7) are available for different applications and bit rates. The basic algorithm for all these versions is the same and is very similar to the other video compression standards.
The proposed algorithm is based on temporal filtering of image sequences with short symmetric kernel filters (SSKFs)[7-8], which are well known for their simplicity. In this paper, we use four SSKFs filters each with 4-taps and with decimation factor of 4:1 instead of two SSKFs filters each of 2-taps and with decimation factor of 2:1 used in classical 3D - decomposition algorithms[7-8]. The temporal filtering removes the redundancy in temporal domain. On the other hand, the pyramid coding (PC) is used for subband decomposition in the spatial domain. The vector quantization (VQ) and the absolute moment block truncation code (AMBTC) will be used to encode the spatial domain subbands.

2. 3-D decomposition of the video sequence

Practical video compression relies on techniques to reduce the amount of data required to represent a video sequence without any appreciable loss of information that can affect the visual quality of image. Our aim in this paper is to introduce an algorithm that compress the video sequence with a reduced bit rate and highest fidelity while keeping the computational complexity to a minimum to allow for easy hardware implementation. The complexity of the proposed algorithm is less than the standard MPEG-1 and MPEG-2 algorithms.
Since our approach to the video compression problem is based on progressive transmission, the multiresolution representation of the signals is required. The idea of multiresolution is that a coarser approximation to the signal is refined step by step until the desired resolution is obtained. An elaborate discussion on 3-dimensional decomposition of the video signals, using pyramid method for spatial decomposition, is given in this section.
A group of video sequences (four frames each) is decomposed into subbands in the temporal and spatial domains. The temporal frequencies are restricted to four subbands by passing four consecutive frames through four band pass filters of 4-taps each and with decimation factor of 4:1. By applying pyramid decomposition on these temporal subbands, nine spatial subbands are produced. In the next sub-sections, the temporal and spatial domain decomposition will be discussed in more details.

2.1 Temporal frequency decomposition

The 4-tap Haar basis functions (SSKFs filters) are used for temporal frequency decomposition. These filters have no phase or amplitude distortion and belong to a class of perfect reconstruction filters. The coefficients of SSKFs filters used in this research are given

---

[4] Digital pictures representation, compression, and standard, Plenium Press (Netravali & Haskell, 1995).
[5] Image and video compression standards: algorithms and architectures, Kluwer Academic Publishers (Bhaskaran & Konstantinidides & Hewlett Packard Laboratories, 1996).
[6] Digital compression of still images and video, Academic Press (Clarke, 1995).
[7] Subband coding of video for packet networks, Optical Engineering, vol. 27, no. 7, pp. 574-586, (Karlsson & Vetterli, July 1988).
[8] Pyramid coding of video signals for progressive transmission, CISST'97 International Conference, pp-392-398, (Dantwala et al., June 30 - July 3, 1997).

in Table 1. The frequency responses of these filters are shown in Figure 1. $H_0(e^{j\omega})$ is the low pass filter, $H_3(e^{j\omega})$ is the high pass filter, while $H_1(e^{j\omega})$ and $H_2(e^{j\omega})$ are the band pass filters. The 3-dB bandwidth for these filters is approximately $\pi/4$.

	Lowpass filter	**Bandpass filters**		**Highpass filter**
N	**$h_0(n)$**	**$h_1(n)$**	**$h_2(n)$**	**$h_3(n)$**
0	0.5	0.5	0.5	0.5
1	0.5	0.5	-0.5	-0.5
2	0.5	-0.5	-0.5	0.5
3	0.5	-0.5	0.5	-0.5

Table 1. SSKFs Coefficients for Haar filters.

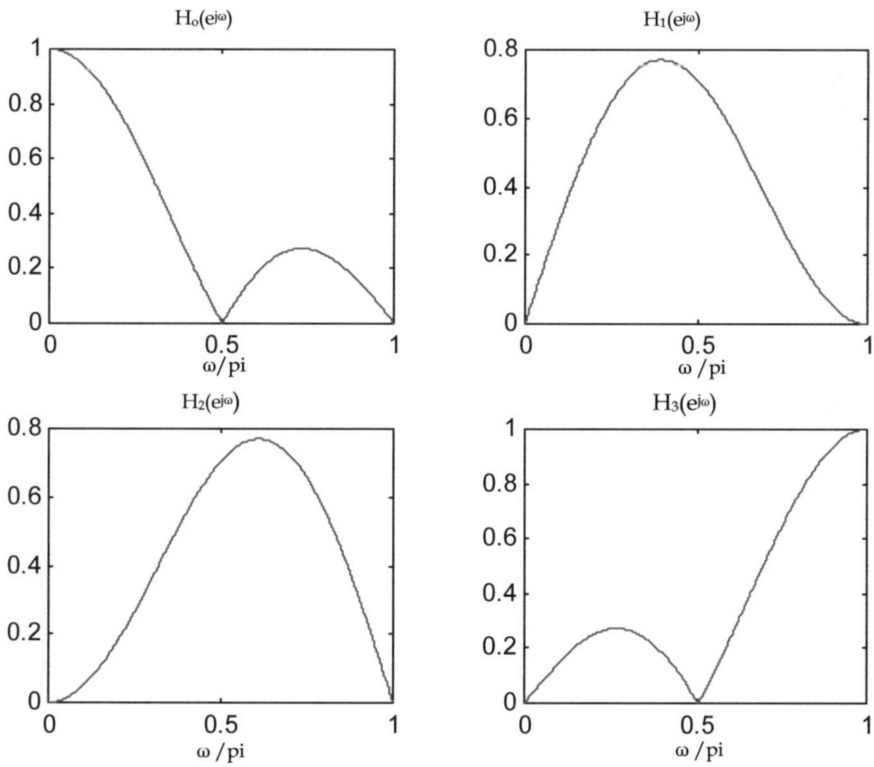

Fig. 1. Frequency response of 4-tap Haar filters.

The video sequence with four consecutive frames is decomposed in the temporal domain by passing these frames through the 4-tap Haar filters as shown in Figure 2.
The second four frames of Miss America sequence, that contains clear motion of the eyes, are filtered using SSKFs filters. These filters decompose the sequence into four temporal subbands. Namely, temporal low-low (T_{LL}), temporal low-high (T_{LH}), temporal high-low

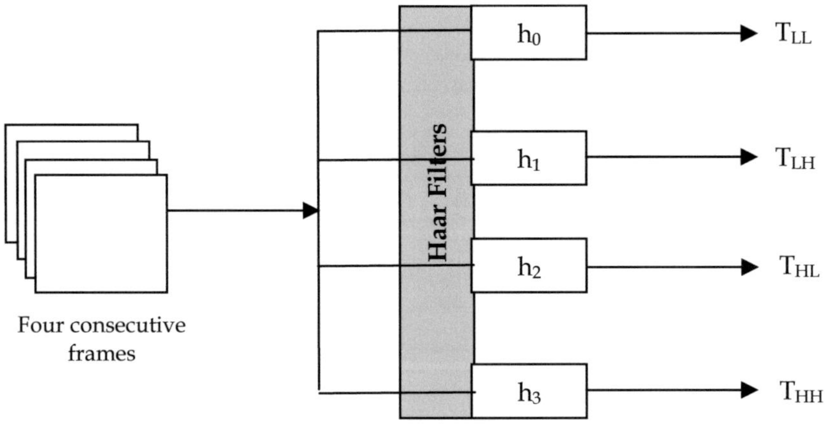

Fig. 2. Temporal filtering process using 4-tap Haar filters.

(T_{HL}) and temporal high-high (T_{HH}) subbands. Figure 3 shows the original and the filtered frames. It can be seen from this figure that the subband T_{LL} contains most of the image sequence information, while the subband T_{LH} contains most of the motion information in the four frames. The subbands T_{HL} and T_{HH} contain the edge information, which are relatively spares in the nature. Figure 3 (b) shows that the information of the temporal T_{LL} subband is highly correlated since it is only an average of the four frames, while the temporal (T_{LH}, T_{HL} and T_{HH}) subbands are of low correlated data. Compression is achieved since instead of transmitting four highly correlated frames of the video at 8 bpp each, only one frame with highly correlated data (T_{LL}) at high bit rate will be transmitted. The other frames (T_{LH}, T_{HL} and T_{HH}) with low correlated information will be transmitted with very low bit rate.

The average entropy is calculated for the original and the decomposed four frames. Table 2 shows the average entropy for the original and the temporal filtered frames of Miss America sequence. From this table, it is clear that the multiresolution decomposition process results in lower entropy than that of the original images. From Shannon's theory, the entropy for a signal can be minimized by decomposing this signal into sub-signals using orthogonal bases. Therefore, the calculated entropy is act as a lower measure for the information to be encoded[9].

Original frames	Entropy	Temporal frames	Entropy
Frame 4	5.66	T_{LL}	5.78
Frame 5	5.68	T_{LH}	2.39
Frame 6	5.66	T_{HL}	2.09
Frame 7	5.65	T_{HH}	2.11
Average	5.66	Average	3.1

Table 2. The average entropy for the four frames before and after the decomposition.

[9] A mathematical theory of communication, Bell System Tech. J.. Vol. 27, pp. 379-423, and pp. 623-656 (Shannon, July. 1948a, Oct. 1948b).

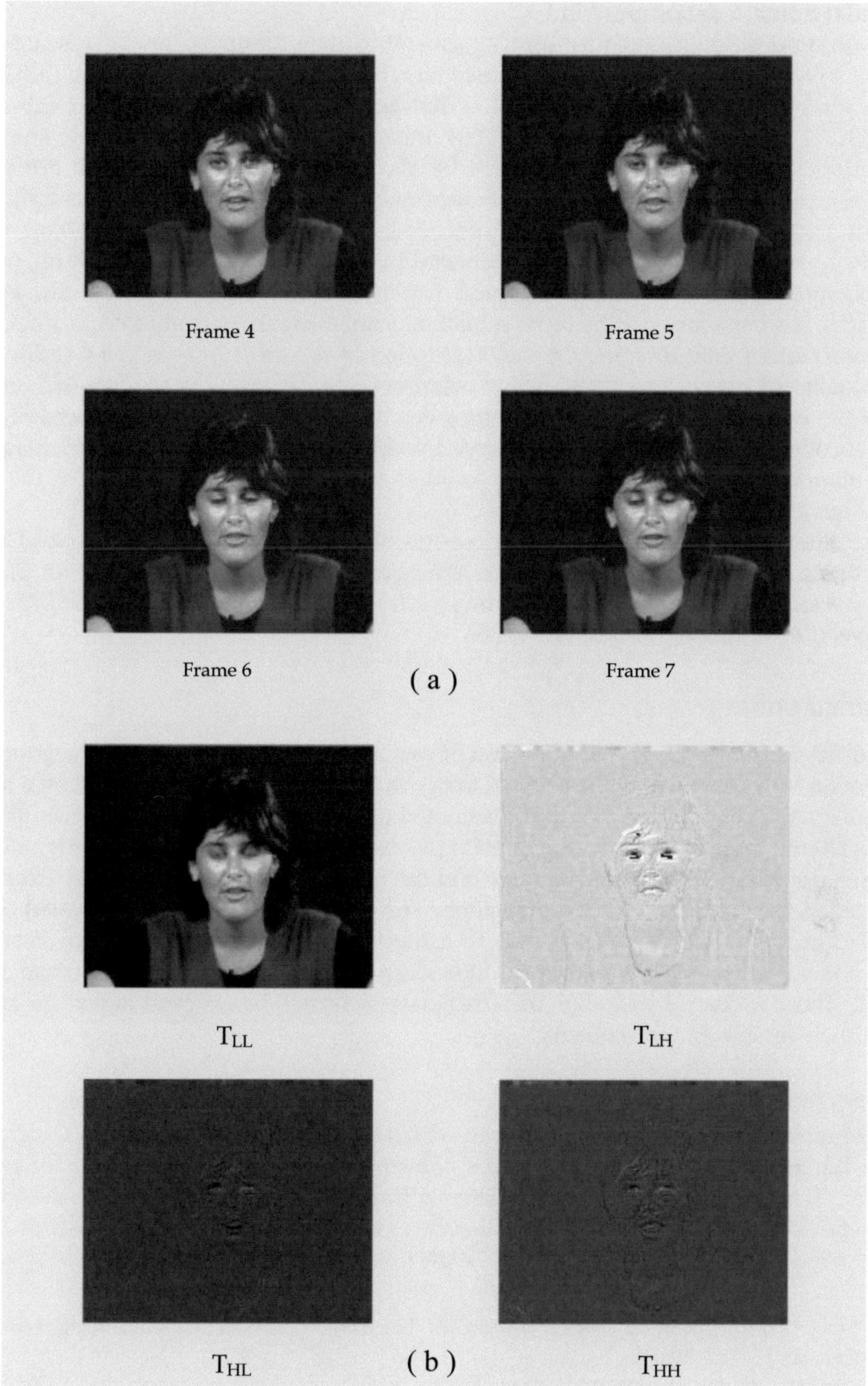

Fig. 3. (a) Original and (b) Temporal filtered frames of the second four frames of Miss America sequence.

2.2 Spatial domain decomposition

Spatial decomposition techniques aim at achieving data compression by discarding the redundant or visually non-perceptual information in an image. Subband coding (SBC) is one such scheme where the image spectrum is divided into a set of uncorrelated sub-spectra, and each of the sub-spectrums is treated individually depending on the amount of information it carries. The low-frequency bands with more energy content are given a higher priority as compared to the high frequency bands with low energy contents[10].

The four frames can be independently encoded using any image compression method available for still images. Since we are interested in multiresolution decomposition, pyramid decomposition method has been adopted for spatial domain decomposition. Pyramid coding (PC) has been found to be more robust to channel errors as compared to SBC[8]. This is so because neither data loss nor channel corruption in the error images has a serious effect on the quality of the reconstructed image. Moreover, lower bit rates are possible for PC as most of the energy of the pyramid structure lies in the lowest resolution baseband, which can be encoded at high bit rates to preserve maximum information without increasing the overall bit rate of the compressed image. Another advantage of the PC scheme is the ease of filter design as compared to SBC [10].

Subband filters are designed under the constraints of perfect reconstruction and narrow transition band. Both of these constraints are relaxed in PC as it makes use of bandpass images for reconstruction [10]. Because of these advantages, this research uses PC for spatial decomposition of images, instead of the SBC.

3. Pyramid coding

Burt and Adelson have suggested a method of pyramid coding that is suitable for progressive transmission[11]. In this method, the original image is filtered to be down-sampled by a factor of 2. The image thus obtained serves as a decimated image of the original. Then, the decimated image is filtered to be interpolated by a factor of 2 to have the same size of the original image. The difference between the original image and the interpolated one generates an error image. This is called the first level PC decomposition. This process can be further repeated over the decimated image to obtain higher levels. To achieve compression, the difference images and the decimated image are bit allocated depending on the amount of information in each subband. Those subbands with high information content will be assigned higher bit rate than those with lower information content.

3.1 24-tap filter

In [12], a 24-tap FIR filter has been introduced with a nominal bandwidth of $\pi/4$, which would allow a higher decimation factor than the conventional Gaussian filter used for pyramid coding [11]. The special property of this filter is that the passband ripples are designed for passband flatness. This ensures that the filter has as little in-band ripples as possible. It has a nominal bandwidth of $\pi/2M$ where M is the decimation factor (M = 4).

---

[10] Video Signal Transmission for IS-95 Environment, Electronic Letters, Vol. 36, no. 5, pp. 465-466 (Al-Asmari et al., 2nd March 2000).

[11] The Laplacian Pyramid as a compact Image Code, IEEE Trans Communication., vol. COM-31, no. 4 pp. 532-540, (Burt & Adelson, April 1983).

[12] Optimum Bit Rate Pyramid Coding with Low Computational and Memory Requirements, IEEE Trans. Circuit and Systems for video Tech., vol. 5, no. 3 pp. 182-192,(Alasmari, June 1995).

By using a pyramidal coding scheme which basically follows a rate of change of 4 instead of 2 as used in the conventional pyramid coding, the number of samples to be encoded are 20% less than the conventional pyramidal samples[12-13]. Another advantage of this filtering technique is that the 24-tap FIR filter involves 33% fewer computations as compared to the Gaussian filter when FFT algorithm is used. The third advantage of this filter is the lower entropy obtained when compared with that found when the Gaussian filter is applied[12].

4. The adopted spatial domain filtering techniques

The four temporal subbands (T_{LL}, T_{LH}, T_{HL} and T_{HH}) resulting from the temporal filtering process are further decomposed in the spatial domain using pyramid coding as shown in Figure 4. The temporal subband (T_{LL}) is further decomposed into three subbands using the

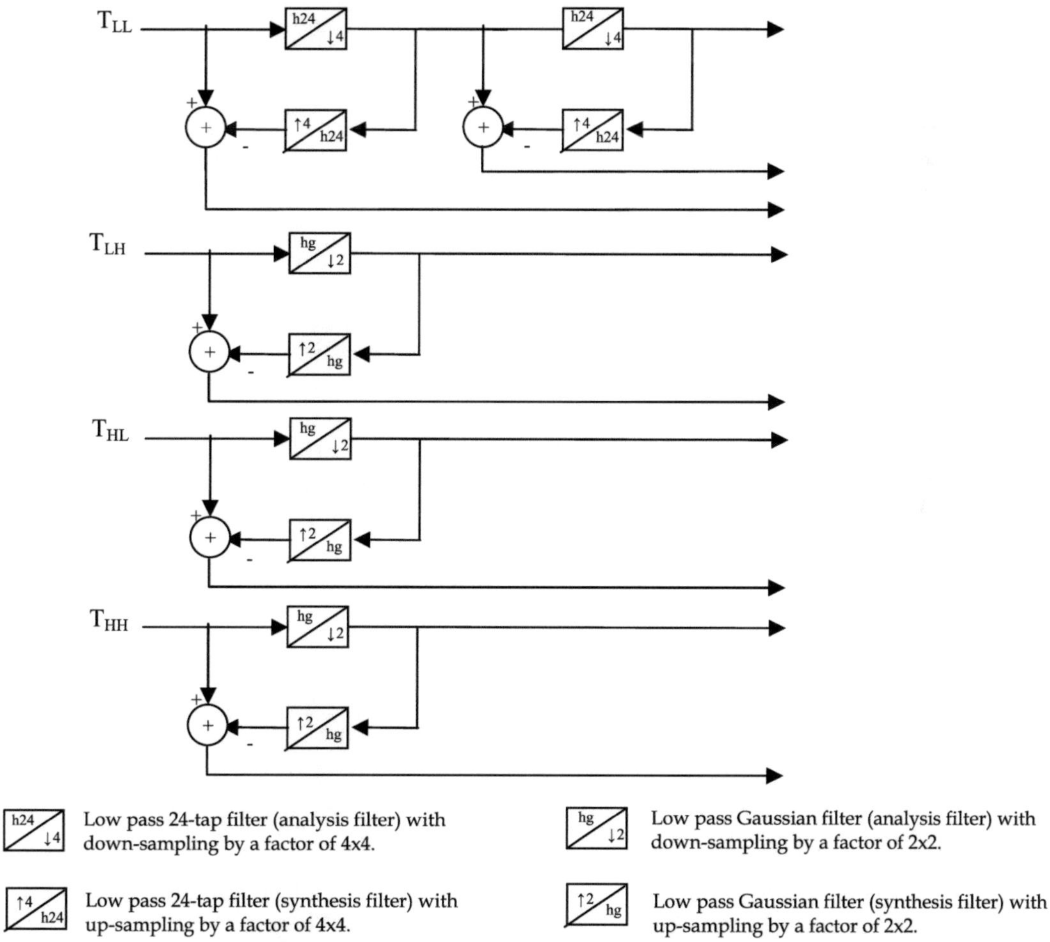

Fig. 4. Spatial decomposition for the temporal subbands using pyramid coding.

---

[13] Low complexity subband encoding for HDTV images, IEEE J. Select. Areas Commun., vol. 11, no. 1, pp. 77-87 (Coppisetti et al., Jan. 1993).

24-tap filter. It is found that the 24-tap filter will not give a good performance when used to decompose the temporal (T_{LH}, T_{HL} and T_{HH}) bands due to the spares nature of the information in these subbands[10]. The Gaussian filter given in[11] is used to decompose these subbands. Figures 5, 6, 7, and 8 show the spatial subbands for the temporal bands of Miss America sequence using the pyramid coding concept.
Fig. 5 shows the spatial pyramid decomposition of the temporal T_{LL} subband. Two levels of pyramid coding have been applied for this temporal subband. The decimated image (band 1), which contains most of T_{LL} subband information, is of dimension 18 × 22 pixels. The difference images of this band (band 2 and band 3) contain edge components and are of dimension 72 × 88 pixels and 288 × 352 pixels; respectively.

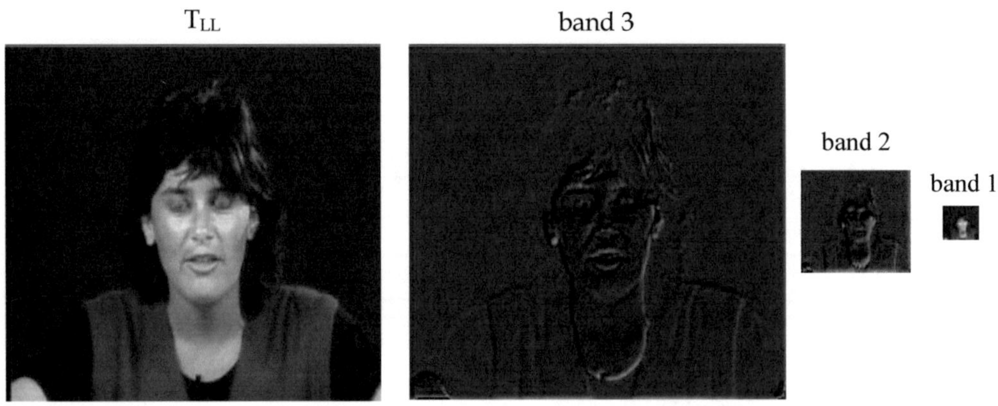

Fig. 5. Spatial subbands for the temporal low-low band.

The spatial pyramid decomposition of the temporal T_{LH} subband is shown in Figure 6. One level pyramid coding has been applied for this temporal subband. The decimated image of this band (band 4) is of dimension 144 × 176 pixels. The difference image (band 5) is of dimension 288 × 352 pixels.

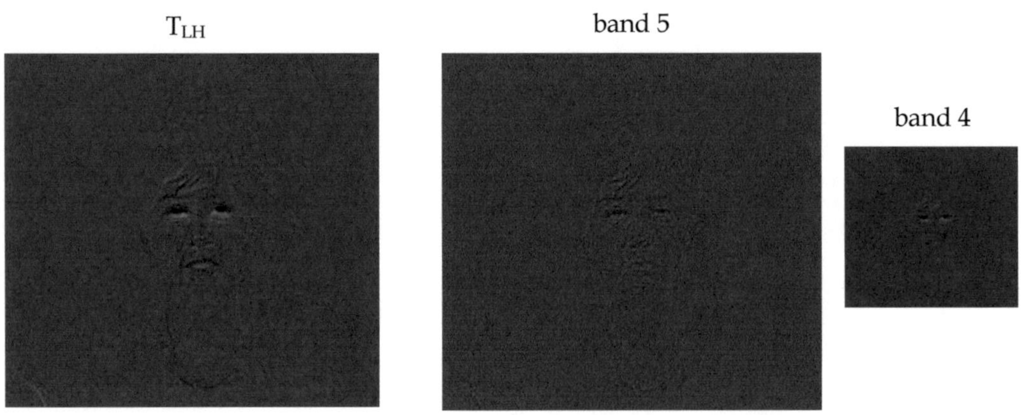

Fig. 6. Spatial subbands for the temporal low-high band.

In Figure 7 the spatial pyramid decomposition of the temporal T_{HL} subband is shown. One level pyramid coding has been applied for this temporal subband. The decimated image (band 6) is of dimension 144 × 176 pixels while the difference image (band 7) is of dimension 288 × 352 pixels.

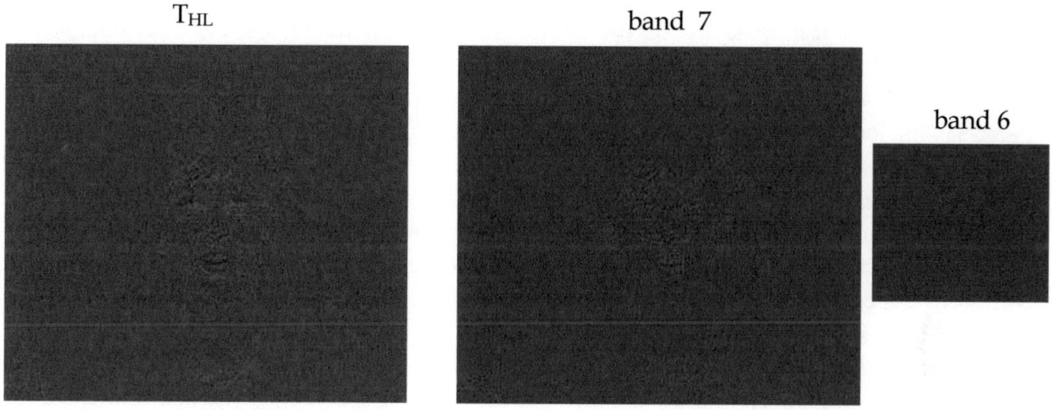

Fig. 7. Spatial subbands for the temporal high-low band.

Fig. 8 shows the spatial pyramid decomposition of the temporal T_{HH} subband. One level pyramid coding has been applied for this temporal subband. The decimated image (band 8) is of dimension 144 × 176 pixels and the difference image is of dimension 288 × 352 pixels.

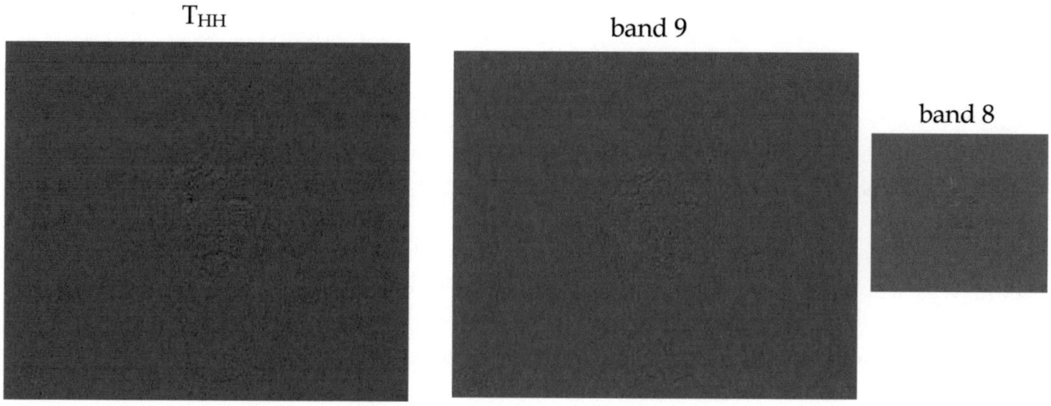

Fig. 8. Spatial subands for the temporal high-high band.

5. Local adaptive vector quantization

Once the original image has been decomposed and the redundancy in the data removed, the next step in the image compression problem is to encode the constituent bands. It has been found that most of the energy signal resides in the lower spatial frequency subands, namely bands 1, 2, and 3. Subbands 4, 5, 6, 7, 8, and 9, which corresponding to the high frequencies, carry most of the motion and edge information and acts as a motion detector. Thus, by accurate coding of low spatial-temporal bands, the spatial details of the original image are conserved. Unlike the majority of the works on the structuring of VQ codebooks, the primary goal of this work is to make the codebook simple and robust to the motions which occur in video sequences and which are seldom capture from a single training sequence. Therefore, the local adaptive vector quantization (LAVQ) [14] is adapted to encode some of the spatial subbands.

A simple and effective one-pass image compression algorithm is provided by the local adaptive vector quantization (LAVQ) [15]. The encoder has a codebook containing codewords (vectors). Each of these codewords is assigned an index corresponding to its position in the codebook. The image is scanned block by block. Each time, a block is taken and compared to the stored codewords. If there is a codeword sufficiently close to the image block (within the pre-decided error) the index itself is sent, and that codeword is moved to the top of the codebook in both transmitter and receiver. If the codebook search is complete without accepted codeword, a special index is sent and followed by the block itself. Now, this block is considered a new codeword and is placed at the top of the codebook. All other codewords are pushed down, and if the number of codewords exceeds the maximum allowed, the last codeword is lost [14]. The LAVQ algorithm maintains the most recently used vectors in the codebook in order of last usage. This allows the LAVQ algorithm to be quick and efficient for any image to be encoded without codebook training. New codewords are generated more often in regions containing edges and fine features, while blank regions are coded with fewer new codewords. Therefore, LAVQ is suitable for the high bands where the correlation is low. The properties of one-pass and high speed codebook generation and encoding are the two main advantages of LAVQ[14].

5.1 Adaptive dead zone for the high subbands

Before we apply the LAVQ on the spatial subbands, a dead zone for each subband based on the number of occurrence of the pixels around zero value is selected. Then, the band is divided into vectors. The number of zero vectors after applying the dead zone will be increased.

So, instead of encoding and sending all vectors, we just encode and send the non-zero vectors with its location. Figure 9 shows an example for band 5 before and after applying the dead zone concept. This process reduces the number of vectors to be transmitted to 20% - 30% of that needed if the dead zone approach is not adopted.

---

[14] Analysis of Coding and Compression strategies for Data Storage and Transmission, Ph. D. thesis, california Instiute of Technology (Sayano, 1992).

[15] Image compression scheme using improved basic-LAVQ and optimized VLC, J. King Saud Univ., Vol. 8, Eng. Sci. (2), pp. 251-266 (Al-Asmari et al., 1996).

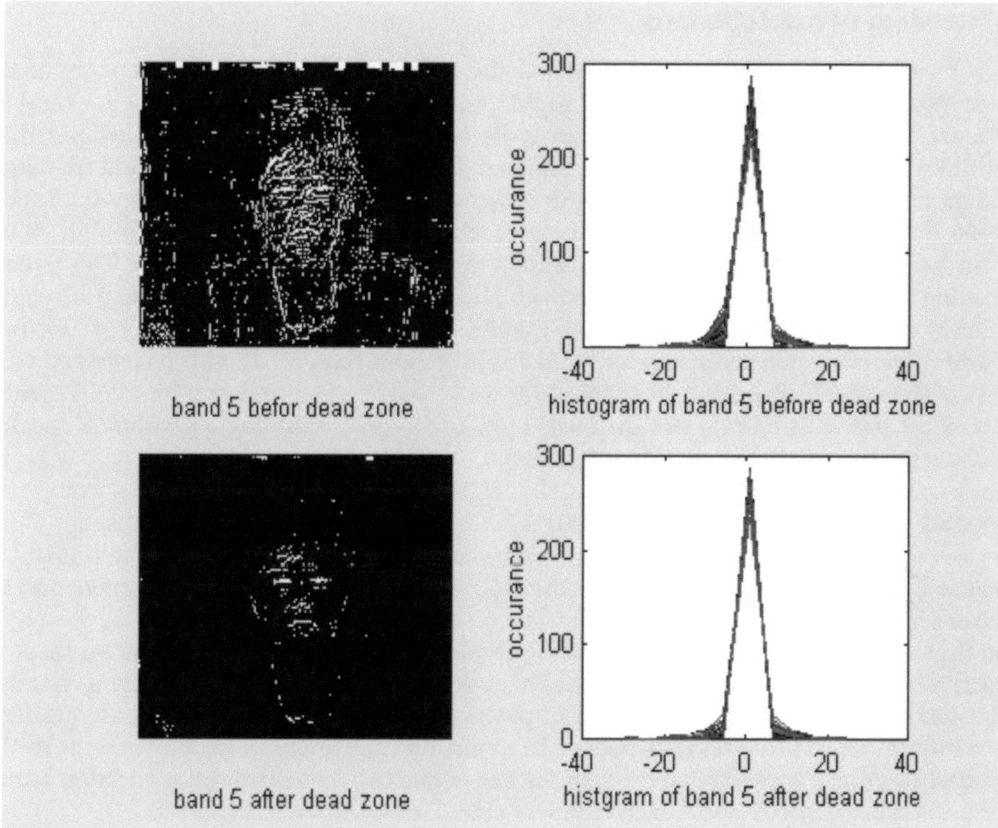

Fig. 9. Example of dead zone process for band 5.

5.2 Searching method for the LAVQ

The difference (error) between the image vectors and the codebook vectors can be calculated using LAVQ searching method concept as follow:

$$d_m = \left(\sum_{j=1}^{cd} \frac{(V_i(j) - V_m(j))^2}{cd} \right)^{1/2} \quad (m = 1,2,...C_s \text{ and } i = 1,1+C_d,1+2C_d...,mxn) \tag{1}$$

Where
d_m is the root mean square error (RMSE).
V_i is the image vector.
V_m is the codebook vector.
c_s is the codebook size.
c_d is the codeword dimension.

The RMSE (d_m) will be compared with a pre-decided threshold error (V_{th}). If d_m is less than this threshold, then the index of the codebook vector with lowest error will be transmitted and this vector is moved to the top of the codebook in both transmitter and receiver. Otherwise, the image vector will be transmitted and placed at the top of the codebook.

6. Encoding of the subbands

High bit allocation is assigned for the baseband (band 1) since most of the energy of the decomposed T_{LL} image is concentrated in this band. For the high bands (band 2 - band 9), different encoding algorithms are design to be tested for these bands. The first encoding algorithm is to test the LAVQ for all the high bands (band 2 - band 9). The second technique is to encode some of these bands using the edge detection concept, then applay the LAVQ on the detected information. The third approach is to encode some of these high bands using the absolute moment block truncation coding (AMBTC) algorithm[16]. The overall encoding algorithm is decided based on the highest performance in terms of the peak signal to noise ration (PSNR) and the visual quality for the encoded subband. For the first algorithm, those bands reconstructed with PSNR greater than 51 dB will be encoded with LAVQ. The second algorithm is adapted for those subbands encoded with PSNR greater than 40 dB and with bit rate less than 0.06 bpp. The overall encoding algorithm is decided based on the best performance for each subband.

The second level in the pyramid has the high frequency content of the decomposed temporal T_{LL} subband. From the simulation results of the previous three algorithms,
it is found that AMBTC algorithm will give the best performance for this subband (band 2) because it is highly correlated than the other subbands. The mean, absolute moment and bit map are transmitted for each subblock.

The first difference level (band 3) in the pyramid has the minimum information most of which is concentrated around the edges. This information is encoded by applying an edge detection approach to find the location of pixels that are perceptually important and then transmitting only these encoded pixels. To avoid the transmission of the position of the encoded locations, a predicting scheme for the edges of band 3 from the encoded bands (band 1 and band 2) is adapted at the receiver side. This is shown in Figure 10.

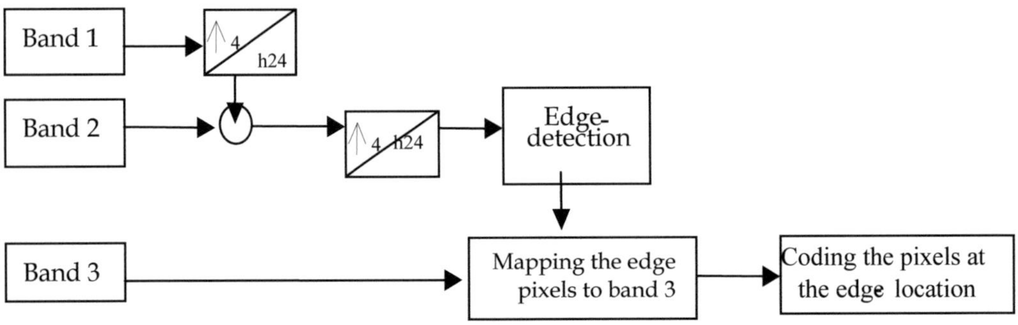

Fig. 10. Coding of Edge-detection for band 3.

Before encoding, the baseband is interpolated to the second level and added to band 2. Then, the result is further interpolated to the size of band 3. Edge-detection is applied to this up-sampled version and the corresponding pixels from band 3 are formed into vectors to be encoded for transmission. At the receiver, similar process is repeated by upsampling the encoded baseband to be added to the encoded band 2. Then, these two subbands are up-

[16] Absolute moment block truncation coding and application to color images, IEEE Trans. on Commun., Vol. COM-32, pp-1148-1157 (Lemma & Mitchell, Oct. 1984).

sampled to have the same size as band 3. This partially reconstructed version of the original image is used for edge-detection, which gives the location of the vectors of the band 3 that are encoded. Once the locations are known, the encoded vectors are suitably placed to form band 3. Thus, using this approach, no side information needs to be sent for the encoded areas of the first difference image level and an average of only 4 % to 5% of this level needs to be encoded. Thus, more compression is achieved by edge-detection instead of coding the entire band. After edge-detection, the data is encoded by using LAVQ.
The decomposed subbands (band 4 and band 5) of the temporal (T_{LH}) subband are encoded using the LAVQ for band 4 and the edge-detection approach for band 5. Band 4 is interpolated to the size of band 5. Then, the edge-detection technique is applied to the interpolated version and the corresponding pixels from band 5 are formed into vectors to be transmitted. At the receiver, this process is repeated by interpolating the decoded band 4 to the size of band 5. Then, edge-detection is taken for this band to decide the location of the received vectors for band 5. The same decoding process is adapted for bands 6 and 7 to get the temporal T_{HL} subband. Band 8 and band 9 formed the temporal T_{HH} subband. Band 9 has extremely low energy content and the sparse information carried in this band is not significant for the final image reconstruction. Thus, it can be safely discarded. Band 8 is encoded using the LAVQ algorithm. At the receiver, this band is interpolated to get the temporal T_{HH} subband.
The subbands encoded using LAVQ have different codebooks sizes and vectors (codewords) dimension. The choice of the codebook size and the codeword dimension depends on many factors such as the important of the information to be transmitted, the correlation between the data in each band, and the size of the band to be encoded. Band 4, for example, is more important than band 8 because it has some of the motion information, and also used at the receiver as a detector to encode band 5. Therefore, some care shall be given to this band. The codebook size is selected to be 128 codewords each of dimension 4. Band 6 and band 8 have most of the edges information, which already emphasized by encoding band 7. Therefore, a codebook with smaller size and a codeword of bigger dimension than that of band 4 can be adapted. From the simulation results, we find that the codebook of size 64 with codeword dimension of 8 will give an excellent reconstructed video sequence quality.
Since the encoded vectors corresponding to the edge-detection concept are the only information used to reconstruct band 3, band 5, and band 7, then, these vectors shall be quantized with lowest possible MSE. Therefore, codebooks of size 64 and codewords of dimension 4 pixels are selected to encode those subbands. Table 3 shows the encoding techniques, PSNR, and bit rate for Miss America sequence.

	Encoding technique	**PSNR**	**Avg. Bit rate (bpp)**
Band 1	AMBTC	45	0.0027
Band 2	AMBTC	43.37	0.02536
Band 3	LAVQ + Edge-detection	40.3749	0.0543
Band 4	LAVQ	52.6049	0.0133
Band 5	LAVQ + Edge-detection	47.1512	0.0061
Band 6	LAVQ	54.2208	0.0123
Band 7	LAVQ + Edge-detection	40.9862	0.0086
Band 8	LAVQ	51.7706	0.0145
Average		37.2	**0.137**

Table 3. The average bit rates and PSNR for Miss America sequence with $V_{th} = 9$.

7. Simulation results

The compression algorithm is tested on three video sequences with different motions and backgrounds. The first sequence is Miss America sequence with slow motion and static background. In this sequence, the only moving objects are the lips and head. The second sequence with moderate motion and noisy background is the Salesman sequence. The man's head and hand are moving faster than Miss America sequence and with noisy background. The third sequence with fast motion than the man's sequence is Walter sequence. All of these sequences were 256 level gray-scale images with dimension of 288 x 352 pixels per frame at the rate of 30 frames /s and 8 bits per pixel. These sequences are standard and are used by many researchers. The only way to check the performance of our proposed algorithm is to test it on such images and compare the results with other compression algorithms.

7.1 Calculating the bit rates

The baseband (band 1 with 18×22 pixels) and band 2 (with 72×88 pixels) are encoded using AMBTC because the information in those subbands is highly correlated.
Band 1 and band 2 are divided into sub-blocks to be encoded by using AMBTC algorithm. The average bit rate needed to encode each band is calculated as follow:

$$Bitrate = \frac{(B_m + B_{h-l}) \times \left(\frac{\frac{l_1}{4^n} \times \frac{l_2}{4^n}}{B_d}\right)}{l_1 \times l_2} \quad (2)$$

Where B_m is the bit-map,B_{h-1} is the required bits to encode the high and the low mean, B_d is the sub-block dimension, $l_1 \times l_2$ is the original image frame dimension, and n is the pyramid level number (n = 1, for first level, and n = 2 for second level). In this paper, B_d is selected to be 3x3 for band 1, and 4x4 for band 2. The high mean and the low mean for band 1 are encoded at 8 bits each, while for band 2, the high mean and the low mean are encoded at 6 and 4 bits; respectively.
The bit rate calculation for the Miss America sequence according to equation (2) is shown below for four frames of the original image sequence; namely, frame 4,5,6 and frame 7. These frames are considered to have the highest motion among this test sequence.

$$Bitrate(band1) = \frac{(9+16) \times \frac{18 \times 22}{3 \times 3}}{288 \times 352} = \frac{0.01085}{4} = 0.0027bpp \quad (3)$$

$$Bitrate(band2) = \frac{(16+10) \times \frac{72 \times 88}{4 \times 4}}{288 \times 352} = \frac{0.10156}{4} = 0.0253bpp \quad (4)$$

The second encoding technique (edge detection + LAVQ) is used to encode bands 3, 5, and 7. First, the edge concept is applied for those bands. Then, those pixels corresponding to the positions represented with "1" are encoded using the LAVQ technique.
The first algorithm (LAVQ) is found to be of high performance for bands 4,6 and 8 since the motion and edges information are presented in these bands. The average bit rate for each band can be calculated using the following formula:

$$Bitrate = \frac{(X \times b) + (Y \times ((cd \times 8) + b))}{l_1 \times l_2} \quad (5)$$

Where X is the number of matched codewords, b is the number of bits needed to encode the index, Y is the number of non-matched codewords, and cd is the dimension of codeword.

Since the eight subbands represent four frames, then the bit rate for each frame is given by the sum of the bit rates for each band divided by a factor of four.

Simulation results on these sequences can be discussed based on three main factors: peak signal to noise ration (PSNR), bit per pixel (bpp) and visual quality. The PSNR in decibel (dB) is given by;

$$\text{PSNR} = 10\log_{10}\left(\frac{255^2}{MSE}\right) \quad (6)$$

Where MSE is the mean square error written as follow;

$$\text{MSE} = \frac{1}{mxn}\sum_{i=1}^{m}\sum_{j=1}^{n}(X_{ij} - \tilde{X}_{ij})^2 \quad (7)$$

where;

m is the number of rows.

n is the number of columns.

$\tilde{X}$ is the reconstructed pixel value.

Table 4 shows the average bit rate and average PSNR with different pre-decided thresholds error (V_{th}) for the three sequences. These thresholds are compared with the RMSE (dm) that result from LAVQ searching method. The bigger the V_{th} the lower number of non-matched (Y) codewords will be. This will reduce the average bit rate required for transmission as given in equation (5). However, the quality of the reconstructed image will be effected. Therefore, a compromised between the bit rate and the required visual quality shall be decided.

		Miss America	**Salesman**	**Walter**
V_{th} = 6	**PSNR**	37.34	36.5	35.6
	Bpp required	0.143	0.172	0.207
	Bit rate	0.435 Mbps	0.523 Mbps	0.629 Mbps
V_{th} = 9	**PSNR**	37.2	36.31	35.42
	Bpp required	0.137	0.161	0.198
	Bit rate	0.416 Mbps	0.489 Mbps	0.602 Mbps
V_{th} = 12	**PSNR**	36.9	36.2	35.15
	Bpp required	0.13	0.154	0.191
	Bit rate	0.395 Mbps	0.468 Mbps	0.58 Mbps

Table 4. Performance characteristics for different test sequences.

Three different thresholds have been tested in this study. The best result in terms of PSNR (dB) is given at V_{th} = 6. However, at this threshold the bit rate requirement is higher than that at V_{th} > 6. At V_{th} = 12, the bit rate for the three sequences is very low. It has been found from the simulation results that the visual quality of the reconstructed sequences is excellent at V_{th} = 12. Figure 11 shows the original and the reconstruction of the second four frames of Miss America sequence at V_{th} =12. The visual quality of the reconstructed sequence is the same as the original. From the simulation, it can be concluded that this compression algorithm is capable of compressing a video sequences of different motions.

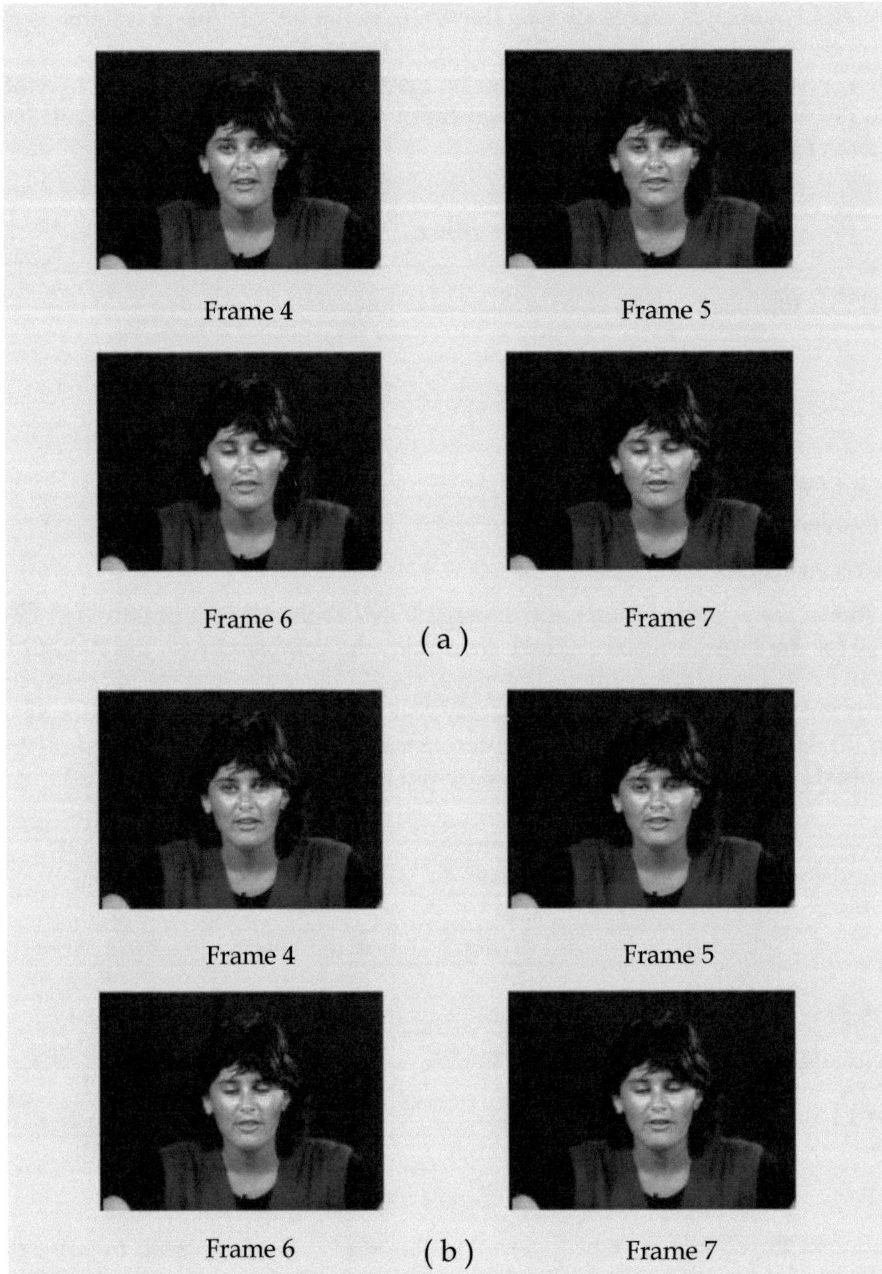

Fig. 11. (a) Original and (b) Reconstructed frames of the second four frames of Miss America sequence at V_{th} = 12.

The PSNR (dB) via the number of frames is demonstrated for the three sequences at different thresholds. Also the average bit rate (bpp) versus the number of frames is presented for 16 frames of the test video sequence. Since four frames are simulated as one group at a time, only 4 different bit rates will be observed. However, the subband T_{LL} is transmitted first. Then, band T_{LH} which is the second important subband regarding the information contents. This approach will be followed until all the subbands are transmitted. Accumulative calculation for the bit rate is then adopted in order to plot the bit rate curves. Figure 12 shows the overall performance in terms of PSNR (dB) and bit rate (bpp) of the proposed algorithm for Miss America sequence.

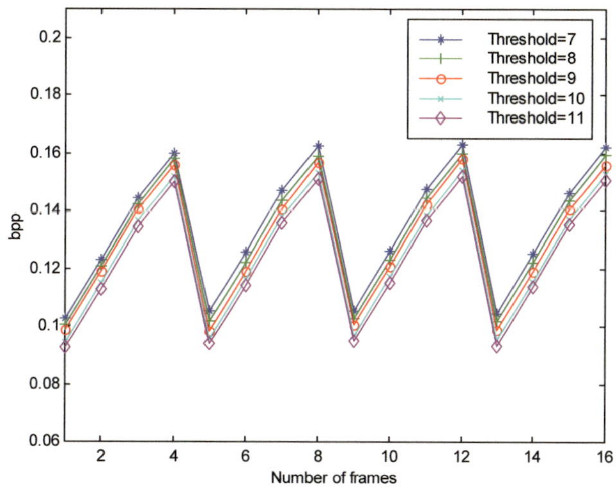

(a)

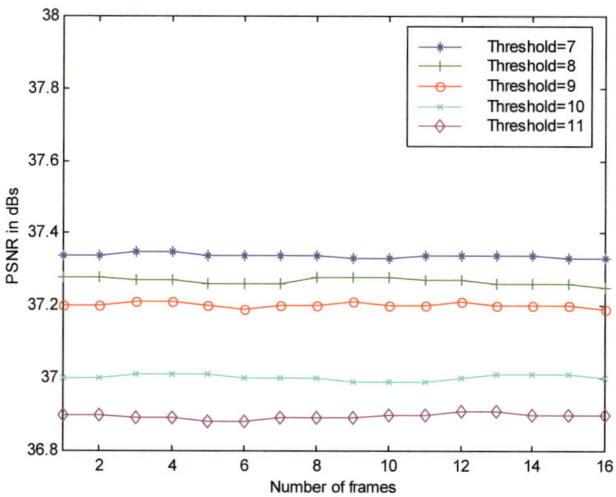

(b)

Fig. 12. Performance curves. (a) PSNR vs. number of frames for Miss America sequence. (b) bpp vs. number of frames for Miss America sequence.

8. Performance evaluation

The performance evaluation of the proposed algorithm is done in two stages. First, it is compared with the performance of MPEG standard algorithm. Second, it is compared with some existing research works in this field using multiresolution decomposition concept.

8.1 Comparison with MPEG-1

In[17], we have tested MPEG-1 for the monochrome Miss America sequence at 30 frames/second. The results are produced for CIF (288 × 352) image format. The PSNR is 37 dB and the bit rate is 0.343 bpp[17]. The proposed algorithm in this paper achieves 36.9 dB at 0.13 bpp. At approximately the same PSNR, the saving in bit rate is about 56% as shown in Table 5. The visual quality is excellent in both MPEG-1 and the proposed technique. However, the encoder/decoder of MPEG-1 is more complex than our scheme. MPEG-1 based on a coder uses the DCT transform for the intraframe and the motion compensation (MC) for the interframe. Studies reveal that if there are many moving objects in the image, each moving in a different direction, the search technique becomes computationally complex, involving larger storage and delay problems[17].

	MPEG-1	KARL [7]	NEHAL [8]	Al-Asmari [10]	Al-Asmari [17]	This Method
Interframe Coding	Motion compensation	Temporal 2-tap filtering SSKFs	Temporal 2-tap filtering SSKFs	Temporal 2-tap filtering SSKFs	Motion compensation	Temporal 4-tap filtering SSKFs
Intraframe Coding	DCT - Transform (JPEG)	SBC + ADPCM and PCM	PC + DPCM or BTC	PC + FSCL (VQ)	AMBTC and quantizetion	PC + AMBTC + LAVQ
Average PSNR	37 dB	36.9 dB	36.5 dB	36.52 dB	37 dB	36.9 dB
Bpp	0.343	0.434	0.273	0.25	0.2	0.13
Relative complexity	Complex	Moderate	Low	Moderate	Moderate	Low
Comments	Excellent quality with moderate bit rate	Good Quality at high bit rate	Competitive quality with low bit rate	Excellent quality with low bit rate	Excellent quality at Low bit rate	Excellent quality with very low bit rate

Table 5. Comparison with different compression methods.

8.2 Comparing with other works

The performance of the proposed algorithm is compared with the results obtained in related works in[7-8], [10], and[17] in terms of PSNR, bit rate, and complexity. The comparison between those algorithms is presented in Table 5. Karlsson and Vetterli in[7], and Nehal, et al. in[8] have suggested schemes for progressive transmission using temporal filtering with 2-tap symmetric short kernel filters (SSKFs). The reconstruction quality is very good. For[7], the PSNR is 36.9 dB with an average bit rate of 0.434 bpp while for[8] the PSNR is 36.5 dB and the bit rate is 0.273 bpp. Al-Asmari, et al. in [10] have suggested an algorithm for video compression. The 2-tap SSKFs filters are used for temporal domain and pyramid coding for intraframe. The decomposed bands are encoded using VQ called frequency selective competitive learning (FSCL). This technique used the neural network concept to design the

[17] Low Complexity Video Compression Algorithm Using AMBTC, Proceeding of IEEE Military communication conference, Atlantic city, NJ (Al-Asmari et al., 31 Oct. - 3 Nov. 1999).

codebook for the vector quantization. This algorithm gives an excellent image quality for the Miss America sequence at an average bit rate of 0.25 bpp and PSNR 36.52 dB. This algorithm is considered to be of higher complexity than our algorithm because of the codebook design. In [17], the authors present a coder based on a combination of AMBTC for intraframe and MC for interframe. They produce results for the monochrome Miss America sequence. For the CIF format (i.e. 288 × 352) at 30 frames/sec, they achieve approximately 37 dB at 0.2 bpp. The disadvantage of this algorithm is the use of motion compensation for fast motion video sequence. For the same video sequence, the proposed algorithm in this paper gives a higher PSNR (37.2 dB) and a lower bit rate (0.13 bpp) than those algorithms for a coder with lower complexity.

9. Conclusion

The results presented here are better than other coding schemes, which are published using almost the same coding technique concept. The 3-D decomposition does not make unrealistic assumptions about the data, as do methods based on motion compensation (MC). Moreover, coding and decoding for the proposed algorithm are of comparable and relatively low complexity. The robustness obtained by adapting the LAVQ for the codebook has been discussed. The results reported in this paper are independent of which sequence is used to produce the codebook.

This scheme is faster than MPEG algorithms and other existing technique based their encoder on VQ concept since no need for training set or codebook generation. This scheme will be an optimal choice for real time transmission. It is well suited for progressive transmission of the video sequence and for browsing moving images via the Internet.

LAVQ technique gives good performance with those bands, which are highly uncorrelated, and with spark information. Bit rate is varying from 0.13 to 0.191 bpp depending on the nature of the sequence. Different video sequences have been tested and show very good image quality with PSNR in the range of 36.9 to 35.15 dB and with bit rate range from 0.395 Mbps to 0.58 Mbps as shown in table 4.

10. References

Al-asmari Awad Kh. (1995), *Optimum Bit Rate Pyramid Coding with Low Computational and Memory Requirements*, IEEE Trans. Circuit and Systems for video Tech., vol. 5, no. 3 pp. 182-192, (June 1995).

Al-Asmari Awad Kh., Ahmed Abobakr & Al-Doweesh Abdullah (1996), *Image compression scheme using improved basic-LAVQ and optimized VLC, J.* King Saud Univ., Vol. 8, Eng. Sci. (2), pp. 251-266.

Al-Asmari Awad Kh., Aryai Deepali, & Kwatra Subhash C. (2000), *Video Signal Transmission for IS-95* Environment, Electronic Letters, Vol. 36, no. 5, pp. 465-466, 2nd March 2000.

Al-Asmari Awad Kh., Dave Sameep & Kawatra Subhash C. (1999), *Low Complexity Video Compression Algorithm Using AMBTC*, Proceeding of IEEE Military communication conference, Atlantic city, NJ, (31 Oct. - 3 Nov).

Al-Asmari Awad, Singh Vinay & Kawatra Subhash (June 28 - July 1 CIST 99), *Hybrid coding of images for progressive transmission over a digital cellular channel*, CISST'99

International Conference on Imaging Science, Systems and Technology, Monte Carlo resort, Las Vegas, Nevada, USA, PIN 128C.

Bhaskaran Vasudev, Konstantinidides Konstantions & Hewlett Packard Laboratories (1996), *Image and video compression standards: algorithms and architectures,* Kluwer Academic Publishers.

Burt P. & Adelson E. (1983), *The Laplacian Pyramid as a compact Image Code,* IEEE Trans Communication., vol. COM-31, no. 4 pp. 532-540, (April 1983).

Child J. (July 1993), *Realtime video compression poses challenge to designers and vendors alike,* Computer Design, vol. 32, no. 7, pp. 67-70.

Clarke.R. J., (1995) *Digital compression of still images and video,* Academic Press.

Coppisetti N., Kwatra S. C., & Al-asmari A. Kh. (1993), *Low complexity subband encoding for HDTV images,* IEEE J. Select. Areas Commun., vol. 11, no. 1, pp. 77-87, (Jan. 1993).

Dantwala Nehal, Kwatra Subhash C. & Al-Asmari Awad Kh. (June 30 – July 3 - CISST'97), *Pyramid coding of video signals for progressive transmission,* CISST'97 International Conference, pp-392-398.

Karlsson .G. & Vetterli. M. (July 1988), *Subband coding of video for packet networks,* Optical Engineering, vol. 27, no. 7, pp. 574-586.

Lemma Maximo D. & Mitchell O. R. (1984), *Absolute moment block truncation coding and application to color images,* IEEE Trans. on Commun., Vol. COM-32, pp-1148-1157, (Oct. 1984).

Netravali. Arun . N & Haskell Barry G. (1995), *Digital pictures representation, compression, and standard,* Plenium Press.

Sayano M. (1992), *Analysis of Coding and Compression strategies for Data Storage and Transmission,* Ph. D. thesis, california Instiute of Technology.

Sayood Khalid (1996), *Introduction to data compression,* Morgan Kaufmann Publishers Inc., San Francisco, California.

Shannon.C. E (Oct. 1948), *A mathematical theory of communication,* Bell System Tech. J.. Vol. 27, pp. 379-423, July. 1948 and pp. 623-656.

8

Low Complexity Implementation of Daubechies Wavelets for Medical Imaging Applications

Khan Wahid
University of Saskatchewan, Canada

1. Introduction

The Discrete Wavelet Transform (DWT) has extensively been used in a wide range of applications, including numerical analysis, image and video coding, pattern recognition, medical and telemetric imaging, etc. The invention of DWT decomposition by Mallat (Mallat, 1998) shows that the DWT can be viewed as a multiresolution decomposition of signal. This means it decomposes the signal into its components in different frequency bands. The Inverse DWT does the opposite, i.e. it reconstructs the signal from its octave band components. After its inclusion in JPEG2000 compression standard (Seo & Kim, 2007), significant research has been done to optimize the DWT implementation to reduce the computational complexity. Among a wide range of wavelets, the Daubechies wavelets include members ranging from highly localized to highly smooth and can provide excellent performance in image compression (Daubechies, 1992). Among the family members, the first two - Daubechies 4-tap (DAUB4) and Daubechies 6-tap (DAUB6) - are popular choices in medical imaging applications.
While compressing medical images, the key here is to preserve as much critical information as possible in the reconstructed image so that accurate diagnosis is possible. There have been several efficient implementations of wavelet filters proposed for applications in image processing (Lee & Lim, 2006; Martina & Masera, 2007; Acharyya et al., 2009; Shi et al., 2009; Lai et al., 2009). But, the use of conventional fixed-point (FP) binary (or any other weighted) representation for implementing discrete wavelet coefficients (that are irrational in nature) introduces round-off or approximation errors at the very beginning of the process. The error is due to the lack of exact representation of the irrational numbers that form the coefficient basis. These errors tend to expand as the calculations progress through the architecture, degrading the quality of image reconstruction (Wahid et al., 2003). A lossless mapping technique, known as Algebraic Integer Quantization (AIQ), can be used to minimize the approximation error and efficiently compute the DAUB4 and DAUB6 coefficients (Wahid et al., 2004). The AIQ scheme is divided into two parts: the first stage is based on factorization and decomposition of transform matrices exploiting the symmetric structure. After the decomposition, we map the irrational transform basis coefficients using multidimensional algebraic integers that results in exact representation and simpler implementation. As a result, less error is introduced in the computation process that yields significantly better

reconstruction of images while keeping critical information, making the scheme suitable for medical and telemetric imaging applications.

As a case study, we apply the scheme to several medical images, such as endoscopic, ultrasound, x-ray, CT-scan images and evaluate the performance. The chapter is organized as follows: Previous related works are presented next. Section 3 presents a brief introduction to Daubechies wavelets. In Section 4, we explain the AIQ scheme applied to Daubechies wavelets. Then the simulation and synthesized results of the case study are summarized in Section 5. Finally, we conclude the work in Section 6.

2. Past work

Lewis and Knowles proposed an architecture for Daubechies wavelets without multipliers (Lewis & Knowles, 1991). A major drawback was that it was heavily dependent on the properties of only one specific wavelet, DAUB4 tap coefficients. At the same time, Aware Inc. came out with a chip called Wavelet Transform Processor (WTP) (Aware, 1991). It essentially consists of a 4-tap filter (4 Multiply-Accumulate cells) and some external memory with control but no specific features that can take advantage of the DWT structure rather it relies heavily on the software to compute the DWT. It is also a complex design requiring extensive user control. Parhi and Nishitani proposed two architectures, folded and digit serial, for 1D DWT (Parhi & Nishitani, 1993). These architectures do not easily scale with the filter size and the number of octaves computed. The number of multipliers is higher, and hence the silicon area is large. In (Vishwanath et al., 1995), the authors proposed linear systolic array architecture. Paek and Kim in proposed recursive and semi-recursive architectures for DWT which has several drawbacks like large area (hardware cost), scheduling control overhead and incomplete data-bus utilization (Paek & Kim, 1998).

Most of the research work to reduce the hardware complexity is inclined towards multiplierless implementations by maneuvering the filter banks (Lee & Lim, 2006; Martina & Masera, 2007; Acharyya et al., 2009) or using lifting schemes (Shi et al., 2009; Lai et al., 2009; Huang et al., 2004). However, in these designs, the use of conventional FP binary representation results in erroneous computation process and degrades image reconstruction. In this chapter, we present an efficient low-cost implementation of the DAUB filters with a demonstration of performance advantages on medical images and noisy environment.

3. Daubechies wavelets

This section provides a brief introduction to Daubechies wavelets. This class of wavelets includes members ranging from highly localized to highly smooth - Daubechies-2 (DAUB2 with two coefficients) to Daubechies-20 (DAUB20 with 20 coefficients) and also provides excellent performance in image compression (Daubechies, 1992). The Daubechies wavelet coefficients are based on computing wavelet coefficients, C_n (where, n = 0, 1, 2,..., N-1 and N is the number of coefficients) to satisfy the following conditions (Mallat, 1998):

1. The conservation of area under a finite length signal $x(t)$: $\sum C_n = 2$
2. The accuracy conditions: $\sum(-1)^n n^m C_n = 0$ (where m = 0, 1, 2,..., p-1 and $p = N/2$)
3. The perfect reconstruction conditions: $\sum_n C_n^2 = 2$ and $\sum_n C_n C_{n+2m} = 0$

Then the low-pass filter is $h(n) = \frac{C_n}{2}$ and the high-pass filter is $g(n) = (-1)^{n+1} h(n - N - 1)$. One of the simplest and most localized members is the DAUB6 which has six coefficients:

$$C_0 = \frac{(1+z_1+z_2)}{16\sqrt{2}} \qquad C_1 = \frac{(5+z_1+3z_2)}{16\sqrt{2}} \qquad C_2 = \frac{(10-2z_1+2z_2)}{16\sqrt{2}}$$

$$C_3 = \frac{(10-2z_1-2z_2)}{16\sqrt{2}} \qquad C_4 = \frac{(5+z_1-3z_2)}{16\sqrt{2}} \qquad C_5 = \frac{(1+z_1-z_2)}{16\sqrt{2}} \tag{1}$$

Where, $z_1 = \sqrt{10}$ and $z_2 = \sqrt{5+2\sqrt{10}}$. For an 8x8 input data, the DAUB6 forward transform matrix (using an assumption of periodicity) is shown in Eq. (2):

$$\psi_6(C) = \begin{bmatrix} C_0 & C_1 & C_2 & C_3 & C_4 & C_5 & 0 & 0 \\ C_5 & -C_4 & C_3 & -C_2 & C_1 & -C_0 & 0 & 0 \\ 0 & 0 & C_0 & C_1 & C_2 & C_3 & C_4 & C_5 \\ 0 & 0 & C_5 & -C_4 & C_3 & -C_2 & C_1 & -C_0 \\ C_4 & C_5 & 0 & 0 & C_0 & C_1 & C_2 & C_3 \\ C_1 & -C_0 & 0 & 0 & C_5 & -C_4 & C_3 & -C_2 \\ C_2 & C_3 & C_4 & C_5 & 0 & 0 & C_0 & C_1 \\ C_3 & -C_2 & C_1 & -C_0 & 0 & 0 & C_5 & -C_4 \end{bmatrix} \tag{2}$$

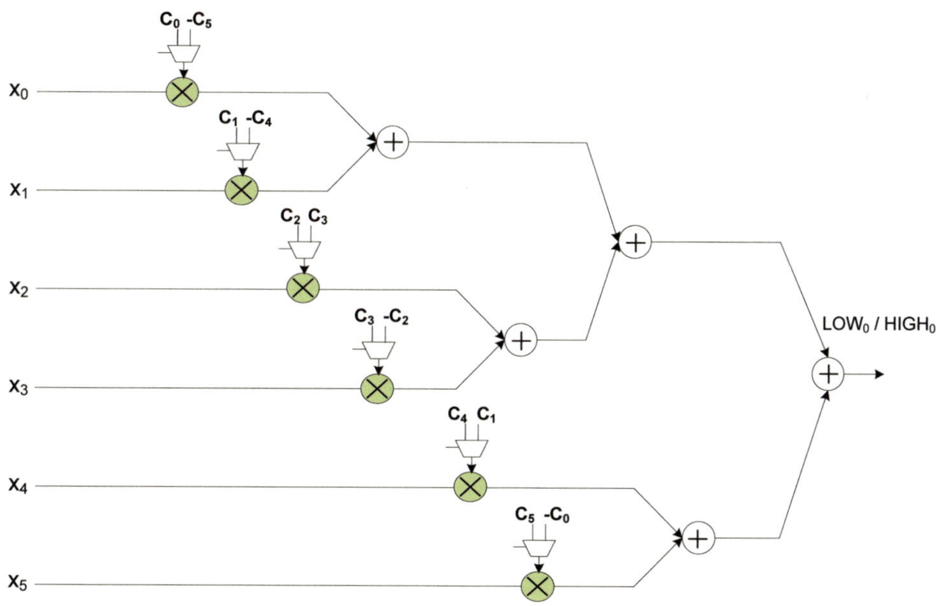

Fig. 1. FP-based DAUB6 filter architecture.

The structure of the matrix uses the set of coefficients, $\{C_0, C_1, ..., C_5\}$ as a smoothing filter (low-pass) and the set, $\{C_5, -C_4, ..., -C_0\}$ as a non-smoothing filter (high-pass). The DWT is invertible and orthogonal - the inverse transform, when viewed as a matrix, is simply the transpose of the forward transform matrix. So, basically we need only 2 sets of multiply-accumulate (MAC) cells each containing 6 multipliers and 5 adders where partial products are computed separately and subsequently added. However, it can be seen that, by introducing additional control circuitry, the same multipliers can be used for both low-pass and high-pass filtering. As a result, the number of multipliers can be reduced to 6 instead of 12. Fig. 1 shows the signal flow graph of the conventional finite-precision (FP) implementation of Eq. (2), where x_i is the input data vector. Since all the coefficients are fixed, for a fixed precision, we can in fact replace all the multipliers by adders and shifters. As a result, the total equivalent additions required to compute the 1-D DAUB6 filter is 44.

4. AIQ-based algorithm

Algebraic integer (AI) is defined by real numbers that are roots of monic polynomials with integer coefficients (Wahid et al., 2004). As an example, let $\omega = e^{\frac{2\pi j}{16}}$ denote a primitive 16th root of unity over the ring of complex numbers. Then ω satisfies the equation: $x^8 + 1 = 0$. The ring $Z(\omega)$ can be regarded as consisting of polynomials in ω of degree 7 with integer coefficients. The elements of $Z(\omega)$ are added and multiplied as polynomials, except that the rule $\omega^8 = -1$ is used in the product to reduce the degree of powers to below 8.

In summary, algebraic integers of an extension of degree n can be assumed to be of the form:

$$a_0\omega_0 + a_1\omega_1 + ... + a_{n-1}\omega_{n-1} \tag{3}$$

Where, $\{\omega_0, \omega_1, ..., \omega_{n-1}\}$ is called the AI basis and the coefficients a_i are integers. The process of mapping with AI is known as Algebraic Integer Quantization (AIQ).

The AIQ technique is useful in computing discrete transforms as first explored by Cozzens and Finkelstein (Cozzens & Finkelstein, 1985). In their work, the algebraic integer number representation, in which the signal sample is represented by a set of (typically four to eight) small integers, combines with the Residue Number System (RNS) to produce processors composed of simple parallel channels. The analog samples must first be quantized into the algebraic integer representation and the final algebraic integer result converted back to an analog or digital form. In between these two conversions, the algebraic integer representation must be converted into and out of two levels of RNS parallelism.

4.1 AIQ-based Daubechies wavelets

Now we present the concept of AIQ to encode the DAUB6 coefficients. First of all, consider the polynomial of two variables:

$$f(z_1, z_2) = \sum_{i=0}^{1}\sum_{j=0}^{1} a_{ij} z^i{}_1 z^j{}_2 = \begin{bmatrix} a_{00} & a_{10} \\ a_{01} & a_{11} \end{bmatrix} \begin{bmatrix} 1 & z_2 \\ z_1 & z_1 z_2 \end{bmatrix} \tag{4}$$

So the corresponding coefficients, a_{ij}, are encoded in the form $\begin{bmatrix} a_{00} & a_{10} \\ a_{01} & a_{11} \end{bmatrix}$. Then all the DAUB6 coefficients are exactly encoded (scaled by $16\sqrt{2}$) and shown below in Eq. (5):

$$C_0 = \begin{bmatrix} 1 & 1 \\ 1 & 0 \end{bmatrix} \quad C_1 = \begin{bmatrix} 5 & 1 \\ 3 & 0 \end{bmatrix} \quad C_2 = \begin{bmatrix} 10 & -2 \\ 2 & 0 \end{bmatrix}$$
$$C_3 = \begin{bmatrix} 10 & -2 \\ -2 & 0 \end{bmatrix} \quad C_4 = \begin{bmatrix} 5 & 1 \\ -3 & 0 \end{bmatrix} \quad C_5 = \begin{bmatrix} 1 & 1 \\ -1 & 0 \end{bmatrix} \tag{5}$$

The obvious advantages of this approach are: a) Very small dynamic range (numbers ranging from 0 to 10); b) Multiplication by a constant is very easy and efficient (only 1 addition is required in most cases; so, multiplication can be eliminated by add/shift algorithm); and c) We have 3 parallel channels through which data flows independently (since a_{11} is zero for all) and also a very simple scheduling is needed. No quantization errors would be incurred. Fig. 2 shows the signal flow graph of the AIQ-based scheme that requires 42 adders.

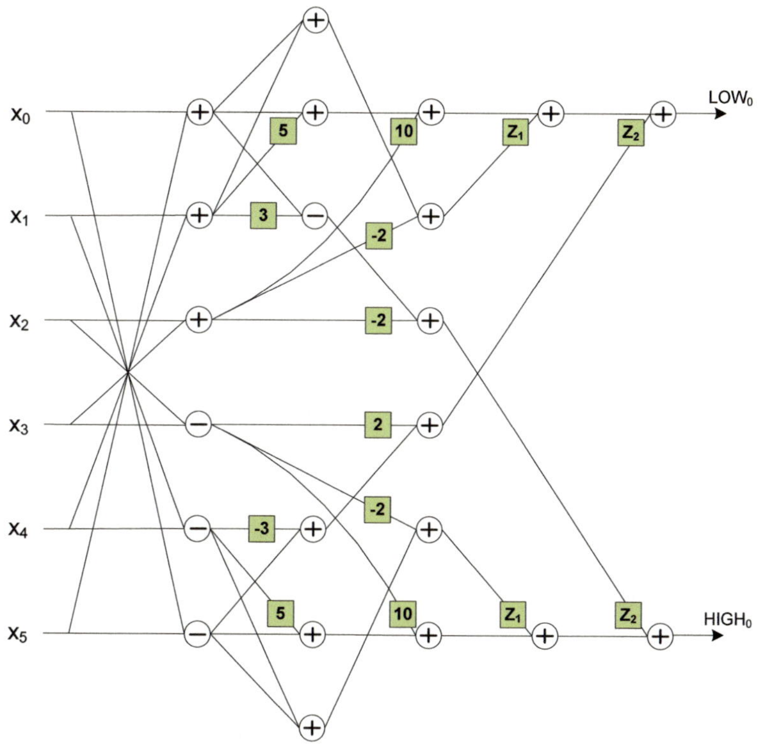

Fig. 2. AIQ-based DAUB6 filter architecture.

The encoding scheme can be easily applied to DAUB4 coefficients. In that case, we need a 2nd degree polynomial of one variable:

$$f(z_3) = a_0 + a_1 z_3 + a_2 z^2{}_3 \quad (6)$$

Where, $z_3 = \sqrt{3}$. As a result, the error-free mapping of DAUB4 coefficients can computed as given below (scaled by $4\sqrt{2}$):

$$C_0 = 1 + z_3;\ C_1 = 3 + z_3;\ C_2 = 3 - z_3;\ C_3 = 1 - z_3 \quad (7)$$

4.2 Hardware implementation

The AIQ-based architecture is coded in Verilog and prototyped onto Xilinx VirtexE FPGA to assess the performance. A precision of 8-bit is used in the multipliers to minimize the hardware and optimize the operation, which is completed in one clock cycle (CC). Table 1 presents the comparison of the synthesized results along with the fixed-point (FP) designs. It can be seen from the table that the AIQ scheme for both DAUB4 (D4) and DAUB6 (D6) costs lesser hardware resources and has lower critical path delay; in case of DAUB4, the savings is even higher.

Scheme	Fixed-point		AIQ		Overall savings (%)	
	D4	D6	D4	D6	D4	D6
Datapath	4	6	3	6	25	0
Adders	32	44	16	42	50	5
LUTs	268	364	124	340	54	7
Registers	422	520	200	494	53	5
Critical path	Tm+2Ta	Tm+3Ta	5Ta	6Ta	--	--
Frequency (MHz)	98	112	148	120	--	--

[1]Xilinx VirtexE (xcv300epq240-8); D4 = DAUB4; D6 = DAUB6; Tm = latency for multiply operation; Ta = latency for addition operation

Table 1. FPGA[1] implementation and hardware comparison.

A key advantage of the AIQ approach is error reduction. In order to better understand the sources of error induction, we present in Fig. 3 the entire process of digital computation process. Here each arrow represents one key stage in the computation. In case of FP-based approach, there are three stages of error accumulation (or induction). In stage 1, the quantization (or approximation) error is introduced due to the lack of finite representation of transform basis coefficients that are irrational numbers. The error gets larger and larger in later stages as the process continues.

However, in AIQ-based approach, there is only one stage of error induction at the end: in stage 1, the basis coefficients are mapped with algebraic integers (that is error-free); then all the required computations take place (that is also error-free) using the AI representation. Finally, the data is converted back to binary (in stage 3) where some errors may be introduced; but these errors are much less compared to FP-approach, and are introduced very late in the computation process, and hence less affect the quality of image reconstruction.

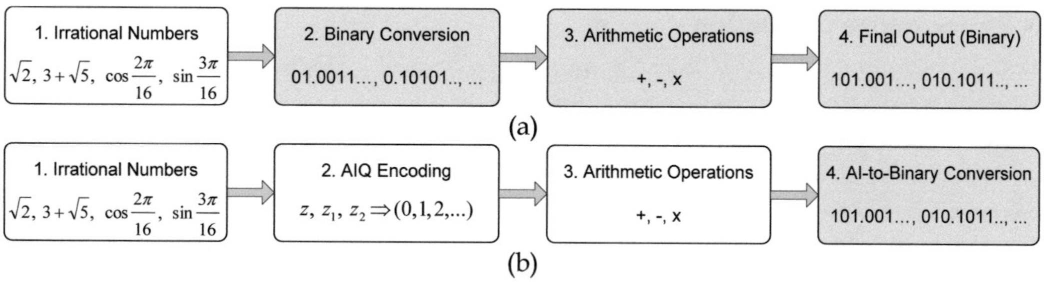

Fig. 3. Stages in computation process (error induced in shaded blocks): (a) FP approach; (b) AIQ approach.

Moreover, the error introduced at the final stage in AIQ approach can be further minimized using higher precision AIQ multipliers. We have performed an error analysis that shows the error incurred for different bit-length of the AIQ multipliers (in Fig. 4). The error is computed taking a multiplier of 16-bit width as reference. The signed digit representation (for 8-bits) is shown below in Eq. (8):

$$\begin{aligned} z_1 &= \sqrt{10} \approx 11.001010 = 3 + 2^{-3} + 2^{-5} \\ z_2 &= \sqrt{5+2\sqrt{10}} \approx 100.\bar{1}0\bar{1}00 = 4 - 2^{-1} - 2^{-3} \\ z_3 &= \sqrt{3} \approx 10.0\bar{1}00\bar{1}0 = 2 - 2^{-2} - 2^{-5} \end{aligned} \tag{8}$$

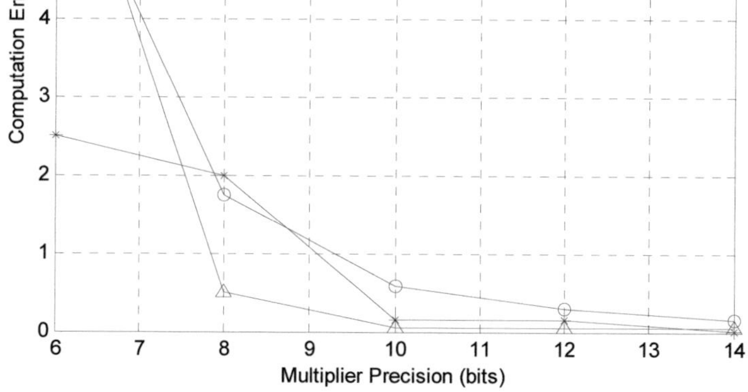

Fig. 4. Computation error in AIQ multipliers.

5. Performance evaluation

The AIQ-based algorithm to compute the Daubechies Wavelet Transform is intended to be used in applications where the quality of image reconstruction is critical, such as biomedical imaging, telemedicine, capsule endoscopy (Wahid et al., 2008), etc. Due to the error-free nature of integer mapping, the AIQ approach results in a much better reconstruction compared to conventional binary approach. Here, we present the results of our study, where we apply the scheme to several standard benchmark and medical images, such as endoscopic, ultrasound, x-ray, CT-scan images and evaluate the performance.

The section is divided into four sub-sections. In the first section, we evaluate the performance of the AIQ scheme for standard images followed by the analysis of medical images. Next, we show the performance of the scheme in a noisy environment. Finally, the results are compared with existing works related to medical image compression. In all these cases, we have used peak-signal-to-noise-ratio (PSNR) as the visual quality assessment index which is given by Eq. (9):

$$PSNR = 20 \times \log_{10} \frac{255}{\sqrt{\frac{1}{M \times N} \sum_{n=1}^{N} \sum_{m=1}^{M} \left(x_{m,n} - x'_{m,n} \right)^2}} \tag{9}$$

Where, M and N are the image width and height namely; x and x' are the original and reconstructed component values namely.

5.1 Performance analysis on standard images

Here, we perform 1-D forward transform on the benchmark "Goldhill" image followed by the inverse transform to get the original image back. No compression was performed, so the image quality degradation is purely due to arithmetic quantization effects. Different hardware precision (number of bit) is used where a full adder is considered as the unit for the hardware cost, and making a simple assumption of a hardware cost of n for an n-bit word (this will be a best case comparison for the fixed-point binary implementation). The results are shown in Fig. 5 and 6.

As shown in Fig. 5(a), the PSNR of the reconstructed image gets higher with the increased bit precision which is expected. In all cases, the AIQ performs much better that FP, i.e., the data recovery rate is higher, especially in lower bit rate region. In other words, for a fixed level of distortion, the number of bits required to transmit the transformed coefficients of AIQ approach would be less than those required for FP technique.

In Fig. 5(b), we present an analysis of reconstruction quality (in PSNR) with the cost of implementation. An interesting comparison is to select similar hardware cost and then compare the reconstruction performance. As an example, for same hardware cost of 150, compare the PSNR of both FP (44dB) and AIQ implementation (82dB). In this case the difference in the PSNR is 38dB in favour of AI – that is for similar cost of implementation, the AIQ scheme produces much better image reconstruction. On the other hand, for same PSNR, say 60 dB, AIQ scheme (95) requires around three times less hardware than FP implementation (270).

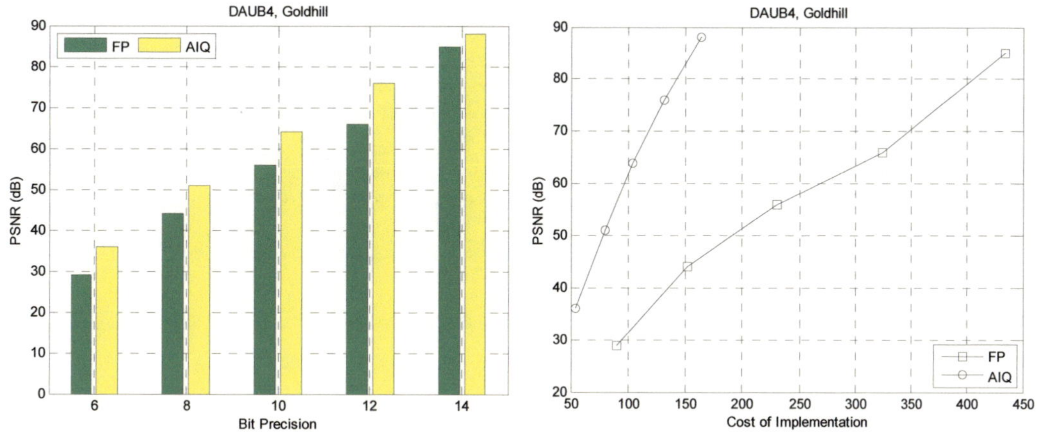

(a) (b)

Fig. 5. Performance analysis of DAUB4 - FP vs. AIQ: (a) PSNR vs. Precision; (b) PSNR vs. Hardware cost.

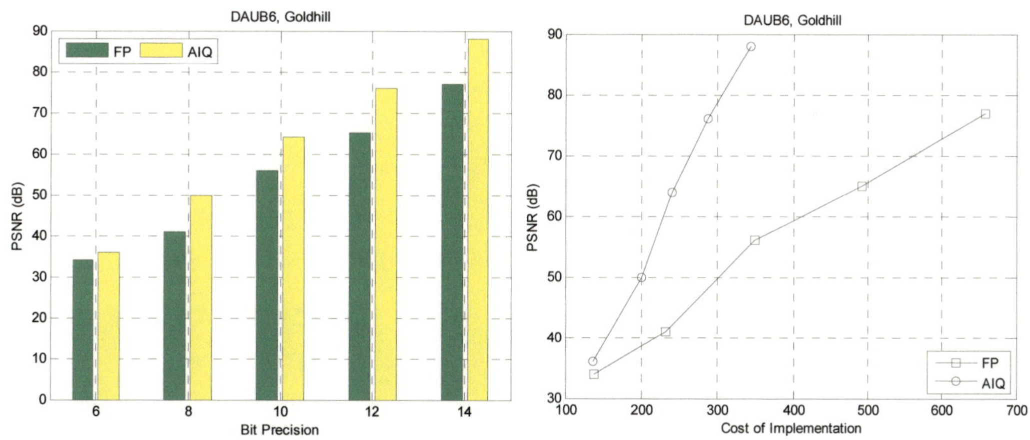

(a) (b)

Fig. 6. Performance analysis of DAUB6 - FP vs. AIQ: (a) PSNR vs. Precision; (b) PSNR vs. Hardware cost.

Same kind of superiority is seen for DAUB6 (Figure 6) too. So, not only an improvement in image reconstruction quality is obtained but also hardware cost is reduced. Fig. 7 shows the image reconstruction for a 8-bit FP vs. a 14-bit AIQ for DAUB4. The difference in PSNR is about 45dB and the level of improvement is quite noticeable.

(a) Original (b) PSNR = 43dB (c) PSNR= 88dB

Fig. 7. (a) Original goldhill image; (b) Reconstructed image using FP scheme (8-bits); (c) AIQ scheme (14-bits).

5.2 Performance analysis on medical images

We have performed an exhaustive simulation using several medical images, such as, X-ray, CT-scan, Ultrasound (US) and endoscopic images, and the results are presented in Table 2 (showing for two cases of bit precision: 8-bits and 12-bits). In all cases, the AIQ-based scheme produces a high PSNR and outperforms the conventional approach by a far margin. Some sample original and reconstructed images are shown in Fig. 8 – 11. In most cases, the difference in PSNR is around 8dB with noticeable level of improvement.

		D4-FP	D4-AIQ	D6-FP	D6-AIQ
CT	8 bit	44.4	52.5	41.1	49.3
	12 bit	66.7	76.6	65.5	76.6
Endoscopic	8 bit	44.8	51.8	41.4	50.8
	12 bit	67.1	76.0	66.1	75.9
US	8 bit	48.0	55.9	44.8	53.7
	12 bit	70.4	79.9	69.0	79.9
X-ray	8 bit	43.3	50.1	39.9	49.2
	12 bit	65.5	74.1	64.5	74.1

Table 2. Quality of reconstruction (in terms of PSNR in dB) for medical images.

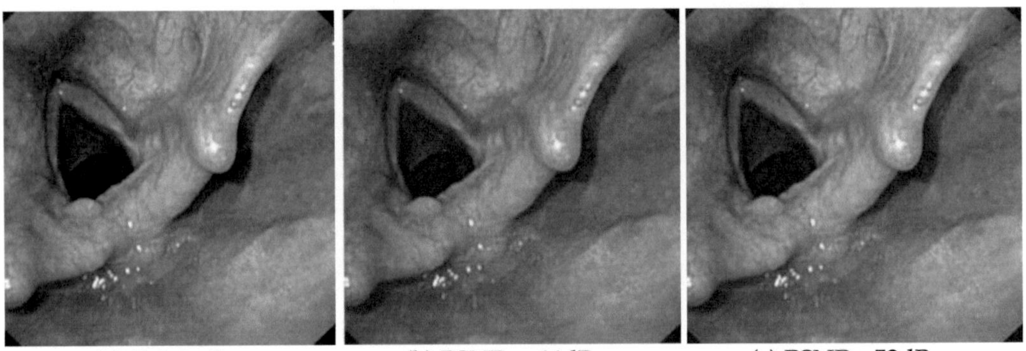

(a) Original (b) PSNR = 44dB (c) PSNR= 52dB

Fig. 8. (a) Original endoscopic image; (b) Reconstructed image using FP scheme; (c) AIQ scheme.

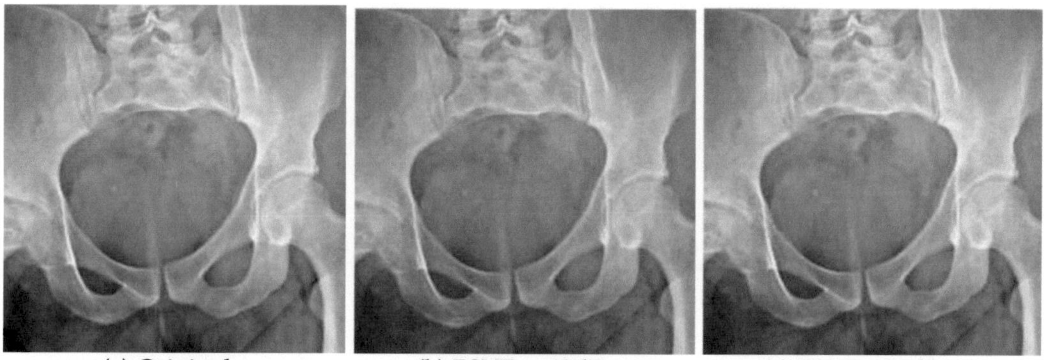

(a) Original (b) PSNR = 43dB (c) PSNR= 50dB

Fig. 9. (a) Original x-ray image; (b) Reconstructed image using FP scheme; (c) AIQ scheme.

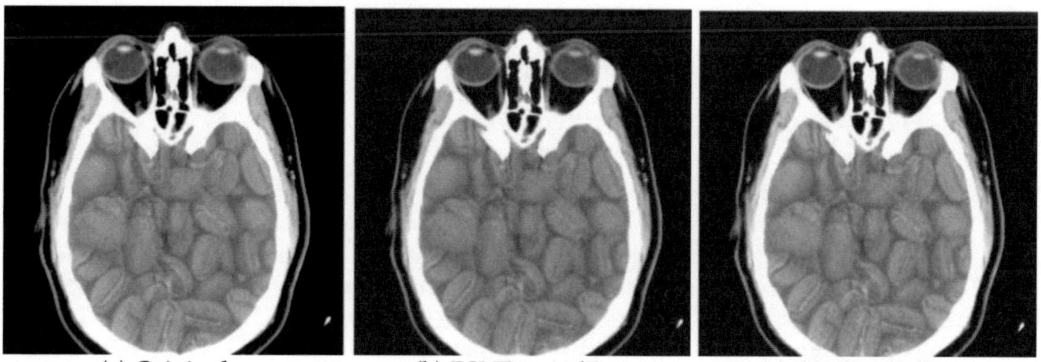

(a) Original (b) PSNR = 44dB (c) PSNR= 53dB

Fig. 10. (a) Original CT-scan image; (b) Reconstructed image using FP scheme; (c) AIQ scheme.

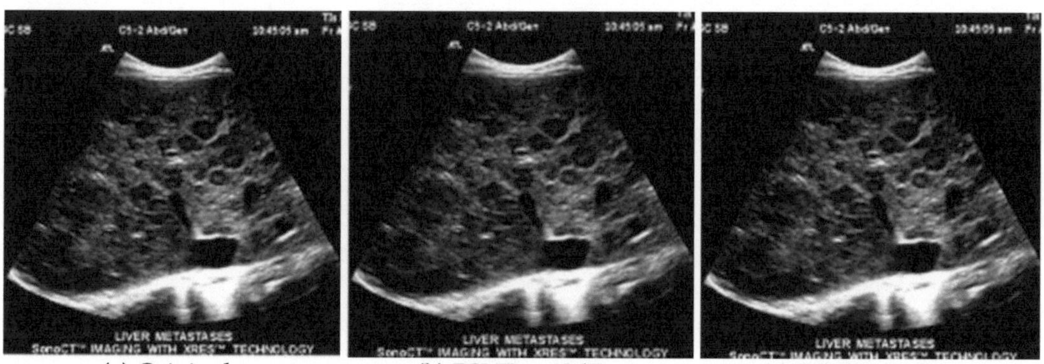

(a) Original (b) PSNR = 48dB (c) PSNR= 56dB

Fig. 11. (a) Original US image; (b) Reconstructed image using FP scheme; (c) AIQ scheme.

5.3 Performance analysis on noisy images

As a final study, the AIQ algorithm is tested under a noisy environment. The Gaussian white noise and Poisson noise are added to the images of all types, and the performance is compared with the FP implementation. The results are tabulated in Table 3 (all using 8-bit precision). Like previous cases, due to less error accumulation in the computation process, the AIQ-based approach is seen to have performed better than FP approaches even in a noisy environment.

Noise	Algorithm	PSNR (dB)				
		Goldhill	US	X-ray	Endoscopic	CT
Gaussian	D4 - FP	43.9	47.5	43.1	44.6	44.4
	D4 - AIQ	51.4	55.5	50.0	51.6	52.4
	D6 - FP	40.6	44.3	39.7	41.3	41.1
	D6 - AIQ	49.9	53.2	49.3	50.6	49.7
Poisson	D4 - FP	44.1	47.6	43.2	44.8	44.6
	D4 - AIQ	51.6	55.6	50.0	51.8	52.5
	D6 - FP	40.7	44.5	39.8	41.5	41.3
	D6 - AIQ	50.1	53.4	49.3	50.9	49.9

Table 3. Quality of reconstruction in noisy environment.

5.4 Comparative analysis

In order to show the effectiveness of the AIQ approach, the algorithm is compared with some compression standards: JPEG, JPEG2000, and existing algorithms targeted to medical imaging. Since there is no benchmark for medical images, we have conducted the experiment with benchmark images like "Lena", "Barbara" and "Goldhill". Table 4 summarizes the comparison results (all using 8-bit precision with 0.25 bits per pixel). From the table, it is clearly observed that the error-free algorithm performs competitively compared to other existing compression schemes.

Algorithm	Lena	Barbara	Goldhill
HS-HIC (Mohammed, 2008)	35.0	26.1	30.5
Hybrid (Yu & Mitra, 1997)	35.0	31.5	32.9
JPEG (Wahid et al., 2008)	32.4	27.7	29.7
JPEG2000 (Seo & Kim, 2007)	34.1	28.8	30.5
OB-HIC (Mohammed & Abd, 2010)	35.9	32.8	33.8
D4-AIQ	44.9	45.0	35.8
D6-AIQ	43.2	43.6	35.3

Table 4. Comparative analysis (in terms of PSNR in dB) of the AIQ scheme.

6. Conclusion

In this chapter, we have presented an efficient approach to compute Daubechies wavelet transforms that is based on encoding the basis set of forward transform coefficients using algebraic integers. The AIQ approach not only reduces the number of arithmetic operations, but also reduces the dynamic range of the computations. Because of error-free mapping in the earlier stages, less error is introduced in the system, as compared to FP implementation, that results in much better data reconstruction. The performance is validated using standard and medical images in both normal and noisy conditions. In all cases, the AIQ-based approach outperforms the conventional FP scheme by far margin. The rate of data recovery is very high while preserving critical information that makes the scheme suitable for medical and telemetric imaging applications.

7. Acknowledgement

The author would like to acknowledge the Natural Science and Engineering Research Council of Canada (NSERC) for its support to this research work. The author is also indebted to the Canadian Microelectronics Corporation (CMC) for providing the hardware and software infrastructure used in the development of this design.

8. References

Acharyya, A., Maharatna, K., Al-Hashimi, B., Gunn, S. (2009), Memory reduction methodology for distributed arithmetic based DWT/IDWT exploiting data symmetry, IEEE Trans. on Circuits and Systems II, vol. 56, no. 4, pp. 285-289.

Aware Inc., (1991) Aware Wavelet Transform Processor WTP) Preliminary, Cambridge, MA.

Cozzens, J. and Finkelstein, L. (1985) Computing the Discrete Fourier Transform using Residue Number Systems in a Ring of Algebraic Integers, IEEE Transactions on Information Theory, vol. 31, pp. 580-588.

Daubechies, I., (1992) Ten lectures on wavelets, SIAM, 1992.

Huang, C., Tseng, P., and Chen, L., (2004) Flipping structure: an efficient VLSI architecture for lifting based discrete wavelet transform, IEEE Trans. Signal Process., vol. 52, no. 4, pp. 1080–1089.

Lai, Y., Chen, L., Shih, Y. (2009) A high-performance and memory-efficient VLSI architecture with parallel scanning method for 2-D lifting-based discrete wavelet transform, IEEE Trans. on Consumer Electronics, vol. 55, no. 2, pp. 400 - 407.

Lee, S. and Lim, S., (2006) VLSI design of a wavelet processing core, IEEE Trans. Cir. Syst. Video Tech., vol. 16, pp. 1350-1360.

Lewis, A. and Knowles, G. (1991) VLSI Architecture for 2D Daubechies Wavelet Transform without Multipliers, IEE Electronics Letters, vol. 27, no. 2, pp. 171-173.

Mallat, S., (1998) A wavelet tour of signal processing, New York: Academic.

Martina, M. and Masera, G., (2007) Multiplierless, folded 9/7-5/3 wavelet VLSI architecture," IEEE Trans. Cir. Syst. II, 54, pp. 770-774, 2007.

Mohammed, U. (2008), Highly scalable hybrid image coding scheme, Digital Signal Processing, Science Direct, vol. 18, pp. 364–374.

Mohammed, U. and Abd-elhafiez, W. (2010), Image coding scheme based on object extraction and hybrid transformation technique, Int. J. of Engineering Science and Technology, vol. 2, no. 5, pp. 1375–1383.

Paek, S. and Kim, L. (1998) 2D DWT VLSI Architecture for Wavelet Image Processing, IEE Electronics Letters, vol. 34, no. 5, pp. 537-538.

Parhi, K. and Nishitani, T. (1993) VLSI Architectures for Discrete Wavelet Transforms, IEEE Transactions on VLSI Systems, vol. 1, no. 2, pp. 191-202.

Seo, Y. and Kim, D. (2007) VLSI architecture of line-based lifting wavelet transform for motion JPEG2000, IEEE J. Solid-State Circuits, vol. 42, no. 2, pp. 431-440.

Shi, G., Liu, W., Zhang, L., Li, F. (2009) An efficient folded architecture for lifting-based discrete wavelet transform, IEEE Trans. on Circuits and Systems II, vol. 56, no. 4, pp. 290-294.

Vishwanath, M., Owens, R. and Irwin, M. (1995) VLSI Architectures for the Discrete Wavelet Transform, IEEE Transactions on Circuits and Systems - II, vol. 42, no. 5, pp. 305-316.

Wahid, K., Dimitrov, V., Jullien, G. (2004) VLSI architectures of daubechies wavelet transforms using algebraic integers, J. of Circuits, Sys., and Comp., vol. 13, no.6, pp. 1251-1270.

Wahid, K., Dimitrov, V., Jullien, G. and Badawy, W. (2003) Error-Free computation of daubechies wavelets for image compression applications, Elect. Lett., vol. 39, no. 5, pp. 428-429.

Wahid, K., Ko, SB. and Teng, D., (2008) Efficient hardware implementation of an image compressor for wireless capsule endoscopy applications, Proc. of the IEEE Int. Joint Conf. on Neural Net., pp. 2762-2766.

Yu, T., and Mitra, S. (1997), Wavelet based hybrid image coding scheme, Proc. IEEE Int Circuits and Systems Symp, vol. 1, pp. 377–380.

9

Discrete Wavelets on Edges

Alexandre Chapiro[1], Tassio Knop De Castro[1], Virginia Mota[2], Eder De Almeida Perez[2], Marcelo Bernardes Vieira[2] and Wilhelm Passarella Freire[2]

[1]Instituto de Matemática Pura e Aplicada,
[2]Universidade Federal de Juiz de Fora
Brazil

1. Introduction

Human life is closely tied to signals. These signals are present everywhere - listening to music is possible because of audible sound signals traveling through air, reading a book is feasible due to light waves bouncing off objects and interpreted by our bodies as visual images, electromagnetic waves allow us to communicate through the radio or wireless Internet.
Signal Processing is an area of electrical engineering and applied mathematics that deals with either continuous or discrete signals. Particularly, Image Processing is any kind of Signal Processing where the input is an image, such as a digital photograph. The underlying essence of Image Processing lies in understanding the concept of what is an image and studying techniques for the manipulation of images with the use of a computer. While these explanations may seem quite generic, the importance of Image Processing in the modern world is undeniable and progress in this field is very desirable.

1.1 Images

The concept of an image can initially be mathematically defined as a function $f : S \to C$ that goes from a certain space S (such as $\mathbb{R}^2$, for instance) to a space C of colors that can be perceived by the human eye. This definition does not exhaust all of the possible meanings of this word, but will be enough for this chapter. When working on a computer, however, both the domain and counter-domain of the image-function must be discrete. The most common representation of an image in Image Processing thus consists of taking a discrete subset of S - S' and a function that associates the values of S' to a certain subset of C - C'. In this way, an image I can be thought of as a discrete function $I : S' \to C'$.
In this work and in Image Processing in general, the kind of image we are most interested in is a digital image, usually obtained through a digital camera or generated by a computer. As the previous mathematical definition, digital images are discrete, that is they are composed of a finite number of elements. A digital image can be thought of as a mosaic of colors taken form a certain set. In mathematical terms, a digital image can be represented via a matrix $M \in M_{n,m}$, composed of numbers that represent colors that can be shown by modern electronic devices, such as televisions, computer monitors and projectors. Each element of this matrix is called a pixel (this name comes from the words 'picture element').
It is important to understand the concept of color. Initially, color is a sensation produced by the human brain when it receives certain visual stimuli. This input is given by electromagnetic radiation (or light) in a set wavelength that is called the visible spectrum. A typical human eye will respond to wavelengths from about 390 to 750 nm. Theoretically speaking, the space

of all visible colors, as given by their wavelengths is of infinite dimension, and thus not fit for a computer. This limitation is bypassed through the study of the human vision.
Scrutiny of the human eyes shows that they contain two different kinds of photo-receptor cells that allow vision. These cells are rods and cones. Rods are very sensitive to light, being mostly responsible for night vision and have little, if any, role in color vision. Cones on the other hand are of three types (Short, Medium and Long), each covered in a different photo-sensitive pigment. These pigments respond differently to incoming light wavelengths. A chart showing the response of each kind of cone to light can be seen below in Figure 1.
By using the knowledge above, modern visual devices are built so that they emit light at only three different wavelengths, specifically suited to excite each cone in a known way. This allows devices to create a wide range of visible colors. While its not possible to re-create all possible color sensations using only these three colors, the difference when using modern technology is mostly imperceptible. Thus we have arrived at the discretization of the color space used for digital images. These colors can now be codified as certain finite amounts taken in small intervals of these three primary colors. A schematic of a digital image can be seen in Figure 2.

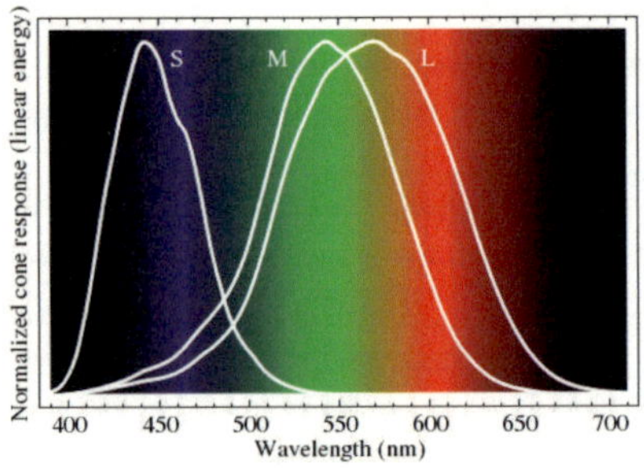

Fig. 1. Human eye response curves. (Image in Public Domain)

Fig. 2. Raster Image. (Image in Public Domain)

1.2 Applications of Image Processing

Image Processing has seen a great variety of methods developed in the last fifty years. These techniques are greatly diverse and are present in various aspects of human daily life, as well as other important scientific fields.
Some typical tasks in Image Processing involve text or pattern recognition by a computer (machine vision), like identifying individuals from photographs, for instance using their face, retina or fingerprints. In this last case, a specialized camera is used to create a digital image of a person's fingers. This image is then analyzed by a computer program that searches for patterns, which are larger characteristics of the ridges in the skin, and minutia - smaller details

such as ends and bifurcations of said ridges. Figure 3 shows a program extracting information from a finger photograph and Figure 4 shows a fingerprint recognition device being used.

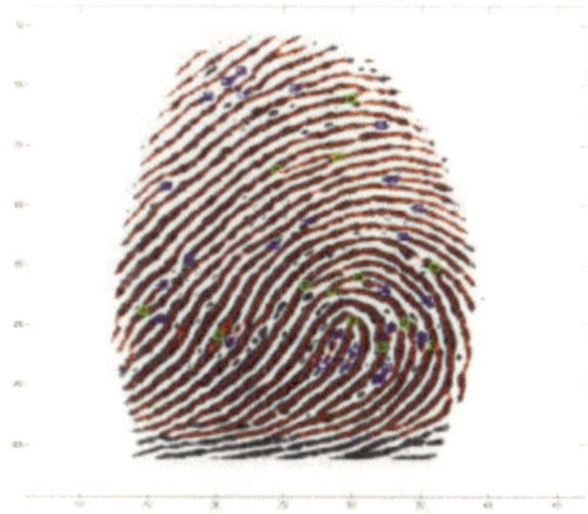

Fig. 3. Human fingerprint analysis. (Image in Public Domain)

Fig. 4. Biometric reading device. (Image in Public Domain)

Other applications involve various methods of obtaining valuable data from several image sources, such as satellites or other sensors in order to discover important characteristics. Several software products such as Photoshop (trademark of Adobe Systems Incorporated) and GIMP (trademark of The GIMP Development Team) rely on common Image-Processing techniques to alter or improve the quality of images. An example of this is High Dynamic Range imaging - a method that blends the information from several differently exposed digital photographs in order to obtain a better view of the scene. An excellent source of information on this topic can be found at (Max Planck Institut fur Informatik, n.d.). See Figure 5 below for an example.

Image Processing can be used to allow cars and other machines to operate automatically by interpreting the information of a video-camera and determining the shapes or movement of objects on the visible scene. An example of a new technology that involves heavy use of Image-Processing in this way is the new Kinect gaming system developed by Microsoft for the Xbox360 console. This device is comprised of three cameras, two of which serve the purpose of analyzing the distance of objects on the scene from the device using an infrared laser. These images are then processed so that the system is able to separate the location of the players from the background or other objects in a process called segmentation (Shotton et al., 2011). An image of this device can be seen on Figure 6. An example of image segmentation can be seen in Figure 7, where the frog is separated from the background.

These and other applications show the importance of Image Processing as a field of research. A good overview of the whole field of Image Processing can be found in (Velho et al., 2008).

Fig. 5. An example of HDR creation from multiple differently-exposed images. (Source exposures by Grzegorz Krawczyk)

Fig. 6. The Kinect gaming device. (Image in Public Domain)

Fig. 7. An example of image segmentation. The frog is being segmented from the background.

Some more information on interesting applications of this field and otherwise can be found in (Acharya & Ray, 2005).

2. A quick glance at wavelet transforms applied to edge detection

The first mention of wavelets appeared in (Haar, 1911). But only in the 1980s did Stephane Mallat (Mallat, 1989) spearheaded the use of wavelets in his work with digital image processing. Inspired by this work, Yves Meyer (Meyer, 1987) constructed the first non-trivial wavelets, which were differentiable, unlike Haar wavelets. They did not, however, have compact support. A few years later, Ingrid Daubechies (Daubechies, 1988) used the works of Mallat to construct a set of orthonormal bases of wavelets with compact support. These works of Daubechies are the foundation of the current use of wavelets in Image Processing. More historical information on wavelets can be found in (Daubechies, 1992).

There are plenty of uses of wavelets in image processing. For example, in 1994 (Fröhlich & Weickert, 1994) presented an algorithm to solve a nonlinear diffusion equation in a wavelet basis. This equation has the property of edge enhancement, an important feature for image processing. More applications in edge detection are shown later in this chapter. The JPEG 2000 image coding system (from the Joint Photographic Experts Group) uses compression techniques based on wavelets. In (Walker, 2003) the author describes a wavelet-based technique for image denoising. Applications of the wavelet transform to detect cracks in frame structures is presented by (Ovanesova & Suárez, 2004). Wavelet transforms have an important role in multiresolution representations in order to effectively analyze the content of images. Multiresolution will be introduced later in this chapter.

2.1 Wavelet Transforms

While the Fourier transform decomposes a signal over sine functions with different frequencies, the wavelet transform decomposes a signal onto translated and dilated versions of a wavelet. Figure 8 shows both a sine wave for the Fourier transform and a wavelet for wavelet transform.

Fig. 8. A sine wave and a wavelet (image from (Radunivić, 2009))

Unlike the Fourier transform, the wavelet transform can capture both frequency and location information.
A wavelet is a function $\psi \in L^2(\mathbb{R})$ with a zero average:

$$\int_{-\infty}^{+\infty} \psi(t)dt = 0 \tag{1}$$

This function is normalized $\|\psi\| = 1$, and centered in the neighborhood of $t = 0$. A family of time-frequency atoms is obtained by scaling ψ by s and translating it by u:

$$\psi_{u,s}(t) = \frac{1}{\sqrt{s}}\psi\left(\frac{t-u}{s}\right) \tag{2}$$

Thus, the Continuous Wavelet Transform (CWT) of a function f at a scale $s > 0$ and translated by $u \in \mathbb{R}$ can be written as:

$$Wf(u,s) = \int_{-\infty}^{+\infty} f(t)\frac{1}{\sqrt{s}}\psi^*\left(\frac{t-u}{s}\right)dt \tag{3}$$

In the field of image processing we are interested in wavelets which form a base of $L^2(\mathbb{R}^2)$ to represent images. If we have an orthonormal wavelet basis in $L^2(\mathbb{R})$ given by ψ with the scaling function ϕ, we can use

$$\begin{aligned}\psi^1(x_1,x_2) &= \phi(x_1)\psi(x_2),\\ \psi^2(x_1,x_2) &= \psi(x_1)\phi(x_2),\\ \psi^3(x_1,x_2) &= \psi(x_1)\psi(x_2),\end{aligned} \tag{4}$$

to form an orthonormal basis in $L^2(\mathbb{R}^2)$ (Mallat, 1999):

$$\left\{\psi^1_{j,p},\ \psi^2_{j,p},\ \psi^3_{j,p}\right\}_{[j,p]\in\mathbb{Z}^3} \tag{5}$$

where ψ^1 corresponds to variations along rows, ψ^2 corresponds to variations along columns and ψ^3 corresponds to variations along diagonals.
It is computationally impossible to analyze a signal using all wavelet coefficients. Thus, for discrete computations, we have to use a Discrete Wavelet Transform (DWT), that is a wavelet transform for which the wavelets are discretely sampled (Mallat, 1999).
Let $f[n] = f(n)$ be the discrete signal of size N. Its discrete wavelet transform is computed at scales $s = a^j$. A discrete wavelet scaled by a^j is defined by:

$$\psi_j[n] = \frac{1}{\sqrt{a^j}}\psi\left(\frac{n}{a^j}\right) \tag{6}$$

The DWT can then be written as a circular convolution $\bar{\psi}_j[n] = \psi_j^*[n]$:

$$Wf(n,a^j) = \sum_{m=0}^{N-1} f[m]\psi_j^*[m-n] = f \star \bar{\psi}_j[n] \tag{7}$$

A wavelet transform computed up to a scale a^J is not a complete signal representation (Mallat, 1999). We need to add the low frequencies $Lf[n,d]$ corresponding to scales larger than d. A discrete and periodic scaling filter is computed by sampling the scaling function $\phi(t)$ defined by:

$$\phi_J[n] = \frac{1}{\sqrt{a^J}}\phi\left(\frac{n}{a^J}\right) \tag{8}$$

Let $\bar{\phi}_j[n] = \phi_j^*[n]$. The low frequencies are carried by:

$$Lf[n,a^J] = \sum_{m=0}^{N-1} f[m]\phi_j^*[m-n] = f \star \bar{\phi}_J[n] \tag{9}$$

As we can see in the Equations 6 and 9, the DWT is a circular convolution. In that way, we will have lowpass and highpass filters which form a bank of filters. Figure 9 shows the discrete wavelet transform for 3 scales. $h_\psi(n)$ is a highpass filter and h_ϕ is a lowpass filter. This form is known as Fast Wavelet Transform (FWT).

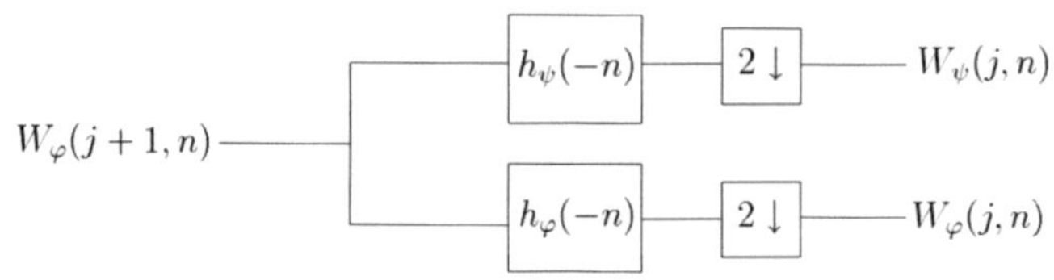

Fig. 9. Fast Wavelet Transform for 1 dimension Mallat (1999)

As we saw before, in the field of image processing we are interested in two dimensional signals. For two dimensions, the DWT of a function $f(x_1, x_2)$ of size $M \times N$ can be written as:

$$W_{\phi}(j_0, m, n) = \frac{1}{\sqrt{MN}} \sum_{x_1=0}^{M-1} \sum_{x_2=0}^{N-1} f(x_1, x_2) \phi_{j_0,m,n}(x_1, x_2)$$
$$W_{\psi}^{i}(j, m, n) = \frac{1}{\sqrt{MN}} \sum_{x_1=0}^{M-1} \sum_{x_2=0}^{N-1} f(x_1, x_2) \psi_{j,m,n}^{i}(x_1, x_2) \quad (10)$$

where $i = \{1, 2, 3\}$
Similar to Figure 9, we can express the FWT in two dimensions like the Figure 10.

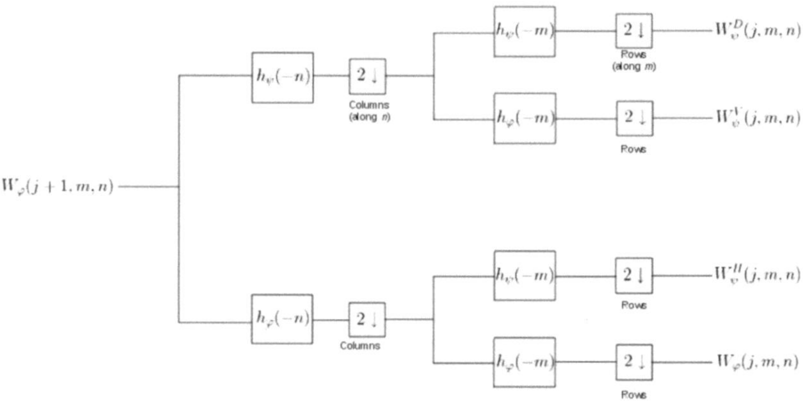

Fig. 10. Fast Wavelet Transform for 2 dimensions Mallat (1999)

For more information on the theory of multiresolution and high-frequency in images, read Section 3.

3. Multiresolution and high frequency in images

Multiresolution Analysis is a very efficient way to process different levels of detail in an image. Detecting and assessing discontinuities of an image allows one to detect its borders, edges and peaks.

3.1 What are high-frequencies?

An image is composed by the sum of its components of low and high frequencies. Low frequencies are responsible for the general smooth areas, while high frequencies are responsible for details, like edges and noise Gonzalez & Woods (2006).
A filter that attenuates high frequencies is called a lowpass filter. A filter that has the opposite characteristic, i.e., highlights high frequencies, is called highpass filter. As we saw on previous sections, in a Discrete Wavelet Transform we have a filter h_{ϕ} that corresponds a lowpass filter and a filter h_{ψ} that corresponds a highpass filter.
The Figure 11 shows an example of applying a lowpass filter and a highpass filter on a image. Therefore, high frequencies on images can be used for several applications which need the details of an image, such as detecting edges, corners and textures.

3.2 Multiresolution analysis

A multiresolution analysis of the space $L^2(\mathbb{R})$ consists of a sequence of nested subspaces such that
$\{0\} \cdots \subset V_0 \subset V_1 \subset \cdots \subset V_n \subset V_{n+1} \subset \cdots \subset L^2(\mathbb{R})$
with some important properties. The most important characteristics that we consider in the context of image processing for high frequency assessment are:

Fig. 11. Results of lowpass and highpass filters. The first image is the original, the second is the result of a lowpass filter and the third is the result of a highpass filter

- Regularity

  The subspace V_0 is generated as the linear combination of integer shifts of one or a finite number of generating functions $\phi_1, \ldots, \phi_r$. These generating functions are called scaling functions. Usually those functions must have compact support and be piecewise continuous.
- Completeness

  those nested subspaces fill the whole space $L^2(\mathbb{R})$, and they are not too redundant. So, the intersection of these subspaces should only contain the zero element.

This concept, applied to image processing and wavelets, justifies the successful use of image pyramids in the context of high frequency detection.

3.3 Image pyramids

A simple, but powerful, structure to represent images at more than one resolution is the image pyramid Burt & Adelson (1983). Basically, it is a collection of decreasing resolution images arranged in the shape of a pyramid (Figure 12).

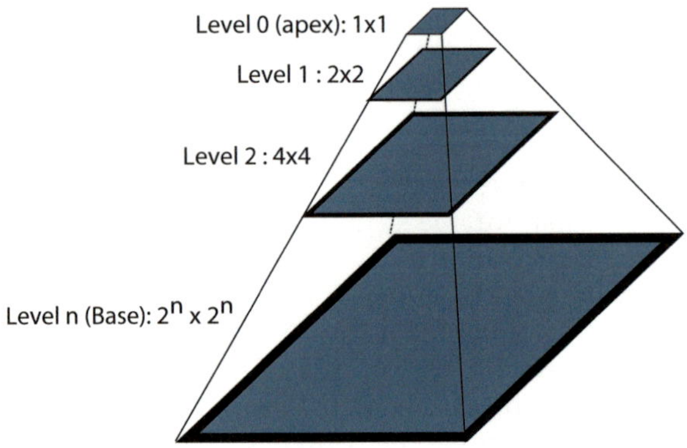

Fig. 12. Image Pyramid.

The idea behind image pyramids is to generate a number of images corresponding to the response of a bank of filters at different scales. There are many different types of filters that can be used for this purpose.

One special family of filters consists of Wavelets. They are constructed from a mother wavelet. A family is constructed by dilating and translating the mother wavelet by different quantities. The main advantage of using this family of functions over the Fourier transform is that wavelets respond very well to discontinuities, i.e, high frequencies. The most know wavelet families are the Haar, Daubechies, Coiflet, and Symmlet.

The Daubechies family is of particular interest because it is fractal in nature, and the Haar family, although very simple, can be very useful in many applications.
In practical terms, the base of the pyramid is the image which we want to filter in various scales, and each level of the pyramid above the base is produced by filtering it and generating an image with half of its width and height.
Using wavelet and scale functions, the nested subspaces of scale and detail are produced. The horizontal, vertical and diagonal details of a subspace V_{i+1} are the information that cannot be represented in V_i (Figure 13).

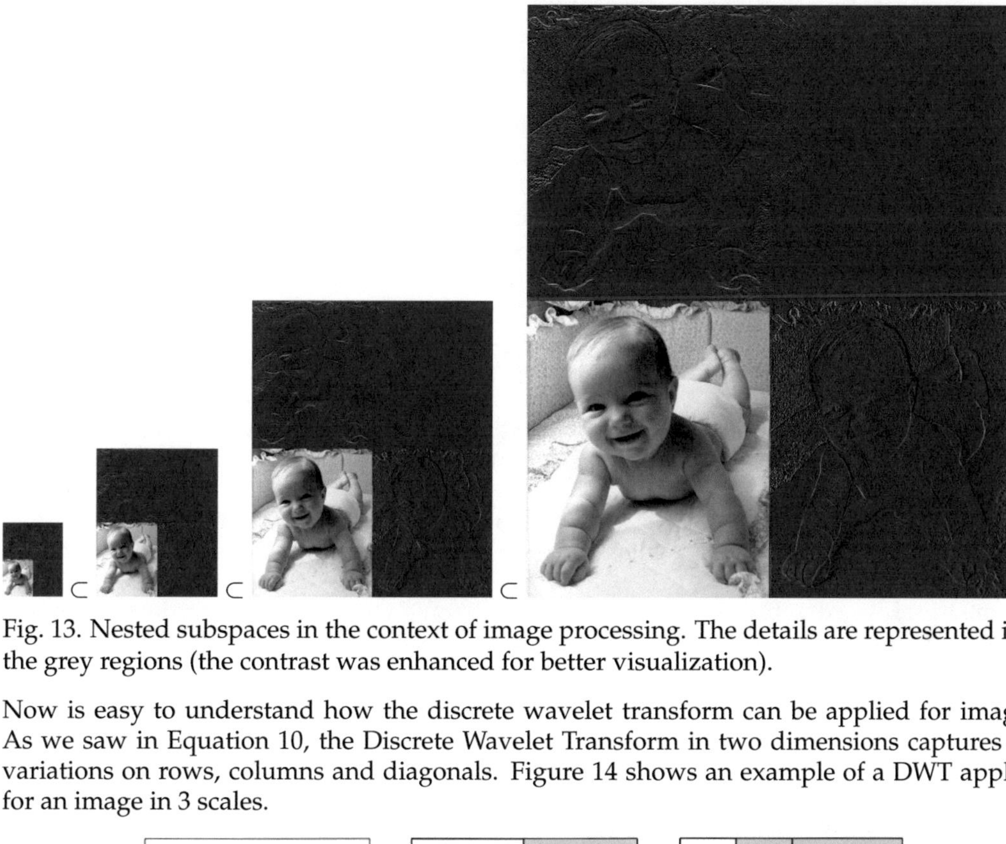

Fig. 13. Nested subspaces in the context of image processing. The details are represented in the grey regions (the contrast was enhanced for better visualization).

Now is easy to understand how the discrete wavelet transform can be applied for images. As we saw in Equation 10, the Discrete Wavelet Transform in two dimensions captures the variations on rows, columns and diagonals. Figure 14 shows an example of a DWT applied for an image in 3 scales.

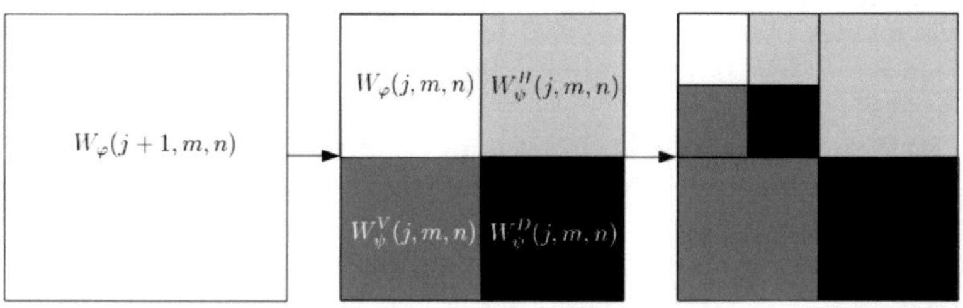

Fig. 14. The result decomposition of a blank image using a discrete Wavelet Transform for 1 and 2 scales Gonzalez & Woods (2006)

Section 4.2 describes a method which produces a pyramid of a chosen image and processes the correspondent details in every scale. This allows us to detect discontinuities in a very precise and adaptative approach.

3.4 Edge detectors using multiresolution and discrete wavelet transform

Many works use multiresolution as a step to gather specific image information on a single scale. The idea is to combine the information present at several scales, as appearance is related to the scale of the observation, so a scene should be described at multiple scales.

The first ones to formalize this concept were Witkin (1983) and Koenderink (1984) with the idea of scale-space linear filtering. The principle is to convolve the original image by a family of Gaussians of increasing variance related to the studied scale, and then to progressively eliminate the smallest structures in the image.

However, this approach suffers from several drawbacks such as blurred edges and the edges at the coarse scale are shifted. Multiple nonlinear diffusion filters have been suggested to overcome these drawbacks. More elaborated approaches have been suggested to accelerate the resolution, such as wavelet-based ones.

Recent works still use the idea of convolution by a family of Gaussians (Sumengen & Manjunath (2005), Zhang et al. (2010)) and nonlinear diffusion filters(Tremblais & Augereau (2004)). Other works are wavelet-based, as can be seen in (Belkasim et al., 2007), (Shih & Tseng, 2005), (Han & Shi, 2007), Brannock & Weeks (2006) and Heric & Zazula (2007).

Sumengen & Manjunath (2005) create an Edgeflow vector field where the vector flow is oriented towards the borders at either side of the boundary. To create this vector field, they use a fine to coarse strategy. In that way, the proposed method favors edges that exist at multiple scales and suppress edges that only exist at finer scales. The strength of the edges are represented by the strength of the vectors at the edge location where the vector field changes its direction. This method is also used to multi-scale image segmentation.

Tremblais & Augereau (2004) present a new explicit scheme to the linear diffusion filtering which preserves edges. A fast filtering algorithm is then combined with a simple multiscale edge detection algorithm.

For Zhang et al. (2010), the one pixel width edge is more accurate than other edge detection. So, they explore the zero-crossing edge detection method based on the scale-space theory.

For image segmentation, Belkasim (Belkasim et al., 2007) uses a wavelet-based image analysis scheme based on extracting all objects in the image using their borders or contours. The size of the contour can then be used to define the level of resolution and hence the extent of the analysis.

Shih (Shih & Tseng, 2005) argue that edge extraction based only on a gradient image will produce a bad result with noise and broken edges. In order to solve this problem, they combine an edge detector with a multiscale edge tracker based on the discrete wavelet transform.

In Han (Han & Shi, 2007), the wavelet transform plays an important role in the task of decomposing a texture image into several levels. Once a decomposition level is chosen, textures are then removed from the original image by the reconstruction of low frequencies only.

The problem for Brannock & Weeks (2006) is to automatically detect edges. To determine its efficacy, the 2D discrete wavelet transform is compared to other common edge detection methods. They conclude that the discrete wavelet transform is a very successful edge-detection technique, especially when utilizing auto-correlation.

Heric & Zazula (2007) present a novel edge detector based on the wavelet transform and signal registration. The proposed method provides an edge image by a time-scale plane based edge detection using a Haar wavelet. Then, this edge image is used in a registration procedure in order to close the edge discontinuities and calculate a confidence index for the detected contour points.

4. The DWT applied to high-frequency assessment from multiresolution analysis

In this section, we present a practical use of wavelets for visualization of high frequency regions of a multiresolution image. Our approach combines both multiresolution analysis and orientation tensor to give a scalar field representing multiresolution edges. Local maxima of this scalar space indicate regions having coincident detail vectors in multiple scales of wavelet decomposition. This is useful for finding edges, textures, collinear structures and salient regions for computer vision methods. The image is decomposed into several scales using the DWT. The resulting detail spaces form vectors indicating intensity variations which are adequately combined using orientation tensors. A high frequency scalar descriptor is then obtained from the resulting tensor for each original image pixel.

4.1 Orientation tensor

One way of estimating salient regions in image processing is to use multiresolution to capture global and local brightness variations. Even in a non-redundant wavelet decomposition, local and global borders occurring in the same region may carry useful information. The problem lies in combining this global information into a single image. In this way, we can capture the multivariate information of several scales and color channels using orientation tensors (Knutsson, 1989).

A local orientation tensor is a special case of non-negative symmetric rank 2 tensor, built based on information gathered from an image. As shown by Knutsson (Knutsson, 1989), one can be produced by combining outputs from polar separable quadrature filters. Because of its construction, such a tensor has special properties and contains valuable information about said image.

From definition given by Westin (Westin, 1994), orientation tensors are symmetric, and thus an orientation tensor T can be decomposed using the Spectral Theorem as shown in Equation 11, where λ_i are the eigenvalues of T.

$$T = \sum_{i=1}^{n} \lambda_i T_i \tag{11}$$

If T_i projects onto a m-dimensional eigenspace, we may decompose it as

$$T_i = \sum_{s=1}^{m} e_s e_s^T \tag{12}$$

where $\{e_1, ..., e_m\}$ is a base of $\mathbb{R}^m$. An interesting decomposition of the orientation tensor T (Westin, 1994) is given by

$$T = \lambda_n T_n + \sum_{i=1}^{n-1} (\lambda_i - \lambda_{i+1}) T_i \tag{13}$$

where λ_i are the eigenvalues corresponding to each eigenvector e_i. This is an interesting decomposition because of its geometric interpretation. In fact, in $\mathbb{R}^3$, an orientation tensor T decomposed using Equation 13 can be represented by a spear (its main orientation), a plate and a ball

$$T = (\lambda_1 - \lambda_2)T_1 + (\lambda_2 - \lambda_3)T_2 + \lambda_3 T_3 \tag{14}$$

A $\mathbb{R}^3$ tensor decomposed by Equation 14, with eigenvalues $\lambda_1 \geq \lambda_2 \geq \lambda_3$, can be interpreted as following:

- $\lambda_1 \ggg \lambda_2 \approx \lambda_3$ corresponds to an approximately linear tensor, with the spear component being dominant.

- $\lambda_1 \approx \lambda_2 \ggg \lambda_3$ corresponds to an approximately planar tensor, with the plate component being dominant.
- $\lambda_1 \approx \lambda_2 \approx \lambda_3$ corresponds to an approximately isotropic tensor, with the ball component being dominant, and no main orientation present

Consider two orientation tensors A and B and its summation $T = A + B$. After the decomposition of T using Equation 14, the component $(\lambda_1 - \lambda_2)T_1$ is an estimate of the collinearity of the main eigenvectors of A and B.

4.2 Proposed method

The method proposed in (de Castro et al., 2009) uses high frequency information extracted from wavelet analysis. Given an input image I, for each scale j and position $p \in I$, we create a vector $v_{j,p}$ as follow:

$$v_{j,p} = [I \cdot \psi^1_{j,p}, I \cdot \psi^2_{j,p}, I \cdot \psi^3_{j,p}]^T \tag{15}$$

This vector contains the high frequency value at vertical, horizontal and diagonal directions of the image I at the position p and scale j. Simmetric rank 2 tensors are then created as

$$M_{j,p} = v_{j,p} v^T_{j,p} \tag{16}$$

We find the final tensor $M_{0,p}$ for each pixel of the original image using

$$M_{0,p} = \sum_{j=1}^{n_j} k_j M_{j,p} \tag{17}$$

to combine the tensors obtained at each scale j, where n_j is the number of scales and $k_j \in \mathbb{R}$ is the weight assigned to each scale, given by

$$k_j = \frac{\sum_{n=1}^{n_p} Trace\left(M_{j,n}\right)}{\sum_{k=1}^{n_j} \sum_{n=1}^{n_p} Trace\left(M_{k,n}\right)} \tag{18}$$

where n_p is the number of pixels and $Trace(M_{j,p})$ is the sum of the eigenvalues of $M_{j,p}$. The trace represents the amplification driven by the tensor to the unit sphere and is a good estimator of its importance. Thus, the tensor sum is weighted by the proportion of energy of each scale in the multiresolution pyramid.

In order to find $M_{j,p}$ in Equation 17, we use bilinear interpolation of the tensor values, relative to each position p in the initial image, at the subsampled image at scale j to find the resulting tensor $M_{j,p}$ for each pixel of the initial image. This is depicted in Figure 15, where tensors are represented as superquadric glyphs whose longer axis shows the main direction.

Note that the tensor presented in Equation 17 is a $3x3$ positive symmetric matrix with real coefficients, and thus we may apply Equation 14. We then find the main orientation component (spear) of the final orientation tensor for each pixel of the input image. This component indicates the collinearity of the interpolated tensors and provides interesting results.

4.2.1 Implementation

The proposed algorithm consists of three main steps: a discrete wavelet transform (Barnard, 1994; Mallat, 1999), a tensor field computation and a weighted sum of the computed tensors. The whole process is illustrated in Figure 16.

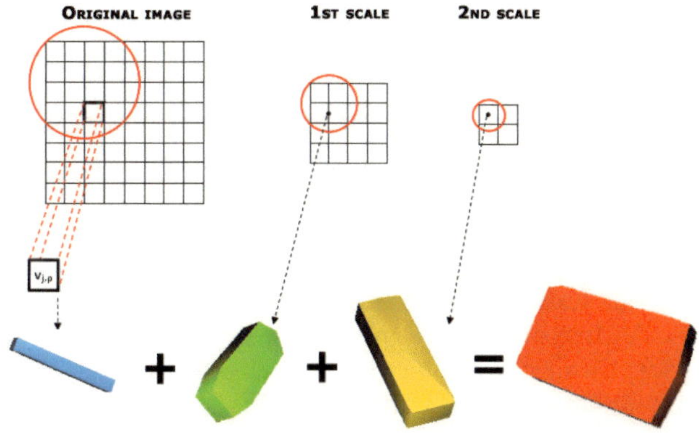

Fig. 15. A tensor is computed for each pixel in original image by a weighted sum of corresponding tensors in each scale. In this example, two wavelet decompositions are performed.

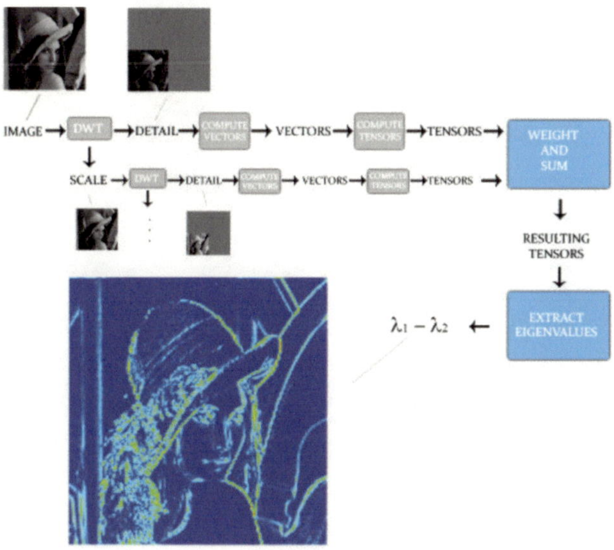

Fig. 16. Example of the proposed algorithm using Daubechies1 to decompose the image into two scales.

The number of scales to be used is a parameter of the algorithm. The DWT splits the image into three detail components and one scale component in the beginning of each iteration. In the next iteration, the same process is applied, using the resulting scale component as the input image.
For each pixel of the input image, its correspondent position at the current scale is computed with subpixel precision for each resolution. The four nearest pixels in a given resolution are used to compute the final tensor. The vectors $v_{j,p}$ described in Equation 15 are computed for each of these pixels and then used to compute four spear type tensors. The final tensor for the subpixel position is obtained by combining these four tensors with bilinear interpolation. The pixel tensor is computed by combining the n_j tensors as showed in Equation 17.
The pixel tensors are decomposed and their eigenvalues are then extracted. The values $\lambda_1 - \lambda_2$ are computed and normalized to form the output image. Color images are split

into three monochromatic channels (Red, Green and Blue) and the proposed algorithm is applied to each channel separately. The tensors for each color channel are summed before eigen decomposition.
The complexity of the whole process is $O(n_j \cdot n_p)$, where n_j is the number of analyzed scales and n_p the amount of input pixels. Thus, this is an efficient method that can be further parallelized.

4.2.2 Experimental results

The proposed method was tested with several images and using several wavelets functions (de Castro et al., 2009). A piece of the experiments is shown in Figure 17. The DWT is applied with different analyzing Daubechies filters and number of scales. The Church's ceiling is formed by coincident frequencies on its geometric details. These details can be better observed in Figure 17c.

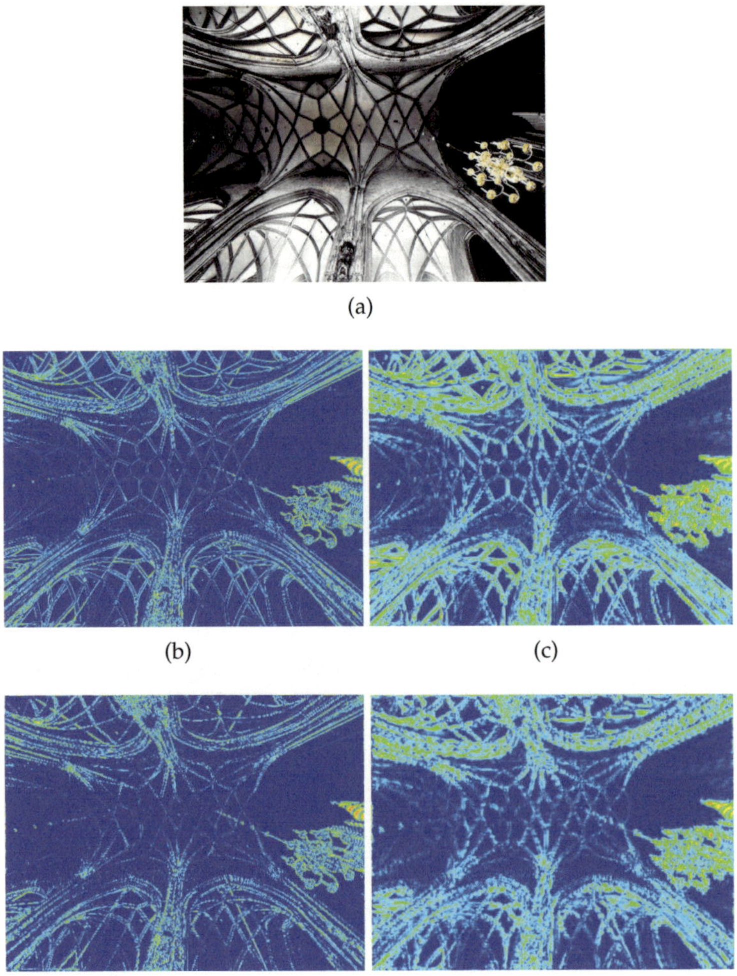

(a)

(b) (c)

(d) (e)

Fig. 17. (a) input image. (b) $\lambda_1 - \lambda_2$ with Daubechies1 and 1 scale. (c) Daubechies1 and 3 scales. (d) Daubechies3 and 1 scale. (e) Daubechies3 and 3 scales.

A better estimation of soft edge transitions is obtained by changing the analyzing filter from Daubechies1 to Daubechies3. Figures 17b and 17d illustrate this behavior.
In general, it can be noted that this method highlights high frequencies occurring in the same region at different scales. We used thermal coloring with smooth transition from blue to red, where blue means absence of high frequencies, and red means presence of high frequencies. The green regions also indicate high frequencies, but less intense than those indicated by red regions. The red regions provide the better higher frequencies estimation tensors.

4.2.3 Conclusion

We presented an overview of discrete wavelets and multiresolution applied to edge detection. We also presented a method for high frequency assessment visualization using these powerful tools. The method is based on the DWT decomposition and detail information merging using orientation tensors. This multiresolution analysis showed to be suitable for detecting edges and salient areas in an image. The experimental results show that the high frequency information can be inferred by varying the DWT filters and number of scales. Coincident frequencies in space domain are successfully highlighted. By tuning the number of scales, one may infer texture feature regions. The $\lambda_1 - \lambda_2$ scalar field is one of the most used orientation alignment descriptors. However, other relations can be extracted from final tensors. This method can be easily parallelized, the use of technologies like GPGPUs and multicore CPUs turns it attractive for high performance applications.

5. References

Acharya, T. & Ray, A. K. (2005). *Image Processing - Principles and Applications, First Edition*, Wiley InterScience.

Barnard, H. J. (1994). *Image and Video Coding Using a Wavelet Decomposition*, PhD thesis, Delft University of Technology, Department of Electrical Engineering, Information Theory Group, P.O.Box 5031, 2600 GA, Delft.

Belkasim, S., Derado, G., Aznita, R., Gilbert, E. & O'Connell, H. (2007). Multi-resolution border segmentation for measuring spatial heterogeneity of mixed population biofilm bacteria, *Computerized Medical Imaging and Graphics* 32.

Brannock, E. & Weeks, M. (2006). Edge detection using wavelets, *Proceedings of the 44th annual Southeast regional conference*, ACM-SE 44, ACM, New York, NY, USA, pp. 649–654.

Burt, P. J. & Adelson, E. H. (1983). The laplacian pyramid as a compact image code, *IEEE Transactions on Communications* 31: 532–540.

Daubechies, I. (1988). Orthonormal bases of compactly supported wavelets, *Communications on Pure and Applied Mathematics* 41(7): 909–996.

Daubechies, I. (1992). *Ten lectures on wavelets*, Society for Industrial and Applied Mathematics, Philadelphia, PA, USA.

de Castro, T. K., de A. Perez, E., Mota, V. F., Chapiro, A., Vieira, M. B. & Freire, W. P. (2009). High frequency assessment from multiresolution analysis., *ICCS (1)*, Vol. 5544 of *Lecture Notes in Computer Science*, Springer, pp. 429–438.

Fröhlich, J. & Weickert, J. (1994). Image processing using a wavelet algorithm for nonlinear diffusion.

Gonzalez, R. C. & Woods, R. E. (2006). *Digital Image Processing (3rd Edition)*, Prentice-Hall, Inc., Upper Saddle River, NJ, USA.

Haar, A. (1911). Zur theorie der orthogonalen funktionensysteme, *Mathematische Annalen* 71: 38–53. 10.1007/BF01456927.

Han, Y. & Shi, P. (2007). An adaptive level-selecting wavelet transform for texture defect detection, *Image Vision Comput.* 25(8): 1239–1248.

Heric, D. & Zazula, D. (2007). Combined edge detection using wavelet transform and signal registration, *Image Vision Comput.* 25: 652–662.

Knutsson, H. (1989). Representing local structure using tensors, *The 6th Scandinavian Conference on Image Analysis*, Oulu, Finland, pp. 244–251. Report LiTH–ISY–I–1019, Computer Vision Laboratory, Linköping University, Sweden, 1989.

Koenderink, J. J. (1984). The structure of images, *Biological Cybernetics* 50(5): 363–370–370.

Mallat, S. (1999). *A Wavelet Tour of Signal Processing, Second Edition (Wavelet Analysis & Its Applications)*, Academic Press.

Mallat, S. G. (1989). A theory for multiresolution signal decomposition: the wavelet representation, *IEEE Transactions on Pattern Analysis and Machine Intelligence* 11: 674–693.

Max Planck Institut fur Informatik, M. (n.d.). http://www.mpi-inf.mpg.de/resources/hdr/.

Meyer, Y. (1987). Principe d'incertitude, bases hilbertiennes et algèbres d'opérateurs. (The uncertainty principle, Hilbert base and operator algebras)., Sémin. Bourbaki, 38ème année, Vol. 1985/86, Exp. Astérisque 145/146, 209-223 (1987).

Ovanesova, A. V. & Suárez, L. E. (2004). Applications of wavelet transforms to damage detection in frame structures, *Engineering Structures* 26(1): 39 – 49.

Radunivić, D. (2009). *WAVELETS from MATH to PRACTICE*, Springer.

Shih, M. & Tseng, D. (2005). A wavelet-based multiresolution edge detection and tracking, *IVC* 23(4): 441–451.

Shotton, J., Fitzgibbon, A., Cook, M., Sharp, T., Finocchio, M., Moore, R., Kipman, A. & Blake, A. (2011). Real-time human pose recognition in parts from a single depth image.

Sumengen, B. & Manjunath, B. S. (2005). Multi-scale edge detection and image segmentation, *European Signal Processing Conference (EUSIPCO)*.

Tremblais, B. & Augereau, B. (2004). A fast multi-scale edge detection algorithm, *Pattern Recogn. Lett.* 25: 603–618.

Velho, L., Frery, A. & Gomes, J. (2008). *Image Processing for Computer Graphics and Vision, First Edition*, Springer.

Walker, J. S. (2003). Tree-adapted wavelet shrinkage, Vol. 124 of *Advances in Imaging and Electron Physics*, Elsevier, pp. 343 – 394.

Westin, C.-F. (1994). *A Tensor Framework for Multidimensional Signal Processing*, PhD thesis, Department of Electrical Engineering Linköping University.

Witkin, A. P. (1983). Scale-Space Filtering., *8th Int. Joint Conf. Artificial Intelligence*, Vol. 2, Karlsruhe, pp. 1019–1022.

Zhang, M., Li, X., Yang, Z. & Yang, Y. (2010). A novel zero-crossing edge detection method based on multi-scale space theory, *Signal Processing (ICSP), 2010 IEEE 10th International Conference on*, pp. 1036 –1039.

10

Discrete Wavelet Transform and Optimal Spectral Transform Applied to Multicomponent Image Coding

Isidore Paul Akam Bita[1], Michel Barret[2], Florio Dalla Vedova[1], Jean-Louis Gutzwiller[2] and, Dinh-Tuan Pham[3]
[1]*LUXSPACE Sarl, Chateau de Betzdorf, Betzdorf*
[2]*SUPELEC, Information Multimodality and Signal Team, 2, rue E. Belin, Metz*
[3]*Jean Kuntzmann Laboratory, 51 rue des Mathématiques, Grenoble Cedex 9*
[1]*Luxembourg*
[2,3]*France*

1. Introduction

These last years, research activities on multicomponent image compression have been expanded, due to the development of multispectral and hyperspectral image sensors which supply larger and larger amount of data. The end-users of such images become also more numerous and have various needs and various applications. The future earth observation systems, for instance, will use multi-, super- and hyper- spectral image sensors with higher resolutions leading to bigger amount of transmitted data. However the channel bandwidth for transmission is limited and therefore there is an interest of conceiving compression systems (onboard and on the ground) of multicomponent images which are not application dependent and which are compatible with the diversity of end-users' needs. The components of a multicomponent image generally represent the same scene with different views depending on the wavelength. For data from different sensors, a preliminary step of image registration is therefore required as there is a high degree of dependence (or redundancies) between the various components: the usual spatial redundancy (between different pixels in each component) and the spectral redundancy (between the components).

During the past two decades, different solutions have been proposed for multicomponent image coding. A solution currently adopted consists of using two different transformations, each with the goal of reducing only one of the two redundancies. In (Dragotti et al., 2000), a 2-D discrete wavelet transform (DWT) is used to reduce the spatial redundancies in each component while the Karhunen Loève transform (KLT) is applied to reduce the spectral ones. In that paper, the quantization and entropy coding are achieved thanks to the well known SPIHT (Set Partitioning in Hierarchical Trees) codec by Said and Pearlman (Said & Pearlman, 1996) in its original version and in a modified version including VQ (vector quantization). In the same way, with the use of the 2-D DWT of (Antonini et al., 1992) (usually called the Daubechies 9/7), the authors of (Vaisey et al., 1998) use a lattice VQ with a stack run coder as quantization and entropy coding. More recently in (Rucker et al., 2005), the KLT associated with the Daubechies 9/7 2-D DWT and with EBCOT (Taubman, 2000; Taubman & Marcellin, 2002) for quantizing and entropy coding has been tested on

hyperspectral images with different bit-allocations between components. It is shown that the Post Compression Rate-Distortion (PCRD) optimizer of EBCOT applied across multiple bands gives the best rate-distortion performance. Another solution consists of using a 3-D DWT for reducing both the spatial and spectral redundancies with only one transform. This approach is generally applied to hyperspectral images as in (Christophe et al., 2006). An overview of 3-D wavelet-based techniques and more can be found in (Fowler & Rucker, 2007). The two above mentioned solutions are compatible with the JPEG2000 Part 2 standard. The JPEG2000 standard is well known and well spread today. Moreover the KLT used in JPEG2000 Part 2 is considered as the best existing lossy compression techniques for hyperspectral images at medium and high bit rates (Du & Fowler, 2007; Penna et al., 2007). The KLT consists in a Principal Component Analysis (PCA), well known of statisticians, where all the components are kept. However, the rather great computational complexity of the KLT hinders its adoption in practice — specially on satellite platforms — and recent works propose different solutions in order to pass round this problem. One approach consists in reducing the complexity of the covariance matrix computation. This is done by randomly sampling the entire image in order to obtain a small sample of the pixels' population on which the covariance matrix is computed (Du & Fowler, 2008; Penna et al., 2007). Another approach consists in computing a kind of KLT average on a set of images (the learning basis) issued from only one sensor and using it on other images obtained with the same sensor. This sub-optimal transform is called exogenous KLT in (Thiebaut et al., 2006) and the computational complexity of the second approach is compatible with satellite platforms. Both approaches are fruitful: the rate-distortion performance sacrifice compared with the true KLT is very slight, whereas the computational burden is significantly reduced. In the second approach, the exogenous KLT matrix is known by the decoder, hence there is no need to transmit it.
It is well known that the KLT can be suboptimal in transform coding when the data are not Gaussian. Now, under only the high resolution quantization hypothesis, nearly everything is known about the performance of a transform coding. Nevertheless, the optimal transform computation is generally considered as a difficult task and the Gaussian assumption is then used in order to simplify the calculation. Recently, the problem of computing the optimal coding transform associated with scalar variable-rate quantizers for still images was resolved under high-resolution quantization hypothesis, with mean square error as distortion and without the Gaussian assumption (Narozny et al., 2005; 2008). However, for the JPEG2000 Part2 compression scheme, the previous optimal transform computation cannot be directly applied to obtain the optimal spectral transform, because of the 2D DWT presence—see the criterion (15) in Section 4, which depends on subband statistics—. In (Akam Bita et al., 2010a), the authors solved both the problems of computing an optimal spectral transform (OST), with the constraint of orthogonality and without any constraint but invertibility, for that compression scheme, when the 2D DWT has fixed coefficients and under the only high resolution quantization hypothesis. They showed that on hyperspectral images, the orthogonal OST, called OrthOST, performs slightly but significantly better than a KLT at low, medium and high bit-rates and that the gain obtained by removing the orthogonality constraint in the computation of the OST is not significant. Further, it is not widely known that even when the input data are Gaussian, the KLT is not optimal in the above mentioned compression scheme. Indeed, after the 2D DWT, the variance of the wavelet coefficients depends on the subband they belong to (even for Gaussian data) and the KLT does not capture these various variances, while the EBCOT coder with its PCRD optimizer performing simultaneously across all the codeblocks from the entire image take them into

account. In (Akam Bita et al., 2010b), the authors introduced an orthogonal spectral transform (called JADO for Joint Approximate Diagonalization under Orthogonality constraint) using only second order statistics that has not this shortcoming, and that is optimal at high bit-rates for the JPEG2000 Part 2 compression scheme, when the data are Gaussian. They showed on natural hyperspectral images that JADO (resp. OrthOST) performs slightly but significantly better than the KLT (resp. JADO). The main drawback of the OSTs is their heavy computational cost, which is much higher than the one of a KLT or JADO (which both have roughly the same complexity).

In order to reduce the complexity of a codec based on OrthOSTs, the authors of (Akam Bita et al., 2008; 2010c; Barret et al., 2009) used the same strategy as in (Thiebaut et al., 2006): they replaced the OrthOST, which must be computed for each new encoded image, with an *exogenous* quasi optimal spectral transform. This last transform is an OrthOST computed once and for all on a learning basis constituted of images from only one spectrometer and which is then applied to any image to be coded stemming from the same spectrometer. Using either the JPEG2000 codec called Verification Model version 9 (JPEG2000, 2001) or the Bit Plane Encoder (BPE (CCSDS-1, 2007)) recommended for satellite image compression (Yeh et al., 2005) by the CCSDS (Consultative Committee for Space Data Systems), they showed that this strategy yielded good performances, sometimes better than the (non exogenous) KLT ones, in terms of bit-rate versus distortions. Four different distortions were considered: Signal to Noise Ratio (SNR), Maximum Absolute Difference (MAD), Mean Absolute Error (MAE) and Maximum Spectral Angle (MSA). Indeed, it is well-known that providing the mean square error as one distortion only is not sufficient to assess the quality of a codec for hyperspectral images (Christophe et al., 2005). However in the simulations presented in (Akam Bita et al., 2008; 2010c; Barret et al., 2009) when the VM9 is used, the computational complexity of the EBCOT coder associated with its PCRD optimizer is very high, and when the BPE is applied to encode each component of the transformed image, the complexity of the algorithm for optimal allocation between components is also very high. In both cases, the computational complexity is too high for a compression system on-board a satellite. In (Barret et al., 2011), the authors present a low complexity hyperspectral image coder based on exogenous OrthOST and zerotrees well adapted to OrthOST.

It is important to note that the point of view presented in this chapter — i.e., a compression scheme for hyperspectral images that is independent of the end-user application — is no longer justified at very low bit-rates (lower than 0.5 bits per pixel and per band). For more details on low-bit rates hyperspectral compression see (Chang et al., 2010c).

In this chapter, we study the question of an optimal linear transform for reducing spectral redundancies under high resolution and variable rate constrained quantization hypothesis, when a 2-D DWT — with fixed coefficients — is applied to each component to reduce spatial redundancies and one scalar quantizer per subband and per component is used. This compression scheme, described in Section 2, is compatible with the JPEG2000 Part 2 standard. The asymptotic expression of the mean square error distortion associated with that compression scheme is given in Section 3. In Section 4, we clarify the criterion minimized by such an optimal spectral transform with mean square error distortion and we show the link between the criterion and the mutual information contrast used in Independent Component Analysis (ICA). In Section 5, we derive a criterion minimized by an OrthOST under Gaussian data assumption. Moreover, we describe in Section 6 the quasi-Newton algorithms used for the minimization of the criterion, either with the constraint of an orthogonal transform or with no constraint but invertibility or with the constraint of an orthogonal transform and the assumption of Gaussian data. The two first algorithms are derived from an algorithm by Pham `ICAinf` described in (Pham, 2004) that performs ICA. Then in Section 7, performances of these transforms and comparisons with the KLT are given for multi- and hyper-spectral satellite images, with the four above mentioned different measures of distortion. Finally, in Section 8 we introduce quasi-optimal OrthOSTs, called *exogenous*, that have not the main drawback of heavy computational cost and we compare their performances in lossy coding with OrthOSTs.

2. Description of the separable compression scheme

2.1 Conventions and notations

We consider a multicomponent image $\mathbf{X}$ with N components $\mathbf{X}_1, \ldots, \mathbf{X}_N$. Each component $\mathbf{X}_i$ is a 2-D image with N_r rows and N_c columns. To simplify the notations and the mathematical expressions, we assume that each component is written as a row vector by scanning all its pixels row by row (for example). Then $\mathbf{X}$ is a $N \times L$ matrix, with $L = N_r N_c$. In the following, depending on the context, we shall interpret $\mathbf{X}_i$ as a 2-D image or as a row vector of dimension L. For a square matrix $\mathbf{M}$, the expressions $\det \mathbf{M}$, $\operatorname{tr} \mathbf{M}$ and $\operatorname{diag}(\mathbf{M})$ denote respectively its determinant, its trace and the diagonal matrix obtained with its diagonal elements.
In the following compression scheme, the 2-D DWT has fixed coefficients (in our tests, the Daubechies 9/7 DWT is always used), but the spectral linear transform is adapted to the data. We denote $\mathbf{W}$ the invertible $L \times L$ matrix associated with the 2-D DWT.

2.2 The separable scheme

The separable scheme is compatible with the JPEG2000 Part 2 standard. It can be described as follow:

- *Coding*. The same 2-D DWT is applied to each component $\mathbf{X}_i$ in order to reduce the spatial redundancies and a linear transform $\mathbf{A}$ is applied between the components in order to reduce the spectral redundancies. The result of the 2-D DWT applied to the entire image $\mathbf{X}$ is $\mathbf{X}\mathbf{W}^T$ and the transformed coefficients are the elements of the matrix $\mathbf{Y} = \mathbf{A}\mathbf{X}\mathbf{W}^T$. For each component, the wavelet coefficients of each subband are regrouped according to a fixed scan that does not depend on the component. This re-ordering corresponds to the right multiplication of $\mathbf{X}\mathbf{W}^T$ by a permutation matrix $\mathbf{P}^T$. We can suppose without loss of generality that $\mathbf{P}$ is the identity, otherwise we could replace $\mathbf{W}$ with $\mathbf{P}\mathbf{W}$. This partitioning can be written $\mathbf{X}\mathbf{W}^T = [(\mathbf{X}\mathbf{W}^T)^{(1)} \ldots (\mathbf{X}\mathbf{W}^T)^{(M)}]$, where M is the number of subbands. Then, the transformed coefficients $\mathbf{Y} = [\mathbf{Y}^{(1)} \ldots \mathbf{Y}^{(M)}]$ (where $\mathbf{Y}^{(i)} = \mathbf{A}(\mathbf{X}\mathbf{W}^T)^{(i)}$) are quantized and entropy coded with one quantizer per subband and per component (see § 7.1).
- *Decoding*. Let $\mathbf{Y}^q$ denote the matrix with the same dimension as $\mathbf{Y}$ containing the dequantized transformed coefficients. The mathematical inverse transforms are applied to $\mathbf{Y}^q$ in order to reconstruct an approximation $\widehat{\mathbf{X}} = \mathbf{A}^{-1}\mathbf{Y}^q\mathbf{W}^{-T}$ of the original image $\mathbf{X}$.

We can remark that the order of the transformations (i.e., applying first the DWT then $\mathbf{A}$, or first $\mathbf{A}$ then the DWT) has no effect on the result, since $\mathbf{Y} = \mathbf{A}(\mathbf{X}\mathbf{W}^T) = (\mathbf{A}\mathbf{X})\mathbf{W}^T$. This is why that scheme is called *separable*.

3. Expression of the distortion

In lossy or quasi-lossless coding, the quantization leads to irreversible loss of information, therefore the decoded image $\widehat{\mathbf{X}}$ is an approximation of the original image and in order to quantify the quality of the reconstructed image, it is necessary to introduce a measure of distortion. In this section we give, under various hypotheses, the relation that links the distortion between $\mathbf{X}$ and $\widehat{\mathbf{X}}$ to the quantizers distortions, when the distortion is the mean square error:

$$D_a(\mathbf{X}, \widehat{\mathbf{X}}) = \frac{1}{NL} \|\mathbf{X} - \widehat{\mathbf{X}}\|^2 \quad \text{with} \quad \|\mathbf{X} - \widehat{\mathbf{X}}\|^2 = \sum_{i=1}^{N} \sum_{k=1}^{L} (X_i(k) - \widehat{X}_i(k))^2. \tag{1}$$

We begin by recalling the solution of the problem in a simple general case (Gersho & Gray, 1992; Taubman & Marcellin, 2002).

3.1 A simple general case

Lemma 3.1. *Let $\mathbf{X}$ be a real random vector with N components and $\mathcal{A}$ be an invertible matrix of order N. The transformed vector $\mathbf{Y} = \mathcal{A}\mathbf{X}$ is quantized and dequantized in $\mathbf{Y}^q$. The original vector $\mathbf{X}$ is approximated by $\widehat{\mathbf{X}} = \mathcal{A}^{-1}\mathbf{Y}^q$ and let $\mathbf{b} = \mathbf{Y} - \mathbf{Y}^q$ be the quantization noise. Then, the end-to-end distortion $D = \frac{1}{N}\mathrm{E}(\|\mathbf{X} - \widehat{\mathbf{X}}\|^2)$, where E denotes the mathematical expectation, satisfies the relation $D = \frac{1}{N}\,\mathrm{tr}\left[\mathrm{E}(\mathbf{b}\mathbf{b}^T)\mathcal{A}^{-T}\mathcal{A}^{-1}\right]$.*

Proof: We have $\mathbf{X} - \widehat{\mathbf{X}} = \mathcal{A}^{-1}\mathbf{b}$ and $\|\mathcal{A}^{-1}\mathbf{b}\|^2 = \mathbf{b}^T\mathcal{A}^{-T}\mathcal{A}^{-1}\mathbf{b} = \mathrm{tr}[\mathcal{A}^{-1}\mathbf{b}\mathbf{b}^T\mathcal{A}^{-T}] = \mathrm{tr}[\mathbf{b}\mathbf{b}^T\mathcal{A}^{-T}\mathcal{A}^{-1}]$, therefore $D = \frac{1}{N}\mathrm{E}(\|\mathcal{A}^{-1}\mathbf{b}\|^2) = \frac{1}{N}\,\mathrm{tr}\left[\mathrm{E}(\mathbf{b}\mathbf{b}^T)\mathcal{A}^{-T}\mathcal{A}^{-1}\right]$. ■

Further, we may need the following assumption, that can be deduced from high resolution quantization hypothesis (Gersho & Gray, 1992) (this point is recalled in Subsection 3.2).

$\mathcal{H}_1$: *The components of the quantization noise are zero mean and uncorrelated.*

Theorem 1. *1. With the hypotheses of Lemma 3.1 and assuming $\mathcal{H}_1$, the distortion becomes*

$$D = \frac{1}{N} \sum_{i=1}^{N} \alpha_i D_i, \tag{2}$$

where $D_i = \mathrm{E}(b_i^2)$ is the quantizer distortion of the ith component $\mathbf{Y}_i$ of $\mathbf{Y}$ and, with $\mathbf{e}_i$ the ith canonical vector of $\mathbb{R}^N$ and $(\mathcal{A}^{-1})_{ij}$ the element of $\mathcal{A}^{-1}$ located on row i and column j, we have

$$\alpha_i = \sum_{j=1}^{N} (\mathcal{A}^{-1})^2_{ji} = \|\mathcal{A}^{-1}\mathbf{e}_i\|^2. \tag{3}$$

2. The assertion 1. holds without the assumption $\mathcal{H}_1$ if $\mathcal{A}^{-T}\mathcal{A}^{-1}$ is diagonal, e.g. if $\mathcal{A}$ is orthogonal.

Proof: The assumptions in 1. or 2. state that at least one of the two matrices $\mathcal{A}^{-T}\mathcal{A}^{-1}$ and $\mathrm{E}(\mathbf{b}\mathbf{b}^T)$ is diagonal. Hence the trace of their product is equal to the sum of the products of their diagonal elements. ■

3.2 Justification of the assumption $\mathcal{H}_1$

We recall here well known results that can be found e.g. in (Gersho & Gray, 1992). The assumption $\mathcal{H}_1$ can be justified under the following conditions. C_1: the random vector $\mathbf{Y} = (Y_1, \ldots, Y_N)^T$ has a continuous probability density function (pdf) $f_\mathbf{Y}$; C_2: separable high-rate quantization is achieved, meaning that the quantization steps $\mathbf{h} = (h_i)_{1 \le i \le N}$ of the N components are small with respect to the variations of $f_\mathbf{Y}$ (i.e. $f_\mathbf{Y}(\mathbf{y} + \mathbf{h}) \simeq f_\mathbf{Y}(\mathbf{y})$, $\forall \mathbf{y} \in \mathbb{R}^N$) and C_3 : for any cell S of the separable N-D quantizer, the dequantized value $\mathbf{Y}^q$

associated with S is the iso-barycenter of S. Indeed, if the three conditions C_1, C_2 and C_3 hold, then the pdf $f_{\mathbf{Y}}$ can be considered as quasi constant in the hypercube $\mathbf{Y}^q + \prod_{i=1}^{N}[-h_i/2, h_i/2]$. Further, the conditional law of the quantization noise $\mathbf{b} = \mathbf{Y} - \mathbf{Y}^q$ knowing the dequantized value $\mathbf{Y}^q$ satisfies $f_{\mathbf{b}|\mathbf{Y}^q}(\mathbf{u}) \simeq 1/\prod_{i=1}^{N} h_i$ if $\mathbf{u} \in \prod_{i=1}^{N}[-h_i/2, h_i/2]$, 0 otherwise. We see that the conditional pdf $f_{\mathbf{b}|\mathbf{Y}^q}$ does not depend on the quantized value $\mathbf{Y}^q$, hence it is equal to $f_{\mathbf{b}}$, the pdf of $\mathbf{b}$. Further the components of $\mathbf{b}$ are zero mean and (quasi) independent since their joint density is approximatively equal to the product of their marginal densities.

3.3 The separable subband scheme

In the following, the symbols $\mathbf{X}$, $\mathbf{Y}$ and $\mathbf{Y}^q$ refer again to the matrices defined in Section 2 and $\mathcal{A}$ denotes the matrix of the linear transform that associates $\mathbf{Y}$ with $\mathbf{X}$. We are going to apply the formulae of the general simplified case to the separable scheme. The actual distortion D_a given in relation (1) is an estimation of the distortion

$$D(\mathbf{X}, \widehat{\mathbf{X}}) = \mathrm{E}[D_a(\mathbf{X}, \widehat{\mathbf{X}})] = \frac{1}{NL}\,\mathrm{E}[\|\mathbf{X} - \widehat{\mathbf{X}}\|^2]. \tag{4}$$

Now, in order to express the relation (3) in terms of the DWT $\mathbf{W}$ and the spectral transform $\mathbf{A}$, it is important to note first that the canonical basis of the space of matrices of dimension $N \times L$ is the family of matrices $\mathbf{e}_{i,k} = \mathbf{e}_i \mathbf{e}_k^{'T}$ $(1 \le i \le N, 1 \le k \le L)$, with $\mathbf{e}_i$ (resp. $\mathbf{e}_k^{'}$) the ith (resp. k^{th}) vector of the canonical basis of $\mathbb{R}^N$ (resp. $\mathbb{R}^L$). Therefore, the weighting factor α_i in relation (3) depends here on the two indices i and k: $\alpha_{ik} = \|\mathcal{A}^{-1}\mathbf{e}_{i,k}\|^2$. Then, let

$$w_i = \|\mathbf{A}^{-1}\mathbf{e}_i\|^2 \qquad (1 \le i \le N), \tag{5}$$

we have $\mathcal{A}^{-1}\mathbf{e}_{i,k} = \mathbf{A}^{-1}\mathbf{e}_i\mathbf{e}_k^{'T}\mathbf{W}^{-T}$ and $\|\mathcal{A}^{-1}\mathbf{e}_{i,k}\|^2 = \mathrm{tr}[\mathbf{A}^{-1}\mathbf{e}_i\mathbf{e}_k^{'T}\mathbf{W}^{-T}\mathbf{W}^{-1}\mathbf{e}_k^{'}\mathbf{e}_i^T\mathbf{A}^{-T}] = \mathbf{e}_i^T\mathbf{A}^{-T}\mathbf{A}^{-1}\mathbf{e}_i\mathbf{e}_k^{'T}\mathbf{W}^{-T}\mathbf{W}^{-1}\mathbf{e}_k^{'}$ and finally

$$\alpha_{ik} = \|\mathcal{A}^{-1}\mathbf{e}_{i,k}\|^2 = w_i\|\mathbf{W}^{-1}\mathbf{e}_k^{'}\|^2. \tag{6}$$

Therefore, according to Theorem 1, under assumption $\mathcal{H}_1$ we have

$$D(\mathbf{X}, \widehat{\mathbf{X}}) = \frac{1}{NL}\sum_{i=1}^{N}\sum_{k=1}^{L} w_i\|\mathbf{W}^{-T}\mathbf{e}_k^{'}\|^2\,\mathrm{E}[(Y_i(k) - Y_i^q(k))^2]. \tag{7}$$

Now, for any subband m $(1 \le m \le M)$, let K_m be the number of columns in $\mathbf{Y}$ corresponding to that subband and let

$$\pi_m = \frac{K_m}{L} \qquad (1 \le m \le M) \tag{8}$$

be the ratio of wavelets coefficients that belong to it. If k $(1 \le k \le L)$ refers to a column indice of the matrix $\mathbf{Y}$ located in that subband and if we assume that

$\mathcal{H}_2$: *for any component i $(1 \le i \le N)$, the distortion* $\mathrm{E}[(Y_i(k) - Y_i^q(k))^2] = D_i^{(m)}$ *does not depend on the spatial position k in the subband m,*

(which is the case under high resolution quantization hypothesis), then equation (7) becomes

$$D(\mathbf{X}, \widehat{\mathbf{X}}) = \frac{1}{N}\sum_{i=1}^{N}\sum_{m=1}^{M} \pi_m w_i \omega_m D_i^{(m)} \quad \text{with} \quad \omega_m = \frac{1}{K_m}\sum_{k}\|\mathbf{W}^{-T}\mathbf{e}_k^{'}\|^2, \tag{9}$$

where in the last summation, the range of k consists in the columns of $\mathbf{Y}$ with the subband m. Or, by adopting a different perspective, if we assume that

$\mathcal{H}_3$: *the weight* $\|\mathbf{W}^{-1}\mathbf{e}_k\|^2 = \omega_m$ *does not depend on the spatial position k in the subband m,*

then equation (7) becomes

$$D(\mathbf{X},\widehat{\mathbf{X}}) = \frac{1}{N}\sum_{i=1}^{N}\sum_{m=1}^{M}\pi_m\omega_m w_i D_i^{(m)} \quad \text{with} \quad D_i^{(m)} = \frac{1}{K_m}\sum_k \mathrm{E}[(Y_i(k) - Y_i^q(k))^2], \tag{10}$$

where in the last summation, the range of k consists in the columns of $\mathbf{Y}$ with the subband m.

Remark 1. *The condition $\mathcal{H}_3$ is satisfied by dyadic wavelets having Finite Impulse Response (FIR) synthesis filters, when edge effects are neglected (for more details see e.g. (Usevitch, 1996; Woods & Naven, 1992)).*

Lastly, we can notice that the actual distortion D_a given in equation (1) satisfies

$$D_a(\mathbf{X},\widehat{\mathbf{X}}) = \frac{1}{NL}\,\mathrm{tr}[(\mathbf{X}-\widehat{\mathbf{X}})(\mathbf{X}-\widehat{\mathbf{X}})^T] = \frac{1}{NL}\,\mathrm{tr}[\mathbf{A}^{-1}(\mathbf{Y}-\mathbf{Y}^q)\mathbf{W}^{-T}\mathbf{W}^{-1}(\mathbf{Y}-\mathbf{Y}^q)^T\mathbf{A}^{-T}],$$

therefore if we assume

$\mathcal{H}_4$: *the DWT is orthogonal, i.e.* $\mathbf{W}\mathbf{W}^T = \mathbf{I}_L$, *with* $\mathbf{I}_L$ *the identity matrix of dimension L,*

then $D_a(\mathbf{X},\widehat{\mathbf{X}}) = \frac{1}{NL}\,\mathrm{tr}[\mathbf{A}^{-1}(\mathbf{Y}-\mathbf{Y}^q)(\mathbf{Y}-\mathbf{Y}^q)^T\mathbf{A}^{-T}] = \frac{1}{NL}\sum_{m=1}^{M}\mathrm{tr}[\mathbf{A}^{-1}(\mathbf{Y}^{(m)}-\mathbf{Y}^{q(m)})(\mathbf{Y}^{(m)}-\mathbf{Y}^{q(m)})^T\mathbf{A}^{-T}]$.

Remark 2. *The hypothesis $\mathcal{H}_4$ is roughly satisfied with the approximately orthogonal Daubechies 9/7 DWT (indeed, a simulation shows that the infinity norm of the diagonal, and respectively the off diagonal, elements of $\mathbf{W}^T\mathbf{W} - \mathbf{I}_L$ is worth 0.42 and 0.16, for five levels of decomposition on a 1-D signal of length 512).*

Now, $\frac{1}{K_m}(\mathbf{Y}^{(m)} - \mathbf{Y}^{q(m)})(\mathbf{Y}^{(m)} - \mathbf{Y}^{q(m)})^T$ is the actual autocorrelation matrix of the m-th subband quantization noise. If we assume

$\mathcal{H}_1'$: in each subband, the actual autocorrelation matrix of the quantization noise is diagonal, i.e., $\frac{1}{K_m}(\mathbf{Y}^{(m)} - \mathbf{Y}^{q(m)})(\mathbf{Y}^{(m)} - \mathbf{Y}^{q(m)})^T = \mathrm{diag}(D_1^{(m)},\ldots,D_N^{(m)})$ $(1 \le m \le M)$,

then we have

$$\begin{aligned}
\mathrm{tr}[\mathbf{A}^{-1}\,\mathrm{diag}(D_1^{(m)},\ldots,D_N^{(m)})\mathbf{A}^{-T}] &= \sum_{i=1}^{N} w_i D_i^{(m)}\\
D_a(\mathbf{X},\widehat{\mathbf{X}}) &= \frac{1}{N}\sum_{m=1}^{M}\pi_m\,\mathrm{tr}[\mathbf{A}^{-1}\,\mathrm{diag}(D_1^{(m)},\ldots,D_N^{(m)})\mathbf{A}^{-T}]\\
D_a(\mathbf{X},\widehat{\mathbf{X}}) &= \frac{1}{N}\sum_{i=1}^{N}\sum_{m=1}^{M}\pi_m w_i D_i^{(m)}.
\end{aligned} \tag{11}$$

Moreover, if we assume $\mathcal{H}_4$ and

$\mathcal{H}_5$: *the spectral transform* $\mathbf{A}$ *is orthogonal, i.e.* $\mathbf{A}\mathbf{A}^T = \mathbf{I}_N$,

then

$$D_a(\mathbf{X},\widehat{\mathbf{X}}) = D_a(\mathbf{Y},\mathbf{Y}^q). \tag{12}$$

Let us state these results in the following theorem.

Theorem 2. *With the notations of Section 2.2, the end-to-end distortion of the separable scheme is given by:*

- *equation (9) under the assumptions* $\mathcal{H}_1$ *and* $\mathcal{H}_2$*;*
- *equation (10) under the assumptions* $\mathcal{H}_1$ *and* $\mathcal{H}_3$*;*
- *equation (11) under the assumptions* $\mathcal{H}_1^{'}$ *and* $\mathcal{H}_4$*;*
- *equation (12) under the assumptions* $\mathcal{H}_4$ *and* $\mathcal{H}_5$*.*

Remark 3. *1. The assumptions* $\mathcal{H}_1$ *and* $\mathcal{H}_1^{'}$ *are consequences of high resolution quantizations (see Subsection 3.2). They can also be deduced from the condition of statistical independence of the transformed components, since if the components of* $\mathbf{Y}$ *are independent, then the components of the quantization noise* $\mathbf{Y} - \mathbf{Y}^q$*, which is generally centered, are uncorrelated.*

2. *A method for the computation of the weighting wavelet coefficients* ω_m $(1 \leq m \leq M)$ *can be found in (Usevitch, 1996; Woods & Naven, 1992).*
3. *Since the assumptions* $\mathcal{H}_1^{'}$, $\mathcal{H}_1, \ldots, \mathcal{H}_4$*, are only approximatively satisfied, the equalities (9–13) are only approximations. However, we observed on many experiments that these approximations are very good for bit-rates greater than* 0.25 *bits per pixel and per band.*

We search the optimal spectral transform (that is the one which minimizes the total bit-rate for a given end-to-end distortion) which adapts to the data, assuming high resolution quantizations hypotheses and 2-D DWT with fixed coefficients, i.e., which do not adapt to the data. As already mentioned, in our tests we always used the Daubechies 9/7 DWT. First, we derive the criterion minimized by an optimal spectral transform. We emphasize the fact that we do not assume Gaussian data and that generally in the literature this assumption is made in order to clarify the criterion (coding gain) maximized by the optimal transform. However, the Bennett's formula and the optimal bit allocation between quantizers formula on which our criteria are based are well-known and therefore it is straightforward to deduce these criteria from well-known results. Our major innovation consists especially in the computation of the optimal transforms, since this computation is generally presented as a difficult task in classical transform coding and has never been done in the case of the separable scheme which is JPEG2000 compatible.

4. Criteria for optimal transforms under high resolution quantizations

We recall the extension of the Bennett's formula which can be stated as follows: if X is a real random variable quantized under the high resolution hypothesis, then the bit-rate of quantized variable X^q is well approximated by $H(X) - \frac{1}{2}\log_2(cD)$, where $H(X)$ is the differential entropy of X, D is the distortion (expected mean square error) introduced by the quantization and c is a constant depending on the quantization, e.g., for uniform scalar quantization $c = 12$ (Gray & Neuhoff, 1998). Hence, if $R_i^{(m)}$ denotes the quantizer bit-rate associated with component i and subband m, the Bennet's approximation gives

$$R_i^{(m)} \simeq H(Y_i^{(m)}) - \frac{1}{2}\log_2(cD_i^{(m)})$$

and the total bit-rate $R = \frac{1}{N}\sum_{i=1}^{N}\sum_{m=1}^{M}\pi_m R_i^{(m)}$ satisfies

$$R \simeq \frac{1}{N}\sum_{i=1}^{N}\sum_{m=1}^{M}\pi_m\left[H(Y_i^{(m)}) - \frac{1}{2}\log_2(cD_i^{(m)})\right]. \tag{13}$$

The problem now consists in minimizing R under the constraint (given by Theorem 2)

$$\frac{1}{N}\sum_{i=1}^{N}\sum_{m=1}^{M}\pi_m\omega_m w_i D_i^{(m)} \leq D_t \tag{14}$$

for a given end-to-end distortion D_t. In other words, for a target end-to-end distortion D_t, how can the quantizer distortions $D_i^{(m)}$ be distributed in each subband of each component in order to minimize the total bit-rate? It is a classical problem in compression, called optimal bit allocation (Gersho & Gray, 1992), that can be solved as follows. According to relation (13), when the spectral and spatial transforms $\mathbf{A}$ and $\mathbf{W}$ are given, the differential entropies $H(Y_i^{(m)})$ and the factors w_i and ω_m are given. Then, the total bit-rate is minimized if and only if $\prod_{i=1}^{N}\prod_{m=1}^{M}(D_i^{(m)})^{\frac{\pi_m}{N}}$ is maximized, that is if and only if

$$\left[\prod_{i=1}^{N}\prod_{m=1}^{M}\left(D_i^{(m)}\right)^{\frac{\pi_m}{N}}\right]\left[\prod_{i=1}^{N}w_i\right]^{\frac{1}{N}}\left[\prod_{m=1}^{M}\omega_m^{\pi_m}\right] = \prod_{i=1}^{N}\prod_{m=1}^{M}\left(\omega_m w_i D_i^{(m)}\right)^{\frac{\pi_m}{N}}$$

is maximized. Now the mean inequality states the last expression (which is a geometric mean) is not greater than the arithmetic mean corresponding to the left member of inequality (14), with equality if and only if all the terms in the summation are equal. Hence, the minimization holds when $D_i^{(m)} = D_t\omega_m^{-1}w_i^{-1}$ for all m and i. That leads to

$$R \simeq \sum_{m=1}^{M}\pi_m\left[\frac{1}{N}\sum_{i=1}^{N}\left\{H(Y_i^{(m)}) + \frac{1}{2}\log_2 w_i\right\} + \frac{1}{2}\log_2\omega_m\right] - \frac{1}{2}\log_2(cD_t)$$

and since w_i is the ith diagonal element of $\mathbf{A}^{-T}\mathbf{A}^{-1}$, the other terms ω_m do not depend on $\mathbf{A}$, we obtain the following theorem.

Theorem 3. *For the separable scheme when the 2-D DWT has fixed coefficients, if high resolution quantizations hypotheses are assumed, then the optimal spectral transform* $\mathbf{A}$ *is an* $N \times N$ *matrix that minimizes the criterion:*

$$C_2(\mathbf{A}) = \sum_{j=1}^{N}\sum_{m=1}^{M}\pi_m H(Y_j^{(m)}) + \frac{1}{2}\log_2\det\operatorname{diag}(\mathbf{A}^{-T}\mathbf{A}^{-1}). \tag{15}$$

Remark 4. *Since* $\sum_{m=1}^{M}\pi_m = 1$*, the criterion* $C_2(\mathbf{A})$ *can be expressed as*

$$\begin{aligned} C_2(\mathbf{A}) &= \sum_{m=1}^{M}\pi_m\left[\sum_{i=1}^{N}H(Y_i^{(m)}) - \log_2|\det\mathbf{A}|\right] + \frac{1}{2}\log_2\left[\frac{\det\operatorname{diag}\left(\mathbf{A}^{-T}\mathbf{A}^{-1}\right)}{\det(\mathbf{A}^{-T}\mathbf{A}^{-1})}\right] \\ &= \sum_{m=1}^{M}\pi_m C_{ICA}^{(m)}(\mathbf{A}) + C_O(\mathbf{A}), \end{aligned} \tag{16}$$

where, for $1 \leq m \leq M$, $C_{ICA}^{(m)}(\mathbf{A}) = \sum_{i=1}^{N}H(Y_i^{(m)}) - \log_2|\det\mathbf{A}|$ *is the criterion to minimize when performing only ICA to the N components of the transformed coefficients that belong to the subband m. Pham (Pham, 2004) used that criterion to perform the algorithm* `ICAinf`.

Remark 5. *It results of Hadamard's inequality, that the term* $C_O(\mathbf{A}) = \frac{1}{2}\log_2 \frac{\det \operatorname{diag}(\mathbf{A}^{-T}\mathbf{A}^{-1})}{\det(\mathbf{A}^{-T}\mathbf{A}^{-1})}$ *is always positive or null (Narozny et al., 2008) and vanishes if and only if* $\mathbf{A}$ *is a matrix whose columns are pairwise orthogonal, therefore it can be seen like a kind of measure of deviation to orthogonality.*

The relation (16) shows that the criterion $C_2(\mathbf{A})$ takes into consideration the fact that one quantizer per subband and per component is allocated. It is also important to notice that the criterion $C_2(\mathbf{A})$ involves the transformed coefficients $\mathbf{Y}$. Therefore, even for the separable scheme (where the order of processing between the 2-D DWT and the spectral transform does not matter), the search of the optimal spectral transform must be done *after* the 2-D DWT.
Note that the separable compression scheme does not take into account the difference of statistics between subbands, since the same spectral transform is applied to all the subbands. Moreover it is well known that after a DWT some redundancies remain between adjoining wavelets coefficients. In (Akam Bita et al., 2010a), the authors introduced the subband compression scheme, that uses as many optimal spectral transforms as subbands in order to capture the difference of statistics between subbands, and the mixed subband compression scheme, that captures both redundancies between adjacent wavelet coefficients and the difference of statistics between subbands. Their experiments on hyperspectral images showed that these variants of the separable scheme, which are not JPEG2000 compatible, perform finally worse than the separable scheme because of the increasing of memory size occupied by the optimal spectral transforms in the bit stream.
Lastly, note that the algorithm that computes a KLT is customarily applied first to the image before the DWT, but this would be equivalent to applying it after the DWT (i.e. to the DWT coefficients) if the DWT is orthogonal (as is often the case or at least nearly so in practice[1]). But then it will not distinguish subbands: the DWT coefficients are considered as coming from a same (Gaussian) distribution, regardless of the subband they belong to. We feel that the higher performance — shown in § 7 — of criterion (15) over the criterion $\frac{1}{2}\log_2 \prod_{j=1}^{N} \operatorname{var}(Y_j)$, which leads to the KLT, is due primarily to the fact that it treats each subband separately rather than that treating the distribution in each subband as non Gaussian. This is logical since, after any DWT, the energy in each subband depends on the power spectrum of the input signal. It is important to notice that there is no contradiction in the fact that the criterion (15) treats each subband separately, while the same spectral transform $\mathbf{A}$ is applied to all the subbands. The idea is then to introduce the distinction between subbands but retain the (approximate) Gaussian assumption used by the KLT. The distribution of all the wavelet coefficients (with no distinction between subbands) is a mixture of distributions of the coefficients in the subbands. It can be shown that the kurtosis of the mixed distribution is higher than the average kurtosis of the individual distributions. In particular, mixture of Gaussian distributions has always a positive kurtosis, unless all the individual distributions are the same. Thus the wavelet coefficients, regardless of the subband they belong to, have a positive kurtosis even if in each subband their distribution is Gaussian. The above consideration suggests modifying the criterion (15) by treating the transformed coefficients in each subband m as having a Gaussian distribution *with differing variance for different* m. The transformation minimizing this modified criterion is no longer optimal, but can be nearly so if the distribution in each subband is not too far from Gaussian. This is not an unrealistic situation: the wavelet coefficients in a subband is the (decimated) output of a bandpass filter which tends to produce more Gaussian output than input, due to the reasoning (given e.g. in (Papoulis, 1984) section 8-5) that yields to the proof of the Central Limit Theorem. The advantage of the modified criterion is that it avoids

[1] See Remark 2.

the entropy estimation and uses only second order statistics. Thus its minimization requires much less computer resources than using (15).

5. A simplified criterion using only second order statistics

Let $H^{-}(Z) = \log_2 \sqrt{\mathrm{var}(Z) 2\pi e} - H(Z)$ denote the negentropy of Z (which is the difference of entropy between a Gaussian distribution with variance $\mathrm{var}(Z)$ and the distribution of Z), it is non negative and vanishes if and only if Z is Gaussian. The criterion (15) can be rewritten for orthogonal[2] matrices

$$C_{\perp}(\mathbf{A}) = -\sum_{i=1}^{N}\sum_{m=1}^{M} \pi_m H^{-}(Y_i^{(m)}) + \frac{1}{2}\sum_{i=1}^{N}\sum_{m=1}^{M} \pi_m \log_2[\mathrm{var}(Y_i^{(m)}) 2\pi e]. \tag{17}$$

An analysis of criterion (17) shows that it takes into account two phenomena: 1) the non Gaussianity of the transformed coefficients $Y_i^{(m)}$ for $1 \leq m \leq M$ and $1 \leq i \leq N$ — this is controlled by the first term — and 2) the inhomogeneity of the variances in the subbands — this is controlled by the second term. It is natural to explore the case where the second phenomenon is the most important, since the DWT tends to render the variables more Gaussian. In practice, this condition is generally roughly satisfied, except in the LL subband (a subband of lowest resolution) for which the weighting coefficient π_m is generally small. Thus, if we neglect the variation, induced by the spectral transform $\mathbf{A}$, of the first term in the right member of equation (17), and if we consider only orthogonal matrices $\mathbf{A}$, then the optimal transform minimizes the new criterion

$$C'(\mathbf{A}) = \frac{1}{2}\sum_{i=1}^{N}\sum_{m=1}^{M} \pi_m \log_2[\mathrm{var}(Y_i^{(m)})]. \tag{18}$$

Furthermore if we assume in each component the transformed coefficients have all the same variance, regardless of the subband they belong to, then the criterion (18) becomes $\frac{1}{2}\log_2\left[\prod_{i=1}^{N} \mathrm{var}(Y_i)\right]$, leading to the KLT.

In the following, we express criterion (18) in terms of the covariance matrices of the wavelets coefficients $\mathbf{X}\mathbf{W}^T = \left[(\mathbf{X}\mathbf{W}^T)^{(1)} \; (\mathbf{X}\mathbf{W}^T)^{(2)} \; \cdots \; (\mathbf{X}\mathbf{W}^T)^{(M)} \right]$ located in the same subband. The matrix $(\mathbf{X}\mathbf{W}^T)^{(m)}$ is of dimension $N \times \pi_m L$. Its columns can be considered as different realizations of a random vector of dimension N whose covariance matrix is denoted $\mathbf{C}^{(m)}$. Now, $\mathbf{Y} = \mathbf{A}\mathbf{X}\mathbf{W}^T$ can be written $\mathbf{Y} = [\mathbf{Y}^{(1)} \cdots \mathbf{Y}^{(M)}]$, where $\mathbf{Y}^{(m)} = (\mathbf{A}\mathbf{X}\mathbf{W}^T)^{(m)}$ is a matrix whose columns can also be considered as different realizations of a random vector having $\mathbf{A}\mathbf{C}^{(m)}\mathbf{A}^T$ as covariance matrix. With these notations, we have $\prod_{j=1}^{N} \mathrm{var}(Y_j^{(m)}) = \det \mathrm{diag}(\mathbf{A}\mathbf{C}^{(m)}\mathbf{A}^T)$ and hence the new criterion becomes

$$C'(\mathbf{A}) = \frac{1}{2}\sum_{m=1}^{M} \pi_m \log_2 \det \mathrm{diag}(\mathbf{A}\mathbf{C}^{(m)}\mathbf{A}^T) \tag{19}$$

to be minimized with respect to $\mathbf{A}$, under the constraint that it is orthogonal.

[2] The orthogonality constraint will be justified in § 7 in which we find that minimizing (15) with and without this constraint yields almost the same performances. With the orthogonality constraint, the second term in (15) vanishes.

The FG algorithm in (Flury & Gautschi, 1986) can be used to minimize the above criterion. We have developed a slightly different algorithm (called JADO) which is briefly described in Appendix 6.3.

6. Minimization of the criteria for the separable scheme

We explain now three algorithms that minimize the criterion (15), one with no constraint but invertibility, another with the constraint of orthogonality and the third with the constraints of orthogonality and Gaussian data. To simplify some mathematical expressions we shall use the Neperian logarithm instead of the base two logarithm until the end of this section.

6.1 The algorithm OST

As in (Pham, 2004) and (Narozny et al., 2008), the algorithms of minimization are based on a quasi-Newton method with the relative gradient and a simplified relative Hessian. Starting with a current estimator $\mathbf{A}$, the method consists of expanding $C_2(\mathbf{A} + \mathcal{E}\mathbf{A})$ with respect to the matrix $\mathcal{E} = [\mathcal{E}_{ij}]$ up to the second order, in a neighborhood of $\mathcal{E} = \mathbf{0}_N$ (the null matrix), and then minimizing the resulting quadratic form in $\mathcal{E}$ to obtain a new estimate. Using the results of (Pham, 2005) it is straightforward to deduce that the Taylor expansion up to the second order of $C_{ICA}^{(m)}(\mathbf{A} + \mathcal{E}\mathbf{A})$ can be approximated as follows

$$C_{ICA}^{(m)}(\mathbf{A} + \mathcal{E}\mathbf{A}) = C_{ICA}^{(m)}(\mathbf{A}) + \sum_{1 \leq i \neq j \leq N} \mathrm{E}[\psi_{Y_i^{(m)}}(Y_i^{(m)})Y_j^{(m)}]\mathcal{E}_{ij}$$
$$+ \frac{1}{2} \sum_{1 \leq i \neq j \leq N} \{\mathrm{E}[\psi^2_{Y_i^{(m)}}(Y_i^{(m)})]\,\mathrm{E}[Y_j^{(m)2}]\mathcal{E}_{ij}^2 + \mathcal{E}_{ij}\mathcal{E}_{ji}\} + \cdots, \qquad (20)$$

where the function $\psi_{Y_i^{(m)}}$ is equal to the derivative of $-\log p(y_i^{(m)})$ — $p(y_i^{(m)})$ denoting the probability density function of $Y_i^{(m)}$ — and is known as the score function. Let $\mathbf{M} = \mathbf{A}^{-T}\mathbf{A}^{-1}$. In (Narozny et al., 2008), the Taylor expansion of $C_O(\mathbf{A} + \mathcal{E}\mathbf{A})$ is given up to the second order, however it is quite involved and it is simplified into

$$C_O(\mathbf{A} + \mathcal{E}\mathbf{A}) \approx C_O(\mathbf{A}) - \sum_{1 \leq i \neq j \leq N} \frac{M_{ji}}{M_{ii}}\mathcal{E}_{ji} + \frac{1}{2} \sum_{1 \leq i \neq j \leq N} \left[\frac{M_{jj}}{M_{ii}}\mathcal{E}_{ji}^2 + \mathcal{E}_{ji}\mathcal{E}_{ij}\right] + \cdots \qquad (21)$$

by neglecting the non diagonal elements of $\mathbf{M} = [M_{ij}]$ in the second order terms of the Taylor expansion.
Using the approximation (21), the equality (20) and the relation (16) we obtain

$$C_2(\mathbf{A} + \mathcal{E}\mathbf{A}) = C_2(\mathbf{A}) + \sum_{1 \leq i \neq j \leq N} \left[\sum_{m=1}^{M} \pi_m E\left[Y_j^{(m)} \psi_{Y_i^{(m)}}\left(Y_i^{(m)}\right)\right] - \frac{\mathbf{M}_{ij}}{\mathbf{M}_{jj}}\right]\mathcal{E}_{ij}$$
$$+\frac{1}{2} \sum_{1 \leq i \neq j \leq N} \left[\sum_{m=1}^{M} \pi_m \mathcal{E}_{ij}^2 E\left[Y_j^{(m)2}\right] E\left[\psi^2_{Y_i^{(m)}}\left(Y_i^{(m)}\right)\right] + \frac{M_{ii}}{M_{jj}}\mathcal{E}_{ij}^2 + 2\mathcal{E}_{ij}\mathcal{E}_{ji}\right]. \qquad (22)$$

The quadratic form associated to this last expansion is positive definite. One iteration of the algorithm is first to solve the following equation

$$\begin{bmatrix} \Psi_{ij} & 2 \\ 2 & \Psi_{ji} \end{bmatrix} \begin{pmatrix} \mathcal{E}_{ij} \\ \mathcal{E}_{ji} \end{pmatrix} = \begin{pmatrix} \Phi_{ij} \\ \Phi_{ji} \end{pmatrix}, \qquad (23)$$

with $\Phi_{ij} = \frac{M_{ij}}{M_{jj}} - \sum_{m=1}^{M} \pi_m E[\psi_{Y_i^{(m)}}(Y_i^{(m)})Y_j^{(m)}]$ and $\Psi_{ij} = \sum_{m=1}^{M} \pi_m E[\psi^2_{Y_i^{(m)}}(Y_i^{(m)})]E[Y_i^{(m)2}] + \frac{M_{ii}}{M_{jj}}$ and then to replace the current solution $\mathbf{A}$ with $\mathbf{A} + \mathcal{E}\mathbf{A}$. Since the diagonal elements of $\mathcal{E}$ are undetermined, they are arbitrarily fixed to zero. For the practical computation of the algorithm, we replace $\psi_{Y_i^{(m)}}$ with its estimator $\widehat{\psi}_{Y_i^{(m)}}$ that is described in (Pham, 2005) as well as the estimator of the differential entropy. The mathematical expectations are replaced with simple empirical means. We call `OST` (*Optimal Spectral Transform*) the algorithm described above and OST the optimal transform returned by this algorithm.

6.2 The algorithm `OrthOST`

To minimize the criterion (15) with the constraint that the solution is an orthogonal matrix, it is important to note, as in (Narozny et al., 2008), that if $\mathbf{A}$ is orthogonal, then $\mathbf{A} + \mathcal{E}\mathbf{A}$ remains orthogonal when $\mathbf{I} + \mathcal{E}$ is also orthogonal. This condition is satisfied up to the first order if $\mathcal{E}$ is an antisymmetrical matrix, since then $(\mathbf{I} + \mathcal{E})^T(\mathbf{I} + \mathcal{E}) = \mathbf{I} + \mathcal{E}^T\mathcal{E}$. Using that condition, the expansion (22) becomes

$$C(\mathbf{A} + \mathcal{E}\mathbf{A}) = C(\mathbf{A}) + \sum_{m=1}^{M} \sum_{1 \le i < j \le N} \pi_m \left\{ E[Y_j^{(m)} \psi_{Y_i^{(m)}}(Y_i^{(m)})] - E[Y_i^{(m)} \psi_{Y_j^{(m)}}(Y_j^{(m)})] \right\} \mathcal{E}_{ij} +$$

$$\frac{1}{2} \sum_{1 \le i < j \le N} \left[\sum_{m=1}^{M} \pi_m \left\{ E[Y_j^{(m)2}] E[\psi^2_{Y_i^{(m)}}(Y_i^{(m)})] + E[Y_i^{(m)2}] E[\psi^2_{Y_j^{(m)}}(Y_j^{(m)})] \right\} - 2 \right] \mathcal{E}_{ij}^2. \quad (24)$$

The matrix $\mathcal{E}$ is calculated in that case according to

$$\mathcal{E}_{ij} = \frac{\sum_{m=1}^{M} \pi_m \left\{ E[Y_i^{(m)} \psi_{Y_j^{(m)}}(Y_j^{(m)})] - E[Y_j^{(m)} \psi_{Y_i^{(m)}}(Y_i^{(m)})] \right\}}{\sum_{m=1}^{M} \pi_m \left\{ E[Y_j^{(m)2}] E[\psi^2_{Y_i^{(m)}}(Y_i^{(m)})] + E[Y_i^{(m)2}] E[\psi^2_{Y_j^{(m)}}(Y_j^{(m)})] \right\} - 2}. \quad (25)$$

Actually, $\mathbf{A} + \mathcal{E}\mathbf{A}$ obtained in this way is not a true orthogonal matrix. This can be overcome by replacing $\mathbf{A} + \mathcal{E}\mathbf{A}$ with $e^{\mathcal{E}}\mathbf{A} = (\mathbf{I} + \mathcal{E} + \mathcal{E}^2/2! + \cdots)\mathbf{A}$, which is orthogonal and differs from $\mathbf{A} + \mathcal{E}\mathbf{A}$ only by second order terms. We call `OrthOST` (*Orthogonal Optimal Spectral Transform*) this algorithm and OrthOST the orthogonal transform returned by the algorithm. The case where the spectral transform is constrained to be orthogonal is particularly interesting because the weightings which depend on the linear transform are all equal to one.

6.3 The `JADO` (Joint Approximate Diagonalization under Orthogonality constraint) algorithm

Given K positive definite (complex) matrices $\mathbf{C}_1, \ldots, \mathbf{C}_K$ associated with positive weights w_1, $\ldots, w_K$, the `JADO` algorithm aims to find a unitary matrix $\mathbf{B}$ which minimizes

$$C(\mathbf{B}) = \sum_{k=1}^{K} w_k \log \det \operatorname{diag}(\mathbf{B}\mathbf{C}_k\mathbf{B}^*) \quad (26)$$

where * denotes the hermitian operator. This algorithm differs only slightly from FG algorithm in (Flury & Gautschi, 1986). However, its derivation in (Flury & Gautschi, 1986) is complex and difficult to understand. Here we provide briefly a much simpler derivation.

The idea is to make successive Givens rotations, each time on a pair of rows of $\mathbf{B}$, the ith row $\mathbf{B}_{i\cdot}$ and the jth row $\mathbf{B}_{j\cdot}$, say:

$$\begin{bmatrix} \mathbf{B}_{i\cdot} \\ \mathbf{B}_{j\cdot} \end{bmatrix} \leftarrow \mathbf{T}_{ij} \begin{bmatrix} \mathbf{B}_{i\cdot} \\ \mathbf{B}_{j\cdot} \end{bmatrix}, \tag{27}$$

where $\mathbf{T}_{ij}$ is a 2×2 unitary matrix, chosen so that the criterion is decreased. The processing of all the $\frac{K(K-1)}{2}$ pairs is called a sweep. The algorithm consists of repeated sweeps until convergence is achieved.

The decrease of the criterion (26) induced by (27) is

$$\sum_{k=1}^{K} w_k \log \left[(\mathbf{B}_{i\cdot}\mathbf{C}_k\mathbf{B}_{i\cdot}^*)(\mathbf{B}_{j\cdot}\mathbf{C}_k\mathbf{B}_{j\cdot}^*) \Big/ \det \operatorname{diag} \left(\mathbf{T}_{ij} \begin{bmatrix} \mathbf{B}_{i\cdot} \\ \mathbf{B}_{j\cdot} \end{bmatrix} \mathbf{C}_k \begin{bmatrix} \mathbf{B}_{i\cdot}^* & \mathbf{B}_{j\cdot}^* \end{bmatrix} \mathbf{T}_{ij}^* \right) \right].$$

A natural idea is to chose $\mathbf{T}_{ij}$ to maximize this decrease, but there is no closed form formulae for that. Our idea is to maximize a lower bound of it instead. Since for $a > 0, b \geq 0, \log(a/b) \geq 1 - b/a$, the above decrease can be seen to be bounded below by

$$2(w_1 + \cdots + w_K) - \mathbf{T}_{ij;1\cdot}\mathbf{P}\mathbf{T}_{ij;1\cdot}^* - \mathbf{T}_{ij;2\cdot}\mathbf{Q}\mathbf{T}_{ij;2\cdot}^*, \tag{28}$$

where $\mathbf{T}_{ij;1\cdot}$ and $\mathbf{T}_{ij;2\cdot}$ are the first and second rows of $\mathbf{T}_{ij}$ and

$$\mathbf{P} = \sum_{k=1}^{K} \frac{w_k}{\mathbf{B}_{i\cdot}\mathbf{C}_k\mathbf{B}_{i\cdot}^*} \begin{bmatrix} \mathbf{B}_{i\cdot} \\ \mathbf{B}_{j\cdot} \end{bmatrix} \mathbf{C}_k [\,\mathbf{B}_{i\cdot}^* \ \mathbf{B}_{j\cdot}^*\,]; \quad \mathbf{Q} = \sum_{k=1}^{K} \frac{w_k}{\mathbf{B}_{j\cdot}\mathbf{C}_k\mathbf{B}_{j\cdot}^*} \begin{bmatrix} \mathbf{B}_{i\cdot} \\ \mathbf{B}_{j\cdot} \end{bmatrix} \mathbf{C}_k [\,\mathbf{B}_{i\cdot}^* \ \mathbf{B}_{j\cdot}^*\,].$$

Since $\mathbf{T}_{ij;2\cdot}$ has unit norm and is orthogonal to $\mathbf{T}_{ij;1\cdot}$, it must be of the form $e^{i\alpha}\overline{\mathbf{T}}_{ij;1\cdot}\mathbf{J}$ where α is some phase angle, $\overline{x}$ denotes the complex conjugate of x and $\mathbf{J}$ is the 2×2 matrix with 0 on the diagonal and $1, -1$ on the anti-diagonal. Thus $\mathbf{T}_{ij;2\cdot}\mathbf{Q}\mathbf{T}_{ij;2\cdot}^* = \overline{\mathbf{T}}_{ij;1\cdot}\mathbf{J}\mathbf{Q}\mathbf{J}^*\overline{\mathbf{T}}_{ij;1\cdot}^*$, but since the above left hand side is real (as $\mathbf{Q}$ is hermitian), it also equals $\mathbf{T}_{ij;1\cdot}\mathbf{J}\overline{\mathbf{Q}}\mathbf{J}^*\mathbf{T}_{ij;1\cdot}^*$. Therefore expression (28) can be rewritten as $2(w_1 + \cdots + w_K) - \mathbf{T}_{ij;1\cdot}(\mathbf{P} + \mathbf{J}\overline{\mathbf{Q}}\mathbf{J}^*)\mathbf{T}_{ij;1\cdot}^*$. Maximizing it with respect to the unitary matrix $\mathbf{T}$ thus amounts to minimizing $\mathbf{T}_{ij;1\cdot}(\mathbf{P} + \mathbf{J}\overline{\mathbf{Q}}\mathbf{J}^*)\mathbf{T}_{ij;1\cdot}^*$ with respect to the vector of unit norm $\mathbf{T}_{ij;1\cdot}$. The solution is that $\mathbf{T}_{ij;1\cdot}$ is (up to a factor of unit modulus) the normalized left eigenvector of the smallest eigenvalue of $\mathbf{P} + \mathbf{J}\overline{\mathbf{Q}}\mathbf{J}^*$. Since $\mathbf{T}_{ij;2\cdot}$ is orthogonal to $\mathbf{T}_{ij;1\cdot}$ it is the other eigenvector. Finally, $\mathbf{T}_{ij}$ is the matrix formed by the left eigenvectors of $\mathbf{P} + \mathbf{J}\overline{\mathbf{Q}}\mathbf{J}^*$. Its elements can be computed explicitly in closed form as follows. We note that the off diagonal elements of $\mathbf{J}\overline{\mathbf{Q}}\mathbf{J}^*$ is the negative of those of $\mathbf{Q}$ while the diagonal elements are those of $\mathbf{Q}$ *in reverse order*. Thus $\mathbf{J}\overline{\mathbf{Q}}\mathbf{J}^* = \operatorname{tr}(\mathbf{Q})\mathbf{I} - \mathbf{Q}$ where tr denotes the trace. Since the addition of a multiple of the identity matrix does not change the eigenvectors, $\mathbf{T}_{ij}$ is also the matrix formed by the left eigenvectors of $\mathbf{P} - \mathbf{Q}$. One can now recognize that the rotation (27) is the same as an iteration in the G loop of the FG algorithm. However, it differs from our `JADO` algorithm in that it repeats (27) with the same pair i, j (but with the newly computed $\mathbf{B}_{i\cdot}$ and $\mathbf{B}_{j\cdot}$) until convergence (the G loop) and only then another pair i, j is considered. We feel that this is not efficient since the decrease of the criterion will be very small near the end of the G loop. We call JADOST the transform returned by the algorithm.

6.4 Computational complexity of the optimal transforms

We give here a rough estimation of the number of operations required for the computation of the two first algorithms described above, taking into account only multiplications and divisions. The differential entropies and the score functions are calculated according to a method explained in (Pham, 2005). The computational complexity of each of these quantities is O(NrL), where r is the number of bins in the binned kernel density estimation. In general $r \ll L$ and for most cases r belongs to the interval $[30\,,\,60]$. At each iteration, the criterion and the matrix $\mathcal{E}$ must be computed. The complexity of the criterion computation is O($NrL + N^3$). For the calculation of the matrix $\mathcal{E}$, we first need to compute the score function. The complexity of the matrix $\mathcal{E}$ computation (including the score function computation) is O($NrL + N^2L$). Finally, the complexity of one iteration is O($NrL + N^2L + N^3$). In practice, the convergence of the algorithm is usually obtained after p iterations, $p \in [20\,,\,60]$. Generally $N \ll L$ and the total computational complexity is $\mathrm{O}(p(NrL + N^2L))$. The computational complexities of `OrthOST` is the same. We recall that for the computation of a KLT, this complexity is $O(LN^2)$. The JADOST and KLT computation complexities are roughly the same.

7. Experimental results

In this section we present the performances in image compression of the optimal transforms described in the previous sections.

7.1 Description of the tests

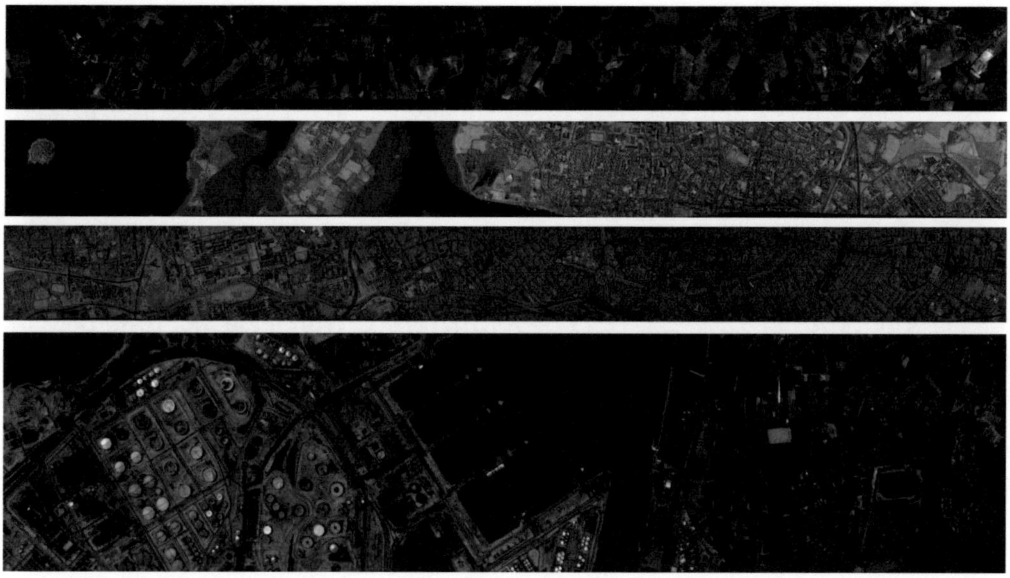

Fig. 1. From up to down *Moissac, Vannes, Toulouse, Port-de-Bouc*

We tested two kinds of multicomponent images: multispectral ones and hyperspectral ones. The multispectral images are[3] PLEIADES simulations of French cities with $N = 4$ components and coded on $N_b = 12\,$bpppb: *Moissac* with $N_c \times N_r = 320 \times 3152$, *Port-de-Bouc* with

[3] These images have been given by the French Space Agency CNES (Centre National d'Etudes Spatiales). They are described on the web site `http://smsc.cnes.fr/PLEIADES/`.

$N_c \times N_r = 320 \times 1376$, *Toulouse* with $N_c \times N_r = 352 \times 3816$, *Vannes* with $N_c \times N_r = 352 \times 3736$, ... The hyperspectral images are[4] AVIRIS images (*Moffett*, *Cuprite* and *Jasper*) with $N = 224$ components from the visible to the infrared and coded on $N_b = 16$ bpppb. They are originally acquired with $N_r \times N_c = 512 \times 624$, but for the simulations we kept only the 512 leftmost columns. Some images used in our tests are shown in figures 1 and 2. As already

Fig. 2. From left to right: *Moffett*, *Jasper* and *Cuprite*

mentioned, the 2-D DWT used in all our experiments is the Daubechies 9/7 which proved to be efficient in lossy image compression (Antonini et al., 1992; Taubman & Marcellin, 2002). For simplicity, we used only uniform scalar quantizers with a dead zone twice as large as the quantization step. The performances are evaluated in terms of bit-rate versus end-to-end distortion. For hyperspectral images, we considered four distortions. A first one is the mean square error (MSE) expressed in terms of the Signal to Noise Ratio, SNR $= 10\log_{10}(\sigma^2/D)$ where D is the actual end-to-end MSE distortion and $\sigma^2 = \sum_{i=1}^{N}\sum_{n=1}^{L}(X_i(n) - \mu)^2/(NL)$ is the empirical variance of the initial image with the empirical mean of the image $\mu = \sum_{i=1}^{N}\sum_{n=1}^{L} X_i(n)/(NL)$. A second distortion is the maximal absolute difference (MAD $= \max\{|X_i(n) - \widehat{X}_i(n)| : 1 \leq i \leq N \text{ and } 1 \leq n \leq L\}$), a third one is the maximum spectral angle MSA $= \max\left\{\text{acos}\left(\frac{\sum_{i=1}^{N} X_i(n)\widehat{X}_i(n)}{\sqrt{\sum_{i=1}^{N} X_i^2(n)\sum_{i=1}^{N}\widehat{X}_i^2(n)}}\right) : 1 \leq n \leq L\right\}$ and the last one is the mean absolute error (MAE $= \sum_{i=1}^{N}\sum_{n=1}^{L}|X_i(n) - \widehat{X}_i(n)|/(NL)$). With these four distortions, one can estimate the performances of a codec on usual applications of hyperspectral images, like classifications and targets detections (Christophe et al., 2005). For multispectral images, we considered only the MAD and the MSE distortions, the last one being expressed in terms of Peak of Signal to Noise Ratio, PSNR $= 10\log_{10}[(2^{N_b} - 1)^2/D]$, where D is the actual end-to-end MSE distortion and N_b is the number of bits per pixel and per band (bpppb) of the initial image. The bit-rate, expressed in bpppb, was measured on the actual bit stream obtained with the JPEG2000 coder EBCOT (Taubman, 2000) and its PCRD optimizer applied across components for optimal bit allocation. We used the Verification Model version 9.1 (VM9 (JPEG2000, 2001)) codec developed by the JPEG2000 group. The coefficients of $\mathbf{A}^{-1}$ (the inverse matrix of the optimal spectral transform) and the mean of each component are stored in the bitstream as `float32` data (this costs $32(N+1)/L$ bpppb). A difference exists between the aimed bit-rate and the actual bit-rate obtained with the VM9. In our tests, this difference does not exceed ± 0.001 bpppb and thus the precision of the PSNR is about ± 0.05 dB.

[4] These images have been downloaded from the NASA web site `http://aviris.jpl.nasa.gov/`.

7.2 Bit-rate versus distortion performances

In this subsection, we discuss and compare the bit-rate versus distortion performances of different spectral transforms. Table 1 presents the bit-rate of different transforms versus the

	PSNR (dB)								MAD							
bit-rate	0.25	0.50	0.75	1.00	1.50	2.00	2.50	3.00	0.25	0.50	0.75	1.00	1.50	2.00	2.50	3.00
	Moissac															
Id	36.37	39.59	41.93	43.89	47.22	50.16	52.93	55.66	**691**	366	253	187	108	68	49	38
KLT	38.61	42.39	45.24	47.63	51.51	54.49	56.98	59.44	716	381	**214**	**135**	79	48	32	25
JADOST	38.54	42.30	45.14	47.52	51.39	54.42	56.98	59.47	700	**357**	298	137	79	**46**	**31**	24
OrthOST	38.67	42.50	45.35	47.72	51.55	54.55	57.11	59.60	818	399	229	145	**78**	47	33	24
OST	**38.69**	**42.55**	**45.43**	**47.80**	**51.62**	**54.59**	**57.15**	**59.65**	745	496	215	138	**78**	48	32	**23**
	Port-de-Bouc															
Id	30.36	33.68	36.14	38.25	41.93	45.27	48.43	51.52	1198	653	544	361	198	135	85	64
KLT	**33.47**	37.74	40.88	43.45	47.53	50.89	53.82	56.53	922	513	**297**	**230**	139	**74**	**50**	35
JADOST	33.26	37.56	40.73	43.32	47.47	50.91	53.93	56.68	922	**504**	324	256	135	75	52	32
OrthOST	33.42	37.80	41.05	43.71	47.90	51.31	54.28	56.99	885	513	305	237	**122**	77	51	**31**
OST	33.46	**37.85**	**41.12**	**43.78**	**48.00**	**51.40**	**54.36**	**57.06**	**866**	557	351	256	129	82	53	35
	Vannes															
Id	39.25	42.89	45.67	47.99	51.77	54.80	57.51	60.11	603	269	178	109	63	42	29	21
KLT	41.36	45.71	48.78	51.11	54.38	56.82	59.24	61.79	482	219	148	86	51	33	**24**	18
JADOST	41.83	46.15	49.16	51.42	54.61	57.09	59.53	62.06	368	214	**134**	**84**	48	**29**	**24**	19
OrthOST	41.90	46.27	49.29	51.54	54.71	57.18	59.62	62.16	**354**	**190**	135	91	46	30	25	18
OST	**41.94**	**46.34**	**49.35**	**51.59**	**54.74**	**57.22**	**59.68**	**62.20**	393	204	138	88	**45**	33	25	**16**
	Strasbourg															
Id	30.82	34.19	36.73	38.91	42.70	46.09	49.20	52.13	1357	877	546	353	205	118	86	60
KLT	**32.51**	**36.59**	39.77	42.49	46.99	50.58	53.51	56.08	1041	927	**438**	403	184	90	52	**38**
JADOST	32.47	36.51	39.65	42.33	46.78	50.36	53.33	55.92	1082	**872**	543	371	189	85	56	45
OrthOST	**32.51**	**36.59**	39.78	42.50	47.01	50.61	53.55	56.11	**1010**	948	449	404	178	87	**50**	**38**
OST	32.49	**36.59**	**39.79**	**42.53**	**47.07**	**50.67**	**53.60**	**56.17**	1149	904	455	**289**	**162**	**81**	55	42
	Montpellier															
Id	32.17	35.23	37.59	39.62	43.17	46.30	49.17	51.95	1216	630	406	292	168	117	77	54
KLT	34.09	37.75	40.60	43.03	47.20	50.69	53.63	56.18	747	488	340	248	143	75	49	34
JADOST	34.09	37.72	40.55	42.99	47.15	50.62	53.55	56.13	782	501	**323**	245	124	81	51	36
OrthOST	34.08	37.90	40.92	43.46	47.72	51.16	54.01	56.55	**681**	**454**	338	255	**127**	**68**	47	**32**
OST	**34.14**	**37.99**	**41.01**	**43.56**	**47.79**	**51.21**	**54.06**	**56.60**	704	483	332	**239**	**127**	**68**	**46**	33
	Perpignan															
Id	33.71	36.90	39.34	41.43	45.04	48.17	51.04	53.78	984	526	332	230	158	89	62	42
KLT	36.51	40.44	43.29	45.60	49.33	52.36	54.99	57.52	726	435	245	172	**84**	**54**	41	29
JADOST	36.55	40.51	43.37	45.69	49.43	52.44	55.07	57.60	715	388	234	172	90	58	39	30
OrthOST	36.59	40.59	43.48	45.83	49.61	52.66	55.30	57.82	721	**371**	**232**	165	94	**54**	**37**	30
OST	**36.60**	**40.60**	**43.49**	**45.84**	**49.62**	**52.67**	**55.32**	**57.85**	**645**	383	292	**164**	94	55	38	**28**

Table 1. Bit-rate (in bpppb) versus PSNR (in dB) and versus MAD of different spectral transforms on multispectral images (best results are bolded). The bit-rate was computed with the VM9.

two distortions PSNR and MAD on six multispectral images and Tables 2 and 3 show the bit-rate of different transforms versus the four distortions SNR (in dB), MAE, MAD and MSA (expressed in degree °) on three hyperspectral images. All the 2-D DWT was applied with five levels of decomposition. We observe the well-known fact that spectral transforms perform significantly better than the identity matrix (i.e., no spectral transform), especially for hyperspectral images. Indeed, on six multispectral images (see Table 1) the average gains

	SNR (dB)								MAE						
bit-rate	0.25	0.50	0.75	1.00	1.50	2.00	2.50	3.00	0.50	0.75	1.00	1.50	2.00	2.50	3.00
	Moffett														
Id	25.45	30.37	33.97	36.94	41.78	45.76	49.15	52.01	24.32	16.93	12.52	7.62	5.02	3.48	2.51
KLT	44.21	47.68	50.08	51.97	54.76	57.10	59.21	61.04	3.83	3.03	2.49	1.82	1.39	1.07	0.85
JADOST	45.13	48.39	50.70	52.50	55.17	57.47	59.53	61.30	3.54	2.83	2.35	1.74	1.33	1.03	0.82
OrthOST	45.31	**48.57**	**50.87**	52.61	55.28	57.57	59.62	61.37	**3.47**	**2.78**	**2.32**	**1.72**	1.31	1.02	0.81
OST	**45.32**	48.56	**50.87**	**52.62**	**55.30**	**57.64**	**59.77**	**61.63**	**3.47**	**2.78**	**2.32**	**1.72**	**1.30**	**1.00**	**0.79**
	Cuprite														
Id	29.99	33.48	36.12	38.41	42.44	45.99	49.19	52.11	26.07	19.85	15.60	10.13	6.89	4.83	3.47
KLT	47.79	50.46	52.55	54.16	56.76	59.07	61.26	63.27	3.96	3.23	2.73	2.04	1.55	1.19	0.92
JADOST	48.22	50.85	52.86	54.42	56.97	59.27	61.44	63.43	3.80	3.13	**2.65**	1.99	1.51	1.16	0.90
OrthOST	48.25	50.88	**52.89**	**54.44**	56.99	59.29	61.46	63.44	**3.79**	**3.12**	**2.65**	**1.98**	1.51	1.16	0.90
OST	**48.26**	**50.89**	**52.89**	**54.44**	**57.01**	**59.34**	**61.56**	**63.60**	**3.79**	**3.12**	**2.65**	**1.98**	**1.50**	**1.14**	**0.88**
	Jasper														
Id	21.34	24.83	27.56	29.92	34.01	37.67	41.09	44.33	64.84	34.39	26.82	17.23	11.52	7.89	5.49
KLT	42.93	46.49	48.61	50.37	53.18	55.56	57.72	59.66	4.04	3.27	2.72	1.99	1.51	1.16	0.91
JADOST	43.56	46.89	48.97	50.67	53.43	55.78	57.91	59.83	3.87	3.15	2.63	1.94	1.47	1.13	0.89
OrthOST	43.66	46.94	49.02	50.73	53.47	55.81	57.94	59.85	3.85	3.13	2.62	1.93	1.46	1.13	0.88
OST	**43.70**	**46.96**	**49.05**	**50.74**	**53.50**	**55.87**	**58.03**	**60.01**	**3.84**	**3.12**	**2.61**	**1.92**	**1.45**	**1.11**	**0.87**

Table 2. Bit-rate (in bpppb) versus SNR (in dB) and versus MAE of different spectral transforms on hyperspectral images. The bit-rate was computed with the VM9.

of the KLT, JADOST, OrthOST and OST on Identity are respectively 3.6 dB, 3.6 dB, 3.8 dB and 3.8 dB. On three hyperspectral images (see Table 2) the average gains of the KLT, JADOST, OrthOST and OST on Identity are respectively 15.9 dB, 16.3 dB, 16.3 dB and 16.4 dB. Moreover, we can notice that the optimal transforms OrthOST and OST perform always a little better than the KLT at medium and high bit-rates: on six multispectral (resp. three hyperspectral) images the average gains of OrthOST and OST on KLT are about 0.23 dB and 0.28 dB (resp. 0.43 dB and 0.49 dB). On the multispectral images, we observed that JADOST performs roughly as the KLT for MSE distortion, sometimes slightly better, sometimes slightly worse, at any rate. On six images, the average gain of JADOST on the KLT is negligible (about 0.02 dB) at medium and high bit-rates (from 0.25 to 3 bpppb), whereas the average gain of OrthOST on JADOST is about 0.21 dB at the same rates. Nevertheless, on hyperspectral images, JADOST performs slightly but significantly better than the KLT for the four distortions tested at medium and high bit-rates (see Tables 2 and 3) and nearly reaches the OrthOST scores with a significantly lower computational complexity. The average gain of JADOST on the KLT (resp. OrthOST on JADOST) is 0.37 dB (resp. 0.07 dB) on the range $[0.25\,\text{bpppb}\,,\,3\,\text{bpppb}]$. Further, we can remark that there is an insignificant difference of performances between OrthOST and OST. This can be explained by the fact that transforms minimizing the criterion (16) must have a small value for $C_O(\mathbf{A})$, i.e., they must be close to orthogonality (see Remark 5). Therefore there is no advantage to use OST rather than the orthogonal transform OrthOST. In examining the MAD distortion we observe that on the multispectral images tested, at medium bit-rates (i.e. between 0.25 and 1.5 bpppb), OrthOST performs worse than the KLT (see Table 1). On the other hand, on the three hyperspectral (AVIRIS) images tested, for all the distortions measured, at medium and high bit-rates, JADOST and OrthOST perform *always* better than the KLT (see Tables 2 and 3). This is a nice finding, since the optimality of OrthOST is justified only for the MSE distortion and at high bit-rates.

	MSA (°)								MAD							
bit-rate	0.25	0.50	0.75	1.00	1.50	2.00	2.50	3.00	0.25	0.50	0.75	1.00	1.50	2.00	2.50	3.00
	Moffett															
Id	12.12	6.82	3.94	2.66	1.29	0.85	0.52	0.36	1676	781	492	1259	183	62	32	20
KLT	1.43	0.87	0.57	0.37	0.20	0.15	0.12	0.10	392	211	119	67	24	14	8	7
JADOST	1.15	0.59	0.42	0.27	0.19	**0.14**	**0.11**	**0.09**	279	120	67	44	18	12	8	**6**
OrthOST	0.96	**0.47**	**0.31**	**0.25**	**0.18**	**0.14**	**0.11**	**0.09**	261	**77**	49	**33**	**18**	**10**	8	**6**
OST	**0.86**	0.50	0.32	**0.25**	**0.18**	**0.14**	**0.11**	**0.09**	**207**	101	**46**	37	19	12	**7**	**6**
	Cuprite															
Id	5.30	2.81	2.20	1.57	1.01	0.59	0.40	0.26	659	360	253	185	110	62	61	40
KLT	0.42	0.25	0.22	0.15	0.12	**0.08**	**0.07**	0.06	154	135	100	54	26	16	10	8
JADOST	0.33	0.25	**0.16**	**0.14**	**0.10**	**0.08**	**0.07**	**0.05**	**112**	**109**	61	39	20	**11**	**9**	**7**
OrthOST	**0.32**	0.25	0.17	**0.14**	**0.10**	**0.08**	**0.07**	**0.05**	113	110	61	**37**	22	**11**	**9**	**7**
OST	0.35	**0.24**	**0.16**	**0.14**	**0.10**	**0.08**	**0.07**	**0.05**	113	**109**	**58**	42	**17**	**11**	**9**	**7**
	Jasper															
Id	18.20	12.53	7.88	5.70	3.87	2.14	1.41	1.01	1907	1220	732	559	241	160	84	55
KLT	0.91	0.53	0.43	0.34	0.26	0.20	0.15	0.12	225	151	82	57	30	15	10	7
JADOST	0.87	**0.51**	0.44	0.33	**0.24**	0.19	0.15	0.12	157	91	56	51	**20**	**11**	9	7
OrthOST	0.83	**0.51**	**0.40**	0.33	**0.24**	0.19	0.15	0.12	157	**84**	**46**	**34**	23	13	9	7
OST	**0.79**	**0.51**	0.41	**0.32**	**0.24**	**0.18**	**0.14**	**0.11**	**156**	86	48	**34**	22	14	**8**	**6**

Table 3. Bit-rate (in bpppb) versus MSA (in degree °) and versus MAD of different spectral transforms on hyperspectral images for the separable scheme. The bit-rate was computed with the VM9.

As already mentioned, the main drawback of the OrthOSTs returned by `JADO` and `OrthOST` algorithms is their heavy computational costs. In the next section we introduce quasi-optimal orthogonal spectral transforms.

8. Performances of exogenous quasi-optimal spectral transforms

8.1 Exogenous quasi-optimal spectral transforms

When one gets a set of images coming from one (and only one) spectrometer sensor, it is possible to compute an exogenous OrthOST from a learning basis extracted from this set. Generally, images from one spectrometer have the same number of bands and the same number of rows. However, the number of columns may vary. To compute an *exogenous* OrthOST, we first split the set of all images in two disconnected sets, one consisting of several images and which becomes the learning basis $\mathcal{L}$, the other constituted of the remaining images and which becomes the test subset. Then, all the images of the learning basis are connected band per band and row per row to construct a single virtual large image $\mathbf{X}$ having the same numbers of bands and rows as any image from the spectrometer and a large number of columns. This image is used as input of the OrthOST algorithm described in (Akam Bita et al., 2010a) and the output is the exogenous OrthOST associated with the learning basis $\mathcal{L}$. The exogenous KLT and exogenous JADOST are calculated similarly.

8.2 Performance comparison between exogenous and non exogenous OrthOSTs

In our tests, we used 10 images[5] (shown in Figure 3) from the imaging spectrometer MERIS on-board the satellite ENVISAT. This fifteen spectral bands spectrometer operates in the solar

[5] The images were acquired via the Data Disseminated System (http://dwlinkdvb.esrin.esa.it/DDS/) thanks to ESA/ESRIN.

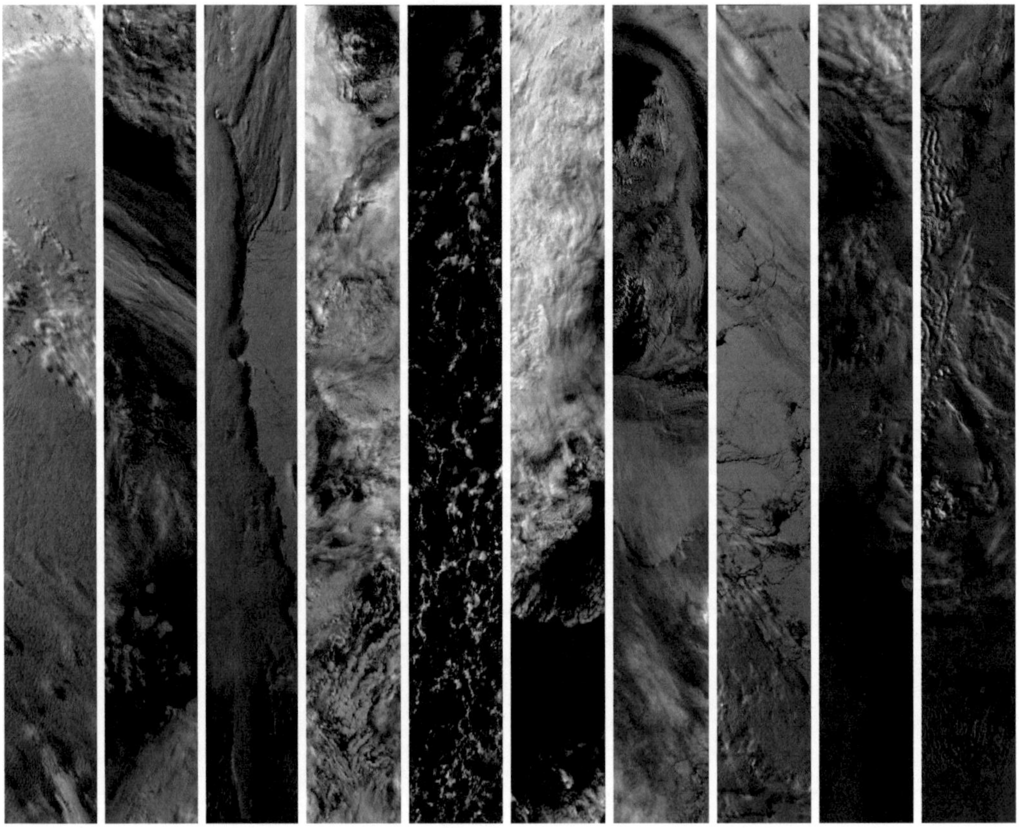

Fig. 3. Fifth component (corresponding approximately to the band [555 nm, 565 nm]) of the hyperspectral images MERIS, numbered 1–4, 6, 8, 10, 13, 15–16, from left to right

reflective spectral range of visible and near infrared light. Each band has a programmable width and a programmable location in the 390 nm to 1040 nm spectral range. As mentioned in (MERIS, 2006) the instrument scans the Earth's surface by the push-broom method, CCD arrays provide spatial sampling in the across-track direction, while the satellite's motion provides scanning in the along-track direction. The scene is imaged simultaneously across the entire spectral range, through a dispersing system, onto the CCD array. Therefore there is no problem of deregistration on the MERIS images. The ten images of our tests have all the same dimensions: $N_r = 128$, $N_c = 1121$ and $N = 15$. They are originally coded on $N_b = 16$ bpppb and they were acquired with the same fifteen spectral bands. To construct exogenous KLT and exogenous OrthOST, we split the ten MERIS images in two disconnected sets, one constituted of seven images (the learning basis), the other constituted of the three remaining images (the test subset). We considered 13 various learning bases, denoted $\mathcal{L}_i$ $(1 \leq i \leq 13)$ which are presented in Table 4. The bit-rate is computed with the Verification Model version 9 (VM9 (JPEG2000, 2001)). Note that the exogenous transforms are fixed (i.e., they do not adapt to the encoded image), hence they are known by the decoder and have not to be transmitted. However, in the lossy compression results given in Table 5 with the VM9, the inverse of the spectral transform is coded in the bit-stream (it costs less than 0.001 bpppb).

	$\mathcal{L}_1$	$\mathcal{L}_2$	$\mathcal{L}_3$	$\mathcal{L}_4$	$\mathcal{L}_5$	$\mathcal{L}_6$	$\mathcal{L}_7$	$\mathcal{L}_8$	$\mathcal{L}_9$	$\mathcal{L}_{10}$	$\mathcal{L}_{11}$	$\mathcal{L}_{12}$	$\mathcal{L}_{13}$
Meris1	×	×		×		×	×	×		×		×	×
Meris2	×	×		×		×		×	×	×	×		×
Meris3	×	×			×	×	×		×	×	×		×
Meris4	×	×	×	×	×		×	×		×	×	×	
Meris6	×		×	×	×	×	×			×	×	×	
Meris8	×		×	×	×			×	×	×		×	×
Meris10	×		×		×	×	×	×	×		×	×	
Meris13		×	×				×	×	×	×	×	×	×
Meris15		×	×	×	×	×	×		×		×		×
Meris16		×	×	×	×	×		×	×			×	×

Table 4. Various learning bases, denoted $\mathcal{L}_i$ ($1 \leq i \leq 13$) and constituted of seven MERIS images each

In Table 5 we present the performances obtained with two images when the learning basis varies. Among all the tests we made, we chose to show the best and worst cases obtained with an exogenous OrthOST. For this, the PSNR of a spectral transform is compared to that obtained with the KLT by subtracting, and we considered that difference of PSNR at 1 bpppb. The best and worst cases correspond respectively to the tested images *MERIS2* and *MERIS8*. We can see that for *MERIS2*, the exogenous OrthOST performs significantly better than the KLT at all rates for both MSE and MAE global distortions. Whereas for both MAD and MSA local distortions, exogenous OrthOST and KLT have roughly the same performance, the winner depending on the bit-rate. A more interesting result is the worst case: at bit-rates not greater than 1 bpppb, the worst exogenous OrthOST performs worse than the worst exogenous KLT and this trend is reversed for bit-rates larger than 1.0 dB. Moreover, the loss of PSNR compared to the KLT is 4.3 dB at 1 bpppb, however, the difference of PSNR between the KLT and identity (i.e., no spectral transform) is particularly high here (30 dB). For the other eight tested images, the loss of PSNR of the **worst** exogenous OrthOST with respect to the KLT, is not greater that 2.5 dB, at all bit-rates. Moreover, it is always smaller than the loss of PSNR of the **best** exogenous KLT with respect to the KLT. An example is shown in Fig. 4, where the bit-rate is computed either with the VM9 or the Bit Plane Encoder (BPE) (CCSDS-1, 2007) recommended by the CCSDS (Yeh et al., 2005). In order to compute the bit-rate with the BPE, we proceeded as follows: first, for each transformed component we computed a few hundred points of the graph that links mean square error to bit-rate, then we applied the algorithm by Shoham and Gersho (Shoham & Gersho, 1988) to optimally allocate distortions between components for given maximal total bit-rates.

In average on the 10 images, the loss of PSNR of the **worst** exogenous OrthOST with respect to the KLT is significantly smaller than the one of the **best** exogenous KLT (see Table 6). It is no longer the case for exogenous JADOST. We observed the importance of the learning basis, whose influence can range from 0 dB to −4 dB. In other words, when the learning basis is well chosen (depending on the scene and not only on the spectrometer), one can expect a loss of PSNR of an exogenous OrthOST with respect to the KLT not greater than 0.4 dB. Whereas, when it is badly chosen, the same loss of PSNR should be limited to 4 dB. However, these values are only indicative and should not be considered definitive, because they were obtained on a set of 10 MERIS images, which was not proven to be statistically significant.

We observed good performances of exogenous OrthOST used with the VM9 and in (Akam Bita et al., 2010c) the authors observed that, associated with the BPE and the optimal bit allocation

	PSNR (dB)							MAD						
bit-rate	0.25	0.50	0.75	1.00	1.50	2.00	3.00	0.25	0.50	0.75	1.00	1.50	2.00	3.00
	MERIS2													
Id	39.40	42.13	44.20	45.99	49.22	52.26	58.26	5878	3271	2369	2226	1258	850	443
KLT	54.87	63.81	69.60	73.66	79.29	83.02	88.39	1407	564	229	140	65	27	13
JADOST	55.65	65.04	70.53	74.49	80.02	83.66	88.92	1309	465	197	134	56	26	13
OrthOST	55.65	65.41	71.15	75.23	80.66	84.17	89.33	1354	397	189	119	48	22	12
exo3_KLT	54.11	62.36	67.79	*71.85*	77.77	81.86	87.53	1392	511	256	159	72	37	16
exo3_JADOST	55.11	64.01	69.53	73.46	78.82	82.78	88.23	1313	434	228	121	191	37	15
exo3_OrthOST	55.35	64.48	70.15	**74.18**	79.71	83.40	88.72	1267	476	240	134	53	28	13
exo5_KLT	54.08	62.37	67.89	**72.04**	78.05	82.11	87.69	1326	536	325	154	68	41	15
exo5_JADOST	55.12	64.01	69.54	73.48	79.08	82.88	88.30	1289	398	228	**117**	58	28	13
exo5_OrthOST	55.36	64.46	70.11	*74.13*	79.70	83.42	88.74	1314	497	257	134	49	26	12
exo7_KLT	54.69	62.92	68.09	72.00	77.79	81.84	87.52	1226	602	265	*183*	66	43	16
exo7_JADOST	55.22	63.97	69.14	*72.88*	78.32	82.26	87.86	1236	524	244	*165*	64	39	14
exo7_OrthOST	55.61	64.94	70.32	**74.18**	79.57	83.25	88.60	1418	504	238	**128**	56	28	13
exo12_KLT	54.13	62.37	67.83	71.95	77.99	82.07	87.66	1432	513	312	**152**	68	42	15
exo12_JADOST	55.13	64.02	69.54	**73.50**	79.08	82.87	88.30	1289	435	258	136	52	30	14
exo12_OrthOST	55.35	64.48	70.14	74.15	79.72	83.42	88.73	1305	481	221	*139*	47	30	13
	MERIS8													
Id	35.22	38.02	40.17	42.11	45.67	49.06	55.71	9723	5652	4123	3068	2050	1313	626
KLT	53.85	62.69	68.09	72.11	77.71	81.48	87.18	2638	1192	411	228	87	37	17
JADOST	54.21	63.68	69.39	73.44	78.83	82.35	87.91	2838	709	262	148	50	31	15
OrthOST	54.2	63.86	69.61	73.7	79.07	82.58	88.12	2773	705	305	130	51	26	15
exo2_KLT	52.22	59.49	64.16	68	73.95	78.34	84.79	3501	1504	608	*400*	149	51	24
exo2_JADOST	51.19	58.64	63.66	**67.83**	73.93	78.83	85.2	3536	1608	646	321	501	59	21
exo2_OrthOST	50.54	58.19	63.46	*67.8*	74.39	78.95	85.29	3446	1471	592	326	133	46	20
exo6_KLT	52.62	59.99	64.57	**68.16**	73.81	78.24	84.77	2813	973	471	**255**	115	59	23
exo6_JADOST	52.3	59.46	63.86	*67.4*	73.16	77.43	84.44	2670	1077	547	312	138	229	23
exo6_OrthOST	51.57	59.7	64.95	**68.96**	75.01	79.36	85.6	2871	1195	482	**290**	91	51	20
exo7_KLT	52.49	59.68	64.18	*67.83*	73.63	78.06	84.59	2887	1013	469	287	126	70	23
exo7_JADOST	52.28	59.45	63.85	67.44	73.31	77.92	84.6	2689	980	543	*328*	135	70	22
exo7_OrthOST	51.71	59.29	64.16	68.03	74.14	78.69	85.11	2768	1147	451	326	115	51	22
exo11_KLT	52.56	59.87	64.43	68.06	73.76	78.16	84.67	2885	876	459	**255**	104	68	24
exo11_JADOST	52.28	59.49	63.94	67.6	73.49	78.08	84.7	2610	961	525	**290**	126	67	23
exo11_OrthOST	51.89	59.59	64.64	68.73	75.01	79.44	85.68	2909	1130	441	*346*	131	47	19
	MSA (in °)							MAE						
	MERIS2													
Id	34.94	24.67	19.57	14.91	10.70	8.05	4.37	503.5	377.8	302.7	248.5	173.7	123.3	62.17
KLT	8.63	2.91	1.62	1.36	0.42	0.23	0.14	87.50	31.02	15.88	10.03	5.41	3.58	1.93
JADOST	10.41	2.66	1.54	0.83	0.38	0.22	0.11	80.46	27.18	14.45	9.22	4.99	3.33	1.82
OrthOST	9.47	2.55	1.57	1.07	0.44	0.21	0.11	80.22	25.87	13.43	8.48	4.65	3.15	1.73
exo3_KLT	10.26	4.19	2.05	**1.16**	0.54	0.28	0.13	95.35	36.85	19.79	*12.44*	6.43	4.09	2.13
exo3_JADOST	8.42	3.33	1.75	1.19	0.51	0.30	0.13	85.27	30.56	16.17	10.35	5.66	3.69	1.97
exo3_OrthOST	9.07	3.27	1.63	1.10	0.38	0.25	0.11	83.01	28.91	15.06	9.52	5.17	3.44	1.86
exo5_KLT	10.12	3.89	2.06	*1.38*	0.54	0.30	0.13	95.60	36.72	19.50	**12.18**	6.24	3.98	2.10
exo5_JADOST	8.61	3.59	1.96	**1.00**	0.49	0.28	0.12	85.21	30.49	16.12	10.31	5.55	3.64	1.95
exo5_OrthOST	9.03	3.25	1.49	1.08	0.41	0.24	0.12	82.71	28.94	15.10	*9.56*	5.18	3.43	1.86
exo7_KLT	8.59	3.79	1.89	1.37	0.53	0.32	0.13	89.55	34.46	19.04	12.20	6.40	4.10	2.14
exo7_JADOST	9.72	2.95	1.67	*1.29*	0.47	0.27	0.13	84.59	30.68	16.86	*11.01*	6.03	3.91	2.06
exo7_OrthOST	10.33	2.78	1.56	**0.90**	0.43	0.24	0.12	80.62	27.32	14.70	**9.49**	5.24	3.49	1.89
exo12_KLT	9.41	4.17	2.46	1.23	0.54	0.29	0.13	95.20	36.77	19.67	12.30	6.28	3.99	2.10
exo12_JADOST	8.45	3.23	1.89	1.25	0.45	0.26	0.13	85.00	30.51	16.15	**10.30**	5.55	3.65	1.95
exo12_OrthOST	8.97	3.20	1.57	*1.25*	0.39	0.26	0.12	82.91	28.88	15.07	9.54	5.17	3.43	1.86
	MERIS8													
Id	35.69	29.24	28.75	19.75	15.56	10.93	6.22	796.1	584.5	461.4	373.3	250.6	170.83	80.01
KLT	8.34	2.81	1.54	1.02	0.5	0.28	0.14	95.77	33.84	18.52	11.93	6.47	4.25	2.22
JADOST	8.39	2.28	1.29	0.74	0.36	0.24	0.13	92.49	30.45	16.06	10.28	5.71	3.86	2.04
OrthOST	7.71	2.96	1.25	0.77	0.36	0.25	0.11	92.67	29.82	15.68	10.02	5.56	3.76	1.99
exo2_KLT	8.2	3.92	2.53	*1.5*	0.63	0.34	0.17	113.61	46.49	27.87	18.44	9.75	6.04	2.93
exo2_JADOST	10.53	4.81	3.14	**1.44**	0.68	0.39	0.17	128.47	52.80	29.90	**18.97**	9.61	5.71	2.79
exo2_OrthOST	12.27	4.97	2.61	1.53	0.81	0.34	0.16	138.68	56.09	30.87	*19.22*	9.33	5.65	2.76
exo6_KLT	8.31	4.16	1.84	**1.29**	0.71	0.41	0.17	109.55	44.79	26.67	**18.02**	9.84	6.09	2.94
exo6_JADOST	8.75	4.22	2.17	1.46	0.85	0.45	0.18	113.05	46.89	28.35	19.25	10.47	6.55	3.05
exo6_OrthOST	10.18	3.47	1.87	**1.24**	0.55	0.35	0.17	123.22	47.09	25.79	16.51	8.67	5.39	2.67
exo7_KLT	8.84	3.97	2.06	1.35	0.71	0.46	0.19	110.39	45.8	27.74	*18.67*	10.06	6.21	3
exo7_JADOST	8.10	3.58	2.00	*1.76*	0.71	0.45	0.17	113.27	46.72	28.58	*19.26*	10.32	6.30	3.00
exo7_OrthOST	9.89	4.05	2.28	*1.76*	0.68	0.38	0.19	120.79	48.94	28.22	18.41	9.52	5.8	2.82
exo11_KLT	8.18	4.12	1.95	1.3	0.68	0.46	0.18	110.01	45.14	27.14	18.32	9.93	6.15	2.97
exo11_JADOST	8.93	3.42	2.07	1.69	0.70	0.38	0.19	113.56	46.76	28.29	**18.97**	10.13	6.20	2.96
exo11_OrthOST	9.8	4.25	1.97	1.56	0.6	0.33	0.15	118.26	47.54	27.19	**17.15**	8.69	5.34	2.64

Table 5. Bit-rate (in bpppb) vs PSNR (in dB), vs MAD, vs MSA and vs MAE of various spectral transforms on two images. The exo*i*_KLT, exo*i*_JADOST and exo*i*_OrthOST correspond respectively to exogenous KLT, JADOST and OrthOST computed with the learning basis $\mathcal{L}_i$. The best (resp. worst) results of exogenous transforms at 1.0 bpppb are bolded (resp. in italics).

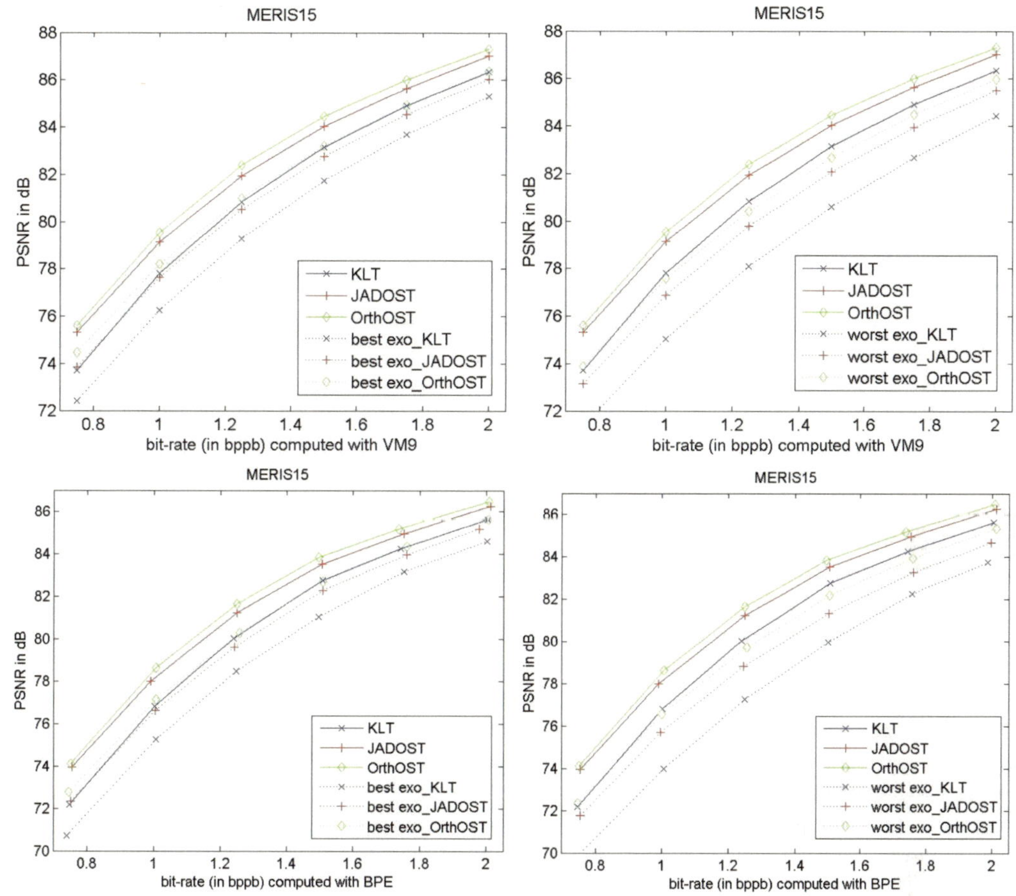

Fig. 4. PSNR (in dB) versus bit-rate (in bpppb) for various spectral transforms (KLT, JADOST OrthOST and (left) best exogenous KLT, best exogenous JADOST, best exogenous OrthOST or (right) worst exogenous KLT, worst exogenous JADOST, worst exogenous OrthOST). The image is *MERIS15* and the bit-rate is computed with first row: the VM9, second row: the BPE.

bit-rate (in bpppb)	0.25	0.50	0.75	1.00	1.50	2.00	3.00
mean (in dB) {PSNR(KLT) − worst exogenous PSNR(OrthOST)}	0.67	1.19	1.56	1.68	1.49	1.15	0.86
mean (in dB) {PSNR(KLT) − worst exogenous PSNR(JADOST)}	0.56	1.32	1.99	2.29	2.25	1.89	1.40
mean (in dB) {PSNR(KLT) − best exogenous PSNR(KLT)}	1.02	1.83	2.34	2.51	2.27	1.82	1.4

Table 6. Comparison of the averaged losses of PSNR with respect to the KLT for the worst exogenous OrthOST, the worst exogenous JADOST and the best exogenous KLT. The worst and best exogenous transforms are selected at 1.00 bpppb. The averages are computed on the ten images.

algorithm by Shoham and Gersho (Shoham & Gersho, 1988) for quantization and entropy coding, exogenous OrthOST still performs well (see Fig. 4). However, the VM9 and the Shoham and Gersho algorithm both have a too high computational complexity for a coder on-board a satellite. In (Gutzwiller et al., 2009), the authors propose an extension to multicomponent images of the well-known 2-D SPIHT encoder that has not the shortcoming of a high computational cost for bit-rate allocation.

9. Conclusion

In this chapter, we have studied the problem of finding optimal spectral transforms associated with fixed 2D discrete wavelet transforms in coding of multi- and hyper-spectral images, for a compression scheme that is compatible with the JPEG2000 Part 2 standard. We clarified the criterion that gives, when minimized, an optimal transform under high-rate entropy constraint scalar quantization hypothesis and when one scalar quantizer per subband and per component is applied. We showed the link between the criterion and the mutual information contrast used in independent component analysis. We derived a criterion minimized by an orthogonal optimal transform when the data are Gaussian. Then we gave three algorithms that return the spectral transforms that minimize the JPEG2000 compatible criterion, two under the constraint of orthogonality — one of which assuming Gaussian data — and the third with no constraint, but invertibility. Finally, we have tested the optimal transforms on satellite multi- and hyper-spectral images and found that for hyperspectral images the orthogonal optimal transform OrthOST and JADOST performs a little better than the KLT for four distortion measures that permit to evaluate the performances of the codec in applications of hyperspectral images like classifications or target detections. However the computational complexity of the optimal transform is too heavy for actual applications. Last we have presented the exogenous orthogonal quasi-optimal spectral transforms, that have a significantly smaller complexity, and their performances in lossy coding. In future works, we will study the problem of designing optimal spectral filters (i.e. a convolutive rather than an instantaneous mixture) in lossy compression of multi- and hyper-spectral images.

10. References

Akam Bita, I. P., Barret, M., Dalla Vedova, F. & Gutzwiller, J.-L. (2008). Onboard compression of hyperspectral images using an exogenous orthogonal quasi-optimal transform, *Proceedings of On-Board Payload Data Compression Workshop*, Noordwijk (The Netherlands).

Akam Bita, I. P., Barret, M. & Pham, D.-T. (2010a). On optimal transforms in lossy compression of multicomponent images with JPEG2000, *Signal Processing* Vol. 90(No. 3): 759–773.

Akam Bita, I. P., Barret, M. & Pham, D.-T. (2010b). On optimal orthogonal transforms at high bit-rates using only second order statistics in multicomponent image coding with JPEG2000, *Signal Processing* Vol. 90(No. 3): 753–758.

Akam Bita, I. P., Barret, M., Vedova, F. D. & Gutzwiller, J.-L. (2010c). Lossy and lossless compression of MERIS hyperspectral images with exogenous quasi-optimal spectral transforms, *Journal of Applied Remote Sensing* Vol. 4: 1–15.

Antonini, M., Barlaud, M., Mathieu, P. & Daubechies, I. (1992). Image coding using wavelet transform, *IEEE Transactions on Image Processing* Vol. 1(No. 2): 205–220.

Barret, M., Akam Bita, I. P., Gutzwiller, J.-L. & Dalla Vedova, F. (2009). Lossy hyperspectral image coding with exogenous quasi optimal transforms, *Proceedings Data Compression Conference*, Snowbird (USA), pp. 411–419.

Barret, M., Gutzwiller, J.-L. & Hariti, M. (2011). Low complexity hyperspectral image coding using exogenous orthogonal optimal spectral transform (OrthOST) and degree-2 zerotrees, *IEEE Transactions on Geoscience and Remote Sensing* Vol. 49(No. 5).

CCSDS-1 (2007). Image data compression, *Report concerning space data system standards, CCSDS 120.1-G-1, Green book* .

Chang, C.-I., Ramakrishna, B., Wang, J. & Plaza, A. (2010). Low-bit rate exploitation-based lossy hyperspectral image compression, *Journal of Applied Remote Sensing* Vol. 4: 1–24.

Christophe, E., Léger, D. & Mailhes, C. (2005). Quality criteria benchmark for hyperspectral imagery, *IEEE Transactions on Geoscience and Remote Sensing* Vol. 43(No. 9): 2103–2114.

Christophe, E., Mailhes, C. & Duhamel, P. (2006). Best anisotropic 3-D wavelet decomposition in a rate-distortion sense, *Proceedings of International Conference on Acoustic, Speech and Signal Processing*, Toulouse (France), pp. II–17–20.

Dragotti, P. L., Poggi, G. & Ragozini, A. R. P. (2000). Compression of multispectral images by three-dimensional SPIHT algorithm, *IEEE Transactions on Geoscience and Remote Sensing* Vol. 38(No. 1): 416–428.

Du, Q. & Fowler, J. E. (2007). Hyperspectral image compression using JPEG2000 and principal component analysis, *IEEE Geoscience and Remote Sensing Letters* Vol. 4: 201–205.

Du, Q. & Fowler, J. E. (2008). Low-compexity principal component analysis for hyperspectral image compression, *International Journal of High Performance Computing Applications* Vol. 22: 438–448.

Flury, B. N. & Gautschi, W. (1986). An algorithm for simultaneous orthogonal transformation of several positive definite symmetric matrices to nearly diagonal form, *SIAM Journal on Scientific and Statistical Computing* Vol. 7(No. 1): 169–184.

Fowler, J. E. & Rucker, J. T. (2007). chap 14: 3D wavelet-based compression of hyperspectral imagery, *in* C.-I. Chang (ed.), *Hyperspectral Data Exploitation: Theory and Applications*, John Wiley & Sons, Hoboken.

Gersho, A. & Gray, R. M. (1992). *Vector quantization and signal compression*, Kluwer Academic Publisher.

Gray, R. M. & Neuhoff, D. L. (1998). Quantization, *IEEE Transactions on Information Theory* Vol. 44(No. 6): 2325–2384.

Gutzwiller, J.-L.and Hariti, M., Barret, M., Christophe, E., Thiebaut, C. & Duhamel, P. (2009). Extension du codeur SPIHT au codage d'images hyperspectrales, *Proceedings of Colloquium COmpression et REprésentation des Signaux Audiovisuels (CORESA)*, Toulouse (France).
URL: *http://liris.cnrs.fr/Documents/Liris-4087.pdf*

JPEG2000 (2001). JPEG2000 verification model 9.1 (technical description), *ISO/IEC JTC 1/SC 29/WG 1 WG1 N2165* pp. 1–213.

MERIS (2006). MERIS detailed instrument description, *European Space Agency* .
URL: *http://envisat.esa.int/instruments/meris/*

Narozny, M., Barret, M., Pham, D.-T. & Akam Bita, I. P. (2005). Modified ICA algorithms for finding optimal transforms in transform coding, *Proceedings of IEEE International Symposium on Image and Signal Processing and Analysis*, Zagreb (Croatie), pp. 111–116.

Narozny, M., Barret, M. & Pham, D.-T. (2008). ICA based algorithms for computing optimal 1-D linear block transforms in variable high-rate source coding, *Signal Processing* Vol. 88(No. 2): 268–283.

Papoulis, A. (1984). *Probability, Random Variables, and Stochastic Processes*, McGraw-Hill.

Penna, B., Tillo, T., Magli, E. & Olmo, G. (2007). Transform coding techniques for lossy hyperspectral data compression, *IEEE Transactions on Geoscience and Remote Sensing* Vol. 45(No. 5): 1408–1421.

Pham, D.-T. (2004). Fast algorithms for mutual information based independent component analysis, *IEEE Transactions on Signal Processing* Vol. 52(No. 10): 2690–2700.

Pham, D.-T. (2005). Entropy of random variable slightly contaminated with another, *IEEE Signal Processing Letters* Vol. 12(No. 7): 536–539.

Rucker, J. T., Fowler, J. E. & Younan, N. H. (2005). JPEG2000 coding strategies for hyperspectral data, *Proceedings of International Geoscience and Remote Sensing Symposium*, Seoul (Korea), pp. 128–131.

Said, A. & Pearlman, W. A. (1996). A new, fast and efficient image codec based on set partitioning in hierarchical trees, *IEEE Transactions on Circuits and Systems for Video Technology* Vol. 6(No. 3): 243–250.

Shoham, Y. & Gersho, A. (1988). Efficient bit allocation for an arbitrary set of quantizers, *IEEE Transactions on Acoustics, Speech, and Signal Processing* Vol. 36(No. 9): 1445–1453.

Taubman, D. S. (2000). High performance scalable compression with EBCOT, *IEEE Transactions on Image Processing* Vol. 9(No. 7): 1158–1170.

Taubman, D. S. & Marcellin, M. W. (2002). *JPEG2000: Image Compression Fundamentals, Standards and Practice*, Kluwer Academic, Place of publication.

Thiebaut, C., Lebedeff, D., Latry, C. & Bobichon, Y. (2006). On-board compression algorithm for satellite multispectral images, *Proceedings of Data Compression Conference*, Snowbird (USA), pp. 28–30.

Usevitch, B. (1996). Optimal bit allocation for biorthogonal wavelet coding, *Proceedings of Data Compression Conference*, Snowbird (USA), pp. 387–395.

Vaisey, J., Barlaud, M. & Antonini, M. (1998). Multispectral image coding using lattice VQ and the wavelet transform, *Proceedings of IEEE International Conference on Image Processing*, Chicago (USA), pp. 307–311.

Woods, J. W. & Naven, T. (1992). A filter based bit allocation scheme for subband compression of HDTV, *IEEE Transactions on Image Processing* Vol. 1(No. 3): 436–440.

Yeh, P. S., Armbruster, P., Kiely, A., Masschelein, B., Moury, G. & Schafer, C. (2005). The new CCSDS image compression recommendation, *Proceedings of IEEE Aerospace Conference*, Big Sky (USA), pp. 1–8.

Part 3

Discrete Wavelet Transforms for Watermaking

11

Watermarking-Based Image Authentication System in the Discrete Wavelet Transform Domain

Clara Cruz Ramos, Rogelio Reyes Reyes, Mariko Nakano Miyatake and Héctor Manuel Pérez Meana
SEPI ESIME Culhuacan, National Polytechnic Institute of México, México City, México

1. Introduction

Nowadays, digital images and video are gradually replacing their conventional analog counterparts. This is quite understandable because digital format is easy to edit, modify, and exploit. Digital images and videos can be readily shared via computer networks and conveniently processed for queries in databases. Also, digital storage does not age or degrade with usage. On the other hand, thanks to powerful editing programs, it is very easy even for an amateur to maliciously modify digital media and create "perfect" forgeries. It is usually much more complicated to tamper with analog tapes and images. Tools as digital watermarks help us establish the authenticity and integrity of digital media and can prove vital whenever questions are raised about the origin of an image and its content.

A digital watermarking technique embeds an invisible signal with an imperceptible form for human audio/visual systems, which is statistically undetectable and resistant to lossy compression and common signal processing operations. So far there some content authentication of digital image methods, which can be classified in two groups: watermarking based technique (Hsu & Wu, 1999) and digital signature based technique (Friedman, 1993). Some authors had written about digital image authentication systems (Wong, 1998; Holiman & Memos, 2000; Wong & Memon 2001; Celik, et al, 2002; Monzoy, et al, 2007; Cruz, et al, 2008; Cruz, et al, 2009; Hernandez, et al, 2000; Lin & Chang 2001; Maeno, 2006; Hu & Chen, 2007; Zhou, et al, 2004; Lu & Liao 2003) and are classified in three categories: complete authentication, robust authentication and content authentication (Liu & Steinebach, 2006). Complete authentication refers to techniques that consider the whole piece of multimedia data and do not allow any manipulation (Yeung & Mintzer, 1997; Wu & Liu, 1998). Because the non-manipulable data are like generic messages, many existing message authentication techniques can be directly applied. For instance, digital signatures can be placed in the LSB of uncompressed data, or the header of compressed data. Then, manipulations will be detected because the hash values of the altered content bits may not match the information in the altered digital signature.

We define robust authentication as a technique that treats altered multimedia data as authentic if manipulation is imperceptible. For example, authentication techniques, that tolerate lossy compression up to an allowable level of quality loss and reject other manipulations, such as tampering, belong to this category.

Content authentication techniques are designed to authenticate multimedia content in a semantic level even though manipulations may be perceptible. Such manipulations may include filtering, color manipulation, geometric distortion, etc. We distinguish these manipulations from lossy compression because these perceptible changes may be considered as acceptable to some observers but may be unacceptable to others.

A common objective for authentication is to reject the crop-and-replacement process that may change the meaning of data. Many robust watermarking techniques in literature are designed to be robust to all manipulations for copyright protection purpose. They usually fail to reject the crop-and–replacement process so that they are not suitable for robust authentication and content authentication.

An authentication system can be considered as effective if it satisfies the following requirements:

1. Sensibility: The authenticator is sensitive to malicious manipulations such as crop-and-replacement.
2. Robustness: The authenticator is robust to acceptable manipulations such as lossy compression, or other content-preserving manipulations.
3. Security: The embedded information bits cannot be forged or manipulated. For instance, if the embedded watermarks are independent of the content, then an attacker can copy watermarks from one multimedia data to another.
4. Portability: Watermarks have better portability than digital signatures because the authentication can be conducted directly from only received content.
5. Identification of manipulated area: Users may need partial information. The authenticators should be able to detect location of altered areas, and verify other areas as authentic.

Regardless of security issues, watermarking capacity is determined by invisibility and robustness requirements. There are three dimensions shown in Figure 1. If one parameter is determined, the other two parameters are inversely proportional. For instance, a specific application may determinate how many bits of message are needed. After the embedded amount is decided, it always exists a trade-off between visual quality and robustness which must be considered. Robustness refers to the extraction of embedded bits with an error probability equal to or approaching zero. Watermark imperceptibility (invisibility) represents the quality of watermarked image respect to the original one. In general, if we want to make our watermark more robust against attacks then a longer codeword or larger codeword amplitudes will be necessary to provide better error-resistence. However, visual quality degradation cannot be avoided. Another scenario may be that with a default visual quality, there exists a trade-off between the information quantity of embedded message and robustness. For instance, the fewer the message bits are embedded, the more redundant the code word can be. Therefore, the code word has better error correction capability against noise.

It is difficult for an authenticator to know the purpose of manipulation. A practical approach is to design an authenticator based on the manipulation method. In this work, we design an authenticator which accepts format transformation and lossless compression (JPEG). The authenticator rejects replacement manipulations because they are frequently used for attacks. Our authenticator does not aim to reject or accept, in absolute terms, other manipulation methods because the problem of whether they are acceptable or not depends on applications.

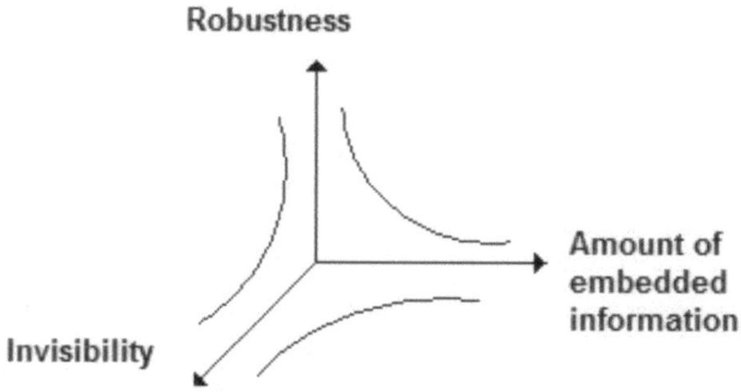

Fig. 1. Parameters of watermarking: Robustness, information quantity of embedded message and invisibility.

2. Previous techniques for robust authentication and content authentication

In Paquet, Ward & Pitas, 2003, a novel watermarking scheme to ensure the authenticity of digital images is presented. Their authentication technique is able to detect malicious tampering of images even if they have been incidentally distorted by common image processing operations. The image protection is achieved by the insertion of a secret author's identification key in the wavelet coefficients by their selective quantization. Their system uses characteristics of the human visual system to maximize the embedding energy while keeping good perceptual transparency and develop an image-dependent method to evaluate, in the wavelet domain, the optimal quantization step allowing the tamper proofing of the image. The nature of multiresolution discrete wavelet decomposition allows the spatial and frequency localization of image tampering. Experimental results show that system can detect unauthorized modification of images.

Kundur & Hatzinakos (Kundur & Hatzinakos, 1999), presented a fragile watermarking technique for the tamper proofing of still images. A watermark is embedded in the discrete wavelet domain by the quantization of the corresponding wavelet coefficients. The Haar wavelet is used for the image decomposition and a pseudo-random binary sequence is generated by a secret identification key. The rounding of the DWT coefficients to even or odd quantization steps embeds the zeros or ones of the watermark. The embedding locations are stored in the coefficient selection key, *ckey*. In addition, an image-dependent quantization key, *qkey*, is introduced to improve security against forgery and monitor specific changes to the image.

In the same line a digital image authentication procedure that allows the detection of malicious modifications, while staying robust to incidental distortion introduced by compression is presented in Yu, et al., 2000. A binary watermark is embedded in the wavelet transform domain. The insertion is again done by the even or odd quantization of selected wavelet coefficients. To increase the robustness of the scheme to image processing operations, the authors proposed to make the embedded watermark more robust by rounding the mean value of weighted magnitudes of wavelet coefficients to quantization levels specified by the predetermined function Q(x,q). The same function is also used in the blind detection process to retrieve the watermark privately by reversed quantization. In order to distinguish malicious tampering from incidental distortion, the amount of modification on wavelet coefficients introduced by incidental versus malicious tampering is modeled as Gaussian distributions with small vs. large variance. The probability of watermark detection error due to incidental alterations is shown to be smaller than the probability of watermark detection error due to malicious tampering because they produce comparatively smaller variance difference with the embedded marks. The authors argue that this grants a certain degree of robustness to the system and show that their method is able to authenticate JPEG compressed images without any access to the original unmarked image. However, the degree of image compression allowed by the detection procedure is not stated and the selection procedure of quantization parameters is not explained either.

In this work we develop a content authentication technique using imperceptible digital watermarking which is robust to malicious and incidental attacks for image authentication, embedding a digital signature as watermark. A digital signature is a set of features extracted from an image, and these features are stored as a file, which will be used later for authentication. To avoid the extra bandwidth needed for transmission of the signature in a conventional way; having extracted the digital signature we applied the discrete wavelet transform (DWT) to the image to embed the watermark in the sub band of lowest frequency, because we want the watermark insertion to be imperceptible to the Human Visual System and robust to common image processing such as JPEG compression and noise contamination. The proposed system is able to extract the watermark in full blind detection mode, which does not have access to the original host signal, and the watermark extracted has to be re-derived from the watermarked signal, this process increases the system security.

In the security community, an integrity service is unambiguously defined as one which insures that the sent and received data are identical. Of course, this binary definition is also applicable to image, however it is too strict and not well adapted to this type of digital document. Indeed, in real life situations images will be transformed, their pixel values will therefore be modified but not the actual semantic meaning. In other words, the problem of image authentication is released on the image content, for example: when modifications of the document may change its meaning or visually degrade it. In order to provide an authentication service for still images, it is important to distinguish between malicious manipulations, which consist of changing the content of the original image (captions, faces, etc.) and manipulations related to the usage of an image such as format conversion, compression, noise, etc.

Unfortunately this distinction is not always clear; it partly depends on the type of image and its usage. Indeed the integrity criteria of an artistic master piece and a medical image will not be the same. In the first case, a JPEG compression will not affect the perception of the image, whereas in the second case it may discard some of the fine details which would render the image totally useless. In the latter case, the strict definition of integrity is required. We applied the proposed algorithms in to grayscale and color no medical images.

3. Proposed watermarking algorithm

The figure 2(a) shows a general block diagram to the watermark insertion where we can see that original image is divided in non-overlapping blocks, we extracted a digital signature from each block then we insert a signature as watermark in the same block, finally all the watermarked blocks form the watermarked image. Figure 2(b) shows a general block diagram to the watermark extraction process from the watermarked block where we can see that is not necessary to now the original image to extract the digital signature. Finally in the verification process we compare the extracted watermark and the digital signature to determine if the image has been modified, or not.

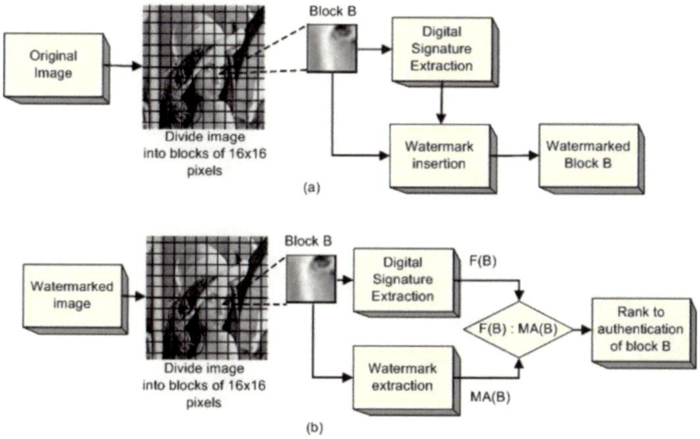

Fig. 2. (a) Watermark insertion system; (b) Watermark extraction system.

3.1 Digital signature generation

The algorithm used to extract the digital signature was proposed in Fridrich, 1999, and used by Chen, et al., 2001. The goal of this algorithm is to make a method for extracting bits from image blocks so that all similarly looking blocks, whether they are watermarked or attacked, will produce almost the same bit sequence of length N. Method is based on the observation that if a low-frequency DCT coefficient of an image is small in absolute value, it cannot be made large without causing visible changes to the image. Similarly, if the absolute value of a low-frequency coefficient is large, we cannot change it to a small value without influencing the image significantly. To make the procedure key-dependent, we replace DCT modes with low-frequency DC-free (i.e., having zero mean) random smooth patterns generated from a secret key (with DCT coefficients equivalent to projections onto the patterns). For each image, we calculate a threshold Th so that on average 50% of projections have absolute value larger than Th and 50% are in absolute value less than Th. This will maximize the information content of the extracted N bits.

Given an image I, we divide it into blocks of 16x16 pixels (for large images, larger block sizes could be used) as showed in Figure 3. Using a secret key K (a number uniquely associated with an author, movie distributor, or a digital camera) we generate N random matrices with entries uniformly distributed in the interval [0, 1]. Then, a low-pass filter is repeatedly applied to each random matrix to obtain N random smooth patterns. All patterns are then made DC-free by subtracting the mean value from each pattern. Considering the block and the pattern as vectors, the image block B is projected on each pattern P_i, $1 \leq i \leq N$ and its absolute value is compared with a threshold *Th* to obtain N bits b_i:

$$if|B.Pi| < Th \quad bi = 0$$

$$if|B.Pi| \geq Th \quad bi = 1 \tag{1}$$

Since the patterns P_i have zero mean, the projections do not depend on the mean gray value of the block and only depend on the variations in the block itself. The distribution of the projections is image dependent and should be adjusted accordingly so that approximately half the bits b_i are zeros and half are ones. This will guarantee the highest information content of the extracted N-tuple. This adaptive choice of the threshold becomes important for those image operations that significantly change the distribution of projections, such as contrast adjustment.

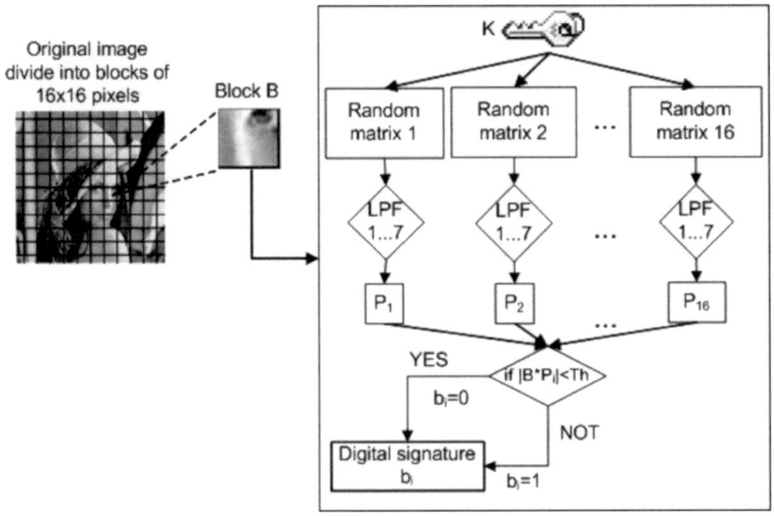

Fig. 3. Digital signature extraction process.

3.2 Wavelet transform for image signals

Two-dimensional DWT leads to a decomposition of approximation coefficients at level j in four components: the approximation at level j + 1, and the details in three orientations (horizontal, vertical, and diagonal).

Figure 4 describes the basic decomposition steps for images.

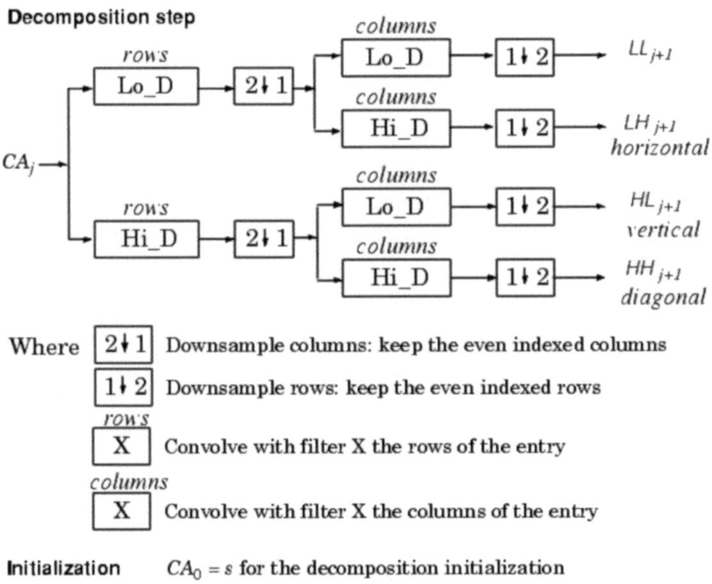

Fig. 4. Subband decomposition using 2D-DWT.

The subbands labeled LH_1, HL_1, and HH_1 represent the finest scale wavelet coefficients. In the present work, the wavelet transform is realized with Daubechies Wavelets of order 2. Using this wavelets, the image is decomposed into four subbands: LL_1, LH_1, HL_1 and HH_1.

3.3 Watermark embedding algorithm

Because we want the embedded watermark to be imperceptible to the Human Visual System (HVS) and robust to common image processing such as JPEG compression and contamination, we implement the algorithm proposed by Inoue, et al. 2000. In this method information data can be embedded in the lowest frequency components of image signals by using controlled quantization process. The data is then extracted by using both the quantization step-size and the mean amplitude of the lowest frequency components without access to the original image.

Once the digital signature is extracted, we applied the discrete wavelet transform (DWT) to embed the watermark, the subband $LL_1(i,j)$ is divided into small subblocks B_k with the size of $b_x \times b_y$ and calculate the mean M_k of the wavelet coefficients of B_k. A quantization step-size which is called the embedded intensity Q=5 is used, then we calculate the mean of the wavelet coefficients of B_k. The watermark information is embedded into the subblock B_k modifying the quantization value q and adds δM_k to the wavelet coefficients of B_k, as described in detail (Inoue, et al. 2000). Finally we construct the watermarked image using the inverse wavelet transform.

Figure 5 illustrates the embedding process; the data w_k =0 or 1 into a subblock B_k when b_x=b_y =2 and Q =5.

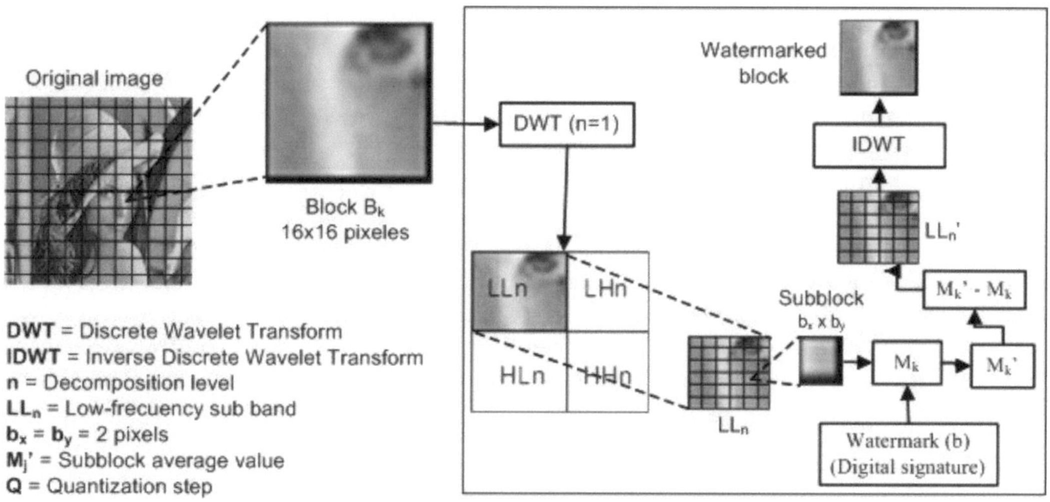

Fig. 5. Watermark insertion process.

3.4 Watermark extracting algorithm

We can extract the embedded data w by using the parameters n (decompose level), b_x, b_y, Q and LM′. Let I′ be the watermarked image, we decompose I′ for the scale 1 and obtain the lowest frequency components $LL_1'(i,j)$. Then we divide $LL_1'(i,j)$ into subblocks B_k with the size of $b_x x b_y$ and compute the mean M_k' of B_k and find the quantization value S from

$$S = int[(M_k') \, / \, Q\,] \tag{2}$$

Then, we extract the embedded binary data w_k as follows: if S is an even number, then w_k =0, otherwise w_k =1.

3.5 Authentication process

After the watermark w_k and the digital signature sequences are extracted from the watermarked image I′, we determines a threshold (Th_v) to decide using an XOR operation if the block is tampered or not, which is expressed in equation (3).

$$if \begin{cases} \sum \widetilde{w_k} \otimes \widetilde{b_k} \leq Th_v \ authentic\ block \\ \sum \widetilde{w_k} \otimes \widetilde{b_k} \geq Th_v \ modified\ block \end{cases} \tag{3}$$

Threshold Th_v was determined through trial and error; resulting value of Th_v was 4, it means that if bits number of digital signature extracted of the block authenticated has at least 12 of 16 bits equal, the block is consider as authentic else it is consider as modified. Although the block is considered modified, sometimes you do not get the same 16-bit digital signature extracted with respect to the original signature can be caused by any intentional modification, which is why we proposed the following process check.

3.6 Verification process

After the watermark w_k from the watermarked image I′ is extracted, we compare it with the digital signature extracted from I′. If they have some different blocks we make an "difference image" (I_{dif}).

According to evaluation carried out using 200 images, in authentication process, the following conclusion was reached: when error blocks are present in regions non intentional modified, these blocks are presented in isolation, as shown in figures 6(a,b), however in the case of images modified intentionally error blocks are detected in concentrated form as shown in figures 6(c,d), so when error blocks are detected isolated, means that region is authentic otherwise it is non-authentic. Therefore to establish a criterion to determine whether the change at a block is intentional or unintentional, we define the following rule:

If there are more than three consecutive error blocks in the region of I_{dif} the image was intentionally modified, otherwise the change was made by common signal processing as JPEG compression or noise. Applying the concept of connectivity between the 8 neighbors of error blocks, it can help us to identify intentionally modified regions of which are not. This criterion is represented mathematically by the equation (4).

$$region \begin{cases} Authentic\ \ if\ \tilde{B} \leq 3 \\ Tampered\ \ if\ \tilde{B} > 3 \end{cases} \tag{4}$$

were $\tilde{B}$ represents an error block, so if there are more than three consecutive error blocks in the region, it has been intentionally modified.

(a) Isolated error blocks

(b) Isolated error blocks

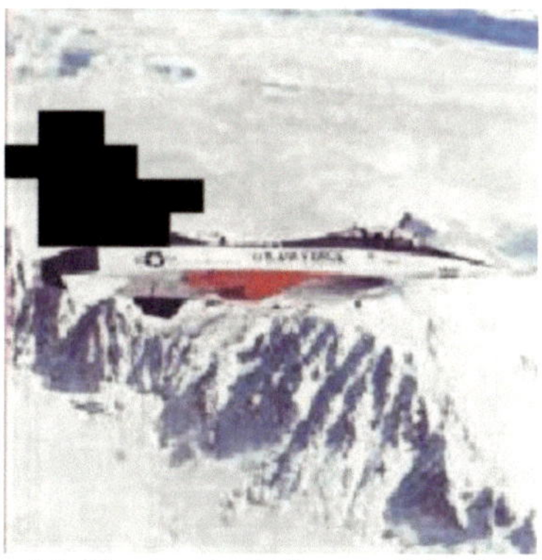

(c) Concentrated error blocks

(d) Concentrated error blocks

Fig. 6. (a,b) Non intentional modified image; (c,d) Intentionally modified image.

4. Experimental results

4.1 Digital signature robustness

To evaluate the robustness of the bit extraction procedure, we subjected the test image "Barbara" with 512x512 pixels and 256 gray levels to various image processing operations available in specialized commercial image manipulation software (we used Photoshop). The test image "Barbara" had 1024 blocks of 16x16 pixels. We extracted N=16 bits from each block for the original image and the manipulated image and calculated the average number of error over all 1024 blocks. The results are shown in Table 1.

Image name	Shine (%)	Average number of error bits
Barb_100	10	0
Barb_200	20	0
Barb_300	30	0
Barb_400	40	0
Barb_500	50	0
	Contrast (%)	
Barb_10	10	0
Barb_20	20	0
Barb_30	30	0
Barb_40	40	0
Barb_50	50	0
Ecualization		0.015
JPEG compression		
Quality factor		Average number of error bits
20, 25, 30, 35, 40, 45, 50, 55, 60, 65, 70, 75, 80, 85, 90, 95 and 100		2.15, 1.98, 1.78, 1.69, 1.51, 1.35, 1.30, 1.22, 1.11, 1.08, 0.98, 0.91, 0.75, 0.67, 0.5, 0.36 and 0.07
Impulsive noise		
Intensity	PSNR	Average number of error bits
0.0010	35.8258	0.58
0.0020	32.3782	0.98
0.0030	30.8060	1.16
0.0040	29.6593	1.23
0.0050	28.6105	1.87
0.0060	27.8483	2.01
0.0070	27.1725	2.22
0.0080	26.5314	2.53
0.0090	26.0121	2.85
0.0100	25.6005	2.92

Table 1. Average number of error recovered bits out of 16 bits after some image processing operations.

4.2 Semi-fragile watermark system performance

In order to confirm that the proposed digital watermark system is effective, we implemented some numerical experiments with attacks such as JPEG compression, impulsive and Gaussian noise and photomontage. Experimental results show that the algorithm is capable to determine whether the image has been altered. The algorithm was evaluated using 200 standard images. These images are 8 and 24 bits per pixel (bpp) grayscale and color images, which were 512x512 and 128x128 pixels in size showed in figure 7.

Another advantage of this algorithm is that the size and texture of the image doesn´t affect on the correct operation of the system.

(a) 8 bits per pixel (bpp) grayscale image

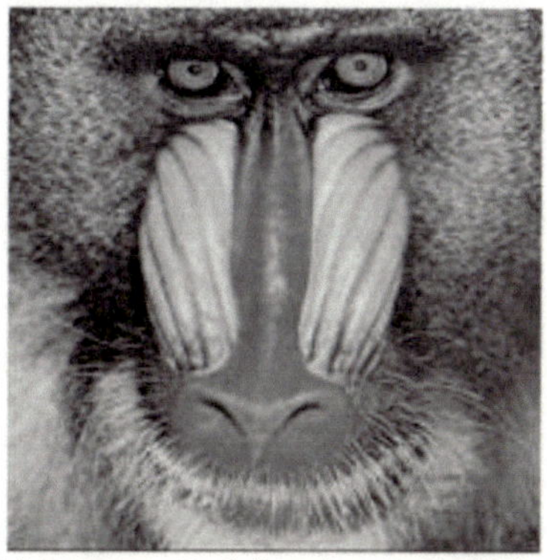

(b) 8 bits per pixel (bpp) grayscale image

(c) 24 bits per pixel (bpp) color image

(d) 24 bits per pixel (bpp) color image

Fig. 7. Some images used in the experimental process.

4.2.1 Watermarked image quality

In our system we use the peak signal to noise ratio (PSNR) to mesure the degradation of the image quality caused by watermarking, this value is given by (5),

$$PSNR_{dB} = 10\, log_{10} \frac{255^2}{\delta_q^2} \tag{5}$$

where δ_q^2 is the mean square of the difference between the original image and the watermarked one.

Figure 8 shows some examples of original images (in grayscale and color) together with their respective watermarked images and PSNR values, where we can see that watermarked images are to perceptually very similar to the original version. In table 2 PSNR values of some grayscale and color images are shown, where we can observe that the average PSNR value in the grayscale image is 45 dB's and in the color image is 50 dB's, so we can conclude that degradation in the watermarked image is not perceptible.

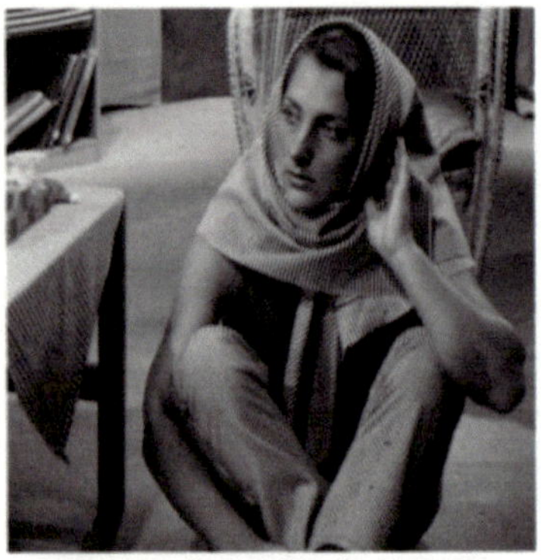

Original grayscale image

Watermarked grayscale image PSNR=45 dB

Original color image

Watermarked color image PSNR=49.80 dB

Fig. 8. Watermarked image quality.

Grayscale watermarked image	PSNR (dB´s)	Color watermarked image	PSNR (dB´s)
Barbara	45.059944	Plane	49.806491
Boat	44.966452	Mountain	49.848597
Bridge	45.007931	Lake	49.810409
Camera	45.056509	Chiles	49.853756
Chiles	45.003896	People	49.848703
Goldhill	44.959921	Lena	49.815038
Lena	44.958274	Home	50.342928
Baboon	45.041577	Girl	49.568472
Bird	44.962013		

Table 2. PSNR values of some grayscale and color watermarked tested images.

4.2.2 Robustness against JPEG compression

The authenticator is sometimes expected to pass only those images that are compressed by JPEG up to a certain compression ratio or quality factor (fc). For example, if the image is JPEG compressed below to image quality 75 (The Mathworks, 2008), the image is acceptable, otherwise, if it is more compressed, it will fail the test. The argument for failing highly compress images is that such images usually have poor quality and should not be considered as authentic. To satisfy this need, we calculate the increase of the number of the "different" signature bits after compression (error blocks). The number of the error blocks increases if the image is more compressed. We can set a threshold on this change to reject those images that have too many error blocks.

If the error blocks are isolated, we apply equation (4) to determinate if those blocks are result of a JPEG compression, however, if they are concentrated we are talking about an intentional attack. We called to this process "verification" and it helps us to differentiate between an intentional or non intentional attack.

Figure 9 shows the extracted results from the authentication JPEG compressed watermarked images with quality factors higher than 75 and their corresponding verified image; we can see that compressed images with quality factors higher than 75 have their error blocks (white blocks) isolated; consequently, before the verification process they are considered as not attacked.

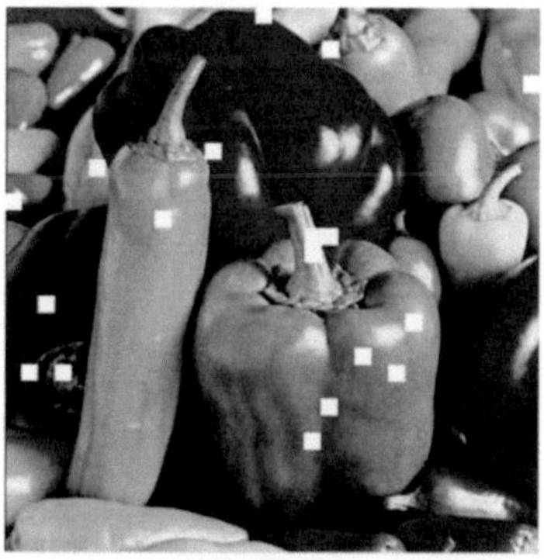

Error blocks of "chiles", with fc=75
Authenticated image

Verified image
(not attacked)

Error blocks of "boat", with fc=80
Authenticated image

Verified image
(not attacked)

Fig. 9. Tampered regions detection of the JPEG compressed images.

Table 3 shows some compression ratio where the JPEG compressed watermarked image is considered as authentic by the system. In this table we can see that in grayscale watermarked images were considered as authentic when their quality factor of JPEG compression was higher than 75 and in the color compressed images with a quality factor higher than 70.

4.2.3 Robustness against additive and Gaussian noise

We contaminate watermarked image with different levels of additive and Gaussian noise to simulate the communication channel noise. Tables 4 and 5 show the highest density and variance value of additive and Gaussian noise in grayscale and color images before the system considers the error blocks detected as intentionally tampered, these results indicate that the system is efficient in front of impulsive noise attacks because it supports a density= 0.002 which produces a PSNR average value equal to 32 dB between watermarked image and contaminated watermarked image; a similar case occurs whit the Gaussian noise; the highest variance that the system accepts is 0.00011 before it considered watermarked contaminated image as intentionally modified.

	Quality factor	Error blocks	Original size/ compresion	Bits/ pixel
Grayscale watermarked images				
Boat	80	5	257k/38.7k	1.20
Bridge	75	18	65k/14.6k	1.79
Camera	80	14	65k/10.3k	1.26
Chiles	75	18	257k/31.4k	0.97
Lena	75	4	65k/10.5k	1.29
Baboon	80	24	257k/72.1k	2.24
Bird	80	11	65k/7.56k	0.93
Color watermarked images				
Plane	70	13	193k/11k	0.45
Home	70	5	193k/9k	0.37
Girl	75	17	193k/10k	0.41
Chiles	65	17	193k/14k	0.58
Lake	70	14	193k/14k	0.58
Lena	65	2	193k/11k	0.45
Mountain	75	12	193k/12k	0.49
People	70	11	193k/9k	0.37

Table 3. Compression ratio of some JPEG compressed images considered as authentics.

Grayscale watermarked image	Density	Error blocks	PSNR (dB´s)	Color Watermarked image	Density	Error Blocks	PSNR (dB´s)
Barbara	0.002	27	32.6765	Plane	0.0016	9	33.0454
Boat	0.002	30	32.9256	Home	0.0016	15	33.5461
Bridge	0.002	17	32.1300	Girl	0.0015	18	32.4259
Camera	0.002	36	32.4250	Chiles	0.0024	8	31.4738
Chiles	0.002	26	32.0939	Lake	0.0018	7	32.0180
Goldhill	0.002	11	32.3100	Lena	0.0025	12	31.1327
Lena	0.002	14	32.0448	Mountain	0.0015	18	33.0446
Baboon	0.002	24	32.7793	People	0.0015	26	32.2085
Bird	0.0009	18	35.7967				

Table 4. Test to resistance to impulsive noise from grayscale and color watermarked images.

Grayscale watermarked image	Variance	Error blocks	PSNR (dB´s)	Color Watermarked image	Variance	Error blocks	PSNR (dB´s)
Barbara	0.00011	48	39.5594	Plane	0.00031	14	35.2396
Boat	0.0001	36	40.0032	Home	0.00027	15	35.5625
Bridge	0.00014	22	38.8350	Girl	0.00027	20	35.9495
Camera	0.00011	29	39.5884	Chiles	0.00033	21	35.1859
Chiles	0.00011	37	39.5761	Lake	0.00027	10	35.5499
				Lena	0.00031	16	35.2449
				Mountain	0.00027	24	35.5431
				People	0.00027	23	35.8596

Table 5. Test to resistance to gaussian noise from grayscale and color watermarked images.

4.2.4 Robustness against photomontage

Of course, an important aspect of our system is its ability to localize tampered regions into the image. For that reason, we have tampered the previously watermarked Bird and lake images and evaluated the ability of our system to detect. We found that the ability of our system to detect tampering is excellent (Figure 10) because our system detected correctly which group of blocks were modified intentionally and which were not into the watermarked image, based on the assumption explained in section 2.5. To tamper the images we used Photoshop. Figures 10(a) to 10(d) show the results of this evaluation in grayscale images and figures 10(e) to 10(g) the results of color images. Figures 10(c) and 10(g) show by white blocks the tampered detected by our system where we can see that its location is correct comparing 10(a) vs. 10(b) and 10(e) vs. 10(f) where the first are the watermarked images and the others are the tampered watermarked images. Finally in figure 10(d) we see that the verification is working well because it eliminates the isolated error blocks which were caused by the processing image.

5. Conclusion

The transition from analog to digital technologies is widely used, with the higher capacity of storage devices and data communication channels, multimedia content has become a part of our daily lives. Difital data is now commonly used in many areas such as education, entertainment, journalism, law enforcement, finance, health services, and national defense. The low cost of reproduction, storage, and distribution has added an additional dimension to the complexity of the problem. In a number of applications, multimedia needs to be protected for several reasons. Watermarking is a group of complementary technology that has been identified by content provider to protect multimedia data.

In this paper we have successfully developed a robust digital signature algorithm which is used as a semi-fragile watermarking algorithm for image authentication. The highest advantage of this combination besides the digital signature robustness and the watermark image imperceptibility, is that is not necessary an additional band width to transmit the digital signature, since this is embedded in the host image as a watermark. Besides to the extraction and authentication process, we propose a verification process, which helps us to differentiate between an intentional or non intentional modification applying the concept of connectivity between the 8 neighbors of error blocks.

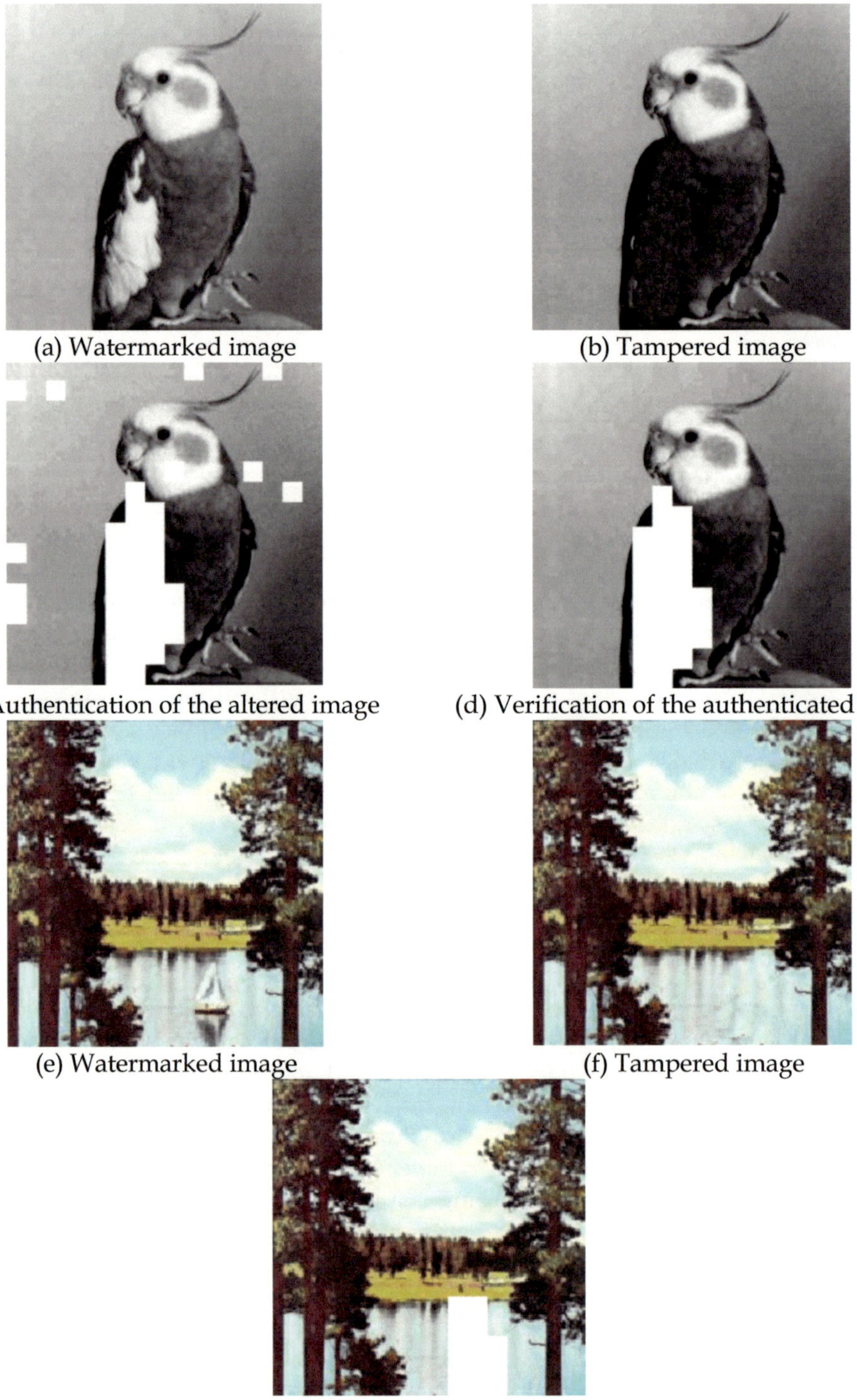

(a) Watermarked image (b) Tampered image

(c) Authentication of the altered image (d) Verification of the authenticated image

(e) Watermarked image (f) Tampered image

(g) Authentication of the altered image

Fig. 10. Authentication and verification process of a tamper watermarking grayscale and color image.

Numerical experiments show that this algorithm is robust to JPEG lossy compression, the lowest acceptable JPEG quality factor is 75 for grayscale images and 70 for color images. In the case of impulsive noise, verification system determines that a watermarked image has no-intentional modification if its density value is less than 0.002 which produce a PSNR average value equal to 32 dB between watermarked image and contaminated watermarked image; a similar case occurs with the Gaussian noise; the highest variance that the system accept is 0.00011 before it consider watermarked contaminated image as intentionally modified.
An important characteristic of this system besides its robustness against common signal processing is its capacity to detect the exact tampered locations, which are intentionally modified. Several watermarking systems using digital signature had been reported but they aren't robust to JPEG compression neither to modifications caused by common signal processing.
Finally it is important to mention that the watermarked images generated by the proposed algorithm are secure because the embedded watermarks are dependent on their own content.

6. Acknowledgment

This work is supported by the National Polytechnic Institute of México.

7. References

Celik, M.; Sharma, G.; Saber, E. & Tekalp, A. (2002), Hierarchical Watermarking for Secure Image Authentication with Localization, *IEEE Transactions on Image Processing*, Vol. 11, No. 6, pp. 585–595.

Chen, T.; Wang, J. & Zhou, Y. (2001), Combined Digital Signature and Digital Watermark Scheme for Image Authentication, *Info-tech and Info-net, 2001. Proceedings. ICII 2001 - International Conferences on*, Vol. 5, pp. 78-82, Print ISBN: 0-7803-7010-4.

Cruz, C. ; Reyes, R.; Nakano M. and Pérez, H. (2009), Image Authentication Scheme Based on Self-embedding Watermarking, *CIARP '09 Proceedings of the 14th Iberoamerican Conference on Pattern Recognition: Progress in Pattern Recognition, Image Analysis, Computer Vision, and Applications*, ISBN: 978-3-642-10267-7.

Cruz, C.; Reyes, R.; Mendoza, J.; Nakano, M. and Pérez, H. (2008), A Novel Verification Scheme for watermarking based Image Content Authentication Systems, *Telecommunications and Radio Engineering*, vol. 67, no. 19, pp. 1777-1790, 2008, ISSN:0040-2508, http://begelhouse.com

Fridrich, J. (1999), Robust Bit Extraction from Images, Proceedings of IEEE International Conference on Multimedia Computing and Systems (ICMCS'99), Vol. 2, pp. 536-540, ISBN:0-7695-0253-9.

Friedman, G.L. (1993), The Trustworthy Digital Camera: Restoring Credibility to the Photographic Image, *IEEE Transactions on Consum. Elec.*, Vol. 39, pp. 905–910.

Hernández, V. ; Cruz, C. ; Nakano M. and Pérez, H. (2000), Algoritmo de Marca de Agua Basado en la DWT para Patrones Visualmente Reconocibles, *IEEE Latin America Transactions*, Vol. 4, No. 4, June 2006.

Holiman, M. & Memos N. (2006), Counterfeiting Attacks on Oblivious Block-Wise Independent Invisible Watermarking Scheme, *IEEE Transactions on Image Processing,* Vol. 9, No. 3, pp. 432-441.

Hsu, C. T. & Wu, J.I. (1999). Hidden Digital Watermarks in Images, IEEE *Transactions on Image Processing,* Vol. 8, pp. 58–68.

Hu, Y. & Chen, Z. (2007), An SVD-Based Watermarking Method for Image Authentication, *Proceedings of the Sixth International Conference on Machine Learning and Cybernetics,* pp. 1723-1728, Hong Kong, 19-22 August (2007).

Inoue, H.; Miyazaki, A. & Katsura, T. (2000), A Digital Watermark for Images Using the Wavelet Transform, *Journal Integrated Computer-Aided Engineering,* Vol. 7, No. 2, pp. 105-115.

Kundur, D. & Hatzinakos, D. (1999). Digital watermarking for telltale tamper proofing and authentication, *Proceedings of the IEEE,* Vol. 87, No.7, pp. 1167–1180.

Lin, C. & Chang S. (2001), A Robust Image Authentication Method Distinguishing JPEG Compression from Malicious Manipulation, *IEEE Transactions on Circuits and systems of Video Technology,* Vol. 11 No. 2, pp. 153-168.

Liu, H. & Steinebach, M. (2006), Semi-Fragile Watermarking for Image Authentication with High Tampering Localization Capability, Proc. of Int. Conf. Automated Production of Cross Media Content for Multi-Channel Distribution, ISBN:0-7695-2625-X.

Lu, C. & Liao, H. M. (2003), Structural Digital Signature for Image Authentication: An Incidental Distortion Resistant Scheme, *IEEE Transactions on Multimedia,* Vol. 5, No. 2, pp. 161-173.

Maeno, K.; Sun, Q.; Chang, S. & Suto, M. (2006), New Semi-Fragile Image Authentication Watermarking Techniques Using Random Bias and Nonuniform Quantization, *IEEE Trans. on Multimedia,* Vol. 8, No. 1, pp. 32-45.

Monzoy, M.; Salinas, M.; Nakano, M. & Pérez, H. (2007), Fragile Watermarking for Color Image Authentication, *4th Int. Conf. Electrical and Electronic Engineering (ICEEE 2007),* pp. 157-160.

Paquet, H. A.; Ward, R. K. & Pitas, I. (2003). Wavelet packets-based Digital Watermarking for Image Verification and Authentication, *Journal Signal Processing - Special section: Security of data hiding technologies archive,* Vol. 83 Issue 10, Amsterdam, The Netherlands.

The Mathworks. Inc. (2008), Imwrite: Functions (Matlab functions references), Matlab help, Ver. 7.6.0.324.

Wong, W. P. (1998), A Public Key Watermark for Image Verification and Authentication, *Proceedings of the IEEE Int. Conf. Image Processing,* pp. 425-429.

Wong, W. P. & Memon, N. (2001), Secret and Public Key Image Watermarking Schemes for Image Authentication and Ownership Verification, *IEEE Transactions on Image Processing,* Vol. 10, No. 10, pp. 1593-1601.

Wu, M. & Liu, B. (1998), Watermarking for image authentication, *Image Processing, 1998. ICIP 98. Proceedings. International Conference on.* Vol. 2, pp. 437–441, Print ISBN: 0-8186-8821-1

Yeung, M. & Mintzer, F., (1997), An Invisible Watermarking Technique for Image Verification, *Image Processing, International Conference on,* Vol. 2, pp. 680, ISBN: 0-8186-8183-7.

Yu, G.J. ; Lu, C.-S. ; Liao, H.-Y. M. & Sheu, J.-P. (2000). Mean quantization blind watermarking for image authentication, *IEEE International Conference on Image Processing (ICIP'2000),* Vol. III, pp. 706–709, Vancouver, BC, Canada.

Zhou, X.; Duan, X. & Wang, D. (2004), A Semi-Fragile Watermark Scheme for Image Authentication, Proc. of Int. Conf. Multimedia Modeling Conference, pp. 374 – 377, Print ISBN: 0-7695-2084-7.

12

Application of Discrete Wavelet Transform in Watermarking

Corina Nafornita and Alexandru Isar
"Politehnica" University of Timisoara, Romania

1. Introduction

Proliferation of multimedia data on the Internet and the ease of copying this data have brought an interest for copyright protection (Cox et al., 2002). During transmission, data can be protected using encryption; however after decrypting it, it is no longer protected. As an alternative to encryption, watermarking has been proposed as a means of identifying the owner, by secretly embedding an imperceptible signal into the host signal (Cox, 2005) – see Fig. 1.

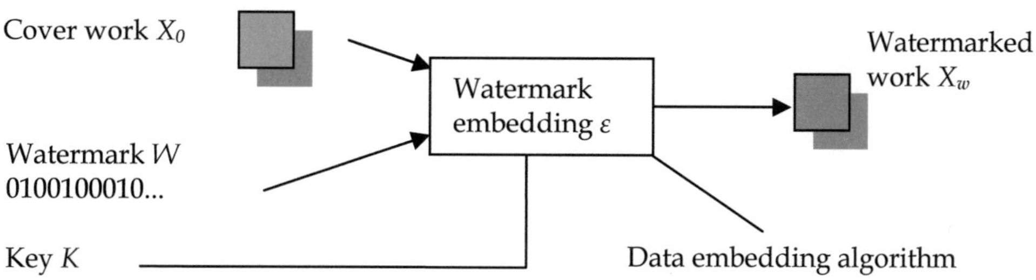

Fig. 1. Watermark embedding. The watermark is embedded using a secret or public key, making invisible changes to the cover work.

The main properties of a watermarking system are perceptual transparency, robustness, security, and data hiding capacity (Cox et al., 1997). Some of the terms used in watermarking are (Cox et al., 2002):

- The original data where the watermark is to be inserted is referred to as host or cover work.
- The hidden information is called payload.
- Visible watermarks are visual patterns (images, logos) inserted or overlaid on images/video. Visible watermarks are applied to photos publicly available on the web, to prevent commercial use of such images. One example of visible watermarking has been implemented by IBM for the Vatican library (Braudaway et al., 1996).
- Most watermarking systems involve making the watermark imperceptible.
- The key is required for embedding the watermark. If the same key is used for retrieving the watermark, the system is private, while if another key is used to retrieve it, the system is known as public.

- If the cover work is required at the detector, the system is informed (non-blind); if it's not required at the detector, the system is blind.
- Watermarking systems are robust or fragile. Robust watermarks should resist any modifications and are designed for copyright protection. Fragile watermarks are designed to fail whenever the cover work is modified and to give some measure of the tampering. Fragile watermarks are used in authentication.

Most of existing watermarking systems proposed in the literature can be classified depending on the watermarking domain, where the embedding takes place: spatial domain techniques (Nikolaidis & Pitas, 1998), where the pixels are directly modified, or transform domain techniques.

The majority of watermarking algorithms operate based on the spread spectrum (SS) communication principle. A pseudorandom sequence is added to the host signal in some critically sampled domain and the watermarked signal is obtained by inverse transforming the modified coefficients. Typical transform domains are the Discrete Wavelet Transform (DWT), the Discrete Cosine Transform (DCT) and the Discrete Fourier Transform (DFT). The DWT based algorithms usually produce watermarked images with the best balance between visual quality and robustness due to the absence of blocking artefacts (Nafornita, 2008).

Watermarks can be robust or fragile, depending on the application. For copyright protection, robustness is required. This can be assured with encoding of the watermark using a repetition code or an error correcting code. Robustness is increased with the increase of the correction capacity of the code. Despite of their efficient use in telecommunications, turbo codes have been rarely used in watermarking (Abdulaziz et al., 2002, Serdean et al., 2003, Balado & Perez-Gonzalez, 2001, Nafornita et al., 2009).

At the embedding side, the watermark can be added to coefficients of known robustness (large valued coefficients) or perceptually significant regions (Cox, 2005), such as contours and textures of an image. This can be done empirically, selecting larger coefficients (Cox et al., 1997) or using a thresholding scheme in the transform domain (Podilchuk & Zeng, 1998, Nafornita et al., 2005). Another approach is to insert the watermark in all coefficients of a transform, using a variable strength for each coefficient (Barni et al., 2001). Hybrid techniques, based on compression schemes, embed the watermark using a thresholding scheme and variable strength (Podilchuk & Zeng, 1998). The performance of such a system depends on the quality of the wavelet transform.

This chapter will focus on the application of the wavelet transforms in robust watermarking for static images. We will present the classical techniques of watermarking; starting with the spread spectrum DCT based watermarking system proposed by Cox et al. (Cox et al., 1997) and continuing with those proposed in the wavelet domain.

Other wavelet transforms as the Double Tree Complex Wavelet Transform (DTCWT) (Selesnick et al., 2005) or the Hyperanalytic Wavelet Transform (HWT) (Nafornita et al., 2008, Firoiu et al., 2009) could also be considered. The advantages of such transforms compared to DWT are: quasi-shift invariance and enhanced directional selectivity. The data hiding capacity increases with the increase of redundancy (4x for DTCWT and HWT). We will compare the efficiency of those wavelet transforms in watermarking.

2. Watermarking methods

Most techniques embed the watermark in a transform domain as mentioned before. Early techniques have used the Discrete Cosine Transform. One of the most influential watermarking works is a spread spectrum approach proposed in (Cox et al., 1997). They argue that the watermark be placed explicitly in the perceptually most significant components of the data, and that the watermark be composed of random numbers drawn from a Gaussian distribution $\mathcal{N}(0,1)$, in order to make it invisible and robust to attacks:

$$v'(i) = v(i)(1 + \alpha w(i)) \tag{1}$$

where $v(i)$ is the DCT coefficient to be watermarked, $w(i)$ is the watermark bit, α is the embedding strength and $v'(i)$ is the watermarked coefficient. Detection is made using the similarity between the original W and extracted $\hat{W}$ watermarks:

$$\text{sim}(W,\hat{W}) = \frac{\hat{W} \cdot W}{\sqrt{\hat{W} \cdot \hat{W}}} \tag{2}$$

The fact that the transform is performed over the entire image increases the computation time. Other methods have been proposed that use the block-based DCT transform, just like in the JPEG compression (see for example Podilchuk & Zeng, 1998).

Other authors have proposed the use of the Discrete Fourier Transform or its variant - the Fourier-Mellin transform. This is useful in order to perform phase modulation between the watermark and the original signal (Ó Ruanaidh et al., 1996). The phase is more important than the amplitude; hence it will be difficult for an attacker to remove the watermark. Phase modulation often possesses superior noise immunity in comparison with amplitude modulation. Many watermarking techniques use DFT amplitude modulation because the watermark will be translation invariant. The DFT is more often used in its derived forms such as the Fourier-Mellin transform. This Fourier-Mellin transform approach has arisen out of the need for Rotation, Scale and Translation invariant (RST-invariant) watermarking techniques. It involves creating a Log Polar map of the DFT amplitudes of the image, where the embedding takes place. This method is said to be extremely RST invariant and uses a RST invariant watermark (Lin et al., 2001, Ó Ruanaidh & Pun, 1998).

3. Watermarking using wavelets

3.1 Discrete wavelet transform methods

There are different approaches to embed the watermark in the wavelet domain. Almost all methods rely on masking in some way the watermark, either by selecting a few coefficients, or using adaptive embedding strength.

Podilchuk & Zeng, 1998 propose an image-adaptive (IA) approach. They use the just difference noticeable difference (JND) to determine the image dependent perceptual mask for the watermark. They applied this method in both DCT and wavelet domain:

$$I^{*}_{u,v} = \begin{cases} I_{u,v} + JND_{u,v} \times w_{u,v}, & \text{if } I_{u,v} > JND_{u,v} \\ I_{u,v}, & \text{otherwise} \end{cases} \tag{3}$$

$I_{u,v}$ are the coefficients of the original image, $w_{u,v}$ are the watermark bits, and $JND_{u,v}$ are the JND values computed using visual models. In the case of DCT, they are computed using Watson's perceptual model; for the wavelet domain, the weight is computed for each frequency band based on typical viewing conditions. Detection is made using correlation between the image difference and the watermark sequence. This method is more robust than the spread-spectrum method by Cox et al., 1997. Although more robust than IA-DCT, the IA-W method does not take into account perceptual significant regions, so the watermark can be erased from perceptually insignificant coefficients. For example, low-pass filtering will affect the watermark inserted in high frequency components.

Xia et al., 1998 propose a watermarking algorithm using the Haar mother wavelet, and two levels of decomposition. A pseudo-random sequence is added to the highest coefficients not located in the lowest resolution:

$$f'(m,n) = f(m,n) + \alpha \cdot f(m,n)^{\beta} w_i \tag{4}$$

where α is the watermark strength, and β is the amplification for large coefficients. This algorithm concentrates most of the energy in edges and textures, which are the coefficients in detail subbands. This increases the invisibility of the watermark, because human observers are less sensitive to change in edges and textures compared to changes in smooth areas of an image. More watermarks are inserted in each subband, and detection is done hierarchically, for each resolution level, using intercorrelation between original watermark and the difference of the two images. The method is robust to a series of distortions, but low-pass and median filtering affect the watermark.

Kundur & Hatzinakos, 1998 use the Daubechies wavelet family to compute the DWT on three levels of decomposition. The watermarking algorithm selects in a pseudo-random manner the embedding locations from the detail subbands. The authors state that the spread-spectrum technique is not appropriate for transmitting the watermark because the correlator used for watermark detection is not effective in the presence of fading. Hence, they use quantization for embedding the watermark bits. To increase robustness, they use a reference watermark in order to estimate if the watermark bit has been embedded (Kundur & Hatzinakos, 2001).

One of the popular methods is the one proposed by Barni et al., 2001. The watermark is masked according to the characteristics of the human visual system (HVS), taking into account the texture and the luminance content of all the image subbands. For coefficients corresponding to contours of the image a higher strength is used, for textures a medium strength is used and for regions with high regularity a lower strength is used, in accordance with the analogy water-filling and watermarking (Kundur, 2000).

The image I, of size $2M \times 2N$, is decomposed into 4 levels using Daubechies-6 wavelet mother, where I_l^{θ} is the subband from level $l \in \{0, 1, 2, 3\}$, and orientation $\theta \in \{0, 1, 2, 3\}$ (horizontal, diagonal and vertical detail subbands, and approximation subband). A pseudorandom binary (±1) sequence is casted into 2D binary watermarks, each of size $MN/4^l$, x_l^{θ}. The watermark is embedded in all coefficients from level l=0 by addition

$$\tilde{I}_l^{\theta}(i,j) = I_l^{\theta}(i,j) + \alpha w_l^{\theta}(i,j) x_l^{\theta}(i,j) \tag{5}$$

where α is the embedding strength and $w_l^{\theta}(i,j)$ is half of the quantization step:

$$q_l^{\theta}(i,j) = \Theta(l,\theta)\Lambda(l,i,j)\Xi(l,i,j)^{0.2} \tag{6}$$

as it is presented in the following figure.

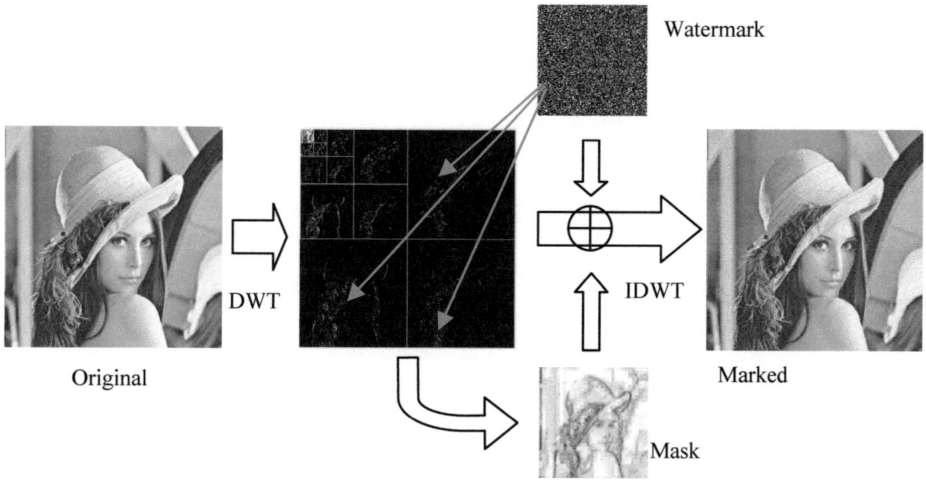

Fig. 2. Watermark embedding in the wavelet domain (Barni et al., 2001). The watermark is embedded in the first resolution level using a perceptual mask.

This is a product of three factors: sensitivity to noise, local brightness and texture activity around a pixel. They are computed as follows:

$$\Theta(l,\theta)=\begin{Bmatrix}\sqrt{2}, & \theta=1\\ 1 & \text{otherwise}\end{Bmatrix}\cdot\begin{Bmatrix}1.00 & l=0\\ 0.32 & l=1\\ 0.16 & l=2\\ 0.10 & l=3\end{Bmatrix} \tag{7}$$

$$\Lambda(l,i,j)=1+L'(l,i,j) \tag{8}$$

$$L(l,i,j)=I_3^3\left(1+\lfloor i/2^{3-l}\rfloor,1+\lfloor j/2^{3-l}\rfloor\right)\Big/256 \tag{9}$$

$$\begin{aligned}\Xi(l,i,j)=&\sum_{k=0}^{3-l}16^{-k}\sum_{\theta=0}^{2}\sum_{x,y=0}^{1}\left[I_{k+l}^{\theta}\left(y+i/2^k,x+j/2^k\right)\right]^2\\ &\cdot\mathrm{Var}\left\{I_3^3\left(1+y+i/2^{3-l},1+x+j/2^{3-l}\right)\right\}_{\substack{x=0,1\\ y=0,1}}\end{aligned} \tag{10}$$

The texture activity around a pixel is composed by the product of two contributions; the first is the local mean square value of the DWT coefficients in all detail subbands and the second is the local variance of the 4th level approximation image. Both are computed in a small 2×2 neighborhood corresponding to the location (*i, j*) of the pixel. The first contribution is the distance from the edges, and the second one is the texture. This local variance estimation is computed with a low resolution.

Detection is made using the correlation between the marked DWT coefficients and the watermarking sequence to be tested for presence (the original image is not needed):

$$\rho(l)=4^l\sum_{\theta=0}^{2}\sum_{i=0}^{M/2^l-1}\sum_{j=0}^{N/2^l-1}\tilde{I}_l^{\theta}(i,j)x_l^{\theta}(i,j)\Big/(3MN) \tag{11}$$

The correlation is compared to a threshold $T_\rho(l)$, computed to grant a given probability of false positive detection, using the Neyman-Pearson criterion. For example, for $P_f \le 10^{-8}$, the threshold is $T_{\rho(l)} = 3.97\sqrt{2\sigma^2_{\rho(l)}}$, with $\sigma_{\rho(l)}{}^2$ the variance of the wavelet coefficients, if the image was watermarked with a code Y other than X,

$$\sigma^2_{\rho(l)} \approx \left(4^l/(3MN)\right)^2 \sum_{\theta=0}^{2} \sum_{i=0}^{M/2^l-1} \sum_{j=0}^{N/2^l-1} \left(\tilde{I}_l^\theta(i,j)\right)^2. \tag{12}$$

Barni's method is quite robust against common signal processing techniques like filtering, compression, cropping and so on. However, because embedding is made only in the last resolution level, the watermark information can be easily erased by an attacker. Nafornita, 2008 proposed a pixel-wise mask allowing insertion of the watermark in lower resolution levels. The third factor of the texture is estimated using the local standard deviation of the original image computed on a rectangular moving window $W(i,j)$ of $W_S \times W_S$ pixels, centered on each pixel $I(i,j)$. This criterion of segmentation finds its contours, textures and regions with high homogeneity. The local mean is:

$$\hat{\mu}(i,j) = W_S^{-2} \sum_{I(m,n)\in W(i,j)} I(m,n) \tag{13}$$

The local variance is given by:

$$\hat{\sigma}^2(i,j) = W_S^{-2} \sum_{I(m,n)\in W(i,j)} \left(I(m,n) - \hat{\mu}(i,j)\right)^2 \tag{14}$$

The local standard deviation is the square root of this local variance. The texture for a considered DWT coefficient is proportional with the local standard deviation of the corresponding pixel from the host image. We denote this local standard deviation image with S, and the local mean image with U. Embedding is made in the subband s, level l; the size of the texture matrix must agree with the size of the subband. Hence, the approximation image at the lth decomposition level is used. This compression can be realized exploiting the separation properties of the DWT. To generate the mask required for the embedding into the detail subimages corresponding to the lth decomposition level, the DWT of the local standard deviation image is computed (making l+1 iterations). The required mask will be the approximation subimage from level l, denoted S_l^3, normalized to the local mean, also compressed in the wavelet domain, U_l^3. This is illustrated in Fig. 3. One difference between the watermarking method proposed by Nafornita, 2008 and the one proposed by Barni et al., 2001, is given by the computation of the local variance – the second term – in (10). To obtain the new values of the texture, the local variance of the image to be watermarked is computed, using the relations (13) and (14). The local standard deviation image is decomposed using one iteration wavelet transform, and only the approximation image is kept. Relation (10) is then replaced with:

$$\Xi(l,i,j) = \sum_{k=0}^{3-l} 16^{-k} \sum_{\theta=0}^{2} \sum_{x,y=0}^{1} \left[I_{k+l}^{\theta}\left(y + i/2^k, x + j/2^k\right)\right]^2 \cdot S_l^3(i,j)/U_l^3(i,j) \tag{15}$$

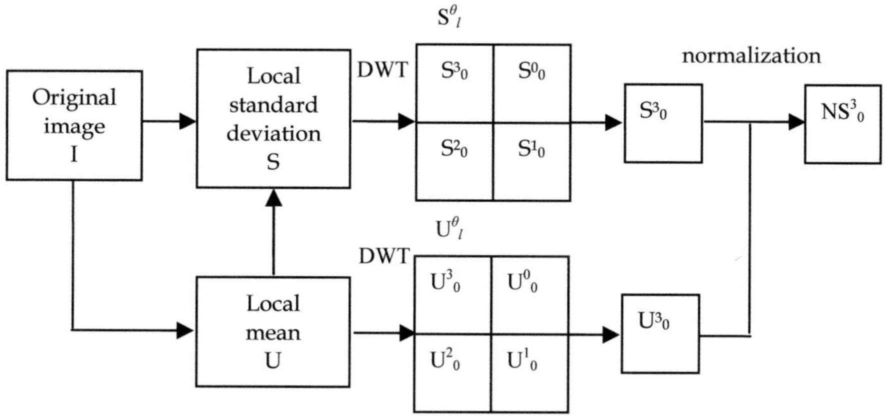

Fig. 3. Watermark embedding. The watermark is embedded using a secret or public key, making invisible changes to the cover work.

The second difference is that the luminance mask is computed on the approximation image from level l, where the watermark is embedded. The DWT of the original image using l decomposition levels was computed and the approximation subimage corresponding at level l was separated, obtaining the image I_l^3. The luminance content is computed using:

$$L(l,i,j) = I_l^3(i,j)/256 \tag{16}$$

Since both factors are more dependent on the resolution level in the method proposed by Barni, the noise sensitivity function becomes:

$$\Theta(l,\theta) = \begin{Bmatrix} \sqrt{2}, & \theta = 1 \\ 1, & \text{otherwise} \end{Bmatrix} \begin{Bmatrix} 1.00 & l \in \{0,1\} \\ 0.66 & l = 2 \end{Bmatrix}. \tag{17}$$

It was considered the ratio between the correlation $\rho(l)$ in Eq. (11) and the image dependent threshold $T_\rho(l)$, hence the detector was viewed as a nonlinear function with a fixed threshold. In Nafornita, 2007a, three detectors are used, to take advantage of the wavelet hierarchical decomposition. The watermark presence is detected,

1. from all resolution levels, "all_levels",
2. separately from each resolution level, considering the maximum detector response from each level, "max_level",
3. separately from each subband, considering the maximum detector response from each subband, "max_subband".

Evaluating the correlations separately per resolution level or subband can be sometimes advantageous. In the case of cropping, the watermark will be damaged more likely in the lower frequency than in the higher frequency, while lowpass filtering affects more the higher frequency than lower ones. Layers or subbands with lower detector response are discarded. This type of embedding combined with new detectors is more attack resilient to a possible erasure of the three subbands watermark. The detector "all_levels" evaluates the watermark's presence on all resolution levels:

$$d_1 = \rho_{d1}/T_{d1} \tag{18}$$

where the correlation ρ_{d1} is given by:

$$\rho_{d1}=\sum_{l=0}^{2}\sum_{\theta=0}^{2}\sum_{i=0}^{M/2^l-1}\sum_{j=0}^{N/2^l-1}\tilde{I}_l^{\theta}(i,j)x_l^{\theta}(i,j)\Bigg/\left(3MN\sum_{l=0}^{2}4^{-l}\right) \tag{19}$$

The threshold for $P_f \leq 10^{-8}$ is $T_{d1}=3.97\sqrt{\sigma_{\rho d1}^2}$, with:

$$\sigma_{\rho d1}^2\approx\sum_{l=0}^{2}\sum_{\theta=0}^{2}\sum_{i=0}^{M/2^l-1}\sum_{j=0}^{N/2^l-1}\left(\tilde{I}_l^{\theta}(i,j)\right)^2\Bigg/\left(3MN\sum_{l=0}^{2}4^{-l}\right)^2 \tag{20}$$

The second detector "max_levels" considers the responses from different levels, as $d(l)=\rho(l)/T(l)$, with $l\in\{0, 1, 2\}$, and discards the detector responses with lower values:

$$d_2=\max_l\{d(l)\} \tag{21}$$

The third detector considers the responses from different subbands and levels, as $d(l,\theta)$ the ratio $\rho(l,\theta)/T(l,\theta)$, with $l,\theta\in\{0, 1, 2\}$, and discards the detector responses with lower values,

$$d_3=\max_{l,\theta}\{d(l,\theta)\} \tag{22}$$

The correlation and threshold are computed with the same rationale on one subband, indicated by its orientation and level.

3.2 Complex wavelet transform methods

The discrete wavelet transform is useful to embed the watermark because the visual quality of the images is very good. However, it has three main disadvantages (Kingsbury, 2001): lack of shift invariance, lack of symmetry of the mother wavelets and poor directional selectivity. Caused by the lack of shift invariance of the DWT, small shifts in the input signal can produce important changes in the energy distribution of the wavelet coefficients. Due to the poor directional selectivity for diagonal features of the DWT the watermarking capacity is small. The most important parameters of a watermarking system are robustness and capacity. These parameters must be maximized. These disadvantages can be diminished using a complex wavelet transform (Kingsbury, 2000, 2001).

A very simple implementation of the Hyperanalytic Wavelet Transform, (HWT), recently proposed (Adam et al., 2007) has a high shift-invariance degree versus other quasi-shift-invariant wavelet transforms (WT) at same redundancy. It has also an enhanced directional selectivity. All the WTs have two parameters: the mother wavelets (MW) and the primary resolution (PR), (number of iterations). The importance of their selection is highlighted in Nason, 2002. Another appealing particularity of those transforms, coming from their multiresolution capability, is the interscale dependency of the wavelet coefficients.

We present in the next paragraphs a new implementation of HWT (Adam et al., 2007) and its application to watermarking (Nafornita et al., 2008). The watermark capacity was studied in Moulin & Mihcak, 2002, where an information-theoretic model for image watermarking and data hiding is presented. Models for geometric attacks and distortion measures that are invariant to such attacks are also considered. The lack of shift invariance of the DWT and its poor directional selectivity are reasons to embed the watermark in the field of another WT.

To maximize the robustness and the capacity, the role of the redundancy of the transform used must be highlighted first. An example of redundant WT is represented by the tight frame decomposition. In Hua & Fowler, 2002 are analyzed the watermarking systems based on tight frame decompositions. The analysis indicates that a tight frame offers no inherent performance advantage over an orthonormal transform (DWT) in the watermark detection process despite the well known ability of redundant transforms to accommodate greater amounts of added noise for a given distortion. The overcompleteness of the expansion, which aids the watermark insertion by accommodating greater watermark energy for a given distortion, actually hinders the correlation operator in watermark detection. As a result, the tight-frame expansion does not inherently offer greater spread-spectrum watermarking performance. This analytical observation should be tempered with the fact that spread-spectrum watermarking is often deployed in conjunction with an image-adaptive weighting mask to take into account the human visual model (HVM) and to improve perceptual performance. Another redundant WT, the DTCWT, was already used for watermarking (Loo & Kingsbury, 2000). The authors of this paper prove that the capacity of a watermarking system based on a complex wavelet transform is higher than the capacity of a similar system that embeds the watermark in the DWT domain. Many authors (e.g. Daugman, 1980) have suggested that the processing of visual data inside our visual cortex resembles filtering by an array of Gabor filters of different orientations and scales. The proposed implementation of HWT is efficient, has only a modest amount of redundancy, provides approximate shift invariance, has better directional selectivity than the 2D DWT and it can be observed that the corresponding basis functions closely approximate the Gabor functions. So, the spread spectrum watermarking based on the use of an image adaptive weighting mask applied in the HWT domain is potentially a robust solution that increases the capacity.

3.2.1 A new implementation of the Hyperanalytic Wavelet Transform

The hypercomplex mother wavelet associated to a real mother wavelet $\psi(x,y)$ is:

$$\begin{aligned}\psi_a(x,y) &= \psi(x,y) + i\mathcal{H}_x\{\psi(x,y)\} + \\ &+ j\mathcal{H}_y\{\psi(x,y)\} + k\mathcal{H}_x\{\mathcal{H}_y\{\psi(x,y)\}\}\end{aligned} \tag{23}$$

where $i^2 = j^2 = -k^2 = -1$, and $ij = ji = k$ (Davenport, 2008). The HWT of the image $f(x,y)$ is:

$$HWT\{f(x,y)\} = \langle f(x,y), \psi_a(x,y)\rangle. \tag{24}$$

The 2D-HWT of the image $f(x,y)$ can be computed using the 2D-DWT of its associated hypercomplex image:

$$\begin{aligned}&HWT\{f(x,y)\} = DWT\{f(x,y)\} + \\ &iDWT\{\mathcal{H}_x\{f(x,y)\}\} + jDWT\{\mathcal{H}_y\{f(x,y)\}\} + \\ &+kDWT\{\mathcal{H}_y\{\mathcal{H}_x\{f(x,y)\}\}\} = \\ &\langle f_a(x,y), \psi(x,y)\rangle = DWT\{f_a(x,y)\}.\end{aligned} \tag{25}$$

HWT uses four trees, each implemented by 2D-DWT, being adequate to a multi-wavelet environment (Firoiu et al., 2009). $\mathcal{H}_x$ is the Hilbert transform computed across lines and $\mathcal{H}_y$ across columns (Fig. 4). The HWT coefficients are organized in two sequences of complex coefficients separated by the sign of their preferential orientation, with 6 subbands, 3 of positive orientations and 3 of negative orientations ±atan(1/2), ±π/4 and ±atan(2):

$$\begin{aligned} z_{\pm} &= z_{\pm r} + j z_{\pm i} \\ &= \left({}_{f}D^{1,2,3} \mp {}_{\mathcal{H}_y\{\mathcal{H}_x\{f\}\}}D^{1,2,3} \right) + j\left({}_{\mathcal{H}_x}D^{1,2,3} \pm {}_{\mathcal{H}_y}D^{1,2,3} \right). \end{aligned} \tag{26}$$

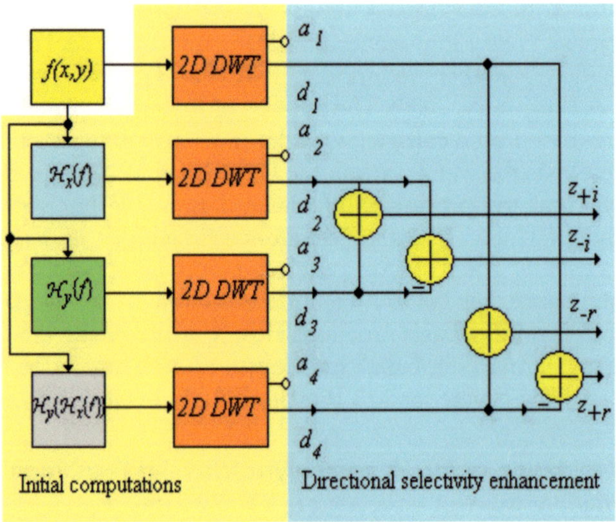

Fig. 4. The new HWT implementation architecture.

3.2.2 Watermarking using the Hyperanalytic Wavelet Transform

Adapting the strategy already described in the previous paragraph to the case of HWT, a new method was proposed in Nafornita et al., 2008. The first three wavelet decomposition levels are used and the watermark is embedded into the real coefficients with positive and negative orientations, z_{+r} and z_{-r}, respectively. In this case the relations already described in the previous paragraph were used independently for each of these two images. The same message was embedded in both images, using the mask from Nafornita, 2007a. The difference is that the orientations or preferential directions are in this case: atan(1/2), π/4, atan(2) (respectively for θ = 0, 1, 2), for the image z_{+r} and -atan(1/2), -π/4, -atan(2), (θ=0, 1, 2) for the image z_{-r} . At the detection side, we consider the pair of images (z_{+r}, z_{-r}), thus having twice as much coefficients than the standard approach, and θ takes all the possible values, ±atan(1/2), ±π/4, ±atan(2).

3.3 Results and comparisons

We will compare in the following watermarking systems based on DWT with the ones based on complex WTs, namely the HWT.

3.3.1 Results for methods based on the discrete wavelet transform

In Nafornita et al., 2006a, the system proposed by Barni et al. was modified, using the texture mask in (15). The image Barbara is watermarked with various values of the embedding strength α. The binary watermark is embedded in all the detail wavelet coefficients of the first resolution level. Watermarked Barbara for α=1.5 is shown in Fig. 5.

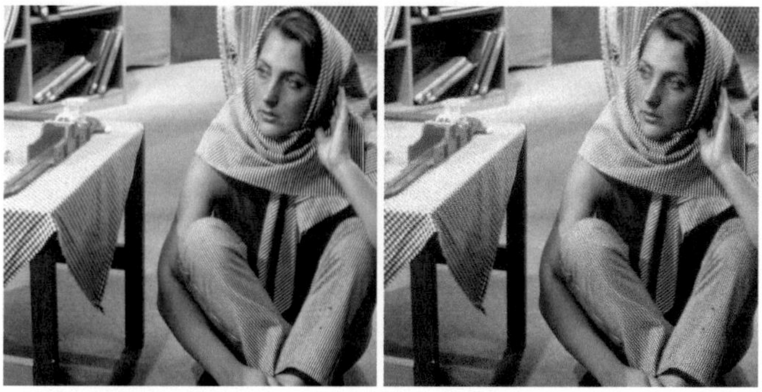

Fig. 5. Original and watermarked Barbara images with α = 1.5.

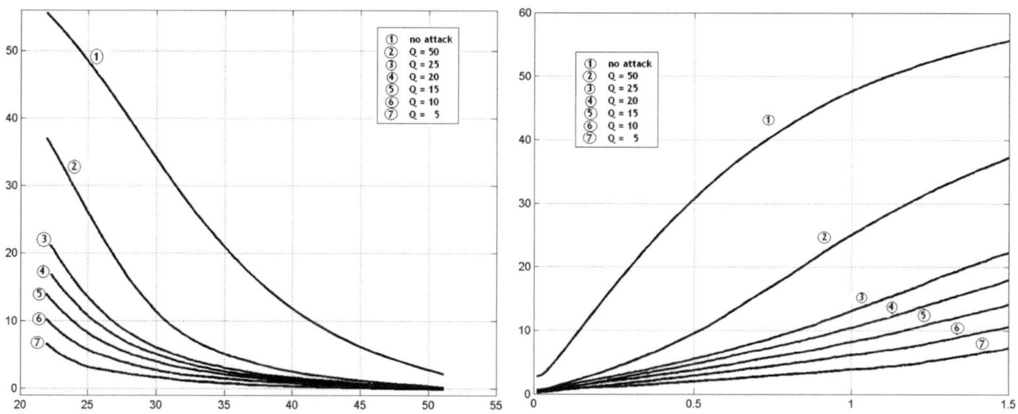

Fig. 6. Left: The ratio ρ/T as a function of the PSNR between the marked and the original images, for different quality factors, JPEG compression. Right: Ratio ρ/T as a function of embedding strength, for different quality factors, JPEG compression. P_f is set to 10^{-8}.

Fig. 6 shows results for JPEG compression, for different quality factors: the ratio ρ/T is plotted as a function of the peak signal-to-noise ratio (PSNR) between the marked (un-attacked) image and the original one, and respectively as a function of α. The probability of false positive detection is set to 10^{-8}. If this ratio is greater than 1 then the watermark is positively detected. Generally, for a PSNR higher than 30 dB, the original image and watermarked one are considered indistinguishable. For compression quality factors higher or equal than 25 the distortion introduced by JPEG compression is tolerable. For PSNR in the range of 30-35 dB, of practical interest, the watermark is detected for all significant compression quality factors. Increasing the embedding strength, the PSNR of the watermarked image decreases, and the ratio ρ/T increases. The watermark is still detectable even for very small values of α. For the quality factor Q=5 (or a compression ratio CR=32), the watermark is still detectable even for α=0.5. Fig. 7 shows the detection of a true watermark for various quality factors, in the case of α=1.5; the threshold is well below the detector response. In Table 1 we give a comparison between the two methods, for the Lena image, α=1.5 in the case of JPEG compression with a quality factor of 5 (compression ratio of 46).

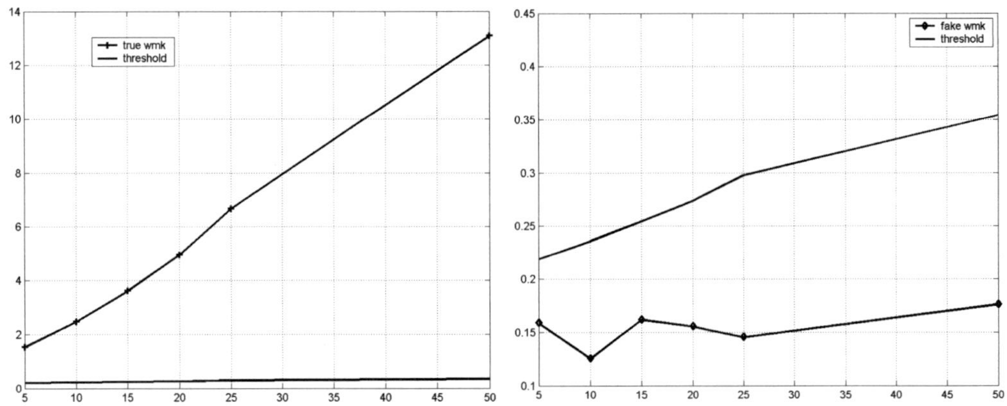

Fig. 7. Left: Detector response ρ, threshold T, as a function of different quality factors (JPEG compression). The watermark is successfully detected. P_f is set to 10^{-8}. Right: Highest detector response, ρ_2, corresponding to a fake watermark and threshold T. The threshold is above the detector response.

	Nafornita et al., 2006a	Barni et al., 2001
ρ	0.3199	0.038
T	0.0844	0.036
ρ_2	0.0516	0.010

Table 1. A comparison for JPEG compression with a compression ratio CR = 46.

The detector response for the original embedded watermark ρ, the detection threshold T, and the second highest detector response ρ_2 are given. P_f was set to 10^{-8} and 1000 marks were tested. The detector response is higher than in Barni's case.

Fig. 8. Original image Lena; mask from Nafornita et al., 2006b and Barni's mask for level l=0. The masks are the complementary of the real ones.

In Nafornita et al., 2006b, Barni's method is modified, using the texture mask in (15), as well as the luminance factor in (16). The masks obtained are shown in Fig. 8. The improvement is clearly visible around edges and contours. The method is applied in two cases, when the watermark is inserted in level 0 only and when it's inserted in level 1 only. JPEG compression is again considered. The image Lena is watermarked at level l=0 and respectively at level l=1 with α ranging from 1.5 to 5. The binary watermark is embedded in all the detail wavelet coefficients of the resolution level, l as previously described. For α=1.5, the watermarked images, in level 0 and level 1, as well as the image watermarked using Barni's mask, are shown in Fig. 9. Obviously the quality of the watermarked images are preserved using the new pixel-wise mask. The PSNR values are 38 dB (level 0) and 43 dB (level 1), compared to Barni's method, with a PSNR of 20 dB.

Fig. 9. Watermarked images, α =1.5, for Nafornita et al., 2006b, level 0 (PSNR = 38 dB); level 1 (43 dB); for Barni et al., 2001, level 0 (20 dB).

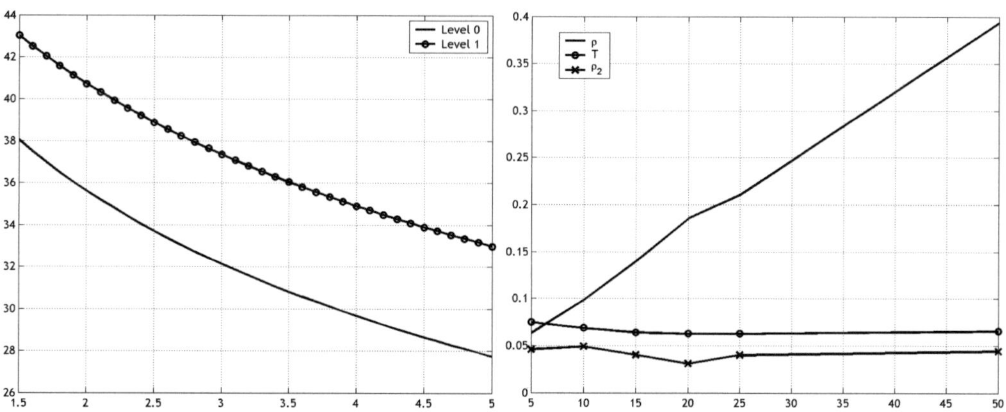

Fig. 10. Left: PSNR as a function of α. Embedding is made either in level 0 or in level 1.Right: Detector response ρ, threshold T, highest detector response, ρ_2, corresponding to a fake watermark, as a function of different quality factors (JPEG compression). The watermark is successfully detected. P_f is set to 10^{-8}. Embedding was made in level 0.

PSNR values are shown in Fig. 10(left) as a function of the embedding strength. The watermark is still invisible, even for high values of α. Fig. 11 gives the results for JPEG compression. In all experiments, the probability of false positive detection is set to 10^{-8}. The

watermark is successfully detected for a large interval of compression quality factors. For PSNR values higher than 30 dB, the watermarking is invisible. For quality factors Q≥10, the distortion introduced by JPEG compression is tolerable. For all values of α, the watermark is detected for all the significant quality factors (Q≥10). Increasing the embedding strength, the PSNR of the watermarked image decreases, and ρ/T increases. For the quality factor Q = 10 (or a compression ratio CR = 32), the watermark is still detectable even for low values of α.
Fig. 10(right) shows the detection of a true watermark from level 0 for various quality factors, for α=1.5; the threshold is below the detector response. The selectivity of the watermark detector is also illustrated, when a number of 999 fake watermarks were tested: the second highest detector response is shown, for each quality factor. False positives are rejected.
In Table 2 a comparison between Nafornita et al., 2006b and Barni et al., 2001, can be seen for JPEG compression with Q=10 (compression ratio of 32). The detector response for the original watermark ρ, the detection threshold T, and the second highest detector response ρ_2, when the watermark was inserted in level 0 are given. The detector response is higher than for Barni et al.

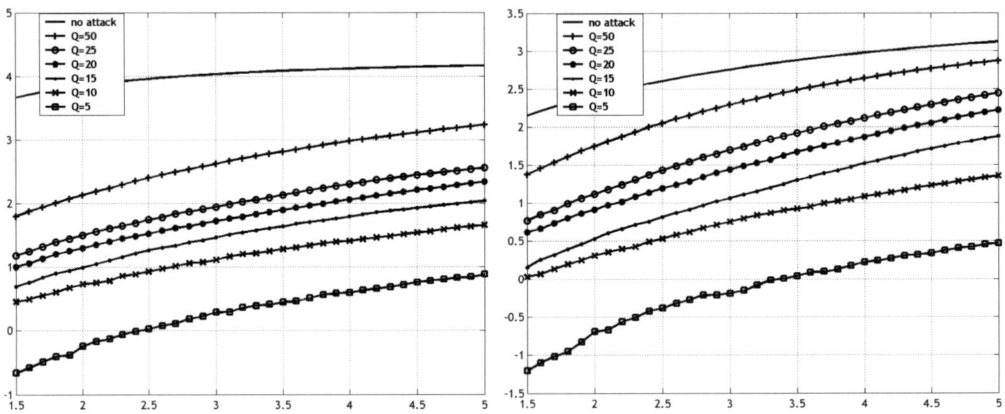

Fig. 11. Ratio ρ/T as a function of the embedding strength α. The watermarked image is JPEG compressed with different quality factors Q. P_f is set to 10^{-8}. Embedding was made in level 0 (left), and in level 1 (right).

	Nafornita et al., 2006b	Barni et al., 2001
ρ	0.0750	0.062
T	0.0636	0.036
ρ_2	0.0461	0.011

Table 2. A comparison for JPEG compression with a compression ratio CR = 32.

The method in Nafornita, 2007a allows embedding of the watermark in all resolution levels, except the last one (low resolution). Three types of detectors are used, as described in paragraph 3.1. Various images of size 512x512, have been watermarked at levels $l \in \{0, 1, 2\}$ using the new mask. The embedding strength is α=1.5. Based on human observation and the peak-signal-to-noise ratio, PSNR, the images are indistinguishable from the original ones. For Barni et al. method, a watermark is embedded in all the detail wavelet coefficients of the first resolution level, l=0, for α=0.2, that results in a similar image quality (see Fig.12). This has been concluded in Nafornita, 2007b, where by limiting the watermark strength such that the PSNR is 35 dB and in average the percentage of affected pixels is less than 25%, the quality of the images is greatly improved. Girod's model has been used for determining the location and number of affected pixels (Girod, 1989). For instance, in Barni's case, the watermarked image with α=0.2 has a PSNR of 36.39 dB, 11.84% affected pixels, compared to the one watermarked with α=1.5 has a PSNR of 20 dB, and all pixels are affected. What is kept constant for comparison are the 2D watermarks embedded in the first level, and the image quality. The method Nafornita, 2007a cannot be compared with the one in Barni et al., 2001 when the watermark is embedded in all resolution levels, simply because their mask isn't suited for embedding in other levels than the highest resolution level. Results for some of the standard images from the USC SIPI Image Database are given.

Fig. 12. (left) Original image Lena, (middle) Watermarked images for Nafornita, 2007a, α=1.5, PSNR=36.86 dB, (right) Barni et al., 2001, α=0.2, PSNR=36.39 dB.

Table 3 includes PSNR values for the two cases. For the first detector, an estimate of the false positive probability is shown for the image Lena, before and after JPEG compression attack, with quality factor Q=10, as a function of the detection thresholds, $T_{\rho 1}$. The threshold values have been computed using as estimate the variance of the ρ_1 obtained from experiments. The mean PSNR for the twelve images is 34.16 dB for the proposed method (Nafornita, 2007a) and 34.06 dB for Barni's method.

Detector response vs. attack	Nafornita, 2007a			Barni's method
	1-All levels	2-Max level	3-Max subband	
JPEG compression, Q=10	2.38	1.98	1.44	1.75
Median filtering, M=5	1.32	1.12	1.46	0.25
Scaling, 50%	4.06	5.21	5.76	1.85
Cropping, 512x512 -> 32x32	0.68	0.98	1.73	1.48
Gamma correction, γ=2	20.32	29.19	28.06	32.54
Motion blur, L=31, θ=11	1.98	5.48	8.04	6.14

Table 3. Resistance to different attacks, for Nafornita, 2007a method. The detector response is a mean value of different responses.

Tests were made for JPEG compression, median filtering, cropping, resizing, gamma correction and blurring. Table 3 shows the mean values of the detector responses for each attack. A particular attack parameter is chosen where the watermark is still detectable by at least one detector. For compression, the method in Nafornita, 2007a successfully detects the watermark at Q=10. The 1st detector is better in all cases. This new method has better results than Barni's technique. The watermark of both methods survived in all images for median filtering with kernel sizes up to 3. For kernel size 5, the watermark of Nafornita, 2007a using the first and third detector is detectable; Barni's method fails to detect the watermark. In the case of scaling to 50%, the watermark was successfully detectable in both cases, with better results for Nafornita, 2007a. The third detector has the best performance in detecting the mark. The watermark of Nafornita, 2007a was successfully detected in the cropped image of 32x32, only with the third detector, which proves its efficiency. Barni's method detects the watermark with similar detector responses as in the case of the third detector. As expected for normalized correlation detection, both methods are practically insensitive to gamma correction adjustment. For the motion blur attack, both methods have successfully detected the watermark in all cases. Detector 3 has slightly better results than the others.

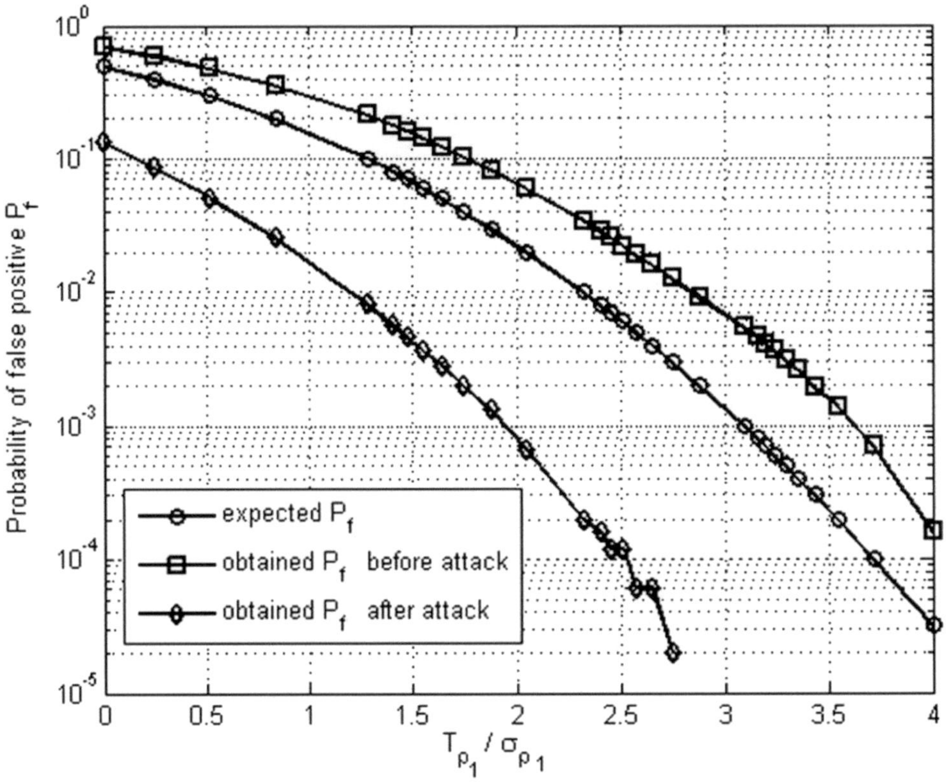

Fig. 13. Experimentally evaluated probability of false positive P_f vs. $T_{\rho 1}/\sigma_{\rho 1}$, the ratio between the detection threshold and standard deviation of the correlations in the case where an incorrect watermark was embedded. The theoretical trend is also shown ('o' marker). Tests were made on Lena, before and after JPEG compression with quality factor 10, using 5×10^4 different watermarks.

For the first detector, the probability of false positive was estimated by searching many different watermarks into one watermarked image, Lena. Each threshold $T_{\rho 1}$ was set in such a way to grant a given value of P_f. The trial was repeated for values of P_f ranging from 10^{-1} through 10^{-4}. In total 5×10^4 watermarks per image have been tested. The estimation has been done before any type of manipulation and after JPEG compression, with quality factor 10. The estimated P_f is plotted in Fig. 13 versus the ratio $T_{\rho 1}/\sigma_{\rho 1}$ between the detection thresholds and standard deviations of correlations for the case corresponding to certain estimates of this probability of false positive. This case corresponds to the situation where the image is watermarked with a code Y other than X.

Surprisingly, the estimated false alarm P_f, is lower in the case of compression than in the case of no attack, for the same detection threshold. This can be explained by the fact that before compression, the empirical pdf of the correlations in the case for an incorrect watermark is embedded, was not Gaussian. Although the two empirical pdf's are closer after the attack, they are still very good separated and the empirical pdf for an incorrect watermark has the mean below zero, compared to the equivalent one before - which is centered on zero. Thus setting a particular threshold can indeed result in a lower false alarm after attack. Similar results were obtained for Barbara, and for the same attack.

For the first detector, the obtained probability of false positive is close to the expected one. The assumption that the wavelet coefficients from different levels and subbands are i.i.d. is thus reasonable and the detector has a good performance.

3.3.2 Results for methods based on the Hyperanalytic Wavelet transform

In Nafornita et al., 2008 the watermark is embedded in the HWT domain, in all levels (0, 1 and 2) and all orientations (positive and negative). The test image is Lena, of size 512x512. For $\alpha=1.5$, the watermarked image has a PSNR of 35.63 dB. The original image, the corresponding watermarked image and the difference image are presented in Fig. 14.

Fig. 14. Original and watermarked images with method (Nafornita et al., 2008), for $\alpha=1.5$, PSNR=35.63 dB; Difference image, amplified 8 times.

The watermarked images have been exposed at some common attacks: JPEG compression with different quality factors (Q), shifting, median filtering with different window sizes M, resizing with different scale factors, cropping with different areas remaining, gamma correction with different values of γ, blurring with a specified point spread function (PSF) and perturbation with AWGN with different variances.

Resistance to unintentional attacks, for watermarked image Lena, can be compared to the results obtained using the watermarking methods in Barni et al., 2001 and Nafornita, 2007a analyzing Table 4. For the method in Nafornita, 2007a, the same watermark strength, 1.5 is used and the watermark is embedded in all three wavelet decomposition levels, resulting in a PSNR of 36.86 dB. For the method in Barni et al., 2001, the watermark strength 0.2 is used and the embedding is made only in the first resolution level, resulting in a similar quality of the images (PSNR=36.39 dB).

Attacks vs. detector response	DWT-Nafornita, 2007a			DWT-Barni et al., 2001	HWT-Nafornita et al., 2008		
	all levels	max level	max subband		all levels	max level	max subband
Before attack	21.57	39.12	33.60	**44.31**	24.78	43.18	26.30
JPEG, Q=50	5.45	6.76	5.02	6.22	6.25	**7.87**	4.85
JPEG, Q=25	3.02	3.67	2.60	3.03	3.23	**4.19**	2.62
JPEG, Q=20	2.55	3.08	2.09	2.38	2.72	**3.58**	2.33
Shift, *li*=128, *co*=128	21.57	39.12	33.59	**44.31**	24.78	43.18	26.30
Median filter, M=3	4.29	4.58	4.87	1.57	4.59	**5.42**	4.37
Median filter, M=5	**1.66**	1.24	2.27	0.59	1.61	1.64	1.49
Resizing, 0.75	9.53	15.86	15.64	14.09	10.93	**19.34**	14.67
Resizing, 0.50	4.21	5.72	5.75	2.31	4.56	6.14	**8.71**
Cropping, 256x256	7.40	12.14	17.10	**18.08**	8.68	15.20	13.82
Cropping, 128x128	3.11	4.66	**8.31**	8.01	3.53	6.04	6.86
Cropping, 64x64	1.10	1.72	**4.45**	3.92	1.32	2.47	3.71
Gamma correction, γ=1.5	22.18	39.76	33.74	43.04	25.31	**43.61**	26.45
Gamma correction, γ=2	22.59	39.70	32.98	42.43	25.62	**43.24**	25.88
Blur, L=31, β=11	2.69	7.81	**9.56**	9.05	3.05	9.18	7.55

Table 4. Resistance to different attacks, for HWT based method compared to DWT based methods.

Special attention was paid to the shifting attack. First the watermarked image was circularly shifted with *li* lines and *co* columns, obtained the attacked image $(\tilde{I}_t)$. Supposing that the numbers *li* and *co* are known, the messages at level l are circularly shifted with $li/2^l$ lines and $co/2^l$ columns obtaining the new messages $(x_t)_l^\theta$. Next the watermark was detected using the image $(\tilde{I})_t$ and the messages $(x_t)_l^\theta$. The values obtained for *li*=128 and *co*=128 are presented in Table 4.

From the results, it is clear that embedding in the real parts of the HWT transform yields in a higher capacity at the same visual impact and robustness. In fact the results obtained in Nafornita et al., 2008 are slightly better than the results obtained with the DWT-based methods in Nafornita et al., 2008 and Barni et al., 2001 for JPEG compression, median filtering with window size M=3, resizing and gamma correction. For the other attacks the results obtained are similar with the results of the watermarking methods based on DWT. The case of the shifting attack is very interesting. In this case the robustness of the watermarking method is given by two properties: the shift invariance degree of the WT used and the masking ability. All the methods compared in Table 4 are very robust against the shifting attack. The values of the ratios between the correlations and the image dependent thresholds obtained before and after the shifting attack are equal for all the methods compared in Table 4. So, the ability of masking seems to be more important than the shift invariance degree of the WT used for the conception of counter-measures against the shifting attack, when the numbers of lines and columns used for the attack are already known. Of course, the detection of these numbers must also be realized, for the implementation of a strategy against the shifting attack.

4. Conclusion

In a watermarking system, robustness evaluation should be made if invisibility criteria are satisfied. For this purpose, perceptual watermarks are being used to overcome the issue of robustness against invisibility. In the literature, there was proposed a blind spread spectrum technique that uses a perceptual mask in the wavelet domain, taking into account the noise sensitivity, texture and the luminance content of all image subbands. We described new techniques proposed by the authors, based on the modifications of this perceptual mask, in order to increase robustness, while still maintaining imperceptibility. Moreover, using the new mask, information is successfully hidden in the lower frequency levels, thus increasing the capacity and making the watermark more robust to common attacks that affect both high frequencies and low frequencies of the image. A good balance between robustness and invisibility of the watermark is achieved when embedding is made in all detail subbands for all resolution levels, except the coarsest level; this can be particularly useful against erasure of high frequency subbands containing the watermark in Barni's system.

A nonlinear detector with fixed threshold - as ratio between correlation and the image dependent ratio - has been used; three watermark detectors were proposed in Nafornita, 2007a that take advantage of the hierarchical wavelet decomposition: 1) from all resolution levels, 2) separately from each level, considering the maximum detector response for each level and 3) separately from each subband, considering the maximum detector response for each subband. This has been advantageous for cropping, scaling and median filtering where the 3rd detector shows improved performance. We tested our methods against different attacks, and found out that it is better than Barni's method. The behavior of our methods can be explained by the fact that we have used a better estimate of the mask and we took advantage of the diversity of the wavelet decomposition. The effectiveness of the new perceptual mask is appreciated by comparison with Barni's method. Simulation results show the superiority of the proposed methods (Nafornita et al., 2006a, b, Nafornita, 2007a).

The HWT is a very modern WT as it has been formalized only two years ago. A very simple implementation of this transform has been used, which permits the exploitation of the mathematical results and of the algorithms previously obtained in the evolution of wavelets theory. It does not require the construction of any special wavelet filter. It has a very flexible structure, as we can use any orthogonal or bi-orthogonal real mother wavelets for the computation of the HWT. The presented implementation leads to both a high degree of shift-invariance and to an enhanced directional selectivity in the 2D case. An ideal Hilbert transformer was considered. A new type of pixel-wise masking for robust image watermarking in the HWT domain has been presented (Nafornita et al., 2008). Modifications were made to two existing watermarking technique proposed in Barni et al., 2001 and Nafornita, 2007a, based on DWT. These techniques were selected for their good robustness against the usual attacks. The method is based on the method in Barni et al., 2001, with some modifications. The first modification is in computing the estimate of the variance, which gives a better measure of the texture activity. An improvement is also owed to the use of a better luminance mask. The third improvement is to embed the watermark in the detail coefficients at all resolutions, except the coarsest level, making the watermark more attack resilient. The HWT embedding exploits the coefficients z_{+r} and z_{-r}.

The simulation results illustrate the effectiveness of the proposed algorithms. The methods were tested against different attacks (in terms of robustness). The HWT based watermarking method is similar and in some cases outperforms the DWT based methods, but it has a superior capacity than the DWT based methods.

As a future research direction, the statistical properties of the HWT will be used to improve the watermark detection.

5. References

Abdulaziz, N.; Glass, A.; Pang, K.K. (2002). Embedding Data in Images Using Turbo-Coding, *6th Symposium on DSP for Communication Systems*, 28-31 Jan. 2002, Univ. of Wollongong, Australia.

Adam, I.; Nafornita, C.; Boucher, J.-M. & Isar, A. (2007). A New Implementation of the Hyperanalytic Wavelet Transform, *Proc. of IEEE Symposium ISSCS 2007*, Iasi, Romania, '07, 401-404.

Balado F. & Perez-Gonzalez, F. (2001). Coding at the Sample Level for Data Hiding: Turbo and Concatenated Codes, *SPIE Security and Watermarking of Multimedia Contents*, San Jose CA, 22-25 Jan. 2001, San Jose CA , USA, 2001, 4314, 532-543.

Barni, M.; Bartolini, F. & Piva, A (2001). Improved wavelet-based watermarking through pixel-wise masking, *IEEE Trans. Image Processing*, 10, 5, May 2001, 783 - 791.

Braudaway, G.W.; Magerlein, K.A. & Mintzer, F. (1996). Protecting publicly available images with a visible watermark, *Proc. SPIE – Int. Soc.Opt. Eng.*, vol. 2659, pp.126 - 133, 1996.

Cox, I. (2005). Robust watermarking, *ECRYPT Summer School on Multimedia Security*, Salzburg, Austria, Sept. 22, 2005

Cox, I.; Killian, J.; Leighton, T. & Shamoon, T. (1997). Secure Spread Spectrum Watermarking for Multimedia, *IEEE Trans. Image Processing*, 6, 12, 1997, 1673-1687

Cox, I.; Miller, M. & Bloom, J. (2002). *Digital Watermarking*, Morgan Kaufmann Publishers, 2002

Daugman, J. (1980). Two-dimensional spectral analysis of cortical receptive field profiles, *Vision Res.*, 20, '80, 847-856.

Davenport, C. (2008). Commutative Hypercomplex Mathematics, Available from: http://home.comcast.net/~cmdaven/hyprcplx.htm.

Firoiu, I.; Nafornita, C.; Boucher, J.–M. & Isar, A. (2009). Image Denoising Using a New Implementation of the Hyperanalytic Wavelet Transform, *IEEE Transactions on Instrumentation and Measurements*, vol. 58, Issue 8, August 2009, pp. 2410-2416.

Girod, B. (1989). The information theoretical significance of spatial and temporal masking in video signals, *Proc. SPIE Human Vision, Visual Processing, and Digital Display*, vol. 1077, pp. 178–187, 1989.

Hua, L. & Fowler, J. E. (2002). A Performance Analysis of Spread-Spectrum Watermarking Based on Redundant Transforms, *Proc. IEEE Int. Conf. on Multimedia and Expo*, Lausanne, Switzerland, '02, vol. 2, 553–556.

Kingsbury, N. (2001). Complex Wavelets for Shift Invariant Analysis and Filtering of Signals, *Applied and Comp. Harm. Anal.* 10, '01, 234-253.

Kingsbury, N. (2000). A Dual-Tree Complex Wavelet Transform with improved orthogonality and symmetry properties, *Proc. IEEE Conf. on Image Processing*, Vancouver, '00, paper 1429.

Kundur, D. (2000). Water-filling for Watermarking?, *Proc. IEEE Int. Conf. On Multimedia and Expo*, NY, 1287-1290, Aug. 2000.

Kundur, D. & Hatzinakos, D. (1998). Digital Watermarking using Multiresolution Wavelet Decomposition, *Proc. IEEE Int. Conf. On Acoustics, Speech and Signal Processing*, Seattle, Washington, Vol. 5, pp. 2969-2972, May 1998.

Kundur, D. & Hatzinakos, D. (2001). Diversity and Attack Characterization for Improved Robust Watermarking, *IEEE Transactions on Signal Processing*, Vol. 49, No. 10, 2001, pp. 2383-2396.

Lin, C. Y.; Wu, M.; Bloom, J. A.; Cox, I. J.; Miller, M. L. & Lui, Y. M. (2001). Rotation, Scale, and Translation Resilient Watermarking for Images, *IEEE Trans. On Image Processing*, 10, 5, May 2001

Loo, P. & Kingsbury, N. (2000). Digital Watermarking Using Complex Wavelets, *ICIP* 2000.

Moulin, P. & Mihcak M.K. (2002). A Framework for Evaluating the Data-Hiding Capacity of Image Sources, *IEEE Trans. Image Processing*, 11(9), '02, 1029-1042.

Nafornita, C.; Isar, A. & Borda, M. (2005). Image Watermarking Based on the Discrete Wavelet Transform Statistical Characteristics, *Proc. IEEE EUROCON* 2005, Serbia & Montenegro, 943-946.

Nafornita, C. (2008). *Contributions to Digital Watermarking of Still Images in the Wavelet Transform*, Ph.D. thesis, Feb. 2008, Technical University of Cluj-Napoca, Romania.

Nafornita, C.; Isar, A.; Kovaci M. (2009). Increasing Watermarking Robustness using Turbo Codes, *IEEE International Symposium on Intelligent Signal Processing* WISP 2009, Budapest, Hungary, 26-28 August 2009.

Nafornita, C.; Firoiu, I.; Boucher, J.-M. & Isar, A. (2008). A New Watermarking Method Based on the Use of the Hyperanalytic Wavelet Transform, *Proc. SPIE Europe: Photonics Europe, vol. 7000: Optical and Digital Image Processing 70000W*, pp.70000W-1-70000W-12, ISBN 97808194 71987, Strasbourg, April, 2008.

Nafornita, C. (2007). A New Pixel-Wise Mask for Watermarking, *Proc. of ACM Multimedia and Security Workshop*, 2007, Dallas, TX, USA.

Nafornita, C.; Isar, A. & Borda, M. (2006). Pixel-wise masking for watermarking using local standard deviation and wavelet compression, *Scientific Bulletin of the Politehnica Univ. of Timisoara, Trans. on Electronics and Communications*, 51(65), 2, pp. 146-151, ISSN 1583-3380, 2006.

Nafornita, C.; Isar, A. & Borda, M. (2006). Improved Pixel-Wise Masking for Image Watermarking, *Multimedia Content Representation, Classification and Security*, September 11-13, 2006, Istanbul, Turkey, Lecture Notes in Computer Science, Springer-Verlag, 2006, pp. 90-97.

Nafornita, C. (2007). Robustness Evaluation of Perceptual Watermarks, *IEEE Int. Symposium on Signal, Circuits and Systems ISSCS 2007*, 12-13 July 2007, Iasi, Romania.

Nason, G.P. (2002). Choice of wavelet smoothness, primary resolution and threshold in wavelet shrinkage, *Statistics and Computing*, 12, '02, 219-227.

Nikolaidis, N. & Pitas, I. (1998). Robust Image Watermarking in the Spatial Domain, *Trans. Signal Processing*, Vol. 66, No. 3, pp. 385-403, 1998.

Ó Ruanaidh, J.J.K. & Pun, T. (1998). Rotation, Scale and Translation Invariant Spread Spectrum Digital Image Watermarking, *Signal Processing*, 66(1998), pp. 303-317.

Ó Ruanaidh, J.J.K; Dowling, W.J.; Boland, F.M. (1996). Phase watermarking of digital images, *Proc. IEEE Int. Conf. Image Processing*, 1996, pp. 239-242.

Podilchuk, C. & Zeng, W. (1998). Image-Adaptive Watermarking Using Visual Models, *IEEE Journal on Selected Areas in Communications*, 16, 4, May 1998, 525-539

Selesnick, I. W.; Baraniuk, R. G. & Kingsbury, N. (2005). The Dual-tree Complex Wavelet Transform - A Coherent Framework for Multiscale Signal and Image Processing, *IEEE Signal Processing Magazine*, 22(6):123-151, November 2005.

Serdean, C.V.; Ambroze, M.A.; Tomlinson, M. & Wade, J.G. (2003). DWT based high-capacity blind video watermarking, invariant to geometrical attacks, *IEE Proc.-Vis. Image Signal Process.*, 150, 1, Feb. 2003.

Xia, X.; Boncelet, C. G. & Arce, G. R. (1998). Wavelet Transform Based Watermark for Digital Images, *Optics Express*, Vol. 3, No. 12, 1998, pp. 497-505.

Part 4

Discrete Wavelet Transform Algorithms

Shift Invariant Discrete Wavelet Transforms

Hannu Olkkonen and Juuso T. Olkkonen
Department of Applied Physics, University of Eastern Finland, Kuopio,
VTT Technical Research Centre of Finland, VTT,
Finland

1. Introduction

The discrete wavelet transform (DWT) has an established position in processing of signals and images in research and industry. The first DWT structures were based on the compactly supported conjugate quadrature filters (CQFs) (Smith & Barnwell, 1986; Daubechies, 1988). However, a drawback in CQFs is related to the nonlinear phase effects such as image blurring and spatial dislocations in multi-scale analyses. On the contrary, in biorthogonal discrete wavelet transform (BDWT) the scaling and wavelet filters are symmetric and linear phase. The biorthogonal filters (BFs) are usually constructed by a ladder-type network called lifting scheme (Sweldens, 1988). The procedure consists of sequential down and uplifting steps and the reconstruction of the signal is made by running the lifting network in reverse order. Efficient lifting BF structures have been developed for VLSI and microprocessor environment (Olkkonen et al. 2005; Olkkonen & Olkkonen, 2008). The analysis and synthesis filters can be implemented by integer arithmetics using only register shifts and summations. Many BDWT-based data and image processing tools have outperformed the conventional discrete cosine transform (DCT) -based approaches. For example, in JPEG2000 Standard (ITU-T, 2000), the DCT has been replaced by the lifting BFs.

One of the main difficulties in DWT analysis is the dependence of the total energy of the wavelet coefficients in different scales on the fractional shifts of the analysed signal. If we have a discrete signal $x[n]$ and the corresponding time shifted signal $x[n-\tau]$, where $\tau \in [0,1]$, there may exist a significant difference in the energy of the wavelet coefficients as a function of the time shift. Kingsbury (2001) proposed a nearly shift invariant method, where the real and imaginary parts of the complex wavelet coefficients are approximately a Hilbert transform pair. The energy (absolute value) of the wavelet coefficients equals the envelope, which provides smoothness and approximate shift-invariance. Selesnick (2002) observed that using two parallel CQF banks, which are constructed so that the impulse responses of the scaling filters have half-sample delayed versions of each other: $h_0[n]$ and $h_0[n-0.5]$, the corresponding wavelets are a Hilbert transform pair. In z-transform domain we should be able to construct the scaling filters $H_0(z)$ and $z^{-0.5}H_0(z)$. For design of the scaling filters Selesnick (2002) proposed a spectral factorization method based on the half delay all-pass Thiran filters. As a disadvantage the scaling filters do not have coefficient symmetry and the nonlinearity interferes with the spatial timing in different scales and prevents accurate statistical correlations. Gopinath (2003) generalized the idea for N parallel

filter banks, which are phase shifted versions of each other. Gopinath showed that increasing N the shift invariance of the wavelet transform improves. However, the greatest advantage comes from the change $N = 1$ to 2.
In this book chapter we review the methods for constructing the shift invariant CQF and BF wavelet sequences. We describe a dual-tree wavelet transform, where two parallel CQF wavelet sequences form a Hilbert pair, which warrants the shift invariance. Next we review the construction of the BF wavelets and show the close relationship between the CQF and BF wavelets. Then we introduce a novel Hilbert transform filter for constructing shift invariant dual-tree BF banks.

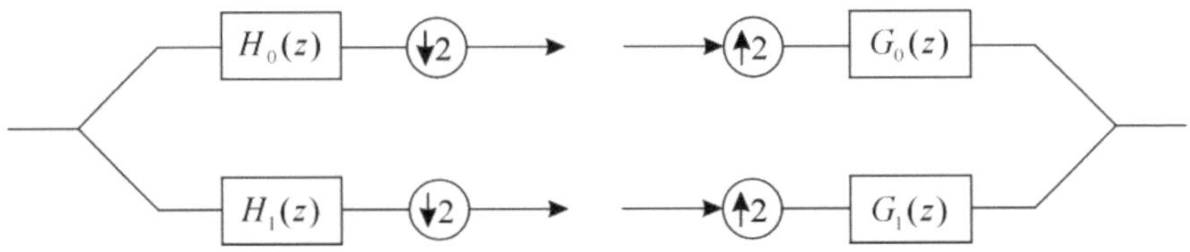

Fig. 1. The analysis and synthesis parts of the real-valued CQF DWT bank.

2. Design of the shift invariant CQF

The CQF DWT bank consists of the $H_0(z)$ and $H_1(z)$ analysis filters and $G_0(z)$ and $G_1(z)$ synthesis filters for N odd (Fig. 1)

$$\begin{aligned} H_0(z) &= (1+z^{-1})^K P(z) \\ H_1(z) &= z^{-N} H_0(-z^{-1}) \\ G_0(z) &= H_1(-z) \\ G_1(z) &= -H_0(-z) \end{aligned} \tag{1}$$

where $P(z)$ is a polynomial in z^{-1}. The scaling filter $H_0(z)$ has the Kth order zero at $\omega = \pi$. The wavelet filter $H_1(z)$ has the Kth order zero at $\omega = 0$, correspondingly. The filters are related via the perfect reconstruction (PR) condition

$$\begin{aligned} H_0(z)G_0(z) + H_1(z)G_1(z) &= 2z^{-N} \\ H_0(-z)G_0(z) + H_1(-z)G_1(z) &= 0 \end{aligned} \tag{2}$$

The tree structured implementation of the real-valued CQF filter bank is described in Fig. 2. Let us denote the frequency response of the z-transform filter as

$$H(z) = \sum_n h_n z^{-n} \Rightarrow H(\omega) = \sum_n h_n e^{-j\omega n} \tag{3}$$

Correspondingly, we have the relations

$$\begin{aligned} H(-z) &\Rightarrow H(\omega - \pi) \\ H(-z^{-1}) &\Rightarrow H^*(\omega - \pi) \end{aligned} \tag{4}$$

where * denotes complex conjugation. In M-stage CQF tree the frequency response of the wavelet sequence is

$$W_M(\omega) = H_1(\omega/2)\prod_{k=2}^{M} H_0(\omega/2^k) \tag{5}$$

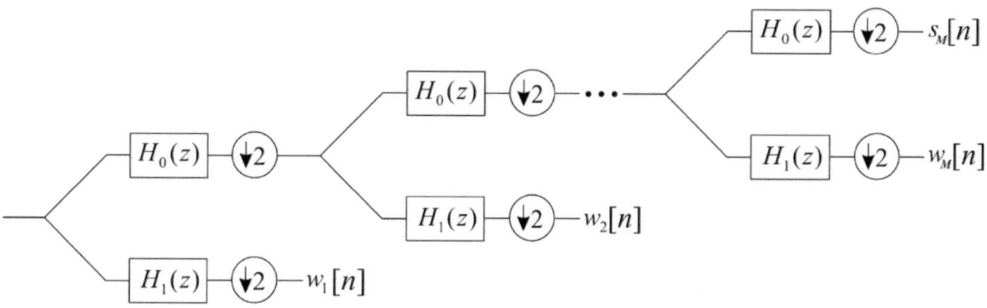

Fig. 2. The tree structured implementation of the real-valued CQF DWT, which yields the wavelet sequences $w_1[n], w_2[n] ... w_M[n]$ and one scaling sequence $s_M[n]$.

Next we construct a phase shifted parallel CQF filter bank consisting of the scaling filter $\bar{H}_0(z)$ and the wavelet filter $\bar{H}_1(z)$. Let us suppose that the scaling filters in parallel CQF trees are related as

$$\bar{H}_0(\omega) = e^{-j\phi(\omega)} H_0(\omega) \tag{6}$$

where $\phi(\omega)$ is a 2π periodic phase function. Then the corresponding CQF wavelet filters are related as

$$H_1(\omega) = e^{-j\omega N} H_0^*(\omega - \pi) \tag{7}$$

and

$$\bar{H}_1(\omega) = e^{-j\omega N} \bar{H}_0^*(\omega - \pi) = e^{-j\omega N} e^{j\phi(\omega-\pi)} H_0^*(\omega - \pi) = e^{j\phi(\omega-\pi)} H_1(\omega) \tag{8}$$

We may easily verify that the phase shifted CQF bank (6,8) obeys the PR condition (2). Correspondingly, the frequency response of the M-stage CQF wavelet sequence is

$$\begin{aligned}\bar{W}_M(\omega) &= \bar{H}_1(\omega/2)\prod_{k=2}^{M} \bar{H}_0(\omega/2^k) = e^{j\phi(\omega/2-\pi)} H_1(\omega/2)\prod_{k=2}^{M} e^{-j\phi(\omega/2^k)} H_0(\omega/2^k) \\ &= e^{j\phi(\omega/2-\pi)} e^{-j\sum_{k=2}^{M}\phi(\omega/2^k)} H_1(\omega/2)\prod_{k=2}^{M} H_0(\omega/2^k) = e^{j\theta} W_M(\omega)\end{aligned} \tag{9}$$

where the phase function

$$\theta = \phi(\omega/2 - \pi) - \sum_{k=2}^{M} \phi(\omega/2^k) \tag{10}$$

If we select the phase function $\phi(\omega)$ in (6) as

$$\phi(\omega) = \omega / 2 \tag{11}$$

the scaling filters (6) are half-sample delayed versions of each other. By inserting (11) in (10) we have

$$\theta = \frac{\omega / 2 - \pi}{2} - \omega \sum_{k=2}^{M} \frac{1}{2^{k+1}} = -\frac{\pi}{2} + \frac{\omega}{2^{M+1}} \tag{12}$$

The wavelet sequences (5,9) yielded by the CQF bank (1) and the phase shifted CQF bank (6,8) can be interpreted as real and imaginary parts of the complex wavelet sequence

$$W_{MC}(\omega) = W_M(\omega) + j\bar{W}_M(\omega) \tag{13}$$

The requirement for the shift-invariance comes from

$$\bar{W}_M(\omega) = \mathcal{H}\{\psi_M(\omega)\} \tag{14}$$

where $\mathcal{H}$ denotes the Hilbert transform. The frequency response of the Hilbert transform operator is defined as

$$\mathcal{H}(\omega) = -j\,\mathrm{sgn}(\omega) \tag{15}$$

where the sign function is defined as

$$\mathrm{sgn}(\omega) = \begin{cases} 1 \; for \; \omega \geq 0 \\ -1 \; for \; \omega < 0 \end{cases} \tag{16}$$

In this work we apply the Hilbert transform operator in the form

$$\mathcal{H}(\omega) = e^{-j\pi/2}\,\mathrm{sgn}(\omega) \tag{17}$$

Our result (12) reveals that if the scaling filters are the half-sample delayed versions of each other, the resulting wavelet sequences are not precisely Hilbert transform pairs. There occurs a phase error term $\omega / 2^{M+1}$, which depends both in frequency and the stage M of the wavelet sequence. In sequel we describe a novel procedure for elimination this error. We move the phase error in front of the phase shifted CQF tree using the equivalence described in Fig. 3. Then the error term reduces to $\omega / 2$. The elimination of the error term can be made by prefiltering the analyzed signal by the half-sample delay operator $D(z) = z^{-1/2}$, which has the frequency response $D(\omega) = e^{-j\omega/2}$. The total phase function is then for $-\pi \leq \omega \leq \pi$

$$\theta(\omega) = \angle D(\omega) - \pi / 2 + \omega / 2 = -\pi / 2 \tag{18}$$

which warrants that the M-stage CQF wavelet sequence and the phase error corrected sequence are a Hilbert transform pair.

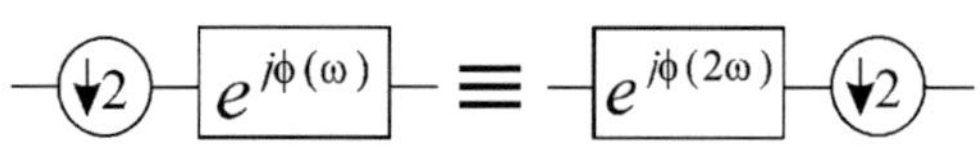

Fig. 3. The two equivalents for transferring the phase function in front of the phase shifted CQF tree.

3. Biorthogonal discrete wavelet transform

The first DWT structures were based on the compactly supported conjugate quadrature filters (CQFs) (Smith & Barnwell, 1986), which have unavoided nonlinear phase effects in multi-resolution analyses. On the contrary, in biorthogonal discrete wavelet transform (BDWT) the scaling and wavelet filters are symmetric and linear phase. The two-channel biorthogonal filter (BF) bank is of the general form

$$\begin{aligned} H_0(z) &= (1+z^{-1})^L Q(z) \\ H_1(z) &= (1-z^{-1})^M R(z) \\ G_0(z) &= H_1(-z) \\ G_1(z) &= -H_0(-z) \end{aligned} \tag{19}$$

where the scaling filter $H_0(z)$ has the Lth order zero at $\omega = \pi$. The wavelet filter $H_1(z)$ has the Kth order zero at $\omega = 0$, correspondingly. $Q(z)$ and $R(z)$ are polynomials in z^{-1}. The low-pass and high-pass reconstruction filters $G_0(z)$ and $G_1(z)$ are defined as in the CQF bank. For two-channel biorthogonal filter bank the PR relation is

$$\begin{aligned} H_0(z)G_0(z) + H_1(z)G_1(z) &= 2z^{-D} \\ H_0(-z)G_0(z) + H_1(-z)G_1(z) &= 0 \end{aligned} \tag{20}$$

4. Relationships between CQF and BF wavelet transforms

In the following treatment we use a short notation for the binomial term

$$B_K(z) = (1+z^{-1})^K \tag{21}$$

which appears both in the CQF and BF banks. Using the binomial term the CQF bank can be written as

$$\begin{aligned} H_0(z) &= B_K(z)P(z) \\ H_1(z) &= z^{-N}(-z)^K B_K(-z)P(-z^{-1}) \\ G_0(z) &= z^{-N} z^K B_K(z)P(z^{-1}) \\ G_1(z) &= B_K(-z)P(-z) \end{aligned} \tag{22}$$

For the PR condition of the CQF bank ( ) the following is valid for K odd

$$B_{2K}(z)P(z)P(z^{-1}) - B_{2K}(-z)P(-z)P(-z^{-1}) = 2z^{-N} \tag{23}$$

On the other hand, the PR condition of the BF bank gives

$$B_{L+M}(z)Q(z)R(-z) - B_{L+M}(-z)Q(-z)R(z) = 2z^{-D} \tag{24}$$

Both PR conditions are identical if we state $2K = L + M$. Then we have

$$P(z)P(z^{-1})z^{-N+D} = Q(z)R(-z) \tag{25}$$

The above relation (25) gives a novel way to design of the biorthogonal wavelet filter bank based on the CQF bank and vice versa. The polynomials $Q(z)$ and $R(-z)$ can be found by factoring $P(z)P(z^{-1})$, which is a symmetrical polynomial. The roots of the product filter $P(z)P(z^{-1})$ should be optimally divided so that both $Q(z)$ and $R(-z)$ are low-pass. Then $R(z)$ is high-pass. If the BF bank is known it is easy to factor $Q(z)R(-z)$ into $P(z)$ and $P(z^{-1})$ using some spectral factorization method. An important result is related to the modification of the BF bank (Olkkonen & Olkkonen, 2007a).

Lemma 1: If the scaling filter $H_0(z)$, the wavelet filter $H_1(z)$ and the reconstruction filters $G_0(z)$ and $G_1(z)$ in FB bank (19) have a perfect reconstruction property (20), the following modified FB bank obeys also the PR relation

$$\begin{aligned}\bar{H}_0(z) &= F(z)H_0(z)\\ \bar{H}_1(z) &= F^{-1}(-z)H_1(z)\\ \bar{G}_0(z) &= F^{-1}(z)G_0(z)\\ \bar{G}_1(z) &= F(-z)G_1(z)\end{aligned} \tag{26}$$

where $F(z)$ is any polynomial in z^{-1}. Proof is yielded by direct insertion (26) to PR condition (20).

5. Hilbert transform filter for construction of shift invariant BF bank

In BF bank the shift invariance is not an inbuilt property as in CQF bank. In the following we define the Hilbert transform filter $\mathcal{H}(z)$, which has the frequency response

$$\mathcal{H}(\omega) = e^{-j\pi/2}\operatorname{sgn}(\omega) \tag{27}$$

where $\operatorname{sgn}(\omega) = 1$ for $\omega \geq 0$ and $\operatorname{sgn}(\omega) = -1$ for $\omega < 0$. We describe a novel method for constructing the Hilbert transform filter based on the half-sample delay filter $D(z) = z^{-0.5}$. The classical approach for design of the half-sample delay filter $D(z)$ is based on the Thiran all-pass interpolator

$$D(z) = z^{-0.5} = \prod_{k=1}^{p} \frac{c_k + z^{-1}}{1 + c_k z^{-1}} = \frac{z^{-N}A(z^{-1})}{A(z)} = \frac{c_N + c_{N-1} + \cdots + z^{-N}}{1 + c_1 z^{-1} + \cdots + c_N z^{-N}} \tag{28}$$

where the c_k coefficients are optimized so that the frequency response follows approximately

$$D(\omega) = e^{-j\omega/2} \tag{29}$$

In this work we define the half-sample delay filter more generally as

$$D(z) = \frac{A(z)}{B(z)} \tag{30}$$

The quadrature mirror filter $D(-z)$ has the frequency response

$$D(\omega - \pi) = e^{-j(\omega - \pi)/2} \tag{31}$$

The frequency response of the filter $D(z)D^{-1}(-z)$ is, correspondingly

$$\frac{D(\omega)}{D(\omega-\pi)} = e^{-j\omega/2}e^{j(\omega-\pi)/2} = e^{-j\pi/2} \tag{32}$$

Comparing (27) and using the IIR filter notation (30) we obtain the Hilbert transform filter as

$$\mathcal{H}(z) = \frac{A(z)B(-z)}{A(-z)B(z)} \tag{33}$$

The Hilbert transform filter is inserted in the BF bank using the result of Lemma 1 (26). The modified prototype BF filter bank is

$$\begin{aligned} \bar{H}_0(z) &= \mathcal{H}(z)H_0(z) \\ \bar{H}_1(z) &= \mathcal{H}^{-1}(-z)H_1(z) \\ \bar{G}_0(z) &= \mathcal{H}^{-1}(z)G_0(z) \\ \bar{G}_1(z) &= \mathcal{H}(-z)G_1(z) \end{aligned} \tag{34}$$

The BF bank (34) can be highly simplified by noting the following equivalents concerning on (33)

$$\begin{aligned} \mathcal{H}^{-1}(-z) &= \mathcal{H}(z) \\ \mathcal{H}^{-1}(z) &= \mathcal{H}(-z) \end{aligned} \tag{35}$$

By inserting (35) in (34) we obtain a highly simplified FB bank

$$\begin{aligned} \bar{H}_0(z) &= \mathcal{H}(z)H_0(z) \\ \bar{H}_1(z) &= \mathcal{H}(z)H_1(z) \\ \bar{G}_0(z) &= \mathcal{H}(-z)G_0(z) \\ \bar{G}_1(z) &= \mathcal{H}(-z)G_1(z) \end{aligned} \tag{36}$$

The modified BF bank (36) can be realized by the Hilbert transform filter $\mathcal{H}(z)$, which works as a prefilter for the analysed signal. The Hilbert transform filter $\mathcal{H}(-z)$ works as a postfilter in the reconstruction stage, respectively. The wavelet sequences yielded by the two parallel BF trees can be considered to form a complex wavelet sequence by defining the Hilbert transform operator

$$\mathcal{H}_a(z) = 1 + j\,\mathcal{H}(z) \tag{37}$$

By filtering the real-valued signal $x[n]$ by the Hilbert transform operator results in an analytic signal

$$x_a[n] = x[n] + j\,\mathcal{H}\{x[n]\} \tag{38}$$

whose magnitude response is zero at negative side of the frequency spectrum

$$X_a(\omega) = \begin{cases} 2\,X(\omega) & 0 \le \omega < \pi \\ 0 & -\pi \le \omega < 0 \end{cases} \tag{39}$$

The wavelet sequence is obtained by decimation of the high-pass filtered analytic signal

$$W(\omega) = [X_a(\omega)H_1(\omega)]_{\downarrow 2} = W_a(\omega)_{\downarrow 2} = \frac{1}{2}X_a(\omega/2)H_1(\omega/2) \tag{40}$$

The result (40) means that the decimation does not produce aliasing but the frequency spectrum is dilated by two. The frequency spectrum of the undecimated wavelet sequence $W_a(\omega)$ contains frequency components only in the range $0 \le \omega < \pi$, but the frequency spectrum of the decimated analytic signal has the frequency band $0 \le \omega < 2\pi$. Hence, the decimation does not produce overlapping and leakage (aliasing) to the negative frequency range. A key feature of the dual-tree wavelet transform is the shift invariance of the decimated analytic wavelet coefficients. The Fourier transform of the decimated wavelet sequence of the fractionally delayed signal $x[n-\tau]$ is $\frac{1}{2}e^{-j\omega\tau/2}W_a(\omega/2)$ and the corresponding wavelet sequence is $w[n-\tau/2]$. The energy (absolute value) of the decimated wavelet coefficients is $\frac{1}{2}|W(\omega/2)|$, which does not depend on the fractional delay τ. If the wavelet filter has linear phase the wavelet coefficients are shift invariant in respect to their energy content.
An integer-valued half-delay filter $D(z) = A(z)/B(z)$ is obtained by the B-spline transform (see details Olkkonen & Olkkonen, 2007b). Table I gives the polynomial coefficients for the B-spline orders K=4, 5 and 6. The frequency response of the Hilbert transform filter constructed by the fourth order B-spline (Fig. 4) shows a maximally flat magnitude spectrum. The phase spectrum corresponds to an ideal Hilbert transformer (15).

K	$A(z)$	$B(z)$
4	$\frac{1+6z^{-1}+z^{-2}}{8}$	$\frac{1+4z^{-1}+z^{-2}}{6}$
5	$\frac{1+76z^{-1}+230z^{-2}+76z^{-3}+z^{-4}}{384}$	$\frac{1+11z^{-1}+11z^{-2}+z^{-3}}{24}$
6	$\frac{1+237z^{-1}+1682z^{-2}+237z^{-3}+z^{-4}}{3840}$	$\frac{1+26z^{-1}+66z^{-2}+26z^{-3}+z^{-4}}{120}$

Table I. The half-delay filter polynomials for the B-spline transform order K=4, 5 and 6.

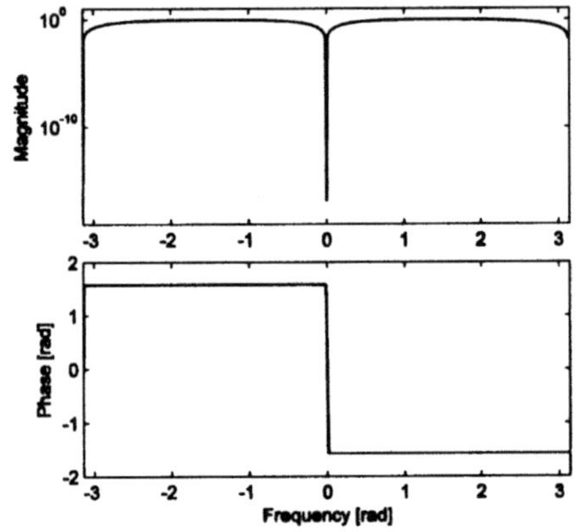

Fig. 4. Magnitude and phase spectra of the Hilbert transform filter yielded by the fourth order B-spline transform.

6. Conclusion

It is well documented that the real-valued DWTs are not shift invariant, but small fractional time-shifts may introduce significant differences in the energy of the wavelet coefficients. Kingsbury (2001) showed that the shift invariance is improved by using two parallel filter banks, which are designed so that the wavelet sequences constitute real and imaginary parts of the complex analytic wavelet transform. The dual-tree discrete wavelet transform has been shown to outperform the real-valued DWT in a variety of applications such as denoising, texture analysis, speech recognition, processing of seismic signals and neuroelectric signal analysis (Olkkonen et al. 2006; Olkkonen et al. 2007b).

Selesnick (2002) made an observation that a half-sample time-shift between the scaling filters in parallel CQF banks is enough to produce the shift invariant wavelet transform. In this work we reanalysed the condition and observed a phase-error term $\omega / 2^{M+1}$ (12) compared with the ideal phase response $\theta(\omega) = -\pi / 2$. The phase error attains s highest value at high frequency range and small stage M of the wavelet sequence. Fortunately, we showed in this book chapter that the phase error term can be cancelled by adding a half-delay prefilter in front of the CQF chain. For this purpose the half-delay filter $D(z) = A(z) / B(z)$ (30, Table I) constructed by the B-spline transform (Olkkonen & Olkkonen, 2007a) is well suited. In addition, there exists many other design methods for half-delay filters (see e.g. Laakso et al. 1996; Johansson & Lowenborg, 2002; Pei & Tseng, 2003; Pei & Wang, 2004; Tseng, 2006).

In multi-scale DWT analysis the complex wavelet sequences should be shift invariant. This requirement is satisfied in the Hilbert transform-based approach (Olkkonen et al. 2006, Olkkonen et al. 2007b), where the signal in every scale is Hilbert transformed yielding strictly analytic and shift invariant transform coefficients. The procedure needs FFT-based computation which may be an obstacle in many digital signal processor realizations. To avoid this we conducted the novel shift invariant dual-tree BF bank (36) based on the Hilbert transform filter (33). This highly simplified BF bank is yielded by *Lemma 1* and the equivalence (35) of the Hilbert transform filter (33). In many respects the BF bank (36) outperforms the previous nearly shift invariant DWT approaches.

7. References

Daubechies, I. (1988). Orthonormal bases of compactly supported wavelets. *Commmun. Pure Appl. Math.*, Vol. 41, 909-996.

ITU-T (2000) Recommend. T.800-ISO DCD15444-1: *JPEG2000 Image Coding System. International Organization for Standardization*, ISO/IEC JTC! SC29/WG1.

Johansson, H. & Lowenborg, P. (2002). Reconstruction of nonuniformy sampled bandlimited signals by means of digital fractional delay filters, *IEEE Trans. Signal Process.*, Vol. 50, No. 11, pp. 2757-2767.

Kingsbury, N.G. (2001). Complex wavelets for shift invariant analysis and filtering of signals. *J. Appl. Comput. Harmonic Analysis.* Vol. 10, 234-253.

Laakso, T., Valimaki, V., Karjalainen, M. & Laine, U.K. (1996). Splitting the unit delay. Tools for fractional delay filter design, *IEEE Signal Processing Magazine*, pp. 30- 80.

Olkkonen, H., Pesola, P. & Olkkonen, J.T. (2005). Efficient lifting wavelet transform for microprocessor and VLSI applications. *IEEE Signal Process. Lett.* Vol. 12, No. 2, 120-122.

Olkkonen, H., Pesola, P., Olkkonen, J.T. & Zhou, H. (2006). Hilbert transform assisted complex wavelet transform for neuroelectric signal analysis. *J. Neuroscience Meth.* Vol. 151, 106-113.

Olkkonen, H. & Olkkonen, J.T. (2007a). Half-delay B-spline filter for construction of shift-invariant wavelet transform. *IEEE Trans. Circuits and Systems II.* Vol. 54, No. 7, 611-615.

Olkkonen, H., Olkkonen, J.T. & Pesola, P. (2007b). FFT-based computation of shift invariant analytic wavelet transform. *IEEE Signal Process. Lett.* Vol. 14, No. 3, 177-180.

Olkkonen, H. & Olkkonen, J.T. (2008). Simplified biorthogonal discrete wavelet transform for VLSI architecture design. *Signal, Image and Video Process.* Vol. 2, 101-105.

Pei , T. S.C. & Tseng, C.C. (2003). An efficient design of a variable fractional delay filter using a first-order differentiator, *IEEE Signal Processing Letters*, Vol. 10, No. 10, pp. 307-310.

Pei , S.C. &and Wang, P.H. (2004). Closed-form design of all-pass fractional delay, *IEEE Signal Processing Letters*, Vol. 11, No. 10, pp. 788-791.

Selesnick, I.W. (2002). The design of approximate Hilbert transform pairs of wavelet bases. *IEEE Trans. Signal Process.* Vol. 50, No. 5, 1144-1152.

Smith, M.J.T. & Barnwell, T.P. (1986). Exaxt reconstruction for tree-structured subband coders. *IEEE Trans. Acoust. Speech Signal Process.* Vol. 34, 434-441.

Sweldens, W. (1988). The lifting scheme: A construction of second generation wavelets. *SIAM J. Math. Anal.* Vol. 29, 511-546.

Tseng,C.C. (2006). Digital integrator design using Simpson rule and fractional delay filter, *IEEE Proc. Vision, Image and Signal Process.*, Vol. 153, No. 1, pp. 79-85.

14

Condition on Word Length of Signals and Coefficients for DC Lossless Property of DWT

Masahiro Iwahashi[1] and Hitoshi Kiya[2]
[1]*Nagaoka University of Technology, Niigata,*
[2]*Tokyo Metropolitan University, Tokyo,*
Japan

1. Introduction

A discrete wavelet transform (DWT) has been widely applied to various digital signal processing techniques. It has been designed under a certain condition such as perfect reconstruction, aliasing cancellation, regularity, vanishing moment, etc. This article introduces a new condition referred to "DC lossless". It guarantees lossless reconstruction of a constant input signal (DC signal) instead of rounding of signal values and coefficient values inside a transform. The minimum word length of the values under the new condition is theoretically derived and experimentally verified.

Since JPEG 2000 algorithm based on the discrete wavelet transform (DWT) was adopted as an international standard for digital cinema video coding [1], high speed and low power implementation of a DWT has been becoming an issue of great importance [2,3]. In designing a DWT, its coefficient values and signal values are assumed to be real numbers. However, in implementation, they are rounded to rational numbers so that they are expressed with finite word length representation in binary digit. Therefore it is inevitable to have rounding errors inside a DWT processing unit.

In this article, we derive a condition on word length of coefficient values and that of signal values of a DWT such that the transform becomes lossless for a DC signal. Under this condition (DC lossless condition), it is theoretically guaranteed that an output signal contains no error in spite of rounding of coefficients and signals inside the DWT. We treat the irreversible 9-7 DWT adopted by the JPEG 2000 for lossy coding of image signals as an example.

In case of the 5-3 DWT in JPEG 2000 for lossless coding, benefiting from its lifting structure [4-6], lossless reconstruction of any signal is guaranteed even though signals and coefficients are rounded. On the contrary, it does not hold for the 9-7 DWT because of scaling for adjusting DC gain of a low pass filter in a forward transform [7]. However, we have pointed out that it became possible to be lossless for a DC signal under a certain condition on word length of coefficients and signals [8].

This DC lossless condition is a necessary condition for the regularity which has been analyzed by numerous researchers to improve coding performance of a transform. When the regularity is not satisfied, the DWT has some problems such as a checker board artifact which is observed in a reconstructed signal as unnecessary high frequency noise in flat or smooth region of a signal [9]. It also brings about DC leakage which decreases the coding gain of a transform [10].

The regularity has been structurally guaranteed for a two channel quadrature mirror filter bank (QMF) [9] and the DCT [10] respectively. However, since these previous methods were based on the lattice structure, these are not directly applicable to the lifting structure of the 9-7 DWT. Beside these relations to the regularity, the DC lossless condition itself is also considered to be important for white balancing of a video system in which the DC signal is used as a reference input for calibration [11].

This article aims at deriving the DC lossless condition theoretically and clarifying the minimum word length of signals and coefficients. In conventional analysis, errors due to shortening of word length of signals (signal errors) were described as 'additive' to a signal [7,12]. They were treated as independent and uniformly distributed white noise. On the other hand, errors due to rounding of coefficients (coefficient errors) were described as 'multiplicative' to a signal and evaluated with the sensitivity [13-15]. It should be noted that the signal error and the coefficient error have been treated independently. Unlike those conventional approaches, we utilize mutual effect between rounding of signals and that of coefficients. Introducing a new model which unifies the coefficient error and the signal error, we define tolerance for those errors as a parameter to simultaneously control both of word length of signals and that of coefficients.

As a result of our theoretical analysis, the minimum word length of signals and that of coefficients inside the lifting 9-7 DWT are derived under the DC lossless condition. We confirm that the minimum word length derived by our analysis is shorter than that determined by a conventional approach. We also confirm that the DWT under the condition does not have the checker board for a DC signal.

This article is organized as follows. Chapter 2 defines a rounding operation and a rounding error, describes their basic properties in algebraic approach, and derives 'addition' formula and 'multiplication' formula of the rounding (modulo) operation. Application of these formulas to scaling of a signal value is introduced in chapter 3. Chapter 4 introduces the DC lossless DWT. Its usefulness is also described. Derivation process of conditions on word length of signals and coefficients is described in chapter 5. The new condition derived from the basic properties in chapter 2 is summarized in chapter 6. Other related condition derived from a conventional approach is also summarized. Theoretical results are verified and the minimum word length of the DC lossless DWT is clarified in chapter 7. This article is concluded in chapter 8.

2. Rounding operation and its basic formulas

This chapter introduces basic properties of the rounding operation focusing on 'quotient', rather than 'remainder', in modulo operation. So far, 'remainder' had been attracted numerous mathematicians' attention and various basic properties were found such as the Chinese remainder theorem in the commutative algebra (commutative ring theory). On the contrary, 'quotient' plays an important role as a 'practical' value in finite word length implementation in modern computer systems. This chapter introduces an algebraic approach of expressing 'quotient' as a practical value, and 'remainder' as a rounding error, so that it can be applied to analyzing exact behavior of rounding errors in a complex calculation procedure.

2.1 Definition of rounding operation and rounding error

In a digital calculation system, all the values of both of signals and coefficients are calculated and stored as a binary digit with finite word length. In this article, we treat a case such that a value x is expressed with a fixed point binary expression as

$$x = \sum_{p=-F}^{I-1} b_p 2^p, \quad b_p \in \{0,1\}, \quad I \geq 1, \quad F \geq 0, \quad I \in \mathbf{Z}, \quad F \in \mathbf{Z} \tag{1}$$

where b_p, $p \in$ {$-F, \cdots, I-1$), is a set of binary digit for a value x. It has I bit integer part including one sign bit and F bit fraction part. Hereinafter, F is referred to as word length of a value x. This F bit value x has a range expressed as

$$x \quad \in [-2^{I-1}, 2^{I-1} - 2^{-F}] \quad \in [-2^{I-1}, 2^{I-1}). \tag{2}$$

For example, in case of I=1 and F=2, the maximum value is x=0.75 for $[b_0\ b_{-1}\ b_{-2}]$=[0 1 1], and the minimum value is x=-1.00 for $[b_0\ b_{-1}\ b_{-2}]$=[1 0 0].

When an F bit signal value is multiplied with a coefficient value, in a convolution of a filtering process in DWT for example, a resulting signal value has longer word length than its original value. Therefore it is rounded to F bit again. So far there are various types of rounding operations [16]. In this article, we deal with the rounding operation defined by

$$R_0[x] = \lfloor x + 2^{-1} \rfloor \quad or \quad R_0[x] = x' - (x' \bmod 1) \quad for \quad x' = x + 2^{-1} \tag{3}$$

as an example. This rounding operation generates a rounding error. We denote it as

$$\Delta_0[x] = x - R_0[x] \quad or \quad \Delta_0[x] = \left\{ (x + 2^{-1}) \bmod 1 \right\} - 2^{-1}. \tag{4}$$

Expanding these expressions to an F bit case, we can define the rounding operation and the rounding error as

$$\begin{cases} R_F[x] = R_0[x 2^F] 2^{-F} \\ \Delta_F[x] = \Delta_0[x 2^F] 2^{-F} \end{cases} \tag{5}$$

for an F bit word length implementation case.

Fig.1 illustrates rounding operations expressed by these equations. The term $R_F[x]$ is a quotient, and $\Delta_F[x]$ (= x - $R_F[x]$) is related to a remainder. The former is an actual value treated in a digital system under a finite word length implementation, and the latter is a rounding error. We are now trying to develop an algebraic expression approach to exactly trace a practical value and a rounding error in a convolution processing inside a DWT.

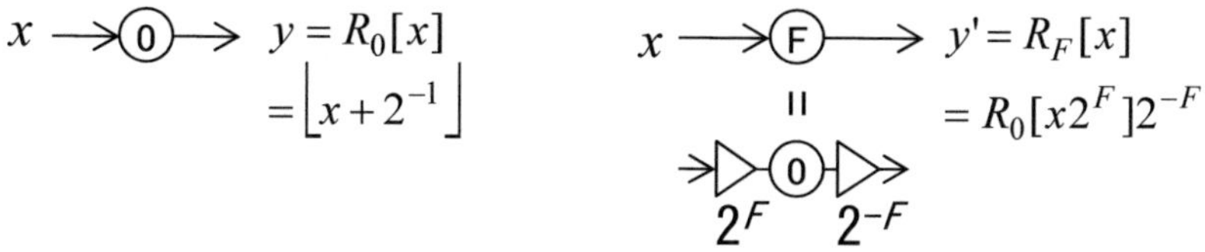

(a) integer (b) F bit fraction

Fig. 1. Definition of the rounding operation and the rounding error. (a) An integer implementation case. (b) An F bit word length implementation case.

2.2 Basic properties of the rounding operation

Since a convolution includes additions and multiplications, we should know behavior of an addition of two values x and y. Resulting value is $R_F[x+y]$ and its rounding error is $\Delta_F[x+y]$. A multiplication result $R_F[xy]$ and its error $\Delta_F[xy]$ should be also investigated.
First of all, let's derive basic properties of the rounding operation starting with an obvious property;

$$y \in \mathbf{Z} \rightarrow R_0[x+y] = R_0[x] + y \quad for \quad x \in \mathbf{R}. \tag{6}$$

It represents that only a real number x can be rounded if y is an integer to calculate a rounded value of $x+y$. In this case, its rounding error becomes

$$y \in \mathbf{Z} \rightarrow \Delta_0[x+y] = \Delta_0[x] \qquad for \quad x \in \mathbf{R}. \tag{7}$$

It suggests that an integer y can be ignored when only the rounding error is considered in an analysis. There is another obvious property;

$$R_0[x] = 0 \leftrightarrow x \in [-2^{-1}, 2^{-1}). \tag{8}$$

Since the range of a rounding error is

$$\Delta_0[x] \in [-2^{-1}, 2^{-1}), \tag{9}$$

we can add two more identities;

$$\begin{cases} R_0[\Delta_0[x]] = 0, \\ \Delta_0[\Delta_0[x]] = \Delta_0[x]. \end{cases} \tag{10}$$

The equations above for F=0 can be straightforwardly extended to an F≠0 case as follows.

$$y2^F \in \mathbf{Z} \rightarrow \begin{cases} R_F[x+y] = R_F[x] + y \\ \Delta_F[x+y] = \Delta_F[x] \end{cases} \quad for \quad x \in \mathbf{R} \tag{11}$$

$$R_F[x] = 0 \leftrightarrow x \in [-2^{-1-F}, 2^{-1-F}) \tag{12}$$

$$\Delta_F[x] \in [-2^{-1-F}, 2^{-1-F}) \tag{13}$$

$$\begin{cases} R_F[\Delta_F[x]] = 0 \\ \Delta_F[\Delta_F[x]] = \Delta_F[x] \end{cases} \tag{14}$$

In addition, Eq.(12) can be extended to a more general case with an integer n as

$$R_F[x] = n2^{-F} \leftrightarrow x2^F \in \left[-2^{-1}+n, \ 2^{-1}+n\right) \quad for \quad n \in \mathbf{Z}. \tag{15}$$

2.3 Basic formulas of the rounding operation

Utilizing the basic properties in Eqs.(11)-(14), we can derive an addition formula and a multiplication formula of a practical value (quotient) of the rounding operation as follows.

Addition formula

$$R_F[x+y]=R_F[x]+R_F\left[y+\Delta_F[x]\right] \quad for \quad x,y\in\mathbf{R} \tag{16}$$

Proof:

$$\begin{aligned}&R_F\left[x+y\right]\\&=R_F\left[R_F[x]+\Delta_F[x]+y\right] &\leftarrow(4)\\&=R_F[x]+R_F\left[\Delta_F[x]+y\right] &\leftarrow(11)\end{aligned}$$

Q.E.D.

Multiplication formula

$$R_F[xy]=R_F\left[xR_F[y]\right]+R_F\left[x\Delta_F[y]+\Delta_F\left[xR_F[y]\right]\right] \quad for \quad x,y\in\mathbf{R} \tag{17}$$

Proof:

$$\begin{aligned}&R_F[xy]\\&=R_F\left[x\Delta_F[y]+xR_F[y]\right] &\leftarrow(4)\\&=R_F\left[x\Delta_F[y]+\Delta_F\left[xR_F[y]\right]+R_F\left[xR_F[y]\right]\right] &\leftarrow(4)\\&=R_F\left[x\Delta_F[y]+\Delta_F\left[xR_F[y]\right]\right]+R_F\left[xR_F[y]\right] &\leftarrow(11)\end{aligned}$$

Q.E.D.

Formulas for a rounding error (remainder) can be also derived as

$$\begin{cases}\Delta_F[x+y]=\Delta_F\left[\Delta_F[x]+\Delta_F[y]\right]\\ \Delta_F[xy]=\Delta_F\left[\Delta_F[x]R_F[y]+R_F[x]\Delta_F[y]+\Delta_F[x]\Delta_F[y]\right]\end{cases} \tag{18}$$

for real numbers x and y. These formulas have following variations;
Addition formula

$$y2^F\in\mathbf{Z} \;\rightarrow\; \begin{cases}R_F[x+y]=\ R_F[x]+y\\ R_F[x+y]=-\Delta_F[x]+x+y\\ \Delta_F[x+y]=\ \Delta_F[x]\end{cases} \tag{19}$$

Multiplication formula

$$y2^F\in\mathbf{Z} \;\rightarrow\; \begin{cases}R_F[xy]=\ R_F\left[\Delta_F[x]y\right]+R_F[x]y\\ R_F[xy]=-\Delta_F\left[\Delta_F[x]y\right]+xy\\ \Delta_F[xy]=\ \Delta_F\left[\Delta_F[x]y\right]\end{cases} \tag{20}$$

Especially when two kinds of word lengths are mixed in a signal processing, the following variation of the multiplication formula is conveniently applied to analyzing behavior of signals and errors in a pair of encoder and decoder [17].

$$R_{F_2}\left[xR_{F_1}[y]\right] = R_{F_2}[xy] + R_{F_2}\left[-x\Delta_{F_1}[y] + \Delta_{F_2}[xy]\right] \quad (21)$$

Proof:

$$\begin{aligned} & R_{F_2}\left[xR_{F_1}[y]\right] \\ &= R_0\left[-x\Delta_{F_1}[y]2^{F_2} + xy2^{F_2}\right]2^{-F_2} \\ &= R_0\left[-x\Delta_{F_1}[y]2^{F_2} + \Delta_0[xy2^{F_2}] + R_0[xy2^{F_2}]\right]2^{-F_2} \\ &= R_0\left[-x\Delta_{F_1}[y]2^{F_2} + \Delta_0[xy2^{F_2}]\right]2^{-F_2} + R_0[xy2^{F_2}]\,2^{-F_2} \\ &= R_{F_2}\left[-x\Delta_{F_1}[y] + \Delta_{F_2}[xy]\right] + R_{F_2}[xy] \end{aligned}$$

Q.E.D.

3. Application of the formulas to basic signal processing

This chapter applies the formulas to some basic signal processing cases.

3.1 Mapping invariant condition

Fig.2 illustrates a scaling of a signal value x with a coefficient value h. As illustrated in Fig.2(a), this processing maps an input value x to an output value y^* with an ideal (infinite word length) coefficient value h. Note that x has F bit word length. Output value of the multiplication is also rounded to F bit (y^* has F bit word length). In implementation, as illustrated in Fig.2(b), a coefficient value h is also rounded to W bit word length (h' has W bit word length). We aim at finding the minimum word length W of a coefficient h' such that the mapping is invariant (y -y^* =0).

$h \in$ real number $\quad\quad h' \in$ rational number

$W \to \infty$ [bit] $\quad\quad W \to$ **min.** [bit]

(a) assumption (b) implementation

Fig. 2. Scaling of a signal value x with a coefficient value h. (a) This processing maps x to y^* with h under a given F. (b) A mapped y should be equal to y^* even though h is rounded to h'.

In case of Fig.2(b), an input value x is multiplied by a rounded value $R_W[h]$ (=h') of a given coefficient h. The result $R_W[h]x$ is rounded to $R_F[R_W[h]x]$ (=y). When it is the same as $R_F[hx]$ (=y^*), the mapping of x is invariant. It means that effect of rounding of h is nullified. This mapping invariant case is expressed as

$$E_m = 0 \quad for \quad \begin{cases} E_m = R_F\left[R_W[h]x\right] - R_F[hx] \\ R_W[h] = h - \Delta_W[h] \end{cases}. \quad (22)$$

From the basic properties, the mapping invariant condition is derived as

$$\Delta_W[h]x - \Delta_F[hx] \in \left(-2^{-1-F}, 2^{-1-F}\right]. \tag{23}$$

Proof:

$$\begin{aligned}
&R_F\left[R_W[h]x\right] - R_F[hx] \\
&= R_F\left[hx - \Delta_W[h]x\right] - R_F[hx] \\
&= R_F\left[\Delta_F[hx] - \Delta_W[h]x\right] + R_F[hx] - R_F[hx] \\
&= R_F\left[\Delta_F[hx] - \Delta_W[h]x\right] \\
&= 0
\end{aligned}$$

$$\therefore \quad \Delta_F[hx] - \Delta_W[h]x \in \left[-2^{-1-F}, 2^{-1-F}\right)$$

Q.E.D.

The Eq.(23) also means

$$\begin{cases} \Delta_W[h] \in \left(\dfrac{\Delta_F[hx] - 2^{-1}}{x}, \dfrac{\Delta_F[hx] + 2^{-1}}{x}\right], & x > 0 \\ \Delta_W[h] \in \left[\dfrac{\Delta_F[hx] + 2^{-1}}{x}, \dfrac{\Delta_F[hx] - 2^{-1}}{x}\right), & x < 0 \end{cases} \tag{24}$$

which gives tolerance to the rounding error of a coefficient [8]. This is the mapping invariant condition on word length W of a coefficient under a given word length F of signals. It represents exact (not approximated) behavior of rounding errors.
Unlike the condition above, a sufficient condition can be derived by substituting the upper bound of errors and signals;

$$\left|\Delta_W[h]\right| < 2^{-1-W}, \quad \left|\Delta_F[hx]\right| < 2^{-1-F}, \quad |x| < 2^{I-1}, \tag{25}$$

to Eq.(23). It results in the condition described as

$$W > F + I - 1. \tag{26}$$

This condition is too strict and requires too long word length to guarantee the mapping invariance. In both cases of Eq.(24) and Eq.(26), the mapping invariant condition determines the minimum of word length W of a coefficient under a given word length F of signals.

3.2 Lossless condition on a scaling pair

Fig.3 illustrates a pair of two multipliers. In Fig.3(a), an input signal x has F_2 bit word length. It is scaled with a coefficient h_1, and its output value y is rounded to F_1 bit. It is re-scaled with a coefficient h_2 ($=1/h_1$), and its final output value w is rounded to F_2 bit. This scheme is embedded in a forward transform and a backward transform of DWT for example. It is required to regain w exactly the same as x, under a given word length set of F_1 and F_2. Note that rounding errors due to finite word length expression of coefficients h_1 and h_2 can be ignored as far as the mapping invariant condition is satisfied.

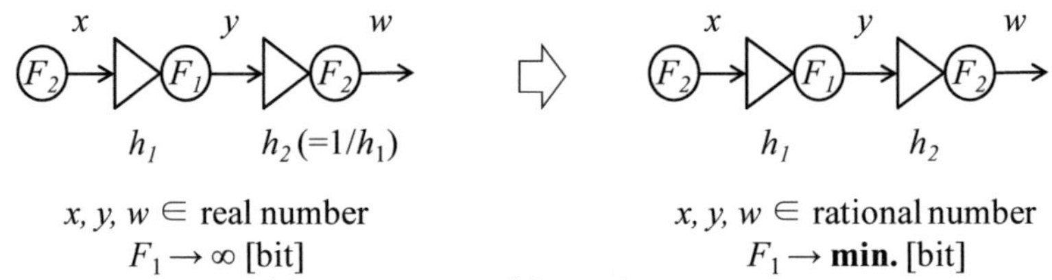

(a) assumption (b) implementation

Fig. 3. Scaling pair has two coefficients h_1 and h_2 (=$1/h_1$). (a) Output w is exactly the same as its original x. (b) This lossless property is guaranteed under a condition on F_1 and F_2.

We apply the formulas and the properties to derive the condition on F_1 and F_2. The lossless case in Fig.3(b) is described as

$$E_p = 0 \quad for \quad \begin{cases} E_p = R_{F_2}\left[h_2 R_{F_1}[h_1 x]\right] - x \\ h_1 h_2 = 1 \end{cases}. \tag{27}$$

From the basic properties, the lossless condition on a scaling pair is derived as

$$h_2 \Delta_{F_1}[h_1 x] \in \left(-2^{-1-F_2},\ 2^{-1-F_2}\right]. \tag{28}$$

Proof:

$$\begin{aligned} & R_{F_2}\left[h_2 R_{F_1}[h_1 x]\right] - x \\ & = R_0\left[-h_2 \Delta_{F_1}[h_1 x] 2^{F_2} + h_2 h_1 x 2^{F_2}\right] 2^{-F_2} - x \\ & = R_0\left[-h_2 \Delta_{F_1}[h_1 x] 2^{F_2}\right] 2^{-F_2} + x - x \\ & = R_{F_2}\left[-h_2 \Delta_{F_1}[h_1 x]\right] \\ & = 0 \end{aligned}$$

$$\therefore\ -h_2 \Delta_{F_1}[h_1 x] \in \left[-2^{-1-F_2},\ 2^{-1-F_2}\right)$$

Q.E.D.

This condition determines the word length F_1 and F_2 of signals for an input value x. It represents exact condition such that total accumulated rounding error is nullified by the rounding just after the final multiplier with h_2. As a result, the original value x is recovered as the final output without any loss.

Unlike the exact condition above, a sufficient condition can be derived by analyzing the upper bound as follows.

$$\left| h_2 \Delta_{F_1}[h_1 x] \right| < \left| h_2 \right| 2^{-1-F_1} < 2^{-1-F_2} \tag{29}$$

As a results, when the sufficient condition given by

$$F_1 > F_2 + \log_2 \left| h_2 \right| \tag{30}$$

holds, the scaling pair becomes lossless. However this condition is too strict and requires too long word length of signals.

4. Application of the formulas to DWT

This chapter introduces the DC lossless DWT [8, 18]. Definition and its usefulness are also described. The algebraic approach based on the formulas is applied to derive conditions on word length of signals and coefficients. Derivation process is described in chapter 5.

4.1 DWT and its word length of signals and coefficients

Fig.4 illustrates the irreversible 9-7 DWT of the JPEG 2000 standard [1]. The forward transform in Fig.4(a) decomposes an input signal $x(n)$, $n \in \mathrm{N}$, $\mathrm{N}=\{n \mid 1,2, \cdots, L\}$ into band signals $y_1(m)$ and $y_2(m)$, $m \in \mathrm{M}$, $\mathrm{M}=\{m \mid 1,2, \cdots, L/2\}$. The backward transform in Fig.4(b) reconstructs the signal $w(n)$ from the band signals. In the figure, z^{-1} and $\downarrow 2$ indicate the delay and the down sampler respectively.

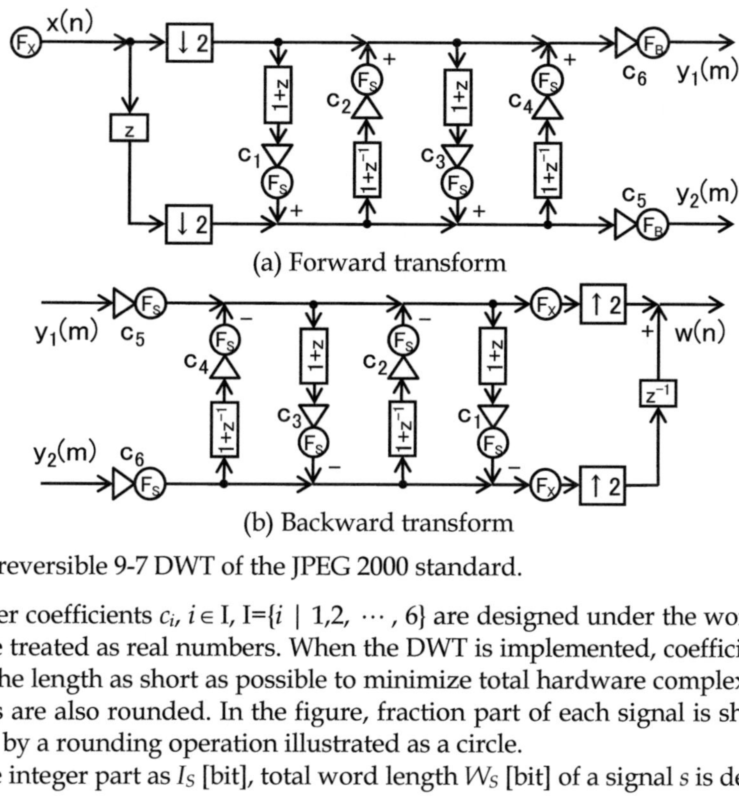

Fig. 4. The irreversible 9-7 DWT of the JPEG 2000 standard.

The multiplier coefficients c_i, $i \in \mathrm{I}$, $\mathrm{I}=\{i \mid 1,2, \cdots, 6\}$ are designed under the word length long enough to be treated as real numbers. When the DWT is implemented, coefficient values are rounded to the length as short as possible to minimize total hardware complexity. Similarly, signal values are also rounded. In the figure, fraction part of each signal is shortened to F_S, F_B or F_X [bit] by a rounding operation illustrated as a circle.

Denoting the integer part as I_S [bit], total word length W_S [bit] of a signal s is defined as

$$W_S = I_S + F_S + 1 \tag{31}$$

including 1 [bit] for the sign part. Similarly, total word length W_C [bit] of a coefficient c is defined as

$$W_C = I_C + F_C + 1\,. \tag{32}$$

In Fig.4, fraction part of the input signal $x(n)$ is given as F_X [bit]. Inside the DWT, fraction part of the signals are rounded to F_S [bit] just after each of all the multiplications with c_i, $i \in \mathrm{I}$. Output signals from the forward and backward transforms are rounded to F_B [bit] and F_X [bit] respectively. Note that we do not truncate integer part of signals and that of coefficients. We are determining F_S and F_C such that the DC lossless property is satisfied.

4.2 Definition of DC lossless property and its necessity

In this article, we define the DC lossless as the conjunction of the following two propositions:

$$\forall n \in \mathrm{N}, \forall m \in \mathrm{M} \left(\, x(n) = d \;\; \rightarrow \;\; y_1(m) = d \;\; \wedge \;\; y_2(m) = 0 \, \right) \tag{33}$$

$$\forall n \in \mathrm{N}, \forall m \in \mathrm{M} \left(\, y_1(m) = d \;\; \wedge \;\; y_2(m) = 0 \;\; \rightarrow \;\; w(n) = d \, \right) \tag{34}$$

for a given constant value d with F_X [bit] fraction part. When the proposition in Eq.(33) holds, the DWT has no DC leakage for the DC input signal with value d. Similarly, when the proposition in Eq.(34) is true, the reconstructed signal $w(n)$ contains no checker board artifact for the DC input signal. In the following chapters, we investigate the minimum fraction part of signals F_S [bit] which guarantees the DC lossless for given F_X and F_B [bit]. We also investigate the minimum fraction part F_{C_i} [bit] of a coefficient c_i, $i \in \mathrm{I}$ with flexibility of trading off the signal error and the coefficient error.

Fig.5(a) illustrates an example of a video system. It contains an encoder and a decoder which are composed of a forward DWT and a backward DWT. In white balancing, a camera and a display are calibrated with a constant valued input signal (DC signal) [11,19]. Therefore, it is useful for this calibration if the forward DWT and its backward do not generate any error. In this case, the camera and the display can be calibrated ignoring existence of the encoder and the decoder as illustrated in Fig.5(b). Namely, the DC lossless condition provides a low complexity DWT useful for the white balancing.

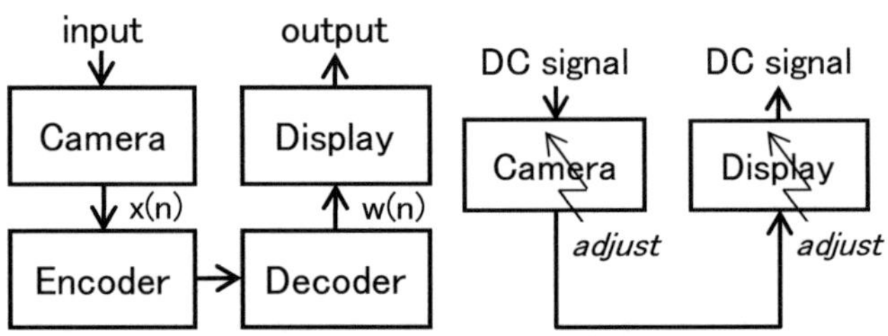

(a) video system (b) calibration

Fig. 5. The DC lossless property is useful for white balancing in a video system.

In addition, the DC lossless condition is a necessary condition for the regularity which controls smoothness of basis functions and coding performance of a transform. A DWT under the regularity does not generate the checker board artifact or the DC leakage. Harada et. al. analyzed a condition for the regularity of a two channel quadrature mirror filter bank (QMF) [9]. They confirmed that a QMF under the condition has reduced checker board artifact for an input step signal. It is expanded to a multirate system under short word length expression [20]. The regularity was structurally guaranteed for a biorthogonal linear phase filter bank [21,22] and the DCT [10] respectively. However, since these previous methods are based on factorization of a transfer function including $(1+z^{-1})$ or $(1-z^{-1})$ in the lattice structure, these are not directly applicable to the lifting structure of the 9-7 DWT in Fig.4.

In this article, we derive the DC lossless condition theoretically in chapter 5, and determine the minimum word length of signals and that of coefficients under the condition in following chapters.

5. Derivation of condition for the DC lossless DWT

This chapter describes derivation process of the DC lossless condition.

5.1 New model for error analysis

Fig.6(a) illustrates a multiplier in the DWT circuit. An input value s has F_S [bit] fraction part and multiplied by a coefficient c'. The coefficient is originally designed as a real number c. It is rounded to a rational number c' in implementation. It produces the coefficient error:

$$\Delta c = c - c' . \tag{35}$$

Just after the multiplication, the signal is rounded to s' with F_S [bit] fraction part as

$$s' = R_{F_S}[c's] \quad = c's + e' \tag{36}$$

where e' is the signal error. From Eq.(35) and (36), the final output becomes

$$s' = cs - \Delta cs + e' . \tag{37}$$

where cs is the ideal output. This conventional model, illustrated in Fig.6(b), describes the coefficient error Δc as multiplicative to the signal s [13-15], and the signal error e' as additive [7,12]. In addition, these errors are treated independently as mutually uncorrelated noises.

Unlike these existing approaches, as illustrated in Fig.6(c), we describe the coefficient error e'' as

$$\begin{cases} s' = R_{F_S}[cs] + e'', \\ e'' = R_{F_S}\left[\Delta_{F_S}[cs] - \Delta_{F_C}[c]s\right]. \end{cases} \tag{38}$$

From Eq.(15), we utilize the fact that e'' is observed as a 'particle';

$$e'' \cdot 2^{F_S} = p \tag{39}$$

where p is an integer. Given the tolerable maximum to an integer p, word length of the coefficient c can be controlled independently of other coefficients in other sections inside the DWT. Furthermore, denoting the signal error as e' similarly to Eq.(36), the output value is described as

$$\begin{cases} s' = cs + e \\ e = e' + e'' \end{cases} \tag{40}$$

where

$$\begin{cases} e' = -\Delta_{F_S}[cs] \\ e'' = R_{F_S}\left[\Delta_{F_S}[cs] - \Delta_{F_C}[c]s\right] \end{cases} \tag{41}$$

as illustrated in Fig.6(d). In this new model, both of the coefficient error e'' and the signal error e' are unified to the error e. Utilizing Eqs.(13) and (15), its absolute value is limited to

$$|e| \le (p + 2^{-1})2^{-F_S} . \tag{42}$$

Note that the parameter p to control word length of a coefficient c is included in this equation. It is equivalent to

$$2^{-F_C + F_S + I_S - 1} \le p \tag{43}$$

where its proof is given in appendix.
Benefitting from this inequality, it becomes possible to consider mutual effect of the coefficient error and the signal error.

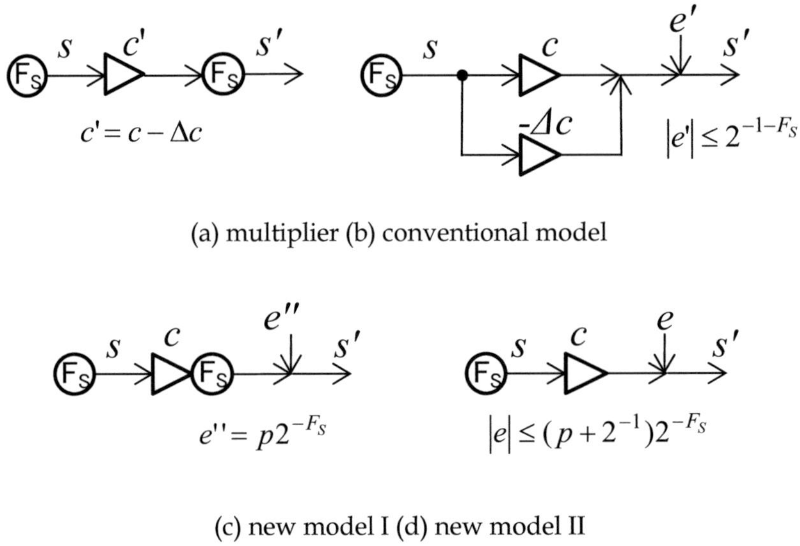

Fig. 6. A multiplier in the DWT and its models for error analysis.

Inside the forward DWT, the error e is propagated and added up with other errors from other multipliers. When its maximum absolute value is less than 2^{-1-F_B} , the total error is nullified by the rounding at the final output of the forward DWT. In this article, we utilize this nullification of errors at output of the DWT to derive a condition on word length such that the DC lossless defined by Eq.(33) and (34) is satisfied.

5.2 DC equivalent circuit

When the input signal is restricted to a DC signal, $x(n)$ can be described as a scalar x independent of n. The delay z^{-1} can be treated as 1 and $(1+z^{-1})$ can be replaced by 2. Therefore, instead of the circuits in Fig.4, we can use their equivalent circuits for a DC input signal in Fig.7 to derive the condition.

In Fig.7(a), a scalar x with F_X [bit] fraction part is multiplied by the rational numbers c_i, $i \in \mathrm{I}$ and rounded to F_S [bit]. Finally, the signals are rounded to F_B [bit] at its output to produce two scalars $[y_1\ y_2]$. The unified errors inside the circuit are described as

$$e_i = e_i' + e_i'' \text{ , } i \in \mathrm{I} \tag{44}$$

where

$$\begin{cases} e_i' = -\Delta_{F_S}[c_i s_i] \\ e_i'' = R_{F_S}\left[\Delta_{F_S}[c_i s_i] - \Delta_{F_C}[c_i] s_i\right] \end{cases}$$

$$\begin{bmatrix} s_1 & s_3 & s_5 \\ s_2 & s_4 & s_6 \end{bmatrix} = \begin{bmatrix} 2x & 2(x+s'_2) & s_4 \\ 2(x+s'_1) & 2(s_2+s'_3) & s_3+s'_4 \end{bmatrix}$$

$$s'_i = c_i s_i + e_i = R_{F_S}[c_i s_i] .$$

Similarly, for the backward transform in Fig.7(b), errors are described as

$$f_i = f_i' + f_i'' \text{ , } i \in \mathrm{I} \tag{45}$$

where

$$\begin{cases} f_i' = -\Delta_{F_S}[c_i t_i] \\ f_i'' = R_{F_S}\left[\Delta_{F_S}[c_i t_i] - \Delta_{F_C}[c_i] t_i\right] \end{cases}$$

$$\begin{bmatrix} t_1 & t_3 & t_5 \\ t_2 & t_4 & t_6 \end{bmatrix} = \begin{bmatrix} 2(t_3-t'_2) & 2(t'_5-t'_4) & y_1 \\ 2(t_4-t'_3) & 2t'_6 & y_2 \end{bmatrix}$$

$$t'_i = c_i t_i + f_i = R_{F_S}[c_i t_i] .$$

Similarly to Eq.(42), these errors are described with the parameters p_i and q_i to control word length of coefficients as

$$| e_i | \leq (p_i + 2^{-1}) 2^{-F_S} \text{ , } i \in \mathrm{I} \tag{46}$$

$$| f_i | \leq (q_i + 2^{-1}) 2^{-F_S} \text{ , } i \in \mathrm{I} \tag{47}$$

for a given word length F_s [bit] of signals.

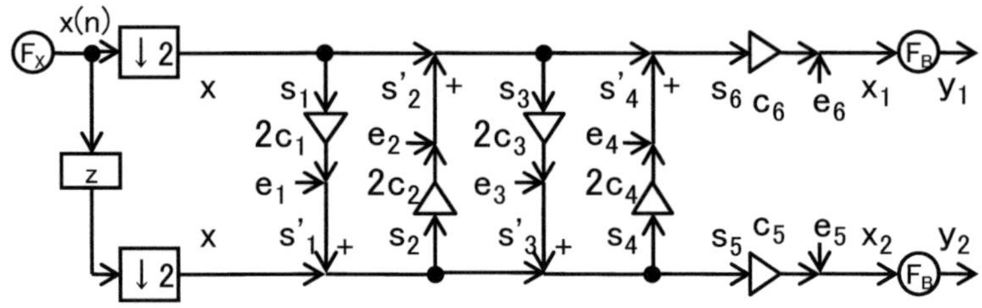

(a) Forward transform

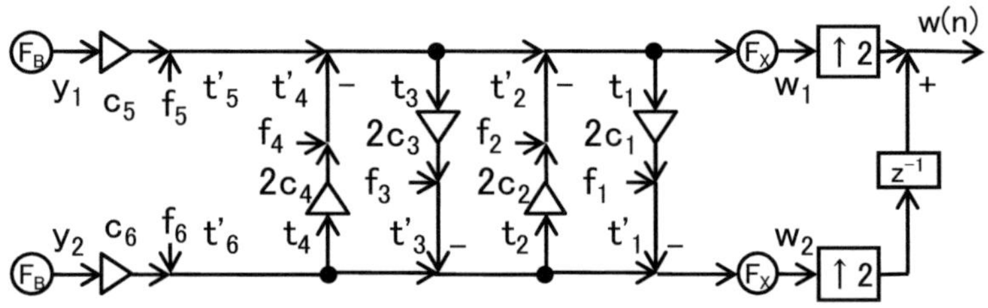

(b) Backward transform

Fig. 7. Equivalent circuits of the DWT for a DC input signal.

5.3 Nullification of accumulated errors

In Fig.7(a), the unified errors in Eq.(46) are propagated and accumulated inside the circuit. When the accumulated errors are nullified by the rounding at output of the forward transform, Eq.(33) is satisfied. In the figure, $\mathbf{Y}_{12}=[y_1\ y_2]^T$ is described as

$$\begin{aligned}\mathbf{Y}_{12} = R_{F_B}\Big[\ &\mathbf{I}_U e_6 + \mathbf{I}_L e_5 + \mathbf{K}\Big(\ \mathbf{I}_U e_4 + \mathbf{H}_4\Big(\ \mathbf{I}_L e_3 \\ &+\mathbf{H}_3\Big(\ \mathbf{I}_U e_2 + \mathbf{H}_2\left(\mathbf{I}_L e_1 + \mathbf{H}_1 \mathbf{I}_{UL} x\right)\Big)\Big)\Big)\Big]\end{aligned} \tag{48}$$

where

$$\mathbf{I}_U = [1\quad 0]^T,\ \mathbf{I}_L = [0\quad 1]^T,\ \mathbf{I}_{UL} = \mathbf{I}_U + \mathbf{I}_L$$

$$\mathbf{H}_{i\in\{1,3\}} = \begin{bmatrix} 1 & 0 \\ 2c_i & 1 \end{bmatrix},\ \mathbf{H}_{j\in\{2,4\}} = \begin{bmatrix} 1 & 2c_j \\ 0 & 1 \end{bmatrix},\ \mathbf{K} = \begin{bmatrix} c_6 & 0 \\ 0 & c_5 \end{bmatrix}.$$

It is described with the unified error matrices $\mathbf{E}_1$ and $\mathbf{E}_2$ as

$$\mathbf{Y}_{12} = R_{F_B}\left[(\mathbf{H}_{e1}\mathbf{E}_1 + \mathbf{H}_{e2}\mathbf{E}_2) + \mathbf{K}\mathbf{H}_{4321}x\right] \tag{49}$$

where

$$\begin{cases} \mathbf{H}_{e1} = [\mathbf{I}_U \quad \mathbf{K}\mathbf{I}_U \quad \mathbf{K}\mathbf{H}_{43}\mathbf{I}_U] \\ \mathbf{H}_{e2} = [\mathbf{I}_L \quad \mathbf{K}\mathbf{H}_4\mathbf{I}_L \quad \mathbf{K}\mathbf{H}_{432}\mathbf{I}_L], \\ \mathbf{H}_{43\cdots} = \mathbf{H}_4\mathbf{H}_3\cdots \end{cases}$$

and

$$\begin{cases} \mathbf{E}_1 = [e_6 \quad e_4 \quad e_2]^T \\ \mathbf{E}_2 = [e_5 \quad e_3 \quad e_1]^T. \end{cases}$$

Similarly, output values $\mathbf{W}_{12}=[w_1\ w_2]^T$ from the backward transform in Fig.7(b) are

$$\mathbf{W}_{12} = R_{F_X}\left[\ (\mathbf{H}_{e3}\mathbf{E}_3 + \mathbf{H}_{e4}\mathbf{E}_4) + (\mathbf{K}\mathbf{H}_{4321})^{-1}\mathbf{Y}_{12}\right] \tag{50}$$

where

$$\begin{cases} \mathbf{H}_{e3} = -[\mathbf{H}_1^{-1}\mathbf{I}_U \quad \mathbf{H}_{123}^{-1}\mathbf{I}_U \quad \mathbf{H}_{1234}^{-1}\mathbf{I}_U] \\ \mathbf{H}_{e4} = -[\mathbf{I}_L \quad \mathbf{H}_{12}^{-1}\mathbf{I}_L \quad \mathbf{H}_{1234}^{-1}\mathbf{I}_L] \\ \mathbf{H}_{12\cdots}^{-1} = \mathbf{H}_1^{-1}\mathbf{H}_2^{-1}\cdots \end{cases}$$

and

$$\begin{cases} \mathbf{E}_3 = [f_2 \quad f_4 \quad f_5]^T \\ \mathbf{E}_4 = [f_1 \quad f_3 \quad f_6]^T. \end{cases}$$

When the DWT is DC lossless, output values of the transforms are

$$\begin{bmatrix} \hat{\mathbf{Y}}_{12} \\ \hat{\mathbf{W}}_{12} \end{bmatrix} = \begin{bmatrix} \mathbf{K}\mathbf{H}_{4321}x \\ (\mathbf{K}\mathbf{H}_{4321})^{-1}\hat{\mathbf{X}}_{12} \end{bmatrix} = \begin{bmatrix} \mathbf{I}_U \\ \mathbf{I}_{UL} \end{bmatrix} x. \tag{51}$$

Using this equation, the accumulated errors are defined as

$$\begin{bmatrix} \mathbf{E}_{y12} \\ \mathbf{E}_{w12} \end{bmatrix} = \begin{bmatrix} \mathbf{Y}_{12} \\ \mathbf{W}_{12} \end{bmatrix} - \begin{bmatrix} \hat{\mathbf{Y}}_{12} \\ \hat{\mathbf{W}}_{12} \end{bmatrix}. \tag{52}$$

Substituting Eqs.(49), (50), (51) and using the property in Eq.(6), we have

$$\begin{bmatrix} \mathbf{E}_{y12} \\ \mathbf{E}_{w12} \end{bmatrix} = \begin{bmatrix} R_{F_B}\left[(\mathbf{H}_{e1}\mathbf{E}_1 + \mathbf{H}_{e2}\mathbf{E}_2)\right] \\ R_{F_X}\left[(\mathbf{H}_{e3}\mathbf{E}_3 + \mathbf{H}_{e4}\mathbf{E}_4)\right] \end{bmatrix}. \tag{53}$$

Applying Eq.(12), it becomes clear that when the conditions;

$$\begin{cases} \left|\mathbf{H}_{e1}\mathbf{E}_1 + \mathbf{H}_{e2}\mathbf{E}_2\right| \le \mathbf{I}_{UL}2^{-1-F_B} \\ \left|\mathbf{H}_{e3}\mathbf{E}_3 + \mathbf{H}_{e4}\mathbf{E}_4\right| \le \mathbf{I}_{UL}2^{-1-F_X} \end{cases} \tag{54}$$

are satisfied, the accumulated errors are nullified by the rounding operations at the final output of each of the forward transform and the backward transform.

6. Derived conditions on word length for the DC lossless DWT

This chapter summarizes the new condition derived from the basic properties in chapter 2, and other related condition derived from a conventional approach.

6.1 Critical condition on word length

Finally, we derive the condition on word length of coefficients and signals such that Eq.(54) is satisfied. Since the unified errors in $\mathbf{E}_1$, $\mathbf{E}_2$, $\mathbf{E}_3$ and $\mathbf{E}_4$ have the maximum in Eqs.(46) and (47) described with the parameters p_i and q_i, the DC lossless condition is also described with the parameters by substituting

$$\begin{cases} \mathbf{E}_1 = \left([p_6 \quad p_4 \quad p_2]^T + \mathbf{I}_3 \cdot 2^{-1} \right) 2^{-F_S} \\ \mathbf{E}_2 = \left([p_5 \quad p_3 \quad p_1]^T + \mathbf{I}_3 \cdot 2^{-1} \right) 2^{-F_S} \\ \mathbf{E}_3 = \left([q_2 \quad q_4 \quad q_5]^T + \mathbf{I}_3 \cdot 2^{-1} \right) 2^{-F_S} \\ \mathbf{E}_4 = \left([q_1 \quad q_3 \quad q_6]^T + \mathbf{I}_3 \cdot 2^{-1} \right) 2^{-F_S} \end{cases} \tag{55}$$

for

$$\mathbf{I}_3 = [1 \quad 1 \quad 1]^T$$

into Eq.(54). This is the condition we derived based on the new model described in section 5.1. We investigate the fraction part F_{Ci} [bit] of a coefficient c_i, $i \in \mathrm{I}$ as the minimum word length under the condition for a DC value x at the word length F_s [bit] of signals.

6.2 Sufficient condition on word length

As an example, in case of all the parameter in Eq.(55) are given as $p_i = q_i = p$ and $F_{Ci} = F_C$ for $\forall\, i \in \mathrm{I}$, the condition in Eq.(54) becomes

$$\begin{cases} \left(\|\mathbf{H}_{e1}\|_{L^1} + \|\mathbf{H}_{e2}\|_{L^1} \right) \cdot 2^{-F_S} (p + 2^{-1}) \le \mathbf{I}_{UL} 2^{-1-F_B} \\ \left(\|\mathbf{H}_{e3}\|_{L^1} + \|\mathbf{H}_{e4}\|_{L^1} \right) \cdot 2^{-F_S} (p + 2^{-1}) \le \mathbf{I}_{UL} 2^{-1-F_X} \end{cases} \tag{56}$$

where $\|\mathbf{H}\|_{L^1}$ denotes a column vector whose component is a sum of absolute value of all components in each row. Substituting coefficients of the 9-7 DWT [1] into Eq.(56), we have

$$\begin{cases} p \le 2^{-1+F_S-G_E} - 2^{-1} \\ G_E = 2.66 \quad \text{[bit]} \end{cases} \tag{57}$$

for $F_X = F_B = 0$. As a result, the DC lossless condition on the word length is given as

$$-\log_2(2^{-\Delta W_C} + 2^{-\Delta W_S}) \ge G_E \tag{58}$$

where

$$[\Delta W_C \quad \Delta W_S] = [F_C - I_S \quad F_S]$$

and G_E is the lower bound. This means a sufficient condition for the DC lossless. Since it is too strict, the word length under this condition is redundant. Unlike this sufficient condition, our critical condition given as Eq.(54) under Eq.(55) determines the word length minimum and necessary for the DC lossless.

7. Simulation results

This chapter verifies theoretically derived conditions, and clarifies the minimum word length of the DC lossless DWT.

7.1 Word length under the sufficient condition

Utilizing the sufficient condition in section 6.2, we calculated the optimized word length under the cost function defined as $J=2^{-1}(F_C+F_S)$. The cost J is minimized for three examples. Ex.1 trades the word length between F_C and F_S, namely $F_C+F_S=$ constant. Ex.2 and Ex.3 are $F_C=F_S$ and $W_C=W_S$ respectively. Results are summarized in table 1. Table 2 summarizes word length of signals and coefficients for an 8 bit system with $W_x=8$ ($I_x=7$ and $F_x=0$). Ex.1 requires $(F_S, F_C)=(4, 12)$ [bit] for signals and coefficients respectively. Ex.2 and Ex.3 require $F_S=F_C=11$ [bit] and $W_S=W_C=14$ [bit] respectively. The condition in Eq.(58) is plotted as a solid line in Fig.8. According to the sufficient condition, it is impossible to be DC lossless for

$$\begin{cases} F_C \le G_E + I_S \\ F_S \le G_E \end{cases} \tag{59}$$

and it is also confirmed by the figure. It guarantees the DC lossless, however the condition is too strict. Therefore the word length is redundant and there is room for further reduction.

	Ex.1 $F_C+F_S=const.$	Ex.2 $F_C=F_S$	Ex.3 $W_C=W_S$
F_C F_S	G_E+1+I_S G_E+1	$G_E+I_S^*$	$G_E+I_C^*+I_S-I_C$ $G_E+I_C^*$
W_C W_S	$G_E+2+I_S+I_C$ G_E+2+I_S	$G_E+I_S^*+1+I_C$ $G_E+I_S^*+1+I_S$	$G_E+I_C^*+I_S+1$
J	$G_E+1+I_S/2$	$G_E+I_S^*$	$G_E+I_C^*+(I_S-I_C)/2$

$I_S^*=\log_2(2^{I_S}+1)$, $I_C^*=\log_2(2^{I_C}+1)$

Table 1. Theoretically derived word length under the sufficient condition for DC lossless. F_S and F_C denote fraction part of signals and coefficients. I_S and I_C denote integer part of signals and coefficients. $W_S=I_S+F_S+1$, $W_C=I_C+F_C+1$, J is a cost function.

	Ex.1 $F_C+F_S=const.$	Ex.2 $F_C=F_S$	Ex.3 $W_C=W_S$
F_C F_S	11.66 3.66	10.67	11.25 4.25
W_C W_S	13.66 12.66	12.67 19.67	13.25
J	7.66	10.67	7.75

Table 2. Word length calculated with equations in table 1 for $W_x=8$ [bit].

7.2 Word length under the critical condition

In Fig.8, a cross "×" indicates a pair (F_S, F_C) which satisfies the critical condition in section 6.1 for any 8 bit integer x with W_X=I_X=8 and F_X=0. Here in after, we denote an input DC value to a video system as

$$x_{in} = x - 2^{I_X - 1} \tag{60}$$

where x is an input value to the DC equivalent circuit in Fig.7. The minimum of F_C for each F_S is indicated as a broken line. It is clear that the word length derived by the critical condition is shorter than that determined by the sufficient condition. For example in Fig.8(a), the fraction part F_S (= F_C) is reduced from 11 [bit] to 9 [bit] for Ex.2. The word length is not shortened for Ex.1 and Ex.3. In case of Fig.8(b), F_S (= F_C) is reduced from 13 [bit] to 12 [bit] for Ex.2. (F_S, F_C) is reduced from (14, 4) to (13, 3) or (12, 4) for Ex.1. W_S (= W_C) is reduced from 16 [bit] to 15 [bit] for Ex.3. It is confirmed that the word length is shortened due to the analysis in this article.

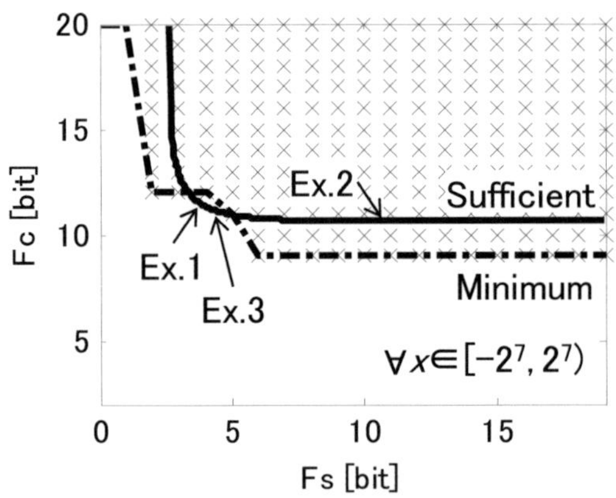

(a) $\forall x_{in} \in [0, 2^8)$, $W_X = 8$ [bit]

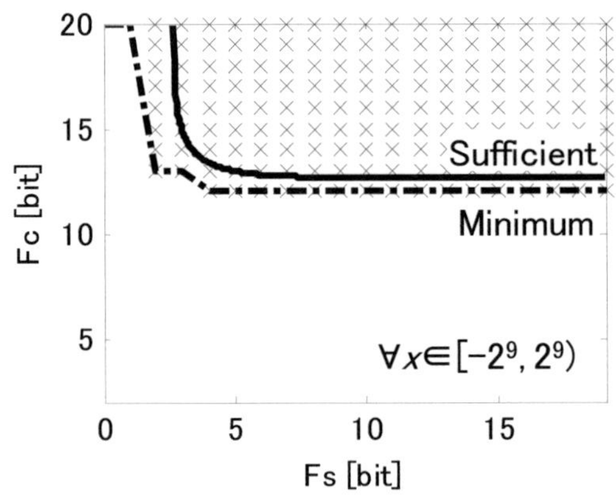

(b) $\forall x_{in} \in [0, 2^{10})$, $W_X = 10$ [bit]

Fig. 8. Word length under the two conditions. "×" indicates (F_S, F_C) such that the DWT becomes DC lossless.

7.3 Word length for a specific value

Fig.9(a) and Fig.9(b) illustrate the word length under the conditions for the black value "16" and the white value "235" respectively. These specific values are utilized in white balancing of an 8-bit video system [19]. For example, (F_S, F_C) is reduced from (4, 12) in Fig.8(a) to (2, 9) in Fig.9(a) for Ex.1. Table 3 summarizes the minimum word length for these specific input DC values [23]. It is observed that the word length can be reduced by limiting input DC signals to a specific value. Fig.10 indicates the minimum word length F_C of coefficients for an input value x at a given word length F_S of signals. This is an example at (F_S, W_X)=(3, 8). The sufficient condition gives the same word length for any of input values. Unlike this conventional statistical analysis, our analysis gives the minimum word length shorter than that determined by the sufficient condition for each of input DC values.

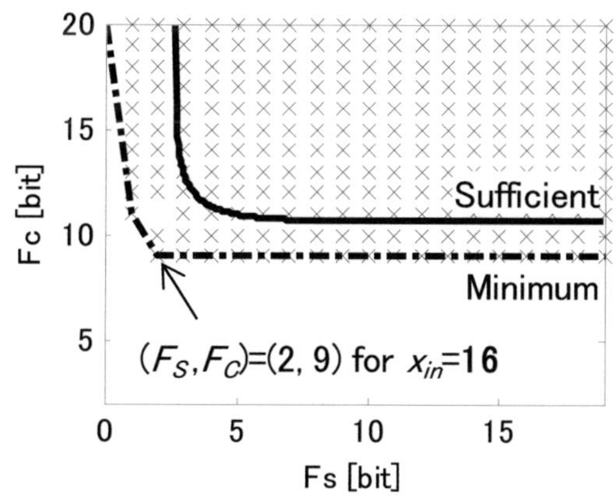

(a) black value

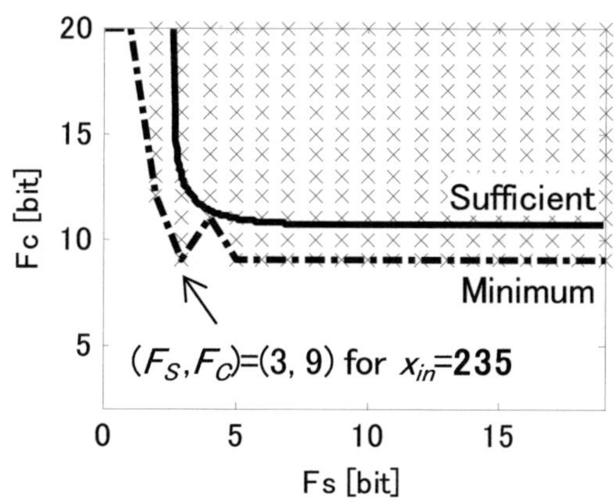

(b) white value

Fig. 9. Word length under the two conditions for a specific value used in white balancing.

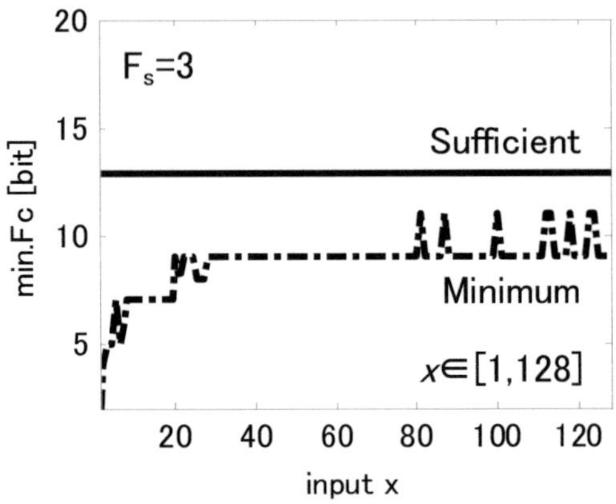

Fig. 10. The minimum word length of coefficients for each of input DC values at (F_S, W_X)=(3, 8). According to the sufficient condition, the word length is too long.

forward transform and backward transform					
input DC values		signals		coefficients	
		integer I_S [bit]	fraction F_S [bit]	integer I_C [bit]	fraction F_C [bit]
W_X=8 bit	sufficient	8	4	2	12
	any $x_{in}\in[0,2^8)$		2		12
	x_{in}= 16 (black)		2		9
	x_{in}=235 (white)		3		9
W_X=10 bit	sufficient	10	4	2	14
	any $x_{in}\in[0,2^{10})$		2		13
	x_{in}= 64 (black)		0		8
	x_{in}=940 (white)		0		12

Table 3. The minimum word length for a specific value for white balancing of a video system.

7.4 Optimum word length assignment

Since we described tolerance for the unified errors as parameters p_i and q_i in Eq.(46) and (47), it becomes possible to simultaneously control both of word length of signals and that of coefficients. Table 4 summarizes these parameters for an input value 16 and the word length of signals at F_S=2 [bit] as an example. It indicates that $[p_1\ p_2\ \cdots\ p_6]$ in Eq.(46) are [0 0 0 0 0 1] for the word length of coefficients at F_C=9 [bit]. In this case, all the coefficients c_i in the forward transform have the same length. It is worth paying attention to the fact that the parameter p_1 is the same for F_C=9, 8 and 7 [bit] for example. It means that word length of the coefficient c_1 can be reduced from 9 to 7 [bit] without any influence to the errors. Therefore, word length [F_{C1} F_{C2} ⋯ F_{C6}] of coefficients [c_1 c_2 ⋯ c_6] can be reduced from [9 9 9 9 9 9] to [7 9 7 4 6 4] according to the table.

Table 5 summarizes results of this optimum word length assignment for the forward transform. Comparing to table 3, it is observed that word length of coefficients is reduced from 9.00 [bit] to 6.17 [bit] on average for an input value x_{in}=16. Table 6 summarizes results for the backward transform. In this case, the word length is furthermore shortened. It is observed that c_6 and c_4 can be omitted since y_2 is equal to zero under the DC lossless. Fig.11 illustrates image signals reconstructed by the DWT which does not satisfy the DC lossless condition. It demonstrates the checker board artifact for reference. It is confirmed that total word length is furthermore shortened utilizing the tolerance parameters p_i and q_i introduced in this article.

F_C	p_1	p_2	p_3	p_4	p_5	p_6	y_1-x	y_2
9	**0**	**0**	**0**	**0**	**0**	**1**	**0**	**0**
8	**0**	-3	**0**	**0**	**0**	0	-1	-1
7	**0**	-3	**0**	**0**	**0**	0	-1	-1
6	7	12	-8	**0**	**0**	2	6	6
5	7	-18	10	**0**	1	0	-7	-5
4	-21	-18	9	**0**	-2	**1**	-10	-12
3	35	107	7	25	9	-28	63	70

Table 4. Tolerance parameters in Eq.(46) and (47) for x_{in}=16 and F_S=2 as an example.

forward transform									
input values		signals	coefficients						
		F_S	F_{C1}	F_{C2}	F_{C3}	F_{C4}	F_{C5}	F_{C6}	*ave.*
W_X=8	x_{in}= 16 (B)	2	7	9	7	4	6	4	**6.17**
	x_{in}=235 (W)	3	9	7	9	9	1	4	**6.50**
W_X=10	x_{in}= 64 (B)	0	7	9	7	1	1	4	**4.83**
	x_{in}=940 (W)	0	7	11	-1	1	1	4	**3.83**

Table 5. The minimum word length of coefficients in the forward transform for a specific values x_{in} for a given word length of signals F_S.

backward transform									
input values		signals	coefficients						
		F_S	F_{C1}	F_{C2}	F_{C3}	F_{C4}	F_{C5}	F_{C6}	*ave.*
W_X=8	x_{in}= 16 (B)	2	9	9	7	0	8	0	**5.50**
	x_{in}=235 (W)	3	9	9	7	0	8	0	**5.50**
W_X=10	x_{in}= 64 (B)	0	7	9	7	0	8	0	**5.17**
	x_{in}=940 (W)	0	7	12	8	0	8	0	**5.83**

Table 6. The minimum word length of coefficients in the backward transform for a specific values x_{in} for a given word length of signals F_S.

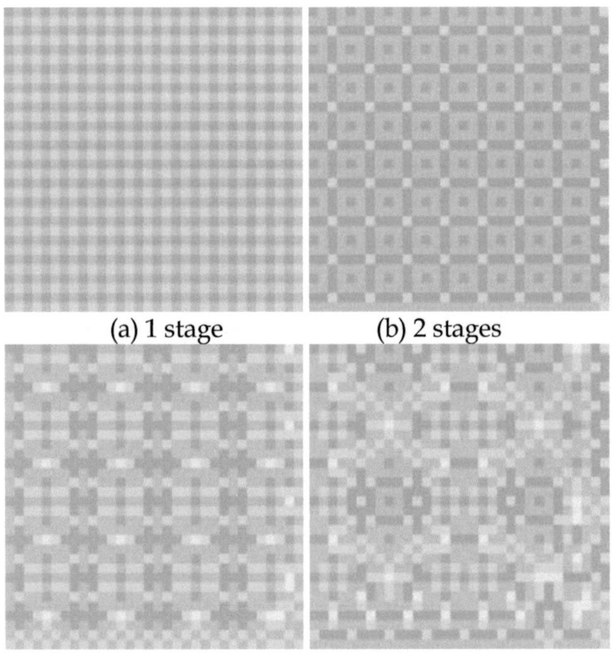

(a) 1 stage (b) 2 stages

(c) 3 stage (d) 4 stages

Fig. 11. Example of reconstructed images for 128^2 pixel DC input image with x=10. Intensity is multiplied by 16.

8. Conclusions

Introducing a new model which unifies the coefficient error and the signal error, and utilizing the nullification of the accumulated errors, this article theoretically derived a condition on word length of signals and coefficients such that the 9-7 DWT of JPEG 2000 becomes lossless for a DC input signal. It was confirmed that the minimum word length derived by the newly introduced 'critical' condition was shorter than that determined by a conventionally well known 'sufficient' condition. It was also confirmed that the DWT under the condition does not have the checker board for a DC signal. Analysis in this article contributes to build a low complexity DC lossless DWT.

9. Appendix

Proof of Eq.(43)
Eq.(39) with Eq.(41) means

$$\left|\Delta_{F_S}[cs]-\Delta_{F_C}[c]s\right| \le (p+2^{-1})2^{-F_S} \tag{A.1}$$

according to Eqs.(13) and (15). Applying the triangle inequality to the left hand side, we have

$$\left|\Delta_{F_S}[cs]-\Delta_{F_C}[c]s\right| \le \left|\Delta_{F_S}[cs]\right| + \left|\Delta_{F_C}[c]\right|\left|s\right| . \tag{A.2}$$

According to Eq.(13), each terms in the right hand side are described as

$$\begin{cases} \left|\Delta_{F_S}[cs]\right| \le 2^{-1-F_S} \\ \left|\Delta_{F_C}[c]\right| \cdot \left|s\right| \le 2^{-1-F_C}2^{I_S} \end{cases} \tag{A.3}$$

Therefore (A.2) and (A.3) under (A.1) means

$$2^{-1-F_S} + 2^{-1-F_C}2^{I_S} < (p+2^{-1})2^{-F_S}$$

and finally we have Eq.(43) as

$$2^{-F_C+F_S+I_S-1} \le p .$$

Q.E.D.

10. References

[1] ISO/IEC FCD15444-1, "JPEG2000 image coding system," March 2000.
[2] Descampe, et.al., "A flexible hardware JPEG 2000 decoder for digital cinema," IEEE Trans. circuits, systems on video technology, vol.16, issue 11, pp.1397-1410, Nov. 2006
[3] Bing-Fei Wu, Chung-Fu Lin, "Memory-efficient architecture for JPEG 2000 coprocessor with large tile image, IEEE Trans. circuits and systems II, vol.53, issue 4, pp.304-308, April 2006.
[4] H. Kiya, M. Yae, M. Iwahashi, "Linear phase two channel filter bank allowing perfect reconstruction", IEEE Proc. international symposium on circuits and systems (ISCAS), no.2, pp.951-954, May 1992.
[5] W. Sweldens, "The lifting scheme: A custom-design construction of biorthogonal wavelets," Technical Report 1994:7, industrial mathematics initiative, department of mathematics, university of South Carolina, 1994.
[6] M. L. Bruelers, A. W. M. van den Enden, "New Networks for Perfect Inversion and Perfect Reconstruction," IEEE Journal of selected areas in communications, vol.10, no.1, pp.130-137, Jan.1992.

[7] M. Reza, Lian Zhu, "Analysis of error in the fixed-point implementation of two-dimensional discrete wavelet transforms," IEEE Trans. circuits and systems, fundamental theory and applications, vol.52, issue 3, pp.641-655, March 2005.
[8] Kiya , M. Iwahashi, O. Watanabe, "A new class of lifting wavelet transform for guaranteeing losslessness of specific signals," IEEE international conference, acoustics, speech, and signal processing (ICASSP), pp.3273-3276, March 2008.
[9] Y. Harada, S. Muramatsu, H. Kiya, "Two channel QMF bank without checker board effect and its lattice structure," IEICE Trans. on fundamentals, vol.J80-A, no.11, pp.1857-1867, Nov. 1997.
[10] Wei Dai, T. D. Tran, , "Regularity-constrained pre- and post- filtering for block DCT-based systems," IEEE Trans. signal processing, vol.51, Issue 10, pp.2568- 2581, Oct. 2003.
[11] Hirakawa, T. W. Parks, "Chromatic adaptation and white balancing problem," IEEE Proc. international conference, image processing (ICIP), vol. III, pp.984-987, Nov. 2005.
[12] Grangetto, et.al., "Optimization and implementation of the integer wavelet transform for image coding," IEEE Trans. Image Processing, vol.11, Issue 6, pp. 596-604, June 2002.
[13] Xiao, et.al., "Coefficient sensitivity and structure optimization of multidimensional state-space digital filters," IEEE Trans. circuits, systems I, vol.45, issue 9, pp.993-998, 1998.
[14] S. Yamaki, M. Abe, M. Kawamata, "A closed form solution to L2-sensitivity minimization of second-order state-space digital filters subject to L2-scaling constraints," IEICT Trans. fundamentals of electronics, communications and computer sciences, vol.E91A, no.7, pp.1697-1705, July 2008.
[15] Y. Tonomura, S. Chokchaitam, M. Iwahashi, "Minimum hardware implementation of multipliers of the lifting wavelet transform," IEEE Proc. international conference, image processing (ICIP), pp.2499-2502, Oct. 2004.
[16] IEEE Standard 754-1985, IEEE standard for binary floating-point arithmetic.
[17] M. Iwahashi, H. Kiya, "Finite word length error analysis based on basic formula of rounding operation", the international symposium on intelligent signal processing and communication systems (ISPACS), no.86, pp.49-52, Dec. 2008.
[18] M. Iwahashi, H. Kiya, "Word length condition for DC Lossless DWT," Asia pacific signal and information processing association (APSIPA) annual summit and conference, no.TA-P2-6, pp.469–472, Oct. 2009.
[19] The society of motion picture and television engineers, "Standard for television, 1920x1080 image sample structure, digital representation and digital timing reference sequences for multiple picture rates", SMPTE 274 M-2005, Feb.2005.
[20] H. Iwai, M. Iwahashi, K. Kiya, "Methods for avoiding the checkerboard distortion caused by finite word length error in multirate system", IEICE Trans. fundamentals, vol. E93-A, no.3, pp.631-635, March, 2010.
[21] S. Oraintara, T.D. Tran, T.Q. Nquen, "A class of regular biorthogonal linear-phase filterbanks: Theory, structure, and application in image coding," IEEE Trans. signal processing, vol.51, no.12, pp.3220-3235, Dec.2003.
[22] Y. Tanaka, M. Ikehara, "First order linear phase filter banks with regularity constrains for efficient image coding," IEICE Trans. fundamentals, vol. J91-A, no.2, pp.192-201, Feb. 2008.
[23] M. Iwahashi, H. Kiya, "A lossless condition of lifting DWT for specific DC values", IEEE International Conference on Acoustics, Speech, and Signal Processing (ICASSP), pp.1458-1461, March 2010.

15

Wavelet-Based Analysis and Estimation of Colored Noise

Bart Goossens, Jan Aelterman, Hiêp Luong, Aleksandra Pižurica and Wilfried Philips
Ghent University - TELIN-IPI-IBBT
Belgium

1. Introduction

Digital imaging devices inevitably produce images corrupted with noise. The noise originates from the sensors and analogue circuitry in the camera. In order to have better and sharper images and also for commercial reasons, there is a recent tendency to further increase the image resolution. Nowadays, cameras with more than 20 megapixels are not uncommon. To reach such a high number of megapixels, the area of the sensor elements must be decreased and correspondingly the elements become more sensitive to noise, resulting in a lower image quality due to noise.

During the last decades, the use of image processing techniques has become widespread. The increasing processing power of computers allows for more sophisticated techniques that are better adapted to the classes of images under consideration (e.g. photographic images or medical images). This also allows for new classes of techniques that alleviate the physical limitations of the sensor elements by means of post-processing such as denoising. Because of power and hardware complexity constraints, the post-processing techniques implemented by camera manufacturers are based on simplistic assumptions with respect to the assumed noise model: for example, while it is well known that photon signals are *Poisson* distributed, the techniques most often rely on a white *Gaussian* noise model. In practice, such model mismatches generally lead to inferior denoising results. Also, many factors cause the noise in practice to be colored instead of white (i.e. with a flat power spectrum). For example, the image formation is often a reconstruction process based on an insufficient number of samples, and missing samples need to be estimated using interpolation techniques (e.g. Bayer pattern demosaicing). Doing so, the noise becomes colored. A technique that is designed to remove white Gaussian noise may offers a image quality: either some noise artifacts may be left in the image, or the noise is suppressed too much, leading to an overblurred image.

The obvious solution to this problem is to adapt existing techniques to use a colored noise model that is well matched to the underlying sensor characteristics and/or reconstruction. Therefore, estimation of the noise statistics is indispensable. Stationary colored noise (or correlated noise) is completely described by its Power Spectral Density (PSD). The noise PSD describes the power distribution of the noise in frequency space and can be estimated by using the Discrete Fourier Transform (DFT). However, noisy images also contain information other than noise (e.g. edges and textures), and directly estimating the PSD through the DFT will yield seriously biased estimates caused by the signal presence. Alternatively, the PSD could be estimated from noise-only patches in the image. However, not all images contain such patches and also the number of noise samples that can be used for this task is often too limited to yield reliable PSD estimates. Hence, more specialized techniques are needed.

The discrete wavelet transform (DWT) is an important tool for developing such techniques. The DWT provides a non-uniform partitioning of the space-frequency plane, which allows positional information of structures to be included in the estimation. This is not possible with the DFT, since the DFT cannot recover information at specified positions in the image.

In this chapter, we investigate the estimation of colored noise. First, we discuss a number of origins for colored noise in images. Next, we explain the importance of wavelets in solving the estimation problem. To proceed, it is necessary to know how the wavelet-domain and spatial-domain autocorrelation functions are related to each other, since we are aiming at estimating the wavelet-domain autocorrelation function. Because the wavelet transform in general does not fully decorrelate signals as we will explain, noise-free wavelet coefficients with significant magnitudes can still be found near high-frequent transitions in the signals (for example, near edges in images). To benefit from prior knowledge in a statistical estimation approach, we will discuss a number of wavelet domain prior models. Two iterative EM-based techniques will be presented, to estimate the wavelet-domain autocorrelation function. Next, we will explain how the parameters of a parametric noise PSD can be estimated using the presented tools. Finally, we will give a number of experimental results for the proposed techniques.

1.1 From white noise to colored noise

Throughout this chapter, we will consider a stationary additive Gaussian noise process:

$$y(\boldsymbol{p}) = x(\boldsymbol{p}) + w(\boldsymbol{p}) \tag{1}$$

where $x(\boldsymbol{p})$ is a pixel intensity of a noise-free image at position $\boldsymbol{p} \in \mathbb{Z}^2$, $y(\boldsymbol{p})$ is the corresponding observed pixel intensity and $w(\boldsymbol{p})$ is a zero-mean additive noise component. $w(\boldsymbol{p})$ and $x(\boldsymbol{p})$ are mutually statistically independent. We will further assume that the samples $w(\boldsymbol{p})$ are generated by a (wide-sense) spatial stationary process w, in which the correlation between two noise samples only depends on the position difference between the two noise samples, but not on their absolute position. Consequently, w can be completely described by the mean and the autocorrelation function.

A wide-sense stationary random process w obeying the above conditions is called *white* if its autocorrelation function is a Dirac delta function:

$$R_w(\boldsymbol{p}) = \mathrm{E}\left[w(\boldsymbol{p}')\overline{w(\boldsymbol{p}+\boldsymbol{p}')}\right] = \delta(\boldsymbol{p}). \tag{2}$$

For colored noise, neighboring noise samples are *not* statistically independent, hence spatial dependencies exist between these samples. Their dependencies can be characterized by the autocorrelation function of the noise, which is - for colored noise - different from the Dirac delta function.

The PSD is a related descriptor of colored noise. More specifically, the PSD describes how the noise energy is distributed in frequency space. According to the Wiener-Khinchin theorem, the *power spectral density* is the (discrete time) Fourier transform of the autocorrelation function

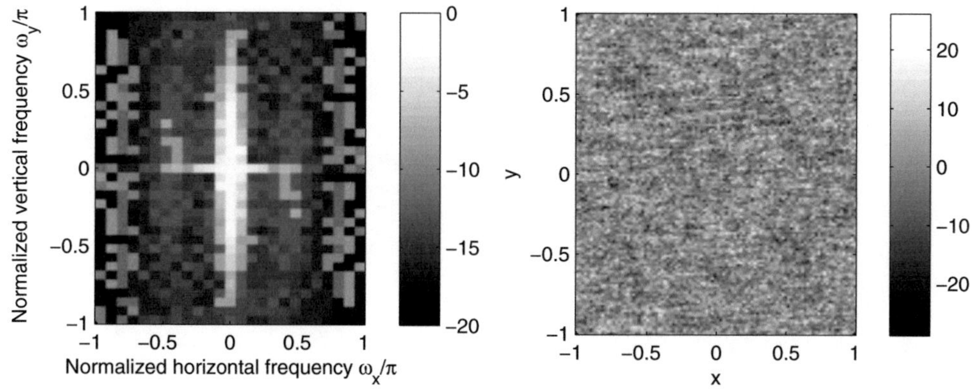

(a) (b)

Fig. 1. Noise in PAL broadcasting. (a) Power Spectral Density [dB], (b) Noise signal (containing horizontal stripe patterns due to correlations).

$R_w(\boldsymbol{p})$:

$$P_w(\boldsymbol{\omega}) = \sum_{\boldsymbol{p}\in\mathbb{Z}^2} R_w(\boldsymbol{p}) \exp\left(-j\boldsymbol{\omega}^T\boldsymbol{p}\right). \tag{3}$$

White noise has a flat PSD: $P_w(\boldsymbol{\omega}) = 1$. Suppose a filter with frequency response $H(\boldsymbol{\omega}) \neq 1$ is applied to the noise signal, then the resulting PSD $P_w^{'}(\boldsymbol{\omega})$ becomes Baher (2001):

$$P_w^{'}(\boldsymbol{\omega}) = P_w(\boldsymbol{\omega}) \left|H(\boldsymbol{\omega})\right|^2. \tag{4}$$

Clearly, the PSD $P^{'}(\boldsymbol{\omega})$ is subjected to the filter magnitude response $|H(\boldsymbol{\omega})|$. Hence one can think of correlated noise as white noise subjected to linear filtering. In analogy with the term *"white noise"* the resulting term is called *"colored noise"* (or *correlated* noise, because the filtering introduces correlations in the noise samples).

In practical circumstances, there are a number of origins of colored noise in images:

- *Phase Alternating Line (PAL) television*: the noise in PAL television images is a good example of colored noise. The correlations between the noise samples are caused by several mechanisms, such as deinterlacing Kwon et al. (2003), demodulation and filter schemes. In Figure 1, the PSD of a noise patch from a PAL broadcast is shown. Here, there is a high concentration of energy in the lower horizontal frequencies, leading to horizontal stripes and artifacts.

- *Color interpolation (demosaicing)*: modern digital cameras use a rectangular arrangement of photosensitive elements. In this matrix arrangement, photosensitive elements of different color sensitivity are placed in an interleaved way. This allows sampling of full color images without the use of three arrays of photosensitive elements. One popular example is the Bayer pattern Bayer (1976). Color interpolation (or demosaicing) is the process of estimating the values of missing photosensitive elements.

- *Post-processing techniques*: image noise often becomes correlated by the use of post-processing techniques, e.g., image quality enhancement techniques, sharpening filters, digital zoom functions of cameras, JPEG compression...

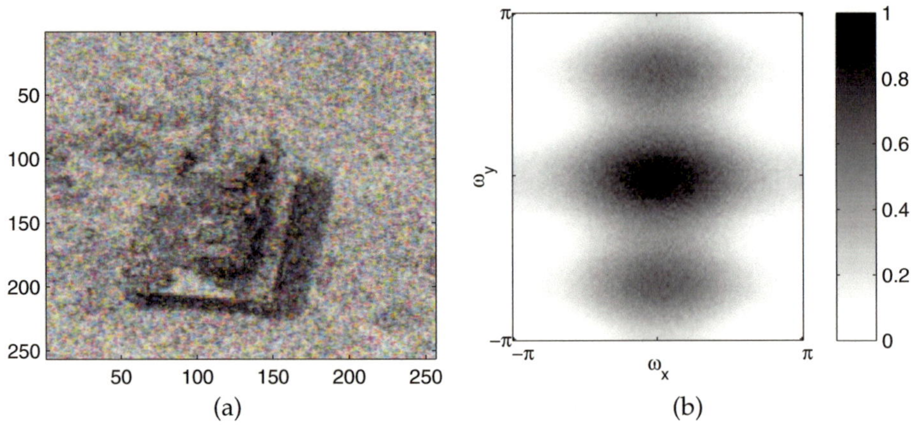

Fig. 2. (a) Image corrupted with colored noise caused by demosaicing (b) PSD of the noise in the green color channel of (a).

- *Thermal cameras*: images captured by thermal cameras of the push broom or whisk broom type often exhibit streaking noise artifacts, mainly caused by detector and sampling circuitry Aelterman, Goossens, Pižurica & Philips (2010). This kind of noise can be approximated using a $1/f$ frequency characteristic (called *pink* noise) Borel et al. (1996). Pink noise also frequently arises in image sensors that acquire pixel data in time.
- *Medical imaging*: in computed tomography (CT), noise correlations are introduced by the specific reconstruction technique that is being used. Noise created by the backprojection algorithm (without reconstruction filter) is called *ramp-spectrum* noise, and has an $1/f$ frequency characteristic. Noise in magnetic resonance imaging (MRI) is traditionally considered *white* Nowak (1999); Pižurica et al. (2003), although many MRI scanner manufacturers have included a wide range of techniques to allow for shorter scanning times (mainly to avoid patient motion artifacts in the images). To name a few: K-space subsampling, partial Fourier, elliptical filtering Aelterman, Deblaere, Goossens, Pižurica & Philips (2010). The use of these techniques results in correlated noise in the reconstructed MRI images.

In Figure 3 another example is shown of an image corrupted with colored noise. The colored noise was artificially generated by subjecting white noise to a filter with magnitude response $\sqrt{P(\boldsymbol{\omega})}$ and subsequently by adding the filtered noise to the images.

2. Wavelets for the estimation of colored noise

Spatially stationary colored noise can be directly specified through its mean and autocorrelation function and/or power spectral density. Given an observed noise signal $w(\boldsymbol{p})$, the estimation of these parameters is then a relatively simple task by, e.g., using the sample mean and sample autocovariance estimates. However, in practice, it often happens that the observed signal also contains information other than noise, this underlying signal is unknown and it is the signal that we eventually want to estimate. Hence, we are observing $y(\boldsymbol{p})$ instead of $w(\boldsymbol{p})$. The estimation of the noise statistics from the signal $y(\boldsymbol{p})$ is then considerably more difficult.

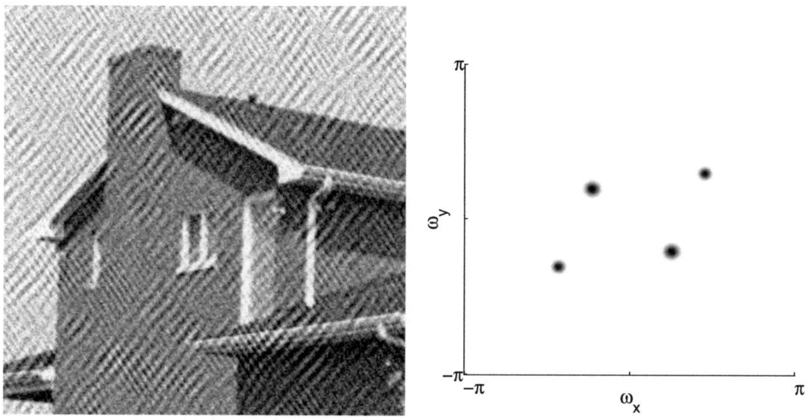

(a) (b)

Fig. 3. Illustration of the noise PSD: (a) Image with correlated noise, (b) The noise PSD (in frequency domain, the center of the image is the origin of frequency space, white corresponds with low noise powers, black with high noise powers).

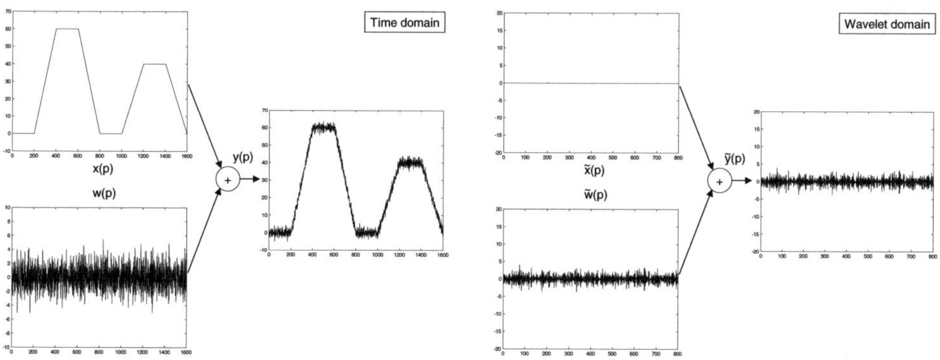

(a) (b)

Fig. 4. Example of a piecewise linear signal with correlated noise. Our goal is to estimate the noise power spectrum from the corrupted signal $y(\mathbf{p})$. (a) The signals in time domain, (b) The finest scale of the wavelet transform of the signals (Daubechies' wavelet with 2 vanishing moments was used).

This problem is illustrated in Figure 4 for a piecewise linear signal corrupted with correlated Gaussian noise. While the noise statistics can be easily estimated from $w(\mathbf{p})$, we only have the degraded signal $y(\mathbf{p})$ at our disposal, which also contains an unknown signal component. A straightforward solution is then to first estimate the signal $\hat{x}(\mathbf{p})$, to subtract it from $y(\mathbf{p})$ and finally to estimate the noise statistics from the difference $y(\mathbf{p}) - \hat{x}(\mathbf{p})$. However, *optimal* estimation of $x(\mathbf{p})$ from $y(\mathbf{p})$ requires knowledge of the noise statistics on its own, so we have a chicken-and-egg problem. The common approach is then to use iterative techniques, which first estimate $\hat{x}(\mathbf{p})$ and then later refine this estimate $\hat{x}(\mathbf{p})$ when better estimates for the noise parameters become available.

In this chapter, we will take a different approach by relying on the properties of *wavelets*. The wavelet transform Daubechies (1992); Mallat (1999) analyzes signals according to different

scales and at different points in time. Starting from a fixed mother wavelet $\psi(t)$, the input signal is correlated with time-shifted and time-stretched (dilated) versions of this wavelet. Correlations with wavelets with a large dilation factor then give the coarse features of the signal, while correlations with wavelets with small dilation factors give the fine signal details. Because the wavelet basis functions are well localized in time or space (this is in contrast to the basis functions of e.g., the Fourier transform), wavelets are ideal candidates for analyzing non-stationary signals, having statistical properties that vary in time (or space).
The Daubechies wavelets are a class of orthogonal wavelets for which the number of vanishing moments for a given support is maximal. More specifically, the n-th moment of a real-valued wavelet function $\psi(t)$ is defined by:

$$\mu_n = \int_{-\infty}^{+\infty} t^n \psi(t) dt. \tag{5}$$

The Daubechies wavelet of support $2N$ (with N vanishing moments) will have moments $\mu_n = 0$ for $0 \leq n < N$. Now, let us denote the time-shifted and dilated basis functions of $\psi(t)$ by:

$$\psi_{a,b}(t) = \frac{1}{\sqrt{a}} \psi\left(\frac{t-b}{a}\right) \tag{6}$$

where a is the dilation factor, b is a time shift, and the constant $1/\sqrt{a}$ is an energy normalization factor. The continuous wavelet transform of a signal $f \in L^2(\mathbb{R})$ is defined by:

$$\mathcal{W}f(a,b) = \int_{-\infty}^{+\infty} f(t)\psi_{a,b}(t) \mathrm{d}t. \tag{7}$$

Now, suppose that a signal is linear on a region larger than the support $S(a)$ of the wavelet function $\psi_{a,b}(t)$:

$$f(t) = c \cdot t \quad \text{if } |t - b| \leq S(a).$$

For Daubechies wavelets with at least two vanishing moments ($N \geq 2$), the corresponding wavelet coefficient $\mathcal{W}f(a,b)$ will be zero:

$$\begin{aligned}
\mathcal{W}f(a,b) &= \int_{-\infty}^{+\infty} c \cdot t\psi_{a,b}(t)\mathrm{d}t \\
&= \frac{c}{\sqrt{a}} \int_{-\infty}^{+\infty} t\psi\left(\frac{t-b}{a}\right) \mathrm{d}t \\
&= c\sqrt{a} \int_{-\infty}^{+\infty} (at' + b)\, \psi\left(t'\right) \mathrm{d}t' \\
&= ca^{3/2} \int_{-\infty}^{+\infty} t'\psi\left(t'\right) \mathrm{d}t' + cba^{1/2} \int_{-\infty}^{+\infty} \psi\left(t'\right) \mathrm{d}t' \\
&= 0
\end{aligned}$$

In the remainder of this chapter, for the ease of notation, we will consider one particular wavelet subband (with scale a) at a time and we will denote the corresponding wavelet coefficients by a tilde: for example $\tilde{x}(\boldsymbol{p})$ are the wavelet coefficients for that particular scale of $x(\boldsymbol{p})$. The process can then be repeated for other subbands as well. Let us now apply a

Daubechies wavelet transform to the piecewise linear signal from Figure 4(a). The result is shown in Figure 4(b) for the finest scale of the DWT[1]: because of the vanishing moments of the wavelet, the wavelet coefficients $\tilde{x}(\boldsymbol{p})$ are zero, except at the positions where the derivative of $x(\boldsymbol{p})$ does not exist. At these positions, the wavelet coefficients have a negligibly small magnitude. This nicely illustrates the sparsifying properties of the DWT for this type of signal. Correspondingly, the wavelet coefficients $\tilde{y}(\boldsymbol{p})$ are (approximately) $\tilde{w}(\boldsymbol{p})$, which means that the chicken-and-egg problem is solved: the noise statistics can be directly estimated from $\tilde{y}(\boldsymbol{p})$! More specifically, the wavelet domain autocorrelation function of $w(\boldsymbol{p})$ can in this case be estimated based on the following relationship:

$$R_{\tilde{w}}(\boldsymbol{p}) \approx R_{\tilde{y}}(\boldsymbol{p}) = \mathrm{E}\left[\tilde{y}(\boldsymbol{p}')\overline{\tilde{y}(\boldsymbol{p}+\boldsymbol{p}')}\right]. \tag{8}$$

It then suffices to compute the sample autocorrelation function of $\tilde{y}(\boldsymbol{p})$. There are now two issues remaining, which we will explain in the remainder of this Chapter:

1. The autocorrelation function of a signal in the wavelet domain (e.g. a for particular wavelet subband) is not the same as the autocorrelation function of a signal in time domain. Nevertheless, there exists a simple relation between both, as we will explain in Section 3.

2. Most real-life signals are not piecewise linear functions or piecewise polynomials. For such signals, the wavelet coefficient magnitudes may become non-negligible, causing serious biases to the final noise estimates. An example of a frequency modulated signal with maximal frequency at half length of the signal, is given in Figure 5. Because of the high local bandwidth of the signal at this time position, the wavelet is not able to cancel out the signal, resulting in wavelet coefficients with a large magnitude. Consequently, the approximation $\tilde{y}(\boldsymbol{p}) \approx \tilde{x}(\boldsymbol{p})$ does not hold anymore. However, it can be seen in Figure 5(b) that this phenomenon is well localized in time, hence, because the noise process is assumed to be stationary, a plausible solution would be to estimate the noise statistics from the wavelet coefficients $\tilde{y}(\boldsymbol{p})$ that have a small underlying components $\tilde{x}(\boldsymbol{p})$ (ignoring the outliers in Figure 5(b)). In Section 4 we will discuss solutions that generalize this idea by using a statistical prior model for wavelet coefficients.

So far, we discussed the estimation of colored noise for one dimensional signals. The reasoning can also be extended to higher dimensional signals, such as images. To illustrate this, a noisy image together with its DWT are shown in Figure 6. It can be seen that the wavelet subbands (LH, HL and HH in Figure 6) predominantly contain information on the noise, with exception in the areas of textures and edges (the fine hairs of the mandrill). In these areas, the (noise-free) wavelet coefficients $\tilde{x}(\boldsymbol{p})$ still have a relatively large magnitude, but this phenomenon is localized - in the surrounding smooth regions the wavelet coefficients $\tilde{y}(\boldsymbol{p})$ mostly consist of noise.
For higher dimensional signals, the DWT is usually computed by using basis functions that are tensor products of one dimensional wavelets and one dimensional scaling functions. While this approach can efficiently deal with point-wise singularities (e.g. bumps, dots, ...), most structures in images are line-like singularities with a given direction. However, the DWT can not well adapt to the arbitrary direction of the singularity: for example, the

[1] Note that for other scales the plots are similar.

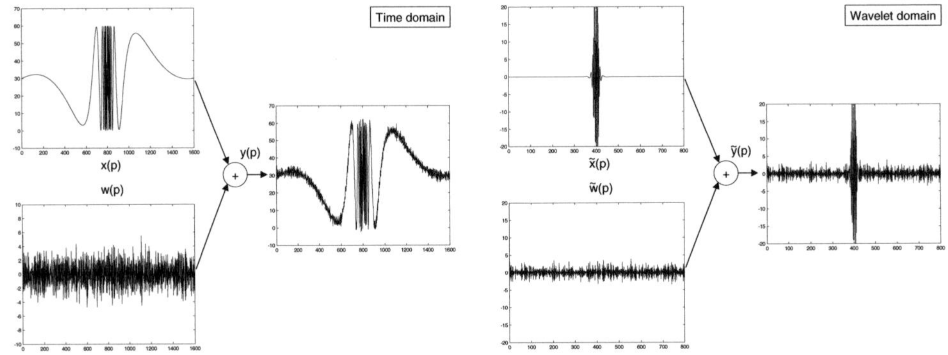

(a) (b)

Fig. 5. Example of a non-piecewise linear signal with correlated noise. Our goal is to estimate the noise power spectrum from the corrupted signal $y(\boldsymbol{p})$. (a) The signals in time domain, (b) The finest scale of the wavelet transform of the signals (Daubechies' wavelet with 2 vanishing moments was used).

transform can not make a distinction between features oriented at +45° and -45°. This is known as the *checkerboard* problem of the DWT: due to the separability of the higher dimensional wavelets, these wavelets appear as a checkerboard pattern which does not have a dominant direction. Consequently, many nonzero wavelet coefficients may be needed to represent a line singularity at an arbitrary orientation. To overcome this limitation there has recently been a lot of interest in transforms that offer a better *directional selectivity*. Examples are steerable pyramids Simoncelli et al. (1992), dual-tree complex wavelets Selesnick et al. (2005a), Marr-like wavelet pyramids Van De Ville & Unser (2008), 2-D (log) Gabor transforms Fischer et al. (2007); Lee (1996), contourlets Do & Vetterli (2005), ridgelets Candès (1998); Do & Vetterli (2003), curvelets Candès et al. (2006) and shearlets Guo & Labate (2007). These transforms are designed to have better sparsifying properties so that our outlier problem in Figure 5(b) is alleviated (but not solved).
In the next subsections we will focus on the DWT as a primary multiresolution decomposition tool, however, the same reasoning can also be applied to more recently developed transforms.

3. From time-domain to wavelet-domain autocorrelation functions

Because our goal is to estimate the autocorrelation function of noise in the wavelet domain, it is very useful to know how the wavelet-domain and time-domain autocorrelation functions are related to each other. When the autocorrelation function of the input signal is known, a simple Monte-Carlo based technique is to generate colored noise with this given autocorrelation function, then to transform the noise to the wavelet domain (or other multiresolution transform domain) and subsequently to estimate the autocorrelation function in this domain Portilla et al. (2003). While such computational method is attractive from an implementation point of view, it does not bring a direct analytical relationship between both autocorrelation functions. We will see in Section 6 that an analytical relationship will prove to be very useful when estimating parametric noise PSDs.
Let us consider the wavelet analysis filterbank shown in Figure 7(a), where a signal with z-transform $\tilde{F}_1(z)$ is filtered by a wavelet filter $G(z)$ and a scaling filter $H(z)$. Both signals

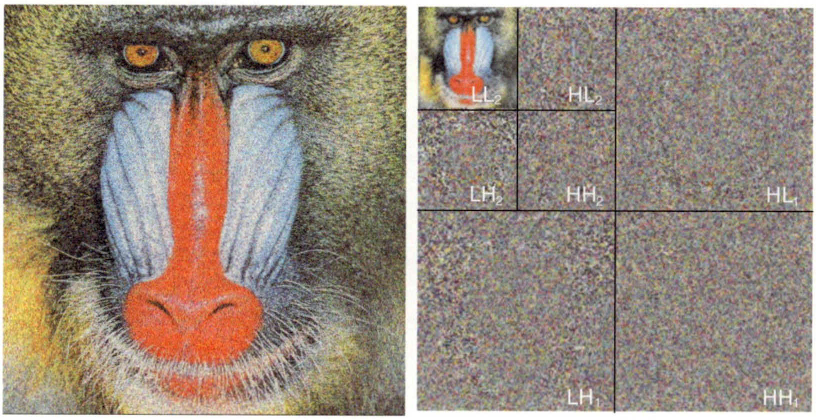

(a) (b)

Fig. 6. (a) *Baboon* image with noise, (b) DWT of the image.

are subsequently decimated by a factor of two. The analysis is iterated on the scaling coefficients $F_2(z)$. Now, the input signal has an autocorrelation function in the z-domain defined by $\tilde{R}_1(z) = E\left[\tilde{F}_1(z)\tilde{F}_1(z^{-1})\right]$. The filtered signals then have autocorrelation functions respectively $\tilde{R}_1(z)G(z)G(z^{-1})$ and $\tilde{R}_1(z)H(z)H(z^{-1})$. Decimating the resulting signals by a factor 2 leads to the signal with autocorrelation function Goossens et al. (2010):

$$\begin{aligned}
R_1(z) &= E\left[F_1(z)F_1(z^{-1})\right] \\
&= \frac{1}{2}\left(\tilde{R}_1\left(z^{\frac{1}{2}}\right)G\left(z^{\frac{1}{2}}\right)G\left(z^{-\frac{1}{2}}\right) + \tilde{R}_1\left(-z^{\frac{1}{2}}\right)G\left(-z^{\frac{1}{2}}\right)G\left(-z^{-\frac{1}{2}}\right)\right), \\
R_2(z) &= E\left[F_2(z)F_2(z^{-1})\right] \\
&= \frac{1}{2}\left(\tilde{R}_1\left(z^{\frac{1}{2}}\right)H\left(z^{\frac{1}{2}}\right)H\left(z^{-\frac{1}{2}}\right) + \tilde{R}_1\left(-z^{\frac{1}{2}}\right)H\left(-z^{\frac{1}{2}}\right)H\left(-z^{-\frac{1}{2}}\right)\right).
\end{aligned} \tag{9}$$

Hence, the wavelet-domain autocorrelation function $R_1(z)$ can be directly computed from the autocorrelation function of the input signal $\tilde{R}_1(z)$ and the wavelet and scaling filters. This involves two simple convolutions and a decimation operation of the input autocorrelation function $\tilde{R}_1(z)$. For subsequent decompositions (coarser scales of the wavelet transform), this process can be iterated by re-inserting $\tilde{R}_1(z) = R_2(z)$ in (9).

To show that this reasoning also applies to other wavelet transforms, we will briefly discuss the adaptation to the dual-tree complex wavelet transform (DT-CWT) Kingsbury (2001) in one dimension. Extension to higher dimensions is then straightforward. The 1D DT-CWT is implemented using two parallel DWT filter banks, the first filter bank uses the real parts of the complex wavelet and scaling filters (respectively $G_1(z)$ and $H_1(z)$), while in the second filter bank, the imaginary parts of the wavelet and scaling filters (respectively $G_2(z)$ and $H_2(z)$) are applied. Finally, the output of both filter banks are mixed together (see the right square in Figure 7(b)), applying a 45° rotation in the complex plane. This last step is in fact only necessary in 2D (or higher dimensions), where complex wavelets are constructed using tensor products of 1D complex wavelets. The translation of the resulting complex-valued filter banks to parallel real-valued filter banks then automatically results into this phase modulation in the complex plane (for more details, see Selesnick et al. (2005b)). Defining

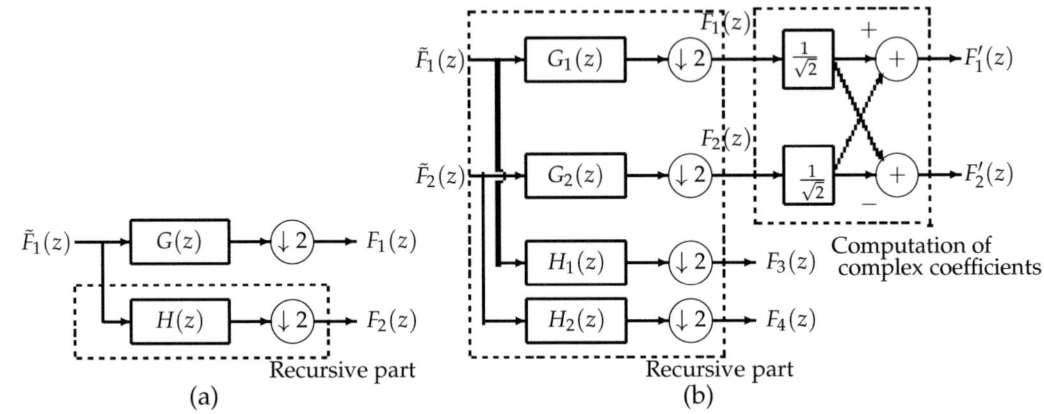

Fig. 7. Analysis filterbank for (a) the DWT, (b) the DT-CWT.

$\tilde{R}_2(z) = E\left[\tilde{F}_2(z)\tilde{F}_2(z^{-1})\right]$, application of (9) to the DT-CWT leads to the following equations:

$$\begin{aligned}
R_1(z) &= E\left[F_1(z)F_1(z^{-1})\right] = \frac{1}{2}\left(\tilde{R}_1\left(z^{\frac{1}{2}}\right)G_1\left(z^{\frac{1}{2}}\right)G_1\left(z^{-\frac{1}{2}}\right) + \tilde{R}_1\left(-z^{\frac{1}{2}}\right)G_1\left(-z^{\frac{1}{2}}\right)G_1\left(-z^{-\frac{1}{2}}\right)\right)\\
R_2(z) &= E\left[F_2(z)F_2(z^{-1})\right] = \frac{1}{2}\left(\tilde{R}_2\left(z^{\frac{1}{2}}\right)G_2\left(z^{\frac{1}{2}}\right)G_2\left(z^{-\frac{1}{2}}\right) + \tilde{R}_2\left(-z^{\frac{1}{2}}\right)G_2\left(-z^{\frac{1}{2}}\right)G_2\left(-z^{-\frac{1}{2}}\right)\right)\\
R_3(z) &= E\left[F_3(z)F_3(z^{-1})\right] = \frac{1}{2}\left(\tilde{R}_1\left(z^{\frac{1}{2}}\right)H_1\left(z^{\frac{1}{2}}\right)H_1\left(z^{-\frac{1}{2}}\right) + \tilde{R}_1\left(-z^{\frac{1}{2}}\right)H_1\left(-z^{\frac{1}{2}}\right)H_1\left(-z^{-\frac{1}{2}}\right)\right)\\
R_4(z) &= E\left[F_4(z)F_4(z^{-1})\right] = \frac{1}{2}\left(\tilde{R}_2\left(z^{\frac{1}{2}}\right)H_2\left(z^{\frac{1}{2}}\right)H_2\left(z^{-\frac{1}{2}}\right) + \tilde{R}_2\left(-z^{\frac{1}{2}}\right)H_2\left(-z^{\frac{1}{2}}\right)H_2\left(-z^{-\frac{1}{2}}\right)\right)\\
S_{1,2}(z) &= E\left[F_1(z)F_2(z^{-1})\right] = \frac{1}{2}\left(\tilde{S}_{1,2}\left(z^{\frac{1}{2}}\right)G_1\left(z^{\frac{1}{2}}\right)G_2\left(z^{-\frac{1}{2}}\right) + \tilde{S}_{1,2}\left(-z^{\frac{1}{2}}\right)G_1\left(-z^{\frac{1}{2}}\right)G_2\left(-z^{-\frac{1}{2}}\right)\right) \qquad (10)
\end{aligned}$$

where $\tilde{S}_{1,2}(z)$ is the cross-power spectrum between $\tilde{F}_1(z)$ and $\tilde{F}_2(z)$: $\tilde{S}_{1,2}(z) = E\left[\tilde{F}_1(z)\tilde{F}_2(z^{-1})\right]$. The final autocorrelation functions (after the complex phase modulation) are computed from $R_1(z)$, $R_2(z)$ and $S_{1,2}(z)$, as follows:

$$\begin{aligned}
R_1'(z) &= E\left[F_1'(z)F_1'(z^{-1})\right] = \frac{1}{2}\left(R_1(z) + R_2(z)\right) + \frac{1}{2}\left(S_{1,2}(z) + S_{1,2}(z^{-1})\right),\\
R_2'(z) &= E\left[F_2'(z)F_2'(z^{-1})\right] = \frac{1}{2}\left(R_1(z) + R_2(z)\right) - \frac{1}{2}\left(S_{1,2}(z) + S_{1,2}(z^{-1})\right). \qquad (11)
\end{aligned}$$

In Algorithm 1, an OCTAVE/MATLAB program is given for computing the autocorrelation functions in case of the DWT and DT-CWT, according to (9) and (10)-(11). In this program, the variables `lo` and `hi` respectively signify the scaling and wavelet coefficients. It can be seen that all operations are linear operations, which makes it possible to express the conversion from time-domain to wavelet-domain as a matrix multiplication applied to the input autocorrelation coefficient vector.

In Figure 8, an example of a parametric autocorrelation function and its DWT decomposition, according to (9), is shown. Due to the cone of influence (Mallat, 1999, p. 174), the support size of the autocorrelation function decreases when increasing the wavelet scale (i.e., when analyzing finer scales). Interesting to note is the envelope of the noise variance in the wavelet domain: the noise variance is identical to the noise autocorrelation function evaluated in the origin (which is in this case also the maximum of the autocorrelation function). When one modifies the center band frequency of the noise PSD in Figure 8(b), this also directly

Algorithm 1 OCTAVE/MATLAB program for computing wavelet domain autocorrelation functions.

```
f = [1 2 1];   % input autocorrelation function
% discrete wavelet transform (DWT)
lo = conv(f, conv(h, h(end:-1:1)));
hi = conv(f, conv(g, g(end:-1:1)));
lo = lo(1:2:end); hi = hi(1:2:end);

% dual-tree complex wavelet transform (DT-CWT)
lo1 = conv(f, conv(h1, h1(end:-1:1)));
hi1 = conv(f, conv(g1, g1(end:-1:1)));
lo2 = conv(f, conv(h2, h2(end:-1:1)));
hi2 = conv(f, conv(g2, g2(end:-1:1)));
cr1 = conv(f, conv(h1, h2(end:-1:1))); % cross-correlation
cr2 = conv(f, conv(h2, h1(end:-1:1)));
lo1 = lo1(1:2:end); lo2 = lo2(1:2:end); % decimations
hi1 = hi1(1:2:end); hi2 = hi2(1:2:end);
cr1 = cr1(1:2:end); cr2 = cr2(1:2:end);
hi1_out = 0.5*(hi1+hi2)+0.5*(cr1+cr2); % complex phase modulation
hi2_out = 0.5*(hi1+hi2)-0.5*(cr1+cr2);
```

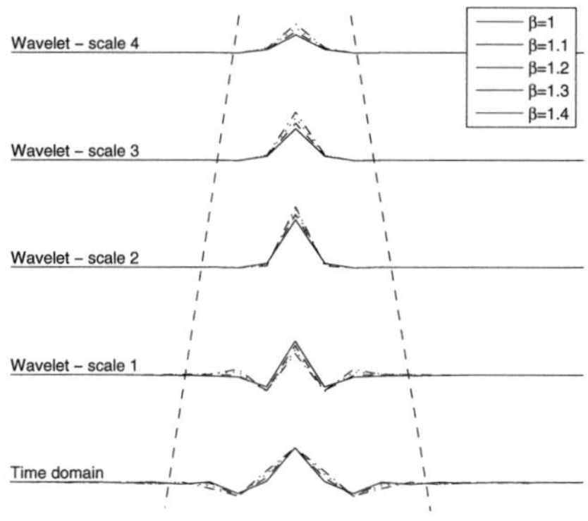

(a)

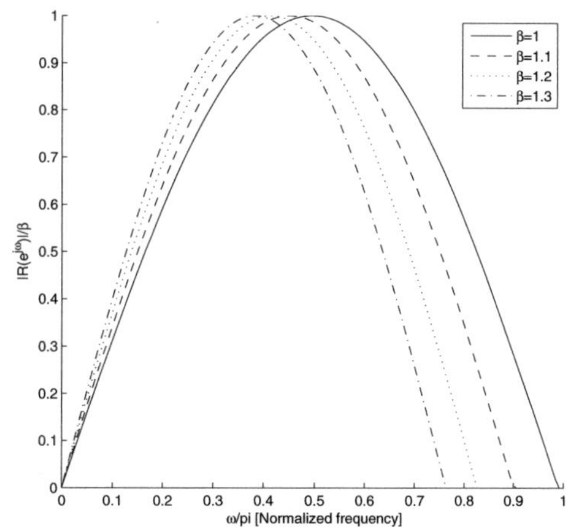

(b)

Fig. 8. (a) Wavelet analysis of the autocorrelation function (in z-domain) $R(z) = \sum_n \frac{\beta^2}{\pi(n^2-\beta^2)}\left(1+\cos\left(\frac{\pi n}{\beta}\right)\right) z^n$ across different scales and for different values of β. Daubechies' wavelet with two vanishing moments was used. (b) Power spectral density $R(e^{j\omega})$ for different values of β.

influences the noise variances of the individual wavelet subbands (see Figure 8(a)), due to the frequency-selective behavior of the wavelets at different scales. For example, increasing the parameter β has as effect that the noise variance at wavelet scale 4 decreases. This also suggests that, when a thresholding strategy (e.g. soft/hardthresholding) would be used to suppress the colored noise process, the thresholds would need to be level-dependent, e.g., as proposed by Johnstone and Silverman Johnstone & Silverman (1997).

4. Statistical priors for noise estimation

As already illustrated in Figure 5, the DWT will in general not fully suppress the signal. Consequently, wavelet-based noise estimation techniques need to take into account that the wavelet coefficients contain a non-negligible signal component. One of the earliest and well-known wavelet-based noise estimation techniques is the MAD estimator from Donoho, which estimates the noise standard deviation as follows Donoho & Johnstone (1995):

$$\hat{\sigma} = \frac{\text{Median}_{\boldsymbol{p}}\left(|\tilde{y}(\boldsymbol{p})|\right)}{0.6745}. \tag{12}$$

The estimator gives level dependent estimates of the noise standard deviation in every wavelet subband. Based on robust statistics, the non-zero signal coefficients are considered to be *outliers*. By computing a median instead of a more traditional mean, the outlier influences in the end result are significantly reduced.

In this chapter, we are interested in estimating the noise *correlations* or *covariances* (next to the noise standard deviation), therefore the estimator (12) can not directly be used. For this purpose, a general class of robust S estimators for the covariance (see, e.g., Campbell et al. (1998); Pena & Prieto (2001)) can be used. These estimators detect outliers after finding projections that maximize the kurtosis of the data. An illustration of such a technique is given in Figure 9: the robust S estimators attempt to estimate the covariance of the noise (the black dots in Figure 9). In this case this is equivalent to determining the sizes of the axes and the orientation of the ellipse shown in the figure (the ellipse can be seen as an isocontour of the probability function of the data). Because of the presence of outliers (the crosses in Figure 9), this is not a trivial task. The robust estimation techniques then try to identify the outliers, in an iterative process.

While robust S estimators are unfamiliar with the structure of the data they are applied to, in our application, we have some more information on the data that we can take into our advantage. In particular, due to the sparsifying properties of the chosen multiresolution transform, the identification of the outliers (signal components) is somewhat easier: the multiresolution transform already performs a projection to maximize the kurtosis. Instead of relying on robust statistics, we will incorporate prior knowledge on the noise-free wavelet coefficients to further improve the estimation performance using Bayesian techniques. Our noise estimation approach will then consist in 1) specifying a statistical prior distribution for the noise-free signal coefficients, 2) maximum likelihood estimation of the unknown noise covariance matrix.

In the next subsections, we will briefly review a number of statistical models for noise-free wavelet coefficients and we will explain how these models can be used to perform noise estimation.

4.1 The generalized Laplace distribution

It has been found in several studies Field (1987); Mallat (1989) that histograms of wavelet coefficients (or generally coefficients of bandpass filtered images) have a highly kurtotic shape. An example is shown in Figure 10(a)-(b) for the *Baboon* image: the wavelet coefficient histogram reveals a sharp peak and a heavy tail. The sample kurtosis of the wavelet coefficients (6.98) is much higher than the theoretical kurtosis of a Gaussian distribution (which is 3). Several authors Antonini et al. (1992); Chang et al. (1998); Mallat

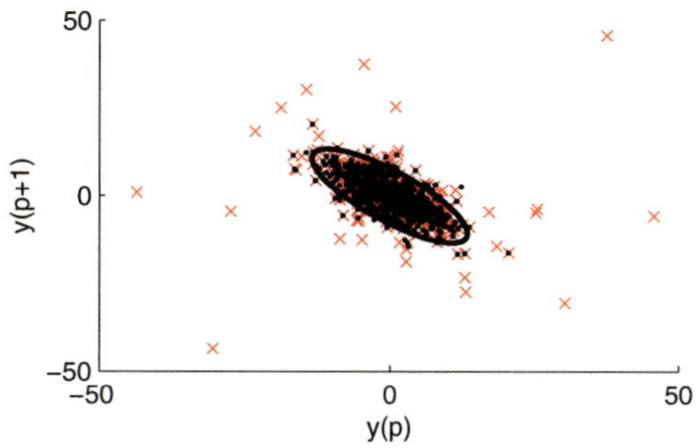

Fig. 9. Joint histogram of neighboring wavelet coefficients for Figure 5(b). Black dots are noise coefficients, crosses are the outliers due to signal presence.

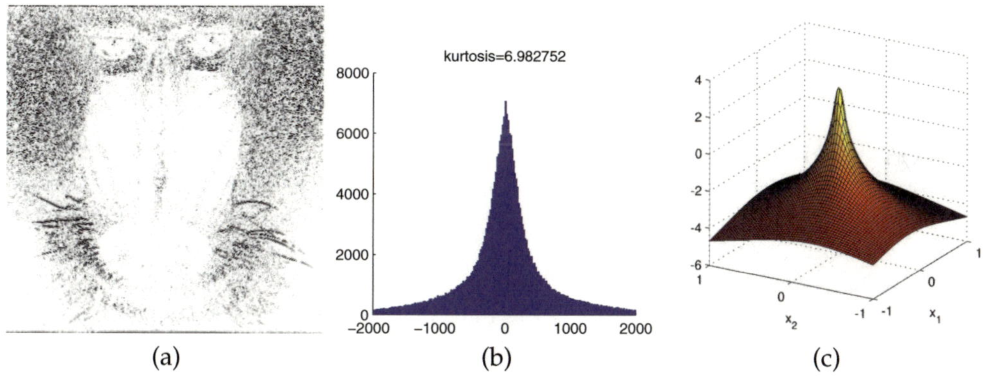

Fig. 10. (a) wavelet subband LH_1 of the *Baboon* image (*black* corresponds to a large coefficient magnitude, *white* to small magnitudes, the contrast of the image was enhanced to better reveal the details), (b) histogram of the wavelet coefficients in (a), (c) multivariate Gaussian Scale Mixture distribution.

(1989); Moulin & Liu (1999); Simoncelli & Adelson (1996) proposed to use a *generalized Laplace* distribution (GLD, also known as *generalized Gaussian* distribution) to model the kurtotic behavior of wavelet coefficients. The GLD is defined as:

$$f_{\tilde{x}}(\tilde{x}) = \frac{\nu}{2s\Gamma(1/\nu)} \exp\left(-\left|\frac{\tilde{x}}{s}\right|^{\nu}\right), \tag{13}$$

where $\Gamma(x) = \int_0^{+\infty} t^{x-1}e^{-t}\mathrm{d}t$ is the Gamma function. The parameter s is scale parameter of the distribution, which controls the variance of the distribution. The parameter ν is a shape parameter that is related to the kurtosis of the distribution, given by:

$$\kappa = \frac{\Gamma(5/\nu)\Gamma(1/\nu)}{\Gamma^2(3/\nu)} - 3. \tag{14}$$

The shape parameter ν is typically in the range [0.5, 1]. Because in practice, the actual value of this parameter is unknown, the parameter value is usually estimated from the observed data. This may be done using the maximum likelihood method or the method of moments Srivastava et al. (2003).

4.2 Elliptically symmetric distributions and Gaussian Scale Mixtures

The GLD from (13) is a univariate distribution that can well model highly kurtotic histograms of wavelet coefficients, however this distribution does not allow capture correlations between different observations $\tilde{x}$. This can be achieved by using multivariate distributions, where dependencies between neighboring wavelet coefficients can be modeled. For these densities, a neighborhood of a fixed size (e.g. 3×3 in 2D) is defined around every wavelet coefficient. Next, every neighborhood[2] can be represented by a vector, e.g., by using column stacking. In the following, we will use bold letters $\tilde{\boldsymbol{x}}(\boldsymbol{p})$, $\tilde{\boldsymbol{w}}(\boldsymbol{p})$, $\tilde{\boldsymbol{y}}(\boldsymbol{p})$ to denote neighborhood vectors extracted by column stacking. Statistical studies Portilla et al. (2003); Srivastava et al. (2003) have indicated that, next to the kurtotic behavior, the noise-free wavelet coefficients are typically symmetric around the mode and the joint histograms have elliptical contours. This suggests the use of elliptically symmetric distributions (ESD) to model these characteristics. The ESD is defined by Kotz & Kozubowski (2001):

$$f_{\tilde{\boldsymbol{x}}}\left(\tilde{\boldsymbol{x}}\right) = k_d \left|\boldsymbol{C}_x\right|^{-1/2} g\left(\left|\left(\tilde{\boldsymbol{x}} - \mathbf{m}\right) \boldsymbol{C}_x^{-1} \left(\tilde{\mathbf{x}} - \mathbf{m}\right)\right|^{1/2}\right), \tag{15}$$

where $\mathbf{m}$ is the mean of the distribution (typically $\mathbf{m} = \mathbf{0}$), $g(u)$ is a real-valued function (called density generator function), d is the length of $\tilde{\boldsymbol{x}}$ and k_d is a proportionality constant. A multivariate extension of the GLD is obtained by using the following density generator function Kotz et al. (2000): $g(u) = \exp\left(-|u|^{\nu}\right)$. The resulting distribution is known as the multivariate exponential power distribution (EPD). For our modeling task, the EPD has a number of practical limitations: 1) the marginal densities of the distribution are not EPD-distributed and 2) for estimation purposes, the exponential power ν often leads to integral expressions that are analytically intractable.

Wainwright & Simoncelli (2000) noted that when the wavelet filter responses are normalized by dividing by the square root of the local variance, the statistics of the normalized coefficients are approximately Gaussian. The Gaussian Scale Mixture (GSM), see Figure 10(c), was then proposed to account both for the correlations and the variability in local variance of the wavelet coefficients. A random variable $\tilde{\boldsymbol{x}}$ is GSM distributed if it can be written as the product of a zero mean Gaussian random vector $\tilde{\boldsymbol{u}}$ and a scalar positive random variable $\sqrt{z}$ Andrews & Mallows (1974):

$$\tilde{\boldsymbol{x}} \stackrel{\mathrm{d}}{=} \sqrt{z}\tilde{\boldsymbol{u}} \tag{16}$$

where $\stackrel{\mathrm{d}}{=}$ denotes equality in distribution. The scalar variable z is not observed and is therefore also called 'hidden' multiplier or mixing variable. Because of scaling ambiguity between $\sqrt{z}$ and $\tilde{\boldsymbol{u}}$, the hidden multiplier is often assumed to be normalized such that $\mathrm{E}\left[z\right] = 1$. Prior distributions for z include Jeffrey's *non-informative*[3] prior Portilla et al. (2003), the *log-normal* prior Portilla & Simoncelli (2001), the *exponential* distribution Selesnick (2006) and the *Gamma* distribution Fadili & Boubchir (2005); Srivastava et al. (2002).

[2] Quite often, the neighborhoods are chosen to be overlapping, despite of the fact that this destroys the mutual independence of the different neighborhood vectors. This is done to arrive at a sufficiently large number of neighborhood vectors (for example, for a 3×3 neighborhood, the number of vectors will be multiplied by 9), which will generally result in more reliable estimates.

[3] Note that in this case, the mathematical expectation $\mathrm{E}\left[z\right]$ does not exist.

The GSM also belongs to the family of ESDs. The density generator function is given by:

$$g(x) = \int_0^{+\infty} f_z(z) z^{-\frac{d}{2}} \exp\left(-\frac{1}{2z}x^2\right) \mathrm{d}z. \tag{17}$$

For some hidden multiplier densities $f_z(z)$ a closed-form expression can be found for $g(x)$, although most often, numerical integration is performed over a closed interval. In Gómez et al. (2008) it has been shown that the EPD is also a GSM distribution, for some values of the shape parameter $\nu \in]0,1]$. However, the distribution $f_z(z)$ depends on d and has a complicated analytical expression (see Gómez et al. (2008)).

4.3 Other prior distributions

In literature, several other prior distributions for noise-free wavelet coefficients have been proposed. For example, the *Student-T* distribution Tzikas et al. (2007), *Alpha-stable* distributions Achim et al. (2001); Nikias & Shao (1995) and the *Cauchy* distribution Rabbani et al. (2006). All these heavy tailed distributions have a GSM representation, hence studying general GSMs automatically covers all of these distributions. Next, a complex extension of the Gaussian Scale Mixture density has been proposed for modeling complex-valued wavelet coefficients in Vo et al. (2007). This *complex GSM* distribution is a special case of the GSM distribution, with a special condition imposed to the covariance matrix of the distribution. Next to GSMs, *mixtures of a Gaussian distribution and a point mass at zero* were used in Abramovich et al. (1998); Clyde et al. (1998), *mixtures of two Gaussian distributions* in Crouse et al. (1998); Fan & Xia (2001); Romberg et al. (2001) and *mixtures of truncated or quasi-Laplace distributions* in Pižurica & Philips (2006); Shi & Selesnick (2006).

5. Noise covariance estimation techniques

In this Section, we will use the GSM prior distribution from Section 4 to design a noise covariance estimation technique. We therefore start from the signal-plus-noise model from equation (1). The assumed addititivity of the signal and noise leads to an equivalent expression in the wavelet domain:

$$\tilde{\boldsymbol{y}}(\boldsymbol{p}) = \tilde{\boldsymbol{x}}(\boldsymbol{p}) + \tilde{\boldsymbol{w}}(\boldsymbol{p}), \tag{18}$$

where $\tilde{\boldsymbol{w}}(\boldsymbol{p})$ is spatially stationary Gaussian distributed vector of length d with mean $\mathbf{0}$ and covariance $\boldsymbol{C}_{\tilde{w}}$. Due to the assumed noise stationarity, the covariance matrix $\boldsymbol{C}_{\tilde{w}}$ has dimensions $d \times d$ and is directly related to the noise autocorrelation function $R_{\tilde{w}}(\boldsymbol{p})$: the covariance between two coefficients at positions $\boldsymbol{p}$ and $\boldsymbol{q}$ only depends on the difference in location between both positions:

$$(\boldsymbol{C}_{\tilde{w}})_{\boldsymbol{p},\boldsymbol{q}} = R_{\tilde{w}}(\boldsymbol{q} - \boldsymbol{p}) \tag{19}$$

where vector-valued indices in $(\boldsymbol{C}_{\tilde{w}})_{\boldsymbol{p},\boldsymbol{q}}$ are used as a short notation for their respective column-stacked ordening. By (19), the estimation of the noise autocorrelation function is equivalent to the estimation of the covariance $\boldsymbol{C}_{\tilde{w}}$. Next, the noise-free coefficients are GSM distributed with covariance matrix $\boldsymbol{C}_{\tilde{x}}$. For the GSM model, we have $\tilde{\boldsymbol{x}}|z \sim \mathcal{N}(\mathbf{0}, z\boldsymbol{C}_{\tilde{u}})$. Consequently, the density of $\tilde{\boldsymbol{y}}$ is a specific case of a Gaussian mixture model:

$$\tilde{\boldsymbol{y}}|z \sim \mathcal{N}\left(\boldsymbol{0}, z\boldsymbol{C}_{\tilde{u}} + \boldsymbol{C}_{\tilde{w}}\right) \tag{20}$$

where the signal covariance is also unknown. We remark that this matrix can be eliminated relying on $\boldsymbol{C}_{\tilde{u}} + \boldsymbol{C}_{\tilde{w}} = \boldsymbol{C}_{\tilde{y}}$ (this directly follows from (1), when $\mathrm{E}[z] = 1$):

$$\tilde{\boldsymbol{y}}|z \sim \mathcal{N}\left(\boldsymbol{0}, z\boldsymbol{C}_{\tilde{y}} + (1-z)\boldsymbol{C}_{\tilde{w}}\right). \tag{21}$$

The signal-plus-noise covariance matrix can be estimated using the method of maximum likelihood: $\widehat{\boldsymbol{C}_{\tilde{y}}} = \frac{1}{N}\sum_{\boldsymbol{p}} \tilde{\boldsymbol{y}}(\boldsymbol{p})\tilde{\boldsymbol{y}}^T(\boldsymbol{p})$, with N the number of coefficients in the considered wavelet subband.

5.1 Generalized Expectation-Maximization algorithm

In Portilla (2004), a Generalized Expectation-Maximization (GEM) algorithm is given to estimate the noise covariance matrix. Based on an initial estimate of the noise covariance (typically chosen as $\boldsymbol{C}_{\tilde{w}}^{(0)} = c\boldsymbol{C}_{\tilde{y}}$, with $0 < c < 1$ a constant), the noise covariance matrix is iteratively updated according to the following rule:

$$\boldsymbol{C}_{\tilde{w}}^{(i+1)} = \frac{\sum_{\boldsymbol{p}} \mathrm{P}\left(z < z_0|\tilde{\boldsymbol{y}}(\boldsymbol{p}), \Theta^{(i)}\right) \tilde{\boldsymbol{y}}(\boldsymbol{p})\tilde{\boldsymbol{y}}^T(\boldsymbol{p})}{\sum_{\boldsymbol{p}} \mathrm{P}\left(z < z_0|\tilde{\boldsymbol{y}}(\boldsymbol{p}), \Theta^{(i)}\right)}, \tag{22}$$

where i is the iteration index and $\Theta^{(i)}$ denotes the GSM model parameters at iteration i and where z_0 is a small positive constant. Equation (22) can be motivated by the observation that for z sufficiently small, $\boldsymbol{C}_{\tilde{y}|z} = \boldsymbol{C}_{\tilde{w}}$. The posterior probability that $z < z_0$, conditioned on an observation vector $\tilde{\boldsymbol{y}}(\boldsymbol{p})$, i.e., $\mathrm{P}\left(z < z_0|\tilde{\boldsymbol{y}}(\boldsymbol{p}), \Theta^{(i)}\right)$ is then used as a weight in the averaging process. We can understand this as follows: $\mathrm{P}\left(z < z_0|\tilde{\boldsymbol{y}}(\boldsymbol{p}), \Theta^{(i)}\right)$ represents the probability that a given observation vector contains a negligible signal component. The estimated noise covariance is then the average over all sample covariances $\widetilde{\boldsymbol{y}(\boldsymbol{p})}\tilde{\boldsymbol{y}}^T(\boldsymbol{p})$, weighted by the probability that the considered sample contains a negligible signal component.
Because the updating rule (22) is not guaranteed to increase the likelihood of the data, at every iteration it is checked if this new covariance estimate results in a higher likelihood: $Q(\Theta^{(i)}, \Theta^{(i+1)}) > Q(\Theta^{(i)}, \Theta^{(i)})$, with $Q(\Theta^{(i)}, \Theta)$ the expected log-likelihood function of the data:

$$\begin{aligned} Q(\Theta^{(i)}, \Theta) &= \mathrm{E}\left[\log f_{z|\tilde{\boldsymbol{y}}}\left(z|\tilde{\boldsymbol{y}}, \Theta\right)|\tilde{\boldsymbol{y}},\ \Theta^{(i)}\right] \\ &= \sum_{\boldsymbol{p}} \int_0^{+\infty} f_{z|\tilde{\boldsymbol{y}}}\left(z|\tilde{\boldsymbol{y}}(\boldsymbol{p}), \Theta^{(i)}\right) \log f_{z|\tilde{\boldsymbol{y}}}\left(z|\tilde{\boldsymbol{y}}(\boldsymbol{p}), \Theta\right) \mathrm{d}z. \end{aligned} \tag{23}$$

In case the expected log-likelihood (23) decreases, it is proposed in Portilla (2004) to perform a gradient ascent step:

$$\begin{aligned} \boldsymbol{C}_{\tilde{w}}^{(i+1)} &= \boldsymbol{C}_{\tilde{w}}^{(i)} + \lambda \left.\frac{\partial Q(\Theta^{(i)},\Theta)}{\partial \boldsymbol{C}_{\tilde{w}}}\right|_{\boldsymbol{C}_{\tilde{w}}=\boldsymbol{C}_{\tilde{w}}^{(i)}} \\ &= \boldsymbol{C}_{\tilde{w}}^{(i)} + \frac{\lambda}{2} N \int_0^{+\infty} f_z(z)\,(1-z)\boldsymbol{C}_z^{-1}(\boldsymbol{I} - \widehat{\boldsymbol{C}_z}\boldsymbol{C}_z^{-1})\mathrm{d}z, \end{aligned} \tag{24}$$

where

$$\boldsymbol{C}_z = z\boldsymbol{C}_{\tilde{y}} + (1-z)\boldsymbol{C}_{\tilde{w}}, \tag{25}$$

$$\widehat{\boldsymbol{C}_z} = \frac{\sum_{\boldsymbol{p}} f_{z|\tilde{y}}\left(z|\tilde{\boldsymbol{y}}(\boldsymbol{p}),\Theta^{(i)}\right)\tilde{\boldsymbol{y}}(\boldsymbol{p})\tilde{\boldsymbol{y}}^T(\boldsymbol{p})}{\sum_{\boldsymbol{p}} f_z\left(z|\tilde{\boldsymbol{y}}(\boldsymbol{p}),\Theta^{(i)}\right)}. \tag{26}$$

Although a good fitting to the data was reported in Portilla (2004), the technique requires the relatively costly evaluation of the expected log-likelihood function (23). Another issue is the choice of the constant z_0. In Portilla (2004), this was solved by using a discrete GSM mixture for the hidden multiplier density $f_z(z)$. By assigning a non-zero probability mass at $z = 0$, the probability $\mathrm{P}\left(z = 0|\tilde{\boldsymbol{y}}(\boldsymbol{p}),\Theta^{(i)}\right)$ is guaranteed to be non-zero.

5.2 Constrained EM algorithm using augmented Lagrangian optimization

In this subsection, we present a novel, alternative estimation method that does not need evaluation of the expected log-likelihood function. First, we assume a discrete hidden multiplier density $\mathrm{P}(z = z_k) = \alpha_k$, with $k = 1,...,K$. The parameters can be initialized in a manner similar to Portilla et al. (2003):[4]

$$\begin{aligned} z_k &= \exp\left(-3 + 7(k-1)/(K-1)\right), \quad k = 1,...,K \\ \alpha_k &= 1/K. \end{aligned} \tag{27}$$

In contrast to the GEM algorithm, where $\boldsymbol{C}_{\tilde{w}}$ is optimized directly, we take a slightly different approach. We rely on the fact that the density $f_{\tilde{\boldsymbol{y}}}(\tilde{\boldsymbol{y}})$ corresponds to a Gaussian mixture model. This allows us to use the EM algorithm for Gaussian mixtures, with some modifications that we will describe next. Let us denote by $\boldsymbol{C}_k$ the covariance matrices of the mixture components. Because of (20), the mixture covariance matrices should be subject to the constraint $z_k\boldsymbol{C}_{\tilde{u}} + \boldsymbol{C}_{\tilde{w}} = \boldsymbol{C}_k$. Our method now consists of optimizing the expected log-likelihood function (as in a regular EM algorithm Dempster et al. (1977)), but now subject to the GSM constraint:

$$\max_{\Theta} \mathrm{E}\left[\log f_{z|\tilde{\boldsymbol{y}}}(z|\tilde{\boldsymbol{y}},\Theta)\,|\tilde{\boldsymbol{y}},\,\Theta^{(i)}\right] \quad \text{s.t.} \quad z_k\boldsymbol{C}_{\tilde{u}} + \boldsymbol{C}_{\tilde{w}} = \boldsymbol{C}_k \tag{28}$$

To solve this constrained problem, we use the augmented Lagrangian (AL) method. In the AL method, a constrained problem is translated to an unconstrained problem with a Lagrange

[4] Here, values $z_{\min}$ and $z_{\max}$ from (Portilla et al., 2003, p. 1343) are slighly modified to have a good sampling of the continuous pdf $f_z(z)$ with a small number of components K (for example, $K = 6$).

multiplier and an extra penalty term. In our case, the unconstrained problem is given by:

$$\max_{\Theta} \mathrm{E}\left[\log f_{z|\tilde{\boldsymbol{y}}}\left(z|\tilde{\boldsymbol{y}},\Theta\right)|\tilde{\boldsymbol{y}},\ \Theta^{(i)}\right] - 2\sum_{k=1}^{K} \mathrm{Vec}\left[\boldsymbol{a}_k\right]^T \mathrm{Vec}\left[\boldsymbol{C}_k\text{-}z_k\boldsymbol{C}_{\tilde{x}}\text{-}\boldsymbol{C}_{\tilde{w}}\right] - \sum_{k=1}^{K} \lambda_k \left\|\boldsymbol{C}_k\text{-}z_k\boldsymbol{C}_{\tilde{x}}\text{-}\boldsymbol{C}_{\tilde{w}}\right\|_F^2 \tag{29}$$

where $\boldsymbol{a}_k, k = 1, ..., K$ are $d \times d$ matrices of Lagrange multipliers, λ_k are penalty factors, Vec $[\cdot]$ converts a matrix to a column vector (e.g., using column stacking) and $\|\cdot\|_F$ is the matrix Frobenius norm. Taking the derivatives of (29) with respect to $\boldsymbol{C}_x$ and $\boldsymbol{C}_w$ and setting to zero leads to a linear system of equations, in block matrix form:

$$\begin{pmatrix} \mu_2 \boldsymbol{I} & \mu_1 \boldsymbol{I} \\ \mu_1 \boldsymbol{I} & \boldsymbol{I} \end{pmatrix} \begin{pmatrix} \boldsymbol{C}_{\tilde{x}}^{(i+1)} \\ \boldsymbol{C}_{\tilde{w}}^{(i+1)} \end{pmatrix} = \begin{pmatrix} \sum_{k=1}^{K} z_k \left(\lambda_k \boldsymbol{C}_k^{(i)} + \boldsymbol{a}_k\right) \\ \sum_{k=1}^{K} \left(\lambda_k \boldsymbol{C}_k^{(i)} + \boldsymbol{a}_k\right) \end{pmatrix} \tag{30}$$

with $\mu_1 = \sum_{k=1}^{K} \lambda_k z_k$ and $\mu_2 = \sum_{k=1}^{K} \lambda_k z_k^2$. Similarly, maximizing (29) with respect to $\boldsymbol{C}_k$ leads to the following update equation:

$$\boldsymbol{C}_k^{(i+1)} = \frac{\sum_{\boldsymbol{p}} \mathrm{P}\left(z = z_k|\tilde{\boldsymbol{y}}(\boldsymbol{p}),\Theta^{(i)}\right) \tilde{\boldsymbol{y}}(\boldsymbol{p})\tilde{\boldsymbol{y}}^T(\boldsymbol{p}) - 2\lambda_k\left(z_k \boldsymbol{C}_{\tilde{x}}^{(i)} + \boldsymbol{C}_{\tilde{w}}^{(i)} - \boldsymbol{a}_k\right)}{\sum_{\boldsymbol{p}} \mathrm{P}\left(z = z_k|\tilde{\boldsymbol{y}}(\boldsymbol{p}),\Theta^{(i)}\right) - 2\lambda_k}, k = 1, ..., K \tag{31}$$

Additionally, the Lagrange multipliers are updated in every iteration:

$$\boldsymbol{a}_k^{(i+1)} = \boldsymbol{a}_k^{(i)} + \frac{\lambda_k}{2}\left(\boldsymbol{C}_k^{(i+1)} - z_k \boldsymbol{C}_{\tilde{x}}^{(i+1)} - \boldsymbol{C}_{\tilde{w}}^{(i+1)}\right). \tag{32}$$

This process is repeated iteratively until a given convergence criterion has been reached (for example $\left\|\boldsymbol{C}_{\tilde{w}}^{(i+1)} - \boldsymbol{C}_{\tilde{w}}^{(i)}\right\|_F < \epsilon$, with ϵ a small positive number). The penalty weights λ_k are chosen in order to speed up the convergence of the algorithm. In our method, we choose λ_k inversely proportional to z_k: $\lambda_k = z_1/z_k$, with $z_1 < z_2 < \cdots < z_K$. The complete algorithm is summarized in Algorithm 2.

Important to mention is that the above algorithm may fail, if the matrix in the update formula (30) is singular, i.e. if $\mu_1^2 = \mu_2$. It is worthful to note that the kurtosis of the wavelet subband coefficients is given by $3\mu_2/\mu_1^2 - 3$ and becomes zero if $\mu_1^2 = \mu_2$. In this case, the probability density function $f_{\tilde{\boldsymbol{y}}}(\tilde{\boldsymbol{y}})$ is Gaussian, and every component of the GSM model will have the same hidden multiplier value $z_k = \mu_1$, such that also $f_{\tilde{\boldsymbol{x}}}(\tilde{\boldsymbol{x}})$ is Gaussian. Consequently, it becomes impossible to separate the signal from the noise: the highly kurtotic behavior of the noise-free coefficients $\boldsymbol{x}$ can not be exploited. By our specific initialization (27), we actually avoided the latter problem.

The elegance of this algorithm lies in the fact that simple update formulas are being used and that the complete algorithm is guaranteed to converge (albeit to a local maximum of the objective function, as with nearly all EM type of algorithms).

6. Estimation of a parametric noise PSD

In the previous Section, two methods were presented to estimate the noise covariance matrix in the wavelet domain. Although these covariance matrices can be directly used in, e.g., blind

Algorithm 2 Constrained EM algorithm for estimating the noise covariance matrix $\boldsymbol{C}_{\tilde{w}}$.

$\boldsymbol{C}_{\tilde{y}} = \frac{1}{N}\sum_{\boldsymbol{p}} \tilde{\boldsymbol{y}}(\boldsymbol{p})\tilde{\boldsymbol{y}}^T(\boldsymbol{p})$, $\boldsymbol{C}_{\tilde{w}}^{(0)} = \frac{9}{10}\boldsymbol{C}_{\tilde{y}}$, $\boldsymbol{C}_{\tilde{x}}^{(0)} = 0.1\boldsymbol{C}_{\tilde{y}}$, $\boldsymbol{C}_k^{(0)} = z_k\boldsymbol{C}_{\tilde{x}}^{(0)} + \boldsymbol{C}_{\tilde{w}}^{(0)}$, $\alpha_k^{(0)} = \frac{1}{K}$, $\lambda_k = \frac{z_1}{z_k}$.

repeat

$\hat{\alpha}_k^{(i+1)} = \frac{1}{N}\sum_{\boldsymbol{p}} \mathrm{P}\left(z = z_k | \boldsymbol{y}(\boldsymbol{p}), \Theta\right)$, **for** $k = 1, ..., K$

$\boldsymbol{C}_k^{(i+1)} = \dfrac{\sum_{\boldsymbol{p}} \mathrm{P}\left(z=z_k|\tilde{\boldsymbol{y}}(\boldsymbol{p}),\Theta^{(i)}\right)\tilde{\boldsymbol{y}}(\boldsymbol{p})\tilde{\boldsymbol{y}}^T(\boldsymbol{p}) - 2\lambda_k\left(z_k\boldsymbol{C}_{\tilde{x}}^{(i)} + \boldsymbol{C}_{\tilde{w}}^{(i)} - \boldsymbol{a}_k^{(i)}\right)}{\sum_{\boldsymbol{p}} \mathrm{P}\left(z=z_k|\tilde{\boldsymbol{y}}(\boldsymbol{p}),\Theta^{(i)}\right) - 2\lambda_k}$, **for** $k = 1, ..., K$

$\begin{pmatrix} \boldsymbol{C}_{\tilde{x}}^{(i+1)} \\ \boldsymbol{C}_{\tilde{w}}^{(i+1)} \end{pmatrix} = \frac{1}{\mu_2 - \mu_1^2} \begin{pmatrix} \mathbf{I} & -\mu_1\mathbf{I} \\ -\mu_1\mathbf{I} & \mu_2\mathbf{I} \end{pmatrix} \begin{pmatrix} \sum_{k=1}^K z_k\left(\lambda_k\boldsymbol{C}_k^{(i+1)} + \boldsymbol{a}_k^{(i)}\right) \\ \sum_{k=1}^K \left(\lambda_k\boldsymbol{C}_k^{(i+1)} + \boldsymbol{a}_k^{(i)}\right) \end{pmatrix}$

$\boldsymbol{a}_k^{(i+1)} = \boldsymbol{a}_k^{(i)} + \frac{\lambda_k}{2}\left(\boldsymbol{C}_k^{(i+1)} - z_k\boldsymbol{C}_{\tilde{x}}^{(i+1)} - \boldsymbol{C}_{\tilde{w}}^{(i+1)}\right)$ **for** $k = 1, ..., K$

$i \leftarrow i + 1$

until convergence ($\left\|\boldsymbol{C}_{\tilde{w}}^{(i+1)} - \boldsymbol{C}_{\tilde{w}}^{(i)}\right\|_F < \epsilon$).

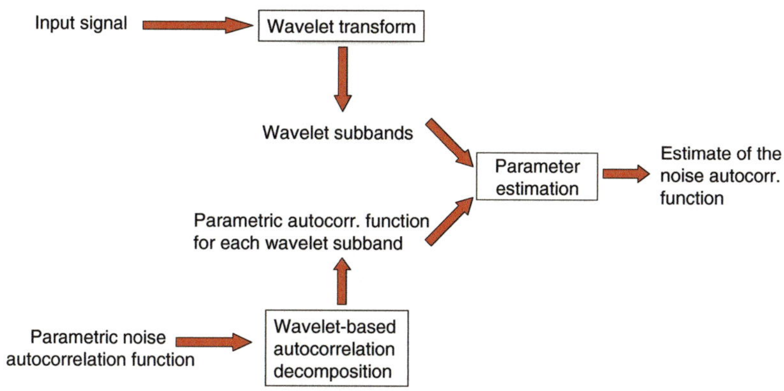

Fig. 11. Overview of the proposed algorithm for the estimation of a parametric noise PSD.

denoising approaches (see Portilla (2004)), the covariance matrices are not directly related to the noise PSD (in the sense that, after estimation of the covariances matrices the noise PSD is still *unknown*). We here present a novel approach to estimate the parameters of a parametric noise PSD based on the covariance matrix estimation methods. As far as the authors are aware of, such a technique does not yet exist. This approach also combines all the different techniques discussed in this Chapter. An overview of our algorithm is given in Figure 11. First, the noise is assumed to have a PSD with an unkown set of parameters $\boldsymbol{\beta}$. Consequently, by the Wiener-Khinchin theorem, the noise autocorrelation function $R_{w,\boldsymbol{\beta}}(\boldsymbol{p})$ is known. The wavelet-domain noise autocorrelation functions can be computed from $R_{w,\boldsymbol{\beta}}(\boldsymbol{p})$, as explained in Section 3. Using the formula (19), the parametric wavelet domain noise covariance matrix

$\boldsymbol{C}_{\tilde{w}}(\boldsymbol{\beta})$ can be found. Defining $\boldsymbol{R}_w(\boldsymbol{\beta}) = \left[R_{w,\boldsymbol{\beta}}(\boldsymbol{p})\right]$, the noise covariance matrix can be expressed in terms of $\boldsymbol{R}_w(\boldsymbol{\beta})$ by using a matrix multiplication:

$$\boldsymbol{C}_{\tilde{w}}(\boldsymbol{\beta}) = \boldsymbol{Q}\boldsymbol{R}_w(\boldsymbol{\beta}) \tag{33}$$

Then, the parameter $\boldsymbol{\beta}$ can be estimated iteratively in every iteration of Algorithm 2. Therefore, we minimize the squared matrix Frobenius norm:

$$\boldsymbol{\beta}^{(i+1)} = \arg\min_{\boldsymbol{\beta}} \left\| \boldsymbol{C}_{\tilde{w}}^{(i+1)} - \boldsymbol{Q}\boldsymbol{R}_w(\boldsymbol{\beta}) \right\|_F^2. \tag{34}$$

Because $\boldsymbol{R}_w(\boldsymbol{\beta})$ is not a linear function in general, this is a non-linear optimization problem, which can be solved using gradient descent or Gauss-Newton techniques. The gradient descent step is given by:

$$\boldsymbol{\beta}^{(i+1)} = \boldsymbol{\beta}^{(i)} + \gamma \left(\boldsymbol{C}_{\tilde{w}}^{(i+1)} - \boldsymbol{Q}\boldsymbol{R}_w\left(\boldsymbol{\beta}^{(i)}\right)\right)^T \boldsymbol{Q} \left. \frac{\partial \boldsymbol{R}_w}{\partial \boldsymbol{\beta}} \right|_{\boldsymbol{\beta}=\boldsymbol{\beta}^{(i)}}. \tag{35}$$

Note that in practice this equation may be iterated several times until convergence in an inner iteration, before the other model parameters are updated. As an example, consider the autocorrelation function from Figure 8, corresponding to the PSD $P(\omega) = \beta \sin(\beta|\omega|)\, I[\beta|\omega| < \pi]$, with $I[\cdot]$ the indicator function. Application of the inverse DTFT gives the spatial autocorrelation function $R_{w,\beta}(n) = \beta^2 \left(1 + \cos\left(\frac{\pi n}{\beta}\right)\right) / \left(\pi(n^2 - \beta^2)\right)$. Its derivative with respect to β is given by:

$$\frac{\partial R_{w,\beta}(n)}{\partial \beta} = \frac{n}{\pi(n^2-\beta^2)^2} \left(\sin\left(\frac{\pi n}{\beta}\right) \pi \left(n^2 - \beta^2\right) + 2\beta n \left(1 + \cos\left(\frac{\pi n}{\beta}\right)\right)\right). \tag{36}$$

Substitution of (36) into (35) then gives the desired update step.

An interesting special case is the estimation of white Gaussian noise, with autocorrelation function $R_{w,\beta}(n) = s\delta(n)$, with s the unknown noise variance. In this case, (34) comprises a least-squares problem, with a linear solution.

7. Experimental results

In this Section, we will compare the performances of the noise estimation methods from Section 5. For this task, both iterative algorithms (the GEM algorithm and the constrained EM algorithm), are initialized using the same set of parameters. The initial values used are given in Algorithm 2 and in (27). The number of mixture components used is 6: $K = 6$. Five images (Barbara, Baboon, Lena, Boats and Peppers) are transformed to the wavelet domain, using the Daubechies wavelet with two vanishing moments. Artificial Gaussian noise with a known (ground-truth) autocorrelation function is added to each LH_1-subband, which allows us to compute the estimation error afterwards. This ground-truth noise autocorrelation function is given by: $\sigma^2\beta^4 \left(1 + \cos\left(\frac{\pi x}{\beta}\right)\right)\left(1 + \cos\left(\frac{\pi y}{\beta}\right)\right) / \left(\pi(x^2 - \beta^2)(y^2 - \beta^2)\right)$, with $\beta = 3/2$ and with $\sigma \in \{1, 5, 10, 15, 25, 50\}$. Then, after every iteration of both algorithms, the log-likelihood function $\log f_{\tilde{\boldsymbol{y}}|\Theta}(\tilde{\boldsymbol{y}}|\Theta)$ and the quadratic error $\left\| \widehat{\boldsymbol{C}_{\tilde{w}}} - \boldsymbol{C}_{\tilde{w}} \right\|_F^2$ are computed, which allows us to compare the performances of both algorithms as function of the iteration number i. Both

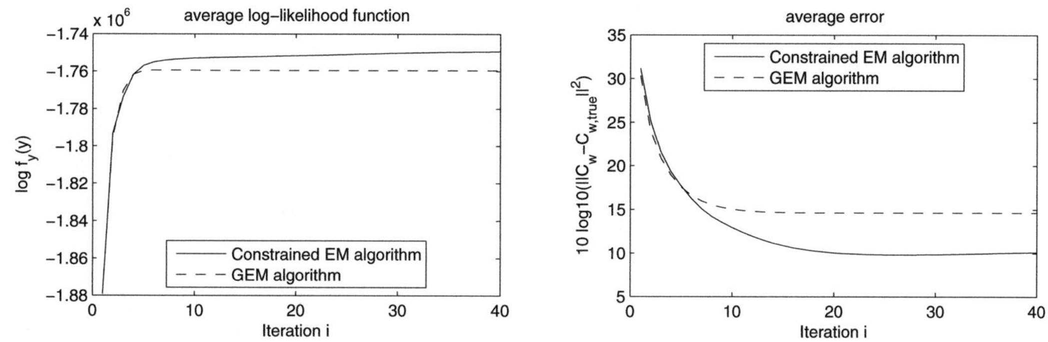

Fig. 12. Comparison of the performance of the GEM algorithm Portilla (2004) and the constrained EM algorithm Subsection 5.2, as a function the iteration number i. Results are averaged over 5 images and 6 noise levels. (*left*) average log-likelihood $\log f_{\tilde{\boldsymbol{y}}|\Theta}(\tilde{\boldsymbol{y}}|\Theta)$, (*right*) average estimation error in logarithmic scale $10\log_{10}\left(\left\|\widehat{\boldsymbol{C}_{\tilde{w}}}-\boldsymbol{C}_{\tilde{w}}\right\|_F^2\right)$.

Table 1. Comparison of the performance of the GEM algorithm Portilla (2004) and the constrained EM algorithm (CEM) from Subsection 5.2, for 5 images and 6 noise levels. Shown is the estimation error in logarithmic scale $10\log_{10}\left(\left\|\widehat{\boldsymbol{C}_{\tilde{w}}}-\boldsymbol{C}_{\tilde{w}}\right\|_F^2\right)$ after 40 iterations.

	$\sigma=1$		$\sigma=5$		$\sigma=10$		$\sigma=15$		$\sigma=25$		$\sigma=50$	
Image	CEM	GEM	CEM	GEM	CEM	GEM	CEM	GEM	CEM	GEM	CEM	GEM
Barbara	**14.25**	14.56	**-12.98**	-11.78	**-26.63**	-23.21	**-29.29**	-28.08	**-36.50**	-31.83	**-37.93**	-35.50
Baboon	**24.02**	28.74	**-3.79**	2.13	**-14.84**	-7.23	**-21.88**	-12.82	**-25.60**	-18.60	**-30.75**	-28.38
Lena	**9.56**	14.42	**-16.77**	-12.23	-23.25	**-23.34**	-29.54	**-29.68**	**-37.99**	-37.17	-38.38	**-38.93**
Boats	**7.72**	9.66	**-17.77**	-16.55	**-30.35**	-26.31	**-30.09**	-28.59	**-35.83**	-32.65	**-37.90**	-37.06
Peppers	**11.28**	17.06	**-14.34**	-9.92	**-24.71**	-21.25	**-30.10**	-27.86	-31.84	**-34.05**	**-40.29**	-36.51
Average	**13.37**	16.89	**-13.13**	-9.67	**-23.96**	-20.27	**-28.18**	-25.41	**-33.55**	-30.86	**-37.05**	-35.28

algorithms maximize the log-likelihood function, note however that this does not necessarily results in minimizing the quadratic error. The results are shown in Figure 12 and Table 1. It can be seen that while the GEM algorithm converges to its final value, on average the constrained EM algorithm is able to reach a solution with a higher log-likelihood function and a lower error. We remark that the objective function is non-convex, such that both algorithms can get trapped in local maxima. Although both algorithms use the same initialization, in most of the experiments (see Table 1) the constrained EM gives a more accurate estimate of the noise covariance matrix.

In Figure 13 and Figure 14, we used the noise estimation method based on the constrained EM algorithm in combination with the BLS-GSM Portilla et al. (2003) denoising method, in order to perform blind noise removal. An undecimated wavelet transform of 3 levels with the Daubechies wavelet with eight vanishing moments was used. The PSD of the Gaussian noise is in the captions of Figure 13 and Figure 14. Clearly, the combined method is well able to distinguish signal information from noise information, leading to a succesful removal of the noise while preserving signal structures.

(a) Original image (b) With artificial noise (PSNR=20.17dB) (c) Denoised (PSNR=41.21dB)

Fig. 13. Blind denoising results (using the BLS-GSM denoising method and the proposed constrained EM noise estimation technique). Noise PSD $P(\boldsymbol{\omega}) \sim \exp(-4000((\omega_x/\pi - 0.1)^2 + (\omega_y/\pi - 0.12)^2))$.

(a) Original image (b) With artificial noise (PSNR=17.25dB) (c) Denoised (PSNR=29.00dB)

Fig. 14. Blind denoising results (using the BLS-GSM denoising method and the proposed constrained EM noise estimation technique). Noise PSD $P(\boldsymbol{\omega}) \sim \exp(-2000((\omega_x/\pi - 0.1)^2 + (\omega_y/\pi - 0.12)^2)) + \exp(-3000((\omega_x/\pi + 0.15)^2 + (\omega_y/\pi - 0.22)^2)) + 10^{-3}$.

8. Conclusion

In this chapter, we investigated the estimation of stationary colored noise, which is most efficiently described in a Fourier basis using the power spectral density (PSD). Because of the time or spatial locality of signal structures, estimation of colored noise is best performed in a transform domain that allows to adapt to the signal locality. We have shown that wavelets are very good candidates for this task: their vanishing moment properties allow us to complete suppress smoothly varying signals, such that efficient noise estimation can directly be performed on a single wavelet subband. However, in practice, signals are not smoothly varying and may contain transitions (such as edges and textures in images). To take this into account, we have presented several prior models for noise-free wavelet coefficients. These prior models are then used in an expectation-maximization algorithm, which gives us an estimate of the noise covariance matrix for a given wavelet subband. We have further shown how this covariance matrix is related to the noise autocorrelation function in spatial or time domain. This relationship can then be used, e.g., to estimate parameters of parametric PSDs, yielding reliable and accurate estimates for noise PSDs. Because noise is present in most real-life signals and images, many signal and image processing methods can be further improved by taking advantage of estimated noise characteristics using techniques as described in this chapter.

9. References

Abramovich, F., Sapatinas, T. & Silverman, B. (1998). Wavelet thresholding via a Bayesian approach, *J. of the Royal Statist. Society B* 60: 725–749.

Achim, A., Bezerianos, A. & Tsakalides, P. (2001). Wavelet-based ultrasound image denoising using an alpha-stable prior probability model, *Proc. International Conference on Image Processing*, Vol. 2, pp. 221–224.

Aelterman, J., Deblaere, K., Goossens, B., Pižurica, A. & Philips, W. (2010). Dual Tree Complex Wavelet-Based Denoising of correlated noise in 3D Magnetic Resonance Imaging. Under revision.

Aelterman, J., Goossens, B., Pižurica, A. & Philips, W. (2010). *Recent Advances in Signal Processing*, IN-TECH, chapter Suppression of Correlated Noise.

Andrews, D. & Mallows, C. (1974). Scale mixtures of normal distributions, *J. Royal Stat. Stoc.* 36: 99–102.

Antonini, M., Barlaud, M., Mathieu, P. & Daubechies, I. (1992). Image coding using wavelet transform., *IEEE Trans. Image Process.* 1(2): 205–220.

Baher, H. (2001). *Analog and Digital Signal Processing*, Wiley, Chichester.

Bayer, B. (1976). Color imaging array, United States Patent 3971065.

Borel, C., Cooke, B. & Laubscher, B. (1996). Partial Removal of Correlated noise in Thermal Imagery, *Proceedings of SPIE*, Vol. 2759, pp. 131–138.

Campbell, N. A., Lopuhaä, H. P. & Rousseeuw, P. J. (1998). On the calculation of a robust s-estimator of a covariance matrix., *Stat Med* 17(23): 2685–2695.

Candès, E. (1998). *Ridgelets: Theory and Applications*, PhD thesis, Departement of Statistics, Stanford University.

Candès, E., Demanet, L., Donoho, D. & Ying, L. (2006). Fast Discrete Curvelet Transforms, *Multiscale modeling and simulation* 5(3): 861–899.

Chang, S. G., Yu, B. & Vetterli, M. (1998). Spatially adaptive wavelet thresholding with context modeling for image denoising, *Proc. IEEE Internat. Conf. on Image Proc.*, Chicago, IL, USA.

Clyde, M., Parmigiani, G. & Vidakovic, B. (1998). Multiple shrinkage and subset selection in wavelets, *Biometrika* 85(2): 391–401.

Crouse, M. S., Nowak, R. D. & Baranuik, R. G. (1998). Wavelet-based statistical signal processing using hidden Markov models, *IEEE Trans. Signal Proc.* 46(4): 886–902.

Daubechies, I. (1992). *Ten Lectures on Wavelets*, Society for Industrial and Applied Mathematics, Philadelphia.

Dempster, A., Laird, N. & Rubin, D. (1977). Maximum likelihood from incomplete data via the EM algorithm, *Journal of the Royal Statistical Society, Series B* 19(1): 1–38.

Do, M. N. & Vetterli, M. (2003). The finite ridgelet transform for image representation, *IEEE Trans. Image Processing* 12(1): 16–28.

Do, M. N. & Vetterli, M. (2005). The contourlet transform: An efficient directional multiresolution image representation, *IEEE Trans. Image Process.* 14(12): 2091–2106.

Donoho, D. L. & Johnstone, I. M. (1995). Adapting to unknown smoothness via wavelet shrinking, *Journal of the American Statistical Association* 90(432): 1200–1224.

Fadili, J. M. & Boubchir, L. (2005). Analytical form for a Bayesian wavelet estimator of images using the Bessel K form densities, *IEEE Trans. on Image Process.* 14(2): 231–240.

Fan, G. & Xia, X. (2001). Image denoising using local contextual hidden Markov model in the wavelet domain, *IEEE Signal Processing Letters* 8(5): 125–128.

Field, D. J. (1987). Relations between the statistics of natural images and the response properties of cortical cells, *J. Opt. Soc. Am. A* 4(12): 2379–2394.

Fischer, S., Šroubek, F., Perrinet, L., Redondo, R. & Cristobal, G. (2007). Self-Invertible 2D Log-Gabor Wavelets, *International Journal of Computer Vision* 75(2): 231–246.

Gómez, E., Gómez-Villegas, M. A. & Marín, J. M. (2008). Multivariate exponential power distributions as mixtures of normal distributions with Bayesian applications, *Communications in Statistics - Theory and Methods* 37(6): 972–985.

Goossens, B., Aelterman, J., Pižurica, A. & Philips, W. (2010). A Recursive Scheme for Computing Autocovariance functions of complex wavelet subbands, *IEEE Trans. Signal Processing* 58(7): 3907–3912.

Guo, K. & Labate, D. (2007). Optimally Sparse Multidimensional Representation using Shearlets, *SIAM J Math. Anal.* 39: 298–318.

Johnstone, I. M. & Silverman, B. W. (1997). Wavelet threshold estimators for data with correlated noise, *Journal of the Royal Statistical Society B* 59(2): 319–351.

Kingsbury, N. G. (2001). Complex wavelets for shift invariant analysis and filtering of signals, *Journal of Applied and Computational Harmonic Analysis* 10(3): 234–253.

Kotz, S., Kozubowski, T. J. & Podgorski, K. (2000). An asymmetric multivariate laplace distribution, *Computational Statistics* 4: 531–540.

Kotz, S. & Kozubowski, T.and Podgorski, K. (2001). *The Laplace Distributions And Generalizations: A Revisit with Applications to Communications, Economics, Engineering, Finance*, Birkhäuser, Boston.

Kwon, O., Sohn, K. & Lee, C. (2003). Deinterlacing using Directional Interpolation and Motion Compensation, *IEEE Trans. Consumer Electronics* 49(1): 198–203.

Lee, T. (1996). Image Representation Using 2D Gabor Wavelets, *IEEE Trans. Pattern Analysis and Machine Intelligence* 18(10): 1.

Mallat, S. (1989). Multifrequency channel decomposition of images and wavelet models, *IEEE Trans. Acoust., Speech, Signal Proc.* 37(12): 2091–2110.

Mallat, S. (1999). *A Wavelet Tour of Signal Processing*, Academic Press.

Moulin, P. & Liu, J. (1999). Analysis of multiresolution image denoising schemes using generalized-gaussian and complexity priors, *IEEE Trans. Info. Theory, Special Issue on Multiscale Analysis* 3(3): 909–919.

Nikias, C. L. & Shao, M. (1995). *Signal Processing with Alpha-Stable Distributions and Applications*, Wiley-Interscience.

Nowak, R. (1999). Wavelet-based rician noise removal for magnetic resonance imaging., *IEEE Trans Image Process* 8(10): 1408–1419.

Pena, D. & Prieto, F. (2001). Multivariate outlier detection and robust covariance matrix estimation, *Technometrics* 43(3): 286–310.

Pižurica, A. & Philips, W. (2006). Estimating the probability of the presence of a signal of interest in multiresolution single- and multiband image denoising., *IEEE Trans. Image Process.* 15(3): 654–665.

Pižurica, A., Philips, W., Lemahieu, I. & Acheroy, M. (2003). A versatile wavelet domain noise filtration technique for medical imaging, *IEEE Trans. Medical Imaging* 22(3): 323–331.

Portilla, J. (2004). Full blind denoising through noise covariance estimation using Gaussian Scale Mixtures in the wavelet domain, *IEEE Int. Conf. on Image Process. (ICIP)* 2: 1217–1220.

Portilla, J. & Simoncelli, E. (2001). Adaptive Wiener Denoising using a Gaussian Scale Mixture Model in the Wavelet Domain, *IEEE Int. Conf. on Image Process. (ICIP)* 2: 37–40.

Portilla, J., Strela, V., Wainwright, M. & Simoncelli, E. (2003). Image denoising using scale mixtures of gaussians in the wavelet domain, *IEEE Transactions on image processing* 12(11): 1338–1351.

Rabbani, H., Vafadust, M., Gazor, S. & Selesnick, I. W. (2006). Image Denoising Employing a Bivariate Cauchy Distribution with Local Variance in Complex Wavelet Domain, *12th Digital Signal Processing Workshop - 4th Signal Processing Education Workshop*, pp. 203–208.

Romberg, J., Choi, H. & Baraniuk, R. G. (2001). Bayesian tree structured image modeling using wavelet-domain Hidden Markov Models, *IEEE Trans. Image Process.* 10(7): 1056–1068. Enter text here.

Selesnick, I. W. (2006). Laplace random vectors, Gaussian noise, and the generalized incomplete Gamma function, *Proc. IEEE Int. Conf. on Image Process.*, pp. 2097–2100.

Selesnick, I. W., Baraniuk, R. G. & Kingsbury, N. G. (2005a). The Dual-Tree Complex Wavelet Transform, *IEEE Signal Processing Magazine* 22(6): 123–151.

Selesnick, I. W., Baraniuk, R. G. & Kingsbury, N. G. (2005b). The Dual-Tree Complex Wavelet Transform, *IEEE Signal Processing Magazine* 22(6): 123–151.

Shi, F. & Selesnick, I. W. (2006). Multivariate Quasi-Laplacian Mixture Models for Wavelet-based Image Denoising, *Proc. Int. Conf. on Image Processing (ICIP)*, pp. 2097–2100.

Simoncelli, E., Freeman, W. T., Adelson, E. H. & Heeger, D. J. (1992). Shiftable Multi-scale Transforms, *IEEE Trans. Information Theory* 38(2): 587–607.

Simoncelli, E. P. & Adelson, E. H. (1996). Noise removal via Bayesian wavelet coring, *Proc. IEEE Internat. Conf. Image Proc. ICIP*, Lausanne, Switzerland.

Srivastava, A., Lee, A. B., Simoncelli, E. & Zhu, S.-C. (2003). On Advances in Statistical Modeling of Natural Images, *Journal of Mathematical Imaging and Vision* 18: 17–33.

Srivastava, A., Liu, X. & Grenander, U. (2002). Universal Analytical Forms for Modeling Image Probabilities, *IEEE Trans. Pattern Analysis and Machine Intelligence* 24(9): 1200–1214.

Tzikas, D., Likas, A. & Galatsanos, N. (2007). Variational bayesian blind image deconvolution with student-t priors, *Proc. IEEE International Conference on Image Processing ICIP 2007*, Vol. 1, pp. I–109–I–112.

Van De Ville, D. & Unser, M. (2008). Complex Wavelet Bases, Steerability, and the Marr-like pyramid, *IEEE Trans. Image Processing* 17(11): 2063–2080.

Vo, A., Nguyen, T. & Oraintara, S. (2007). Image denoising using shiftable directional pyramid and scale mixtures of complex gaussians, *Proc. IEEE International Symposium on Circuits and Systems ISCAS 2007*, pp. 4000–4003.

Wainwright, M. J. & Simoncelli, E. P. (2000). Scale mixtures of Gaussians and the statistics of natural images, *Adv. Neural Information Processing Systems (NIPS 1999)* 12: 855–861.

16

An Adaptive Energy Discretization of the Neutron Transport Equation Based on a Wavelet Galerkin Method

D. Fournier and R. Le Tellier
CEA, DEN, DER/SPRC/LEPh, Cadarache, F-13108 Saint-Paul-lez-Durance France

1. Introduction

The time-independent neutron transport equation derived from the Boltzmann equation with a linear collision kernel models the neutron population in the six dimensional space defined by $\vec{r} \in \mathcal{D}$ the space variable, $\vec{\Omega} \in \mathcal{S}_2$ the direction of motion variable and $E \in \mathcal{B} =]E_{G+1}, E_1[$ the energy variable. It represents the balance between the neutrons entering the hypervolume $d^3rd^2\Omega dE$ about $\left(\vec{r}, \vec{\Omega}, E\right)$ by fission or scattering and those leaving by streaming or any kind of interactions. The unknown is the so-called neutron flux $\phi(\vec{r}, \vec{\Omega}, E) = v(E)n(\vec{r}, \vec{\Omega}, E)$ with $n(\vec{r}, \vec{\Omega}, E)$ the neutron density and $v(E)$ the neutron velocity. The problem is defined in terms of the neutron interaction properties of the different materials *i.e.* the cross sections.

The solution of this equation in a deterministic way proceeds by the successive discretization of the three variables: energy, angle and space. The treatment of the energy variable invariably consists in a multigroup discretization which considers the cross sections and the flux to be constant within a group (*i.e.* a cell of the 1D energy mesh). A pre-homogenization of the cross sections is performed at the library processing level using a spatially independent weighting flux (*e.g.* $1/E$ spectrum in the epithermal range).

With a broad group structure ($\approx$ 100 to 2000 energy groups), this prior homogenization is unsufficient to take into account the case-specific, spatially-dependent, self-shielding effect *i.e.* the flux local depression in the vicinity of resonances that largely affects the neutron balance. As a consequence, a neutron transport calculation has to incorporate a so-called self-shielding model to correct the group cross sections of resonant isotopes. This homogenization stage of a neutron transport calculation is known to be a main source of errors for deterministic methods; as a consequence, an important work has been carried out to improve it. An optimized energy mesh structure (Mosca et al., 2011) in addition to an advanced self-shielding model (Hébert, 2007) is incorporated in state-of-the-art transport codes.

A different treatment for the energy variable based on a finite element approach is the basis of the present work. Such an avenue was proposed in the past by (Allen, 1986) but seldom used in practice. Indeed, finite element methods are commonly based on polynomial function bases which are not appropriate for non-smooth behavior.

Recently, two independent works by (Le Tellier et al., 2009) and (Yang et al., 2010) have proposed wavelet-Galerkin methods to overcome this issue. In this chapter, after a review of these two approaches, we will focus on the development in this framework of adaptive algorithms with a control (at least, partial) of the discretization error. Such algorithms have been partially presented in a previous conference presentation by (Fournier & Le Tellier, 2009) but this book chapter gives a more in-depth presentation and updated numerical results for algorithms that may be of interest for other applications of wavelet-based finite elements. Such algorithms are analyzed in a limited framework (the fine structure flux equation for a single isotope diluted in a mixture of non-resonant isotopes in an infinite homogeneous medium) but the relevant issues regarding their extension in the general case are discussed.

2. Wavelet-Galerkin based energy discretization of the neutron transport equation

2.1 Generalized weak multigroup neutron transport equation

As in (Allen, 1986), the transport equation is discretized starting from the Sobolev spaces

$$W_2^1(\mathcal{D}\times\mathcal{S}_2) = \{\phi \in L_2(\mathcal{D}\times\mathcal{S}_2), \text{ all the weak derivatives of } \phi \in L_2(\mathcal{D}\times\mathcal{S}_2)\}, \tag{1}$$

$$W_2^{1\dagger}(\mathcal{A}) = \left\{\phi \in L_2(\mathcal{A}), \phi \in W_2^1(\mathcal{D}\times\mathcal{S}_2)\right\}. \tag{2}$$

with $\mathcal{A} = \mathcal{D}\times\mathcal{S}_2\times\mathcal{B}$. In particular, the energy variable is discretized as follows. An energy mesh consisting of G groups such that $E_1 > E_2 \cdots > E_{G+1}$ ($I_g =]E_{g+1}, E_g[$) is selected and the finite-dimension space $W^h(\mathcal{A}) \subset W_2^{1\dagger}(\mathcal{A})$ considered is

$$W^h(\mathcal{A}) = \left\{\phi \in W_2^{1\dagger}(\mathcal{A}), \phi(\vec{r},\vec{\Omega},E) = \sum_{g=1}^{G} \Pi_{I_g}(E)\underline{f}^{g\mathrm{T}}(E)\underline{\phi}^g(\vec{r},\vec{\Omega}) \text{ with } \underline{\phi}^g \in \left(W_2^1(\mathcal{D}\times\mathcal{S}_2)\right)^{N_g}\right\}, \tag{3}$$

where Π_{I_g} is the characteristic function of group g, $\underline{f}^g \in \left(L_2(I_g)\right)^{N_g}$ is an orthonormal set of wavelet functions on I_g and the group flux unknowns are the flux wavelet modes *i.e.* $\underline{\phi}^g(\vec{r},\vec{\Omega}) = \int_{I_g} dE\underline{f}^g(E)\phi(\vec{r},\vec{\Omega},E)$.

Within this framework, a Ritz-Galerkin procedure casts the transport equation (written with isotropic scattering and an external source $Q(\vec{r},\vec{\Omega},E)$) in a generalized (weak) multigroup form: $\forall g \in [1,G]$,

$$\left(\vec{\Omega}\cdot\vec{\nabla} + \underline{\underline{\Sigma_t}}^g(\vec{r})\right)\underline{\phi}^g(\vec{r},\vec{\Omega}) = \frac{1}{4\pi}\sum_{g'=1}^{G}\left(\underline{\underline{\Sigma_s}}^{g\leftarrow g'}(\vec{r})\right)\underline{\Phi}^{g'}(\vec{r}) + \underline{Q}^g(\vec{r},\vec{\Omega}), \tag{4}$$

where $\underline{\Phi}^g(\vec{r}) = \int_{\mathcal{S}_2} d^2\Omega\underline{\phi}^g(\vec{r},\vec{\Omega})$ and the source vector is $\underline{Q}^g(\vec{r},\vec{\Omega}) = \int_{I_g} dE\underline{f}^g(E)Q(\vec{r},\vec{\Omega},E)$.

The matrices coupling the flux modes within a group are defined in terms of the total $\Sigma_t(\vec{r},E)$ and scattering transfer $\Sigma_s(\vec{r},E'\rightarrow E)$ cross sections as

$$\underline{\underline{\Sigma_t}}^g(\vec{r}) = \int_{I_g} dE\underline{f}^g(E)\Sigma_t(\vec{r},E)\underline{f}^{g\mathrm{T}}(E), \tag{5}$$

$$\underline{\underline{\Sigma_s}}^g(\vec{r}) = \int_{I_g} dE\underline{f}^g(E)\int_{I_{g'}} dE'\Sigma_s(\vec{r},E'\rightarrow E)\underline{f}^{g\mathrm{T}}(E'). \tag{6}$$

Note that Eq. 5 introduces a coupling between the different modes within a group on the left hand side of the transport equation *i.e.* a coupling of the angular flux projections $\underline{\phi}^g(\vec{r},\vec{\Omega})$ that is not present for the standard multigroup approach.

Two different approaches by (Le Tellier et al., 2009) and (Yang et al., 2010) based on compactly supported Daubechies wavelets (Daubechies, 1992) have been proposed so far to deal with this coupling:

1. in (Yang et al., 2010), a dilation order is fixed and the basis consists in the translates of the associated scaling function; in this case, $\underline{\underline{\Sigma_t}}^g(\vec{r})$ is a band matrix and the mode coupling is limited in such a way that a Richardson iterative scheme can be employed to resolve this coupling.
2. in (Le Tellier et al., 2009), both dilates and translates of the mother wavelet functions are retained in the basis according to a thresholding procedure applied to the discrete wavelet transform of either the total cross section Σ_t or an approximate flux. In this case, the basis selection can be optimized but the modes are tightly coupled; a procedure based on a change of basis through a matrix diagonalization have been proposed to explictly decouple the equations.

This second approach proceeds as follows. Let us consider that the nuclear data are known by their projections on a set of orthonormal functions $\left(g_k^g\right)_{k\in[1,N_g]}$ in each group *e.g.*

$$\Sigma_t(\vec{r},E) = \underline{\hat{\Sigma}_t}^{g\mathrm{T}}(\vec{r})\underline{g}^g(E). \tag{7}$$

At this stage, $\underline{g}^g$ is assumed to be spatially uniform. This condition is satisfied for example if the same set of functions is considered for all the isotopes of a given configuration.
Considering the isomorphism between the Hilbert space $F_g = \mathrm{span}\left(g_1^g \dots, g_{N_g}^g\right)$ and $\mathbb{R}^{N_g}$, we can construct an orthonormal basis $(f_n^g)_{n\in[1,N_g]}$ of F_g in such a way that the different functions f_n^g are Σ_t-orthogonal. Indeed,

$$\underline{\underline{\tilde{\Sigma}_t}}^g(\vec{r}) = \int_{I_g} dE\underline{g}^g(E)\Sigma_t(\vec{r},E)\underline{g}^{g\mathrm{T}}(E) \tag{8}$$

is unitary similar to a diagonal matrix (see (Le Tellier et al., 2009) for more details) *i.e.*

$$\underline{\underline{\tilde{\Sigma}_t}}^g(\vec{r}) = \underline{\underline{C}}^g(\vec{r})\underline{\underline{\Sigma}}_t^g(\vec{r})\underline{\underline{C}}^{g\mathrm{T}}(\vec{r}), \tag{9}$$

with

- $\underline{\underline{C}}^g(\vec{r})$ = a unitary matrix containing the eigenvectors of $\underline{\underline{\tilde{\Sigma}_t}}^g(\vec{r})$,
- $\underline{\underline{\Sigma_t}}^g(\vec{r})$ = a diagonal matrix containing its eigenvalues.

Thus, $\underline{f}^g(\vec{r},E) = \underline{\underline{C}}^{g\mathrm{T}}(\vec{r})\underline{g}^g(E)$.
The problem at this stage is that the diagonalization of this operator depends on the spatial position through $\Sigma_t(\vec{r},E)$ *i.e.* $\underline{f}^g(\vec{r},E)$ depends on $\vec{r}$ and in the general case the discretized streaming operator is no longer diagonal. However, in most of the practical cases, the total cross section is defined as a step function with respect to the space variable *i.e.* a set of uniform media is defined and used to represent the spatial distribution of the nuclear data. Let us consider that the spatial domain $\mathcal{D}$ is split into a set of non-overlapping uniform medium domains *i.e.* $\mathcal{D} = \bigcup_i \mathcal{D}_i$. The total cross section (along with the other nuclear data) is represented as

$$\Sigma_t(\vec{r}, E) = \sum_g \Pi_{I_g}(E) \sum_i \Pi_{\mathcal{D}_i}(\vec{r}) \underline{\hat{\Sigma}_{ti}}^{g\mathrm{T}}(\vec{r}) \underline{g}^g(E), \tag{10}$$

where $\Pi_{\mathcal{D}_i}$ is the characteristic function of $\mathcal{D}_i$ and the flux is expanded as

$$\phi(\vec{r}, \vec{\Omega}, E) = \sum_g \Pi_{I_g}(E) \sum_i \Pi_{\mathcal{D}_i}(\vec{r}) \underline{f}_i^{g\mathrm{T}}(E) \underline{\phi}_i^g(\vec{r}, \vec{\Omega}). \tag{11}$$

For a given i, $\underline{f}_i^g$ is uniform on $\mathcal{D}_i$ and is obtained by diagonalizing $\underline{\underline{\tilde{\Sigma}_{ti}}}^g$ as previously described.

For $\vec{r}$ belonging to a uniform medium domain $\mathcal{D}_i$, Eq. 4 can be written without any complication of the streaming term. In fact, this formulation of the transport equation is similar to the standard multigroup form. In this case, the mode coupling only appears for the conditions at the interface Γ_{ij} between two uniform medium domains $\mathcal{D}_i$ and $\mathcal{D}_j$ along $\vec{\Omega}$. The continuity of $\phi(\vec{r}, \vec{\Omega}, E)$ at $\vec{r} \in \Gamma_{ij}$ implies directly the continuity of $\phi^g(\vec{r}, \vec{\Omega})$ in the standard multigroup case:

$$\phi_j^g(\vec{r}, \vec{\Omega}) = \phi_i^g(\vec{r}, \vec{\Omega}), \tag{12}$$

while, in our case, it translates into

$$\underline{\phi}_j^g(\vec{r}, \vec{\Omega}) = \underline{\underline{C}}_j^{g\mathrm{T}} \underline{\underline{C}}_i^g \underline{\phi}_i^g(\vec{r}, \vec{\Omega}). \tag{13}$$

When crossing an interface between two uniform media domain, a change of basis with respect to the energy expansion has to be performed in order to maintain a diagonal group transport operator over the whole domain.

2.2 Case of study

The numerical study of the proposed algorithms will be limited to the fine structure flux equation for a single isotope diluted in a mixture of non-resonant isotopes in an infinite homogeneous medium in such a way that only the energy variable has to be discretized. The total cross section is written as $\Sigma_t^+ + N^* \sigma_t^*(E)$ considering that Σ_t^+ is constant; $*$ refers to the resonant isotope. Considering $\underline{f}^g(E)$, the σ_t^{*g}-orthogonal and orthonormal basis of F_g, the weak form of the fine structure flux equation is written as

$$\left(\underline{\underline{\sigma_t}}^{*g} + \sigma_d\right) \underline{\phi}^g = \sum_{g'=1}^{G} \underline{\underline{\sigma_s}}^{*g \leftarrow g'} \underline{\phi}^{g'} + \sigma_d \int_{I_g} dE \underline{f}^g(E), \tag{14}$$

In matrix-vector form, this linear system is summarized as

$$H\Phi = S\Phi + Q. \tag{15}$$

We will also consider that the source-flux coupling in Eq. 15 is solved by a simple Richardson iterative scheme under the form

$$H\Phi^{n+1} = S\Phi^n + Q. \tag{16}$$

H^{-1} will be denoted A in the remainder.

2.3 Wavelet-based elements

Let θ be some function in $L_2(\mathbb{R})$. We consider the translates and dilates of θ denoted $\theta_{j,k}$ such that $\theta_{j,k}(x) = 2^{j/2}\theta(2^j x - k)(j \in \mathbb{Z}, k \in \mathbb{Z})$ and $V_j = \text{span}\left\{\theta_{j,k}, k \in \mathbb{Z}\right\}$ the generated linear spaces. θ is called the father wavelet or scaling function and is constructed in such a way that $\left\{V_j, j \in \mathbb{Z}\right\}$ is a multiresolution analysis (MRA) *i.e.*

- $\{\theta_{0,k}, k \in \mathbb{Z}\}$ is an orthonormal system in $L_2(\mathbb{R})$,
- $V_j \subset V_{j+1}, \forall j \in \mathbb{Z}$,
- $\bigcup_{j\geq 0} V_j$ is dense in $L_2(\mathbb{R})$.

Moreover, for convenience, we consider that θ is normalized in such a way that $\int dx\theta(x) = 1$. In this case, defining W_j by $V_{j+1} = W_j \oplus V_j (j \in \mathbb{Z})$, we obtain $L_2(\mathbb{R}) = V_0 \oplus \bigoplus_{j=0}^{\infty} W_j$. The next step is to find a function $\gamma \in W_0$ ($\gamma_{j,k}$ is defined in a same way as $\theta_{j,k}$) such that $\{\gamma_{0,k}, k \in \mathbb{Z}\}$ is an orthonormal basis of W_0. The existence of such a function is guaranteed but it is not unique; in any case, it verifies $\int dx\gamma(x) = 0$. This function is called the mother wavelet. Consequently, $\left\{\gamma_{j,k}, k \in \mathbb{Z}\right\}$ is an orthonormal basis of W_j. Note that the mother wavelet is always orthogonal to the father wavelet.

Within such a framework, any function $\phi \in L_2(\mathbb{R})$ has a unique representation in terms of an L_2-convergent series: (see (Hardle et al., 1997))

$$\phi(x) = \sum_k \alpha_{0,k}\theta_{0,k}(x) + \sum_{j=0}^{\infty}\sum_k \beta_{j,k}\gamma_{j,k}(x), \tag{17}$$

where $\alpha_{j,k}$ and $\beta_{j,k}$ correspond to the orthogonal projection of ϕ on $\theta_{j,k}$ and $\gamma_{j,k}$ respectively. In the present work, we consider for the basis functions $\underline{g}^g$ in each group I_g a subset of $\left((\theta_{0,k})_k, \left(\gamma_{j,k}\right)_{j,k}\right)$ obtained by the sampling, discrete wavelet transform and thresholding of $\sigma_t^{*g}(E)$ or an approximate flux restricted to I_g. This is to be distinguished from the work of (Yang et al., 2010) where the basis is composed of the scaling functions for a given dilation order j *i.e.* $\underline{g}^g = \left(\theta_{j,k}\right)_k$.

In the following, we restrict ourselves to compactly supported wavelets introduced by (Daubechies, 1992) constructed starting from a function $m_0(\xi) = \frac{1}{\sqrt{2}}\sum_k h_k e^{-ik\xi}$ where h_k are real-valued coefficients such that only a finite number M (the support length) of h_k are non-zero. In this context, the MRA obeys

$$\theta_{j-1,l} = \sum_k h_{k-2l}\theta_{j,k}, \tag{18}$$

$$\gamma_{j-1,l} = \sum_k g_{k-2l}\gamma_{j,k}, \tag{19}$$

and the decomposition of a sampled $N-$length signal is obtained efficiently by the discrete wavelet transform (DWT) based on the cascade algorithm proposed in (Mallat, 1989).

Following such a wavelet decomposition, the thresholding consists in replacing Eq. 17 by

$$\phi(x) = \sum_k \alpha_{0,k}\theta_{0,k}(x) + \sum_{j=0}^{J}\sum_k \tilde{\beta}_{j,k}\gamma_{j,k}(x), \tag{20}$$

where $(\tilde{\beta}_{j,k})_{j,k}$ is obtained from $(\beta_{j,k})_{j,k}$ and $\#(\tilde{\beta}_{j,k})_{j,k} \ll \#(\beta_{j,k})_{j,k}$
A natural criterion is to discard coefficients lower than a given cut-off ε *i.e.*

$$\tilde{\beta}_{j,k} = \begin{cases} 0 & \text{if} \quad |\beta_{j,k}| \leq \varepsilon \max_{j,k}(\beta_{j,k}), \\ \beta_{j,k} & \text{otherwise.} \end{cases} \tag{21}$$

This method is called hard thresholding. We refer the interested reader to (Le Tellier et al., 2009) for a comparison of different wavelet filters and thresholding strategies in this context.

3. Adaptivity

In the context of Eq. 16, adaptive algorithms aim at improving the operators discretization during the iterative process by dynamically selecting the basis functions and consequently, optimizing the computational cost and control (at least partially) the error on the final solution. The proposed algorithms aim at reducing the computational cost defined as the sum of the supports size at each iteration:

$$\text{cost} = \sum_{i=1}^{nbIter} \left(\#\Lambda_i^A + \#\Lambda_i^S\right), \tag{22}$$

where Λ_i^S (resp. Λ_i^A) represents the support of operator S (resp. A) at iteration i. Actually, the computational cost required to solve Eq. 16 is directly linked to the size of the operators manipulated: Λ_i^S for the construction of matrix S_i and Λ_i^A the order of the system used for iterations. It justifies the use of Eq. 22 as a measure of the algorithm computational cost.
Our work differs from the approach in (Cohen, 2003) where the goal was to minimize the final support. Here, the purpose is to find a balance between the number of iterations and the support size. In the following, two different algorithms are presented and tested. Both are based on a decomposition of the error in terms of the Richardson iterations residual ($\delta\epsilon^{res}$) and the errors due to the discretization of A and S operators (denoted $\delta\epsilon^A$ and $\delta\epsilon^S$ respectively):

$$\frac{\left\|\Phi^{n+1} - \Phi\right\|}{\left\|\Phi^{n+1}\right\|} \leq \frac{1}{1 - \|AS\|}\left(\delta\epsilon^A + \delta\epsilon^S + \delta\epsilon^{res}\right) = NB. \tag{23}$$

Sections 3.2 and 3.3 explicit this bound for both algorithms. The first version, inspired from (Cohen, 2003), uses two levels of iterations: one in order to increase the support and one to converge the residual. The single-loop algorithm is proposed as a simplification of the first one and a way to correlate the errors on the operators and the residual is detailed.

3.1 Numerical cases of study

As $\|AS\|$ plays an important role in both algorithms presented in Sections 3.2 and 3.3, tests are performed on different isotopes and energy ranges (the energy mesh used for this study contains 172 groups) as presented in Table 1.

Isotope	$\|AS\|$	Energy range (eV)	Energy groups
^{238}U	0.26	6.16 - 7.52	88
^{56}Fe	0.10	1018 - 1230	56
^{16}O	0.01	273.2E3 - 498.9E3	26-29

Table 1. Numerical cases of study for the two adaptive algorithms

3.2 Two-loop algorithm

In this algorithm, an outer iteration loop (index j) is added. At a given iteration j, the following system is solved:

$$\Phi_{j+1}^{n+1} = A_{j+1}\left(S_{j+1}\Phi_{j+1}^{n} + Q\right), \tag{24}$$

with A_{j+1} (resp. S_{j+1}) representing matrix A (resp. S) restricted to Λ_{j+1}^{A} (resp. Λ_{j+1}^{S}) support. The error is given by:

$$\begin{aligned}\Phi_{j+1}^{n+1} - \Phi &= A_{j+1}\left(S_{j+1}\Phi_{j+1}^{n} + Q\right) - A(S\Phi + Q)\\ &= \left(A_{j+1} - A\right)\left(S_{j+1}\Phi_{j+1}^{n} + Q\right) + A\left(S_{j+1} - S\right)\Phi_{j+1}^{n} + AS\left(\Phi_{j+1}^{n} - \Phi\right).\end{aligned} \tag{25}$$

It follows that the relative error can be expressed by Eq. 23 with

$$\delta\epsilon^{S} = \|A\| \frac{\left\|\left(S_{j+1} - S\right)\Phi_{j+1}^{n}\right\|}{\left\|\Phi_{j+1}^{n+1}\right\|}, \tag{26}$$

$$\delta\epsilon^{A} = \frac{\left\|\left(A_{j+1} - A\right)\left(S_{j+1}\Phi_{j+1}^{n} + Q\right)\right\|}{\left\|\Phi_{j+1}^{n+1}\right\|}, \tag{27}$$

$$\delta\epsilon^{res} = \|AS\| \frac{\left\|\Phi_{j+1}^{n+1} - \Phi_{j+1}^{n}\right\|}{\left\|\Phi_{j+1}^{n+1}\right\|}. \tag{28}$$

A main issue is the choice of the matrices S_{j+1} and A_{j+1} or, in other words, the selection of the wavelet supports. The idea in the remainder is to monitor the errors related to the operator discretizations using the numerical residual in order to obtain a relation of the type:

$$\frac{\left\|\Phi_{j+1}^{n+1} - \Phi\right\|}{\left\|\Phi_{j+1}^{n+1}\right\|} \leq K \frac{\left\|\Phi_{j+1}^{n+1} - \Phi_{j+1}^{n}\right\|}{\left\|\Phi_{j+1}^{n+1}\right\|}, \tag{29}$$

where K is a given constant. The error on the flux is thus controlled by the residual at each iteration.

The error on $\delta\epsilon^{S}$ (resp. $\delta\epsilon^{A}$) can be practically controlled by a thresholding on the product $S\Phi^{n}$ (resp. $A\left(S_{j+1}\Phi_{j+1}^{n} + Q\right)$) ensuring:

$$\left\|(S_{j+1} - S)\Phi_{j+1}^{n}\right\| \leq \epsilon_{j+1}^{\prime}\left\|\Phi_{j+1}^{n}\right\|, \tag{30}$$

$$\left\|\left(A_{j+1} - A\right)\left(S_{j+1}\Phi_{j+1}^{n} + Q\right)\right\| \leq \epsilon_{j+1}\left\|\Phi_{j+1}^{n}\right\|. \tag{31}$$

Remaining coefficients give the new supports Λ^S_{j+1} and Λ^A_{j+1} such that $\#\Lambda^S_{j+1} \ll \#\Lambda^S$ and $\#\Lambda^A_{j+1} \ll \#\Lambda^A$ where Λ^S and Λ^A are the support of S and A operators approximated by a large number of coefficients. The localization property of wavelets ensure that these two supports slowly increase when ϵ'_{j+1} and ϵ_{j+1} decrease (see (Cohen, 2003) for more details).
By applying the procedures exposed above to A and S, Eq. 23 becomes:

$$\frac{\left\|\Phi^{n+1}_{j+1} - \Phi\right\|}{\left\|\Phi^{n+1}_{j+1}\right\|} \leq \frac{1}{1 - \|AS\|} \left(\epsilon_{j+1} \frac{\left\|\Phi^{n}_{j+1}\right\|}{\left\|\Phi^{n+1}_{j+1}\right\|} + \epsilon'_{j+1} \|A\| \frac{\left\|\Phi^{n}_{j+1}\right\|}{\left\|\Phi^{n+1}_{j+1}\right\|} + \|AS\| \frac{\left\|\Phi^{n+1}_{j+1} - \Phi^{n}_{j+1}\right\|}{\left\|\Phi^{n+1}_{j+1}\right\|} \right). \tag{32}$$

Note however that the thresholding procedure described for operator A in Eq. 31 cannot be applied in the general context of the spatially-dependent transport equation (Eq. 4). A possibility is to use the same support for operators A and S. Such a solution has been tested in (Fournier & Le Tellier, 2009). Even if the convergence is deteriorated compared to the solution with two different supports for S and A, results are interesting and show that the adaptive algorithms proposed in this book chapter are extensible to the general problem.
As proposed in (Cohen, 2003), a geometrical decreasing sequence $\left(\epsilon_j\right)$ is fixed and iterations on n are performed until the residual becomes inferior to the value imposed by this sequence. To link ϵ_j and ϵ'_j, we ensure that the first two terms defined in Eq. 32 decay at the same rate by imposing:

$$\epsilon'_{j+1} = \frac{\epsilon_{j+1}}{\|A\|}. \tag{33}$$

At a given iteration j, Richardson iterations are carried out in order to ensure:

$$\frac{\left\|\Phi_{j+1} - \Phi_j\right\|}{\left\|\Phi_{j+1}\right\|} \leq \frac{\epsilon_{j+1}}{\|AS\|}. \tag{34}$$

Combining Eqs. 33 and 34 with the bound of Eq. 32 guarantees the convergence of the error:

$$\frac{\left\|\Phi_{j+1} - \Phi\right\|}{\left\|\Phi_{j+1}\right\|} \lesssim \frac{3\epsilon_{j+1}}{1 - \|AS\|}. \tag{35}$$

The devised algorithm is written in pseudocode in Algorithm 1.
The choice of $\left(\epsilon_j\right)$ is arbitrary and some numerical tests have been performed with different values. A possible choice is

$$\epsilon = \frac{\epsilon_{j+1}}{\epsilon_j} = \left\|A_j S_j\right\|,$$

the rate of convergence of Richardson method.
Indeed, two asymptotic behaviours can be observed depending on the ϵ value with respect to $\rho = \|AS\|$ as presented in Figure 1 for ^{16}O where $\rho = 0.01$:

- $\epsilon \gg \rho$ (case $\epsilon = 1/2$ in Figure 1): Richardson iterative scheme converges rapidly (and even in one iteration in the presented case) and the error decreases linearly at the same rate than the sequence (ϵ_j) but it needs many outer iterations. In our example, the slope of the straight line is equal to $0.3 = \log(1/2) = \log(\epsilon)$.

Result: Solve $H\Phi = S\Phi + Q$ thanks to an adaptive procedure
Input : Matrix H, S and vector Q calculated on an "infinite" support
given accuracy tol
Output: Φ: flux solution of $\Phi = H^{-1}(S\Phi + Q)$ at accuracy tol
Data: Λ: support, ϵ: accuracy

$\Phi_0 = 0, \Lambda_0 = \emptyset, \epsilon_0 = 1$;
$j = 0$;
$err = 1$;
while $\epsilon_j \geq tol\ \frac{1-\|AS\|}{3}$ **do**
  $j \leftarrow j + 1$;
  $\epsilon_j \leftarrow \epsilon\epsilon_{j-1}$;
  $\Phi_j^0 \leftarrow \Phi_{j-1}$;
  $n \leftarrow 1$;
  while $err \geq \frac{\epsilon_j}{\|AS\|}$ **do**
    $tmp = S\Phi_{j-1}^{n-1}$;
    $prod = \texttt{Thresholding}(tmp, \epsilon_j)$;
    % *remove smallest coefficients of tmp, guarantee* $\|tmp - prod\| \leq \epsilon_j \left\|\Phi_{j-1}^{n-1}\right\|$
    $R_j^n = prod + Q$;
    $\Lambda^{S_j^n} = \texttt{Support}(R_j^n)$;
    $\Phi_j^n = H^{-1}R_j^n$;
    $\Phi_j^n = \texttt{Thresholding}(\Phi_j^n, \frac{\epsilon_j}{\|H^{-1}\|})$;
    $\Lambda^{A_j^n} = \texttt{Support}(\Phi_j^n)$;
    $err \leftarrow \frac{\left\|\Phi_j^n - \Phi_j^{n-1}\right\|}{\left\|\Phi_j^n\right\|}$;
    $n \leftarrow n + 1$;
  end
  $\Phi_{j+1} = \Phi_j^n$;
end

Algorithm 1: two-loop adaptive algorithm

- $\epsilon \ll \|AS\|$: the number of coefficients kept increases rapidly and several Richardson iterations are necessary to converge at a given support.

$\epsilon = \rho$ seems a good compromise between increasing too slowly the support causing useless iterations and keeping too many coefficients which implies the resolution of a uselessly large linear system.
Figure 2 presents the L^2-error as a function of the cost for ^{238}U and ^{16}O. Showing this two cases is interesting because they exhibit a different spectral radius ($\|AS\| = 0.26$ for ^{238}U and 0.01 for ^{16}O). As ϵ decreases, the cost decreases to a minimum value ($\epsilon = \frac{1}{8}$ for ^{238}U), and then increases again. As ϵ decreases, less iterations are performed which improves the cost; below a given value too large systems are solved and the cost increases (these are the two

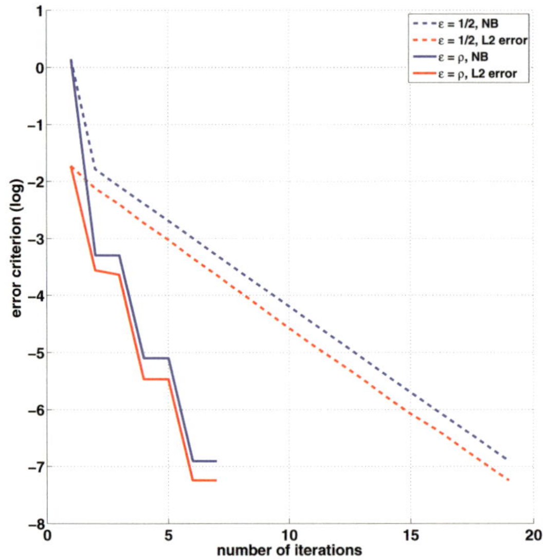

Fig. 1. L^2-error and numerical bound for different ϵ values on groups 26 to 29 of ^{16}O

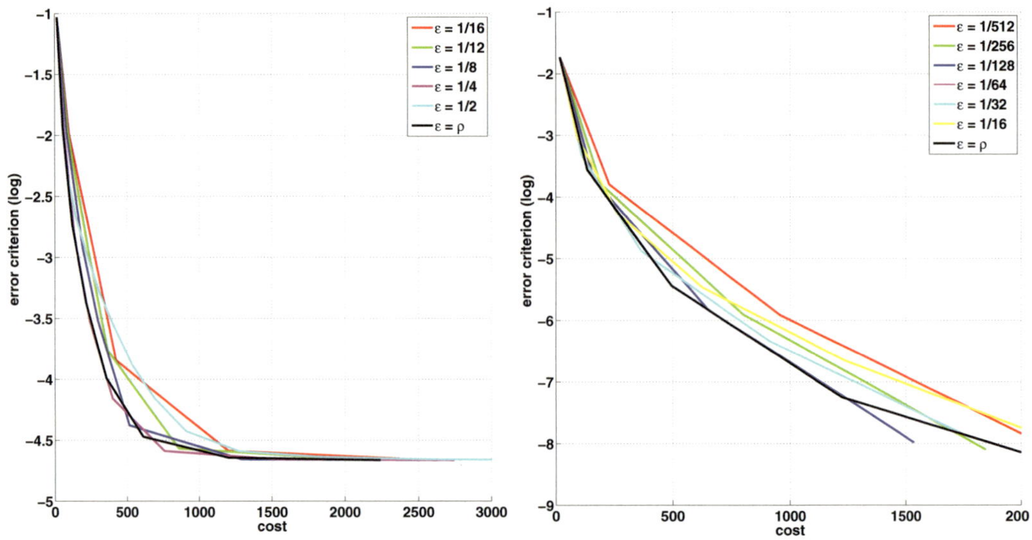

Fig. 2. Relative error versus cost for different ϵ values for group 88 of ^{238}U (left) and for groups 26 to 29 of ^{16}O (right)

behaviours illustrated in Figure 1). Obtaining the value of this minimum is not possible in the general case but let us mention that the use of the spectral radius $\left\|A_jS_j\right\|$ ensures a reasonable cost. Figure 3 further illustrates the evolution of the cost as a function of the parameter ϵ for ^{16}O and confirms the choice of $\left\|A_jS_j\right\|$ to minimize the cost.

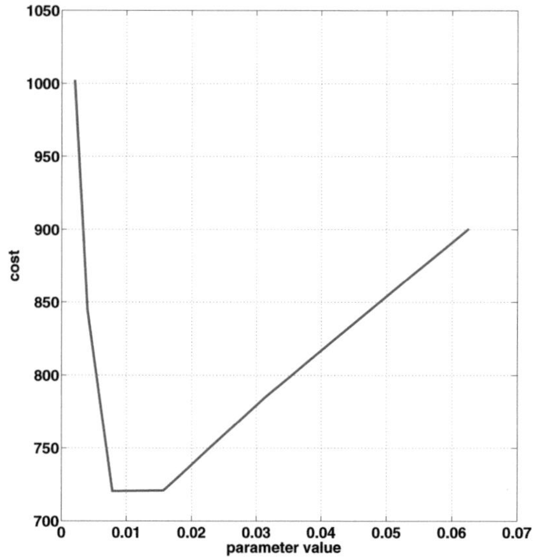

Fig. 3. Cost versus ϵ for a given accuracy of 10^{-6} for groups 26 to 29 of ^{16}O

3.3 Single-loop algorithm

The previous algorithm was directly inspired from Cohen (2003) and uses two levels of iterations which complicate the source iterations. Besides, the choice of the series (ϵ_j) is not obvious even if a geometrical sequence with a common ratio equal to $\left\|A_j S_j\right\|$ gives good results. As a simplification of this algorithm, a one-loop version is proposed, *i.e.* the iterative system is written as:

$$\Phi^{n+1} = A^{n+1}\left(S^{n+1}\Phi^{n} + Q\right). \tag{36}$$

A single loop means that the residual is no longer directly controlled and a strategy to handle this point has to be devised. At a given iteration, the residual is given by:

$$\begin{aligned}\Phi^{n+1} - \Phi^{n} &= A^{n+1}\left(S^{n+1}\Phi^{n} + Q\right) - A^{n}\left(S^{n}\Phi^{n-1} + Q\right)\\ &= \left(A^{n+1} - A^{n}\right)\left(S^{n+1}\Phi^{n} + Q\right) + A^{n}\left(S^{n+1} - S^{n}\right)\Phi^{n} + A^{n}S^{n}\left(\Phi^{n} - \Phi^{n-1}\right).\end{aligned} \tag{37}$$

And the same relationship as the one for the two-loop algorithm holds for the actual error:

$$(I - AS)\left(\Phi^{n+1} - \Phi\right) = \left(A^{n+1} - A\right)\left(S^{n+1}\Phi^{n} + Q\right) + A\left(S^{n+1} - S\right)\Phi^{n} - AS\left(\Phi^{n+1} - \Phi^{n}\right). \tag{38}$$

Substituting $(\Phi^{n+1} - \Phi^{n})$ as given by Eq. 37 in Eq. 38 leads to an error bound given by Eq. 23

with

$$\delta\epsilon^S = \frac{\left\|A\left(\left(S^{n+1}-S\right)-SA^n\left(S^{n+1}-S^n\right)\right)\Phi^n\right\|}{\left\|\Phi^{n+1}\right\|}, \tag{39}$$

$$\delta\epsilon^A = \frac{\left\|\left(\left(A^{n+1}-A\right)-AS\left(A^{n+1}-A^n\right)\right)\left(S^{n+1}\Phi^n+Q\right)\right\|}{\left\|\Phi^{n+1}\right\|}, \tag{40}$$

$$\delta\epsilon^{res} = \left\|ASA^nS^n\right\| \frac{\left\|\Phi^n-\Phi^{n-1}\right\|}{\left\|\Phi^{n+1}\right\|}. \tag{41}$$

Such a bound for the operator-related error $\delta\epsilon^A$ (resp. $\delta\epsilon^S$) is interesting because it takes into account both $\|A_{n+1}-A\|$ (resp. $\|S_{n+1}-S\|$), the distance between the current operator and the complete one, and $\|A_{n+1}-A_n\|$ (resp. $\|S_{n+1}-S_n\|$), the distance between two successive operators. The direct control of the numerical residual with Richardson iterations in the previous algorithm is now "replaced" by the introduction of the distance between two successive operators in the error bounds on A and S. As the first term decreases with n until 0, the second one increases until $\|A-A_n\|$ (resp. $\|S-S_n\|$). Depending on the value of $\|AS\|$, $\left(\left\|A^{n+1}-A\right\|+\|AS\|\left\|A^{n+1}-A^n\right\|\right)$ can be strictly decreasing or presents a minimum or a maximum (Figure 4).

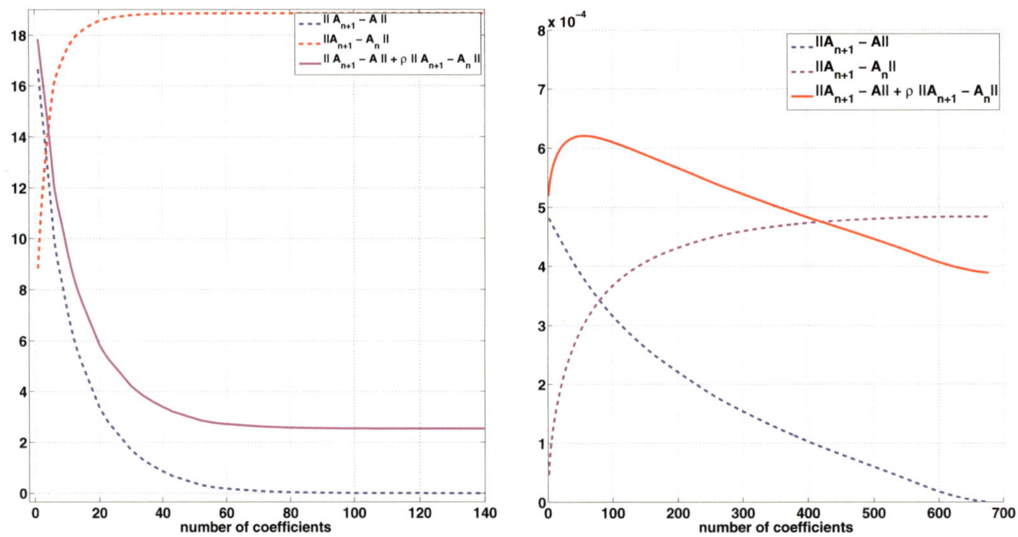

Fig. 4. Comparison of error terms defined in Eq. 40 for group 88 of ^{238}U with $\|AS\| = 0.26$ (left) and with $\|AS\|$ artificially increased to 0.8 (right)

Even if the general behaviour is not known, the initial and final bounds are given by:

$$\delta\epsilon^S_{(S_{n+1}=S)} = \delta\epsilon^S_{fin} = \left\|ASA^n\left(S-S^n\right)\Phi^n\right\|, \tag{42}$$

$$\delta\epsilon^A_{(A_{n+1}=A)} = \delta\epsilon^A_{fin} = \left\|AS\left(A-A^n\right)\left(S^{n+1}\Phi^n+Q\right)\right\|, \tag{43}$$

$$\delta\epsilon^S_{(S_{n+1}=S_n)} = \delta\epsilon^S_{ini} = \left\|A\left(S^n-S\right)\Phi^n\right\|, \tag{44}$$

$$\delta\epsilon^A_{(A_{n+1}=A_n)} = \delta\epsilon^A_{ini} = \left\|\left(A-A^n\right)\left(S^{n+1}\Phi^n+Q\right)\right\|. \tag{45}$$

As $\|AS\| < 1$ (ensuring the convergence of Richardson iterations), it guarantees that $\delta\epsilon^S_{fin} < \delta\epsilon^S_{ini}$ and $\delta\epsilon^A_{fin} < \delta\epsilon^A_{ini}$. These error bounds are at the basis of our algorithm. Three different cases are considered:

- $\delta\epsilon^{res} \in [\delta\epsilon^S_{fin}, \delta\epsilon^S_{ini}]$. It is possible to decrease the error due to operator S discretization to the numerical residual so S^{n+1} is chosen to ensure $\delta\epsilon^S \approx \delta\epsilon^{res}$.
- $\delta\epsilon^{res} < \delta\epsilon^S_{fin}$. Numerical residual is too small to be reached directly. Error on operator S is reduced to
$$\delta\epsilon^S = \alpha\delta\epsilon^S_{ini} + (1-\alpha)\delta\epsilon^S_{fin}, \tag{46}$$
with α fixed in $[0,1]$.
- $\delta\epsilon^{res} > \delta\epsilon^S_{ini}$. The numerical residual is not yet enough converged so the support of operator S is not modified, $S^{n+1} = S^n$.

The same approach is used to treat $\delta\epsilon^A$.
Figure 5 presents the behaviour of the three error terms and the numerical bound defined by Eq. 23. When $\|AS\|$ is low (Figure 5 (left)), Richardson iterations converge rapidly and do not slow the convergence of other terms. When $\|AS\|$ tends to 1 (Figure 5 (right)), more Richardson iterations are needed in order to converge the numerical residual and the operators support grows slowly and stepwise. It explains the decay by step observed for the operator discretization errors in Figure 5 (right).

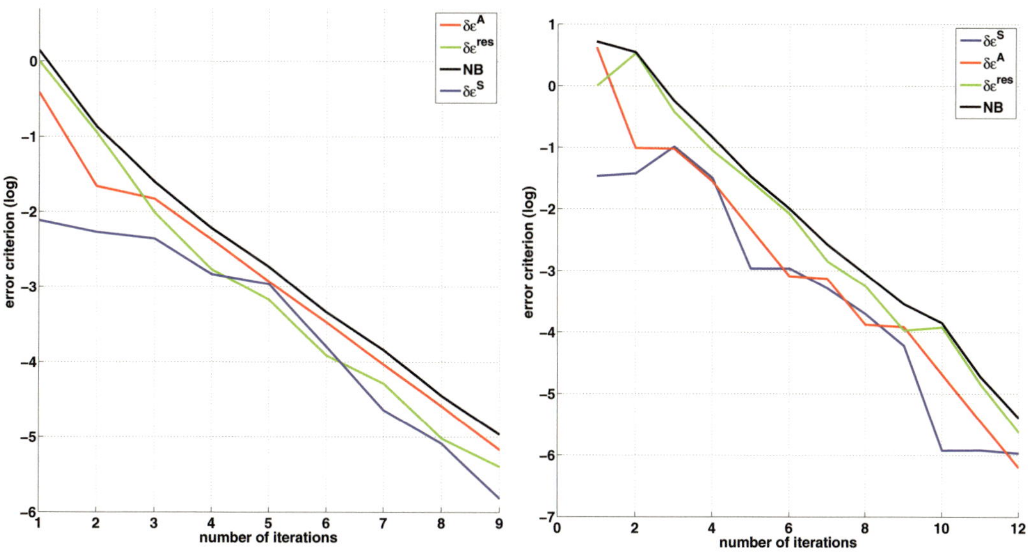

Fig. 5. Comparison of error terms on group 88 of ^{238}U with $\|AS\| = 0.26$ (left) and with $\|AS\|$ artificially increased to 0.8 (right)

The only remaining parameter is α. A numerical study is performed to give us some information about the optimal value.
Figure 6 shows that the choice of this parameter is important regarding the cost of the algorithm. If not enough coefficients are kept at each iteration, the rate of convergence is low which causes an important cost. On the opposite, if a large number is kept, large systems

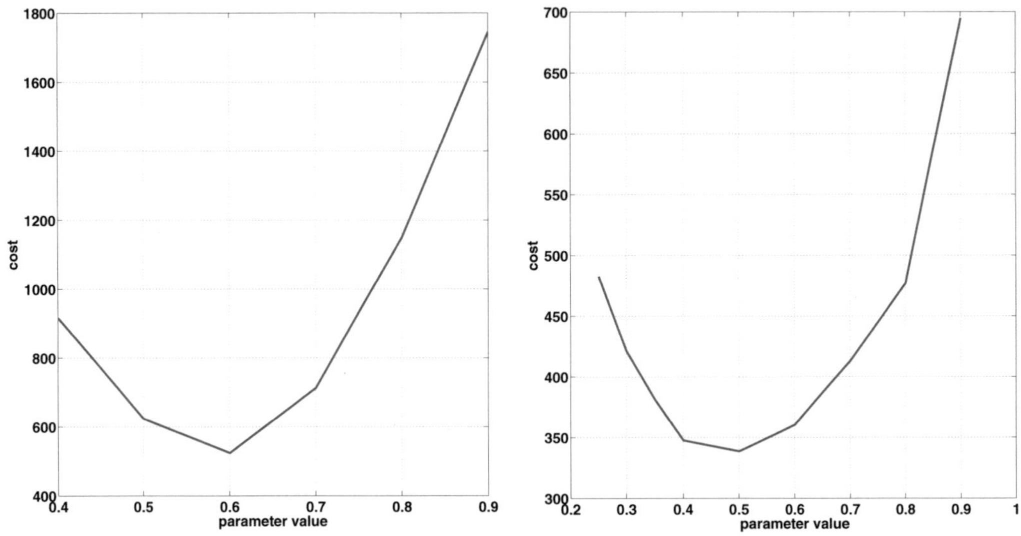

Fig. 6. Cost of the algorithm depending on α for a given accuracy $\epsilon = 10^{-5}$ on group 56 of ^{56}Fe (left) and $\epsilon = 10^{-4}$ on group 88 of ^{238}U (right)

have to be solved. An interesting compromise seems to keep coefficients in order to reduce the error by about half.

3.4 Comparison of the two algorithms

A comparison of the two algorithms and of the non-adaptive strategy is done in this section. All tests are performed by doing hard thresholding on an approximated flux and using symmlets of the 6th order. All strategies are compared as a regard of the number of kept coefficients but also the cost defined by Eq. 22. To make non-adaptive and adaptive strategies comparable, non-adaptive Richardson iterations are stopped when $\delta\epsilon^{res}$ is of the same order as $\delta\epsilon^S + \delta\epsilon^A$ in such a way that the cost of the non-adaptive algorithm is nearly optimal.
Figure 7 (resp. Figure 8) presents results obtained on ^{238}U (resp. ^{56}Fe).
Figures 7 and 8 present coherent results and clearly highlight the interest of the two adaptive algorithms. The use of the spectral radius in the two-loop algorithm and the construction of our single-loop strategy make the convergence nearly independent of the case of study. Moreover, let us recall that the non-adaptive algorithm used in this study exhibits a nearly optimal cost and requires the control of the different error terms ($\delta\epsilon^S$, $\delta\epsilon^A$ and $\delta\epsilon^{res}$) as explained at the beginning of this section.
While both adaptive algorithms exhibit similar performances, the single-loop algorithm presents some advantages. First, the treatment of source iterations is easier with only one level of iteration. Then, the choice of the decreasing series (ϵ_j) is problem-dependent and more difficult to compute compared to the choice $\alpha = 0.5$ in Eq. 46 for the one-loop algorithm.

4. Conclusion

Considering a wavelet-based Galerkin discretization for treating the energy variable in the neutron transport equation, this chapter has proposed two adaptive algorithms for the Richardson iterative scheme that is commonly used to solve the source-flux coupling. While

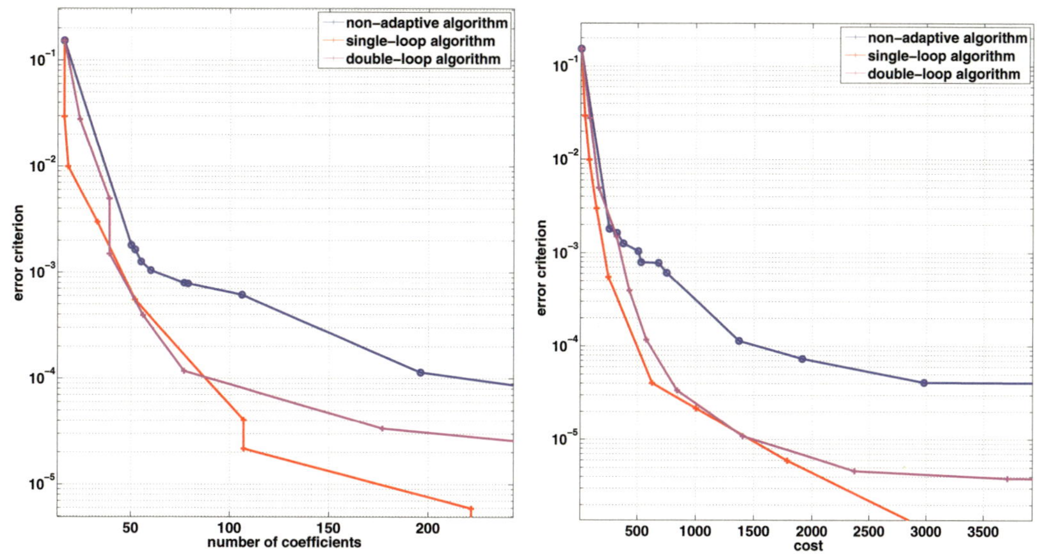

Fig. 7. Algorithms comparison in terms of the convergence (left) and the cost (right) for group 88 of ^{238}U

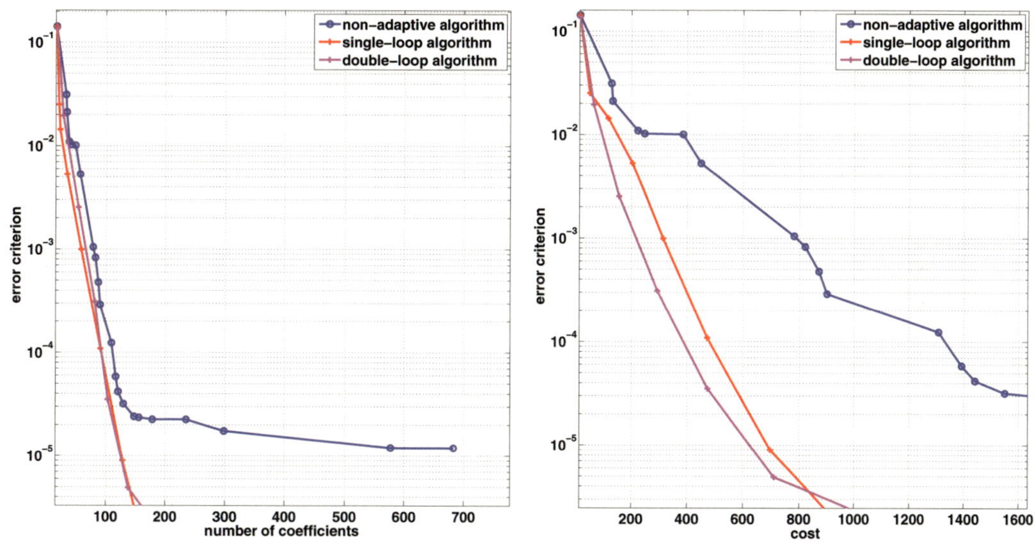

Fig. 8. Algorithms comparison in terms of the convergence (left) and the cost (right) for group 56 of ^{56}Fe

the first algorithm based on two nested loops is a modification of an algorithm previously proposed in the literature, the second one has been devised as a simplification that retains the same convergence properties. Both approaches are based on a formal decomposition of the error into three terms: two of them are related to the operators discretization while the third one is the Richardson residual. The algorithms then consist in a strategy to monitor and relate these three terms in such a way that error can be controlled by the Richardson iterations residual. As a benefit of these algorithms, the accuracy of the final solution is known and the cost to obtain it has been decreased by adapting the size of the system during iterations. The performances of these algorithms have been demonstrated in the restricted framework of the fine structure flux equation in an homogeneous infinite medium. In the context of neutron transport calculations, the modifications necessary for spatially-dependent cases have been mentioned.

5. References

Allen, E. J. (1986). A finite element approach for treating the energy variable in the numerical solution of the neutron transport equation, *Transport Theory and Statistical Physics* **15**(4): 449–478.

Cohen, A. (2003). *Numerical Analysis of Wavelet Methods*, Vol. 32 of *Studies in Mathematics and its Application*, North Holland.

Daubechies, I. (1992). *Ten Lectures on Wavelets*, CBMS-NSF Regional Conference Series in Applied Mathematics, SIAM.

Fournier, D. & Le Tellier, R. (2009). Adaptive algorithms for a self-shielding treatment using a wavelet-based Galerkin method, *Proc. of Int. Conf. on Mathematics, Computational Methods & Reactor Physics M&C 2009*, ANS, Saratoga Springs, USA.

Hardle, W., Kerkyacharian, G., Picard, D. & Tsybakov, A. (1997). Wavelets, approximation and statistical applications, Seminar Paris-Berlin.

Hébert, A. (2007). A review of legacy and advanced self-shielding models for lattice calculations, *Nuclear Science and Engineering* **155**(2): 310–320.

Le Tellier, R., Fournier, D. & Ruggieri, J. M. (2009). A wavelet-based finite element method for the self-shielding issue in neutron transport, *Nuclear Science and Engineering* **163**(1): 34–55.

Mallat, S. G. (1989). A theory for multiresolution signal decomposition: the wavelet representation, *IEEE Transactions on Pattern Analysis and Machine Intelligence* **11**: 674–693.

Mosca, P., Mounier, C., Sanchez, R. & Arnaud, G. (2011). An adaptive energy mesh constructor for multigroup library generation for transport codes, *Nuclear Science and Engineering* **167**(1): 40–60.

Yang, W., Wu, H., Zheng, Y. & Cao, L. (2010). Application of wavelets scaling function expansion method in resonance self-shielding calculation, *Annals of Nuclear Energy* **37**(5): 653–663.